RELIGION AND CULTURE

RELIGION AND CULTURE
CONTEMPORARY PRACTICES AND PERSPECTIVES

RICHARD D. HECHT AND VINCENT F. BIONDO III

Editors

Fortress Press / Minneapolis

RELIGION AND CULTURE
Contemporary Practices and Perspectives

"Religion and Film" by S. Brent Plate has been excerpted from the introduction to S. Brent Plate, *Religion and Film: Cinema and the Re-Creation of the World* (London: Wallflower Press; New York: Columbia University Press, 2008).

"Dreaming in the Contact Zone" by David Chidester is reprinted with permission: *Journal of the American Academy of Religion* 76, no. 1 (March 2008) 27–53
doi:10.1093/jaarel/lfm094 © The Author 2008. Published by Oxford University Press, on behalf of the American Academy of Religion. All rights reserved. For permissions, please e-mail: journals.permis-sions@oxfordjournals.org
Advance Access publication on January 31, 2008
Downloaded from jaar.oxfordjournals.org at Referral based access control for AAR - OUP on September 16, 2010

Cover image: Butter lamps for prayer © iStockphoto.com
Cover design: Alisha Lofgren

Library of Congress Cataloging-in-Publication Data
Religion and culture : contemporary practices and perspectives / edited
  by Richard D. Hecht and Vincent F. Biondo III.
    p. cm.
  Includes index.
  ISBN 978-0-8006-9898-0
  1. Religion and culture. I. Hecht, Richard D. II. Biondo, Vincent F.
  BL65.C8R428 2012
  201'.7—dc23   2011042066

Manufactured in the U.S.A.

17 16 15 14 13 12   1 2 3 4 5 6 7 8 9 10

CONTENTS

PART I
Religion and Culture in the Space of Politics

Contents

GENERAL INTRODUCTION

The essays in this volume describe key facets of the significant interactions between religion and culture. These relationships are constantly in flux historically, although our focus is from the premodern world to the contemporary, or what many would call the "postmodern world." Our vision tries to be global in scope since the processes of religion and culture are not the specific property of the West or any one cultural area. European categories of knowledge, from the Renaissance and Reformation to the Enlightenment and Romanticism, ascribe only one particular form to these relationships. In other parts of the world, concepts of "church and state" or "secularism" have distinctive formulations. For example, we tend to see the impact of secularization as a central factor in differentiating between religion and culture in modern European nations. But this secularization approach is by no means universally shared. In southern Asia and Southeast Asia, secularization has been less influential, despite contrary goals by imperial powers. Instead, anticolonial political movements have harnessed religion, and in this process they reconfigure the religion and culture relationship.

In our global world, where everything seems intensely interconnected, the relationships between religion and culture allow for the maintenance of cultures, histories, and values. Indeed, some might argue that the last decades of the past century and our new century have witnessed a global religious renaissance, which many earlier social theorists might have found surprising since they saw the end of religion coming hand in hand with social and cultural development. And this new religious renaissance runs parallel to the rise of the global world. In the global world, the nation-state has increasingly lost power. New actors, like global businesses, rival the powers of nation-states. New forms of media go beyond the official forms of media that are critical to the legitimacy of nations. Religion is also a global phenomenon. In some cases, religions develop in private homes, but in the global world local franchises or national headquarters can be equally powerful. Religion and culture appear more and more like multinational corporations.

The essays in this book also argue that the meeting points between religion and culture, the complex relationships, are in practices, some which are central to domestic life, while others are intensely public. Practice might be understood as that which forms the possibilities of religion and culture in much the same way as the sculptor works stone or wood, sees their potentialities, and produces an object. We will discuss the role of practice shortly, but we must also point to the multiple perspectives of the scholars who are collected here. Some might identify themselves with the social sciences and others the humanities. They bring different ways of understanding these complex relationships between religion and culture.

FINDING RELIGION AND CULTURE

The very title of this book compels us first to think about the definitions of its two main subjects. We might shy away from definitions, believing that religion and culture are too complex or too variegated to be rendered by meaningful definitions. But let us try to think together about how both might be defined or identified. There are two ways that we can think of religion. First, when we use the term *religion,* we of course refer to the religious traditions of the world, the traditions that all of us already know something about, traditions, for example, like Judaism, Islam, and Buddhism. Our knowledge of these traditions may arise from our experience or may result from having been brought up in one or another tradition or joining a tradition formally or informally. The transformations being wrought by globalization mean that we may now have many of these traditions in our own neighborhoods. Beginning in the early 1990s, radio stations, for example, began to announce the end of the daily fast of Ramadan because of the number of Muslims who populate the American landscape and might need to know when to break fast.

Many scholars object to using singular terms like Buddhism, as if Buddhism in history and today throughout the world is one common tradition. They might identify the two great streams of Buddhist thought and practice, the Mahayana and the Theravadan traditions. Even these must be supplemented by the Buddhist traditions of Japan, which give Buddhism their own Japanese identity. Buddhism, like other religious traditions, also reflects local or ethnic traditions. Driving on Sunset Boulevard as it runs down to the Los Angeles Civic Center, you will pass at least one Chinese Buddhist temple and a Cambodian Buddhist social center, which houses a Cambodian Buddhist temple. Everyone is welcome in both, but the sacred architecture is vastly different. The scholars thus might correct us and say that there are only "Buddhisms" or "Judaisms" or "Hinduisms" because within each there are multitudes of perspectives, positions, and understandings of Buddhism, Judaism, or Hinduism. These differences are not simply "denominations" or different names for the same thing, such as Methodists and Presbyterians. They are fundamentally different worldviews, which may reject other perspectives as inauthentic, false, incomplete, or even heretical.

There is a second way of thinking about religion. Religion is also a complex system of symbols and meanings, which may exist apart from religious traditions. These symbols and meanings may incorporate values and ethics, ways of self and social understanding. Here religion is about the fundamental questions of human existence: What happens when we die? Why are we here? Where do we come from? Why do good people suffer? Who are we? Paul Tillich (1886–1965), one of the great Protestant theologians of the twentieth century, sought to broaden the definition of religion by defining it as "ultimate concern." Those activities, ideas, and ways of being that we think of as ultimately important constituted religion for Tillich. Those matters that are most meaningful to us are expressions of this ultimate concern. And he would not limit this ultimate concern to religious traditions. Other theologians, of course, throughout history have sought to restrict or limit religion. For example, Tillich's contemporary Karl Barth (1886–1968) emphasized how official church institutions, beliefs, creeds, and dogmas provide answers to these fundamental questions. One need go no further than the walls of the church to find these authoritative answers. Tillich thought more expansively about religion so that a wider set of human activities and beliefs that were of ultimate concern to individuals could properly be called "religious." For Tillich, many aspects of culture could reflect this ultimate concern, including contemporary art and film. This meant that culture could be read as religion. Culture was theology.

Tillich was an heir to a long tradition of Protestant thought. Indeed, many students of religion might begin their histories of the modern study of religion with another Protestant theologian, Rudolf Otto (1869–1937), who in 1917 published a slim volume title *Das Heilige* (its English title is *The Idea of the Holy*). Otto began by noting that in many languages of religious traditions, the words that are translated as "holy" or "sacred" suggest something else, that the holy or sacred are a different reality, separate from everything else. He used the phrase *ganz Andere*, "totally Other," to capture this sense of the separation of the holy. Otto thought of his book as being a contribution to the psychology of religion, and thus the human response to the holy was a central element of his discussion. The response to the manifestation of the holy, Otto believed, is always contradictory. He used the term *mysterium tremendum* to describe the overwhelming fear that accompanies this manifestation. But while a human is frightened and repelled by this *mysterium tremendum*, we are also drawn to it, fascinated by it, and hence he called this aspect of the holy, the *fascinans*. We are simultaneously fearful of the holy and simultaneously drawn to it.

Otto believed that the very best example of these two simultaneous experiences—fear and fascination of, and with, the holy—was the well-known narrative of Moses and the burning bush in the book of Exodus (3:1ff). There we are told that Moses was herding the flock of his father-in-law, Jethro, when suddenly a divine messenger appeared to him in a flaming bush, and more important, the bush was not consumed by the fire. He was drawn to it, and as he approached the bush, God called to him, telling him to take off his sandals because the place upon which he stood was *admat kodesh*, which most English translations render as "holy ground." But what fascinated Otto in this text was the more fundamental meaning of a "separate ground" unlike everything around it. The sacred could not be reduced to the world or anything in it. It is something fundamentally different from the immanent world. Yet it can only be experienced through the specificity and particularity of the world. Moses is in the desert with a specific bush on specific ground. Otto's analysis of the sacred remains an important marker for students of religion nearly a century after its publication. The sacred is never abstract, but always experienced, contained, and embodied in local places in conversation with others.

There were contemporaries of Otto who also sought to define religion. Among them, Émile Durkheim (1858–1917) and Sigmund Freud (1856–1939) are among the most important. In 1912, Durkheim published his *The Elementary Forms of Religious Life*, which is one of the foundational works in the modern study of religion. The focus of this long study was the fundamental distinction between the sacred and the profane, which enabled Durkheim to describe how a symbol, or what he called a "collective representation," carried enormous social power that could sustain and unify a community. Many understood Durkheim to suggest that religion was nothing more than a representation of the social, but he is far more complicated. That distinction between sacred and profane was the fundamental distinction in the experiential world, and thus Durkheim began to see its operations throughout the institutions of society or the social world, in law, economy, politics, and the family. Durkheim was not an evolutionary thinker who was interested in how "primitive" religions develop into more advanced religions. Instead, he understood "elementary" to refer to relatively undifferentiated societies, where religious functions could be observed easily and separate from other social functions. Durkheim understood his work as "religious sociology" precisely because he believed that all of society reflected the primary distinction between the sacred and profane.

Freud, however, was interested in human evolution and ultimately the vanquishing of religion as a deep-seated superstition through progress in science and culture. In his first major cultural study, *Totem and Taboo: Some Convergences in the Mental Life of Savages and Neurotics* (1913), Freud agreed that religious symbols hold enormous social power. From his work with patients and from reflecting on some of the same materials that Durkheim used, he was convinced that religious symbols also articulate repressed, powerful emotions such as those regarding parents, love, sex, and our deepest hopes and anxieties. He ingeniously posited that the relationships between humans and their gods were derived from their relationships with their fathers, so that totemism was a repressed cultural and religious form masking the primordial murder of a tyrannical father by his sons. We note in his later cultural works, *The Future of an Illusion* (1927), *Civilization and Its Discontents* (1929), and *Moses and Monotheism* (1937 and 1939) written after World War I and during the rise of Nazism that Freud became increasingly critical of religion's ability to improve peoples' lives in a modern, industrial age. The destruction and violence he witnessed firsthand led Freud to reemphasize an older philosophical distinction between the blind faith of children and the more measured adult recognition of the importance of science and reason. However, his additional suggestion that psychoanalysis had the potential to help people more than religion was bound to offend religious people.

After World War II, the great Romanian scholar Mircea Eliade brought the European discipline of the history of religions to the United States, where he generalized comparatively across cultures and time periods. According to Eliade, human beings require order and orientation in their lives. Religion is made up of the myths and rituals that help us to orient ourselves in time and space. Creation myths, for example, are often narrated during rituals allowing the listeners in the religious community to reexperience the events of creation and to renew the world as it was at creation. Catholics, for example, during the weekly Eucharist remind themselves and relive the foundational meal that stands at the origin of their community and that identifies the simple foods of wine and bread with the blood and body of the Savior. Over the last half of the twentieth century, and beyond, the students of Eliade criticized his theory for being overly dependent upon generalities about complex religious traditions, while also overlooking the importance of particular historical and political contexts. For example, in an essay called "A Pearl of Great Price and a Cargo of Yams," Jonathan Z. Smith points out that religious practices such as those on the island of West Ceram may reenact eternal truths, but they also may respond to recent sociopolitical traumas or what he calls "situational incongruities." In this case, cargo cults, as many anthropologists who have studied the religious traditions and peoples of the South Pacific have called them, may reflect an ancient messianic hope and also be a response to recent colonial encounters with vast disparities in wealth and technology.

One of the founders of the contemporary discipline of religious studies, Ninian Smart (1927–2001), brought together many of the definitions already mentioned into what he called a "dimensional analysis of religion." According to Smart's definition, there is a part of culture that we can call religion when it contains several, but not necessarily all, of these dimensions. Initially, Smart believed that the appropriate number of dimensions was seven, including the mythic, doctrinal, ritual, institutional, ethical, experiential, and aesthetic dimensions. Later, he added the political and the economic, which were vital to understanding how secular ideologies like Communism or nationalism share striking resemblances with religion. Such a move is significant for our purposes since a discussion of both major and minor religious practices requires a broad definition of religion. Ninian Smart's dimensional analysis is ideally suited to help us understand how the sacred is experienced in the practices of men and women in their daily lives.

Though each of these efforts to define religion may prove useful and intriguing, for most scholars of religion and members of religious traditions, religion means more than a specific function or an answer to the question of meaning. Defining culture is equally problematic and elusive. The cultural anthropologist Clifford Geertz (1926–2006) was one of the major figures in his generation to reconceptualize culture. In 1973, he published a collection of some of his most important essays and articles under the title *The Interpretation of Cultures*. This influential volume defined culture as a "semiotic system," which he likened to the human being suspended in webs of meaning and significance spun by himself. Geertz took those webs to be culture, which could be understood through an interpretive quest for their meanings. Culture had become a matter of interpretation whose meanings could appear in the ethnographic method—or what he called "thick description"—described as when anthropologists construct something parallel to the reading of a text or a manuscript that is foreign to its reader, incomplete, with elements that seem completely incoherent, with questionable additions or emendations, and within a commentary tradition that seems impenetrable, but in structured behavior rather than in words. He interpreted religion as an element within this system or one component of the web of culture. Religion was something that was given and awaited interpretation. For example, people are always spinning webs of meaning while drawing upon the cultural resources, or other parts of the web, to produce that meaning.

We might understand Geertz's interpretation of culture and religion by analogy, using the *auteur* theory in film studies. This French word means more than simply "author." *Auteur*, in film studies and in film criticism, refers to films that are dominated by the creative vision of their directors and makers. French filmmakers like François Truffault might initially be thought of when the word *auteur* is used. However, the number of these filmmakers is extensive and not of course limited to French films and their makers. One can think of American filmmakers like Orson Welles, Quentin Tarantino, and Preston Sturges; of Italians like Federico Fellini or Roberto Rossellini; Japanese directors like Akira Kurosawa; and many, many more. It is the creative vision of these filmmakers that is impressed upon the film so strongly that even if you did not know the filmmaker before seeing a film, you might immediately recognize the vision of the director. Indeed, *auteur* films are strikingly different from films that are the result of large studios where the vision of the director or screenwriter is subordinated to other concerns such as run time, audience, or commercial spinoffs. The vision of the filmmaker is analogous to the meaning that is generated from spinning webs. Meaning is what gives reality or the phenomenal world its coherence in the same way that the artistic vision unifies a film and makes it immediately identifiable.

THE "CULTURAL TURN" FROM TEXT TO CONTEXT

The work of the theologians, historians, social theorists, and anthropologists we have discussed has led to an important sea change in scholarship on religion over the past forty years. Indeed, the focus of this volume on religion and culture is a reflection of that change. Scholars of religion have turned more and more to the interactions and relationships between religion and culture, and to do that requires embedding religion in its contexts. Some contemporary scholars refer to this contextualization as "religion in daily life" or "religion in lived experience," or just "lived religion." We will have more to say about this in just a moment. Certainly, the study of religion today is dramatically different than it was forty years ago at one of the great watershed events in the history of the study of religion in the United States. That event was the United States Supreme Court decision in the Schempp v. Abington Township case in 1963. The court ruled that teaching about religion in public schools and state-supported universities and colleges does not violate the constitutional separation of church and state. Justice Thomas Clark, writing for the majority, stated, "It might well be said that one's education is not complete without the study of comparative religion or the history of religion and its relationship to the advancement of civilization. It certainly may be said that the Bible is worthy of study for its literary and historic qualities. Nothing we have said here indicates that such a study of the Bible or of religion, when presented objectively as part of a secular program of education, may not be enacted consistently with the First Amendment."

The court sought to deflect the charge of its ruling being to enshrine a "religion of secularism" by pointing out that the study of the Bible or religion when pursued objectively and within the context of a "secular program of education" is consistent with the First

Amendment. This suggestion was underscored in the concurring opinions of Justices Brennan and Goldberg. Justice Brennan wrote that "the holding of the Court . . . plainly does not foreclose teaching about the Holy Scriptures or about the differences between religious sects in classes in literature or history." Justice Goldberg wrote: "Government must inevitably take cognizance of the existence of religion and, indeed, under certain circumstances the First Amendment may require that it do so. And it seems clear to me from the opinions in the present and past cases that the Court would recognize the propriety of . . . the teaching *about* religion, as distinguished from the teaching *of* religion, in the public schools."

The court's decision led to a dramatic expansion of religion in public universities and colleges in the first two decades after the Schempp decision. In private universities, the study of religion often existed alongside of or was overshadowed by theological education, but the court's decision also had impact here, contributing to an emancipation of the study of religion from its historical-theological context. But it was a more difficult struggle to create ways of studying religion that were not a continuation of theology. The study of religion in the first years after the Schempp decision was oriented toward elite understandings of religious traditions and toward religious "ideas" and the importance of the documents and texts of religious traditions. These texts were often embedded in long traditions of commentary and interpretation by religious leaders, and often these texts with their ideas were explored without deep analysis of their historical, political, economic, cultural, and social contexts. Texts oriented religion to the past and not the present. Here, we must note that the study of religion is not only a humanistic discipline. Sociologists of religion went about their work in the context of the social, but much of the study of religion at the time of the Schempp decision had a commitment to text and ideas, and not their contexts. Today, religion in daily life, or religion in lived experience, has provided a powerful reorientation of the discipline and has given primacy to efforts to reembed religion in the contexts of its practices, including increased attention to the role of ritual, the microenvironments of domestic life and the macrodimensions of public life. In 1978, Ninian Smart spoke to the Wingspread Conference on the state of religious studies sponsored by the Council on the Study of Religion. In his paper, assessing the future directions of the study of religion, Smart called for attention to what he described as "religion on the ground." "Religion on the ground" became an important theoretical concern of his, alongside of his dimensional analysis of religions and his efforts to expand religion to include worldviews. Smart may have been among the first scholars of religion who examined the problem of religion and politics, which today is considered so critical.

The sea change taking place in the study of religion was a reflection of changes taking place in other disciplines, which also sought to recontextualize their explorations of human phenomena. Anthropology, long a discipline of the human past, became increasingly interested in the contemporary; sociology, a discipline that had long understood its practice as limited to the contemporary, became more and more interested in history. As we noted earlier, Clifford Geertz's "thick description" and the hermeneutics of culture pushed the ethnographer deeper and deeper into the contexts of anthropological description and human life. Indeed, the emergence of "cultural studies" or "cultural analysis" challenged disciplinary boundaries by returning to context to reembed culture in its lived experiences. "The cultural turn," as many call this analysis of context, has been one of the most significant transformations of academic disciplines in the last forty years, and the study of religion has also experienced this "cultural turn" no less than other disciplines. Jeffrey Alexander, the distinguished Yale professor of sociology, has explored how this cultural turn can be traced to Durkheim and provides one of the most potent theoretical contributions to the social sciences and the humanities. In the study of religion, the cultural turn has also allowed scholars to see more clearly the limitations of earlier theories and perspectives and thus to formulate and introduce new theoretical constructions that may have been concealed in the earlier emphasis upon textual and idea-oriented study that was inherited from theology. For example, Thomas Tweed notes in his discussion of many significant advances in the study of religion and in other disciplines since the 1970s that we can draw a parallel between the cultural turn and what he and others call the spatial turn. This development in scholarship has positioned spatial constructions of the social world in critical social theory. The cultural turn and the spatial turn have allowed Tweed to introduce a new way to understand religion on the basis of movement, crossing, and dwelling. Once we focus on movement and crossing, we begin to see how religion can be understood as creating and maintaining spatial frames of reference.

The cultural turn had other important results for the study of religion. First, the study of religion turned toward what Smart called the experiential dimension of religion, or how religion was and is experienced by regular people rather than by religious leaders and officials, like priests and rabbis and monks and sheiks, theologians and philosophers, all of whom understand how things are and should be via abstractions of religion. It has become more and more the case that scholars will use, as we noted earlier, the term "lived religion" to recalibrate this focus. David D. Hall, an American religions historian, edited a collection of essays that have had a very significant impact on how American religions are now studied. He titled his collection *Lived Religion in America: Toward a History of Practice*, and in his introduction he set out many of the important factors involved in studying lived religion. He pointed out, for example, that "lived religion" is not the same as popular religion, which often conjures an oppositional relationship between religious authorities and laity. Lived religion is not focused on this opposition between the high and the low within religious traditions. How religions are practiced is the central concern of this focus. The essays in Hall's volume are not longitudinal studies but windows that explore a number of distinctive religious moments in the history of American religions. There are, however, many excellent studies that provide these long historical views of lived religion. Among the best is Jennifer Scheper Hughes's *Biography of a Mexican Crucifix: Lived Religion and Local Faith from the Conquest to the Present*, which examines what has now become the oldest Mexican crucifix and the devotional practices that grew up around this crucifix, apart from the Catholic authorities, from the colonial period to the present. This focus on lived religion will be seen in a number of the essays that have been collected here.

Second, the cultural turn allowed scholars to interpret phenomena that might not have any overt religious characteristics so as to reveal the religious orientations of society. In 1957, the French semiotician and literary theorist Roland Barthes (1915–1980) was a significant trailblazer with his "The World of Wrestling." There, Barthes demonstrated that something as profane as professional wrestling can perform and reveal larger, more sacred cultural and religious realities. Barthes noted, among other "signs," how defeat is total, with its attendant suffering understood as a repetition of the crucifixion of Jesus. Forty years later, the historian of religions Bruce Lincoln returned to Barthes' essay to demonstrate the central of wrestling, in which there are a number of matches in which the bad guys triumph using unscrupulous and sadistic means. They would strangle their opponents, bite them, hit them with chairs and concealed weapons, gouge their eyes, kick them in the groin, throw them against the metal posts that hold the ring's ropes, throw them onto to the mat and stomp them, or throw them out of the ring so that they would crash on the cement floor of the auditorium. All of this was ritually presented to demonstrate that in the final match good would triumph over the evil spectacle that the viewers had seen. The struggle between good and evil in the match is not an intellectual abstraction. At the core of wrestling is ritual reenactment. Another example is Kathryn Lofton's fascinating study of Oprah Winfrey and her company, including her television show, book club, store, magazine, Angel Network, and many other projects. Lofton reads these as providing a way to survive the disorienting plentitude of modernity and the overpowering materiality of the secular world by providing direction and meaning. Her television program is her "ministry," Lofton argues, and her "religiosity, her brand of religion, is non-institutional and non-creedal. The most important part of her ministry is the many lives that have been changed or inspired to change by her television show and multiple spin offs. Oprah functions much like a religious icon, containing and manifesting powers to change lives."

POLITICS, ETHICS, AND AESTHETICS

One of the most important threads running through the new studies of lived religion is practice, or what many have called performance. Religions are matters of practice. Likewise, culture is never an abstraction, but like religion, is a practice. Anthropologists like Talal Asad have questioned how well theories actually explain religion if we understand religion to be a matter of practice. Theory and practice do not necessarily form an unbroken continuum with practice at one end and theory at the other. Religion as practice or performance requires new methods of study, including ethnographic fieldwork and the deep description that we have inherited from Cliford Geertz. Ethnography and fieldwork seem, then, to limit our exploration of religion and culture to the present. But is that true? We think the answer is no. There are many ethnographic accounts from the past two centuries that perhaps can be reread with new interests, attuning our reading to how religions are performed. Of course, we need to be very sensitive to all of the negative baggage that these descriptions contain, such as the dichotomy of "primitive" versus "the developed" or "advanced," which was one way that ethnographers distinguished tribal and traditional religions from Christianity, or interpretive theories that have been discredited, such as "animism."

We suggest here that another way to understand the relationships between religion and culture is to consider the different kinds of spaces in which religion and culture are performed and influence our daily lives. It is in these spaces that lived religion is played out. We will argue that there are three spaces that provide the arenas of performance. In much the same way that the French theorist Michel de Certeau saw three spaces of everyday life, marked by production, consumption, and then a third space between these marked by syntheses, we identify first a space where power and politics are performed, a second space where ethics are performed, and a third space where aesthetics are performed creatively and in response to the first two. All three are social spaces in which performance takes place. In some cases, the performance is acted in physical space, in some cases the performance takes place in temporal space, and finally, some performances are enacted in virtual time and space. Some would argue that the most fundamental distinction is between public and private space. The French sociologist and Marxist social theorist Henri Lefebvre (1905–1991) spent a considerable part of his scholarly career examining and interpreting everyday life and argued that this distinction between public and private collapses because all of our decisions, even those that seem the most private, have significant public implications.

Lefebvre, however, took care to underscore that the relationships between public and private are complex. Significantly, the public and private separation includes the relationship of religion and politics, or what in the United States is commonly referred to as the church-state debate. That debate seeks to balance the powers of the religious traditions or institutions with the state or to restrain their interconnection. This is one of the most hotly contested issues here in the United States and also in many other modern nation-states. Though many of us tend to think of religion as a largely individual matter, we must remember that this is a relatively recent phenomenon that is no older than the Enlightenment tradition in Europe and the United States during the seventeenth, eighteenth, and nineteenth centuries. Enlightenment thinkers sought to separate religion and the public sphere so as to restrict religion, to make it an individual denominational or confessional matter. The citizen of a modern nation-state might have been Catholic or Protestant, but that was not the prime definition of their identity. They were citizens as the state defined them. In their private homes, they would retain a religious identity if they so chose. Prior to the Enlightenment, religion defined identity. It was impossible before the nation-state for identity to be constructed apart from religion. It was the sole frame of reference for questions of identity. Enlightenment thinkers like the Jewish philosopher Baruch Spinoza (1632–1677), Voltaire (1694–1778), and Jean-Jacques Rousseau (1712–1778), among many others, contemplated a nonreligious identity because of the long history of religious warfare in Europe and also because of their commitment to the dictates of reason and universalism. (But despite this separation, we recognize how personal morality influences public morality and how public morality also affects personal morality.) This separation transformed religion. Religion's claim to organize both the public and the private was rejected, and religion became only a private confessional matter. The citizen of the new enlightened world would be defined only by the state.

This was not an easy transition for Christianity and Judaism in Europe and in the Americas. Many of the struggles that we have today between religion and state are the result of that separation. Some might argue that a central problem of the new century will be whether that high wall of separation between church and state will be maintained.

Indeed, there is a multifront culture war going on over the place of religion in the modern state. But it is more than a struggle between science and faith, secularism and religion, or sacred and profane. It is a more complicated struggle involving liberal religious traditions that have normalized the separation and their position in the modern state as particularistic confessions. Small religious minorities cling to the separation in order to protect themselves from the demands of a majoritarian religion. Jews and Catholics in the United States have traditionally been supporters of the separation so as to avoid greater conflicts over the definition of who really is a member of the state and the pressure to conform to the majority Protestant tradition.

Durkheim recognized that the secular nationalism of the nineteenth and twentieth centuries was competing with religious nationalism in providing unifying symbols for the nation-state. Following Durkheim's insight, the sociologist Robert Bellah analyzed this relationship in the use of religious language by US Presidents. In a famous essay published in 1967 titled "Civil Religion in America," Bellah argued that the separation of church and state in the United States provided a social or religious space for the emergence of an elaborate and well-institutionalized civil religion, which was clearly differentiated from church and synagogue. The beginning point for his essay was John Fitzgerald Kennedy's inaugural address on January 20, 1961, where he made reference to God three times.

> "For I have sworn before you and Almighty God the same solemn oath our forebears prescribed nearly a century and three quarters ago," "the belief that the rights of man come not from the generosity of the state but from the hand of God," and "With a good conscience our only sure reward, with history the final judge of our deeds, let us go forth to lead the land we love, asking His blessing and His help, but knowing that here on earth God's work must truly be our own."

Bellah rejected understanding these references as an example of what every American president must do or risk loosing support; nor were these references ceremonial formalities. They told Bellah something important about the nature of religion in American life. Bellah noted that the references are more problematic and more illuminating because Kennedy was a Catholic and chose not to give his references a distinctively Catholic form. Kennedy did not present a doctrinal deity, Bellah pointed out, because this was a matter of his own private religious beliefs; they are not matters relevant in any direct way to the conduct of his public office. Others with different religious views and commitments to different churches or denominations are equally qualified participants in the political process.

The principle of separation of church and state guarantees the freedom of religious belief and association but at the same time clearly segregates the religious sphere, which is considered to be essentially private, from the political one. Given this separation of church and state, Bellah asked, how could the president be justified in using the word "God"? He quickly answered this question—the separation of church and state does not deny the political realm a religious dimension. That separation of the state and particular and private religious claims provided the social space for public religious dimension, and it is the set of beliefs, symbols, and rituals of this public religious dimension that Bellah described as "American civil religion."

Indeed, the force of this civil religion is demonstrated by the theological meanings of Kennedy's statements, especially the third reference, where the young President reiterated that it is the nation's task on earth to work out the blessing of God or that God's work is our work. Bellah described this as an "activist and non-contemplative conception of the fundamental religious obligation," which he believed was associated with American Protestantism. Civil religion had become so much a part of America that it overruled any theology that the president as a Catholic might have wanted to give it. Thus for Bellah the importance of the references is how deeply established civil religion is in the American outlook. Of course, the actual term "civil religion" was drawn from Jean-Jacques Rousseau's *The Social Contract,* where Rousseau explained its central ingredients—the existence of deity, the life to come, reward and punishment for virtue and vice, and exclusion of religious intolerance. But Bellah quickly admitted that there is no necessary causal connection between Rousseau and the founders of the nation. Similar ideas were a part of the climate of the late-eighteenth century, and thus Rousseau and the founders of the nation shared a similar worldview.

Bellah argued that American civil religion has its own myths, rituals, sacred places, and sacred objects. He commented on our myth and how it has integrated traumatic events. The assassination of Abraham Lincoln was understood as a sacrificial death that guaranteed the unity of the nation. The ritual calendar of American civil religion includes Thanksgiving and July 4, and in both celebrations, the myth of the nation is retold to new generations, just as any authoritative myth would be renarrated again in a religious tradition.

By the mid-1970s and in the wake of the divisive Vietnam War and the Watergate scandal, Bellah concluded that American civil religion was an "empty and broken shell." Civil religion was an external covenant in order to guarantee social existence, but this covenant must be loved by the citizens of the nation and not merely obeyed. The spiritual rhythms of the nation did not merely decline during the 1970s, according to Bellah. Rather, the covenant had been betrayed by its most responsible servants. He reasoned that not only had our political leaders betrayed the covenant, but they also did not realize what it was or how that betrayal had affected the entire nation. Their betrayal was much worse, for they knew that there would be no punishment for their breaking of the covenant. The covenant itself had lost any meaning. A decade later, Bellah, along with several colleagues from the University of California, Berkeley, published *Habits of the Heart: Individualism and Commitment in American Life,* where they noted that American civil religion had its own opposite, a religious individualism they called "Sheilaism," after a young nurse by the name of Sheila Larson, who told them, "I believe in God. I'm not a religious fanatic. I can't remember the last time I went to church. My faith has carried me a long way. It's Sheilaism. Just my own little voice." The church-state and civil-religion debates are two examples of how private religion can influence public daily life on a national level. But as civil religion receded, individualistic religion like Sheilaism became more significant.

Though the relationship of religion and politics is a complex one, and debates over the separation of church and state and the line separating the public and private spheres will not be settled once and for all in this volume and its essays, we do hope to provide the raw material that can support the various sides in these debates. The broad definitions of religion outlined above, the Supreme Court decision in the Schempp case, Ninian Smart's call for a study of religion on the ground, and the cultural turn in the study of religion from text to context, attest to the continuing importance of religion and the study of religion in the first decades of the twenty-first century.

According to the theory of everyday life articulated by Henri Lefebvre, and his contemporary the political philosopher Hannah Arendt (1906–1975) would agree, a vital public arena where these living debates are encouraged may contribute to preserving democracy and preventing mass destruction and genocides. In fact, the scholarship on everyday life or daily life emerged after World War II in response to intellectual and historical factors. During the height of the age of empires, or what some scholars mean by "modernity," the initial European followers of the founders of what became the social sciences or human sciences, Marx, Durkheim, Freud, and Weber, emphasized the aspects of their work that coincided with a secularization hypothesis influenced by social evolution. It was tempting for Europeans to connect their military superiority with increased secularization. For many intellectuals, however, two world wars that were "total wars," because civilians had no refuge, and that also included the Nazi destruction of European Jewry with the mass killings of hundreds of thousands of others, were sufficient proof that modernity and progress did not correspond. Instead, modernity came to mean an otherworldly quest for homogeneity, a desire for which scholars of religion were not immune.

The spiritual vacuum, after secularization failed to create peace, has coincided with a new religious pluralism produced by postcolonial immigration since the 1960s. One of the great migrations in world history, which appears to be a permanent global transformation as a result of advances in transportation and communications, is considered by some a threat and by others an opportunity. After analyzing the causes of the rise of Nazism, Hannah Arendt concluded that only a diverse populace who actively participates in politics can prevent other episodes of genocide from occurring in the future.

While Arendt's political analysis of the rise of Nazism does not talk a great deal about the role of religion, her theory of the importance of democratic public spaces for face-to-face communication was also advanced by Lefebvre, who developed a theory of everyday life that includes major traditional religious practices as well as the seemingly minute repetitive details upon which we spend so much time and energy. According to Lefebvre's hypothesis, even decisions as simple as how to get to work or what to eat for breakfast have revolutionary implications for religion and culture. To give only two examples, the importance of automobile transportation in American culture significantly raised the value of oil discovered in Saudi Arabia. The Saudi Arabian government has used some of the funds from American consumers to train religious leaders and translate Islamic texts to be disseminated worldwide. As a result, one particular interpretation of Islamic doctrine has spread widely. Secondly the desire to eat bananas for breakfast resulted in the control of Guatemala by the United Fruit Company during the first half of the twentieth century. This economic and political arrangement contributed to the appeal of liberation theology, which had a direct impact on the official doctrines of the Vatican. Thus the everyday decisions to eat bananas or take the drive-through lane have influenced the religious lives of half of humanity.

We have organized the contributions to this volume according to the three spaces where religion and culture are performed. These include, first, the public, or civil, space of performance competitions and, second, the private space of moral courage and ethical consequence. Of course, the first and second spaces work in tension to synthesize the third, aesthetic space. Power relationships dominate the first space, which can structure the types of performance that are available in the second and third spaces. In the first political space, this volume contains essays that take up issues of conflict and peacebuilding, civil religion, zones of contact, conflict and creativity, science, women, sexuality, and forms of traditional healing. Each of these chapters takes different perspectives on how religion and culture are performed, but each contributes to our understanding of how religions and cultures create societies and communities. The second is private space, which contains the home and domestic space. It is in this second space that individuals are molded. We might think of this creation of individuals using the Catholic educational term *formation*. In the second ethical space, individuals are formed and ideas are performed as a part of that formation. This section includes contributions on economics, nature, tourism, education, and children. The aesthetic third space keeps the public and private, or political and ethical, in creative tension. Aesthetics involve greater creative synthesis than politics or ethics. Consider how a jazz funeral turns the intensely private experience of death into a public event. Or think of how the death of kings, presidents, and other political and cultural figures results in a demand to have these figures viewed in death by the public, so that the public preservation of Elvis Presley's grave at Graceland in Memphis becomes intensely private for individual visitors. Or Maya Lin's Vietnam Veterans' Memorial in Washington successfully draws formerly private, individual mourning into the public space. These creative syntheses prove themselves to be extraordinarily powerful in overturning or subverting the relationships struck in the first and second spaces. Political and intellectual leaders cannot control all creative performance. Here, the third, aesthetic section includes essays on contemporary art, contemporary music, humor, film, material and popular culture, memorialization, and death and dying.

Each part of *Religion and Culture: Contemporary Practices and Perspectives* demonstrates the interweaving of religion and culture. Each chapter helps us to understand why religion cannot be separated or compartmentalized so that it operates only within the walls of religious institutions or during religious events and dates within the calendar. Neither is culture something isolated, belonging to certain classes, groups, and institutions of the social world. Each chapter also demonstrates multiple perspectives in the study of religion. Readers will see how human life is immersed in religion and culture where local daily life practices are laboratories for observing the processes of human meaning-creation.

FOR FURTHER READING

Alexander, Jeffrey C., ed. *Durkheimian Sociology: Cultural Studies*. New York: Cambridge University Press, 1988.

———. *The Meanings of the Social Life: A Cultural Sociology*. New York: Oxford University Press, 2003.

Arendt, Hannah. *The Origins of Totalitarianism*. New York: Harcourt Brace Jovanovich, 1951.

———. *The Human Condition*. Chicago: University of Chicago Press, 1958.

Asad, Talal. *Genealogies of Religion: Discipline and Reasons of Power in Christianity and Islam*. Baltimore: Johns Hopkins University Press, 1993.

Barthes, Roland. *Mythologies*. New York: Farrar, Straus and Giroux, 1972.

Bellah, Robert. "Civil Religion in America." *Daedalus, Journal of the American Academy of Arts and Sciences*, special issue on "Religion in America," 96, no. 1 (1967): 1–21.

———. *The Broken Covenant: American Civil Religion in a Time of Trial*. 1975; repr., Chicago: University of Chicago Press, 1992.

Bellah, Robert, with Richard Madsen, William M. Sullivan, Ann Swidler, and Steven M. Tipton. *Habits of the Heart: Individualism and Commitment in American Life*. Berkeley: University of California Press, 1985.

Certeau, Michel de. *The Practice of Everyday Life*. Berkeley: University of California Press, 1984.

Eliade, Mircea. *Cosmos and History: The Myth of the Eternal Return*. Princeton: Princeton University Press, 1954.

Geertz, Clifford. *The Interpretation of Cultures*. New York: Basic Books, 1973.

Hall, David D. *Lived Religion in America: Toward a History of Practice*. Princeton: Princeton University Press, 1997.

Hughes, Jennifer Scheper. *Biography of a Mexican Crucifix: Lived Religion and Local Faith from the Conquest to the Present*. New York: Oxford University Press, 2010.

Lefebvre, Henri. *The Critique of Everyday Life*, vol. 1, *Introduction*, vol. 2, *Foundations for a Sociology of the Everyday*, vol. 3, *From Modernity to Modernism (Towards a Metaphilosophy of Daily Life)*. Translated by John Moore and Gregory Elliot. New York: Verso, 1991–2005.

Lincoln, Bruce. *Discourse and the Construction of Society: Comparative Studies of Myth, Ritual, and Classification*. New York: Oxford University Press, 1989.

Lofton, Kathryn. *Oprah: The Gospel of an Icon*. Berkeley: University of California Press, 2011.

Ortner, Sherry B., ed., *The Fate of "Culture": Geertz and Beyond*. Berkeley: University of California Press, 1999. The essays collected here by Ortner, Stephen Greenblatt, Renato I. Rosaldo Jr. William H. Sewell Jr., Natalie Zemon Davis, George E. Marcus, and Lila Abu-Lughod where original published as a special issue of *Representations* 59 (Summer 1997).

Smart, Ninian. *Dimensions of the Sacred: An Anatomy of the World's Beliefs.* Berkeley: University of California Press, 1996.

Smith, Jonathan Z. *Imagining Religion: From Babylon to Jonestown.* Chicago: University of Chicago Press, 1982.

Tillich, Paul. *Theology of Culture.* New York: Oxford University Press, 1959.

Tweed, Thomas A. *Crossing and Dwelling: A Theory of Religion.* Cambridge, MA: Harvard University Press, 2006.

Religion and Culture in the Space of Politics

Introduction

The essays in the opening part of *Religion and Culture:* *Contemporary Practices and Perspectives* provide rich descriptions of how religion and culture shape social and political institutions. In this first space of politics and power, ritual practices are social performances that reenact and reinscribe powerful mythic narratives and symbols on a daily, weekly, monthly, or annual basis. Modern nation-states have ritual calendars that create and re-create social solidarity, identity, and unity by invoking the mythic origins of the nation and by providing annual events for collective redemption and renewal.

The integration of politics, religion, and culture is often clearest during the creation and maintenance of national institutions. Émile Durkheim argued in *The Elementary Forms of Religious Life* that a nation or society requires sacred symbols, myths, and rituals to bind people together. The political order is a symbolic order, and Durkheim provided a framework that would later help to understand the formation of religious nationalism. But he was not interested in an exclusivist religious nationalism. As an assimilated French Jew who early in his career had been involved in the development of a modern public educational curriculum in France, Durkheim was interested in advancing inclusive secular and national symbols—rather than specifically Catholic symbols—so that French Protestants, Catholics, and Jews might live together without the centuries'-old animosity, persecution, and warfare that had shaped their relationships for centuries.

The first chapters in this section take Durkheim's understanding of national sacred symbols as their starting point before extending them in different directions. Atalia Omer in chapter 1 compares the role of religion in nationalistic violence in the Middle East, the former Yugoslavia, and southern Asia before describing potential contributions that religions can make toward peacebuilding. In chapter 2 Jason Springs traces Robert Bellah's "civil religion" concept from the Puritans to Martin Luther King Jr. before describing the religious and cultural powers of national holidays and constitutional law. David Chidester examines in chapter 3 how some nineteenth-century theories of religion, from the colonial "contact zone," misrepresented fundamental aspects of Zulu religion and culture that were intended to provide orientation in response to colonial power. In chapter 4 Robert M. Geraci explores how science is involved in resistance to elitism. For many rural peoples, religions remain the primary providers of education and health care so that religious and cultural performances inculcate symbolic languages to be used in populist political movements. Religious opposition to contraception and evolution does not center on women's health or Charles Darwin's theory of natural selection but, as Geraci argues, expresses a desire for the freedom to choose one's own fate against the determination of powerful elites. Particularly in the cases of human cloning and eugenics, a fear arises that an anonymous minimum-wage, outsourced laboratory clerk or health-insurance-form handler will replace an all-powerful God. In the increasingly high-tech world of anonymous bureaucracies, individuals fear their loss of control and significance and sometimes contest the motivations of the wealthiest corporations and the lobbyists and scientists they support.

In chapter 5, Sarah W. Whedon begins her exploration of women with how women were involved in healing practices during the first decades of the Church of Jesus Christ of Latter-day Saints, or Mormons, before taking up issues of political power including menstruation, clothing, marriage, sex and contraception, motherhood, women's deities, money and property, food, household religious practices, and feminist theology. Finally, in chapter 6, Roger Friedland explores the role of men's and women's bodies, including sexuality and gender dynamics, as symbols in nationalist movements. Since 1965, urbanization and immigration have made cities increasingly diverse religiously. At the same time, the Reformation and Enlightenment values of individualism and utilitarianism have made public life more bureaucratic. In response to numerous and competing worldviews in a pluralistic city, people of faith often assert their power over the private sphere of marriage, sexuality, women, children, and the body where they feel more personal control. And yet, very private matters like medical decisions made between a woman and her physician can become national, public issues. The issue of abortion, for example, has become a litmus test within the American conservative movement.

In a world where powerful armies, corporations, scientific researchers, and health care providers are organized bureaucratically, an institutional imperative can put the survival of the institution, or personal profit, before the carrying out of its mission. For the modern citizen, the cultural and religious body situated in physical space becomes the primary source of power and political agency.

1

CONFLICT AND PEACEBUILDING

Atalia Omer

OVERVIEW

Arguably, the most audible expressions of religion are associated with social and political conflicts from civil wars and anticolonial wars of independence and with questions of immigration, toleration, and assimilation in liberal Western democracies. In all these instances, religions are often invoked to justify acts of violence and protest between and within nation-states. Examples include the controversy surrounding the publication of the cartoons of the Prophet Muhammad in the Danish newspaper *Jyllands-Posten* in 2005; the murder of the Dutch film director Theo Van Gogh in 2004 by a Muslim extremist in Amsterdam; the campaign against same-sex marriages (marriage equality) in the United States; the struggle between Sinhalese Buddhists and Tamils in Sri Lanka; Islamicization campaigns, and mobilization of ethnoreligious identities in the Sudan; the tragedy of September 11, 2001; suicide bombings in Palestine/Israel; and the veil controversy in France. These all exemplify the audibility of religion—whether in public debates about the character of the society, as in France

and the United States, or in the dynamics of violent conflict, as in Palestine/Israel, Sri Lanka, and the Sudan. Indeed, to varying degrees, religion sometimes constitutes an integral part of the practice of social protest and civil and international wars. Religion's role is especially obvious when it is invoked to justify acts of violence, such as suicide bombing, and the ritualized executions of such acts. But religion is also evident in generating and challenging conceptions of common identity, such as nationalism.

Because religion undoubtedly plays a role in the dynamics of conflict, it has become clear that religion and religious people (leaders and laypersons) may play a role in peacebuilding as well. This chapter therefore explores religious practices in peacebuilding or conflict transformation. Among other activities, the practice of religious peacebuilding involves engagement in interfaith dialogue, whereby religious individuals across national and ethnic divides discuss the roles of religion in conflict. Such interactions may be transformative in and of themselves, because they often help cultivate interpersonal relationships, challenge stereotypes and received narratives, and embolden a sense of common humanity. The term "religious peacebuilding" is also applied to describe the work of peacemakers whose motivation to act on behalf of victims and for the implementation of peace and justice derives from their particular understanding of a religious tradition. Likewise, the concept of "religious peacebuilding" may resonate with the activities of religious faith-based and/or non-governmental organizations working toward conflict transformation in various contexts. But to study the role of religion in the transformation of conflict, it is imperative to begin by recognizing and analyzing the role of religion in social and political conflict.

RELIGION IN CONFLICT

Clarifying the role of religion in public life and in the formation and reformation of political and social identities is key to understanding the role of religion in conflict and conflict transformation, or peacebuilding.

General Reflections: Is Religion a Cause of Conflict?

The presupposition of the "religious" as an agent of conflict and intolerance is indeed consistent with the basic assumption of an unrevised theory of secularism that assumes the "secular" to signal a neutral space in what the political philosopher John Rawls called "an overlapping consensus" of incompatible "comprehensive doctrines."[1] Thus the converse of this perception of public religion as intolerant and conflictual is the supposition that only the neutralization of religion and minimization of its influence on the political life of the community would curtail this insidious dimension of human history. Notably, the liberal secularist tradition, of which Rawls is the preeminent contemporary voice, was first articulated by John Locke and other

political philosophers of the Enlightenment on the backdrop of the bloody European wars of religion, and it has subsequently maintained a profound suspicion toward political and public expressions of religion. On the surface, this suspicion seems to be vindicated by the evidence of what came to be called "resurgent religion" in the post–Cold War era, but it represents an unrevised framework that does not account for the significant role that religion plays in the formation and reformation of the political in contexts of both peace and war. A more nuanced framework for the analysis of religion in conflict and peacebuilding underscores the public nature of religion and the incoherence of the thesis of governmental neutrality—incoherence most pronounced in zones of conflict defined by ethnoreligious national claims and objectives. This emphasis on the "publicity" rather than the "interiority" of religion suggests a conceptual critique of the normative assertions of the thesis of secularism, which in its unrevised form argues that modernity has necessitated the privatization and eventual disappearance of religion from the "public" or interchangeably "secular" space of social exchanges. Another variation of the discourse of secularism presupposes the values of individualism, liberties, and tolerance, among other hallmarks of the doctrine of modernity, as being ultimately grounded in "Judeo-Christian" roots, thereby feeding into an Orientalist worldview. Both narratives of secularism, according to political theorist Elizabeth Shakman Hurd, inform and delimit international relations theory and practice, and especially the framing of foreign policy with Muslim-majority countries.[2]

To understand the role of religion in peacebuilding, one needs to get a clear understanding of the role of religion in conflict. There are different ways to respond to the question concerning the role of religion in conflict. Pivotal to this inquiry, however, is recognition of the centrality of nationalist agenda. In other words, the analysis of the role of religion in conflict necessitates an exploration of how religious and national identifications interrelate and where they intersect in the ethos and perceptions of nationalist campaigns and mechanisms of socialization. The modern nation is intricately related to religion and culture and to other indices of identity. Benedict Anderson famously explains that the modern nation was *imagined* selectively out of its religious and cultural building blocks.[3] In deploying the notion and act of the imagination, Anderson clearly distinguishes himself from the eminent scholar of nationalism Ernest Gellner and from other Marxist analysts who studied the nation as an invention construed as a mechanism for generating social cohesion from above.[4] Although Gellner's view of nationalism betrays a Marxist functionalist understanding of the nation, Anderson's emphasis on the nation as being *imagined* out of the cultural and religious resources that preceded it shows important continuity and interrelatedness between religious and national conceptions of identity. With that idea, Anderson observes a critical paradox about modern nationalism: its concurrent modernity and perceived antiquity.

Importantly, what the nineteenth-century social theorist Max Weber famously identified as the "elective affinity" between religion, ethnicity, and nationality is not automatic, arbitrary, or inevitable. In his work *Faith in Nation,* which deals with the emergence of nationalisms in Western Europe, Anthony Marx concludes that the processes of erecting centralized state infrastructures, in the three cases of England, France, and Spain, necessitated a policy of a systematic exclusion of what he referred to as the "domestic other."[5] Often state officials capitalized on preexisting prejudices and even violent periodical practices, such as pogroms, as a mode of galvanizing a centralized control over the institutions of the budding premodern state. The exclusion of the domestic others, such as the Huguenots in France and the Jews and Muslims in Spain, implies the concurrent articulation of the nation as aligned with a particular religious or ethnic identification. Notwithstanding these exclusionary origins of the modern nation-state, Anthony Marx argues for a necessary progression toward greater inclusivity, as manifested in Western models of democracy. He uses this argument to suggest that contemporary non-Western nation-states with obvious chauvinistic tendencies are not categorically different from Western liberal democracies but rather only developmentally tardy or at a different stage.

There are obvious problems with this view, not the least of which is its rather paternalistic presuppositions. Yet Marx's analysis brings into sharp contrast a few critical points relevant for the present discussion of religion in conflict and peacebuilding: (1) it relates to the connection between conceptions of nationhood and the construction and reconstruction of states and vice versa; (2) it highlights "power" as a crucial variable of analysis in any attempt to understand why certain conceptions of nationhood became dominant and ingrained in particular given contexts; (3) it illustrates how state infrastructures may indeed effect significant and transformative changes to the definition of membership in the nation; and (4) finally and most importantly for our discussion, Marx's historical study focuses on the instrumental role of religion in the construction of nations. Despite this recognition, his analysis intimates a modernist and unreconstructed position on secularism and liberalism that leads him to suggest a teleological progression from an initial reliance on exclusionary religious identities to the eventual diminishing relevance of religious identity as a factor of membership in the modern liberal nation-state.

In his *Chosen Peoples* and other works on nationalism, Anthony Smith, however, underscores the continuous and persistent role of religion in the formation and reformation of nationalism.[6] "Nationalism," according to Smith, is not a modern phenomenon, but a social consciousness whose roots go back to antiquity and to religious sources. Studying the three cases of Egypt, India, and the United States, Scott Hibbard explores the enduring relevance of religion to political practice and the articulation of national consciousness. Consistent with the already discussed critiques of the secularism thesis, Hibbard observes that, in the three cases he scrutinizes, despite its intentional marginalization in the 1920s during the height of secular ideologies, rather than diminishing in importance, religion (especially illiberal and conservative interpretations of it) has gained momentum.[7] Hibbard explains this phenomenon by looking at religion as "uniquely able to provide a moral sanction for political action."[8] Therefore, he concludes that rather than dichotomizing modernity with so-called fundamentalism, one needs to analyze the "resurgence" of religion as the development of thoroughly modern interpretations and embodiment of tradition, explicitly suited for modern political contexts.[9]

Drawing on the work of social theorist Max Weber, David Little similarly discusses the interrelation between conceptions of religion, ethnicity, and nationality as multidirectional and complex. In other words, a movement away from the exclusionary founding moments of modern nationalisms toward greater inclusivity does not constitute an inevitable move. Nor ought religion to become irrelevant or of a diminishing importance in the liberal secular state. This intricate and multivariable analysis of religion leads Little to a conclusion about the potential constructive role of religion in conflict transformation: to the same degree that religion cannot be singled out as a cause of conflict, it can similarly not be dismissed as irrelevant to conflict and peacebuilding.

> While I agree that defining religion as inherently violent is unsupportable, I disagree that no good use can be found for the concept. In fact, once we better understand what the idea of religion is good for, the more we can appreciate why the pejorative reading is so misguided. We can also better appreciate, I believe, why opposing "the religious" to "the secular" or to the "liberal nation-state," is similarly amiss. The correct conclusion is the rather unsurprising one that religion, properly identified and examined, *may or may not* cause violence; it all depends on the circumstances.[10]

Specific Cases: A Murder in Amsterdam and Murders in Hebron

Ian Buruma describes Mohammed Bouyeri, the murderer of Theo van Gogh, as a

> twenty-six-year-old Moroccan-Dutchman in a gray raincoat and prayer hat, [who] blasts the filmmaker Theo van Gogh off his bicycle on a dreary morning in Amsterdam. He shot him calmly in the stomach, and after the victim had staggered to the other side of the street, shot him several more times, pulled out a curved machete, and cut his throat—"as though slashing a tire," according to one witness. Leaving the machete planted firmly in Van Gogh's chest, he then pulled a smaller knife from a bag, scribbled something on a piece of paper, folded the letter neatly, and pinned it to the body with this second knife . . . . It was in fact a long rambling tract, written in Dutch with few quotations in Arabic, calling for a holy war against the unbelievers, and the deaths of a number of people mentioned by name. The tone was that of a death cult, composed in a language dripping with the imaginary blood of infidels and holy martyrs. The Dutch

is correct but stilted, evidence of the author's lack of literary skill perhaps, but also of several layers of awkward translation.[11]

This chilling description of the murder of Van Gogh points to the role of transnational Islam. It is indeed likely that Bouyeri's indoctrination and exposure to Islamist ideas happened via the Internet and was inspired by various cyber-circulated documented killings of the enemies of Islam.[12] But it also points to the murderer's marginalized social location in Dutch society, and it opens the discussion for complex socioeconomic and cultural exploration of the conditions that led to the execution of such an act of violence. The question that emerges most urgently is whether Bouyeri's allusion to Islam transforms this violent murder into a religious act.

Importantly, the justification of acts of violence through an allusion to biblical or religious warrants is not the domain of Islamists alone. Another example is Baruch Goldstein's massacre in the Cave of the Patriarch (known to Arab-Muslims as the Ibrahimi Mosque) in the West Bank city of Hebron in February 2004 during Ramadan and the Jewish holiday of Purim, which concurred that year. This was a brutal attack on Muslims who prayed at the mosque in the cave. Baruch Goldstein, an Israeli-American settler and member of the extremist Kach movement, opened fire on worshipers. According to Israeli reports, 29 Palestinians were killed and more than 125 wounded. The majority of Israelis and Jews the world over condemned the attack, explaining that such an act constituted a gross violation of Jewish ethics and values. But some sectors of the population began to celebrate Goldstein as a martyr for a cause. For instance, Rabbi Israel Ariel of Gush Emunim (the settlement movement for Greater Israel) eulogized Goldstein as follows.

The holy martyr Baruch Goldstein is from now on our intercessor in the Heavens. Goldstein didn't act as an individual: He heard the cry of the Land [of Israel] which is being stolen from us day after day by the Muslims. He acted in order to relieve that cry of the Land! . . . The Jews will inherit the Land not by any peace agreement but only by shedding blood.[13]

Authentic versus Inauthentic Religion?

The two murderous episodes instigated by Goldstein and Bouyeri bring into the foreground the question whether religion in those cases was the cause of violence or whether it was merely a rhetorical cloak. Because of the explosive rhetorical audibility of religion in conflicts of various natures, the question of the role of religion in conflict surfaced alongside attempts to locate a connection between religion and violence. Some analysts and observers, such as Charles Kimball in *When Religion Becomes Evil,* have rendered religion as a cause of conflict.[14] Other analysts have dismissed it as epiphenomenal, arguing that conflicts that seemed "religious" were *really* indicative of some other underlying cause. Still others have devoted their attention to whether specific religions are inherently more prone to produce violent behaviors than others. In particular, the principle and practice of jihad came into sharp scrutiny for lending itself to public expressions of xenophobia and intolerance in various public contexts. Arguably, in light of the events of September 11, 2001, and other instances of violence committed by Muslims, the Islamic notion of jihad has received disproportional attention, vindicating provocative statements such as "Islam has bloody borders," made by the late Harvard political scientist Samuel Huntington in his famous thesis of "The Clash of Civilizations."[15]

Some critics, such as Christopher Hitchens, who identify themselves as antireligion militants, draw a direct link between religion and violence and are eager to cite the destructive role of religion in various conflict zones around the globe.[16] Apologists of religion react to such accusations by insisting that manifestations of religious violence are in fact inauthentic and constitute aberrations of the true practice and teachings of the religion. Consequently, the Crusades and suicide bombings are classified as distortions rather than expressions of the correct, authentic, and "real" religious orientation."Real religion," it is stressed, is good and peaceful. For instance, in the aftermath of the al-Qaeda-instigated attacks on the World Trade Center and the Pentagon in 2001, King Abdullah II of Jordan said: "What these people stand for is completely against all the principles that Arab Muslims believe in."[17] Sheikh Mohammed Sayed Tantawi of the Al-Azhar mosque of Cairo similarly condemned the appropriation of Islam by extremist Islamists. Addressing a large gathering in 2003, Sheikh Tantawi argued along the same lines: "Extremism is the enemy of Islam. Whereas, jihad is allowed in Islam to defend one's land, to help the oppressed. The difference between jihad in Islam and extremism is like the earth and the sky."[18]

The Complex Role of Religion in Conflict: A Non-reductionist Approach

William Cavanaugh offers a poignant response to those who wish to single out religion as a cause of violence: "The myth of religious violence promotes a dichotomy between *us* in the secular West who are rational and peacemaking, and *them*, the hordes of violent religious fanatics in the Muslim world. *Their* violence is religious, and therefore irrational and divisive. *Our* violence, on the other hand, is rational, peacemaking, and necessary."[19] This conceptual confusion is the reason why religion has often come to be associated with conflict and intolerance and interpreted as an obstacle to peace and justice. This interpretation, Cavanaugh underscores, is incoherent because it depends on a confused and unrevised understanding of religion as absolutist, divisive, and irrational, precluding the possibility that "secular" institutions or ideologies may carry the same attributes and embody similar intensity. Such an oversight betrays an unproblematized view of the "religious" and the "secular" as binaries, a view that has been shown by such theorists as Talal Asad, Russell McCutcheon, Timothy Fitzgerald, and others as incoherent. Recognition of the imperative to problematize the unrevised interpretation of religion and secular as antinomies and appreciation of the interrelatedness of what social theorist Max Weber identified as the "elective affinity" between markers of identity—such as nationality, religion, culture, and ethnicity—constitute key elements in any attempt to analyze the role of religion and religious acts and individuals in conflict and peacebuilding. To begin investigating what religion has to do with conflict and peacebuilding, it is important to challenge dominant interpretations of religion as a matter confined to the domains of private belief and choice. Instead, it is imperative to recognize the complex interconnections among identity markers, such as religion, culture, nationality, and ethnicity, and how they play out in the daily life of individuals and groups.

Such analyses, which identify religion or culture as either a cause or a primary obstacle for conflict resolution and transformation, are reductionist because they overlook the complexity and multidimensionality of social phenomena. Another example of such a reductionist approach to the question of the role of religion in conflict is the critically influential "Clash of Civilizations" thesis previously alluded to, in which Huntington explains the eruption of conflicts in the aftermath of the Cold War as a function of essential incompatibility between what he classifies as Western and non-Western values and worldviews. Similarly, Mark Juergensmeyer, who has distinguished himself as a scholar of religious nationalism and terrorism, views religious nationalism as an ideology or worldview competing with the underlying worldview of the secular nation-state. For Juergensmeyer, religious and secular nationalisms constitute two incompatible "ideologies of order." Other theorists, such as the economist Paul Collier, identify economic motives and greed as the propelling forces of conflict, thereby rendering religion as an irrelevant variable for the analysis of conflict.[20] Yet other analysts of conflict view religion instrumentally, as a vehicle for mobilization on a mass level. Of course, viewing religion as a mobilizing and manipulative force still does not explain *why* the "religious" is so often capable of inciting people into action.

Religion and Nationalism

In his discussion of the conflict in the Bosnia and Herzegovina (B&H) region from 1992 to 1995, Michael Sells offers a poignant critique of the instrumental view of religion as a manipulator used by political elites.[21] He analyzes the use of religious symbols "to create, define, deny, and eliminate a religious other." He underscores that the "use of religious symbols is not necessarily a function of religious observance or commitment." But, he adds, "at some point the manipulator of the symbol becomes manipulated by the symbol. Those who start out using religious symbols instrumentally to gain power or other benefits end up becoming servants of those symbols psychologically."[22] What Sells means is that political campaigns that are based on the manipulation of religious symbols depend *socially* on perpetuating divisiveness (that derives from

rigid religious distinctions) in order to vindicate themselves. Such political campaigns also result in economic systems founded on acts of religiously framed ethnic cleansing and are designed to perpetuate a system that privileges one particular ethnoreligious group. Legally, the ethnoreligious campaign needs to continue selectively unleashing religious and cultural symbols that enable a legal defense and justification of gross violations of human rights and its engagement in illegal acts and war crimes. Hence, in the interest of furthering a political agenda, the manipulators of religious symbols become captive to such symbols.[23]

Sells explains that religious militant ideologies do not erupt onto the scene spontaneously, nor do they generate themselves. In fact, they reflect prolonged processes of intentional cultivation. In the case of B&H, he contends, "It took several years of instrumentalization by people like Franjo Tudjman in Croatia, Slobodan Milosevic in Serbia, and militants within B&H. These leaders instigated violence, used the media to create an atmosphere of fear, recalled past atrocities, and made blanket accusations about their imminent reoccurrence in order to generate the symbolic paradigms of conflict-identity."[24] Sells tells how Serb militants retrieved an ideology of "Christoslavism" that was born of Serb revolutionary engagement with Ottoman rule during the nineteenth century. This ideology of Serb Christoslavism is grounded in the narrative of the Serb Prince Lazar, who gained the status of a martyr as a result of his death at the Battle of Kosovo in 1389 against the Turks. In an effort to articulate Serb opposition to the Ottomans in the nineteenth century, the Battle of Kosovo came to be known as the "Serb Golgotha," making an obvious and emotive allusion to the supposed biblical site of the crucifixion of Jesus near Jerusalem. "Lazar," according to Sells's account, "was explicitly portrayed as a Christ figure in the art and literature, often surrounded by twelve knight disciples (one of whom gave the battle plans to the Turks), ministered by a Mary Magdalena figure."[25] These portrayals of the Battle of Kosovo were revived in the 1980s, upon the crumbling of Yugoslavia. Sells tells the story of the official six hundredth anniversary of the death of Prince Lazar, celebrated in a passion play in 1989 at the actual site of the fateful Battle of Kosovo. Since the construal of Christoslavism in the nineteenth century, the commemoration of the martyrdom of Lazar has become the focal point of St. Vitus Day. In the following excerpt, Sells contends that the commemorative event of 1989 culminated a process of reconceptualizing Serb nationalism and provided a framework for militancy.

> Various elements then flowed together at the 1989 Vidovdan commemoration. Primordial time (the Serb Golgotha), sacred place (the Serb Jerusalem), historical memory (the horrors of World War II), and contemporary fear (the alleged Albanian genocide against Serbs in Kosovo) merged to create a discourse of fear and anger more powerful than any of its parts. Through that period and after it, the Serb Orthodox Church has been united in supporting the religious national project.[26]

One can identify similar dynamics on the Croatian front. The International Criminal Tribunal explained the Croatian policy of "ethnic cleansing" of non-Catholic communities in Herzegovina as a function of a criminal conspiracy instigated by Tudjman (the president of Croatia), Gojko Susak (his defense minister), and Mate Boban (a leader of what is now B&H). Sells argues that the criminal indictment needs to be supplemented with an account of how religious leaders and symbols contributed to generating divisiveness and ethnoreligious conflicts. This amounted to distinguishing among three different groups and construing them as ancient and inevitable enemies. It was also translated into practice: killings, expulsions, and demolition of the others' cultural heritage, including sacred spaces.[27]

Sells concludes that "religious symbols were used not only to define and deny the religious other but also to homogenize the religious self. Croat Catholics who refused to participate in the militia were persecuted or marginalized. Croat Catholic identity was purified by the myth of stable Catholic identity over the centuries (as opposed to historical reality of continual conversions back and forth throughout the history of B&H), by the construction and purification of a Croatian language (as opposed to the common language in the area that had been known as Serbo-Croatian), and by the destruction of evidence of Catholic Croat participation with Islam, Judaism, and Serb Orthodox in the construction of a common civilization."[28]

The case of B&H is by no means unique. Other zones of conflict have exhibited similar patterns and dynamics that resulted in intentional policies that promote ethnoreligious supremacy. This is the case in Sudan's systematic Islamicization and Arabization campaigns, instigated by the Khartoum government. Likewise, in Sri Lanka, the *Mahavamsa*—a Pali text that articulates the vocation of the Sinhala people as the torchbearers of Buddhist teaching—is likewise interpreted to reify the contemporary Sinhala-Tamil dispute. Eva Neumaier explains that such texts as the *Mahavamsa* show "an interdependency between the continuation of the Buddhist teaching, a certain ethnic group, and the land this group occupies whereby they also erase the existence of other ethnic and religiocultural communities within the same spatialhistorical continuum. Thus, these texts provide a rhetoric that offers itself as a voice of ethnoreligious fundamentalism."[29]

Exclusivist interpretations of the nation and perceptions of an existential threat to the group may lead to acts of spontaneous violence, such as the bombing of such religious spaces as mosques, or structural violence, such as the systemic discrimination of minority groups. Although the root causes of ethnoreligious national conflicts are not generally theological or religious, religious spaces tend to transform into highly charged zones that are easily ignited. It is no accident that conflicts often erupt in religious spaces and on religious occasions (such as the previously described commemorations of the death of Prince Lazar). For example, Ariel Sharon's provocative visit to the Dome of the Rock, on the eve of the Jewish New Year in 2000, ignited the emergence of the Second Intifada, or Palestinian uprising, against Israeli military occupation of the Palestinian territories. Sharon legitimized his visit on the ground that the disputed space occupied a crucial location in the narrative of Jewish national self-determination, and thus he claimed, despite protests, to have a natural right to undertake his symbolic visit. Although Sharon's visit did not cause the eruption of the Second Intifada, it provided an explosive occasion that ignited a cycle of devastating violence; and although the sacredness of the Dome of the Rock is relevant to both Palestinian and Israeli conceptions of nationhood, it would be misleading to reduce the various complexities of the conflict to a discussion over theological divergences. Palestinian youths who went to the streets in response to Sharon's provocative visit would not be pacified, nor would subsequent Palestinian struggles be alleviated, through a theological settlement.

However, the fact that such spaces as the Dome of the Rock, or such occasions as St.

The Dome of the Rock atop Temple Mount in Old Jerusalem. Holy to Jews as the site of two ancient temples, the structure atop the Temple Mount has also been a religious site for Islam since the seventh century. (Credit: Wikimedia Commons: http://upload.wikimedia.org/wikipedia/commons/3/34/Temple_Mount_and_Dome_of_the_Rock.jpg)

Vitus Day, can generate explosive acts of violence suggests their relevance to the dynamics of conflict. In some instances, national (secular) spaces, such as the site of the Battle of Kosovo, transform into spaces of sacred significance because of their location in a sacred narrative of belonging. Such sacred national spaces may be as explosive as explicit religious spaces such as the Dome of the Rock. Helpful for this discussion is John Paul Lederach's productive distinction between what he calls an *episode* of conflict and its *epicenter*. The transformation of conflict, Lederach argues, necessitates addressing both the conflictual "episode" and the underlying patterns of relationships that generated it.[30]

Another pertinent example of the intricate relation between religious symbols and chauvinistic interpretations of nationhood is the cultivation by Hindu nationalists of the ideology of Hindutva ("Hinduness"). Hindutva conflates Indian and Hindi identities and thus treats them as synonymous. The implication of this ideological stance is a discriminatory and bellicose approach toward non-Hindi Indians. The concept of Hindutva was first developed by the poet Vinayak Damodar Savarkar (1883–1957), as a rhetorical counter to British colonialism. Subsequent Hindutva formulations came to view India as both a homeland and a holy land, where Christian and Muslim inhabitants are antagonistically categorized as foreigners or invaders.[31] This exclusivist and chauvinistic ideological position, which has been reflected to a certain degree in the platforms of the Bharatiya Janata Party (BJP), carries profound implications for the practice of Indian Hindu nationalists. In 1992, such rhetoric and socialization onto a notion of Hindi supremacy undergirded the tragic demolition, by Hindutva-inspired activists, of the Babri mosque in Ayodhya in the state of Uttar Pradesh. Hindu nationalists legitimated this act of demolition by arguing that the

mosque had been built on and thus violated the site of the birth of the Hindu god Rama. Hindutva draws legitimization for the engagement in violent acts from the Bhagavad Gita's stories of revenge and killing.

Likewise, Jewish settlers in the West Bank legitimize their occupation of Palestinian land and the displacement of Palestinians from their homes through an appeal to the biblical promise of the land to Abraham and the Israelites. To a certain degree, secular Zionism has drawn its legitimacy—as a national project and as a movement of colonization—from the biblical past, as it had reverberated for millennia in the memories, prayers, histories, and cultures of Jews in the diasporas. The words "next year in Jerusalem," recited by the religious Jew, resonate powerfully in the popular Jewish imagination, and the possibility of fulfilling this aspiration of return is nothing less than the fulfillment of a messianic moment. Accordingly, the settlement of the land of Palestine was described as a "return" to the land, and, as such, in the eyes of secular Zionists, it was a redemptive return—one that redeemed the passive character of the diasporic Jew through a process of political self-determination.

Even though the dominant Zionist paradigm has explained this act of return and ingathering of the exiles in the land and the establishment of the modern Israeli nation-state in secular terms—as amounting to the normalization of the Jewish people (making it into a nation like any other nation)—it has nonetheless (not forgetting Smith, Anderson, and Marx's analyses of the role of religion in nationalism)—remained intricately linked to the religious imagination, as a resource for both legitimization and mobilization. When the possibility of settling the Jews in alternative territories, such as Uganda, was dismissed by the Zionist Congress, it was because, for the Zionist movement to reach a mass momentum and popular support, the territory of destination had to be Palestine, a place that has resonated so powerfully in the Jewish popular imagination. This process of normalization is reflective of the internalization of the prevalent anti-Semitic treatment of Jews as a problem and Jewish life as "sickly" in the Europe from which Zionism had emerged as a movement for a national self-actualization. The normalization entailed reinterpreting the theological concepts of return and the ingathering of the exiles in the land of Palestine as events to occur in historical rather than metahistorical time and as a human rather than as a messianic enterprise.

Israeli secularism reinterprets the theologically laden concepts of return and redemption in the land to mean a physical redemption from an existential threat and a history of recurrent prosecutions, as well as a reasserting of full Jewish personhood through a political self-determination. And it reads its Jewish identity as a "cultural" or "ethnic" one. Nevertheless, religious Zionism has reclaimed what it has interpreted as the full theological implications of the Zionist doctrine. Following the events of the War of 1967, in particular, which brought about the occupation of the West Bank and the Gaza Strip, as well as the eventual annexation of East Jerusalem to the Israeli state, religious Zionism has gained saliency. The biblical commandment to settle the land, especially the sacred spaces of Judea and Samaria, has overridden all the other commandments of Judaism. Religious Zionists have perceived their reality as constituting an extraordinary and messianic time, and thus acts of violence, including the displacement of the indigenous Palestinian population, may be vindicated. The cases of Serb and Croat nationalism, the religious Zionist settlement movement, and that of Hindu nationalism illustrate how perceptions of nationalism influence the behavior of nationalists and how the selective interpretation

of the resources of religion and tradition may lead to militant violent acts. Most pertinently, we may identify how the framing and perception of territory as a holy land—to which one has birthrights—legitimates one's attempt at reclaiming that land (regardless of the facts on the ground or others' possibly contradictory claims). Such a profound sense of ownership inspires and validates acts of violence. Notably, the sacralization of territory and its positing as unique, cherished, and worthy of sacrifice are integral features of any form of nationalism—be it French, American, or Zionist. The difference among those instances of nationalism is merely a matter of gradation.

The view of the land as a sacred territory, with unambiguous conceptions of ownership, is closely related to ethnoreligiocentric interpretations of citizenship and membership in the polity. It implies a partial treatment of one group on all levels of sociopolitical and economic life. This inequity entails policies that also privilege the symbols and narratives of one group over and against the collective identities of other inhabitants of the land. Even though the religious dimensions of national identity may be sublimated and secularized, particular interpretations of the resources of religion clearly may provide impetus for engagement in ultranationalist activities, such as the settlement of the Palestinian territories occupied in 1967 and the deadly and violent attacks in India.

The observation earlier of the persistent role of religion in the formation and reformation of conceptions of the nation suggests, however, that there is nothing qualitatively different about explicitly religious interpretations of nationalism. Instead, religious and secular forms of nationalism ought to be viewed and analyzed along a continuum. In the case of Israel, religious concepts, such as return and redemption, and religious narratives, such as the ingathering of the exiles in the land, underscore the idea that, rather than labeling religion as a cause of violence, clashing with the secular liberal worldview of benign nationalism, it is of great importance to articulate first of all how religion and/or group-specific narratives interrelate with nationalist agenda and, second, to determine the possibility of reframing or reconceptualizing this interrelation in the interest of greater peace and justice. One way of stressing this point is to analyze why critiques of an existing regime often draw on religious currency, as in the cases of the Israeli Shas party and the Muslim Brotherhood in Egypt. The argument is that the more chauvinistic the perception of one's claims and narratives is, the greater the potential for violent acts and the greater the likelihood that such acts will be legitimized through appeals to religious symbols, vocabularies, and narratives.

This point is relevant to our discussion because it indicates, first, a complex understanding of the role of religion in conflict. The view of nationalism and religion as intricately connected lends itself to a nonreductionist framework of analysis: religion is not dismissed simply as epiphenomenal or rendered as a cause of conflict in its rejection of the secular state and secular values. But, rather, religion bears directly and immediately on the daily practice of members of the nation, as illustrated in our brief exposition of Hindutva and the theology of Jewish settlers and, to lesser but still important degrees, in the so-called secular interpretation of the *nation*. This is especially the case when national identity is defined primarily in terms of a specific ethnicity or religion, as in Serbia, Croatia, Israel, Sri Lanka, or Sudan.

Even though, in the case of the Israeli settlers, religion is explicitly cited as a resource for the justification of violent acts—that may be understood as an extraordinary necessity to respond to perceptions of an extraordinary time

(messianic time)—nationalism also inspires and necessitates elaborate ritual practices that generate a sense of social cohesiveness in ordinary time. Michael Billig, for instance, coined the term "banal nationalism," which denotes the indispensable role of sublimated everyday practices and images, such as that of the national flag. Benedict Anderson discusses the role of museums and war memorials as sacred national places of pilgrimage. Homi Bhabha discusses the ritualistic reenactment of heroic moments in the nation's history—all these venues provide modes of socializing and instilling certain attitudes and perceptions in the very sense of selfhood of individual members of the society.

Often such attitudes and overarching conceptions of membership are analyzed as "civil religion." Next, we explore how and why the networks of groups, such as the Muslim Brotherhood and Shas, may challenge how cultural and religious resources are utilized in the construction of civil religion and may offer alternative formulations.

Religion and Social Protest

The preceding discussion of the interrelationship between conceptions of nationhood and religious markers of identification exemplifies the role of religion in the construction of modern nationalisms. Because religion has constituted an instrumental aspect of nation-making, it might, unsurprisingly, also play an important role in challenging the premises of an existing nation-state and in affecting its practices. The language of protest against the structures and authorities of the secular modern nation-state thus often assumes and draws on religious vocabularies. This is true in the case of the Muslim Brotherhood in Egypt. The Brotherhood has articulated a clear critique of Egyptian secularism by confronting the selective and instrumental use of

Islam in the construction of Egyptian nationalism by the secularist elites and by providing social services and a network of support for impoverished strata that had frequently been overlooked by the authorities. Islam therefore has provided resources for articulating grievances and a language of protest and critique of the excesses and injustices identified as endemic to a regime that nominally claims an Islamic identity. Furthermore, the network of mosques and community centers has enabled institutional organizing and the building of a support system, providing services to sectors of the society that secular governments have overlooked. This model has been replicated in other contexts, where the resources of religion provide the main currency for counterhegemonic critique and where the institutional infrastructure and spaces of religious communities lend themselves to organizing and mobilization of protest as well as to the implementation of social services.

Frequently, the charitable networks of religious institutions provide social services when governmental infrastructures fail to deliver. In Israel, the case of the educational network of the Shas political party mirrors the model of the Egyptian Brotherhood. Although it is financed by the Israeli government, the party runs its distinct and separate educational system, where it incubates loyalties to a particular sectoral identity and cultivates a potentially subversive social force. Shas is a rabbinically led mass movement that runs on an ethnic ticket, promoting the interests and grievances of Mizrahi Israeli Jews (Israelis who can trace their ancestry, prior to the establishment of the modern state of Israel, to Arab and Islamic countries). The two cases of the Brotherhood in Egypt and of the Shas network in Israel illustrate the processes of what may be called countersocialization, which may result in the eventual transformation of the status quo in their respective societies. This process of

counter-socialization involves the centralization of the religious life over and against the secularist values of the mainstream. In both instances, the movements challenge their respective regimes' ambiguous commitment to a secular nationalism that draws selectively on religious and cultural allegiances and effects change in social attitudes toward religion and politics.

This process of countersocialization occurs in a space that the Israeli historian Emmanuel Sivan calls "the enclave culture." Sivan explains that the ubiquity of secular political systems and societal values generates, in certain religious communities, a sense of being exiled in one's own lands. He cites, for instance, a verse from a popular American Protestant revival hymn— "stranger[s] here, within a foreign land"—the notion of being in "a new Babylonian exile" (the words of the reconstructionist thinker Gary North); and the declaration by an Indian Muslim, Maulana Maududi, and of the Egyptian Sayyid Qutb, of secular Islamic nationalisms and societies as constituting a state of *jahiliyya*, referring to the state of ignorance in pre-Islamic pagan Arabia.[32] In the 1980s, the notion of being exiled in one's own home also comes to the fore in Islamic contexts: Islam is declared to be "'in exile (*ghurba*) in its own lands,' much like it was in Arabia when Muhammad had to flee pagan and hostile Mecca for Medina."[33] Then, just as in the case of Muhammed's *hijra*, or exile, to Medina, the contemporary Muslim also needed to withdraw into the social enclave. This space also distinguishes itself from the broader society linguistically and often exhibits a particular dress code, such as the one observed in Jewish Haredi (orthodox) communities, for instance.

Although the Brotherhood and the Shas party may be classified as domestic agents for domestic transformation of the society and the role of religion therein, religious movements, individuals, and ideas may affect the dynamics of international conflict as well. Often, intra-national configurations and questions of social justice correspond with the patterns of international conflict. In a study of the cases of Sudan/Nigeria, Israel/Palestine, Lebanon, Tibet, and Sri Lanka that were undertaken under the auspices of the US Institute of Peace, ethicist and scholar of international conflict David Little identified a correlation between an ethnocentric or religio-centric definition of citizenship and nationality and a proclivity to engage in violent conflicts. In other words, the more state practices are exclusivist and illiberal, the more the likelihood for violent conflict increases. One way to measure the degree of exclusivity of a nation-state is to study its treatment of religious and cultural minorities. Hence, despite the essential illiberality of the institution of the modern nation state, some instances of nationalism exhibit greater illiberality than others. Often, as in the case of Serbia and Croatia, national exclusivity is articulated through a chauvinistic interpretation of religious and cultural memories and traditions.

The point stressed in our previous discussion of the social phenomenon of nationalism is that nationalism—even in its secularist variety—does not only constitute an analogue to religion (a civil religion) but is also continuously (yet to varying degrees of intensity) interconnected with the religious, with the ethnic and cultural imagination, and with identity indices and memories. This is especially the case in contexts where national identity is defined primarily through ethnoreligious claims, such as those underscored in the ideologies of Zionism, Christoslavism, and Hindutva. So far, the focus of this chapter has not been the benign, conservative, and banal practices designed to socialize the members of a nation-state into a general conception of the good but rather the violent and militant interpretations of nationalism and the types of action that they may entail.

RELIGION AND PEACEBUILDING

Because the complex role of religion in conflict is now underscored, let us turn to a discussion of the role of religion in peacebuilding and conflict transformation.

The Ambivalence of the Sacred

Indeed, religious vocabularies, narratives, and claims have been associated with violent conflicts around the world. Yet religious teachings and religious authorities and individuals have constituted a central, although overlooked aspect of the practice of peacebuilding and conflict transformation. This observation that religion may be not only a factor in conflict, but also a possible source for conflict transformation and peacebuilding, is clearly articulated in Scott Appleby's work *The Ambivalence of the Sacred*.[34] According to Appleby, religion can inspire militant violence and nonviolence to similar degrees of intensity. A developing field of works on the role of religion in peacebuilding agrees with this thesis of the ambivalence of the sacred, and this study undertakes efforts to retrieve resources within various traditions that could inspire peaceful actions and provide an impetus for peacebuilding and reconciliation. The field of religious peacebuilding focuses on the retrieval of such resources from within particular traditions that may affect societal change and conflict transformation. For example, some analysts, such as Mohammed Abu Nimer, articulate a tradition of nonviolent problem-solving in Islam as well as study the efficacy of the practice of interfaith dialogue as a venue for conflict transformation, especially in the Middle East.[35] The practice of interfaith dialogue has entailed the creation of spaces that are conducive for different religious individuals to express how their various interpretations of religion relate to ethnoreligious national conflicts. Scholars such as

Lisa Schirch focus on the transformative potential of rituals involved in efforts to mediate conflicts. Schirch underscores the importance of ritual and symbol in the practice of peacebuilding itself. She argues that "ritual both marks and assists in the process of change. It confirms and transforms people's worldviews, identities, and relationships with others."[36] She adds that "both socializing and transforming rituals are needed for peacebuilding. All cultures have existing, traditional rituals for building relationships, limiting violence, and solving problems. While these traditional rituals often are socializing and preserve the status quo, sometimes peacebuilders can help revive or draw on existing rituals within a culture that can help set the stage for transformational peacebuilding activities and processes."[37] Ritual in peacebuilding can accordingly facilitate the reframing of problems, transform of worldview, identity, relationships, and social structures; generate joint identities that bridge divisiveness at the heart of conflicts; and rehumanize people.[38] Religious people and traditions can play a significant role in such processes. This insight also undergirds the vision and practice of the Interfaith Youth Core, founded by Ebo Patel. This movement focuses on cooperation among people of different faiths and traditions in working toward the common good, and on the capacity of young people to lead the way in a multicultural context such as the North American one. Patel, as suggested in an article in the *New York Times*, views his project of interfaith cooperation as an antidote to the divisiveness and radicalism that may also be attributed to the ethos and realities of multiculturalism, with its often characteristic ghettos and segregated communities.[39] A more global outlook on the question of religion, conflict, and peacebuilding is attempted in an important work by Monica Duffy Toft, Daniel Philpott, and Timothy Shah. In their *God's Century: Resurgent Religion and Global Politics*, the authors empirically study the role of religious actors in conflict and peacebuilding. They conclude that religious actors are "back" and are indeed crucial for setting political agendas worldwide. The authors further underscore that the degree of institutional separation from political structures correlates with the ability of religious actors and institutions to facilitate processes of peacebuilding and conflict transformation (especially in moments of post-mass-atrocity).

Religion and the Reinterpretation of Resources: Specific Examples

Religion may be viewed as an important factor in peacebuilding and conflict transformation on three critical levels. First, it motivates and inspires people to act in a certain way that promotes peace and nonviolence. Second, its institutional infrastructures can lend themselves to grassroots organizing and to cooperation with other nongovernmental networks. Likewise, the prestige of religious leaderships and lay actors may bestow a certain aura of legitimacy on political and institutional processes of postconflict reconciliation and healing. Third, religion and tradition provide ample resources for reinterpreting ethnoreligious definitions of nationhood that result in exclusionary and discriminatory state practices and nonstate aggressions as well.

HINDUISM

Rajmohan Gandhi discusses the resources for peacebuilding found within Hinduism. He explains that the Hindu teachings in the Bhagavad Gita may be interpreted in a bellicose manner, emphasizing the rigid boundaries between antagonistic identities, but also in a manner that enables transcending those boundaries. The Hindu teachings tell the story of the warrior Arjuna, who is convinced by the Krishna to deemphasize the self and personal gains and subsequently engage in fighting out of a selfless duty. Although the Gita has provided grounds for the legitimization of the caste system in India and of the ideology of Hindutva, along with the Vedas and the Upanishads, it has also supplied resources—such as the notions of *ahimsa* ("nonviolence"), *kshama* ("forgiveness"), and *shanti* ("peace")—for nonviolent struggles aimed at the transformation of underlying injustices. For example, the *Atharva Veda* recites the devastation of wars and an aspiration for reconciling with the stranger.

Another source of reconciliatory inspiration is found in the person of Asoka, who ruled India in the third century BCE and who struggled with the consequences of warfare. Suanada Y. Shastri and Yajneshwar S. Shastri explain that "the concept of *ahimsa* in Hindu tradition, includes two ethical ideals: one is the pursuit of the good of humanity (*lokahita*) and the other is devotion to the good of all living beings and the environment (*sarvabhutahita*)."[40] The Aitereya Upanishad stresses the unity of all existence and underscores the importance of overcoming the "sense of duality or separateness" that is at the root of "hatred and violence." "The essence of the Vedantic notion is that the Brahman, the 'pure-consciousness,' is inseparable from its manifestations. To hurt or violate any creature or object in nature is to hurt or violate Brahman itself. This notion of fundamental sameness is the basis for nonviolent action towards all."[41] Likewise, the Hindu epic of the Mahabharata explains the principle of *ahimsa*: "Action which is against one's own desires should also not be done to others. One should never do that to another which one regards as injurious to one's own self. Therefore, one should treat all others as one's own self."[42] Efforts for reconciliation and conflict transformation also draw on Indian Bhakti poetry, which emerged in the fifteenth

century. This genre of Indian poetry, according to Rajmohan Gandhi, emboldens "Hinduism's reconciling, egalitarian, and practical strands. Announcing that Hindus and Muslims worshipped the same God, who valued character more than caste and conduct more than ritual, this poetry fosters Hindu-Muslim accommodation at the grass roots. Loved to this day . . . Bhakti poetry continues to describe the Other as a soul of equal value. Activists for pluralism and peace tap regularly into it."[43]

One celebrated case is exemplified by Mohandas Karamchand Gandhi's nonviolent resistance to British colonialism and proactive encouragement and respect of India's pluralistic landscape. Gandhi's interpretations of the resources of the tradition are antithetical to those central to Hindutva and to the resultant claims for Hindi supremacy. To this effect, Rajmohan Gandhi exclaims: "Gandhi may also be said to have helped liberate Hinduism from the Indian earth. Offering the exact opposite of the 'homeland-holy land' thesis, he helped make Hinduism a matter of the soul rather than of soil, something from India but not chained to India."[44] Gandhi's interpretation of the resources of Hinduism underpinned the basic commitment of the Indian constitution to equality, regardless of religion or caste. Shastri and Shastri explain that "for Gandhi, *ahimsa* meant a transformation of the heart that would result in the freedom of his country and the creation of a casteless society."[45]

The peace scholar and activist David Cortright discusses the immense transnational impact that Gandhi had exerted on the US peace movement. He writes in *Gandhi and Beyond: Nonviolence for an Age of Terrorism*: "The unique approach of Gandhi was his emphasis on mass action. . . . It was Gandhi who discovered in South Africa and India that masses of people could engage in organized nonviolence.

By demonstrating the power of collective disobedience as a force for political change, he turned mass noncooperation into an instrument of political struggle against oppression."[46] Gandhi's legacy has also exerted profound influence on the religious pacifist community: the Quakers, Mennonites, and Brethren. "These pacifist churches," Cortright comments, "were naturally attracted to Gandhi and his use of nonviolence as a means of social change for justice."[47] The transferability of Gandhi's philosophy of nonviolence to different political and religious contexts points to the internal diversity of religious traditions, as well as to the inspiring and motivating force that one's religious orientation can play in generating a mass movement of change.

BUDDHISM

Buddhist teachings also lend themselves to the practice of nonviolent resistance and to an engagement in the processes of conflict transformation and peacebuilding. Christopher Queen notes that among the many resources that Buddhism offers for nonviolent forms of peacemaking are the Four Noble Truths (Pali, *ariya sacca*), which underscore the demand to refrain from inflicting pain on other living beings (the principle of *ahimsa*); *brahmaviharas,* or the practice of compassion; *anatta,* or the doctrines of selflessness; *paticcasamuppada* (interdependence); and *sunyata* (nondualism); as well as the *bodhisattvas,* or the paradigm of enlightened beings who also liberate others from sufferings; the *cakravartin,* or "wheel-turners"; and the *dhammaraja,* or moral leaders who conquer minds and hearts by their virtues rather than physical force.[48] The *Sutta Nipata*—one of the earliest records of Buddhist literature—tells the story of how the Buddha transformed the bellicose meaning of the "wheel-turner," a symbol associated with Indra (lord of the gods who is purported to had

conquered the universe with his war chariot), to a "metaphor of nonviolence—a Peace Wheel."[49]

Like other Indian religions, Buddhism emphasizes the individual dimension of peace. The social ramifications are rendered secondary and dependent upon the process of individual transformation. Eva Neumaier contends that the karmic logic in classical Buddhism may inhibit social and political activism and constitute an obstacle for the role of Buddhism in conflict transformation. Neumaier expresses this problem with urgency: "The tendency to see social problems only as the result of karma, and, thus, to be addressed exclusively within the realm of individual responsibility, seems to have been one important obstacle for Buddhist societies in recognizing inequality, poverty, social strife, and war as moral obligations awaiting concrete solutions."[50] Furthermore, the Buddhist understanding of peace as primarily a "mental quality to be cultivated through meditation and not as a social and ethical responsibility is one of the obstacles that prevented traditional Buddhist institutions and their members from recognizing the potential of Buddhist ethics for building harmony and peace between different social groups and nations."[51]

Although the teachings of the Buddha have viewed karma as profoundly individual and have focused on the attainment of personal enlightenment through a process that entailed an act of withdrawal from society, a thread within Buddhism called "engaged Buddhism" has underscored the social importance of these teachings. Queen relates that "many engaged Buddhists have come to believe that much suffering in the world, particularly of the kind related to poverty, injustice, and war, is caused by the ignorance, cravings, and cruelty of persons other than the sufferer." He also underscores that engaged Buddhists practice nonviolence, generosity, lovingkindness, and selflessness—not in order to attain individual nirvana, but "out of the sense that their deep relatedness to others . . . obligates them to try to relieve that suffering, and that the net effect of such efforts will be a better world for all beings, human, animal, and vegetable."[52] Engaged Buddhism therefore focuses on the transformation of structural and cultural violence through public acts of protest and efforts of mass mobilization. Two celebrated Nobel Peace Prize laureates exemplify this form of engaged Buddhism and the reinterpretation or transformation of the ancient Indian tradition of sacred warfare: His Holiness the Dali Lama of Tibet and Aung San Suu Kyi of Burma.

The cultivation of the nonviolent orientation in Buddhism requires rigorous self-training that enables overcoming hatred, greed, and delusion. The underlying assumption is that the attainment of inner peace also effects outer peace. This process entails traversing the Eightfold Path—from the cultivation of *right views* to the establishment and internalization of foundational *ethical practice* that indicates an ability to apply the right attitude to daily situations. This is what the Vietnamese Zen master Thich Nhat Hanh means when he discusses the notion of "performing peace." Thich Nhat Hanh, one of the most celebrated representatives of "engaged Buddhism," explains in the following excerpt why he and other young Buddhists were compelled to risk and sometimes sacrifice their lives during the war in Vietnam.

> We tried to tell people our perception of the situation: that we wanted to stop the fighting, but the bombs were so loud. Sometimes we had to burn ourselves alive to get the message across, but even then the world could not hear us. . . . We wanted reconciliation, we did not want a victory. . . . Reconciliation is to understand both sides, to go to one side and describe the suffering being endured by the other side, and then to go to the other side

and describe the suffering being endured by the first side.[53]

Thich Nhat Hanh's form of Buddhism is rooted in an understanding of the danger of accepting any doctrine or ideology as absolute. The teachings of his order of Interbeing, or the Tiep Hien, stresses the infallibility of any truth claim, including Buddhist ones: "Do not think the knowledge you presently possess is changeless, absolute truth. Avoid being narrow-minded and bound to present views. Learn and practice nonattachment from views in order to be open to receive others' viewpoints."[54] Integral to Thich Nhat Hanh's notion of "engaged Buddhism" is the impulse to confront and transform social ills and conditions of injustice. Eva Neumaier explains that this approach suggests an alternative and a challenge to classical interpretations of the Buddhist imperative—to be liberated from all forms of attachment, in order to attain enlightenment or nirvana—this is the ideal of *arhant,* which may lead to social and/or political quietism and to a general acquiescence with forms of social injustice. In contrast, the ideal of *bodhisattva* underscores empathy and compassion with the other. A general commitment to transform the suffering of the other may subsequently imply a delay of individual nirvana and social activism.

Religion, Religious Institutions, and the Religious Peacemaker

JUDAISM

The Jewish rabbi and practitioner/scholar of conflict resolution Marc Gopin identifies the imperative to confront and therapeutically engage with the experiences of "loss" in the contexts of violent conflicts as one that is central to the practice of peacebuilding. He subsequently suggests integrating Jewish mourning practices into a theory of conflict resolution. Specifically, he introduces the Jewish ritual of *aveilus* as an integral dimension of the practice of conflict transformation. *Aveilus* is the word referring to the Jewish mourning ritual practice, which includes the reciting of special prayers and periodic active individual and collective/communal remembering of the loss. *Aveilus*, according to Gopin, may be applied as a framework for posttrauma healing. In his attempt to develop a distinctly Jewish approach to the role of religion in peacebuilding, Gopin cites the Golden Rule, as articulated in Leviticus 19:18: "Do not take vengeance, or a bear a grudge. And you must love your neighbor as yourself, I am the eternal God." Gopin interprets this verse to mean that self-love antecedes respect and love to the enemy, or the "other." Hence, the practice of conflict transformation may imply a profound introspective work on oneself. Such introspection, Gopin adds, is especially pertinent to process a history of being a minority that has been discriminated against and persecuted.

Gopin's active role as a religious voice of reconciliation in Palestine/Israel also underscored the imperative to honor the human being, regardless of the predicament in which one is entangled. This enabled him to engage in conversations with individuals labeled as the "enemy" and to recognize the other's sentiment of humiliation and loss.[55] In his attempt to devise a distinctly Jewish approach to peacemaking, Gopin extrapolates what he views as central rabbinic values: "involvement in the suffering of others," "taking responsibility to heal that suffering," a commitment to "social justice" as a religious commandment or *mitsvah*, "constructive social criticism," an awareness of "customs of civility," "discourage excessive wealth," and an internalization of a rabbinic understanding of conflict resolution as "a social *mitsvah*" (the *mitzvah* spelled out in Psalm 34:15: *bakesh*

shalom ve'radfehu, or "seeking peace and pursuing it").[56]

Another peacemaker in the Jewish-Israeli scene, Yehezkel Landau has internalized this explicitly Jewish orientation to the resolution or transformation of the conflict. He explains his maturation as a peacemaker as a consequence of his particular experience of Judaism: "I felt that, as a Jew who identified with the Zionist homecoming, as an interfaith educator, and as someone committed to seeking inclusive justice and the reconciliation of wounded, angry embittered hearts, I might be able to contribute something to the alleviation of people's suffering."[57] Judaism provides a motivating force and an inspiration for Landau's work as a peacemaker in Israel-Palestine. He examines his humanistic approach to Judaism against the realities on the ground, and this examination has compelled him to act in a certain way to promote peace—in an active manner through interfaith engagements and by opening a Jewish-Arab educational center.

For Gopin, Judaism provides this basic framework and motivation, but also, in devising his theory of conflict resolution, he draws on specific Jewish practices and traditions as concrete references for a contemporary adaptation for modern peacebuilding and conflict transformation. He contends that the rabbinic commitment to peacemaking draws on the figure of Aaron, the high priest and the brother of Moses. Aaron has come to symbolize the paradigmatic peacemaker in midrashic literature. For example, *Avot of Rabbi Nathan* reads,

> And thus when two men were in a conflict, Aaron would go and sit with one of them. He would say to him: My son, look at your friend . . . he is tearing at his heart and ripping his clothing. He says, "Woe is me, how can I lift my eyes and see my friend. I am ashamed before him, for it is I who wronged him. And

he [Aaron] would stay with him until he removed all of the jealous rage from his heart. And Aaron would then go to the other man, and say [the same thing]. And when the two would finally meet, they would hug and kiss each other.[58]

Gopin underscores the utmost importance of the mediating role played by Aaron to the process of conflict transformation and reconciliation. He writes: "A key element here is the humility and even self-abnegation of the intermediary. . . . Aaron prepares the parties for a crucial and difficult stage of conflict resolution or, more specifically, reconciliation, which usually involves swallowing a little pride. . . . This . . . is a crucial psychological juncture for conflict resolution."[59] Gopin consequently models the profile of the Jewish peacemaker after Aaron's paradigmatic example of empathetic active listening, patience, humility, and sacrifice.[60]

Yehezkel Landau has indeed internalized this Jewish orientation to peacemaking in Israel-Palestine, and, to this extent, his activities there may be classified as Jewish peacemaking. Jewish peacemaking is also guided by the challenge posed by the rabbinic sages in the midrashic literature: "Who is the strongest of the warriors? He who turns one who hates him into one who loves him."[61] Jewish peacemaking accordingly also centralizes the concept of *teshuva* ("repentance, return") as a framework for thinking and engaging in the process of reconciliation. Engaging in *teshuva,* in this context of conflict transformation, entails "a confession of wrongdoing" in addition to restitution.[62] The *teshuva* also involves "an expression of deep remorse (*harata*), a detailed confession, privately or publicly, of what one has done (*vidui*), and there is finally a commitment to change in the future, to the point of changing one's identity (*kabbalah le-haba*)."[63] The place of forgiveness in the Jewish context is intricately and necessarily linked to this process of repentance, or *teshuvah.*[64]

CATHOLICISM

Although the history of the Catholic Church is entangled with the interrelated histories of forced conversion, persecution of minorities, crusades, colonialism, and discrimination against homosexuals, Catholicism has provided ample resources for both lay and priestly confrontation against situations of injustice. For instance, Catholic social teachings translate to highly motivated religious activism and community and worldwide service by an organization such as the Catholic Peacebuilding Network (CPN). Catholic social teaching promotes "the pursuit of policies that serve the larger public community not just the Church . . . solidarity, the commitment to achieve justice for all people . . . subsidiarity, the dictum that central government should not decide what locally based bodies can determine for themselves . . . the preferential option for the poor, to lift up the condition of 'the least of these' . . . the priority and inviolability of human rights . . . a preferential option for the family as the basic social unit."[65]

David Cortright contends that this form of social Christianity—born out of Pope Leo XIII's encyclical *Rerum Novarum,* issued in 1891 and, as an outcome of the second Vatican Council (1962–1963), most pronouncedly spelled out in Pope John XXIII's encyclical *Pacem in Terris*—enabled framing active commitment to questions of social justice and war prevention as a central component of Catholic life. Vatican II gave an impetus for the emergence of liberation theology, especially prominent in Latin America, which calls for nonviolent action in defense of the poor.[66]

Another example of religion as a motivating force in the practice of peacebuilding is provided by José Inocencio Alas. This El Salvadoran Catholic priest was inspired by the Bible to preach and fight for agrarian reform to benefit the disenfranchised *campesinos* (the mass population of farm laborers). During the 1970s, Alas used the Bible as a main source for extrapolating a social-justice activism that he referred to as the "theology of community organization." A critical influence on Alas was the meeting, in 1968, of the Latin American Catholic bishops at Medellin in Colombia. There they attempted to reflect on the implications of Vatican II to their region. Alas's activism and strong passionate commitment to better the predicament of the poor in El Salvador resulted in his abduction and torture (most likely by the military) and in a life in exile.[67] Alas views his theology of peace as "the constant recreation of the harmony between God and humans, among human beings, and between human beings and the earth."[68]

Appleby cites the Community of Sant'Egidio as another example of a religiously inspired peacemaking network. The Italian community, established in the late 1960s by Andre Riccardi, was in part a response to the Second Vatican Council. For the founders of the community, "Vatican II's identification of the church's mission with the 'joys and hopes, grief and suffering' of all the people of the world, coupled with its exhortation to seek peace and justice as a Christian vocation, meant that the global ('universal') character of the Roman Catholic Church was not merely a historical contingency but a providential gift, enabling new faith communities to find allies, both Catholic and non-Catholic, in virtually every conflict setting imaginable."[69] Hence, the members of Sant'Egidio focused on social services for the poor and marginalized. The community's turn to international humanitarian work developed naturally as an integral part of its mission and interpretation of Vatican II. Sant'Egidio became an important and

recognized player in peacebuilding as a result of its involvement in the case of Mozambique, where, because its credibility was established, the community's members were trustworthy and respected mediators during the peace talks.[70]

Appleby explains that "Sant'Egidio practices nonpartisan social action that underscores its equanimity and commitment to the common good. The community does not seek political or economic power for itself. Heeding Pope John Paul II's call for Catholics to build up civil society, however, the members of Sant'Egidio reject any model of the church that legitimates Catholic withdrawal from public life."[71] Sant'Egidio's commitment to peacebuilding is grounded in the gospel injunction to "Love thy enemy." It does not argue against the jurisdiction of the state and its punitive rights, but, Appleby adds, the community believes that "the religious community operates from a radically different perspective in which all people are sinners and judgment belongs to God." "As Christians, we believe we are obliged to respect the human dignity of a Slobodan Milosevic no less than that of people far less culpable for bloodshed," Sant'Egidio's vice president, Andrea Bartoli, explains. "'Our goal is to understand his point of view—not approve or condemn—but also to search out the grain of reason and goodness we believe persists in even the hardest criminal.'"[72]

Religious Leadership and the Transformation of Conflict

So far we have looked at a few examples that demonstrate the role of religion as a motivating force in the practice of peacebuilding and conflict transformation. Another important dimension for our discussion is the prestige of religious leadership in postconflict healing processes. Appleby argues that, for the capacity of local religious leaders to affect the transformation of conflicts, they need to develop a strategy of peacebuilding that involves forging transnational partnerships and connections with other human-rights and nongovernmental organizations as well as global religious networks. One example of a local-transnational partnership is that of Buddhist peacebuilding in Cambodia. In 1993, Samdech Preah Ghosananda led monks, nuns, and laity in a monthlong march (known as the Dhammayietra or the Pilgrimage of Truth) from Siam Reap to the capital, Phnom Penh. At this time, the Dhammayietra took place at a critical turning point in Cambodian history, prior to the UN-sponsored elections of a new national assembly and government. The march proceeded through dangerous areas of mines and fighting. In this instance, the prestige of Ghosananda and the ability of the Dhammayietra to generate a sizable crowd bestowed added legitimacy to a political recovery process that was already in motion. The following year, participants in Ghosananda's march were caught in a firefight but persisted. Appleby comments that "the Buddhist peace marches were Ghosananda's response to nearly two decades of Cambodians slaughtering Cambodians, despite their shared religious and cultural heritage."[73] Future peacebuilding in Cambodia has built upon the legacy of the Dhammayietra: "For millions of Cambodians the Buddhist community, galvanized by Ghosananda's charismatic leadership, was a powerful source of hope that Cambodia might recover from a quarter century of violence and chaos, dating from the U.S. obliteration bombing during the Vietnam War."[74] A global Buddhist networking and Buddhist nongovernmental organization (NGO) partnership, however, transformed the Dhammayietra: "First, it evolved, according to the anthropologist Monique Skidmore, into 'a new cultural ritual of remembering', which, 'through the creation of new collective memories is allowing

some Cambodians to emerge from the culture of violence.' Second . . . the annual marches had become a force that 'generates solidarity actions by grassroots activists in other parts of the world."[75] The Dhammayietra has thus become a cornerstone for the emergence and cultivation of novel interpretations of membership in the community.

Another notable example of how the prestige of religious leadership affected the dynamics of peacebuilding is the case of South Africa. Partly as a result of the inspiring and charismatic figure of Archbishop Desmund Tutu, the concept of forgiveness became a central motif in the processes involved in the Truth and Reconciliation Commission (TRC) in South Africa. In the context of the TRC, religion has distinguished its role in peacebuilding. Archbishop Tutu underscored the theme of forgiveness, which he has grounded in Christian Scriptures as constituting a crucial dimension in healing the society. Importantly, however, Donald Shriver clarifies a significant distinction between a theological and a social/political notion of reconciliation. He argues that, theologically, reconciliation refers to the reconciliation of humankind and creation with God's self. In contrast, national and social reconciliation constitute a social process that may have some religious and theological tones but should not necessitate interpersonal forgiveness between victims and perpetrators.[76]

Tutu views the TRC venue as offering a "third way," or a compromise between a retributive approach to justice, as envisioned in the International Criminal Court (ICC), and the granting of total amnesty to war criminals and crimes against humanity. Audrey Chapman explains that "this 'third way' is significant for several reasons. Reconciliation usually requires coming to terms with the past, but doing so in a manner that will promote a new political culture and commitment to a shared future."[77] The South African TRC distinguished itself from other TRCs in that it underscored a concept of restorative justice over and against the notion of retribution. "The Christian atmosphere and discourse of the TRC, and particularly archbishop Tutu's frequent framing of issues in terms of repentance and forgiveness, was applauded by some South Africans, for whom Christian ideals had served as an ethical critique of apartheid, but it was distasteful for others." The latter category included commissioners and staff of the TRC, as well as some academics, victims, and victim advocates, who complained about "the imposition of a Christian morality of forgiveness." Regardless of the identified disclaimers, the TRC as structured and orchestrated by Archbishop Tutu exemplifies how religious ideas and individuals can participate in and influence the processes of peacebuilding and social healing and reconciliation.

As the examples of the role of the community of Sant'Egidio in Mozambique and Desmond Tutu in South Africa clearly demonstrate, religious leaders are potentially critical players in peacebuilding not only because of the often prestigious position that they occupy in a society and their established trustworthiness within the community, which is often reinforced by decades of commitment to social services (as practiced by the Muslim Brothers in Egypt for instance), but also because of the frequently intricate interrelation between the religious imagination and popular conceptions of membership in a nation or a society. Hence religious leaders can centrally participate in and contribute to the building of civil society and social institutions that foster cooperation and healing across social, ethnic, and religious divides. Indeed, the political scientist Ashutosh Varshney has concluded, in his study of Indian communal relations, that the formation of multireligious and multiethnic civic associations is crucial for conflict management.[78] Hence, Appleby asserts that "no truly effective methods of conflict resolution can ignore the locally rooted markers of identity over which religions hold sway. Culture, history, memory, authenticity . . . these are the currency of the local peacebuilder."[79]

In summary, this chapter has illustrated that religion plays important and complex roles in the dynamics of conflict and conflict transformation. The first part considers the relation between religion and violence by demonstrating the role of religion in the formation and reformation of collective identities, such as nationalism, and by identifying the place that religion occupies in national conflicts, as defined by ethnoreligious claims. The second part explores the potential role of religion and religious people in the transformation of conflicts and peacebuilding. It is argued that religion is a relevant factor for the analysis of conflict and peacebuilding because it provides motivation to act in a certain way (from leading nonviolent peace marches to murdering innocent worshipers in the Cave in Hebron), institutional frameworks for mobilization (churches, mosques), legitimacy (textual warrants justifying the occupation of a certain territory, the displacement of the "other"), and resources for reinterpreting chauvinistic nationalist claims.

GLOSSARY

Clash of Civilizations: An influential thesis articulated most famously by the political scientist Samuel Huntington, who envisions that, in the post–Cold War era, conflicts will be defined along civilizational lines. Huntington explains the eruption of conflicts in the aftermath of the Cold War as a function of essential incompatibility between what he classifies as Western and non-Western values and worldviews.

Ethnoreligious Nationalism: National identities that are defined through the invocation of exclusive interpretations of religion and ethnicity.

Hindutva: The Hindutva ideology, cultivated by Hindu nationalists in India, conflates Indian and Hindi identities and thus treats them as synonymous. The implication of this ideological stance is a discriminatory and bellicose approach toward non-Hindi Indians.

Religious Peacebuilding: Religious peacebuilding involves engagement in interfaith dialogue where religious individuals across national and ethnic divides discuss the roles of religion in conflict. It is also applied to describe the work of peacemakers whose motivation to act on behalf of victims and for the implementation of peace and justice derives from their particular understanding of a religious tradition.

Serb Christoslavism: An ideology cultivated and retrieved by Slobodan Milosevic and grounded in the narrative of the Serb Prince Lazar, who has gained the status of a martyr as a result of his death at the Battle of Kosovo in 1389 against the Turks.

FOR FURTHER READING

Abu-Nimer, Mohammed, Amal Khoury, and Emily Welty. *Unity in Diversity: Interfaith Dialogue in the Middle East.* Washington, DC: US Institute of Peace Press, 2007.

Almond, Gabriel, Scott Appleby, and Emmanuel Sivan. *Strong Religion: The Rise of Fundamentalisms around the World.* Chicago: University of Chicago Press, 2003.

Anderson, Benedict. *Imagined Communities: Reflections on the Origin and Spread of Nationalism.* New York: Verso, 1991.

Appleby, Scott. *Ambivalence of the Sacred: Religion, Violence and Reconciliation.* Lanham, MD: Rowman and Littlefield, 2000.

———. "Building Sustainable Peace: The Roles of Local and Transnational Religious Actors." In *Religious Pluralism, Globalization, and World Politics*, edited by Thomas Banchoff, 125–54. Oxford: Oxford University Press, 2008.

Buruma, Ian. *Murder in Amsterdam: The Death of Theo van Gogh and the Limits of Tolerance.* New York: Penguin, 2006.

Cavanaugh, William T. "Does Religion Cause Violence? Behind the Common Question Lies a Morass of Unclear Thinking." *Harvard Divinity Bulletin* 35, nos. 2 and 3 (2007).

Chapman, Audrey R. "Truth Commissions as Instruments of Forgiveness and Reconciliation." In *Forgiveness and Reconciliation: Religion, Public Policy, and Conflict Transformation*, edited by S. J. Helmick and G. Raymond, 257–78. Radnor, PA: Templeton Foundation Press, 2001.

Collier, Paul. "Economic Causes of Civil Conflict and Their Implications for Policy." In *Turbulent Peace: The Challenges of Managing International Conflict,* edited by Fen Osler Hampson, Pamella Aall, Chester A. Crocker, 143–62. Washington, DC: United States Institute of Peace Press, 2001.

Cortright, David. *Peace: A History of Movements and Ideas.* Cambridge: Cambridge University Press, 2008.

Gellner, Ernest. *Nations and Nationalism.* Ithaca, NY: Cornell University Press, 1983.

Ghandi, Rajmohan. "Hinduism and Peacebuilding." In *Religion and Peacebuilding,* edited by

Harold Coward and Gordon Smith. Albany: State University of New York Press, 2004.

Gopin, Marc. "Judaism and Peacebuilding." In *Religion and Peacebuilding*, edited by Harold Coward and Gordon Smith, 111–28. Albany: State University of New York Press, 2004.

Hanh, Thich Nhat. "Being Peace." In *Approaches to Peace: A Reader in Peace Studies*, edited by David P. Barash. Oxford: Oxford University Press, 1999.

Hitchens, Christopher. *God Is Not Great: How Religion Poisons Everything*. New York: Twelve, 2007.

Huntington, Samuel. "The Clash of Civilizations." *Foreign Affairs* (1993).

Kimball, Charles. *When Religion Becomes Evil*. San Francisco: HarperOne, 2008.

Lederach, John Paul. *The Little Book of Conflict Transformation*. Intercourse, PA: Good Books, 2003.

Juergensmeyer, Mark. *Terror in the Mind of God: The Global Rise of Religious Violence*. Berkeley: University of California Press, 2003.

———. *Global Rebellion: Religious Challenges to the Secular State, from Christian Militias to al Qaeda*. Berkeley: University of California Press, 2008.

Little, David. "A Double Edged Dilemma." *Harvard Divinity Bulletin* 35, no. 4 (Autumn 2007).

Marx, Anthony. *Faith in Nation: Exclusionary Origins of Nationalism*. Oxford: Oxford University Press, 2003.

Neumaier, Eva. "Missed Opportunites: Buddhism and the Ethnic Strife in Sri Lanka and Tibet." In *Religion and Peacebuilding*, edited

by Harold Coward and Gordon S. Smith. Albany: State University of New York Press, 2004.

Queen, Christopher. "The Peace Wheel: Nonviolent Activism in the Buddhist Tradition." In *Subverting Hatred: The Challenge of Nonviolence in Religious Traditions,* edited by Daniel L. Smith-Christopher, 14–37. Maryknoll, NY: Orbis, 2007.

Rawls, John. *Political Liberalism.* New York: Columbia University Press, 1996.

Schirch, Lisa. *Ritual and Symbol in Peacebuilding.* Sterling, VA: Kumarian, 2005.

Sells, Michael. "Pilgrimage and 'Ethnic Cleansing' in Herzegovina." In *Religion and Nationalism in Iraq,* edited by David Little and Donald Swearer, 145–56. Cambridge, MA: Harvard University Press, 2006.

Shahak, Israel. *The Background and Consequences of the Massacre in Hebron.* 1994. Available at http://www.geocities.com /israel_shahak/1994_2.htm (accessed 2008).

Shastri, Sunanda Y., and Yajneshwar Shastri. "*Ahimsa* and the Unity of All Things: A Hindu View of Nonviolence." In *Subverting Hatred: The Challenge of Nonviolence in Religious Traditions,* edited by Daniel L. Smith-Christopher, 57–75. Maryknoll, NY: Orbis, 2007.

Shriver, Donald. *An Ethic for Enemies: Forgiveness in Politics.* New York: Oxford University Press, 1995.

Smith, Anthony D. *Chosen Peoples: Sacred Sources of National Identity.* Oxford: Oxford University Press, 2003.

Tanenbaum Center for Interreligious Understanding. "An Open House: Yehezkel Landau." In *Peacemakers in Action: Profiles of*

Religion in Conflict Resolution, edited by David Little, 356–81. Cambridge: Cambridge University Press, 2007.

———. "Peasant Power: Jose Inocencio Alas, El salvador." In *Peacemakers in Action: Profiles of Religion in Conflict Resolution,* edited by David Little, 25–52. Cambridge: Cambridge University Press, 2007.

Varshney, Ashutosh. *Ethnic Conflict and Civil Life: Hindus and Muslims in India.* New Haven, CT: Yale University Press, 2002.

2

CIVIL RELIGION

Jason A. Springs

Generally speaking, the term *civil society* refers to all the various practices, institutions, and voluntary associations that fill out the social spaces between the official political apparatus of the government and the private sphere. Examples include schools, voluntary organizations based on religion or ethnicity, churches, sports clubs, unions. Some accounts of civil society include "private" associations, such as the family. In any case, *civil society* is a flexible—and at times even vacuous—term. An examination of religion in civil society might reflect upon the different ways that carriers of the particular religious traditions present in a given society interact within the civil sphere. It might also examine civil society as the space in which religious institutions and practices are formally separated from politics. This essay approaches the topic by examining the complex ways that US civil society institutes certain "religious" dimensions and features for the purposes of legitimating itself and maintaining itself as a cohesive whole. For the purposes of this analysis, the term *civil religion* refers to the religious dimensions and features of civil society.

OVERVIEW: CIVIL RELIGION

This article treats *civil religion* in light of the etymology of its constituent parts—the root *religiare* means "to bind together"; *civitas* refers to the shared, public life of a community of fellow citizens. Used in this way, *civil religion* broadly refers to the practices, symbols, myths, rituals, and consecrated spaces and times that serve to unify and integrate the disparate parts and individuals of a society into a cohesive whole. It also invests that societal whole with overarching significance. Civil religion generates a sense of membership or participation in the society's identity, integrating differences into and legitimating that shared identity and symbolically representing the values that ground and orient the society.

This term applies a *functionalist* definition of religion to the processes that constitute civil society. It is functionalist because the features that constitute a society's civil religion are identified in virtue of the ways they function in the life of that society. The features of civil religion may take the form of symbols, mottos, narratives, and holidays and festivals—usually official, although sometimes informal—that commemorate the origin or founding of the society and reenact the journey by which it came to be what it is. Typically, these represent the values and ideals that the society claims to embody and to which it holds itself collectively responsible.

Conceived in this way, civil religion might not identify with any particular historical religious tradition or employ what is typically considered to be explicitly religious language or symbols. At the same time, however, it need not exclude specific features of various religious traditions that are present in a given society—in as far as those features can be recruited for the purposes of integrating, unifying, legitimating, and amplifying the significance of the public life of a particular society.

For an example of a ritual practice of civil religion common in US civil society, consider standing to observe the national anthem at the start of a baseball game. This action momentarily unifies an otherwise disparate group of people by highlighting—in some cases magnifying—a background identity they share. It illuminates the common allegiances against which more particular team loyalties and regional attachments clash.

Examining such ceremonies and symbols as instances of ritual practice illuminates their more subtle functions. Perhaps they confer a sense of matter-of factness to typically unarticulated notions that US society actually embodies the values by which it claims to identify itself (values such as fair play and equal standing before the rules). Such ceremonies might emotionally confirm the idea that US society is driven by a work ethic of individual effort and achievement, but one that nonetheless aims to contribute to the overall success of the team. They may evoke impressions that the ideals symbolized by the flag and valorized in the lyrics of the national anthem—ideals of individual liberty, courage, and justice—do, in fact, constitute "the American way of life."

Although pregame rituals occur across the full range of athletic events in US society, the example of baseball is uniquely illustrative, because it is associated with the history, leisure, athletic cultures, and civil cohesion of the United States. Its legendary heroes (Babe Ruth, Lou Gehrig, Jackie Robinson, among others) are often taken to personify national motifs: epic might (by which Ruth transformed the game), heroic perseverance in the face of tragic adversity (for which Gehrig is celebrated), and triumph over unjust limitations (Robinson's defeat of racial segregation in major league baseball).[1] At the workaday level, ceremonial observance of the national anthem is a mechanical part of going to a baseball game, no more conspicuous than pausing to sing "Take Me Out to the Ball Game" during the seventh-inning stretch or standing in line at the concession stand. And yet, a common paradox of the practices of civil religion in everyday life is that the deeper and more pervasive the hold by which such rituals, symbols, and stories bind together and unify a society, the more inconspicuous they tend to be. They may appear ordinary, unimportant, or even trite, making it easy for practitioners to be unaware of the influence that they exert.

The usually taken-for-granted symbolic powers of civil religion become anything but mundane under certain circumstances. Because anthems, pledges, and flags function as identity markers for a group or society, they quickly can become charged with conspicuous political significance as objects of patriotic zeal or even nationalist fanaticism. The political valence of such practices surfaced in recent years. Perhaps most notably, during the year following the terrorist attacks of September 11, Major League Baseball stadiums replaced the traditional song of the seventh-inning stretch, "Take Me Out to the Ball Game," with Irving Berlin's "God Bless America." As one commentator remarked, in the seasons following 9/11

> ballparks and stadiums became town squares where much of the ritual of public healing took place. Flags and anthems, no longer perfunctory prelude, emerged as the emotional center of games. Ballparks became home to sacramental ceremony. It seemed natural to salute and sing and cry and then settle in for a game that meant exactly nothing and everything all at once.[2]

Of course, the symbolic sanctity of national and civic identity markers also makes them potential objects for expressing dissent. During the international hockey matches between US and Canadian teams that coincided with the start of the US-led invasion of Iraq in 2003, a stadium of Montréal Canadien hockey fans booed throughout the playing of the US national anthem.[3] Such was perhaps most famously the case at the 1968 Mexico City Olympic Games, when African American sprinters Tommie Smith and John Carlos, Gold and Bronze medalists in the two-hundred-meter race, bowed their heads and raised their fists in the form of the Black Power salute from the medal podium throughout the US National Anthem. At the time, this act was denounced as blasphemous for exploiting a moment considered sacred in the context of US civil religion. Smith and Carlos refused to endorse the ideals that the flag and the anthem purported to represent, given that the social realities in US society were characterized by white supremacy, economic injustice, and violent unrest.[4]

Civil religion presents an instructive case for examining the practice of religion in everyday life. In as far as its ritual and ceremonial practices in civil society can be helpfully understood in broad and everyday terms of "religion," it is because they are simultaneously interwoven with symbols, myths, and meanings. To treat any of these particular ingredients of civil religion in abstraction from the others would result in a partial account. Thus, the following discussion addresses the myths, narratives, symbols, and significances—as well as the practices—that make up civil religion in North American society.

I begin with a historical overview of the events and concepts that have come to constitute the "founding myth" or "myth of origin." I then demonstrate how this mythical framework gives rise to symbols, spaces, and practices that exhibit an "exceptionalist" account of US civil society. The second part of this essay explores how these features of civil religion have exerted themselves in recent decades and what their impact has been on the United States post–September 11.

HISTORY: ROOTS OF CIVIL RELIGION IN THE MYTHICAL ORIGINS OF US SOCIETY

A primary means by which civil religion integrates difference into a shared identity and then legitimates that identity at the level of civil society is by providing a mythical account of the society's origins. In the case of the United States, for instance, a primary "myth of origins" in the popular imagination centers on the story of a group of the earliest European settlers in North America, Puritan Separatists from the Church of England, who fled religious oppression in the early 1600s. Their passage from bondage to freedom led them first to the Netherlands in search of religious freedom and then to North America.

The civic and political practices established by these Puritans were motivated by several motifs from biblical narratives and from specifically Christian theological concepts. Such conceptions included "election," an understanding of having been specially chosen by God; "providence," or a sense of God's intervention in history to fulfill God's purposes; "vocation," or having received a special purpose or "calling" from God within that providential plan, and understanding one's life—or the life of one's group or community—as an instrument by which God works God's purposes in history. These concepts were oriented by the biblical motif of "covenant"—a relationship voluntarily entered into by two parties and based upon the shared commitment that the promises made by each party to the other will be fulfilled. On the basis of these concepts and motifs, the Puritans understood that their fledgling society in the New World had a unique significance in the sight of God and a special role in history. The Puritan Christians, for instance, viewed their flight in 1620 from England through the wilderness to their settlement in the New World as a new form of the people of Israel's flight from slavery in Egypt, as chronicled in the biblical book of Exodus. As the Sons of Israel were led by God across the Red Sea and Sinai wilderness to the promised land of Canaan, so the Puritans understood the God of Abraham, Isaac, and Jacob to have led them safely across the treacherous Atlantic Ocean, to arrive safely in the wilderness of Cape Cod.[5]

Despite what this complex of theological concepts and biblical motifs might suggests, the New England Puritans understood their role in history as much more than special recognition and preferential treatment from their God. Central to the Puritan understanding of covenant with God was a conception of divine judgment. To be named among God's elect conferred profound responsibilities upon them and constrained the ways that they could carry out their errand into the wilderness. At the same time, the New England Puritans understood their duties of faithfulness to be more than matters of personal piety and individual morality. These duties

were equally central to the formation of civil and political practices that the Puritans established in New England. God had commanded them to raise a "city upon a hill" that the eyes of the world would look upon and give glory to God.[6]

With this mission in mind, John Winthrop, governor of the Massachusetts Bay Colony for several terms, invoked the warning of the Hebrew prophets to the people of Israel as a warning that applied directly to the Puritans, in a sermon that he preached en route to the New World. The Puritans, he said, had been called by God to keep the commandments by doing justice, acting mercifully, and walking humbly with God (Micah 6:8). Unfaithfulness would jeopardize the covenant that their God had graciously entered into with them and instead reap God's judgment and wrath. As God sent the Israelites to wander in the wilderness for forty years for their idolatrous worship of the golden calf at the foot of Mount Sinai, if the Puritans were unfaithful to God, their errand into the wilderness would become yet another cautionary tale about what happens when a people trifles with God's blessing.

In practice, many of the Puritans' founding narratives were used to underwrite the spread of the English colonies in the New World. Eventually, those stories came to legitimate the establishment of the United States of America as a sovereign territory and provided a historical narrative that justified its expansion to the Pacific Ocean. This account of its origins became a central feature of the stories and symbols by which the United States—in both state and civil society—has come to represent itself to itself and to the world. Benjamin Franklin and Thomas Jefferson each proposed on separate occasions that the Great Seal of the United States include a depiction of Moses, leading the children of Israel across the Red Sea. Although both proposals were eventually lost in committee, their motivating idea—God's providential leading of the United States (as the "new Israel") through the vicissitudes of history—was included in the final version of the seal. It appears as a single eye, representing God's providential attention to the United States, which sits atop the pyramid featured on the Great Seal. This image appears today on the back of the US one-dollar bill.[7]

In time, explicitly biblical stories and motifs were gradually absorbed into US civil society, and the significance of what were originally tradition-specific narratives, symbols, and theological concepts expanded to accommodate more than meanings that were specific to the Jewish and Christian traditions. They came to be applied in broadly spiritual or mythical ways, to justify political and civic practices and institutions. For instance, what began as a strictly theological understanding of God's providential attention to the United States evolved into a framework of political legitimacy, social integration, and mythic representation known as "American exceptionalism." This framework invested the civic and political life of the American people with extraordinary—or "exceptional"—importance.

American exceptionalism claims that the United States of America has a unique role in the political and social histories of the world. In particular, it is to be unique as a transmitter of such social and civic values as individual freedom and democratic forms of association. It is to be a caregiver to the less fortunate or a defender of the weak against injustice. This concept of American exceptionalism is nowhere more famously symbolized—and still revered by millions of visitors each year—than in the statue, "Liberty Enlightening the World," which stands just inside the entryway to New York Harbor. The sonnet engraved in bronze on the exterior of the statue's pedestal—written in 1883 by poet Emma Lazarus, a daughter of Portuguese

Sephardic Jewish immigrants—attributes to this "Mother of Exiles" an announcement to the world of a type of freedom never seen before and that awaits all who journey to the new world: "'Keep, ancient lands, your storied pomp!' cries she / With silent lips. 'Give me your tired, your poor, / Your huddled masses yearning to breathe free. / The wretched refuse of your teeming shore. / Send these, the homeless, tempest-tost to me. / I lift my lamp beside the golden door!'" This inscription on the Statue of Liberty conveys one version of the exceptionalist framework by which US society portrays the significance of its role in history and understands itself to be unique. Ideally, the liberty it promises is not reserved for the elite or the privileged but is promised to all people. In principle, this is liberty united with justice, in that it views all people as being deserving of freedom, regardless of their station or rank in society, and claims that it will provide each person with the liberty that is his or her due in virtue of shared humanity.

Of course, as often as such ideals are enshrined and heralded in the symbols, rituals, and sacred spaces of civil religion, they have been flouted in practice. Occasionally when severe discrepancies occur between the values that civil religion claims to espouse and its actions, the terms of civil religion have been used to denounce national hypocrisy. Consider, for instance, perhaps the most famous instance of a prophetic use of civil religion—President Abraham Lincoln's second inaugural Address, delivered at the close of the US Civil War. Many Americans had justified slavery with biblical passages and religious justifications. The Confederacy had invoked the Christian God to aid them in a war fought to preserve their alleged right to enslave people. Both sides in the conflict appealed to God's will to vindicate their struggle.

In his second inaugural, Lincoln depicted this tragic conflict within a framework of cosmic

The Statue of Liberty, officially titled Liberty Enlightening the World *and dedicated on October 28, 1886, is a monument commemorating the centennial of the signing of the United States Declaration of Independence. Given to the United States by the people of France, it represents the friendship between the two countries established during the American Revolution. (Photo by Hemera Technologies/www.photos.com.)*

significance by framing it with biblical themes and motifs. He oriented the war by concepts of historical purpose and a higher conception of justice. Lincoln spoke of God's judgment upon a people who had sinned gravely by profiting from the ownership and abuse of other human beings. He invoked Christian Scripture to convey the idea that the North's victory did not place it in a position to mete out judgment upon the defeated; nor did it absolve the victors from God's judgment themselves.

Both read the same Bible and pray to the same God, and each invokes His aid against the other. It may seem strange that any men should dare to ask a just God's assistance in wringing their bread from the sweat of other men's faces, but let us judge not, that we be not judged. The prayers of both could not be answered. That of neither has been answered fully. The Almighty has His own purposes. "Woe unto the world because of offenses; for it must needs be that offenses come, but woe to that man by whom the offense cometh." [Matthew 18:7] If we shall suppose that American slavery is one of those offenses which, in the providence of God, must needs come, but which, having continued through His appointed time, He now wills to remove, and that He gives to both North and South this terrible war as the woe due to those by whom the offense came, shall we discern wherein any departure from those divine attributes which the believers in a living God always ascribe to Him? Fondly do we hope, fervently do we pray, that this mighty scourge of war may speedily pass away. Yet, if God wills that it continue until all the wealth piled by the bondsman's two hundred and fifty years of unrequited toil shall be sunk, and until every drop of blood drawn with the lash shall be paid by another drawn with the sword, as was said three thousand years ago, so still it must be said, "the judgments of the Lord are true and righteous altogether" [Psalm 19:9]. With malice toward none, with charity for all, with firmness in the right as God gives us to see the right, let us strive on to finish the work we are in, to bind up the nation's wounds, to care for him who shall have borne the battle and for his widow and his orphan, to do all which may achieve and cherish a just and lasting peace among ourselves and with all nations.

In these lines, Lincoln interprets the Civil War as an instance of divine judgment upon a wayward nation. Such an interpretation was pivotal for restoring the unity of a society on the brink of being torn apart. The engraved text of this address now orients perhaps the most famous of sacred spaces in US civil society, spanning the north wall of the Lincoln Memorial on the National Mall in Washington, DC. The memorial itself commemorates what is broadly recognized as Lincoln's own "sacrificial death," in exchange for the continued unity of the life of the nation. A few feet away, on the steps of the Lincoln Memorial, are bronze footprints marking another prophet and martyr of US civil religion, Martin Luther King Jr. These footprints mark the spot from which he delivered his "I Have a Dream" speech in 1963. On that occasion, King invoked Lincoln's legacy of issuing the Emancipation Proclamation of black slaves in the United States—to challenge the US legal system and the daily life of US civil society to embody in practice the ideals of liberty, equality, and mutual respect that it claimed to espouse.

SACRED TIME IN US SOCIETY

The founding myths and narratives of US civil religion converge with shared conceptions of "sacred time" in US civil society. Civic holidays are designated to observe, remember, celebrate, mourn, or reenact the pivotal events, values, figures, and narratives that are central to the society's conception of itself. In the United States, civil religion has been instituted in a series of holidays that are set aside to commemorate and celebrate the many people who fought and died while serving the nation and state (Veterans and Memorial Days), pivotal figures and events in the founding narratives (Columbus Day), the survival of the Puritan settlers after their journey to the new world (Thanksgiving), the declaration of independence from Britain (Independence Day). These holidays also honor particular individuals who have been elevated to saintlike status for their devotion and sacrifice to their country (Martin Luther King Jr.'s birthday; Presidents' Day commemoration of the birthdays of George Washington and Abraham Lincoln).

Thanksgiving may be the "high holy day" of US civil religion, in part because it refracts like a prism the nebulous ways that "religion" manifests itself in the civic life of the nation. Instituted by law as a federal holiday, Thanksgiving is officially "secular," that is, not formally affiliated with a particular religious tradition or institution (as are Christmas, Easter, Hanukah, or Ramadan). It commemorates one of society's founding myths of origin that is ritually reenacted at "Thanksgiving dinner."[8] The holiday is oriented around a set of values understood to be rooted in that founding myth. These values purport to provide collective meaning and reflect basic claims about the identity of this particular society, and they do so vaguely enough to encompass both specifically religious and explicitly nonreligious interpretations.

At the same time, the origins of the Thanksgiving holiday were Christian in character and continue to reflect a mythical representation of the Puritans at Plymouth, as previously discussed. Having gathered their first harvest in 1621, the legend goes, the fifty Pilgrims who had survived the treacherous journey and first months in the New World rested and gave thanks to their God for leading them through the wilderness to the new promised land.

The practices of designating days of prayer, giving thanks to God, and even fasting quickly became a common practices in US civil society. On October 3, 1789, President George Washington declared the first Thanksgiving Day observance for the fledgling nation, officially recognizing the "religious" values on which the commemoration centered—gratitude, piety, humility, and rest. Washington declared:

> Whereas it is the duty of all Nations to acknowledge the providence of Almighty God, to obey his will, to be grateful for his benefits, and humbly to implore his protection and favor, and whereas both Houses of congress have by their joint committee requested me to recommend to the People of the United States a day of public thanksgiving and prayer to be observed by acknowledging with grateful hearts the many signal favors of Almighty God especially by affording them an opportunity peaceably to establish a form of government for their safety and happiness.[9]

Although days of thanksgiving and prayer were observed intermittently (not necessarily in autumn, and sometimes more than once per year), this practice was taken with great seriousness, as though the very well-being of the nation depended upon it. Many of Thomas Jefferson's Federalist critics blamed his refusal to designate any official days of fasting and thanksgiving for the outbreak of a yellow fever epidemic that occurred in and around Philadelphia in 1799.[10] Abraham Lincoln designated the Thanksgiving holiday as the final Thursday in November. However, the holiday was not established in its contemporary form until Franklin D. Roosevelt set the next-to-last Thursday of each November as a national holiday in 1939.

The impressionistic and mythical character of the US founding stories enables these tales to orient and reflect popular imagination through various rituals and holidays. It is this same impressionistic quality, however, that conceals divergent and dissenting accounts of the events they portray and hides how these stories have underwritten some of the most destructive chapters in US history. As we saw previously, for instance, the separatist Puritan settlers envisioned their journey to the New World as a reflection of the Israelite's exodus from Egypt to the land of Canaan. When celebrated solely as a narrative of liberation from bondage, the story of the Hebrew people's exodus from slavery obscures the parts of that story that describe the fates of the peoples already living in the land that had been promised to the Hebrews by their God—Canaanites, Hittites, Amorites, Perizzites, Hivits, and Jebusites. The flight from Egypt recounted in the book of Exodus tends to be celebrated in isolation from the story's continuation in Deuteronomy (Chapter 20, in particular). There, God gives the Hebrews a mandate to lay siege to the cities of the inhabitants who are already living in the land, destroying those who do not accept their terms for peace and enslaving those that do.

In a parallel fashion, versions of the Puritans' arrival in the promised land of the New World that prevail in the popular imagination obscure the fact that the alleged uninhabited wilderness in which they arrived was, in fact, already populated by vast numbers of indigenous peoples. Mythic representations of the "First Thanksgiving" of 1621 portray as one of friendship the Puritan affiliation with Wampanoag Indians of Massachusetts. And even though the Pilgrims had entered into treaties with some Native American tribes of the region, assuring some degree of mutual aid in the case that either group came under attack, the full details of the story are much more disconcerting.[11]

In addition to their sense of vocation to settle and subdue the wilderness of the new world, the Pilgrim settlers brought smallpox with them. Between 1633 and 1644, thousands of the indigenous population died from smallpox outbreaks that accompanied the increasing numbers of Puritans settlers (their numbers had reached two thousand by 1632). Although the Puritans offered aid to an Indian population decimated by disease, they did not hesitate to view the epidemic as an act of God on behalf of the chosen people. "If God were not pleased with our inheriting these parts, why did he drive out the natives before us?" John Winthrop wrote in 1634. "And why dothe he still make roome for us, by deminishinge them as we increase?"[12]

Colonists from England brought to the New World King Charles I's "right of discovery"—a provision in British law that permitted a monarch to claim possession of any land not already occupied by Christians. As such, it applied to all the lands on which Native Americans lived and allegedly provided the settlers with legal claim to the lands that they settled.[13] By 1675, the population of New England immigrants had grown to seventy-five thousand whereas the number of Indians in New England diminished to fifteen thousand. Altogether, the displacement of the New England Indian population by European settlers occurred through the combined effects

of epidemics brought by the settlers, settlement expansion, and warfare against the Indians. In 1675, the colonists went to war against large segments of the indigenous population, which largely completed the settlement of New England by the New World colonists. The Puritans were inclined to interpret these events as the unfolding of God's plan for a chosen people who had been called to establish a nation in the new world.

RELIGION IN PUBLIC LIFE: DETACHING PRACTICE FROM BELIEF

The concept of civil religion provides a descriptive category by which to make sense of what has been called the spiritual dimension of the motto *E pluribus unum*, "out of many, one."[14] Somewhat paradoxically, the symbols, rituals, and myths of civil religion could serve such edifying functions in the public life of civil society if religion were legally disestablished. Because it was relieved of the capacity to assert itself coercively, religion was thereby made available to serve, unify, and maintain civil society in informal and cultural ways. Of course, if the symbols, myths, scriptural allusions, and sacred time can be made flexible—to accommodate some degree of ethnic, religious, and cultural diversity in civil society—they can also be employed in ways that divide and exclude. Some argue that the cultural force and social pressures, generated in the name of civil religion, in the United States infringe upon the separation of church and state *in practice*. According to this argument, these pressures institute distinctively theistic (predominantly Christian) practices in civil society, when they ought to be kept as matters of private belief and personal practice. Some of the most difficult challenges to the establishment clause of the First Amendment have occurred over issues of practice of religion in civil society that broadly fall within the category of civil religion.

One of the first tests of the Free Exercise clause occurred in 1879, in the Supreme Court case *Reynolds v. United States*. George Reynolds, a Mormon residing in the territory of Utah, was convicted for marrying multiple wives. He appealed his conviction on the grounds that he was obligated to enter into multiple marriages, owing to his religious duty as a Mormon. The Supreme Court upheld the conviction. The significance of the ruling was not so much its particular result as the court's justification for limiting the way Reynolds practiced his religious beliefs. The laws of the land could restrict certain religious practices, because "laws are made for the government of actions, and while they cannot interfere with mere religious beliefs and opinions, they may with practices." With this, a basic distinction between religious belief and religious practice was written into law. "Belief" on this account operates along the lines of personal opinion—it is an interior act of cognitive commitment or emotional conviction that occurs within the inner recesses of individual conscience. It presumes a clear and distinct division between private conscience and public space. Within the framework established by the court's ruling, a citizen is free to "believe" whatever he or she wants, and the government cannot rightly coerce belief. Religious actions, practices, or institutions, by contrast, are considered to operate in the public space and are thus candidates for restriction. In other words, the laws can restrict what a believer can or cannot actually do in the name of religious conviction or duty, beyond the notion of exercise carved out by the free exercise clause of the First Amendment. The state restrains itself from interfering with religious practices, insofar as participation in them is voluntary and legally uncontroversial. If some practice conflicts with the laws of the land, however, the state is within its right to prohibit or circumscribe that practice.

In justifying its verdict in *Reynolds v. United States,* the court appealed to a letter written by Thomas Jefferson to the Danbury Baptist Association in Connecticut in 1802, which Chief Justice Waite referred to "almost as an authoritative declaration of the scope and effect of the [first] amendment." The letter contains the two lines that have been perhaps as influential, controversial, and contested as the Free Exercise and Establishment clauses themselves. The opinion quoted Jefferson.

Believing with you that religion is matter which lies solely between Man and his God, that he owes account to none other for his faith or his worship, that the legitimate powers of government reach actions only, and not opinions, I contemplate with sovereign reverence that act of the whole American people which declared that their legislature should "make no law respecting an establishment of religion, or prohibiting the free exercise thereof," thus building a wall of separation between Church and State. Adhering to this expression of the supreme will of the nation in behalf of the rights of conscience, I shall see with sincere satisfaction the progress of those sentiments which tend to restore to man all his natural rights, convinced he has no natural right in opposition to his social duties.[15]

Jefferson's reference to a "wall of separation" has been taken by many to capture the limits of religion's role in the political sphere in the United States, as well as in public life and civil society. However, this is an idyllic and highly theoretical articulation of principle of free expression. This principle obscures the informal power and influence that religion exerts.

Jefferson thought that the public practice of certain forms of religion was indispensable for cultivating the civic virtue necessary for the proper functioning of society. In Jefferson's view, the ethical instructions of rationalist

Enlightenment deism was ideal to provide the ethical substance of civil society.[16] Its contents included the moral teachings of Jesus (those that remained after human reason cut away all the claims of "special revelation" and reports of miraculous events in the biblical accounts), the Ten Commandments, and the "the Golden Rule" (Matthew 7:12). Jefferson thought these were basic enough to encompass a great deal of diversity and yet remain fully consistent with the foundational moral principles that are self-evident to natural reason. These basic principles find their most widely recognized articulation in Jefferson's preamble to the Declaration of Independence: "We hold these truths to be self evident, that all men are created equal, that they are endowed by their Creator with certain unalienable rights, that among these are life, liberty and the pursuit of happiness." Jefferson believed the moral dimensions of religion to be indispensable to the operation of a healthy society. In effect, however, this view enshrined a mild form of liberal Protestant Christianity (gradually shading into deism) in the symbols, rituals, and values of the republic.

The practical import of these values is perhaps nowhere better exemplified than in the comment by the then-president-elect Dwight D. Eisenhower that the United States' "form of government makes no sense unless it is founded on a deeply held religious belief, and I don't care what it is."[17] Eisenhower's remark that some deeply held religious belief is necessary to make sense of US government—whatever those beliefs might be—again suggests that the rituals, stories, and practices of US civil religion should be vague enough to accommodate most any particular religious belief. And yet, the mildly theistic elements that are central to civil religion in the United States alienate members of the citizenry, in spite of intention to achieve the opposite. Citizens who explicitly refuse to ascribe to some

"religious affiliation" or a framework of religious beliefs have protested that even society's association with the most broadly construed conception of a God and religion positively excludes them.

Arguably, Eisenhower is the figure who is singly most responsible for the form and content of civil religion in the United States in the latter half of the twentieth century.[18] He oversaw the insertion by the United States Congress of the words "under God" into the Pledge of Allegiance in 1954 ("One nation under God"). He was also pivotal in selecting the phrase "In God we Trust" as the US national motto in 1956, and he vied for its eventual inscription on US currency in 1957. Prior to "In God we Trust," *E pluribus unum* ("out of many, one") had served informally as the national motto. The change overseen by Eisenhower made explicit the tacitly theistic (or deistic) presuppositions of what was required in order to fashion "one from many." Motivated by Cold War patriotism, these additions intended to distinguish the religious heritage and identity of US civil society from the self-described materialist atheism of Soviet Communism.

Criticisms arise that, in practice, the mildly theistic taint of the symbols and rituals of civil religion discriminates against nonbelief or against those who deliberately choose not to affiliate with any religion. Arguably, it sanctions a range of informal exclusions, even though exclusions on the basis of religious affiliation—or refusal thereof—are formally illegal. Legally speaking, for instance, the establishment clause of the First Amendment to the US Constitution prohibits uses of religious criteria to determine whether or not a candidate is eligible to hold public office. Critics ask whether it is even conceivable that a "professing atheist" could be elected to high office in the United States. "We atheists . . . think it bad enough that we cannot run for public office without being disingenuous about our belief in God," the social critic and philosopher Richard Rorty commented in recent years. "No uncloseted atheist is likely to get elected anywhere in the country. We also resent the suggestion that you have to be religious to have a conscience—a suggestion implicit in the fact that only *religious* conscientious objectors to military service go unpunished."[19] In practice, the United States has had enough of a struggle to move beyond a default limitation of its presidents to being adherents of Protestant Christianity. The first Roman Catholic who was elected president, John Fitzgerald Kennedy, was not elected until 1960, and he came under intense scrutiny about whether his allegiance to the pope would interfere with his loyalty to his country. These are cultural and social forces that exert themselves informally and, in practice, often toward the very ends that legal disestablishment is intended to evade. In the remaining pages of this essay, I examine the ways that such social and cultural forces have exerted themselves legally and institutionally in North American civil society.

AUTHORITY: CIVIL RELIGION AFTER SEPTEMBER 11

The diversification of the North American public in terms of ethnicity, religious and cultural background, and language has increased exponentially since the 1960s. This has made it difficult for the earlier variations of the religious dimensions of civic life to suffice any longer as vehicles for social integration of difference into the civic unity promised by "American values." To many, it appears that the "sacred canopy" that previously encompassed, integrated, and legitimated the social, civic, and legal worlds of US society is falling apart at the seams. The increasingly diluted potency of the distinctively Christian symbols, values, and practices that accompanied the heretofore unseen scope of religious, ethnic,

and cultural diversification of US society in the post-Vietnam era has inspired many segments of US Christianity to assert themselves politically and, perhaps more controversially, legally.

The result has been twofold. On one hand, this rapidly increasing diversification has hindered the capacity of the inherited Judeo-Christian symbols, ritual, and myths of civil religion to generate solidarity and integrate difference. The capacities of the traditional symbols and emotional influences to generate an imagined community have diminished and thereby compromised the "religious identity" of the American people as a "Christian nation" or as a "Judeo-Christian civilization." This has inspired an effort to politicize the religious identity of this country, its people, its history, and its role in world affairs. An ebbing cultural dominance has given rise to political and legal assertion, as a means of effecting cultural resurgence, as well as a xenophobic retrenchment of Judeo-Christian values in civic life. Arguably, a new great awakening has occurred in the United States since roughly 1980, one not simply concerned with personal piety and devotion, but a legal and political awakening mobilized in the name of US Judeo-Christian cultural origins and heritage.

In the wake of bitter disappointment over a series of court decisions, legal statutes, and shifts in the cultural ethos of US society,[20] conservative Christians in the United States hoped that electing a self-identified "born again" Christian and active member of a Southern Baptist church to the presidency would vindicate US identity as a "Christian nation" and correct the wayward course of US civil society. President Jimmy Carter, however, disappointed Christian conservatives. In response to Carter's presidency, evangelical televangelist Jerry Falwell formed the political action movement and lobby group calling itself the "Moral Majority," a group that ultimately claimed responsibility for delivering two-thirds of the vote of white evangelical Christians to Ronald Reagan in the 1980 presidential election. This movement took quite literally the mythical and moral dimensions of US civil religion. The Moral Majority mobilized politically in order to reassert culturally the values that were associated with the origins of the United States as a Christian nation, and to institute them legally.[21]

Falwell's Moral Majority understood the "exceptional" role of the United States in history as being grounded in the origins of its Judeo-Christian identity. This identity was something to be defended, at all costs, against the encroachment of multiculturalism and secularism. In the following sermon, directed to the US public, Falwell made his case in terms that are distinctly reminiscent of John Winthrop's jeremiad to his fellow Puritans.

> Our nation's internal problems are direct results of her spiritual condition. America is desperately in need of a divine healing, which can only come if God's people will humble themselves, pray, seek His face, and turn from their wicked ways. . . . It is God Almighty who has made and preserved us as a nation, and the day that we forget that is the day that the United States will become a byword among the nations of the world. We will become nothing more than a memory in a history book, like the many great civilizations that have preceded us. . . . I do not believe that God is finished with America. Yet America has more God-fearing citizens per capita than any other nation on earth. There are millions of Americans who love God, decency, and biblical morality. North America is the last logical base for world evangelization. While it is true that God could use any nation of means possible to spread the gospel to the world, it is also true that we have the church, the schools, the young people, the media, the money, and the means of spreading the Gospel worldwide in

> our lifetime. God loves all the world, not just America. However, I am convinced that our freedoms are essential to world evangelism in this latter part of the twentieth century. I am seeking to rally together the people of this country who still believe in decency, the home, the family, morality, the free-enterprise system, and all the great ideals that are the cornerstone of this nation. . . . But when you ask the average person what can be done about revival in America, he will often reply, "I'm just one person. What can I do anyhow?" As long as the average moral American believes that, the political and social liberals in this society will be able to pass their socialistic legislation at will. We are late, but I do not believe that we are too late. It is time to put our lives on the line for this great nation of ours. . . . I am convinced that God is calling millions of American in the so-often silent majority to join in the moral majority crusade to turn America around in our lifetime.[22]

In the decades that followed, the symbols and rites of civil religion served as trappings for a cultural movement.[23]

These symbols, rites, and stories have achieved nearly sacrosanct status throughout US civil society since the terrorist attacks of September 11, 2001. One explanation for the post–September 11 upsurge in civil-religious devotion states that, as a matter of general sociological principle, during national "times of trial," the symbols, stories, and rituals through which a society understands itself become especially charged with meaning, whether patriotic, nationalistic, or some combination of all of these. These revitalized values might serve as compensatory resources for dealing with periods of national adversity. The perceived common threat to the American way of life, conjoined with a segment of the population united in their commitment to the identity of the United States as a Christian nation or Judeo-Christian civilization, has led to a reassertion of the practices, symbols, and stories of US civil religion.

The clause "One nation under God" in the Pledge of Allegiance was challenged in Federal Appeals court in 2002 as violating the separation of church and state. The suit was filed by a California man—and self-identified atheist—whose daughter attended a Sacramento elementary school where recitation of the pledge was compulsory. Although his daughter was not actually forced to participate in the Pledge of Allegiance (the result of a 1943 Supreme Court ruling that prohibits compulsory participation in the pledge), the girl's father argued nonetheless that the practice infringed upon his daughter's First Amendment protection from being forced to participate in a religious rite. She was required to "watch and listen as her state-employed teacher in her state-run school leads her classmates in a ritual proclaiming that there is a God, and that ours is 'one nation under God.' "

The US Court of Appeals for the Ninth Circuit ruled (2–1) that the clause "One nation under God" was, in fact, unconstitutional, because it violated the First Amendment prohibition of the state's endorsement of any particular religion. Writing for the majority, Judge Alfred T. Goodwin explained that the phrase "under God" is as problematical as the declaration that "we are a nation 'under Jesus,' a nation 'under Vishnu,' a nation 'under Zeus,' or a nation 'under no god,' because none of those professions can be neutral with respect to religion." He continued as follows:

> In the context of the pledge, the statement that the United States is a nation, "under God" is an endorsement of religion. It is a profession of a religious belief, namely, a belief in monotheism. The recitation that ours is a nation "under God" is not a mere acknowledgement that many Americans believe in a deity. Nor is it merely descriptive of the undeniable his-

torical significance of religion in the founding of the republic. Rather, the phase "one nation under god" in the context of the pledge is normative. To recite the pledge is not to describe the United States; instead, it is to swear allegiance to the values for which the flag stands: unity, indivisibility, liberty, justice, and—since 1954—monotheism. The text of the official pledge, codified in federal law, impermissibly takes a position with respect to the purely religious question of the existence and identity of God. . . . "The government must pursue a course of complete neutrality toward religion." Furthermore, the school district's practice of teacher-led recitation of the pledge aims to inculcate in students a respect for the ideals set forth in the pledge, and thus amounts to state endorsement of these ideals. Although students cannot be forced to participate in recitation of the pledge, the school district is nonetheless conveying a message of state endorsements of these ideals when it requires public school teachers to recite, and lead the recitation of, the current form of the pledge.[24]

Had it stood, this decision would have had far-reaching implications. It outlawed the recitation of Pledge of Allegiance in public schools across the nine western states under the court's jurisdiction (Alaska, Arizona, California, Hawaii, Idaho, Montana, Nevada, Oregon, and Washington). At the time, twenty-five states required the pledge as part of the public school day, and six other states advocated that schools incorporate it into their daily schedules. After the terrorist attacks of September 11, lawmaking bodies in seven additional states introduced legislation that would make the pledge obligatory in school.

Upon hearing of the court's ruling, the US Senate unanimously passed a resolution denouncing the court's decision. Congressional representatives protested by convening on the front steps of the US Capitol building to recite, in unison, the Pledge of Allegiance and to sing "God Bless America." The ruling was quickly appealed and ultimately reversed by the Supreme Court on the basis of a technicality. As it turned out, the father who filed the suit lacked standing to sue because he did not have custody of his daughter at the time. The girl's mother did not object to her participation in the recitation of the pledge.

Three years later, another lawsuit was filed, challenging the use of the phrase "under God" in the pledge. A Virginia man, a father of three school-aged children, claimed that use of the phrase "under God" promoted religion unconstitutionally. In contrast to the prior California case, however, this time the suit was motivated by the father's theological convictions: he was a Mennonite. Mennonites are a nonviolent Christian community, originating from the Dutch and German Anabaptists of the Protestant Reformation, that takes its name from its first leader, Menno Simons (1493–1559). Historically, Mennonites have been distinguished by pacifism and principled refusal to participate in forms of state power. They have advocated for the strict separation of church and state and for conscientious objection during periods of war on the basis of Jesus's command in the Sermon on the Mount (Matthew 5:38–39) not to resist evil. As early as 1548, Menno Simons argued for a "separating wall" that should stand between the church and the world—this was long before Thomas Jefferson made the phrase famous.

The suit charged that the invocation of God in the Pledge of Allegiance, in combination with its creedlike affirmation of the values of the US nation state, colluded to form a "civic religion" that he thought encroached upon genuinely religious identity and competed with the specific religious values that he sought to inculcate in his children.[25] The US Fourth Circuit Court of Appeals ruled that recitation of the pledge is a purely patriotic exercise and neither affirms a particular religious view nor functions as a religious act, such as a prayer or the recitation of a creed or incantation. "Undoubtedly, the pledge contains a religious phrase, and it is demeaning to persons of any faith to assert that the words 'under God' contain no religious significance," Judge Karen Williams wrote. "The inclusion of those two words, however, does not alter the nature of the pledge as a patriotic activity."[26]

Another reason for the upsurge in civic piety since the attacks of September 11 has been the positive use of national symbols, rites, and myths by political leaders to consolidate national identity over potentially divisive particular identities in US civil society. Such uses of civil religion seek to cultivate (or to manipulate) popular sentiment in order to mobilize antipathy toward a common enemy. Such mobilization of fear can fund a reactionary willingness to concede to the restriction or suspension of civil liberties (as in the Patriot Act, passed in October 2001) and/or the application of such extreme measures against that enemy as torture and suspension of basic legal protections, such as *habeus corpus,* in the name of protecting "our way of life."

For instance, following the 9/11 terrorist attacks on the World Trade Center and Pentagon, George W. Bush juxtaposed "American values" and "the American way of life" with marginal factions in Islam that are uniquely "militant," frequently referred to as "fanatical Muslims" or "Islamic jihadists." Bush was quick to point out that it is entirely unproblematic to be both a good Muslim and a good American. Extremist Islamic factions, such as the Taliban in Afghanistan, or terrorist Islamic groups, such as Al Qaeda, have hijacked a religion that is essentially peaceful. This refrain is generally followed with the proviso that, at its core, *true* Islam is a religion of peace and that violent struggle in the name of Islam is, in fact, a contortion of that tradition.[27]

As a matter of historical record, the latter claim is false. For example, Islam contains a "just war" tradition of argument that is comparable to the just war tradition in Christianity. In both cases, debate about when it is permissible or necessary to employ force and coercion or enter into violent conflict have been central to mainstream currents in the tradition. Resorting to war or violent means has, at times, been intertwined with the most peaceful features of the tradition. Moreover, Al Qaeda employs just war reasoning that is central to the Islamic tradition in its justifications.[28]

The effect of the rhetorical function of the George W. Bush administration's claims to identify the true and peaceful essence of Islam is to expand the canopy of US civil religion from the Judeo-Christian parameters ascribed to it throughout most of the twentieth century to the even broader category of "Abrahamic faiths" or "religions of the Book." The latter designations refer to the fact that the Torah, the Christian Old Testament, and the Qur'an each identify Abraham as their founding patriarch. These religions share the basic values associated with Western monotheism—respect for the basic sanctity of life, grounded in its creation by a benign and loving Creator who, in turn, mandates mutual respect between individual people associated with "the Golden Rule," and in toleration of difference in the name of neighborly love. Thus, properly understood, "good Islam" fits comfortably under the canopy of "the American way of life" that is grounded in these values. When properly understood—so the argument runs—true Islam should have no difficulty affirming the broadly monotheistic values, rites, and symbols of US civil religion. Conversely, US citizens should have no difficulty affirming their Muslim fellow citizens.

The reality is much more severe. In 2003, sociologist of religion Robert Wuthnow conducted the "Religion and Diversity Survey," which collected and assessed responses and performed in-depth follow-up interviews with a national sample of 2,910 respondents selected to be representative of the US adult population. Seventy-eight percent of the respondents in the survey agreed that the Unites States was founded on Christian principles, and slightly more than that (79 percent) agreed that the United States has been strong because of its faith in God. Fifty-five percent agreed that the democratic form of government in the United States is based on Christianity; just over 73 percent agreed that the United States is still principally a Christian society; and 63 percent agreed that US public schools should teach students the Ten Commandments. Although 85 percent agreed that religious diversity has been good for the United States, 20 to 23 percent of respondents endorsed restricting the basic rights of minority religious groups (Hindus, Buddhists, and Muslims) to meet and worship altogether. Almost four of every ten Americans (38 percent) said that they would support making it more difficult for Muslims to settle in the United States, and 47 and 57 percent, respectively, associated the words "fanatical" and "closed-minded" with Islam. Sixty-six percent of respondents favored the US government "keeping a close watch on the all foreigners in the United States."[29]

Wuthnow takes the results of his survey to reflect a public discourse about religion that is "schizophrenic." He writes as follows.

> On one hand, we say casually that we are tolerant and have respect for people whose religious traditions happen to be different from our own. On the other hand, we continue to speak as if the nation is (or should be) a Christian nation, founded on Christian principles,

and characterized by public references to the trappings of this tradition. This kind of schizophrenia encourages behavior that no well-meaning people would want if they stopped to think about it. It allows the most open-minded among us to get by without taking religion seriously at all. It permits religious hate crimes to occur without much public attention or outcry. The members of new minority religions experience little in the way of genuine understanding. The churchgoing majority seldom hear anything to shake up their comforting convictions. The situation is rife with misunderstanding and, as such, holds little to prevent outbreaks of religious conflict and bigotry. It is little wonder that many Americans retreat into their private worlds whenever spirituality is mentioned. It is just easier to do that than to confront the hard questions about religious truth and our national identity.[30]

Wuthnow concludes that the condition of religion in contemporary US civil society cannot be improved by simply retrieving conceptions of civil religion, as heretofore conceived, and then simply supplementing those with ideals of tolerance and diversity in civic life.

CONCLUSION: FROM CIVIL RELIGION TO PUBLIC RELIGION IN CIVIL SOCIETY

It should be evident from the preceding discussion that the kind of civil religion that has been traditionally understood to unify and legitimate US civil society is, yet again, facing a time of trial (to invoke the language of Robert Bellah, the sociologist most responsible for the form and content of the late twentieth-century discussions of civil religion). Unlike the crisis presented by the Vietnam War era, however, in the face of this trial, late twentieth-century civil religion asserted itself with the brazenness of a newly fashioned fundamentalism. Further exacerbated by September 11, US civil religion in the early twenty-first century risks degenerating into a national cult.

And yet, the more aggressively the "American way of life" is heralded in symbol, song, practice, and (increasingly) law, the more the fraying and unraveling of its viability as an overarching social fabric becomes apparent. Arguably, the symbols, practices, and stories of the civil religion that "held the nation together" do not simply need consolidation or a "new great awakening" (which Bellah hoped for in his time)—but critical rethinking, reframing, and reimagining, an expansion of symbols and reform. If Wuthnow's study indicates anything, it is that religion in US civic life has to become an intentional, multilingual conversation of particular traditions and irreducible identities (religious and nonreligious, theistic and nontheistic) rather than restoration of a single, whole-cloth sacred canopy that professes to encompass the full scope of diverse constituents in their lowest common denominator and in the name of "holding civil society together."

GLOSSARY

American Exceptionalism: The view that the United States has a unique and/or divinely sanctioned role in the political and social history of the world.

Civil Religion: The practices, symbols, myths, rituals, and consecrated spaces and times that serve to unify and integrate the disparate parts and individuals of a society into a cohesive whole. Civil religion also invests that societal whole with overarching significance.

Establishment Clause: Clause in the First Amendment to the US Constitution that prohibits Congress from establishing an official state religion.

Free Exercise Clause: Clause in the First Amendment to the US Constitution that restrains Congress from prohibiting the free exercise of religion.

Wall of Separation: Metaphor used at different times by Thomas Jefferson, Roger Williams, and Menno Simons to describe the partitioning of religion from the political operation of the state.

For Further Reading

Ahlstrom, Sydney. *A Religious History of the American People.* New Haven, CT: Yale University Press, 2004.

Bellah, Robert N. *The Broken Covenant: American Civil Religion in Time of Trial.* Chicago: Chicago University Press, 1992.

———. "Civil Religion in America." *Daedalus* (Winter 1967): 1–21.

Kelsay, John. *Arguing the Just War in Islam.* Cambridge, MA: Harvard University Press, 2007.

Marsh, Charles. *Wayward Christian Soldiers: Freeing the Gospel from Political Captivity.* Oxford: Oxford University Press, 2008.

Pierard, Richard V., and Robert D. Linder. *Civil Religion and the Presidency.* Grand Rapids: Zondervan, 1988.

Wuthnow, Robert. *The Restructuring of American Religion: Society and Faith Since World War II.* Princeton: Princeton University Press, 1989. See especially chapters 10 and 11.

———. *America and the Challenges of Religious Diversity.* Princeton: Princeton University Press, 2005.

3

DREAMING IN THE CONTACT ZONE

Zulu Dreams, Visions, and Religion in Nineteenth-Century South Africa

David Chidester

During the nineteenth century, Zulu-speaking people in South Africa lived in a "contact zone," a space of intercultural engagements shaped by unequal power relations.[1] The advance of British colonialism, which was formalized by the establishment of the colony of Natal in 1843, and extended by British military campaigns, the dispossession of land, and the imposition of new forms of taxation, radically disrupted the indigenous patterns and rhythms of African political, social, and religious life.[2] As in other colonized regions, the world was effectively turned upside down. Although colonialism advanced unevenly and was experienced differently throughout southern Africa, Africans generally became alienated in the land of their birth by the incursions of European settlers and the impositions of a colonial administration. In Natal and Zululand, Christian missionaries played an important role in this massive disruption, providing a haven for African refugees or exiles but also introducing new social divisions between "traditional" and Christian Africans. These divisions were simultaneously spiritual and material.

Material signs of Christianity, such as wearing European clothing, living in square houses, or using a plough to till the land, became indicators of spiritual conversion for a new class of Zulu Christian "believers."[3] At the same time, Africans who tried to adhere to traditional or ancestral ways of life also underwent a transformation that was simultaneously spiritual and material. We can learn something about this transformation through an analysis of dreams.

In recounting his tour of Africa in 1925, the psychoanalyst C. G. Jung recalled a conversation he had about dreams with an African ritual specialist. "I remember a medicine man in Africa," Jung related, "who said to me almost with tears in his eyes: 'We have no dreams anymore since the British are in the country.'" When Jung asked why the British colonial presence had caused Africans to stop dreaming, the diviner answered, "The District Commissioner knows everything. . . . God now speaks in dreams to the British, and not to the medicine-man . . . because it is the British who have the power." For Africans, as Jung concluded, "Dream activity has emigrated."[4] According to Jung's biographer, Frank McLynn, the diviner's point was that Africans were unable to dream under colonial conditions because the European colonial administrator did all their dreaming for them, since "power speaks to power."[5] Certainly, this inability to dream, this dream-loss, represented a spiritual crisis within the most intimate interiority and personal subjectivity of people living under oppressive colonial conditions. But it also reflected broader social, economic, and political realities within which indigenous dreams lost clarity and force in the world.

In British South Africa, the Anglican missionary Henry Callaway studied Zulu dreams, devoting a large part of his book *The Religious System of the Amazulu* to what he called the "subjective apparitions" or "brain sensation" of African dream life.[6] Callaway's remarkable text was produced within a colonial triangle that drew together the force imposed by local colonial officials, the ethnographic research of a Christian missionary, and the information provided by indigenous Africans, most importantly by the Zulu convert Mpengula Mbande, who arguably was the real author of the book. As Mbande collected oral traditions and recorded conversations, he produced the basic material for a text that was not about a single Zulu religious system. Instead, it revealed a dynamic Zulu conflict of interpretations. Nevertheless, *Religious System of the Amazulu* became famous in Europe for providing what anthropologist E. B. Tylor called "the best knowledge of the lower phases of religious belief."[7] As an imperial theorist of religion, Tylor placed Callaway's text at the beginning of human prehistory, as if it provided data of the "lower" and "earlier" stages of religious evolution.[8]

However, if we place this text in its colonial context, we can gain some insight into the spiritual and material dynamics of indigenous dreams in a contact zone. If we return to the Zulu reports, discussions, and debates published in the *Religious System of the Amazulu*, we find a hermeneutics of dreams, with basic principles of interpretation, but also space for indeterminacy. We find an energetics of dreams, linking dreaming to action in maintaining ongoing ritual relations of ancestral exchange, and ancestral presence within the homestead, but we also find colonial conditions of dispossession and displacement that radically disrupted dreaming. And we find a new interreligious subjectivity emerging in this contact zone that changed the terms for interpreting and enacting dreams. Although Jung imagined that under colonial conditions African dreaming had emigrated, the Zulu evidence suggests that dreaming remained a vital medium for negotiating and navigating within a contact zone.

HERMENEUTICS AND ENERGETICS OF DREAMS

Dreams require interpretation. But they might also demand action. Accordingly, we need to pay attention to basic principles of interpretation, the hermeneutics of dreams, but we also need to attend to their practical, dynamic entailments and obligations, a range of active participation that I will call the energetics of dreams.[9]

In the Zulu conversations recorded by Mbande, which form the bulk of Callaway's *Religious System*, we learn the basic principles of an indigenous hermeneutics of dreams. In the interpretation of dreams, according to Mbande, the Zulu had developed basic principles of correlation and contrast for discerning the meaning of dream symbolism.

First, Zulu dream interpretation observed the correlation of summer with good dreams and winter with bad dreams. "People say, summer dreams are true," Mbande observed. By contrast, "winter causes bad dreams." Therefore, in this hermeneutics of dreams, Zulu dream interpretation found a correlation—summer dreams are true, winter dreams are false—which Mbande underscored by reporting that "it is said there is not much that is false in the dreams of summer. But when the winter comes the people begin to be afraid that the winter will bring much rubbish, that is, false dreams." However, in this Zulu hermeneutics of dreams, with its winter rubbish and summer revelations, Mbande introduced an element of indeterminacy by cautioning about summer dreams that Zulu people "do not say they are always true."[10] While the correlation was important in establishing basic principles for interpretation, this indeterminacy was even more important because it opened a space for creative and critical reflection on the potential meaning of dreams.

Second, Zulu dream interpretation observed a principle of contrast, holding that dreaming "goes by contraries."[11] According to a number of Zulu informants recorded in *Religious System*, dreaming of a wedding means that someone will die, while dreaming of a funeral means that someone will get married, or get well, or otherwise flourish. As Mbande related his own experience, he recalled, "I have dreamt of a wedding dance, and the man died; again, I have dreamt of the death of a sick man, but he got well."[12]

In Britain, imperial theorists of religion were intrigued by this principle of contrast. Referring to these Zulu reports, E. B. Tylor noted that "this works out, by the same crooked logic that guided our ancestors, the axiom that 'dreams go by contraries.'"[13] Similarly, Andrew Lang took these reports to indicate that "Dr. Callaway illustrates this for the Zulus," proving that "Savages, indeed, oddly enough, have hit on our theory, 'dreams go by contraries.'"[14]

But the conversations collected in *Religious System* about this hermeneutical principle,

"dreams go by contraries," reveal profound struggles with indeterminacy. Like the correlation of good summer dreams and bad winter dreams, the principle "dreams go by contraries" was true but not always true. As Mbande acknowledged, "I have not yet come to a certain conclusion that this is true; for some dream of death, and death occurs; and sometimes of health, and the person lives."[15] His friend Uguaise Mdunga accepted the principle that dreams go by contraries but then recounted that he had just dreamed of a wedding and a funeral. According to the principle of contraries, "Your dream of a funeral lamentation is good; the dream of a wedding is bad."[16] But what if you dream of both?

As these Zulu deliberations about the hermeneutics of dreams indicate, dreams could be correlated with the seasons, but not always, and dreams could go by contraries, but not always. And sometimes, as Uguaise observed, "sleep has filled my mind with mere senseless images."[17]

This indeterminacy in the interpretation of dreams was related to the uncertainty and instability of daily life under colonial conditions. Dreams were not merely "texts" to be interpreted. They were calls to action. They demanded a practical response, whether through exchanges with ancestral spirits or through asserting ancestral claims on a territory.

In the first instance, as Uguaise Mdunga observed, dreams often required a sacrificial offering for an ancestor, calling the dreamer to action. "You will see also by night, you will dream; the Itongo [ancestor] will tell you what it wishes," he observed. "It will also tell you the bullock it would have killed."[18] This exchange between the living and the "living dead," the ancestors, was a central feature of Zulu religious practice. Dreams were a medium of communication; but they were also a call to action, with detailed attention to the specific ancestral spirit, sacrificial offering, and, of course, the dreaming human being who must be brought into relationship with the deceased ancestor in this exchange.

In the second instance, dreams often required actions to assert or reassert claims on territory, as when dreaming of the dead (or, according to one report, even not dreaming of the dead) required the living to perform certain ritual actions so the dead might be "brought back from the open country to his home."[19] In such ancestral dreams, practical steps had to be taken to reestablish the territorial integrity of domestic space shared by the living and the dead.

These dream-based practices of ritual exchange and territorial orientation suggest that dreams were not only about meaning; they were also about a world of action. Zulu dreams were not merely "subjective apparitions," or "brain sensation," as Henry Callaway would have it. Dreams were objective indicators of a changing world.

BLOCKING DREAMS

Under colonial conditions, the meaning of dreams might have become increasingly uncertain. But the energetics of dreams was radically disrupted. As Africans were deprived of the means of exchange and access to territory, dream life was dramatically altered. Increasingly, according to reports collected in *Religious System*, Africans turned to ritual techniques for blocking dreams because they were unable to fulfill the practical obligations to their ancestors that were conveyed by dreaming. Techniques for blocking dreams included using a black medicinal herb, performing symbolic actions to throw the dream behind (without looking back), and enacting rituals to remove the dream from the home and secure it in a remote place.[20] Conversion to Christianity could also be a technique for blocking ancestral dreams.

In the ritual energetics of exchange, Africans deprived of cattle could not fulfill the requirements of sacrifice. Recounting a recent dream, Uguaise Mdunga noted, "I have seen my brother." His deceased elder brother, appearing in a dream, called for a sacrificial offering, which placed a solemn and sacred obligation on Uguaise to respond. But Uguaise had no cattle. Addressing the spirit of his brother, he cried, "I have no bullock; do you see any in the cattle-pen?" Unable to achieve the necessary exchange, Uguaise could only feel the anger of his brother. "I dreamed that he was beating me," he reported, noting that in further dreams this spirit kept "coming for the purpose of killing me."[21] The result of this blocked exchange, he felt, would only be suffering, illness, and death.

A few decades earlier, European Christian missionaries had complained that they could not gain converts among the Zulu because the people were too wealthy in cattle.[22] Now, ironically, when people had less cattle, ancestors were increasingly appearing in dreams to demand sacrifice. As a result, people dreamed but did not talk about their dreams. As Mbande observed, "although they have dreamed and in the morning awoke in pain, [they] do not like to talk about it themselves; for among black men slaughtering cattle has become much more common than formerly, on the ground that the Idhlozi [ancestor] has demanded them."[23] Under colonial conditions of dispossession, dreams of ancestors calling for cattle apparently increased, but the living, unable to fulfill this exchange, no longer were able to talk about what they had seen in their dreams. Increasingly, Africans sought ritual means to block their dreams, as Callaway observed, "lest the frequent sacrifices demanded should impoverish them."[24]

Under colonial conditions, Africans tried to block their dreams, but their dreams were also blocked by colonial conditions. In addition to calling for sacrificial exchange, dreams also called upon people to keep their ancestors in the home or bring them back to the home. However, for people displaced from their homes, this aspect of the energetics of dreams became very difficult. As Mbande recounted, his own family, which had been displaced by colonial warfare, struggled with their ancestral dreams of home. Forced to flee to another country, they employed the traditional ritual means of transporting ancestors under the sign of snakes. As a symbolic trace of the ancestor, the snake communicated through dreams. As Mbande noted, "Perhaps the snake follows; perhaps it refuses, giving reasons why it does not wish to go to that place, speaking to the eldest son in a dream; or it may be to an old man of the village; or the old queen."[25]

In the case of Mbande's family, however, their ancestral dreams were blocked by the colonial incursions of the Dutch and the British. As they were "flying from the Dutch," the head of the family, Umyeka, dreamed that their paternal ancestor was demanding that they reclaim their home as "it was said to him in a dream, 'Why do you forsake your father?'" But they could not return home, "fearing their feud with the Dutch." Blocked from returning to their ancestral territory, they dreamed of relocating their ancestor. As Mbande recalled, "our father whilst asleep dreamt the chief was talking with him, [saying] it would be well for you to make a bridge for me, that I may cross on it and come home; for I am cold, and the water makes me colder still." With considerable ritual effort, they built a bridge for their ancestor to relocate to a new home. But this dream of a new home was also shattered, as Mbande recounted, because they were soon driven out at the order of the British colonial administrator, Secretary of Native Affairs Theophilus Shepstone.[26] As a result, Mbande reported, "We were scattered and went to other places."[27] The energetics of dreams, therefore, was radically disrupted by such colonial conditions of dispossession and displacement.

INTERRELIGIOUS DREAMS

In *The Religious System of the Amazulu*, a convert at Callaway's mission station who is identified only as James features prominently as a dreamer. After living for over ten years at the Christian mission, James left to pursue his own dreams. Showing all of the symptoms of being called by the ancestors to be a diviner, suffering an illness, Mbande notes, "which is not intelligible among Christians," James went off to live alone, subject to dreams, his body becoming a "house of dreams."[28] When Mbande and his fellow Christian convert Paul went to see him, James related that his initiatory sickness had caused him to leave the mission, noting that "this disease has separated me from you," but he also observed that his dreams had given him new access to the entire world because "there is not a single place in the whole country which I do not know; I go over it all by night in my sleep; there is not a single place the exact situation of which I do not know."[29] In this new freedom, however, his dreams were still blocked. In his dreams, he was told where to find medicinal plants, but he did not find them; he dreamed of antelope telling him where to find an aloe tree, but it was not there. He dreamed of ancestors calling for meat but could "not kill cattle."[30] The word of God and the bell of the church, Mbande advised, would drive away all of these dreams. But James seems to have found these ancestral dreams already blocked. Nevertheless, he continued to dream. As he told Mbande and Paul, "On the night before you came I saw you coming to me, but you were white men."[31] Going by contraries, perhaps, this dream nevertheless suggested that James now perceived these African Christian converts as aliens.

Every night, in dreams, James saw wild animals, dangerous snakes, and rushing rivers. "All these things come near to me to kill me," he said. On the day of his meeting with his Christian friends, James reported that last night he had been attacked by men. As James explained, "I dreamt many men were killing me; I escaped I know not how. And on waking one part of my body felt different from other parts; it was no longer alike all over." As a result, James found, "My body is muddled today."[32] The Zulu term for "muddled"—*Dungeka, Ukudunga*—was a metaphor derived from stirring up mud in water. Although it could be applied to a state of mind, signifying a confusion of mind, it could also be applied to the disturbance of a household by a house-muddler (*Idungandhlu*) or the disturbance of a village by a village-muddler (*Idungamuzi*).[33] All of these meanings, certainly, were at play in the dreams of a Zulu man who experienced his body, his home, his family, and his sense of community stirred up and under attack by forces threatening to kill him.

Mbande reminded James of an old dream, which James had related to Mbande when they were both Christians, in which James crossed a river in a boat of faith and was saved from being killed by wild dogs. In African indigenous religion, the river was a powerful liminal zone in between the sacred space of home, which was built up through ritual relations with ancestors, and the wild, dangerous zones of the bush or forest that contained alien spirits. Mediating between home space and wild space, the river represented both ancestral protection and spiritual danger, a place of potential for both life and death.[34] As James learned during his initiatory sickness, the dreams of a diviner were filled with rushing rivers. Mbande, as a Christian, interpreted these dream rivers as a test of faith. The dreamer, according to Mbande, must cross these rivers in the boat of Christian faith.

Remembering this old dream, in which he had been saved by the boat of faith, James had now arrived at a new interpretation. Yes, James said, "the boat is my faith, which has now sunk into the water. And the dogs which I saw are now devouring me." If he could not be saved by Christian faith, Mbande demanded, "Who will save you?" Nothing, James replied: "I am now dead altogether."[35]

Under colonial conditions in a contact zone, all of the Zulu dreams we have considered bear traces of a changing world, a colonial world in which indigenous people were undergoing dispossession, displacement, and despair. As a result, in the hermeneutics and energetics of dreams, the principles of dream interpretation became increasingly indeterminate and the ways of practically engaging with the demands of dreams by entering into ancestral exchange or affirming ancestral territory became increasingly impossible. These were realities of the colonial situation revealed through dreams.

Disciplining Dreams

Within this interreligious contact zone, new Christian techniques were being developed to block ancestral dreams. In dealing with the case of James, Mbande advised a religious discipline of hearing—listening to the word of God, listening to the bell of the church—as a method for blocking visions. Christian prayer, as well, was a disciplinary technique for counteracting dangerous visions. Mbande's own experience of prayer had required developing a disciplined subjectivity that blocked what Callaway called "subjective apparitions." "As regards those wild animals which a man sees when he is going to pray in secret," Mbande reported, "I too have seen them again and again." According to Mbande, these wild forces arrived in a pattern—snake, leopard, and warrior—to distract the Christian from the sensory focus necessary for prayer. With eyes closed, Mbande felt their approach, as if he heard them saying, "Now he has closed his eyes, and will no longer see me; let me draw near and bite him, or lay hold of him, or stab him." Remaining steadfast in prayer, Mbande heard "a great noise which took away all my courage, and led me to say, 'This is something real . . . now there is coming a great thing to kill me'"[36]—first the snake, with terrifying large eyes; then the leopard, "crackling" through the brush; then the enemy warrior, brandishing a long spear, thrusting the assegai into the body of the praying Christian.

According to Mbande, Christians at prayer faced real dangers from being discovered and attacked by other people who would say, "O, that man is now a believer; I heard him praying; it is well for us to go to the place where he prays, and arouse him, or beat him, that he many not repeat such things."[37] To avoid being discovered, Mbande went out to pray alone before sunrise while most people were still asleep. In the darkness, therefore, the dangerous snake, leopard, and warrior were like phantoms of a dream. Eventually, Mbande realized that he was being attacked by "fantacy" and "deceived by fantasies." But this realization required an extraordinary discipline of the senses, not by employing techniques to block out these dreamlike apparitions, but by surrendering to them. Mbande recounted how he conquered these apparitions by allowing them to seize him, holding steady to feel them through his body.

> And indeed when I was kneeling there came a snake to do as on other days. I said, "No! To-day let me feel by my body that it has already seized me." Then I conquered. There came a huge leopard. I said also to it, "Let me feel by my body." I conquered. There came a man, running to stab me at once. Since I had despised the leopard, I said too of the man, "Let me feel by my body." I conquered him. I

went home having ascended a rock of safety, saying, "O, forsooth I have been hindered by fantasies."[38]

In these nineteenth-century Zulu interreligious reflections, we catch a glimpse of new subjectivities being negotiated in the media of dreams and visions. Putting the matter starkly, indigenous dreams and visions were real because they called for action, requiring practical responses through exchange or relocation. By contrast, following Mbande, Christian converts were called to see through their dreams as heuristic devices, as mere metaphors of the dilemmas of faith. By holding steady, Christians could demystify their visions as mere fantasy. This process of demystification demanded a rigorous discipline of the senses, requiring not only concentration but also endurance in mobilizing the body to withstand dangerous attacks in order to break the hold of fantasy.

We must certainly notice the undercurrent of violence running through these dreams and visions. Spirits come to kill James. Snakes, leopards, and warriors come to kill Mpengula Mbande. Zulu dreams and visions, whether interpreted in traditional or Christian idiom, were undergoing violent transformations under colonial conditions. From a Christian perspective, indigenous dreams and visions had lost their purchase on the world. In a section of Callaway's *Religious System of the Amazulu* entitled "The Diviner Mistaken," the Zulu Christian convert Usetemba Dhladhla related a story about how a Zulu diviner had failed to find and secure the return of a lost cow, "a heifer belonging to Mr. G., my white master."[39] After getting a shilling from Mr. G. to consult the diviner, Dhladhla participated in the traditional divining ritual of questions and responses to learn that the missing heifer was in the thorn country along the Umsunduze River "in the neighborhood of Mr

T." Following the diviner's vision, Dhladhla went off to the thorn country only to learn from people in "native villages" that he was entering an area controlled by "the white man who ate up the cattle of the people that were lost." Dhladhla was afraid to go any further because Mr. T. was a "passionate white man who beats any coloured men whom he does not know if he see them passing through his land. So we went back to Pietermaritzburg without going to T.; and told Mr. G that we had not found the heifer at the place pointed out by the diviner. So he told us to give up the search. We did so, and that was the end of it."[40] According to Henry Callaway, this was a case of a "diviner mistaken," a failure of indigenous African dreams, visions, and divination. But clearly the story provided evidence of colonial violence—appropriation of cattle, control of territory, and practice of torture—that defined the context in which Zulu divination, visions, and dreams were being subjected to a new kind of discipline.

THEORIZING DREAMS

In the academic study of religion, we need to pay close attention to these colonial realities and dreams. A nineteenth-century imperial study of religion, positioned at the center of empire, was committed to erasing these material and spiritual details. E. B. Tylor, for example, used James, the Zulu dreamer, as primary data for building his theory of the origin of religion, animism, as a primitive misunderstanding of the illusions of dreams for the realities of waking life. Citing Callaway's *Religious System*, Tylor invoked the dreams of a Zulu "professional seer" who "becomes as the expressive native phrase is, 'a house of dreams,'" as a classic example of animism because "phantoms are continually coming to talk to him in his sleep."[41] As we have seen, however, this "seer," the Zulu Christian apostate

and struggling diviner, James, was not confused by dreams of spirits coming to talk to him. He was tormented by forces coming to kill him.

In 1871, Henry Callaway presented a paper to the Royal Anthropological Society in London on the results of his research into the dreaming, divination, and religious life of the Zulu of South Africa. Ordinary dreams and extraordinary visions, Callaway proposed, could be explained as "brain-sensation" that took the form of "brain-sight" and "brain-hearing." Brain-sensation, he clarified, is "a condition of brain which, without external causes in operation, is attended by feeling, hearing, and sight, just as it would if there were external causes in operation, capable of producing such sensations." Drawing upon the Zulu accounts and interpretations of such "subjective apparitions," which he had recently published in his *Religious System of the Amazulu*, Callaway illustrated "brain-sensation" through examples of "spectral vision or *brain-sight*" and "*brain-hearing*—that is . . . the same condition of brain as there would be if the sounds actually reached it through the ear."[42]

In the discussion that followed, one member of the society, Walter Cooper Dendy, dismissed Callaway's analysis, complaining that it was "the most prolix and monotonous paper read before the Institute during this session; indeed, it was a real infliction . . . if we hear nothing from south-eastern Africa more rational, the sooner the district is tabooed the better."[43] But the problem with Callaway's analysis was that he did not do justice to his "data" because he reduced the dynamic Zulu hermeneutics and energetics of dreams, which were situated in a colonial contact zone, to a cognitive psychology of "brain-sensation."

Dreaming in the contact zone, as we have seen, cannot be adequately explained as a mentality and certainly not as a "primitive mentality" preserving original cognitive processes of an animism that confused dreaming and waking. In order to distill a primitive religious mentality, E. B. Tylor had to erase all of the social, political, and military conditions under which Henry Callaway was collecting his data. As a matter of method, Tylor insisted on erasing the intercultural exchanges in which this "religious" data was emerging from a contact zone. According to Tylor, "savage religion" had to be abstracted from its living contexts in order to be used in an evolutionary history of human culture that began with primitive animism. "In defining the religious systems of the lower races, so as to place them correctly in the history of culture," Tylor observed in 1892, "careful examination is necessary to separate the genuine developments of native theology from the effects of intercourse with civilized foreigners."[44] Any trace of more advanced religious concepts, such as ideas of deity, morality, or retribution in an afterlife, could only have entered "savage" religion, Tylor argued, through such foreign intercourse with "higher" races. Factoring out colonial contacts, relations, and exchanges, he argued, "leaves untouched in the religions of the lower races the lower developments of animism."[45]

According to this method, therefore, animism appeared as the original religion—the earliest, the lowest—only by erasing the actual colonial situations in which indigenous people lived. As a result, the theory of animism provided an ideological supplement to the imperial project.

Nineteenth-century Zulu dreams were not symptoms of some original "primitive mentality." Instead, they were situated within the violent disruptions of a colonial contact zone. An undercurrent of violence runs through these dreams, as dreamers are threatened by neglected ancestors, enemy warriors, wild animals, or dangerous rivers. As I have proposed, this violent dream imagery can be related to the breakdown

in the religious practices of ancestral exchange and spatial orientation that were important features of African indigenous religion. But some of these dreams, especially the dreams of James, also suggest the interreligious nature of the contact zone, a space in which Africans were negotiating new Christian and indigenous religious understandings of a changing world.

Both of these modes of understanding—indigenous African and African Christian—were erased by E. B. Tylor in abstracting Zulu dreams from the intercultural and interreligious relations of the contact zone. But they were also destined for destruction within his imperial understanding of the mission of a scientific study of religion. Tylor imagined that his anthropological investigations were providing "new evidence and method in theology."[46] But his ethnographic theology, comparing "evidence of religion in all stages of culture,"[47] advanced a discipline of demystification that was not unlike Mpengula Mbande's demystification of dreams and visions as merely fantasy. "It is a harsher, and at times even painful office of ethnography," Tylor asserted, "to expose the remains of crude old culture which have passed into harmful superstition, and to mark these out for destruction."[48] As we have seen, colonial interventions in Zulu dream life, which eroded the material means of ancestral exchange and territorial orientation, had already been far more destructive than E. B. Tylor, from his study at Oxford, could ever have hoped to have been.

However, the colonial situation in South Africa was not only destructive, it was also productive, producing new dreams, and new subjectivities, which have persisted, despite Tylor's attempt to erase their conditions of production and mark them out for destruction. By returning to the colonial hermeneutics of dreams, in all of its indeterminacy, and by returning to the colonial energetics of dreams, with all of its obstacles, we can recover what E. B. Tylor tried to erase and destroy—the reality of dreaming in a contact zone.[49]

ZULU RELIGION

By grounding nineteenth-century Zulu dreaming in colonial situations, I believe we gain a new perspective on an indigenous African religion as a dynamic, fluid, and contested set of resources—interpretive, pragmatic, and energetic resources—that were deployed in a transcultural contact zone. Clearly, this rendering of religion as resources and strategies could be extended more broadly to the analysis of any religious form of life. In the case of Zulu religion, however, such a situated and dynamic rendering is necessary to counteract the characteristic representations of this indigenous African religion as either a "religious system" to be inventoried or a "religious mentality" to be criticized or celebrated.

In the first instance, the notion of a Zulu religious system,[50] echoing the boundaries imposed by the colonial location system or reserve system,[51] has been constructed as an inventory of key features—God,[52] ancestors,[53] sacrifice,[54] divination,[55] and political authority, asserted in collective rituals of fertility[56] and warfare,[57] but also bearing claims to sacred kingship in the lineage of the thoroughly mythologized King Shaka that were most frequently and consistently asserted by British colonizers and imperialists.[58] In the colonial context, however, all of these features of indigenous Zulu religion could not possibly be regarded as elements of a stable system. As religious resources, simultaneously symbolic and material, all of these elements were being deployed during the nineteenth century in complex and contested negotiations under colonial conditions.

God, for example, was at stake and at risk in these negotiations. Almost immediately after they arrived in Natal, the Anglican Bishop J. W. Colenso and the Anglican missionary Henry Callaway became embroiled in an argument over whether the Zulu had any indigenous understanding of a supreme being that was similar to the Christian God. Colenso found that they did, identifying two Zulu terms, uNkulunkulu (the "Great-Great-One") and umvelinqangi (the "First Out-Comer"), which he found equivalent to Yahweh and Elohim of the Hebrew Bible. Disagreeing, Callaway found that the Zulu had no indigenous understanding of God, arguing that uNkulunkulu was actually understood as the original ancestor of the Zulu people. In accounts of the Zulu religious system, this controversy persisted, with some commentators arguing for an indigenous Zulu conception of God[59] and others arguing that Zulu ancestral religion adopted such a concept from the Christian missions.[60] By situating this question in the colonial context, however, we discover a range of Zulu interpretive strategies being deployed along a contested but expanding frontier of British influence and control. Under these conditions, people least affected by these changes tended to regard uNkulunkulu as the original ancestor of their political grouping, while people whose political autonomy had been destroyed interpreted uNkulunkulu as either the original ancestor of all humanity or the supreme being of the world.[61]

As we have seen, ancestors were also at risk, calling for meat from their relatives who had been dispossessed and calling to be brought home by their children who had been displaced. Under these conditions, sacrificial exchange, domestic order, and the divination practiced by ritual specialists were all profoundly affected by British military incursions and colonial interventions. While the British colonial administrator Theophilus Shepstone claimed the sacred mantle of King Shaka, putting himself forward as the

Supreme Chief of all Zulu people,[62] indigenous Zulu religious resources were being deployed and redeployed, mobilized and contested, in a contact zone of intercultural relations and exchanges but also of asymmetrical power relations.

If Zulu religion cannot be reconstructed as a stable system, it also cannot be reduced to a mentality, whether that mentality is critiqued as an unwarranted survival from human prehistory or celebrated as a persistence of an African identity that is "incurably religious."[63] As we have seen, E. B. Tylor based his entire theory of the origin of religion, animism, on the primitive inability to distinguish between dreams and waking consciousness. Citing Zulu data as his best evidence for this original "house of dreams," Tylor also invoked the Zulu as survivals of the "inveterate ignorance" that characterized the primitive mentality of human beings in the earliest phase of evolution. In Tylor's "intellectualist" theory of religion, primitives might have suffered from primordial stupidity, but they exercised their limited intellectual powers to develop explanations of the world in which they lived. As evidence of this primitive mentality, Tylor invoked, once again, Zulu data provided by Henry Callaway's *Religious System of the Amazulu*, quoting Mpengula Mbande, who observed that "we are told all things, and assent without seeing clearly whether they are true or not."[64] However, Mbande's point in this statement was that most Zulu-speaking people had not accepted the truth of the Christian gospel proclaimed by Callaway's mission. Instead of offering "savage" evidence of primordial stupidity, therefore, Mpengula Mbande was announcing his recently acquired Christian commitment. Although Tylor preferred to erase such an entanglement from any reconstruction of "savage" religion, his citation of Mbande as evidence suggests the futility of his enterprise. Everything, even thinking, was thoroughly entangled in colonial relations.

As a strategic counterattack against European denigration of African religion as primitive mentality, John Mbiti's celebration of African religiosity as an all-pervasive spiritual mentality is an understandable but untenable rendering of African religion. According to Mbiti, an indigenous religious mentality pervades every aspect of African life.

> Wherever the African is, there is his religion: he carries it to the fields where he is sowing seeds or harvesting a new crop; he takes it with him to the beer party or to attend a funeral ceremony; and if he is educated, he takes religion with him to the examination room at school or in the university; if he is a politician he takes it to the house of parliament.

In every public sphere of economic, social, and political activity, Africans, according to Mbiti, are essentially religious. "Although many African languages do not have a word for religion as such," Mbiti admitted, "it nevertheless accompanies the individual from long before his birth to long after his physical death."[65] This religious portability, however, is a consequence of precisely the kinds of colonial disruptions that we have considered with respect to Zulu dreaming. Detached from "locative" relations of ancestral exchange and orientation, this "utopian" religiosity can be taken anywhere (or nowhere) as a mobile mentality.[66]

Although cognitive studies in religion have made significant advances in recent years, we are still faced with the challenge of situating mentality in social space.[67] Zulu religion, however rendered, must be more than a generalized mentality. In a discussion of intellectualist theories of religion in which religion is explained as way of explaining and seeking control over the environment, Thomas Lawson and Robert McCauley invoke the Zulu in passing, observing that an intellectualist rendering of religion finds that "the reason the Zulu have a belief in and rites involving the ancestors is that such a belief and the attendant rites enable the Zulu to develop an explanatory theory which not only accounts for any contingency but also permits them to devise means to attempt to control their environment."[68] Based on our brief review of nineteenth-century Zulu dreaming, we must wonder about such an "intellectualist" explanation of Zulu religious mentality as a proto-scientific means of explanation and control. Everything in the nineteenth-century Zulu hermeneutics and energetics of dreams that we have considered suggests that all interpretations were contingent and that the cultural, social, and political environment was out of control. Dreaming, which has been oddly neglected in cognitive studies of religion, might be an important arena for exploring such indeterminacy and chaos in the history of religions.

ZULU DREAMS

Dreams, the most insubstantial medium, which Henry Callaway dismissed as "subjective apparitions," nevertheless mediated substantial and material relations in nineteenth-century Zulu religious life.[69] In conclusion, we can reflect briefly on the colonial mediations of the hermeneutics, pragmatics, and energetics of nineteenth-century Zulu dreaming.

First, dreams were texts to be interpreted. These were multi-sensory texts, evoking a synesthetic engagement[70] and self-involving interpellation[71] of the dreamer into a challenge of sense-making and self-making in a social world. Hermeneutical principles could be drawn upon, principles of correlation and contradiction, with the understanding that these principles were true but not always true. Dreams, therefore, asked questions. Considering a different African context, Ladislav Holy has usefully identified the range of questions raised in the interpretation of dreams:

(1) Should the meaning of the dream be understood as the reversal of its manifest content or not?

(2) Does the dream predict some specific event or is its message merely of general significance?

(3) Should the dream be interpreted intra-textually or should contextual factors be taken into consideration in the proper understanding of its message?[72]

All of these questions, as we have seen, arose in nineteenth-century Zulu dreaming, calling into question whether dreams "go by contraries," bear a specific message, or relate to a practical context. All of these hermeneutical questions, however, were thoroughly embedded in the changing relations and shifting terrains of colonial interventions. Colonialism, therefore, was an integral part of the stuff that indigenous dreams were made of.

Second, dreams were texts to be told. The pragmatics of dreams, which turns private dreams into shared stories, was integral to Zulu religious practices and performances. Dreams provided resources for an oral textuality and performances of that oral textuality provided resources for dreaming. This reciprocal relationship between dreaming and telling can be identified as the crucial motor of the pragmatics of dreaming. In *The Religious System of the Amazulu*, the most extensive account of dream-telling refers to the controversy between the Christian catechist Mbande and the Christian apostate James, who left the mission to become a "house of dreams." Here the Zulu catechist tried to recall the "old dream" of the boat of faith in order to recall the Zulu apostate back to the "old" Christian faith that had only recently arrived and had only recently been abandoned by James. In this pragmatics of dreams, turning "subjective apparitions" into shared narratives, Mbande and James negotiated over the terms and conditions of being a person in a place under colonial relations of power. This particular religious argument, which was conducted by referring to Zulu tradition, but was simultaneously interreligious and transcultural, was pursued in the idiom of recollecting a memorable and definitive dream of the river, the liminal space of pure possibility of transformation and life-threatening danger of dissolution. While Mbande urged James to return to the Christian life of the mission, James insisted, "I am now dead altogether." As this exchange can only suggest, the pragmatics of dreams, by transposing private dreams into public argument, raised issues of life and death for Zulu-speaking people under nineteenth-century colonial conditions.

Finally, dreams were texts that demanded response. As we have seen, the energetics of Zulu dreaming called for responses of ancestral exchange and orientation that were integral to Zulu religious strategies for sustaining ongoing relations between the living and the dead. In the energetics of dreams, Zulu asked not only, "What do dreams mean?" They also had to ask, "What do dreams want?" In this respect, Zulu dreamers anticipated recent theoretical reflection in cultural studies on the demands of visual images in aesthetic, cultural, and religious life. "What do pictures want?", W. J. T. Mitchell has recently asked,[73] a question that has been pursued in research on the demands of visual religious imagery in America,[74] India,[75] and Africa.[76] Under colonial conditions, meeting the demands of dreams—doing what they want by sustaining ancestral exchange and orientation—became increasingly urgent as dispossession and displacement increasingly defined Zulu life. The various responses we have considered, from

indigenous techniques for blocking dreams to Christian conversion, were situated within the colonial crisis of responding to demanding dreams under difficult conditions.

FOR FURTHER READING

Althusser, Louis. "Ideology and Ideological State Apparatuses." In *Lenin and Philosophy and Other Essays*, 170–86. London: New Left Books, 1989.

Benham, Marian S. *Henry Callaway, First Bishop of Kaffraria: His Life History and Work: A Memoir*. London: Macmillan, 1896.

Berglund, Axel-Ivar. *Zulu Thought-Patterns and Symbolism*. London: C. Hurst, 1976.

Burleson, Blake. *Jung in Africa*. New York: Continuum, 2005.

Callaway, Henry. *The Religious System of the Amazulu*. Springvale: Springvale Mission, 1868–70; reprinted Cape Town: Struik, 1970.

———. "On Divination and Analogous Phenomena among the Natives of Natal." *Proceedings of the Anthropological Institute* 1 (1872): 163–183.

Carrasco, David. "Jaguar Christians in the Contact Zone: Concealed Narratives in the Histories of Religions in the Americas." In *Beyond Primitivism: Indigenous Religious Traditions and Modernity*, edited by Jacob K. Olupona, 128–38. London: Routledge, 2004.

Chidester, David. *Word and Light: Seeing, Hearing, and Religious Discourse*. Urbana: University of Illinois Press, 1992.

———. *Savage Systems: Colonialism and Comparative Religion in Southern Africa*. Charlottesville: University of Virginia Press, 1996.

———. "Colonialism." In *Guide to the Study of Religion*, edited by Willi Braun and Russell T. McCutcheon, 423–37. London: Cassell, 2000.

———. "Credo Mutwa, Zulu Shaman: The Invention and Appropriation of Indigenous Authenticity in African Folk Religion." *Journal for the Study of Religion* 15, no. 2: (2002) 65–85.

———. "'Classify and Conquer': Friedrich Max Müller, Indigenous Religious Traditions, and Imperial Comparative Religion." In *Beyond Primitivism: Indigenous Religious Traditions and Modernity*, edited by Jacob K. Olupona, 71–88. London and New York: Routledge, 2004.

———. "Colonialism and Shamanism." In *Shamanism: An Encyclopedia of World Beliefs, Practices and Culture*, edited by Mariko Namba Walter and Eva Jane Neumann Fridman, 2 vols, 1:41–49. Santa Barbara, CA: ABC-Clio, 2004.

———. "Animism." In *Encyclopedia of Religion and Nature*, edited by Bron Taylor and Jeffrey Kaplan, 78–81. New York: Continuum, 2005.

———. "Real and Imagined: Imperial Inventions of Religion in Colonial Southern Africa." In *Religion and the Secular: Historical and Colonial Formations*, edited by Timothy Fitzgerald, 153–76. London: Equinox, 2007.

———. "Zulu Dreamscapes: Senses, Media, and Authentication in Contemporary Neo-Shamanism." *Material Religion* 4, no. 2 (July 2008): 136–58.

Chidester, David, Chirevo Kwenda, Robert Petty, Judy Tobler, and Darrel Wratten. *African Traditional Religion in South Africa: An Annotated Bibliography*. Westport, CT: Greenwood, 1997.

De Heusch, Luc. *Sacrifice in Africa: A Structuralist Approach*. Translated by Linda O'Brien and Alice Morton. Manchester: Manchester University Press, 1985.

Dentan, Robert K. "Ethnographic Considerations in the Cross-Cultural Study of Dreaming." In *Sleep and Dreams: A Sourcebook*, edited by Jayne Gackenbach, 317–58. New York: Garland, 1986.

Doke, C. M., and Vilakazi B. W. *Zulu-English Dictionary*. 2nd ed. Johannesburg: Witwatersrand University Press, 1958.

Du Toit, Brian M. "The Isangoma: An Adaptive Agent Among Urban Zulu." *Anthropological Quarterly* 44, no. 2 (1971): 51–65.

Etherington, Norman. *Preachers, Peasants and Politics in Southeast Africa, 1835–1880: African Christianity in Natal, Pondoland and Zululand*. London: Royal Historical Society, 1978.

———. "Missionary Doctors and African Healers in Mid-Victorian South Africa." *South African Historical Journal* 19 (1987): 77–91.

———. "The 'Shepstone System' in the Colony of Natal and Beyond the Borders." In *Natal and Zululand From Earliest Times to 1910: A New History*, edited by Andrew Duminy and Bill Guest, 170–92. Pietermaritzburg: University of Natal Press, 1989.

———. "Kingdoms of This World and the Next: Christian Beginnings among Zulu and Swazi." In *Christianity in South Africa: A Political, Social and Cultural History*, edited by Richard Elphick and Rodney Davenport, 89–106. Berkeley: University of California Press, 1997.

———. "Outward and Visible Signs of Conversion in Nineteenth-Century KwaZulu-Natal." *Journal of Religion in Africa* 32 (2002): 422–39.

Fanon, Frantz. *Black Skin, White Masks*. Translated by Charles Lam Markmann. New York: Grove, 1967.

Girardot, Norman J. *The Victorian Translation of China: James Legge's Oriental Pilgrimage*. Berkeley: University of California Press, 2002.

Gluckman, Max. "Social Aspects of First Fruits Ceremonies among the South-Eastern Bantu." *Africa* 11 (1938): 25–41.

Guy, Jeff. *The Destruction of the Zulu Kingdom*. London: Longmans, 1979.

———. *The Maphumulo Uprising: War, Law, and Ritual in the Zulu Rebellion*. Scottsville: University of KwaZulu-Natal Press, 2005.

Hamilton, Carolyn. *Terrific Majesty: The Powers of Shaka Zulu and .the Limits of Historical Invention*. Cape Town: David Philip, 1998.

Hexham, Irving, ed. *Texts on Zulu Religion: Traditional Zulu Ideas about God*. New York: Edwin Mellen, 1987.

———. "Lord of the Sky—King of the Earth: Zulu Traditional Religion and Belief in the Sky God." *Sciences Religieuses/Studies in Religion* 10 (1981): 273–78.

Holy, Ladislav. "Berti Dream Interpretation." In *Dreaming, Religion, and Society in Africa,* edited by M. C. Jederej and Rosalind Shaw, 86–99. Leiden: E. J. Brill, 1992.

Horton, Robin. *Patterns of Thought in Africa and the West: Essays on Magic, Science, and Religion*. Cambridge: Cambridge University Press, 1997.

Jederej, M. C., and Rosalind Shaw, eds. *Dreaming, Religion, and Society in Africa*. Leiden: Brill, 1992.

Jung, C. G. *Collected Works*. Translated by R. F. C. Hull. 20 vols. London: Routledge & Kegan Paul, 1964.

Keegan, Timothy. *Colonial South Africa and the Origins of the Racial Order*. Cape Town: David Philip, 1996.

Kiernan, James P. "The Social Stuff of Revelation: Pattern and Purpose in Zionist Dreams and Visions." *Africa* 55, no. 3 (1985): 304–17.

King, Richard. *Orientalism and Religion: Postcolonial Theory, India, and the "Mystic East."* London: Routledge, 1999.

Krige, Eileen Jensen. *The Social System of the Zulus*. London: Longmans Green, 1936.

Lambert, John. *Betrayed Trust: Africans and the State in Colonial Natal*. Scottsville: University of Natal Press, 1995.

Lambert, Michael. "Ancient Greek and Zulu Sacrificial Ritual: A Comparative Analysis." *Numen* 40, no. 3 (1993): 293–18.

Lang, Andrew. *The Making of Religion*. 3rd ed. London: Longman, 1909.

Lawson, E. Thomas, and Robert N. McCauley. *Rethinking Religion: Connecting Cognition and Culture*. Cambridge: Cambridge University Press, 1990.

Lee, S. G. "Social Influences in Zulu Dreaming." *Journal of Social Psychology* 47 (1958): 256–83.

Lewis-Williams, David. *The Mind in the Cave.* London: Thames & Hudson, 2002.

Lohmann, Roger, ed. *Dream Travelers: Sleep Experiences and Culture in the Western Pacific.* New York: Palgrave Macmillan, 2003.

Lopez, Donald, Jr., ed. *Curators of the Buddha: The Study of Buddhism under Colonialism.* Chicago: University of Chicago Press, 1995.

Mannoni, Octave. *Prospero and Caliban: The Psychology of Colonization.* Translated by Pamela Powesland. Ann Arbor: University of Michigan Press, 1990.

Masuzawa, Tomoko. *The Invention of World Religions: Or, How European Universalism Was Preserved in the Language of Pluralism.* Chicago: University of Chicago Press, 2005.

Mbiti, John S. *African Religions and Philosophy.* London: Heinemann, 1969.

———. *Introduction to African Religion.* London: Heinemann, 1975.

McClendon, Thomas. "The Man Who Would Be Inkosi: Civilising Missions in Shepstone's Early Career." *Journal of Southern African Studies* 30, no. 2 (2004): 339–58.

McLynn, Frank. *Carl Gustav Jung: A Biography.* New York: St. Martin's Press, 1997.

Meyer, Birgit. "Religious Sensations: Why Media, Aesthetics, and Power Matter in the Study of Contemporary Religion." Inaugural Lecture at Free University, Amsterdam, 2006.

Mitchell, W. J. T. *What Do Pictures Want? The Lives and Loves of Images.* Chicago: University of Chicago Press, 2005.

Morgan, David. *Visual Piety: A History and Theory of Popular Religious Images.* Berkeley: University of California Press, 1998.

Ngubane, Harriet. *Body and Mind in Zulu Medicine: An Ethnography of Health and Disease in Nyuswa-Zulu Thought and Practice.* London: Academic, 1977.

———. "Aspects of Clinical Practice and Traditional Organization of Indigenous Healers in South Africa." *Social Science and Medicine* 15, no. 2 (1981): 361–65.

Ortiz, Fernando. *Cuban Counterpoint: Tobacco and Sugar.* Translated by Harriet de Onís. New York: Knopf, 1947.

Pinney, Christopher. *"Photos of the Gods": The Printed Image and Political Struggle in India.* London: Reaktion, 2004.

Platvoet, Jan, and Henk J. van Rinsum. "Is Africa Incurably Religious?: Confessing and Contesting an Invention." *Exchange: Journal of Missiological and Ecumenical Research* 32, no. 2 (2003): 123–53.

Poland, Marguerite, David Hammond-Tooke, and Leigh Voigt. *The Abundant Herds: A Celebration of the Nguni Cattle of the Zulu People.* Vlaeberg, South Africa: Fernwood, 2003.

Pratt, Mary Louise. *Imperial Eyes: Travel Writing and Transculturation.* London: Routledge, 1992.

Preston-Whyte, E. M. "Zulu Religion." In *The Encyclopedia of Religion*, edited by Mircea Eliade, 15:591–95. New York: Macmillan, 1987.

Ricoeur, Paul. *Freud and Philosophy: An Essay on Interpretation.* Translated by Denis Savage. New Haven: Yale University Press, 1970.

Smith, Jonathan Z. *Map Is Not Territory: Studies in the History of Religions.* Leiden: Brill, 1978.

Sullivan, J. R. *The Native Policy of Theophilus Shepstone.* Johannesburg: Walker and Snashall, 1928.

Sullivan, Lawrence. "Sound and Sense: Towards a Hermeneutics of Performance." *History of Religions* 11 (1986): 1–33.

Tedlock, Barbara, "Dreams." In *The Encyclopedia of Religion.* 2nd ed. Edited by Lindsay Jones. 2482–91. New York: Macmillan, 2005.

Thwala, J. D., A. L. Pillay, and C. Sargent. "The Influence of Urban/Rural Background, Gender, Age, and Education on the Perception of and Response to Dreams among Zulu South Africans." *South African Journal of Psychology* 30, no. 4 (2000): 1–5.

Tylor, E. B. *Primitive Culture.* 2 vols. London: John Murray, 1871.

———. "On the Limits of Savage Religion." *The Journal of the Anthropological Institute of Great Britain and Ireland* 21 (1892): 283–301.

Van der Veer, Peter. *Imperial Encounters: Religion and Modernity in India and Britain.* Princeton: Princeton University Press, 2001.

Wanger, W. "The Zulu Notion of God according to the Traditional Zulu God-Names." *Anthropos* 18 & 19 (1923–1926): 656–87; 20 (1925): 558–78; 21 (1926): 351–58.

Weir, Jennifer. "Whose Unkulunkulu?" *Africa* 75, no. 2 (2005): 203–19.

Worger, William H. "Parsing God: Conversations about the Meaning of Words and Metaphors in Nineteenth-Century Southern Africa." *Journal of African History* 42, no. 3 (2001): 417–47.

Wylie, Dan. *Savage Delight: White Myths of Shaka.* Pietermaritzburg: University of Natal Press, 2000.

4

SCIENCE

Robert M. Geraci

INTRODUCTION

In 1633 the Roman Catholic Church forced Galileo Galilei (then aged 69 years) to go down on his knees and recant the theory that the Earth orbited the Sun. Galileo, condemned for his insistence that Nicolas Copernicus was right, that the Sun did not revolve around the Earth, has since stood as the prime example of an apparent conflict between theology and scientific inquiry. Of course, those who champion the idea that the Church oppressed Galileo and stood in the way of truth rarely note the fact that Galileo's own experimental observations and proofs for the heliocentric theory were often problematic or that Galileo was enmeshed in seventeenth-century European religious politics.

In fact, Galileo suffered from a considerable number of scientific problems, including the facts that few other people could observe what he could through a telescope (thus nullifying some of his evidence), that at least one of his telescopic observations (his drawing of the moon) was blatantly incorrect, and, even worse, that he rested his defense of the heliocentric theory on the motion of the ocean tides (which is not caused, as Galileo believed, by the conjunction of the Earth's axial and orbital revolutions). Galileo's scientific evidence simply could not provide definite confirmation of the heliocentric theory, which is what he needed. Influential members of the Church, such as Cardinal Bellarmine, were prepared to interpret the Bible liberally should sufficient scientific evidence arise, but Galileo did not have it, nor could he really have obtained it, thanks to his dismissal of Johannes Kepler's (correct) theory that planets move in ellipses around the Sun rather than in circles.

Political problems loomed even larger than scientific problems in the outcome of Galileo's trial. In the middle of the Catholic furor over the Protestant Reformation, any disagreement with Church tradition (and Church tradition favored the geocentric cosmos) looked suspiciously like heresy to certain members of the Catholic hierarchy. No doubt, Galileo exacerbated his problems by offending both professional philosophers and Jesuit theologians, both of whom he considered intellectually inferior to himself. Were it not for the Reformation, however, perhaps Galileo's ideas would have been more welcome in seventeenth-century Italy. At the same time, Galileo insulted Pope Urban VIII (formerly his friend) by having one of the Pope's favorite arguments espoused by the imbecile in his most recent book, *The Dialogue on the Two Chief World Systems* (1632). Galileo's trial was far more than a simple case where dogmatic theologians attacked an honest defender of truth. Indeed, much of what happened in 1632 and 1633 can be tied, not to scientific or theological

Italian scientist Galileo Galilei defended himself before a court of papal judges in 1633, charged with antiscriptural heresy for championing evidence of the pioneering scientific truth that the Earth revolves around the sun. Galileo was convicted and committed to house arrest for the last 8 years of life. In 1992, 350 years after his death, the Roman Catholic Church admitted its error and declared Galileo correct.

problems, per se, but to Galileo's political life and that of his contemporaries.

In some sense, Galileo was right. The Earth does revolve around the Sun. On the other hand, his proof of that was entirely wrong, and thus many of his contemporaries had plenty of reason to doubt him. Scientific truth was—at the time—an open question; Galileo had not settled the matter. It is the politics of the Galileo trial that make the case so interesting. The story of Galileo is not one of monolithic conflict between religion and science. Certainly there were theologians who were steadfastly opposed to the new science, but their voices were almost insignificant compared to other voices whose interests focused upon who Galileo's friends were, how he fit into European politics, and how Galileo related to other philosophers and Church officials (including the Pope).

Based upon misinformed nineteenth-century readings of the Galileo story, it has become commonplace in U.S. life to speak of religion and science being in conflict. Allegedly, we are forced to choose whether science *or* religion will be authoritative in our lives. For many people, believing in particular religions implies that certain scientists are wrong. For others, believing certain scientific positions entails that particular religions are wrong. All too often, we fool ourselves into thinking these are the only two worldviews available to us: either we favor science and denigrate religion, or we support religion and demean science. In both cases, conflict is the story of the day. We should not assume from the Galileo story, however, that religion and science necessarily conflict with one another (although they occasionally do) Instead, the Galileo affair teaches us that we cannot understand the relationship between religion and science without recourse to the politics of daily life. Many different positions are available for the average person. Not everyone feels that religion and science conflict with one another; some people do not even think that the two can conflict with one another (as long as they are understood "properly").

Over the past century, the relationship between religion and science has become increasingly important to scholars, theologians, and lay people. Early approaches to this relationship focused upon ways in which the two domains were fundamentally in conflict, but subsequent research—in Christian and non-Christian communities—demonstrates the inadequacy of such an approach. At different times and among different people, religion and science have held different positions vis-à-vis one another, sometimes conflicting, occasionally ignoring, and even quite frequently mutually supportive of one another.

Prior to the Scientific Revolution, to speak of conflict in religion and science was largely pointless. The Scientific Revolution, which could be dated to have begun as early as 1543 (with the publication of Copernicus's *On the Origin of the Celestial Spheres*), took place primarily in the seventeenth century but extended into the eighteenth and even nineteenth centuries—with advances in chemistry and biology that modernized those fields. With few exceptions, religious institutions in the West nurtured scientific and technological work prior to the Scientific Revolution; thus, even where there were matters of conflict (as in the 1277 condemnation of Aristotelian doctrines), broadly speaking, religion and science worked together in European culture. Even during the Scientific Revolution, religion remained important to key figures, such as Nicholas Copernicus, Galileo Galilei, Robert Boyle, and Isaac Newton. The increasing epistemological relevance of laboratory science and the mathematical approach to understanding the natural world, however, promoted a new sense of individual authority among scientists.

As scientists severed the longstanding connections between their work and the work of theology, fertile ground opened for conflict between religious and scientific interests. Despite this, even after the Scientific Revolution, we cannot speak of a clear conflict between religion and science; we cannot speak of any single relationship between religion and science because the two interact differently among different people, places, and times.

The rapid deployment of new technologies—especially biotechnology, artificial intelligence in computers, and the development of realistic virtual worlds—into society raises new questions for religion and science, questions that increasingly demand a response from the average person, who must live in a world powerfully affected by both religion and science. It is, in fact, the development of new technologies that proves most important in the daily life of religious people in the twenty-first century. Although more esoteric questions relating theology and the hard sciences dominated much of twentieth-century religion and science scholarship and thought, more concrete issues of technology dominate the twenty-first century. The politics of religion, science, and technology are complicated and filled with ambiguities; it is in these politics that the average person engages the three, and, because of these politics, we must continuously reevaluate how religion and science interact.

War and Peace

The belief that religion and science are in conflict gained currency in the late nineteenth century. Championed in different forms by John Draper and Andrew White, the conflict thesis continues to influence modern perceptions of religion-science interactions. Some commentators in the 21st century have eagerly joined this tradition, and books like Richard Dawkins's *The God Delusion* (2006) have sold well. Although the conflict thesis retains strength in society at large, persistent criticism of it has dismantled the conflict thesis in the academic study of religion and science.

In *The History of the Conflict between Religion and Science* (1874), John Draper stood vehemently opposed to the "tyranny" of religion, which he felt was antithetic to scientific reason. Andrew White moderated the conflict thesis in his two-volume *History of the Warfare between Science and Theology in Christendom* (1896), saying that religion and science are not in conflict, but dogmatic theologians and scientists are. It is important to keep in mind that White's aim was to gain acceptability for the secular institution, Cornell University, of which he had been named the first president. As a regular church attendee and member of the Christian faithful, White had no desire to make enemies out of theologians, only to convince them that a secular university did not mark the end of civilization. It was from the real, political interaction of university education and public religion that White's conflict thesis emerged.

Fairly or not, White's work has spearheaded the conflict theory, despite challenges to it in the twentieth century. Reprinted dozens of times and translated into several foreign languages, *The History of the Warfare* has permeated our culture, although its prodigious length (over 900 pages) has perhaps contributed to the belief that White stood in single-minded opposition to religious belief. Thirty years after its publication, the book was so important that John Scopes's lawyer, Clarence Darrow, read it in preparation for the Scopes "Monkey" trial about the teaching of evolution in public school in 1925.

Sustained criticism of White's thesis developed under the academic study of religion and science, as pioneered by Ian Barbour, a physicist and theologian at Carleton College, where he was Bean Professor of Science, Technology, and Society. Barbour developed a four-fold typology of religion-science interactions, claiming that religion and science could (1) be in conflict, (2) be independent of one another, (3) be in dialogue with one another, or (4) be integrated into one worldview. Barbour's typology includes a clear moral teleology, opposing conflict between religion and science while favoring an integrated worldview. This reconciliation agenda—which enabled scientists, theologians, and lay people alike to find an effective way to think through the problems of postwar twentieth-century culture—continues to receive support from various figures in the academic study of religion and science, but it has been disputed by historians.

In their 1995 Gifford Lectures, subsequently published as *Reconstructing Nature* (1998), John Hedley Brooke and Geoffrey Cantor dismiss the typological approach to religion and science as simplistic and incapable of accounting for the lives and actions of real, historical people. According to Brooke and Cantor, a biographical approach reveals that, for any one person—much less for any historical period—religion and science rarely interact the same way twice. The relationship between religion and science "on the ground" is often confusing or even contradictory. Someone who accepts and appreciates the integration of religion and science in one purview, for example, may find the two in conflict in some other area.

Supposedly clear examples of conflict between religion and science appear, upon closer examination, to be rather more complicated than White's simplistic account allows. The story of Galileo demonstrates just how carefully we must tread in examining conflicts between religion and science. White, perhaps more than any other person, contributed to the belief that, in his trial and condemnation of 1633, Galileo

Galilei was a noble defender of truth against the dogmatic and vicious attacks of ignorant churchmen. A complete recounting of Galileo's condemnation must address his scientific difficulties and his political difficulties at least as much as it attends to his theological problems. The conflict thesis, as described by both Draper and White, and the typological approach are both far too narrow and far too simple to provide an accurate description of historical events.

Criticisms of the conflict thesis have carried the day in academic circles, but it remains a powerful part of our cultural makeup. All too often, journalists, politicians, and the public uncritically accept the view that religion and science are at war. This position, fraught with problems, cannot address the ways in which real people practice their religions, think about science, or use their technologies. The interaction of religion and science—sometimes subtle, sometimes not—is never monolithic. History is as unlikely to result in a permanent reconciliation of science and religion as in a total severance of the two.

VARIED RELIGIONS, VARIED RESPONSES

The conflict thesis in religion and science has been largely an aspect of Christian culture because it is in the Christian West that modern science arose. The spread of science and technology to other cultures, however, as happened rapidly throughout the twentieth century, creates opportunity for other cultures to join the dialogue.

Much of the knowledge crucial to the rise of European science emerged in medieval Islam. Muslims translated the Greeks, thereby preserving their knowledge, and improved upon them with their own studies of philosophy, mathematics, optics, chemistry, and physics. For medieval Muslims, there was no conflict between religion and science; both represented the fundamental unity of all things in God. Although certain philosophical positions were disputed (such as in al-Ghazali's influential critique of Greek and Roman philosophy in the eleventh century), science found a welcome home in medieval Islamic culture.

Modern Islamic nations maintain an uneasy relationship with science. Although technological developments have been accepted in the name of modernization and equality (especially with regard to the postcolonial heritage of Islamic countries), mistrust of the West can make this difficult. As in the West (see below), concern over the implications of Darwinian natural selection has led to successful intelligent design movements in many Islamic countries. Resistance to Darwinian evolution has been consistent throughout modern Islamic nations, which have frequently given official sanction to creationist and intelligent design theories. Nearly all contemporary Muslims reject both the Western idea that religion and science can be separated and the subsequent materialism that arose in Euro-American life. Seeing Darwinian evolution as part of European materialism contributed to Muslim resistance to evolutionary biology. Early in the twentieth century, resistance to evolution was relatively passive, accomplished by ignoring evolution whenever possible; more recently, however, creationist and intelligent design approaches to biology have flourished where distrust of secularism and Western politics has increased.

Throughout the ancient and medieval periods, the Chinese made significant use of medicine, pharmacology, astronomy, mathematics, and alchemy/chemistry, often advancing these beyond their Western contemporaries. Chinese inventors created paper, the compass, printing, and gunpowder, although many of these innovations were developed further by Westerners. Taoism pressed the study of alchemy, and the Taoist search for immortality contributed to exercise science and the diagnosis of disease. The Confucian bureaucracy placed great value in astronomical predictions for ceremonial purposes and mathematics in order to improve managerial control over the economy, from taxation to land surveying. After the communist revolution, however, traditional Chinese religions were suppressed in favor of scientific advancement.

Much as cooperation (broadly construed) gave way to isolated elements of conflict in modern Islam, conflict and cooperation between religion and science existed alongside one another in Maoist China. Like medieval Islam, medieval China had a healthy regard for scientific and technological work, but the communist desire for scientific and technological development was paired with a strong distaste for traditional Chinese religion, establishing a hierarchy between the two in the twentieth century. Many considered religious "superstition" anathema to scientific and technological progress, and thus modernization and international significance. At the same time, Maoist ideology suppressed some scientific practices and led to the imprisonment of many scientists during the Cultural Revolution. Opposition to relativity, in addition, was widespread in the early to mid-1950s, when many Chinese found it contrary to the principles of dialectical materialism.

Other nations and religious groups have had few or no problems integrating religious and scientific thought. In Japan, for example, the sacralization of the natural world has promoted the easy integration of robots into Shinto and Buddhist religious life. In the early days of industrial robots, the machines were blessed in rituals by Shinto priests at their installations. Likewise, influential scientists, such as Masahiro Mori, have advocated the belief that robots participate in Buddha-nature; that is, they possess the potential to become Buddhas.

Although Mori may not mean this in the sense of conscious robots meditating and attaining enlightenment, his faith that robots are a part of the sacred experience in the world is a marked departure from the conflict thesis as advocated by Draper or White.

In general, Buddhist nations have adopted modern science without serious conflict. Although there are clear differences in the worldviews adopted in Buddhism and scientific naturalism, they are not necessarily contradictory. The XIV Dalai Lama—the head of Tibetan Buddhism—has defended the scientific understanding of the world, arguing that Buddhist teachings might require revision in the face of scientific progress. At the same time, however, the Dalai Lama has suggested that genetic mutation may not be entirely random but, rather, guided by a causality indiscernible to modern science. Of course, the Dalai Lama does not speak for all Buddhists, and much research remains to uncover the richness of religion-science interactions in Buddhist societies.

Much like the Christians who seek reconciliation of scientific and religious truths in Western debates (see the preceding discussion), many Easterners have found common ground between their traditional religions and the technoscientific contributions of the Western world. The XIV Dalai Lama is a good example of this, as are many leading figures in twentieth- and twenty-first-century Hinduism. Swami Vivekananda (1863–1902), for example, promoted the compatibility of religion and Hindu Advaita thought, giving momentum to the growth of indigenous (as opposed to British colonial) science on the Indian subcontinent.

Despite the goal of reconciling religion and science in India, there are serious problems for Indians. Like the Chinese, ancient and medieval Indians made enormously significant contributions to various sciences, including astronomy, mathematics, architecture, and linguistics, but, as with everyone in the twentieth and twenty-first centuries, Indians must find new ways of thinking in response to modern science. Perhaps the most daunting concern for every Indian as he or she thinks about religion and science is the need to guarantee the birth of at least one son. Sons are important for both religious and economic reasons in India. A daughter leaves the family to work in another household (likely taking with her a dowry), whereas a son stays in the household as a productive member of the family. In addition, sons perform important religious rites upon the deaths of their fathers, without which men cannot progress comfortably through the afterlife. These pressures, combined with the economic strain upon everyday Indian citizens, contributes to abortions and the desire for in vitro fertilization. Hindu authorities frown upon abortion and, although they accept in vitro fertilization, believe that all embryos should be implanted rather than discarded.

Reproductive biotechnology also plays an enormously significant role for modern Jews. Indeed, Jews have only rarely considered there to be a meaningful relationship between modern science and their religious views. Although a few Orthodox Jewish groups have opposed the theory of evolution and the geologic age of the Earth, most modern Jews generally accept scientific advancements and find no difficulty in scientific practice and religious belief. As a result, Jews have made notable contributions in nearly every aspect of twentieth century science, with well over 100 receiving Nobel Prizes for their scientific work (18 percent of all Nobel Prizes between 1901 and 2002 were given to Jews). Jewish scientists almost universally deny that their scientific work is an extension of their Jewish faith or background (many were religiously agnostic or atheist). The numbers clearly indicate, however, that Jewish culture approves and accepts modern scientific work, without necessarily asserting that Jewish theology is identical with it.

Jews have been especially interested in medical research and have contributed to the general acceptance of therapeutic and reproductive biotechnologies. Reproductive technologies, such as in vitro fertilization (opposed by the Catholic Church, for example) have been welcomed as ways for Jews to fulfill the biblical commandment to "be fruitful and multiply" (Gen 1:28). Modern Jews have also wholeheartedly accepted medical progress based in part on the biblical command that "you shall not stand idly by the blood of your fellow" (Lev 19:16). For Jews, preserving life takes precedence over almost any other consideration, so therapeutic biotechnologies—whether these be organ transplants, surgeries, or even genetic manipulations—receive widespread support. Despite their advocacy of therapeutic and reproductive technologies, however, Jewish leaders have not embraced human enhancement projects, such as genetically engineering human beings to be smarter, stronger, or better looking.

Even a cursory look at the interaction of religion and science in different cultures demonstrates that—even if we were to believe in some static entity called science and another static entity called religion, which we should not—the interactions between religion and science vary across time and place. On occasion, conflict and strife appear in the religious and scientific lives of individuals and groups, but just as frequently people hold science and religion in harmony. We still require vastly more ethnographic research before we can fully comprehend the richness of religion-science interactions among non-Christian communities, but we can at least clearly see from our current vantage how those relationships resist easy categories of conflict or cooperation/reconciliation. It was the rise of modern science that provided apparent ground for a conflict between science and religion, but, at the same time, the rise of modern science was itself the result of integrated scientific and religious practices.

THE RISE OF MODERN SCIENCE

Although much of our contemporary outlook traces a conflict of religion and science to the Scientific Revolution (roughly the sixteenth through the eighteenth centuries), the principal actors in the rise of modern science were, by and large, themselves religious. Modern science arose in a Christian environment and was deeply affected by Christian theological aims.

Although there is a very real sense in which the Scientific Revolution was hardly revolutionary, we look upon it as a distinct historical era that was decidedly significant in shaping modern life. The major accomplishments of the Scientific Revolution drew upon preexisting traditions and medieval learning; they did not arise de novo. Nevertheless, from Copernicus forward, the natural philosophers of early modern Europe contributed to a sense of modernity through their own belief that they were doing something new.

We should not confuse the sense of modernity common in the sixteenth and seventeenth centuries with our own understanding of it. Frequently, we speak of modern science as a discipline (or disciplines) committed to empirical study and the understanding of natural causation. Although these were profoundly important to the natural philosophers (the word *scientist* was not coined until the nineteenth century), they were immersed in the religious practices of the day.

Early Modern Natural Philosophy

The natural philosophers of the sixteenth, seventeenth, and even eighteenth centuries engaged in much of what we now think of as pseudo-science—astrology, alchemy, prophecy, demonology, and so forth. Practitioners of these arts were among most eminent practitioners of science, including Francis Bacon, Johannes Kepler, Robert Boyle, and Isaac Newton. Newton, for example, wrote more books of Christian prophecy than of a scientific nature and was a committed alchemist. Although the natural philosophers rejected what they considered to be animism in Aristotelian thought and advocated a turn toward mechanistic explanations of the world, they remained committed to various occult practices and beliefs. In many ways, such practices directly contributed to the development of scientific work. Astrology led Kepler and others to increase their knowledge of facts about the heavens, which helped establish the science of astronomy and contributed to the demise of the Aristotelian worldview. Modern chemistry would have been unthinkable without the knowledge of crystallizations, distillations, acids, and bases that alchemists accumulated. Modern medicine was also profoundly affected by alchemy, especially through the work of Paracelsus, who revolutionized medical practice by insisting upon the healing effects of consuming various minerals.

Christian theology also played a direct role in the rise of modern science. Leading figures in the Scientific Revolution, such as Nicholas Copernicus and Marin Mersenne, were also members of the Catholic holy orders, and the majority of others, Catholic or Protestant, were active churchgoers—who saw their work in light of Christian theology. Scientific inquiry served Christian aims throughout the early modern period: many natural philosophers believed it possible to use scientific knowledge to support belief in the Christian God, and their development of science and technology aimed toward the realization of a divine plan. The desire to prove the existence of God through scientific inquiry is called "natural theology" and was common throughout the Scientific Revolution. As discussed below, natural theology remains a significant element in the intersection of religion and science today. Early modern practitioners of natural theology frequently saw the world as a gargantuan clock. Just as a pocket watch must have a creator, so must the clocklike universe. The natural philosophers, of course, believed the Christian god to be the great clockmaker. Natural theology played a role in the development of chemistry, astronomy, geology, and other sciences. Were it not, for example, for the contributions of physico-theologians who combined biblical theology with a naturalist account for the origins and history of the Earth, modern geology could never have arisen under the auspices of James Hutton, Charles Lyell, and other key figures in the history of geology.

Christian Impulses in Late Modernity

Although science might reveal spiritual truths, according to natural theology, its practitioners also believed that science definitely realized spiritual goals. That is, many early modern Europeans believed that scientific experimentation and technological development were religious practices. The paragon of rationalism and empiricism, Francis Bacon (1561–1626), for example, was deeply affected by his religious beliefs. Bacon believed that the restoration of society must overcome the biblical Fall and was part and parcel with New Testament promises of salvation. Bacon tied scientific (and, to a lesser extent, political) progress to religious promises of salvation and the restoration of knowledge that had been lost in Adam's fall from grace. Scientific advances were the fulfillment of the biblical promise that "many shall go back and forth, and knowledge will increase" (Dan 12:4).[1] On

the frontispiece to the *Instauratio Magna* (*The Great Instauration*, published in 1620), Bacon prints Daniel's eschatological claim to reinforce the apocalyptic theme of the book's title. Seventeenth-century readers would have easily identified the instauration (i.e., renewal or restoration) with the biblical theme of the temple's restoration at the end of time. Natural philosophers believed they were restoring humankind to the perfection of Adam, while preparing the world to battle the Antichrist at the end of the world. In the sixteenth and seventeenth centuries, natural philosophers believed that Adam had had no need of microscopes or telescopes; his moral fall spelled the end of his clear sight and scientific knowledge as well. Some early moderns also believed that Moses and Solomon also possessed broad scientific knowledge; in the *New Atlantis*, Bacon even attributes a book of natural philosophy to Solomon. The closer that they grew to Adam's prelapsarian grace, the stronger they would be in their battle alongside the returned Messiah. From the sixteenth century through the establishment of European governments in the New World, natural philosophers—and, eventually, everyday people—believed that their technoscientific mastery of the world was part of God's plan to establish a new paradise and, finally, conquer the forces of evil with the return of Jesus.

The Christian incentive for technoscientific development was especially significant in US history. The colonists' belief that developing their nation was part of God's plan reinforced the idea that advancing technology was part of the same plan because the two tasks were mutually reinforcing. New technologies made land mastery easier, and the desire to utilize Western resources made technological development a priority. Many twentieth-century technologies continue to find ideological impetus in Christian theology. The historian David F. Noble, in particular, has shown the ways in which Christian theology informed scientific attitudes in atomic weaponry, space exploration, artificial intelligence, and genetic engineering. Noble's thesis—that religious ideology drives techno-scientific innovation, rather than the reverse—is a controversial but vital contribution to the study of religion and science.

The medieval belief that technological progress heralds the end of the world is part of a larger, "postmillenarian" set of Christian beliefs. Christians agree that the book of Revelation predicts a one-thousand-year reign of peace—the "millennium"—but disagree on the mechanics of its arrival. For premillenarians, Jesus will return to Earth prior to the millennium in order to inaugurate the earthly kingdom (hence the *pre-* in premillenarian). Throughout the twentieth and twenty-first centuries, premillenarians have looked to contemporary world events as predictions of the coming of Jesus. Although this has included political events—such as the Cold War, the US war in Iraq, and the persistent conflict over Israel and Palestine—it also includes economics (e.g., the stock market, the price of oil, and inflation), nuclear power, and biotechnology. Postmillenarians believe that Jesus will not return until after the millennium of peace, which means that human action will bring about the millennium and that progress toward it can be measured in earthly terms. The greater our scientific knowledge becomes, the more leisure is produced through our technology, and the closer we are to the millennium. Some believers have even claimed that the predicted millennium has already begun.

Postmillenarian theology championed the growth of science, which subsequently took up the banner of salvation, even as it separated from the monasteries and universities of its Christian origins. Just as faith in human salvation was part and parcel with the rise of modern science, many twentieth-century scientific endeavors continued to work toward the creation of paradise and the immortalization of humankind.

The Emergence of Transhumanism

Often labeled "transhumanism," one strand of modern science has developed into a religion of its own, although it is in essence a repackaging of postmillenarian Christian theology. The two most powerful fields to promise a transcendent future are biotechnology and robotics/artificial intelligence (AI). Biotechnology advocates emphasize the likelihood of curing diseases, halting the aging process, and enhancing human powers through genetic engineering. "Apocalyptic AI" advocates claim that human beings will "upload" their minds into virtual worlds and live forever in a transcendent cyberspace.

Advances in stem-cell technology will enable prodigious medical cures for cases in which death or degeneration would have resulted. Although opposed by many Christian groups in the late twentieth and early twenty-first centuries, stem-cell technologies will soon become theologically acceptable and will likely allow doctors to replace lost organs and cure diseases such as Alzheimer's and Parkinson's. Early in its development, stem-cell technology was opposed by many Christians because the only available source for pluripotent stem cells (the kind of stem cells that can become any other kind of cell, such as a replacement liver or brain cell) was human embryos. Some Christian groups denounced the use of embryos in medical research: they considered such use to be murder, and they feared that scientific use of embryos might embolden those considering abortion. Progress in the creation of pluripotent stem cells from skin cells and from embryos without destroying the embryo, however, promises to defuse the theological controversy.

The medical cures promised by stem-cell advocates are alluring, but they pale in comparison to the soteriological claims of some genetic engineers. Germinal choice technologies, also called recombinant DNA (rDNA) or germline engineering, may someday allow researchers to alter the genetic inheritance of a human being at the blastocyst stage. The blastocyst is an early stage of development in utero, prior to implantation on the uterine wall and the formation of the embryo. Germinal choice technologies could lead to permanent cures for genetically caused diseases (which would no longer be passed on to subsequent generations) or allow for human enhancement. Greater knowledge of our genetic inheritance (and that of other species) might enable us to expand our sensory powers (into the infrared and ultraviolet spectra, for example) or improve our physical and mental abilities. Some advocates, such as University of California–Los Angeles Medical School bioethicist Gregory Stock, believe that the addition of an extra chromosome, which could be turned on and off through chemical means, could alleviate the possibility of unwanted side effects if we change our genetic makeup (though such changes would not be passed on to offspring).

Genetic enhancement is a controversial subject. Although Stock and other "procreative liberty" advocates argue that the benefits of enhancement outweigh the dangers, other commentators, such as Francis Fukuyama and Leon Kass, have been outspoken in their opposition. Detractors of germinal choice technologies usually point toward the dangers of changing an imperfectly understood human genetic makeup and of ignoring the importance of human dignity and human rights. Religious groups have raised concerns about "playing God" and the dangers of hubris.

Of course, transhumanists and their life-extensionist forebears reject the accusations of Fukuyama and Kass as naive and irrational. They argue that the amelioration of human sickness and death can be nothing but good. Their faith in the salvific promises of biotechnology led to popular conferences, scientific research, popular advocacy, and an enormous amount of venture capital. Transhumanists defend their right to self-improvement, arguing that neither individuals nor governments should stand in the way of those who wish to better themselves.

If their faith in the paradise to come were not sufficient to define them as a religious group, some transhumanists have launched actively religious organizations, such as the Society for Universal Immortalism (SUI). The SUI accepts the term "religion" and hopes that it can present transhuman "immortalism" as an attractive alternative to traditional religious beliefs. Whereas other religions promise the good life after death, the SUI promises to provide it now. According to such groups, genetic enhancement—by improving mental and physical strength, adding new powers (such as vision in the infrared spectrum), and eliminating the deleterious effects of aging—is the key to our biological evolution and our religious future.

Despite criticism from both religious and secular groups, transhumanists press for germinal choice technologies that they believe offer permanent relief from the worst aspects of the human condition. Even though we are very far from realizing their dreams, the transhumanists believe that germinal choice technologies will eliminate disease, cease the aging process, and expand our abilities to angelic proportions. This faith follows in the lineage of Christian theology that has penetrated modern science from its earliest days.

As fantastic as the claims of biotechnology can be, they are but the stepping stone to the ultimate aim of transhumanism: an escape from Earth to a paradisiacal virtual world.

"Apocalyptic AI" (as I propose to call it)—the child of science fiction[2] and famed Carnegie Mellon University roboticist Hans Moravec, and subsequently popularized in science fiction and in the work of AI researcher Ray Kurzweil—is the belief that human beings will escape this world by uploading their minds into computers and living in cyberspace forever. Kurzweil has become the champion of these ideas, arguing that the universe moves inevitably toward the imminent triumph of machine life over biological life.

The Apocalyptic AI community argues—following many practitioners of cognitive science and AI—that the human mind is a pattern of activity in the brain. If that pattern could be replicated in a computer, say Moravec and Kurzweil, the computer mind would be identical—until different experiences led to a divergence—with that of the person whose mind had been copied. When the biological person dies, only the immortal computer person would remain. Life in cyberspace, say Moravec and Kurzweil, will be joyous and meaningful. All of us could potentially copy ourselves into virtual reality, thus guaranteeing a powerful new machine culture, where the needs and wants of bodily life will pass away.

The religious promises of transhumanism arose out of the religious context of modern science. Given that theological ideas infused the development of scientific culture, we should be little surprised by the development of an explicitly "scientific" religion. The religion of technology is shared by scientists, researchers, and the general public, although not, of course, by all members of any of these groups. Even many of those who reject transhumanism still maintain a faith that science and technology can produce a perfect or near-perfect world. The intimate ties between Christianity and the rise of modern science have made this faith nearly inevitable.

Of course, even as Christian theology has contributed to technoscientific progress in this way, it has simultaneously established transhumanism as a competing religious worldview. The cooperation of religion and science, therefore, is a complex phenomenon: it is quite common for religion and science to confront each other as competitors while simultaneously providing mutual positive reinforcement.

THE CONTEMPORARY POLITICS OF RELIGION AND SCIENCE

Understanding the intricate ties between religion and science over the past few centuries allows us to think through the current world of religious practice, scientific ideas, and technological innovation. Just as the Galileo example demonstrates that religion-science interactions are often far more complicated than they appear, modern intersections of religion and science require that we account for the many ways in which religion and science can conflict, ignore, or support each other—quite possibly all at the same time. The key technologies and scientific ideas in the contemporary world are biotechnology, the environmental movement, neuroscientific discoveries, modern physics and the mechanization of the world, and the theory of evolution. These can be categorized as local problems, which affect theologians and scholars of religion and science, and global problems, which affect all citizens.

Physics and neuroscience—and their relationship to divine action and human souls—interest theologians and scholars but rarely influence the laity very much. Such concerns—including big bang cosmology, quantum dynamics and the actions of a divine creator, and the relationship between human souls and mechanistic brains—receive substantial scholarly and theological interest yet have very little to say about the actual lives of real people. These esoteric aspects of religion and science are certainly significant for theologians as they wrestle with their understanding of the divine, but they do not play a powerful role in wider culture and should not be allowed to dominate our understanding of religion and science.

The study of religion and science accelerated alongside the enormously important twentieth-century developments in physics. The combination of new scientific theories (relativity and quantum mechanics) and powerful new technologies (atomic power and space exploration) made technoscientific progress enormously significant in theological thought. This significance was further magnified as our greater knowledge of physical processes subsequently furthered astronomical studies and our understanding of cosmic history. All of this combined, in the middle of the twentieth century, to provide an atmosphere ripe for a new way of thinking about religion and science, one that turned away from the nineteenth-century conflict theses.

Physics and Astrophysics

The development of modern physics (including astrophysics) drove the mid-twentieth-century revision of religion-science interpretations. Astronomers and physicists ranked among the leading scientists who sought the reconciliation of science and religion, and major figures from these groups remain deeply invested in the reconciliation agenda. Groups such as the American Scientific Affiliation (founded in 1941 under the auspices of the Moody Bible Institute) and the Institute for Religion in an Age of Science (founded in 1954) promoted the peaceful coexistence and mutual necessity of religion and science, although with very different theological perspectives. In the mid-twentieth century, the reconciliation of science and religion was a popular movement, accepted by both the public and the scientific elite, and it found its way into millions of homes and schools via television shows and documentaries, most notably Frank Capra's *Our Mr. Sun* (1956) and its follow-ups, such as *The Strange Case of Cosmic Rays* (1957), in which Christian theology permeates popularized science.

Progress in astrophysics and, thereby, cosmology, has provided theologians and scientists alike with an effective trope for expounding upon the relationship between religion and science. The development of big bang cosmology (the belief that the universe was once contained in an infinitely dense point of no volume, which violently exploded into an expanding universe) gave scientific respectability to the idea that the world was created at a single moment in time. Many Christian theologians eagerly absorbed this into their nonliteral understanding of the biblical creation narrative, as did Pope Pius XII in his 1951 address to the Pontifical Academy of Sciences. Scientists have also interpreted big bang cosmology through a religious lens. Robert Jastrow, then head of NASA's Goddard Institute for Space Studies, declared that scientists, having climbed the mountain of cosmology, found theologians already there. Although he is personally agnostic, Jastrow has claimed that the "essential" facts in big bang cosmology and the Genesis account are the same; because of this, he continued writing about the connection between astronomy and theology. Nevertheless, his work is understated compared to that of Charles Townes, who believes that astronomy leads to Barbour's integration/reconciliation of religion and science. Townes is a physicist who made fundamental contributions to his home discipline and astronomy and who won the Nobel Prize for Physics and the Templeton Prize for discoveries "about spiritual realities," in addition to a host of other prestigious awards. He believes that the truths of science and religion "must" converge.

As astrophysics expanded our understanding of the cosmos and its laws, the contingency of human life came into question. Given the many universal laws and constants, it is clear the universe is well-adapted to human life. This tautology, the "anthropic principle," has served the aim of religion-science integration. In short, the anthropic principle states that the universe's physical constants are very finely tuned, so as to enable human life; even slight variation in one or more of the natural constants (such as the force of gravity or Planck's constant) would have prevented the formation of a universe where human life was possible. The "strong" anthropic principle, moreover, argues that the laws of nature are such that the evolution of intelligent life is a necessary rather than contingent outcome. Influential figures in religion-science scholarship, such as Arthur Peacocke, have argued that the anthropic principle demonstrates or implies the existence of some powerful figure that controlled the development of the physical universe to enable human life.

One area where physics did have a profound impact upon daily life is the development of atomic power. Not only did mid-twentieth-century futurists imagine a future where atomic power would solve all the problems of the world and usher in a new Eden, but many actually saw atomic weapons as the harbinger of the apocalypse. During the Cold War, some Americans believed that a nuclear holocaust was essential to Jesus's return to Earth, and so they held to political militarism. As with other technological innovations (discussed in the following), the presence of atomic weaponry in religion-science interactions is deeply political, tying together religious beliefs, scientific knowledge, technological inventions, political ideologies, and the worldviews of average citizens.

The Emergence of Emergence

Even as scholars continued exploring the significance of physics for classical theology, developments in biology radically changed the scientific worldview and, thereby, the religion-science dialogue. Struggling against physical reductionism—which argues that all things can be ultimately explained through the laws of physics—physicists, biologists, and, subsequently, religion-science scholars developed the idea of emergent properties. Emergence refers to the presence of different levels of causality that cannot be completely reduced to one another. As one moves up or down the ladder of complexity in a system, new principles might apply; that is, the simplest level of physical laws cannot explain more complicated systems (such as human behavior), because new principles emerge in the complex dynamics of the higher-level systems. Despite their reliance upon the basic laws of physics, these emergent principles cannot be reduced to the laws of simpler systems, because they do not exist in those systems.

Not all scientists or theologians accept emergence as a meaningful account of the natural or supernatural world, but those who do believe that it enables top-down causality. Some theologians, such as Robert John Russell, holder of the Ian Barbour Chair in Science and Religion at the Graduate Theological Union in Berkeley, California, believe that top-down causality enables the Christian God's interaction with the world, as opposed to hierophantic intervention in the world. That is, instead of a world in which only subatomic particles have causal power (through their interactions determined by the laws of quantum mechanics), higher-level systems utilize emergent powers to affect lower levels. Advocates use this claim to defend the significance of human minds—as emergent properties of brains that subsequently affect brain states—and the power of God, who can allegedly affect the material universe from a position that is both "above" and "within" nature.

Neuroscience

Researchers have found that a variety of religious experiences have similar neurocognitive corollaries and, therefore, must be biologically related. This means that there are specific parts of the brain associated with particular religious practices or experiences. Ceremonial rituals, for example, draw upon the autonomic nervous system, which regulates body functions and which intensifies awareness or blissful experiences. In particular, inhibition of the brain's posterior superior parietal lobe may disrupt the individual's sense of self and of spatial location, contributing to a sense of transcendental oneness that might be important for religious faith and practice. Religious people speak of being immersed in God, blissfully disembodied, and at one with everything in the universe. It is quite possible that these experiences can be directly tied to inhibition of the parietal lobe and/or other parts of the brain.

Others in the study of "neurotheology," which explains religious phenomena through recourse to the brain, argue that religion arises from an overactive "agent detection" system in human thinking. They believe that for survival purposes, we are generally well-off attributing intelligence and sentience to objects and animals (for example, the belief that a noise in the dark might be a predator sneaking toward us), and we subsequently cannot disengage this system from presuming the existence of supernatural entities.

Neurological correlates for religious experiences hold explanatory power for the religiously skeptical and faithful alike. Some authors have claimed that religion is nothing but a delusion of the brain, caused by abnormal brain conditions; others argue that the brain quite clearly has the power to observe and connect with the divine, because human beings were created so that they could form such relationships. Although neurobiology clearly affects religious practice, we are far from being able to assert confidently that neuroscience disproves or proves the existence of the various objects of religious speculation.

From Academia to Everyday Life

Studies of religion and science have left the "ivory tower" of academia and increasingly affected the daily lives of real people. Every day, citizens throughout the world read and watch news items about scientific and technological advancements that address their personal morals and their religious affiliations. Religious individuals are far more likely to care about whether prayer helps cancer patients than whether or not the big bang accurately corresponds to the moment when God said "Let there be light!" The environmental crisis and the theory of evolution demand that citizens make religious decisions about what they believe and about what kinds of political choices those beliefs dictate. Such decisions include what party to vote for, what kind of car to drive (and whether to drive at all), how close to work to live, what kind of food to buy, and more. The rapid development of biotechnology and AI likewise challenges religious beliefs and leads to civic action.

Creationism, Intelligent Design, and the Theory of Evolution

The theory of evolution was controversial in US politics throughout the twentieth century, and it remains a topic of concern as we move into the new millennium. First subject to broad public scrutiny of evolution and biblical creation in the Scopes Trial of 1925, the controversy over evolution hits close to home for many US Christians and even for some Jews and Muslims. The fundamental issue is twofold: Should the theory of evolution be taught in public schools if the public opposes it? Should an opposing majority be allowed to dictate that it not be taught? One of these questions has religious implications, but the other is strictly political. The two issues cannot, however, be separated from each other.

Early in the twentieth century, Christians in the United States published a series of pamphlets titled *The Fundamentals*, giving rise to the movement subsequently called fundamentalism. Funded by oil magnates and published by the Bible Institute of Los Angeles, these tracts generally promoted the inerrancy of the Bible, especially with regard to the miracles of Jesus and his virgin birth, but they did not all agree on the subject of evolution. Although not all of *The Fundamentals* tracts discussed evolution, those that did took disparate positions on it. Nevertheless, fundamentalist Christianity eventually became solidly opposed to the theory of evolution, claiming that it undermined Christianity and contributed to public amorality. As public-school attendance increased, the issue became increasingly significant to Christian believers, especially in the southern, midwestern, and western states.

Fundamentalist Christians quickly took on the mantle of creationism, the belief that the biblical God created the world as described in the book of Genesis in the Bible. Creationism was given a scientific mantle by George MacCready Price's *The New Geology* (1927), which was enhanced by Henry Morris and John Whitcomb in *The Genesis Flood* (1961). Even prior to the publication of these books, creationism had gained wide currency in US Christianity and provoked legal prohibitions on the teaching of evolution. Price, Morris, and Whitcomb, however, shaped the creationist worldview more than anyone else. Morris's Institute for Creation Research (founded in 1970) produces a newsletter, popular columns, and scientific essays, of both a technical and a nontechnical nature, which are distributed to Christians throughout the United States.

On March 23, 1925, Governor Peay of Tennessee signed the Butler Act, which stated that "it shall be unlawful for any teacher to teach any theory that denies the Story of Divine Creation of man as taught in the Bible, and to teach instead that man has descended from a lower animal." Although the law passed with broad public support, the governor did not believe that it would be enforced, claiming that the law "will not put our teachers in any jeopardy" and that he could "find nothing of consequence in the books now being taught in our schools with which this bill will interfere in the slightest manner."

The American Civil Liberties Union (ACLU) offered to defend any teacher who wished to challenge the Butler Act, an offer eventually taken up by the citizens of Dayton, Tennessee. Local officials, hoping to boost Dayton's public profile, convinced the substitute biology teacher, John T. Scopes, to stand up in trial. The Scopes Trial quickly blossomed into a nationwide media extravaganza—as populist hero and former Democratic presidential nominee William Jennings Bryan came to assist the prosecution, and the nation's top defense attorney, Clarence Darrow, joined the defense.

In many ways, the Scopes Trial was primarily a battle over the nature of political rights. Bryan stood for the public majority, believing that its will should rule. Darrow and the ACLU fought to protect the rights of individuals, who should not be coerced by "mob politics." Initially, the prosecution sought to paint the defense as enemies of Christianity, but the support of liberal Protestant theologians from all over the United States (especially that of Shailer Matthews, an influential member of the University of Chicago Divinity School) convinced the prosecuting attorneys that a strictly legalistic interpretation of the case would benefit them more. In the end, Scopes was ruled guilty, but Darrow scored a political victory by challenging Bryan to defend his Christian beliefs on the witness stand. Although Bryan's beliefs bore little—if at all—on the case at hand, Darrow encouraged his allies across the nation by maneuvering Bryan into admitting that he does not believe in an exclusively literal interpretation of the Bible and that, indeed, God might have created the world over the course of successive stages (this is commonly called "day-age creationism," where one day for God in the book of Genesis may have been an entire historical age for human beings).

The Scopes Trial did little to resolve the tension over the teaching of evolution. Because it was thrown out by the Tennessee Supreme Court on a technicality, the Scopes case never went to the US Supreme Court as the ACLU hoped it would. The judge in Dayton had issued a $100 fine to Scopes but, according to Tennessee law, only the jury can assign the value of a fine. After the Scopes Trial, advocates for evolution championed Darrow's victory over Bryan on the witness stand and claimed that creationism had been defeated, but creationists continued passing laws and influencing local school boards against the teaching of evolution. Although some antievolution laws failed to pass, in the South and Midwest and West, local regulations carried the day, with no repeals for the next forty years. In the Northeast, citizens came to believe that creationism had been dealt a death blow, as the issue faded from view and the two camps had less and less to do with each other.

In 1957, the Soviets launched Sputnik, which led to enormous fear in the United States. When scientists, believing that Soviet science education must be superior to that of the United States,

looked at nationwide high school curricula, they realized that evolution had been excluded from nearly all biology textbooks. Publishers at the time had not included evolution so as to ensure that creationist states and school districts would still buy their texts. The proevolution camp was shocked out of its belief that creationism had died and began a systematic revision of high school textbooks. As textbook publishers sought to maintain market share against a new book supported by the National Science Foundation, they reintroduced the theory of evolution into texts nationwide. The reemergence of evolution in biology textbooks led to a renaissance in legal wrangling over the teaching of evolution.

The first legal setback to creationism was not until 1968, when the US Supreme Court, in the case of *Epperson v. Arkansas,* declared that laws forbidding the teaching of evolution were illegal. Creationism remained a part of biology teaching in many places, however, until 1987, when, in the case of *Edwards v. Aguillard*, the US Supreme Court considered the teaching of creationism a violation of the First and Fourteenth Amendments and declared it illegal.

After *Edwards v. Aguillard,* the creationist community regrouped under the banner of "intelligent design." Intelligent design proponents claim that the world is orderly in its construction and thus demonstrates the existence of an intelligent agent who ordered it, thereby resurrecting the natural theology of early modernism. Under the leadership of Philip Johnson, who attacked the sole teaching of evolution as ideological rather than scientific, and Michael Behe, who argued that certain molecular structures were irreducibly complex and could not have evolved over the course of time according to Darwinian evolution, the intelligent design movement has advocated a public advocacy "wedge strategy" to force its way into public schools. In *Kitzmiller et al. v. Dover Area Public*

School District et al. (2004), a US Federal District Court refuted the claim that intelligent design is a scientific theory and declared that the Dover School District could not force teachers to assert in class that evolution is a "theory not a fact" and direct the students to a creationist textbook as an alternative.

The case of *Kitzmiller v. the Dover Area Public School District* reflects a growing public feeling that intelligent design belongs in the classroom in order to maintain "fairness." Many Americans believe that students should have an opportunity to hear both sides of the argument before pledging their allegiance to one or the other. According to a 2005 Harris Poll, a majority of those surveyed felt that biology teachers should present all three theories: evolution, creationism, and intelligent design. However, the rhetoric of fairness, employed frequently by intelligent design authors such as Philip Johnson, hides an underlying absence of fairness in the intelligent design agenda. On one hand, it is visibly absurd to force biology teachers to present material that the biology community believes to be "nonbiological." On the other, no advocates of intelligent design or creationism support the teaching in biology classes of non-Christian creation narratives (Hindu, Hopi, or aboriginal Australian narratives, to name just a few possible alternatives). The insistence that Christian cosmogonies deserve equal standing with standard biological interpretation is, contrary to superficial faith in the fairness of teaching multiple perspectives, entirely unfair.

Although the US court system has so far held intelligent design in check, the movement retains broad support in Christian communities and among those citizens who wish the teaching of biology to be "fair." Although intelligent design has almost no scientific supporters (Behe is the only one of significance), the movement's supporters will not likely give up their opposition to evolution. Their wedge strategy means that the battle over evolution will likely remain a matter of public policy and still be subject to regular debate in churches, schools, and courtrooms over the coming century.

Stem-Cell Research

Opposition to stem-cell technology, unlike the evolution and intelligent design controversy, will likely dissipate over the coming decades. Despite this, it has been an explosive issue in twenty-first-century US politics. President George W. Bush acknowledged his conservative Christian constituents by reversing the Clinton-era decision to support human embryonic stem-cell research with federal funds. The Bush administration permitted funding for only those stem-cell lines already in existence and rejected funding any new stem-cell lines. Because the older lines were determined to be defective on several material counts, scientists loudly opposed the Bush administration policy. President Bush also twice vetoed (in 2006 and 2007) Congressional legislation that was supportive of human embryonic stem-cell research.

Proponents of stem-cell research used it as a political lever in 2006, helping unseat several Republican incumbents from the US Congress. Although stem-cell research would affect only a small portion of the US population, opposition to it by the incumbents in Missouri and elsewhere helped doom their reelection campaigns. For citizens watching celebrities such as Michael J. Fox champion the potential of stem-cell research, opposition became a signpost for a fundamental lack of civility or absence of concern for the plight of others. In the election, Senate candidates outspokenly in favor of stem-cell funding won in Maryland, Missouri, New Jersey, and Ohio; opponents also lost in Arizona, California, Indiana, and Pennsylvania.

Given progress in isolating stem cells from skin cells, it is unlikely that stem-cell research will continue to be a hot-button issue in future elections, unless the new technology turns out to be flawed in spite of its initial successes. Nevertheless, the early twenty-first-century stem-cell debates show how religion-science debates can become political concerns.

Stem-cell research will likely depart the political arena, but many related technologies will remain volatile political issues. One of the most prolific political debates of the twentieth and twenty-first centuries was over the issue of abortion; indeed, it is this debate that largely motivated the resistance to stem-cell technologies in the twenty-first century. Those groups who believe that souls enter the world when sperm fertilize eggs will be unlikely to give up their continued opposition to the legalization of abortion.

Abortion

The primary opposition to abortion has come from Christians, despite the historical acceptability of such practices in Christian cultures. Because no one knows for certain how or when human beings acquire souls (assuming that we do), most Christian groups currently support the claim that one should assume the worst—that the soul is there from the beginning. If the embryo or fetus has a soul, aborting it—from this perspective—would be murder. Christians have not always made this assumption, however. Throughout antiquity and during the medieval period, theologians argued over the time of ensoulment.

Whether a modern Christian opposes abortion or accepts it, he or she can find a precedent in antiquity. Some early Christian texts—such as the *Didache* and the *Letter of Barnabus*—prohibited abortion, and the influential Gregory of Nyssa (fourth century) argued that ensoulment was continuous with embodiment. For Gregory, there is no soul without a body and no body without a soul; thus abortion at any time involves killing an ensouled person. But, in the second century, Tertullian argued that ensoulment awaits a humanoid form, and Augustine (fourth to fifth centuries) argued that, because there was no biblical indication as to when God placed the soul into a developing human being, the answer was indecipherable. After consideration, Augustine agreed with Tertullian that the humanly formed fetus has a different status from one that has yet to attain human form. The great medieval Catholic Thomas Aquinas believed that males acquired souls forty days after conception, whereas females acquired them ninety days after conception. Not until 1869 did the Catholic Church formally remove the distinction between an unformed and a formed fetus. At the same time, Protestant Christians generally tolerated (although discouraged) abortion until the rise of fundamentalism in the twentieth century.

The abortion debate has been largely a Christian debate, because few other religions place as much concern on the welfare of the unborn. Like ancient and medieval Christians, most Muslims believe that the unformed fetus is not yet a human person, and in Judaism the unborn are never accorded the same rights as those among the living. Among major non-Western religions, Buddhism is the only religion with a long-standing opposition to abortion, and, in fact, the combination of overpopulation and religious needs has encouraged abortion in some societies. Aside from the economic pressures for raising sons, there are religious reasons why sons are preferable to daughters in many cultures, which increases the likelihood of abortion. The need for sons to perform burial rites, among other duties, ensures that parents desire a son more than a daughter. In China and India, where overpopulation has become a crucial political concern, parents desperate to have a son often abort or abandon female babies.

The anti-abortion crusade has been a Christian movement in the United States; few other religions have gotten involved. This early non-involvement in religion-science issues is not unique to the legalization of abortion, however. For years, few religious groups had much to say about the growing environmental crisis (despite mid-twentieth-century warnings that they needed to play a role), but this distance has eroded as climate change has become one of the twenty-first century's most pressing political issues.

Environmental Concern

In 1967, the historian Lynn White (himself a committed Christian) traced the growing environmental problems of industrial life to a Christian understanding of the biblical command to subjugate the natural world. White argued that Christian missionaries had disenchanted the world by eliminating the belief in spirits and gods of nature and that the triumph of Christianity included a disdain for the world and a belief that the world exists for the sole purpose of serving human ends. White hoped that a turn away from such a Christian theology toward a renewed appreciation for St. Francis, who allegedly preached to birds and converted a dire wolf, would help avert future crises.

The Lynn White thesis, published in the prestigious journal *Science*, had an immediate impact, but it was not without its detractors. The Chinese-American geographer Yi-Fu Tuan was among its more prominent critics. Tuan argued that White had failed to appreciate the difference between a culture's ideals and the reality of its historical activity. Although Chinese religions, such as Taoism and Buddhism, might advocate

harmony with the natural world, as White points out, the history of China shows a flagrant disregard for many aspects of the environment, especially with regard to the Chinese tendency toward deforestation. If Tuan wrote today, no doubt he would point to the Three Gorges Dam and massive Chinese pollution as further evidence that environmental catastrophes are not just a Christian problem. Tuan also argued that, well prior to the Christian conversion, the Roman Empire already exercised more control over the natural environment (through its aqueducts and roads, for example) than was possible for most of Christian history prior to the early modern period. Although environmental problems were prominent in Christian nations, Tuan argued, they were equally likely in developed nations with other religious traditions.

In the United States, Jews and Christians have become vocal in their opposition to a hands-off government policy. In the "Evangelical Call to Civic Responsibility" (2004), conservative Protestant Christians presented a joint position on the need for better protection of the natural world through government intervention. Jewish movements such as eco-kashrut and the Coalition on the Environment and Jewish Life have also taken note of environmental problems and sought to motivate the faithful to greater conservation and political activism. Broad religious support for the environmental movement could pay dividends in industrial nations, where, for the past few decades, religious activity in politics has almost exclusively focused upon the teaching of evolution and anything associated with abortion and embryos.

Harvard biologist Edward O. Wilson, famous for his contributions to sociobiology, wrote *The Creation* (2006) in the hope of finding common ground between religious and scientific activists. Addressing his book to a Southern Baptist preacher (Wilson was raised Southern

Baptist before leaving the faith), Wilson eloquently describes a wide array of environmental problems, from overharvesting of plants and animals to climate change to pollution, which endanger the relatively delicate balance of the natural world. Wilson believes that by harnessing the powers of science and religion toward a common end, the environmental crises of the twentieth and twenty-first centuries might be resolved.

With the National Association of Evangelicals (NAE) calling for environmental action and eminent scientists seeking common ground with them, it is quite possible that environmental politics could grow more prominent in US culture. The NAE accounts for sixty different (generally fundamentalist) Protestant denominations, and the more emphasis that it places upon environmentalism, the more such concerns may take a position alongside abortion and gay marriage in fundamentalist politics and in the daily activity of fundamentalist Christians.

Germinal Choice Technologies

Germinal choice technologies, frequently called germline engineering, refer to the ways in which human beings might permanently alter their genetic heritage. By changing the DNA of a human being at its early stages of development through recombinant DNA techniques, or by adding an extra chromosome with new genes that might be turned on or off by the recipient, scientists believe that we can cure many diseases and perhaps enhance the physical and mental powers of our children.

To a certain extent, the religious response to these nonreproductive biotechnologies can be predicted from past experience with eugenics. Eugenics, the effort to improve the human condition through selective breeding and government-mandated sterilization, had both religious

proponents and detractors. In the United States, some Christians supported eugenics as a way to finish the divine plan for humanity by removing sin and evil; others decried it as cruel and against God's divinely ordained natural order. Loosely speaking, we can expect something very similar as germinal choice technologies change the way human beings are produced.

Some Christian groups (the Roman Catholic Church prominent among them) have continued to oppose in vitro fertilization, by which "test tube" babies are created and then implanted into a human mother. But this technology has gained widespread acceptance in US culture. The fertilization of eggs outside of the womb allows scientists a chance to correct "mistakes" and improve "deficiencies." For example, in early 2008, scientists succeeded in removing the nucleus of one egg and inserting it into a donor egg in order to provide the embryo with healthy mitochondrial DNA.[3] The more we learn to modify our genetic inheritance, the more frequently we will hear accusations of "playing God" and of creating "Frankenstein's monster."

What constitutes playing God? If God created human beings with the powers to improve ourselves, should we consider our technological improvement divinely mandated, as many have believed of technological mastery since the medieval period? Or should we seek to limit ourselves as, perhaps, Adam should have done in the Garden of Eden? These questions—or those very similar—apply to all people of religious faith. The choices they must make, both as voting citizens and as practical decision makers, depend upon how they interpret the relationship between divine will and technology. Should we "pull the plug" from a life-support patient and, if so, when? Should we modify our children to improve their eyesight or musical talent? Should we change the colors of our skin or eyes? Outspoken political commentator Jeremy Rifkin opposes all biotechnologies, because we might easily slide from changing our eyes to changing our skin color to eventually losing sight of our basic humanity. Leon Kass, who chaired the President's Council on Bioethics from 2002 to 2005, believes that we should seek out a "natural norm of health" but stop short of "enhancement." We must also consider the potential political implications of germinal choice technologies. If wealth dictated the availability of genetic improvements, society could be split into two very different groups, thus endangering the legal protections offered in the democratic traditions of the West. Francis Fukuyama, a conservative political thinker, has argued for the regulation of biotechnologies for precisely this reason. The transhumanists, described above, and their "procreative liberty" allies believe that people should decide for themselves what they want for their children.

But if biotechnological promises prove true, free choice may be effectively dissolved. The legal scholar Lori Andrews fears that the widespread use of such technology could lead to the homogenization of the human species, because few parents would want their children to possess socially disadvantageous traits. At the same time, this could heighten racial, ethnic, and sexual prejudices, given that fewer people are born with certain groups' characteristics. And if germinal choice technologies allow for smarter, stronger, healthier children, what parent could refuse them? Even if the first generation parent did so, would his or her children—having seen how the genetically enhanced surpassed his or her own ability in work and play—do likewise? This domino effect, combined with the natural parental desire to give children every possible advantage, might mean that germinal choice technologies would actually destroy "procreative liberty."

The language employed by bioethicists such as Fukuyama, Kass, and Andrews (who is, by profession, a lawyer) actively discourages participation by religious groups. Seeking a "moral Esperanto"[4]—a morality applicable to all human beings regardless of religious affiliation—disenfranchises religious groups, who find their key concepts frequently untenable in bioethical and governmental discussions. The inability of religious groups to argue—on the grounds of souls, divine beings, and possible afterlives—creates a powerful resentment among religious groups to government-sponsored bioethics (often even when the bioethicists, such as Kass or Fukuyama, make recommendations that are closely akin to the positions taken by religious groups).

Religious forces are inclined to oppose genetic enhancement. Jewish authorities have already supported biotechnologies that prevent illness, but they oppose enhancement techniques. Given the emphasis placed upon healing in Jewish life, we can presume that Jewish leaders will continue to condone medical research using stem cells and germinal choice technologies that aim toward the elimination of disease and mental and physical handicaps. It is unlikely, however, that Jewish leaders will reverse course and join those who favor human enhancement. Christian leaders, likewise, will probably oppose enhancement in general. It is well-known, however, that the religious opposition to abortion, for example, does little to stop abortion among the faithful. Even if Jewish and Christian leaders are outspoken in their criticism of genetic enhancement, social competition will pressure parents to disobey in the apparent best interest of their children.

The practice of religion on the ground rarely coincides with the official pronouncements of religious leaders. Many people already find reconciling biotechnological progress and religious practice difficult, and it will remain so as technology advances. The rapid acceptance of in vitro fertilization by most people in US culture seems to indicate that, regardless of institutional religious acceptance, average citizens will continue taking advantage of biotechnological research. Citizens have shown an increasing preference for technologies that promise cures, and they have voiced this preference in voting booths. Political action may well divide populations in modern economies, as some groups put aside the warnings of their religious communities and others attempt to halt research (as happened over stem cells early in the twenty-first century).

Even as we witness the pope announce that certain biotechnologies assault human dignity and we are tempted to declare religion and science once again at war, we must remember that the world is always more nuanced than such easy declarations describe. Not only will actual people frequently believe and act differently from their institutional leaders, but, in other instances, religious leaders will quite possibly support one or more of the technologies that the pope or other Christians happen to oppose. Finally, we must recall how in transhumanism, religion and science march hand in hand (religious promises infuse popularizations of science), whereas the new religion thus formed simultaneously competes with other religious traditions. The world of religion and science is a richly diverse world, which sustains many possible interpretations of biotechnology.

Virtual Religion

The most important debates in religion and science play out in politics; over the next decades, however, new concerns will arise, thanks to the increasing digitalization of culture. The growth of virtual worlds in computer games will reshape the practice of religion worldwide, by encouraging lay power within traditional religions and by presenting a competitive arena for religious life.

In the past century, the religiously faithful have had vastly more opportunity to choose how and when they practice religion, thanks to the pluralization of modern society. Secularization in modern life has led not to the dismantling of religious life, but to the establishment of a "spiritual marketplace," in which religious practitioners can choose those aspects of a given religion that they find most appropriate to their own lives. This democratization of religion creates a competitive world for spiritual institutions, which find that, unlike in the past, they must compete for the patronage of individuals. The competition is about to become a lot stiffer.

The popularity of religion in online life, especially that of massively multiplayer online games (MMOGs) has exploded in recent years, as the population of players has gone from a small crowd of early adopters to include a broad and growing cross-section of modern consumers. Contrary to popular misconception, MMOGs, such as *World of Warcraft*, *EverQuest*, *Star Wars Galaxies*, and *Second Life* (*SL*) are not just for teenage boys. The average *SL* resident, for example, is a thirty-two-year-old female. According to a 2008 study by the Gartner Group, 80 percent of active Internet users will participate in virtual worlds by the year 2012.

Virtual gaming is not just for Americans; indeed, people in eastern and Southeast Asia play online games in greater numbers than do Americans, and new groups have launched efforts to bring virtual reality to developing nations. Uthango, a nongovernmental organization based in Cape Town, South Africa, for example, works to ensure that Africans have a place in and the power to help shape virtual worlds, beginning with *SL*. *Second Life* (as opposed to other online games) is most popular among Americans, but it draws residents from across the world and brings them together in one online world that they can create together.

The world of *SL* is very much like earthly life, with the caveat that residents can fly, teleport, and fabricate anything that their minds and skills allow (by shaping the objects and programming them in *SL*'s proprietary programming language). Residents go to virtual bars, museums, shopping malls, and bordellos; they buy virtual clothes, vehicles, and homes. They make real friends and sustain long-term relationships with people they like, love, and trust. Since free membership was opened in 2006, the user base has gone from a few thousand to a few million by 2008. Over fifty thousand residents come online at any given time as of late 2009, and over one million log on over the course of one month.

Contrary to expectation, all online games promote social relationships, connecting users and forging bonds between them, but "purposeless" games such as *SL* take this sociality one step further—there is really nothing else to do there. In adventure games such as *World of Warcraft*, players can wander alone, slaying monsters and finding treasure, but the highest levels of the games require a wide circle of group and guild memberships. Studies have shown that users who do not form social bonds in the first two or three weeks of play cease returning. In *SL* and similar games, the social relationships have become the almost exclusive aspect of the game. Even though some residents make a living through virtual services, the vast majority return to the world to keep up with the friends they have made there.

In late 2006, shortly after the population of *SL* began its rapid growth, religious groups quickly expanded their presence in this online world, largely through the initiative and governance of laypeople. Churches, synagogues, mosques, and meditation centers sprung up in association with Christianity, Judaism, Islam, Buddhism, and the Hare Krishnas. And, although these virtual buildings are frequently empty (as are earthly temples, most of the time), they quickly acquired adherents, who associate themselves with the group, attend services, and make donations. In one survey, 84 percent of respondents either definitely or probably have a place in *SL*; nearly 40 percent visit religious spaces at least once or twice per month.[5] Clearly, virtual gaming technology adds a new arena for religious practice.

Religious practitioners on *SL* find that virtual religion has important limitations but that it fulfills their spiritual needs. Although Muslims have generally refused to replace the physical *salat* (daily prayers) with virtual prayers, many are known to place their avatars in a prayer posture while they pray. Likewise, no one has yet claimed that the meeting of ten Jews in *SL* constitutes a *minyan*. Nevertheless, the virtually faithful are unanimous in their belief that prayer online is real prayer, aimed at real gods. An individual confined by disease or disability in physical life may find that religion in virtual spaces has become the only kind of practice left to him or her; other practitioners may actively prefer *SL* religious life to conventional religious practices. Some *SL* religious groups, such as Koinonia (United Church of Christ), offer welcoming communities (regardless of gender, sexuality, political persuasion, etc.) that have led some participants to declare, "I wish I could find a church like this in real life!"

The most popular MMOG, *World of Warcraft*, has more than 10 million players worldwide, many of whom experience something akin to the sacred in their gaming lives. Religion separates out time into the sacred (the time of meaning and purpose) and the profane (the daily economic time without true meaning). Practitioners look forward to religious rituals as an escape from the mundane—but also as a promise of fulfillment, in which they join communities that are deeply bonded and participate in activities that are the most meaningful available to people. Games such as *World of Warcraft* allow their players to join groups of adventuring friends, who often have powerful, "mafialike" influence on the lives of the players and who perform heroic deeds—the sort of deeds completely absent from daily life. In some sense, gaming offers daily access to sacred goods (communities, meaning, and purpose). Far from being stereotypical loners, most gamers join up with their online "families" and, while sitting at their computers, sally forth against the forces of evil, defeating demons and rescuing innocents. As their characters progress, the players find themselves deeply enmeshed in a battle to save their characters' universe and the souls of everything living within it. As a consequence, such games operate as "authentic fakes," a term used by the historian of religions David Chidester to refer to secular practices put to sacred work.

Simultaneous to their revision of traditional religious institutions and ideas, online games also create a sacred alternative to them. Many online gamers seek to spend increasing percentages of their time in online worlds; up to 20 percent of polled gamers claim they would like to spend all of their time "in-world." The connection to Apocalyptic-AI promises of mind uploading should be obvious. The games provide a sense of meaningful action (participation in the group, successful completion of quests, clear distinction between good and evil) that individuals often lack in their earthly lives. As they turn to online games to provide them with communities and worldviews, they may well turn away from earthly religious institutions.

Conclusion

Twenty-first-century public life illustrates the importance of studying religion, science, and technology. As we came to better understand the physical laws of nature and, subsequently, our brains, the significance of religion-science interactions grew increasingly obvious. These matters, which have interested scientists, theologians, and academicians, point to the human need for coherent worldviews. For most people, however, a worldview is something acted out, not something settled upon in theological debate. As a consequence, the politically live issues of evolution, environmentalism, and biotechnology demonstrate considerably more about the relationship of religion and science than do the more local concerns over physics and neuroscience. The citizenry has, however, proven that we must commit to the study and understanding of religion and science through its public discourse and political activity. Over the coming decades, understanding the ways in which religious groups, ideas, and practices intersect with scientific groups, ideas, and practices will help us understand our societies and our selves.

Glossary

Apocalyptic AI: A transhumanist system, advocated (principally) by Hans Moravec and Ray Kurzweil, in which vastly intelligent machines are expected to arise by the early to mid-twenty-first century and in which human beings will "upload" their conscious minds into machines in order to live eternally.

Conflict Thesis: The belief that religion and science are at war with one another, chiefly advocated by John Draper and Andrew White in the nineteenth century.

Creationism: The (primarily Christian) belief that the world was created approximately six thousand years ago in a direct act of God and in more or less its present condition. This belief precludes evolution by natural selection and is seen as opposing Darwinian biology.

Geocentric Theory: An astronomical model that hypothesizes that the Earth is the center of the cosmos. Such models were common in Europe after the adoption of Aristotelian philosophy and until the seventeenth-century adoption of the heliocentric model (see entry).

Germinal Choice Technologies: Technologies (such as changing particular genes in an individual or adding an extra chromosome) designed to change the genetic inheritance of the individual permanently.

Heliocentric Theory: An astronomical model that hypothesizes that the Sun is the center of the cosmos. Heliocentric models were occasionally advocated in ancient Greece and were used by some early modern Europeans. Eventually, the heliocentric model became the accepted view of the solar system after the time of Copernicus and Galileo.

Intelligent Design: The belief that the orderly nature of certain aspects of the universe indicates that the universe must have been designed by an intelligent agent. Intelligent design has been criticized as a successor to creationism (see prior discussion), as in the case of *Kitzmiller v. Dover Area Public School District* (2004).

Reconciliation Thesis: The belief that science and theology (usually Christian theology) point toward the same fundamental reality and can, thus, be in agreement with one another when viewed "properly."

Scientific Revolution: A period in European history that is difficult to date precisely but can be seen in the modernization of scientific methods and communities from the sixteenth to the eighteenth centuries.

Stem-Cell Technology: Research with stem cells, the earliest cells in biological development. Because stem cells differentiate into other kinds of cells as the embryo develops, they are considered valuable for resolving otherwise incurable diseases and handicaps. Conflict over the use of embryonic stem cells (stem cells gained from aborted embryos) has been a significant political issue since the late 1990s.

Transhumanism: Religious systems, emerging in the twentieth century, that argue for the plausibility of traditional religious ideas (such as amelioration of the Earth and its inhabitants and the immortality of humankind) through scientific and technological means.

Virtual Worlds: Computer-generated environments shared by users over the Internet. Such worlds include video games such as *World of Warcraft* or *Counterstrike* and social spaces such as *Second Life*.

FOR FURTHER READING

Alexander, Brian. *Rapture: A Raucous Tour of Cloning, Transhumanism, and the New Era of Immortality*. New York: Basic Books, 2003.

Andrews, Lori B. "People as Products: The Conflict between Technology and Social Values." *The Hedgehog Review: Critical Reflections on Contemporary Culture* 4, no. 3 (2002): 45–65.

Barbour, Ian. *Religion and Science: Historical and Contemporary Issues*. San Francisco: HarperSanFrancisco, 1997.

Brooke, John, and Geoffrey Cantor. *Reconstructing Nature: The Engagement of Science and Religion*. New York: Oxford University Press, 1998.

Chidester, David. *Authentic Fakes: Religion and American Popular Culture*. Berkeley: University of California Press. 2005.

Dalai Lama. *The Universe in a Single Atom: The Convergence of Science and Spirituality*. New York: Broadway, 2005.

Draper, John William. *The History of the Conflict between Religion and Science*. New York: D. Appleton, 1874.

Eddis, Tanner. *An Illusion of Harmony: Science and Religion in Islam*. Amherst, NY: Prometheus, 2007.

Ferngren, Gary B. *The History of Science and Religion in the Western Tradition: An Encyclopedia*. New York: Garland, 2000.

Fukuyama, Francis. *Our Posthuman Future: Consequences of the Biotechnology Revolution*. New York: Farrar, Straus and Giroux, 2002.

Furse, Edmund. "A Theology of Robots." Presented at the University of Glamorgan (May 14, 1996). http://www.comp.glam.ac.uk /pages/staff/efurse/Theology-of-Robots /A-Theology-of-Robots.html.

Geraci, Robert M. "Apocalyptic AI: Religion and the Promise of Artificial Intelligence." *Journal of the American Academy of Religion* 76, no. 1 (2008): 138–66.

———. *Apocalyptic AI: Visions of Heaven in Robotics, Artificial Intelligence and Virtual Reality*. New York: Oxford University Press, 2010.

Gilbert, James. *Redeeming Culture: American Religion in an Age of Science*. Chicago: University of Chicago Press, 1997.

Hu, Danian. "The Reception of Relativity in China." *Isis* 98, no. 3 (2007): 539–57.

Jastrow, Robert. *God and the Astronomers,* 2nd ed. New York: W. W. Norton, 2000.

Kurzweil, Ray. *The Age of Spiritual Machines: When Computers Exceed Human Intelligence*. New York: Viking, 1999.

Larson, Edward J. *Summer for the Gods: The Scopes Trial and America's Continuing Debate over Science and Religion*. Cambridge, MA: Harvard University Press, 1997.

Lindberg, David C., and Ronald L. Numbers. *God and Nature: Historical Essays on the Encounter between Christianity and Science*. Berkeley: University of California Press, 1986.

McNight, Stephen A. *The Religious Foundations of Francis Bacon's Thought*. Columbia: University of Missouri Press, 2006.

Merton, Robert K. *Science, Technology and Society in Seventeenth-Century England*. New York: Howard Fertig, 1970.

Moravec, Hans. *Robot: Mere Machine to Transcendent Mind*. New York: Oxford University Press, 1999.

Noble, David F. *The Religion of Technology: The Divinity of Man and the Spirit of Invention*. New York: Penguin, 1999.

Numbers, Ronald. *The Creationists: The Evolution of Scientific Creationism*. Berkeley: University of California Press, 1993.

Nye, David E. *America as Second Creation: Technology and Narratives of a New Beginning*. Cambridge, MA: MIT Press, 2003.

Pennock, Robert T. *Intelligent Design Creationism and Its Critics: Philosophical, Theological and Scientific Perspectives*. Cambridge, MA: MIT Press, 2001.

President's Council on Bioethics. *Beyond Therapy: Biotechnology and the Pursuit of*

Happiness. Washington, DC: The President's Council on Bioethics, 2003.

Roof, Wade Clark. *Spiritual Marketplace: Baby Boomers and the Remaking of American Religion.* Princeton: Princeton University Press, 1999.

Russell, Robert J., William R. Stoeger, and George V. Coyne, eds. *John Paul II on Science and Religion: Reflection on the New View from Rome.* Notre Dame: University of Notre Dame Press, 1990.

Scott, Eugenie. *Evolution vs. Creationism: An Introduction.* Berkeley: University of California Press, 2004.

Shapin, Steven. *The Scientific Revolution.* Chicago: University of Chicago Press, 1996.

Sherwin, Byron. *Golems among Us: How a Jewish Legend Can Help Us Navigate the Biotech Century.* Chicago: Ivan R. Dee, 2004.

Stock, Gregory. *Redesigning Humans: Choosing Our Genes, Changing Our Future.* New York: Houghton Mifflin, 2003.

Taylor, T. L. *Play between Worlds: Exploring Online Game Culture.* Cambridge, MA: MIT Press, 2006.

Tremlin, Todd. *Minds and Gods: The Cognitive Foundations of Religion.* New York: Oxford University Press. 2006.

Tuan, Yi-Fu. "Our Treatment of the Environment in Ideal and Actuality." *American Scientist* 58 (May–June, 1970): 244–49.

Van Huyssteen, J. Wentzel, ed. *Encyclopedia of Science and Religion.* New York: Macmillan, 2003.

Wang, Zuoyue. "Science and the State in Modern China." *Isis* 93, no. 3 (2007): 558–70.

White, Andrew. *The History of the Warfare of Science with Theology in Christendom.* 1896. New York: D. Appleton, 1923.

Wilson, E. O. *The Creation: A Meeting of Science and Religion.* New York: W.W. Norton, 2006.

5

WOMEN

Sarah W. Whedon

INTRODUCTION

It was the mid-1830s and Sarah Studevant Leavitt's daughter Louisa was very ill. Sarah and her family were Mormons, members of the new religion that had been founded a few years before, in 1830, by Joseph Smith, in New York State. When Sarah prayed to God on behalf of the sick Louisa, an angel appeared to her and instructed her to lay her hands on her daughter in the name of Jesus Christ. Sarah complied, the blessing worked, and Louisa was soon well again. Sarah's experience may be the earliest recorded incident of Mormon women laying hands on the sick for healing, a practice that became common for women in the Latter-Day Saints (LDS) Church, but that was nevertheless a subject of scrutiny and debate.

There was a scriptural foundation for this healing practice. In the New Testament book of 1 Corinthians, the apostle Paul describes healing as one of the spiritual gifts available to Christian believers. The Mormon prophet Joseph Smith affirmed the righteousness of these gifts and did not limit their practice by the gender of the believer. In the Mormon Church, only men can enter the priesthood, which empowers them to perform most of the rituals of the Mormon faith. However, one of the rituals that became common for women was laying hands upon other women for healing illnesses. Women would also offer a blessing of washing and anointing for community members who were about to give birth.

Although women were giving healing blessings from the earliest days of the church, men often questioned women's authority to do so. In 1913, the formal church hierarchy first officially doubted the legitimacy of this practice. In 1946, a statement by a prominent male church leader effectively ended women's healing practices, arguing that only members of the priesthood, meaning men, should properly perform such rites. By this time in the twentieth century, most responsibility for healing sick Mormons had already been transferred away from the faith and into the medical profession anyway. Despite the formal restriction, some women continued to exercise this spiritual gift secretively, and they do so to this day.[1]

Issues such as these that the Mormon women faced—relating to women's bodies, motherhood, relationships with other women, domestic spaces of power, and tension with formal religious authority—recur frequently in women's daily religious experience. Although the details of this story are specific to Mormonism, its themes are common in women's practice of religion. Women perform rituals of spiritual healing within the home in many other religious communities as well. Further, women's experiences of struggling to maintain integrity and religious authority in the face of disapproving church institutions are not unique to Mormonism. Finding ways to practice sacred rites despite official sanctions is one route for women to claim their own religious power and self-determination. Women's religious rituals are often outside formal canon and may be considered optional, magical, or otherwise marginal. Likewise, practices identified as folk tradition, syncretism, or superstition are often the religious practices of women. There is also a methodological lesson to be learned from this story. An examination of religious histories, Mormon or otherwise, that looked only at documentation of clergy would miss important parts of women's religious experiences and practices that happen outside the boundaries of religious orthodoxy.

As we unpack these themes, we will find that many of the details that need to be considered seem intensely personal—matters of food or sex, for example. One of the contributions of second-wave feminist thought was the slogan "the personal is political," meaning that that these kinds of intimate personal experiences are actually linked to larger social structures. We need to think about how women's private lives are played out in relationship to public religious and political contexts. Let us now look more closely at the importance of women's daily religious practice, how to delineate this category

of analysis properly, and what details emerge through this study of women's religious lives.

Why Women?

Why should we pay particular attention to women's practices of religion in everyday life? Why separate out this gender? One answer is that, in doing so, we recover a large and historically neglected area of human religious experience. Religion scholars Rita M. Gross and Nancy Auer Falk observe that the study of religion was taught to them as the study of *homo religiosus,* or "religious man," and point out that this framework neglects the study of "religious woman." They argue that "if we are making a genuine effort to recall the whole human experience in religion, it stands to reason that women's experiences must still be a significant part of the picture."[2] We single out women in a project of recovery to mend a gap in what scholars have studied and learned about human religious life.

In seeking to mend this gap, we must consider rituals that women and men practice together as well as those that are performed only by women. In gender-integrated rituals, women may take specific roles or may have their own experiences and interpretations of religion. Alongside men's religious practices, women also often have their own religious observances that may be all but invisible to men in their community or to outside male observers. In many religious cultures, women prepare for and celebrate certain rituals with no participation from men. We consider these different kinds of relationships between women and ritual.

A second answer to the question of why we study women has to do with women's power and social status. Women have often lived as a subordinated class within particular societies, although this experience is not universal, and, in recent years, it has changed a great deal in many parts of the world. The study of women in religion has been framed by notions of patriarchy, meaning that men hold the power in a society, and by the concurrent experience of women's oppression. World religions have historically contributed greatly to the subordination of women as a class. Women are often excluded from or marginalized by orthodox religious practices that are controlled by men. Being unable to access men's rituals can be disempowering to women. Although women quite frequently outnumber men in religious institutions, men usually hold the power and authority. By calling attention to women here, we find ways to understand an imbalance in social and religious power. This information can help women who wish to redress power imbalances in their religious communities.

The relationship between women's religion and women's oppression is not a constant. According to Gross and Falk, religion can harmonize with everyday life, help women bear its difficulties, or draw them out of or help them change it. We can find examples of women's religious practices functioning in all these ways.

The history of women's religious lives parallels that of men's, because women have been a part of every society. Men are certainly players in these stories as well, but different details emerge when we focus on women's beliefs, stories, rituals, and experiences of religion.

WHAT ARE WOMEN?

At first glance, it probably seems obvious what we mean by the word *women*. Ordinarily, it does

BLESSING WAY

In recent years, women in the United States have created new rituals for preparing pregnant women to give birth and for honoring these women's passages into motherhood. These rituals borrow the name "Blessing Way" from a name for Navajo rituals, provoking ethical concerns about cultural appropriation. They offer an alternative to the secular baby shower, and women who choose a Blessing Way say that they want a more spiritual event than the materialism of a baby shower. A Blessing Way of this kind typically involves a gathering of women, led by a friend of the expectant mother, or a ritual specialist hired for the occasion. The ceremonies are adapted for the mother's needs and desires, but certain components are typically included. Storytelling, symbolic burning of fears related to the birth, and stringing together beads for a labor necklace all help prepare a woman for the birth process. Painting the woman's body with henna, foot washing, offering of prayers and blessings, and singing all honor the power and mystery of motherhood and the particular mother's process. These Blessing Ways (sometimes called "Mother Blessings," to distinguish them from Navajo rituals) do not belong to any one religious tradition, although they clearly demonstrate inspiration from contemporary Pagan and Goddess spirituality rituals. The rituals represent creative imagining of new woman-centered practices, addressing a need in women's religious lives.

not even occur to us to question it, and it would likely drain our personal resources if the meaning of *woman* and who belongs in that category were in question on a daily basis. But when we take time to reflect on the term, we discover that determining who is a woman is not as simple as it usually seems.

Women's studies scholars have pointed out at least two different ways of thinking about what makes a woman: biological determinism and social constructionism. On the one hand, biological determinism tells us that women are identifiable by their physiology. Reproductive organs and secondary sex characteristics—such as the presence or lack of facial hair or fatty deposits on the body—help us determine who is a woman. According to this approach, body parts and hormones determine women's beliefs, needs, and behaviors, making biology destiny.

On the other hand, social constructionism argues that the meaning of womanhood changes across history and across cultures and that being a woman is more about learned roles. In the United States, these roles are taught from the moment that the doctor announces "It's a girl!" and puts a pink hat on an infant's head. In this model, we can expect, when we examine different religions, to find that the meaning and practice of womanhood varies greatly.

A combination of these two models helps us most effectively understand what makes womanhood. Realistically, women's lives, including their religious practices and experiences, are probably worked out in a creative mix of biology and culture. For example, the physiological possibility of motherhood is clearly a shaping experience for women across cultures, but the ways in which childbirth is interpreted and ritualized differ widely, as do the ways in which mothering is understood and enacted.

We should also be wary of assuming that there are only two "opposite" genders—male and female. Religions can actually serve to create new ways of identifying women, or even third genders. For example, Hindu *hijras* are male-bodied people who dress and live socially as women. They identify with the deity Siva, a sexually ambiguous figure. Their primary worship is directed, however, at Bahuchara Mata, a goddess in whose name they make blessings of fertility and prosperity to infants and newlyweds. In another kind of gender bending, there are also many religious stories of women cross-dressing or changing gender, such as the Sufi saint Rabi'ah, whose celibacy and religiosity caused her to be perceived as a man. These examples of religious gendering can remind us to remain open-minded when we are looking for who the women are in any given religious society.

The knowledge that women's lives are shaped by different cultural and religious contexts should prompt us to use a wide lens to look for the diversity of women's lives. Just as the term "religious man" was incorrectly assumed to include all religious people, when we think of "woman," we often default to "white, middle-class, adult, American woman." But womanhood is profoundly affected by one's race, class, age, nationality, and other such qualities. The meaning of womanhood is different for a young Afghan Muslim woman than it is for a Chicano Catholic grandmother from Los Angeles. Thinking intersectionally—viewing these intersecting categories as mutually constituting one another—we can see the unique characteristics of particular women's religious lives. We look to examples from many different combinations of such intersections in order to think about women's daily religious lives.

SACRED TIME: THE LIFE COURSE

Women's religious organization of time can take on multiple dimensions. On one end of the spectrum, there are the great epochs of sacred texts, and, at the other end, there are the brief moments of prayer. Let us consider time in terms of how religions shape women's life cycles. Women move from birth, to girlhood, to adulthood, into old age, and finally death. Rites of passage—rituals that mark transitions from one of these stages of life to another—are sometimes celebrated on appropriate occasions during an individual woman's life. This listing of life stages is an imperfect map of all women's lives, because, although there are certain biological facts that women generally share, the ways in which they are interpreted and ritualized differ across cultures and religions. This lifespan perspective, however, enables us to think about how women's religious lives can change in different phases of their lives. In the course of considering women's daily religious lives, we also notice other ways in which sacred time is invoked, in daily prayers, in the celebration of seasonal cycles, and in rituals and taboos around monthly menstrual cycles.

MENSTRUATION

It is not surprising that menstruation is often given special attention, because religions tend to be very concerned with women's bodies and their sexuality. The onset of menses is often the transition point into womanhood for a girl. Some religions honor a girl's first menses with a rite of passage, a ritual that observes and facilitates her transition from one life stage to another. For example, in traditional Native American rituals, multiple days of ceremony, song, and dance instruct the young woman in her new role. The eight-day Apache ceremony, called *Isanaklesh Gotal*, involves a ritual fire, singing, dancing, blessing the girl, a feast, and a period of contemplative isolation for the girl.

Other religions may acknowledge a girl's transition to becoming a woman at about the time of puberty but without explicit links to menstruation. The relatively recent innovation of the Jewish bat mitzvah ritual for a girl, which mirrors the bar mitzvah ritual for a boy, is such a case. In these rituals, the young adult's first public reading from the Torah, the Jewish scriptures, signals passage into adulthood. The girl must study and prepare for the occasion. Depending on the branch of Judaism, the family may also celebrate this event with a large party for the young woman.

In many religions, there are taboos around women's bodily experiences of fertility, including both menstruation and childbirth—for example, in traditional Chinese religion and Japanese Shinto. Similarly, Muslim women do not pray or fast during menstruation. Jewish women who observe traditional practices abstain from sex around menstruation and cleanse themselves after menstruation in a ritual bath called a *mikveh*. This ritual brings women together apart from men, but women also claim that the practices improve their sexual relations with their husbands.

These kinds of fertility taboos usually hinge on notions of menstruation being impure or polluting, but taboos can also signal the perceived power of women's bodies. For example, Daoism views women's menstrual fluid as powerful, not as polluting. Similarly, the Native American Blackfeet of northern Montana considered menstrual blood to be so powerful that male warriors would smear their wives' menstrual blood on themselves as a demonstration of their strength before going into battle. Pliny the Elder reflected a classical view of menstruation as taboo when he wrote that, among the many dangers of menstrual fluid, "contact with the monthly flux of women turns new wine sour, makes crops wither, kills grafts, dries seeds in gardens, causes the fruit of trees to fall off, dims the bright surface of mirrors, dulls the edge of steel and the gleam of ivory, kills bees, rusts iron and bronze, and causes a horrible smell to fill the air."

CLOTHING

As women grow to adulthood and into adult sexuality, religions increasingly tend to regulate their daily bodily practices, even down to the details of dress and hairstyle. Religions often dictate norms of modesty and femininity for women's daily attire and grooming.

Head coverings are a common form of religious clothing. Orthodox Jewish women cover their hair, either with scarves or wigs. In the Christian New Testament, the apostle Paul argues that early Christian women should cover their heads in prayer (and that men should not), perhaps because he is trying to protect the community against accusations of sexual impropriety (see 1 Corinthians 11). Today, women's hats remain a part of appropriate attire for many Christian women who wish to obey this biblical passage. African American churchwomen have a particularly strong culture of church-hat aesthetics.

Appropriate attire for Muslim women has been a topic of much controversy in recent years, especially in cities where Europeans and Middle Easterners interact. In some countries, Muslim women are forced to wear a *hijab,* or headscarf, when in public and during the sexually active years. The purpose of modest dress is to discourage men from thinking of women as sex objects. It also serves to create a kind of sacred space through which a woman can move in privacy, even in public spaces outside her home. In this way, the *hijab* imitates the *harem*, the private inner sanctum of the home that is women's domain. Today, Western women often look pityingly on women who wear veils, assuming that the veil is a symbol of their oppression. In fact, in some Western countries, wearing veils has been banned. But many Muslim women feel that the veil is an important symbol of their cultural and religious identity, and they often choose to wear it even when their communities do not require

it. In some places, veils are markers of wealth, status, and sexual attractiveness, which is the opposite of what many Westerners encounter in the media.

MARRIAGE

Although the onset of menstruation sometimes marks the passage into adulthood for women, marriage is another rite that can signal this transition. Marriage rituals and wedding contracts mark women's entry into married life. The form of these symbols helps create the foundation for daily married life, often the longest stage in a woman's life course.

Contemporary US culture idealizes love marriage, in which partners choose each other based on romantic feeling, but this form of marriage is a relatively late and unusual development in the history of marriage. More commonly, religious cultures structure marriages around community economic and social needs. For example, traditional Chinese marriages are arranged for the production of children, and Hindu marriages tend to be arranged for social purposes as well. There is evidence of polygamy in the Hebrew Bible and in early Christianity; in the early years of Islam, polygyny, marriage of one man to multiple wives, was encouraged in part as a way of dealing with the need for the community to support widows economically.

Marriage customs define appropriate behaviors for wives. In a Hindu wedding, the bride is given to the groom, a male priest directs the rite, and veiled women sing from the sidelines. An ideal Hindu wife who is totally devoted to her husband is called a *pativrata*. Traditionally, Hindu women believe that a husband is required for their own religious salvation. High-caste, menopausal Hindu women perform an expensive ritual called *habisha* that is intended to keep their husbands healthy and alive.

Similarly, in Islam, marriage, *nikah*, involves a contract describing the duties of a husband and wife. In Shi'a Islam, there is a provision for temporary marriage, called *muta'*, that allows for sexual enjoyment without breaking the strict rule against sex outside of marriage, although this practice is widely frowned upon.

The end of marriage can be as consequential for a woman as its beginning. Laws and customs for divorce and widowing can be as critical for women's daily lives as marriage norms. Many religions make divorce difficult for women to obtain, and some make it difficult to live as a divorced woman, often for reasons of economic need. Muslim men, for example, have historically been able to access divorce more easily than women.

For Hindu widows, circumstances have historically been bleak. They could not remarry, wear jewelry, or attend many important rituals, and they were often considered to be evil witches. In Hindu tradition, *sati* means a virtuous woman. A wife could become *sati* by means of immolation on her husband's funeral pyre. In the past, widows chose this practice because they were looked down upon, dependent upon their sons, and required to maintain sexual fidelity to their husbands. As *satis,* however, they would be glorified. Given the constraints placed on widows, it is difficult to see this choice as having been a truly free choice, and this practice is now largely frowned upon.

Most religions have historically allowed little space for women who do not wish to marry because they prefer independence or because they do not desire men sexually. In these traditions, heterosexual marriage is assumed to be the right and best path for adult women and may therefore be compulsory. Sometimes opportunities for religious celibacy have allowed women to escape the demands of marriage, housework, and child-rearing. Catholic convents in the Middle Ages are an example of such a means for women to opt out of an otherwise compulsory role.

SEX AND CONTRACEPTION

Religious authorities usually dictate norms for women's sexuality, including sexual relations, contraception, conception, and child-rearing. The diversity of religious understandings of sexuality range from imagining sex as primarily sinful, or polluted, to sacralizing sex. However, marriage is usually the formal religious precondition for women's sex and sexuality to be socially acceptable.

Seeing women's sexual activity as sacred can take diverse forms. Evangelical women in the United States provide an example of those who sacralize marital sex. Although they frown on sex before marriage, within the context of marriage, they delight in its pleasures and ability to unite a husband and wife. In a different sort of example, the contemporary feminist Pagan movement, with its emphasis on the immanence of divinity and the sacredness of nature, including human bodies, has sacralized sex, particularly queer sex.

Jewish rabbinical laws provide a great deal of structure for married women's sexuality and frame sex in a positive light. They stipulate the *onah*, the husband's martial obligation to provide sexual pleasure for his wife. Jewish laws governing when and how married women may have sex are called *niddah*. By beginning the sexual cycle on a woman's most fertile days, these laws favor reproduction.

Families, mostly in the Middle East and southern Asia, sometimes hold women to very strict sexual moral codes, resulting in "honor killings." A man may kill his wife or female relative to preserve his family's honor if she is suspected of having sex outside of marriage, has been raped, or seeks a divorce. Although Islam has been handed the blame for these murders, honor killings are best understood as driven by cultural norms; Islamic laws do not permit the abuse or murder of women.

Women sometimes resist the sexual and contraceptive rules of their religious traditions. Most Protestants in the United States today favor contraception within marriage, but there is deep division over the issue of women seeking abortions. Similarly, there is a significant gap between the Roman Catholic Church's directives on family planning and their actual implementation by Western women who enjoy sex but cannot or do not wish to raise large families of children. Catholic leadership officially leads the fight against abortion rights, but the laity is split on the issue.

In Japan, women have long practiced abortion. Since the 1970s, Japan has seen a marked increase in Japanese women's participation in *mizuko kuyo*, rituals to appease the hungry ghosts of fetuses aborted even decades before. These rituals are practiced by Japanese women regardless of religious affiliation. Japanese women's growing belief that it is necessary for them to perform these rituals reflects the misogyny in contemporary Japanese culture.

MOTHERHOOD

For many women, the possibility of motherhood is an essential part of religious life. Whether, when, and how a woman mothers greatly affects her daily life and community status, as does whether and how her religion values motherhood. Religions in which women's leadership dominates tend to sacralize maternity, but this is by no means unique to them.

Many religions honor sacred mother figures, but honoring of sacred mothers is imperfectly correlated with honoring of real human mothers. Roman Catholicism reveres the Virgin Mary as the mother of God. The cult of the Virgin Mary is often characterized as furthering the virgin/whore dichotomy that Western women face, in which they are limited to the polarized roles of desexualized mother or sexually active sinner. Among Catholics who revere the Virgin Mary, motherhood is seen as a sacred duty. The Shakers, although they were celibate, used images of motherhood to represent God. The founder and leader of the movement was known as Mother Ann Lee, and she represented the highest ideal of motherhood. For traditional Hindus, motherhood was given much praise in Brahmanical texts, but married women enjoyed little status and often wished for the birth of a son to help secure their status.

Childbirth and the process of becoming a mother are often ritualized and imbued with sacred meaning. Around the world, rituals serve to protect the mother and baby from harm. Israeli Jewish women, like many other women, speak of giving birth and meeting the new baby as a miraculous experience. In the United States, it has been demonstrated that Christian, Jewish, Goddess spirituality, and less formally spiritual women who choose home birth all find religious meaning in the birth process, finding power in procreation. In several traditions, women also engage in rituals following the birth, such as the tradition of ritually burying the placenta.

As mothers, women often bear the bulk of responsibility for raising children and are also usually responsible for children's religious education in the home. Sometimes this responsibility can become a way for women to gain authority outside the home, as with Christian women who teach Sunday school. Teaching in Sunday schools in the nineteenth century, evangelical women in the United States combined the ideal of the virtuous woman with a new stress on right action. In Jewish tradition, however, fathers are responsible for children's education, which is required by conservative interpretations of Jewish law for sons, but not for daughters.

For aging women, the role of mother sometimes transitions to the roles of grandmother and elder. Grandmothers may continue to take part in the care and religious education of children. For example, elderly Oriental Jewish women of Jerusalem concern themselves with care for the ancestors and descendants of their families through a variety of ritual practices.

SYMBOLS: MYTHS AND DEITIES

Religious symbols serve to orient women's religious lives. Myths, the sacred stories of a religious tradition, often provide a framework for understanding who women can be and what they can do. Deities, saints, and other spiritual figures provide models for womanhood. Other kinds of symbols can include images, ritual objects, or elements of sacred narratives.

Deities

Most religions have at their core deities or other sacred beings. Relationships with divine figures are often important for women's identities and participation within a religion. The kinds of relationships available may be dependent on the genders and other qualities of the religion's deities, if any.

In some religions, deity is only or primarily male. At the center of Christian traditions is the male savior Jesus Christ, the son of a God, who is predominantly imagined as male. In Catholicism in particular, the maleness of the divine figure has been used to argue that priests must be male, whereas women may be friends, brides, or lovers of Jesus. The Jewish God is traditionally imagined to have no body and therefore no gender; however, in practice, this divinity is most often spoken of and treated as male.

KUAN YIN

Kuan Yin is the Chinese name for the female bodhisattva of compassion, the most beloved bodhisattva in all eastern Asia, known in Japan as Kannon. A passage of the *Lotus Sutra* in Sanskrit describes a male deity whose name means "all seeing." But, in the Chinese version, the name is translated as Kuan Yin, meaning "all hearing," and the figure is female. She is described as having such great power that calling on her name can keep someone thrown into a great fire from burning, rescue someone from drowning, or save a person from demons. She appears to save those who are in danger, and she provides fearlessness. In art, she is represented in many different ways. Usually, she is seen holding a lotus or a water bottle, but she is also sometimes depicted with many heads, each expressing a different expression that is appropriate to helping with different problems, or she is shown with many arms, each holding a different implement useful for solving different problems. Rarely, she is even made to look like the Virgin Mary, called Maria-Kannon, reflecting Christian influence.

There are goddesses and other holy female figures throughout the world's religions. To name some examples, Roman Catholicism reveres the Virgin Mary as the mother of Jesus Christ; Buddhism recognizes Tara as a goddess and female Buddha, and there are popular female bodhisattvas; and Judaism calls the feminine aspect of God *Shekinah*. In Nigeria, Osun is a Yoruba river goddess. As a representation of the sacredness of water, she is intimately connected to the daily use of water. Osun's waters not only sustain life, but she is also the source of creativity and human procreativity.

The presence of a central female divine figure does not necessarily correlate with high status for women within any given society. On the one hand, in the history of Indian religion, we can see changes in understandings of deities that reflect changes in society. The view of the goddess came to be carefully crafted to reflect the understanding of the human wife as subordinate to her husband. On the other hand, early Daoists saw females as closer to the Dao than males, and the *Dao De Ching* describes the Dao as a Mother. This understanding meant elevated social possibilities for women, and early Daoism created for women important religious offices and convents.

Very few of what religion scholar Susan Starr Sered calls "women's religions"—religious traditions predominantly led and participated in by women—worship a Goddess figure. However, contemporary Pagans and feminist theologians are examples of religious women who frequently imagine deity as a Goddess or as many goddesses. The Wiccan or Pagan Star Goddess is said to speak through the words of the Charge of the Goddess, which, in feminist Pagan author Starhawk's version, includes the words, "I am the soul of nature that gives life to the universe. From me all things proceed and unto Me they must return. Let My worship be in the heart that rejoices, for behold—all acts of love and pleasure

are My rituals." In this passage, the deity is represented as a female, associated with nature, creation and destruction, and sacralizing of love and pleasure. This text is sometimes read in contemporary Pagan ritual, and women take frequent and prominent roles in these rituals.

Myths

Myths and other sacred stories also help locate women in religious life. Myths of origin—which tell how the world came into being and how humans came to be gendered beings living in it—often explicitly or implicitly address the nature of women and their place in that world. Traditions of textual interpretation can be just as important as the sacred text itself. These texts' power comes in part from the attention given them by rabbis, monks, and other religious thinkers.

The Hebrew Bible (called the Old Testament by Christians) contains two stories of God's creation of the first woman, Eve. In the first story, God creates male and female humanity at once, in his image. In the second story, God creates Adam first and then makes his companion Eve out of one of Adam's ribs. The latter story makes woman derivative of man, because Eve was created in support of Adam, the first human.

Jewish traditions also tell stories about Lilith, whose earliest mention is in ancient Sumerian culture. In some stories, Lilith was Adam's first wife, before Eve, but she refused to submit to his will, specifically refusing to take the bottom position during sex, and so lost her place in Eden. Lilith came to be feared as a demon who lies on top of sleeping men, forcing them to have sex with her.

In the Hebrew Bible, the creation story is followed by an account of humanity's fall from grace, in which Adam and Eve eat of the forbidden fruit. Adam is punished with difficult manual labor, and Eve with painful childbirth. Eve's

A statue of the Bodhisattva Kuan Yin in Green Gulch Zen Center near San Francisco, California (c. July 2006).

In the Buddhist creation myth, as the Earth is formed, beings of light begin to eat of it, and out of this meal many distinctions are made. As the savory is distinguished from the bitter, so is the male from the female. When this happens, the woman and man begin to lust for each other, and out of their union comes continued creation of boundaries, now in more negative ways, creating property and drawing boundaries between people. So the man and woman emerge simultaneously, but their difference and thus desire for each other have negative consequences.

SACRED SPACE: HOME AND TEMPLE

When we look at the organization of space for women's daily religious practice, we see frequent emphasis on women's practices in the home. Religious activity at home can give women authority within the domestic sphere and can serve to sacralize all or part of that sphere. From one perspective, associating women with the domestic sphere and men with the public sphere means that women have less power. From another perspective, it simply means that women can exercise their power in more intimate and immediate ways than men.

Victorian Protestant women, for example, were seen as appropriately presiding over home and family. Their supposed natural piety and morality were thought to serve as a counterbalance to their husbands' supposed harsh natures, which were made necessary by their work in the competitive public sphere. The importance of women's religious influence in the domestic sphere was used in the United States to support arguments for prohibition and woman's suffrage, because it was believed that women's natural morality and concern for the home would cause them to vote for measures to protect families.

Across many religions and cultures, women's daily religious lives are played out in

role in the fall into sin has been emphasized over Adam's in Christian history. In this narrative, we can hear echoes of earlier Greek mythology, in which the gods make Pandora as a punishment for the rebellion of Prometheus. Hesiod tells in some detail how she is created to bring sex and death into the world.

Contrastingly, in the Quiche Maya's sacred book, the Popul Vuh, humankind was created by a primordial "mother-father," strikingly naming the mother portion of the figure first in the text. Archaeological evidence, however, suggests that Mayan culture maintained a patriarchal hierarchy.

1 CORINTHIANS 11:2-16

[2]I commend you because you remember me in everything and maintain the traditions just as I handed them on to you. [3]But I want you to understand that Christ is the head of every man, and the husband is the head of his wife, and God is the head of Christ. [4]Any man who prays or prophesies with something on his head disgraces his head, [5]but any woman who prays or prophesies with her head unveiled disgraces her head—it is one and the same thing as having her head shaved. [6]For if a woman will not veil herself, then she should cut off her hair; but if it is disgraceful for a woman to have her hair cut off or to be shaved, she should wear a veil. [7]For a man ought not to have his head veiled, since he is the image and reflection of God; but woman is the reflection of man. [8]Indeed, man was not made from woman, but woman from man. [9]Neither was man created for the sake of woman, but woman for the sake of man. [10]For this reason a woman ought to have a symbol of authority on her head, because of the angels. [11]Nevertheless, in the Lord woman is not independent of man or man independent of woman. [12]For just as woman came from man, so man comes through woman; but all things come from God. [13]Judge for yourselves: is it proper for a woman to pray to God with her head unveiled? [14]Does not nature itself teach you that if a man wears long hair, it is degrading to him, [15]but if a woman has long hair, it is her glory? For her hair is given to her for a covering. [16]But if anyone is disposed to be contentious—we have no such custom, nor do the churches of God.

significant ways in the home. Women's domestic work requires us to consider their relationships to money, property, and earning. We also observe that, in the home, women are often primarily responsible for the preparation of food, maintaining household altars and prayers, and healing sick family members. Yet women also have places in more public spaces of ritual and worship, where gender structures space, power, and belief.

MONEY AND PROPERTY

Women's relationships to money, property, and work are directly related to when and how they spend time in the home, all of which is influenced by religion. Women's authority in the economic sphere makes a big difference in their power at home and beyond. Religion is linked to women's ability to earn, inherit, and own money and property—and even to whether they themselves are considered to be property.

In many contexts, women are constrained in their ability to own, inherit, or earn money. In the United States, women could not legally own money until the mid-nineteenth century and were therefore legally dependent upon husbands and fathers. Even when women may own money, it can have different meaning and value from men's money. There were traditional Pacific Island cultures where men and women actually used different currency.

A dowry, or bride price, is a common feature of marriage rituals. Traditional Chinese engagements include a sum of money given from the groom's family to the bride's family. There is debate over whether this constitutes the sale of the bride or an early transfer of inheritance.

The Laws of Manu, *Manu Smriti*, which set forth the orthodox Hindu laws, prohibit the sale of a woman into marriage but allow women to own property and protect that property from male relatives. They also suggest that women should be honored and cared for, including giving them gifts on holidays as a means of ensuring men's welfare.

Women's manipulation of money in religious contexts includes donating to charities, as well as tithing and donating to religious institutions. In Taiwan, women ritually burn money for the gods in temples and other spaces, using money to connect the earthly and heavenly spheres.

FOOD

The production and distribution of food for daily meals and for special ritual occasions is a domain where women often enjoy power. These practices can include the exercise of social authority, the knowledge of ritual details, and presiding over the pleasure of food. The creation and sharing of food is not just an opportunity for physical nourishment. Sharing meals also fosters social cohesion, and special foods for particular religious observances can also have spiritual meaning.

The center of Jewish life is Shabbat, the sacred time demarcated from sunset on Friday to sunset on Saturday. Shabbat is considered feminine and is celebrated especially by women, who do the lighting of the ritual candles (*hadlikner*), bake *challah*, a special bread, and lead the family in observance of the sacred day. Women are also responsible for maintaining *kashrut*, or dietary laws, in the preparation of food and the feeding of their families throughout the week.

In Protestant churches in the United States, it is usually women, working as individual volunteers or through church women's organizations, who prepare food and drink for coffee hours and church picnics. At the huge US revival-camp meetings of the nineteenth century, this responsibility meant a great deal of cooking work for Protestant women.

Food can be offered to the superhuman as well as to humans. Iranian Shi'ite Muslim women perform a food ritual called *sofreh*. The ritual establishes a relationship with a supernatural being, who accepts food offerings from the women in exchange for which the being offers aid with healing or some other domestic problem.

Abstention from food can also be a way for women to exercise religious power. For example, the evangelical organization Women's Aglow Fellowship instructs women to diet for God as a sign of their faith in him. Medieval Catholic women mystics' fasting and other food practices provided important ways in which they used their bodies in pursuit of religious meaning-making.

HOUSEHOLD ALTARS

In many traditions, women are responsible for maintaining household altars. This responsibility can include setting up altars and keeping them clean; making offerings such as food, flowers, or incense; and conducting prayers. Altars create symbolic pathways of connection between the human and the divine, and household altars encourage relationship between the home or family and the spiritual realms.

Roman Catholic women may keep altars in the home for Jesus, the Virgin Mary, or other beloved saints. Mexican Catholics also build altars, in commemoration of family members who have died, for *El Dia de los Muertos* (the

Day of the Dead), an October holiday. These altars can include images of deceased relatives, marigolds, favorite foods of the deceased, and brightly decorated sugar skulls.

Chinese women are responsible for maintaining proper relationships with ancestors and spirits of the home, making offerings of incense, food, and prayers. They often have a picture or altar for Kuan Yin, a female bodhisattva of compassion. (A bodhisattva is a person who chooses to put off the final stage of enlightenment to help other people become enlightened.) Kuan Yin is attributed with the power to bring children to a woman. She is important, both historically and today, for Chinese women whose status depends on their ability to produce an heir.

In Hindu practice as well, the home is a center of spiritual life, including daily worship (*puja*) performed by women. Indian women also gather together on auspicious occasions, such as a birth or home consecration, to sing all night to their ancestors and to the deities who protect them.

In Korea, women's sacred household objects are less obvious as an altar than in many other parts of the world. Nevertheless, women maintain packets of pine needles, bowls of wine, jars of grain, or other objects in specific places within their houses, as offerings to household gods. Household gods are believed to exist in every house, and such offerings help protect the members of the family.

Women often also have primary responsibility for seasonal festivals that are celebrated within the home. Several Jewish festivals are performed prominently in the home, such as Pesach, which celebrates the Israelites' escape from slavery in Egypt. Hindu women's calendrical festivals tend to focus on the well-being of family and household. Women's domestic rituals at Divali, a Hindu festival of lights, which honors the goddess Lakshmi, extend beyond the rest of the family's celebrations and focus on protecting the family's welfare.

HEALING

As part of caring for home and family, women are often responsible for religiously oriented healing. In religions where women dominate, suffering and healing tend to be particularly prominent themes. These themes are also consistently present in contemporary feminist theology, whether it be Protestant, Catholic, Jewish, Muslim, Buddhist, indigenous, Mormon, or new religious.

Women's healing work takes multiple forms. We have already seen that Mormon women have exercised the blessing of healing the sick through laying on of hands. Catholic women's devotion to saints provides a forum for prayers of healing for themselves and their families. Such prayers might be directed to Saint Jude, the saint of hopeless causes. During illness, traditional Chinese women exorcised the home of evil spirits. Muslim women have historically held the powers of healing and magical practices, such as the ability to ward off *jinn*. In Egypt and the Sudan, Muslim women hold *zar* ceremonies to rid themselves of spirit possession. Mexican women do popular healing, called *curanderismo* (as portrayed in the Rudolfo Anaya novel *Bless Me Ultima*), drawing on Catholic and indigenous Mexican traditions and involving a variety of techniques. *Curanderismo* can include such practices as prayer, fasting, use of magical plants, and altered states of consciousness for diagnosis and curing.

Women's healing work also can include midwifery, facilitating the physical and spiritual processes of childbirth. Indigenous women of the Americas have worked as healers and midwives. West African Sande women use herbal medicine, amulets, and magical remedies to address a variety of fertility needs. Aboriginal Australian women perform childbirth rituals that are characterized by observance of food taboos, spells of protection for the birth, the belief that blood issuing from a woman's genitals is dangerous to men, and segregation of women. Hindu women perform extensive prenatal rituals during pregnancy to ensure the well-being of their unborn children.

Healing has also often been important in new religions in which women are leaders. In nineteenth-century New England, Mary Baker Eddy founded the new religion of Christian Science after an experience of spontaneous healing. Christian Scientists believe that matter is fundamentally an illusion, so healing of the body can come through right thought.

When healing fails, women's rituals may also address death. For example, women, particularly older women, are prominent in the performance of *dügü* and the other death rites of the Black Carib in Central America. Muslim women perform a ritual in the home called *mevlüt,* forty-seven to fifty-two days after a person dies and then annually in the years following. These rituals include gathering of women, readings and teachings (sometimes by a male), weeping, and a meal together.

AT TEMPLE

Thus far, we have focused primarily on the domestic sphere. This is because the gendered power structures of religions often relegate women to the home. In turn, the home becomes a place where women have the most religious authority and responsibility. But women also frequently engage religion in the public sphere, including politics, the marketplace, and places of worship.

Even when men and women worship together, at some places of worship, women and men are physically separated from each other. At mosque, Muslim women stand behind men during the five daily prayers. Muslims usually explain this as an issue of modesty and as a way to keep men from being distracted from prayer by the sight of women. Women usually pray at home, rather than at the mosque, however.

Orthodox Jews also seat men and women separately during worship, and women traditionally may not be counted toward the *minyan,* or quorum of ten people necessary for public prayer. Indeed, there are cases where women cannot understand or even hear the synagogue services, but they choose to attend because they believe the services to be auspicious times to make personal prayers of petition.

Sometimes exclusion or segregation in places of worship causes women to seek out their own sacred spaces. In Morocco, going to saints' tombs is a way for Muslim women to claim the self-determination in their personal and religious lives that is denied them by the orthodox system. Far more women than men visit these tombs, which creates religious spaces where men may feel uncomfortable. From the saints, women seek healing that is more accessible than within the medical system.

AUTHORITY

In recent decades, two major trends in religious authority have made a significant difference for women's daily practice of religion—the development of feminist theology and of new religious fundamentalism. Feminist theology specifically addresses issues of misogyny and of women's oppressions in traditional religions. It also creates liberating theologies for women and destabilizes gender roles in these and new religions. Fundamentalist religious movements have broader concerns than women's roles, but they do pay significant attention to them, creating important changes in women's ways of engaging with their religions and affecting their day-to-day lives.

FUNDAMENTALISM

Religious fundamentalist movements seek to restore an imagined golden age of religion, which believers see as a purer, better time. These movements are responding to the rapid social changes of the modern era, often reacting to experiences of colonialism, industrialization, or poverty. Fundamentalist movements generally concern themselves with women in two major ways. First, they tend to focus on women's domestic roles and attempt to limit their activity in the public sphere. Second, they are usually concerned with control of women's sexuality and with sexual purity, making women's bodies into symbols of the community. Despite the restrictiveness of fundamentalist movements, women may be drawn to fundamentalism for a variety of reasons, ranging from feelings of spiritual alienation to basic economic need.

Fundamentalist movements are not necessarily oppressive of women. Women may find certain kinds of freedoms through fundamentalist religion, feel restricted by the movement, or experience a complicated mixture of freedom and restriction. In Sri Lanka, for example, Buddhist fundamentalism has included efforts to restore an order of nuns and provide new religious opportunities for women. Fundamentalist Protestant women can find community and empowerment in gathering together for prayer, song, and sharing about the work of Jesus Christ in their lives.

Fundamentalist Mormon communities are an interesting case. In 1890, the orthodox Mormon Church (Latter-Day Saints) renounced the nineteenth-century revelation directing members to engage in plural (polygynous) marriage as a key to heavenly salvation, but fundamentalists maintain the practice. These communities are patriarchal, yet women gain power through female networking, in part because sister-wives live and interact with each other on a regular basis, whereas opportunities for interactions with husbands are more limited.

FEMINIST THEOLOGY

In recent decades, women around the world have employed the interpretative and organizational strategies of feminism to reform traditional religious practices and to create new ones. Feminist movements identify gender inequalities in social structures and seek to redress these inequalities. Some feminist women have argued that women's daily religious practices have been limited to the home, which has kept them away from positions of power in churches, synagogues, temples, or mosques. Others have pointed to reclamation of the enormous significance of their activities on the highly localized levels of family and community.

Religion scholar Mary Farrell Bednarowski has analyzed twentieth-century feminist religious thinking and found five common themes: valuing ambivalence in women's identities and experiences; immanence of the sacred; seeing the sacred in the ordinary world; valuing relationship with others; and pervasive healing of injustice and spiritual pain, as much as healing physical bodies. These themes all reflect the fact that women's religious meaning-making derives from the messiness of daily life, more than from rarefied prayer and contemplation.

Many women have made names for themselves as feminist theologians. Judith Plaskow and Tamar Frankiel are examples of prominent Jewish feminist theologians. Rita Gross critiques Buddhism as a feminist. Elisabeth Schüssler Fiorenza is a leading Catholic feminist theologian. Sallie McFague is a Protestant feminist theologian who is also deeply concerned with environmentalism. Amina Wadud has challenged traditional barriers by leading prayers for women in mosques in the United States.

Feminists within established religions not only do interpretative work to render theology through a feminist lens, but they also work to create new rituals that better serve women and work toward women's empowerment. Liturgical change can be as simple (or complex) as changing language to address female as well as male members of a ritual community or to imagining God in feminine as well as masculine ways. Feminists have also struggled to gain greater access to traditional ritual roles, such as those of ministers, priests, and rabbis. Even though they have made great strides, women are still barred from many religious leadership roles. For example, the Catholic Church continues to allow only men to enter into the priesthood.

Women are also creating entirely new rituals for themselves. For example, the Jewish feminist ritual *simhat bat* celebrates and blesses a new daughter. Different forms of the ceremony, generally including community welcoming, naming, and reciting of Scripture, are accepted in Orthodox, Conservative, and Reform Judaism. Goddess spirituality is an entire feminist movement that emphasizes women coming together to create new rituals for celebration, transformation, worship, and ecstatic experience.

The Extraordinary

For some women, everyday life is not so everyday. Thus far, we have focused primarily on practices and experiences of laywomen, but we should also remember exceptional and professional religious women. Women have been ministers, nuns, gurus, shamans, priestesses, missionaries, saints, and prophets. Women can be religious leaders at the front of congregations and communities, or they can be contemplatives and mystics who live in seclusion. Often, taking on one of these extraordinary roles has been

RABI'AH (C. 717–801)

Rabi'ah is revered as one of the greatest of Sufi (Muslim) saints. She escaped the ordinary expectations of women of her time and lived her daily life in extraordinary relationship with God. Rabi'ah described herself as a weak woman, but a consideration of her biography suggests otherwise. She had a conversion experience to Islam as a slave, and later, in her status as a freed slave, she had the ability to refuse marriage and did so several times, claiming that her mystical union with God prevented her from marrying a man. Rabi'ah lived as a recluse and an ascetic, many times refusing offers of gifts. She is said to have performed miracles, such as blowing on her fingertips, which then shed light like a lamp. This saint had an intimate and assertive relationship with God, addressing him thus: "My God, do kings treat a helpless woman this way? You invited me to your house, then killed my donkey in the middle of the journey." The men who wrote about her life were troubled by the idea that so great a religious figure could be female and even suggested that her devotion made it inappropriate to call her a woman.

the only way for women to escape their culture's restrictive demands that they become wives and mothers.

If we were to study extraordinary religious women, we might want to know about the ancient Greek ecstatics known as the Maenads; medieval Christian mystics, such as Hildegard of Bingen; Muslim saints, such as Rabi'ah; or modern religious innovators, such as Ann Lee and Mary Baker Eddy. We might also wish to know about the far less famous women whose religious calling causes them to guide and minister to congregations and other communities every day.

Conclusion

Religion is a powerful force in women's life courses, shaping their experiences of their bodies, their sexuality, their families and communities, and their identities. Myths, symbols, and rituals help them orient themselves in the world and tell stories about who they are as women in relationship to other people, the divine, and the natural world.

Sometimes it is religion that creates or reinforces women's suffering, and sometimes it is religion that provides the antidote and the opportunity for freedom—through salvation, self-determination, or spiritual authority. Religion can dictate how to be a wife and a mother and how to maintain a home ritually in right relationship to the divine. At the same time, religion can provide the tools for women to change their life courses, reorganize their relationships, bring new messages from the divine to their communities, and break out of existing structures that pattern sacred and profane spaces.

If we accept the assertion that women have been structurally in subordinated positions in most cultures, it is natural to ask whether religion improves or worsens the conditions of daily life. The answer is that it has the possibility and power to do both. Careful examination of the religious lives of women in different religious and cultural contexts helps us see the nuances of these daily negotiations of power, privilege, piety, prayer, and prophecy.

Glossary

Biological Determinism: Argument that womanhood is shaped primarily by bodies—hormones, physical features, and reproductive capacities. Distinguished from social constructivism (see entry).

Feminism: Social and political movements to identify and redress social inequalities between men and women. Feminist theology is the religious arm of feminist thought.

Fundamentalism: Conservative movement within any religion that seeks to return to the "fundamentals" of that religion.

Intersectionality: The idea that women and their experiences of oppression are best described by the intersections of their social circumstances—gender, race, class, religion, age, and so on.

Patriarchy: Hierarchical social structure in which men generally hold more power than women.

Social Constructivism: Argument that womanhood is shaped primarily by society—social structures as well as cultural and religious ideals. Distinguished from biological determinism (see entry).

FOR FURTHER READING

Ahmed, Leila. *Women and Gender in Islam*. New Haven, CT: Yale University Press, 1992.

Bednarowski, Mary Farrell. *The Religious Imagination of American Women*. Bloomington: Indiana University Press, 1999.

Eller, Cynthia. *Living in the Lap of the Goddess: The Feminist Spirituality Movement in America*. Boston: Beacon, 1993.

Falk, Nancy Auer, and Rita M. Gross. *Unspoken Worlds: Women's Religious Lives*. 3rd ed. Belmond, CA: Wadsworth, 2001.

Griffith, R. Marie. *God's Daughters: Evangelical Women and the Power of Submission*. Berkeley: University of California Press, 1997.

Sered, Susan Starr. *Priestess, Mother, Sacred Sister: Religions Dominated by Women*. New York: Oxford University Press, 1994.

Sharma, Arvind, ed. *Women in World Religions*. Albany: State University of New York Press, 1987.

Young, Serinity, ed. *An Anthology of Sacred Texts by and about Women*. New York: Crossroad, 1993.

6

SEXUALITY OF RELIGIOUS NATIONALISM

Roger Friedland

Religious nationalism, unlike the capitalist market or the democratic state, has the organization of sexuality at its center.[1] Religious nationalists give primacy to the family, not to democracy or the market, as the social space through which society should be conceived and composed.[2] Familial discourse, with its particularistic and sexual logic of love and loyalty, is pervasive in religious nationalism.

"The family," the Ayatollah Khomeini declared, "is the fundamental unit of society and the main center of growth and transcendence for humanity."[3] Indeed, if one looks at the political programs of Islamic movements, there is no consistent economic policy, nor form of government. The two pillars of contemporary Islamic politics involve, on the one side, a restrictive regulation of sexuality, eliminating it as a public presence and containing it within the family, and, on the other side, the promotion of a welfare state that not only enables families to survive physically, but also especially to care for those—orphans and widows in particular, as enjoined in the Qur'an—who cannot rely on families for support.[4] Islamic politics are a politics of love.

In the United States, the unifying core of Protestant fundamentalism today is likewise its defense of the heterosexual and male-dominated family.[5] For example, Pat Robertson, the founder of the Christian Broadcasting Network, writes, "The basic unit of social, local, national and international organization in God's world order is the family."[6] This is also the message of James Dobson's Christian radio empire, *Focus on Family,* which reaches 500 million listeners throughout the world.[7] Martin Riesebrodt has argued that the defense of the patriarchal family is indeed the core of fundamentalism in general. Fundamentalisms track the origins of societal crisis to the erosion of the family.[8]

Modern nationalism was premised on an abstract individual, all of whom are considered equivalent members of the nation. As Craig Calhoun has pointed out, modern nationalism promotes a categorical identity, not the relational identities that predominate in the organization of kinship.[9] The enemies of the French Revolution railed against this political ontology, this monad—abstract, independent, egoistic, equal.[10] In the primacy they give to defending the patriarchal family, religious nationalists replicate the discourse of the Catholic opponents of the French Revolution that sheared state authority of divine authorship and undercut male property prerogatives within the family.[11] They argued that paternal authority was not only in the nature of things; it was God given. The *anti-philosophes*, as Darrin McMahon has shown, looked to each father as a monarch in miniature, whose authority, like that of the king, should not be subject to revocation by those over whom he was granted dominion. To erode the authority of the patriarch—by instituting civil marriage, legalizing divorce, hemming in the father's authority over his children's property, career, and mate choice—was understood as a figure of and a means for the erosion of the political authority of the king.[12] If marriage were mere contract, morality and political authority would be at risk. There should be no possibility of divorce between a people and the sovereign.

A PATRIARCHAL POLITICS

Some analysts argue that religious regimes, such as that of Iran or Pakistan, center their attention on familial relations because they have failed to reduce unemployment or redistribute wealth, as though family politics were a substitute for or sideshow from the real business of state.[13] This is to miss religious nationalism's distinct ontology of power—as a moral project that derives its authority from divine sources and operates through the family as the basis of social order. The state of the family is taken as the primary criterion for the condition of the state.[14] In Judaism, Christianity, and Islam, the ability to control sexual desire is understood as a template for one's ability and willingness to obey the law. The elemental agents of religious nationalism are gendered and fleshy men and women, not the abstract individuals ordered through

exchange and contract. Its space is the place of family, governed by relations of consubstantiality and caring, not the external, instrumental space of geopolitics, the public sphere, or the market. Religious nationalism is about home and homeland.[15]

Algeria's Islamic Salvation Front, which won national elections in 1991 but was prevented from taking power, made the elimination of female employment part of its program. After it was banned, fundamentalists murdered hundreds of Algerian women for wearing Western clothes, for not wearing a headscarf, for working side by side with men. The Islamic Salvation Front promised to impose the death penalty on those who engaged in sexual relations outside of marriage.[16]

The very first national religious mobilization of the Iranian Islamic forces took place in 1961, after Khomeini spoke at Qum on Ashura, the day of atonement, attacking the shah for having transformed the legal status of women, allowing women into the army, the police, and the judiciary, giving them the vote, and overriding Islamic law such that divorce required mutual consent.[17] Iran's 1979 Islamic Revolution forbade coeducation, closed down the childcare centers, and made the veil obligatory—first in government offices and then in every public place. Women, of whatever age, had to obtain permission of their fathers when they married for the first time.[18]

The Egyptian case suggests that it was not so much the failures of secular nationalism that led to Islamic entry into the public sphere as the modern nationalists' commitments, incomplete as they were, to gender equality.[19] In 1952, Gamal Nasser, who had just come to power as a result of a coup by the Free Officers, vowed to mobilize women as full participants in the project to modernize the country. This decision led the Islamists to break with him, eventuating in their repression. In 1954, Nasser supplanted the *shari'a* courts with a unitary secular state court, thereby expanding women's legal recourse, the immediate response to which was the first assassination attempt by the Muslim Brothers. Sadat's commitment to improving the legal, economic, and political status of women likewise galvanized massive Islamic opposition.

The US fundamentalist embrace of the family is a post–World War II phenomenon. As Margaret Bendroth has shown, during the nineteenth and early twentieth centuries, concern with the family was at the center of mainline Protestantism, a preoccupation that earlier Christian fundamentalists understood as feminized and sentimental.[20] The fundamentalists then viewed the veneration of the family as a diversion from the redemptive tasks at hand. It was only with the rise of middle-class divorce that defense of the family became the central issue for adherents of the Christian Right and the primal medium through which they sought to reconstruct the social order. The polemical series that today constitutes US fundamentalist discourse is organized almost completely around familial issues: divorce, birth control, abortion, feminism, homosexuality, and sex education.

The case of Hindu nationalism at first seems at variance with the pattern. As Amrita Basu notes, the Bharatiya Janata Party (BJP) has not opposed abortion or birth control, nor has it taken particularly conservative positions on adultery or widow remarriage.[21] The BJP has also been a strong advocate of a universal civil code regarding family matters, a code that gives women more rights than do the corresponding religious laws. However, a closer look indicates that Hindu nationalism likewise is committed to the defense of the patriarchal family. The Hindu nationalists' defense of a uniform civil code was animated by their desire to erode the communal rights of the Islamic community, not by their desire to protect the rights of women per se. At the same time that it has fought against the legal force of Islamic family law, the BJP has ferociously defended the practice of *sati,* in which widows are burned alive on the funeral pyre with their husbands, has attacked feminism as a pernicious, Westernizing force that undermines the family, and has sought to censor films and advertisements that display women's bodies.

The BJP, a political party seeking power, depends for the core of its activists and electoral support on the RSS, a religious nationalist organization, which has created an alternative civil society, *the Sangh parivar.* This community espouses a particularly patriarchal worldview. Basu reports on the books espousing the proper role for Hindu women based on Hindu Scripture. That role is one of subordination to men. What should a woman do if her husband beats her? "The wife should think that she is paying her debt to her previous life," replies a religious authority, "and thus her sins are being destroyed and she is becoming pure."[22] Although the BJP's women's organization has brought women into the streets as part of the Hindu nationalist campaign, the women have played subordinate, traditional roles—albeit in a public space. Although the women's organization of the BJP is independent, it has not campaigned against the physical violence to which Indian women are routinely exposed, such as dowry deaths—in which husbands and their families murder their wives on the grounds that the dowry was insufficient, enabling them to remarry and collect yet another dowry.

It is tempting to interpret religious nationalism as sexist reaction, animated by interests in masculine privilege. In accounting for the rise of Islamic fundamentalism in North Africa, Fatima Mernissi, for example, has pointed to the rapid increase of educated and employed women, who not only compete with men for limited employment opportunities but are also able to choose when they marry and to exert more influence within their families on account of the monies they bring home. For men, fundamentalism is understood as a way to win back money and power; for potential rulers, it is a way to reduce unemployment.[23] Martin Riesebrodt likewise interprets the emergence of fundamentalism in both Iran and the United States as a defense of patriarchalism in a world where women have encroached steadily on male prerogatives, an encroachment whose weight falls forcefully on the father inside the family, particularly the sexual regulation of his daughters.[24] Fundamentalism, he argues, is a means to reassert patriarchal structural principles in the family, the economy, and the state.

THE MANLY STATE

The defense of male power is certainly involved here, but religious nationalism is more than a defense of male privilege. Religious nationalism involves both an outraged assault on the effeminization of the collective public body and a celebration of its renewed maleness.[25] Hindu nationalism, for example, repudiates the association of Indian spiritualism with the feminine and seeks to masculinize its men.[26] During the communal violence accompanying the politicization of sacred space, Hindu nationalist women often pressed feminine bangles on men who refused to participate in the fighting.[27] Hindu nationalists draw on a long tradition of Indian cultural nationalism that looks to the physical discipline of men as a technique of creating a strong national subject. M. S. Golwalkar, the leading ideologue of the RSS, wrote the following.

> Let us shake off the present-day emasculating notions and become real living men, bubbling with national pride, living and breathing the grand ideas of service, self-reliance and dedication in the cause of our dear and sacred motherland. . . . Today more than anything else, mother needs such men—young, intelligent, dedicated and more than all virile and masculine. And such are the men who make history—men with capital "M."[28]

The Hindu nationalists have transformed the iconography of Ram, understood as the divine avatar of Vishnu and the originary Indian sovereign. Hindu nationalists have made the mythic ideal of Ram, the warrior-king celebrated in the *Ramayana*, a Sanskrit epic whose recitation in Hindi makes it accessible to all Indians whatever their caste or gender. Speaking of Ram, Kapur writes that, traditionally,

> the rendition of his body and temper is not, for instance, like Shiva or like Krishna. Ram is *udar*, compassionate, benign, and graceful; he is ever-serene and ever-forgiving; he is ever-youthful, boyish almost, with a conspicuous lack of masculine power; and yet, he is the lord of the universe, the *maryada purushottam*.[29]

In Tulsidas's *Ramcharitmanas,* Ram is portrayed as a generous god, immanent in all Hindus, protected by the monkey god Hanuman. By the late 1980s, the Hindu nationalists had made of Ram a muscled warrior, his bow drawn, his image associated with the model of the temple whose rebuilding in Ayodhya would be prepared by such ferocious violence.[30] This refiguring of Ram, of course, was associated with a repudiation of the foundational nonviolent, feminine Gandhian civil culture.[31] In May 1998, one of the first actions of the newly elected Hindu nationalist's government was to detonate a number of nuclear blasts, perceived by India's religious nationalists as a demonstration of India's manliness. Ram had been transmogrified into Rambo.[32]

Likewise US fundamentalists are profoundly concerned with restoring both the difference and the esteem of masculinity, notwithstanding the large role that right-wing Christian women play in carrying forward the evangelical and fundamentalist political agenda. A brief example suffices: Sarah Hinlicky, a Princeton divinity student, writing in *Boundless*, a web magazine for the Christian Right's *Focus on the Family*, describes her visit to a dance club in New York City's Village. When a drunken man, a stranger, attempted to grope her, one of her escorts offered to beat the offender up. She writes as follows.

> The punishment hardly fit the crime, so I declined his offer. But my friend and I were wildly impressed. Neither of us in our lives had met a guy willing to do that for us.[33]

What made it more astounding was that her defender had no romantic entanglement with her, and, in his mid-twenties, he was still a virgin. Her friends all wanted to meet this eminent eligible knight. Hinlicky goes on to argue that premarital sexuality not only robs men of the possibility of finding true love and forming a family, but also,

> Sexuality grips the imagination so because life and death are wrapped up in it. Rightly fulfilled, it creates humanity in both the lovers and their children. Abused, it kills not only physically but spiritually as well.

Religious fundamentalists build the public masculine and the private feminine body. Riesebrodt and Chong write as follows.

> In legalistic-literalist fundamentalism, women tend to be seen as less qualified religiously than men and, at the same time, are prevented from achieving religious qualification by circular, misogynist gender ideology. Where men are seen as heroic, rational, moral, and respon-

sible, women are believed to be intellectually and morally weak, sexually dangerous to men, and polluters of sacred spaces. They are forbidden to interpret sacred texts and preach, or speak, in public.[34]

In US fundamentalist congregations, women predominate numerically but play almost no leadership roles.[35] The voice of public authority is masculine.

It is the female body, particularly its public display, that is the most consistent object of fundamentalist concern. Pointing to the commonalities between Iranian and US fundamentalism, Martin Riesebrodt writes that

> fundamentalism is particularly occupied with the public display of the female body. In both the United States and Iran its themes are the immoral dress of women in public, the creation of a uniform type of decent women's clothing (veiling, national costume), the stimulation of male sexuality by women (dress, films, theatre, swimming pools), and unsupervised contact between the sexes and opportunities for meeting (dance halls, swimming pools, coeducation).[36]

The public status of women's bodies appears to be a critical site and source for religious nationalist political mobilization. "Refusal to wear the veil," declared the Ayatollah Khomeini, "is against the law of God and the Prophet, and a material and moral affront to the entire country."[37]

That religious nationalists concentrate their energies on the female body is not, as Karen Brown has argued, a search "to control the fearsome mute power of flesh" for which women operate as projective screens and metonymic carriers.[38] Sexual desire is integral to power, a relation that social theorists have either erased or instrumentalized.[39] It is the organization of the erotic, not its erasure, that is at issue in religious nationalist movements.[40]

The remasking of the female body is not just imposed by men, but it is also chosen by women. This is particularly the case in countries whose citizens follow Islam, a religion that understands women's sexuality, their desire, as particularly disruptive.[41] In Turkey, for example, women actively participated in the struggle against the government, which had prohibited Turkish women students from wearing the Islamic headscarf,[42] likewise in Iran.[43] Donning Islamic dress, for instance, as Nikki Keddie has noted, enables women to garner more respect from men in public places; it enables them to maneuver better, and it prevents sexual harassment.[44] Religious nationalist movements also create new public spaces—associations, organizations— where women can operate outside the purview of their parents and their husbands.[45] When religious nationalist women participate in religious nationalist politics, moving into public space, they do so in a way that preserves both gender segregation and hierarchy. Amrita Basu notes, for examples, that women were very active in the campaign to "liberate" Ayodhya from the Muslims, but they did so in a way that reenacted women's traditional roles in the public sphere. Women sent the male activists off to battle with food, placed vermilion *tilaks* on their foreheads, surrounded the men to prevent them from being physically attacked by Indian soldiers. Speaking of women's activism, she writes, "Their experience of self-affirmation through self-sacrifice and their empowerment through public activism . . . ultimately renewed their commitment to domestic roles."[46]

Male reaction alone, however, cannot explain religious nationalism's commitment to the patriarchal family. Women, too, find fundamentalism compelling. It is arguable that women, in fact, have been a hidden source of support for religious nationalism. Women find fundamentalism compelling—and not just because of the corrosive powers of unbound flesh. In the United States, for instance, both evangelicalism and fundamentalism draw disproportionately from women, not from men.[47] In Iran, women were major public supporters of Khomeini in his struggle against the shah, and, after the revolution, they delivered their support in the national referendum that secured clerical power over the technocrats managing the transition.[48] Women responded to Khomeini's call to strengthen the nation by giving birth to an average of seven children between 1979 and 1986, causing the population to jump from 34 million to over 50 million.[49] Khomeini himself, who never disenfranchised women after taking power, actually praised their primary role. Indeed, the evidence so far indicates that despite a post-Khomeini wave of mobilization by women, not only at the polls but also for elected office, these women are pushing for social, civil, and political equalities within the framework of an Islamic republic. Not patriarchal power but a moralized family order appears still to organize their claims. It is the primacy of the family that has allowed them to promote birth control and to obtain more flexible working hours for mothers and wives.

Women are attracted by the primacy that religious nationalists give to the family, its affirmation of male familial obligations as a religious duty, and to the language of love. The religious nationalist community also offers a mechanism of social control of men, something that becomes increasingly important as the eyes, the invitations, and the opprobrium that circulate in extended families and long-lived neighborhoods attenuate with geographic migration, the rising incidence of divorce, and the investment of social energy in friendship networks having nothing to do with kinship.

Religious nationalists do not seek a return to the premodern familial structure, with its extended networks of kin loyalties, but to the bourgeois nuclear family. As Lila Abu-Lughod notes in the case of Egyptian Islamists, it is their idealization of a nuclear family grounded in love, an imported Western middle-class notion, that attracts so many Egyptian women to the movement.[50] Women turn to fundamentalism in hopes of finding men who will be good fathers and good husbands, provide for their families, remain with their wives, and contain their sexuality within the family.[51] Female entry into the labor market, mass secular education, the geographic erosion of extended family life and communal social control, and the eroticization of mass culture have all variously created opportunities and constraints that have strained the familial contract.

In the United States, although fundamentalist Christianity typically endorses wifely submission to her husband, it also sacralizes women's role as mothers, who have the time to care for and the will to discipline their children, as well as the passion to keep their husbands. As Linda Kintz discovered in her sojourn among fundamentalist women in the United States, the chance to occupy the sacred status of motherhood was, for many, a refuge from the uncertainty and constant threat of worthlessness they faced in the market.[52] Even though men from the Christian Right dominate the antiabortion movement in the United States, women have provided the bulk of its popular support. These women look to the movement as an integral part of their affirmation of a sexuality that has been domesticated by monogamous marriage and gendered family roles.[53]

THE COUNTRY'S BODY

The nation is understood by the people as a body, a super corpus that is homologous with the individuals of which it is composed. What is the nature of the national body? Collective representation refers to the way societies symbolize their existence, the way the social takes symbolic form, the making of a metaphor. This is true whether the collective representation is a god or a parliament. Collective representation is located in the public sphere. Men have historically dominated the public sphere, their bodies massed, displayed, and sacrificed, as the primary medium and content of collective representation, the way a collectivity exhibits itself to itself and to the world. The public sphere is the locus of the law, where rules binding on all are formulated and enforced. For millennia, the public sphere has been sexed, a masculine space, a space for male bodies.

The public sphere was first defined by its difference from the domestic, a private space identified as feminine, associated with the fleshy motherly matter of reproduction. The property of being a male, of thence of being a subject, someone who did something, was dependent on the fact of owning the reproductive powers of women. Male subjectivity, in other words, was historically constituted through the ownership of women's bodies, bodies housed as and in the property of men, both of those properties—the woman's body and the house—dependent on a law, a *nomos*, defined outside the household, a law that originates in the public sphere, in masculine territory. The house emerges as a bounded space for the institution of marriage, as a means to protect a father's genealogical claims, his line, by isolating the women whose reproductive powers are his property.[54] It is through the construction of houses as private property, houses that house the reproductive powers of women, that men were constituted as public beings, social subjects, who control nature first by controlling the procreative powers of women. In other words, men are made into subjects, agents capable of socially recognized action, by making women into objects whom they exchange between them, the exchange of women being the first economy, a commerce in sexual rights. Being a man depended on the right to have women.

To forge a modern nation, the state depends on an abstract space, upon the bland fact of residence, mere location, to build a universal citizen transcending other group loyalties. Modern citizenship depends on the empty space of the state. Religious nationalism fills that space, the joining of God to the territorial nation, the fusion of two collective representations, a couplet of spirit and matter, a male force joined to a female territorial body.[55]

If religious nationalism is a way to mark the land, to defend or redefine a nation's boundaries, we might interpret religious nationalism's obsessive control of women's bodies as a parallel figuration, the policing of a bodily frontier.[56] Clothing, controlling, and sequestering the female body, taking it out of the sites of collective representation, religious nationalists reassert the maleness of the public body and the femaleness of the territory—as a loved body that must be maintained inviolate, a perpetual possession. Men are to rule both the little house and the big house. In the cosmology of religious nationalism, the nation has two bodies, one political, the second, territorial. Religious nationalists seek to regender these two bodies as male and female, respectively. Theirs is a sexualized politics and a politicized sexuality. Manliness is known by one's capacity to compete for, to penetrate, and to possess the bodies of women. Woman's vagina is, of course, the ultimate sacred space in sexual cosmogony, that which must not be violated, an eroticized template for other divisions. But the estimation of manliness is not validated by women, but by other men.[57]

Woman's body as a token of national territoriality is common in nationalist discourse,

both in the modern and the ancient world.[58] A state is known through its boundaries, through the continuous territory that it controls, by its capacity to regulate the conditions for entry. A woman's bodily purity and state sovereignty are thus parallel symbolic orders. In absolutist Europe, with its celebration of violence as the prerogative of the prince, pictorial, sculptural, and literary renderings of the rape of women were regularly incorporated into the palaces and the ritual spaces of rule as representations of their success in the subjugation of territory.[59] For example, Federigo Gonzaga's Palazzo del Tel in Mantua is chock-full of rape scenes, including Vasari's *Jupiter's Rape of Europa*, to commemorate Duke Cosimo de' Medici's conquest of Piombino and the establishment of a naval base on Elba. In 1583, Francesco de Medici placed Giovanni da Bologna's *Rape of the Sabine* in the Piazza della Signoria as a monument to the Medici's success in subjugating both the citizen and the subject territories of Florence. The violent appropriation of female flesh was understood as the analogue to the territorial conquest of territory.

Indian nationalists have always understood the nation as the body of a woman, typically Bharat Mata, or "mother India." The secular nationalist Jawaharlal Nehru sought to redress this village woman, to "give her" as he noted, "the garb of modernity."[60] For Gandhi, "mother India" was a barefoot widow, a renunciant. The Hindu nationalists understand India as a woman who requires protection from her virile sons.[61] One of the few leading women in the Hindu nationalist movement, Sadhvi Ritamba, conjures the Islamic dismemberment of India as rape. "In Kashmir," she declared, "the Hindu was a minority and was hounded out of the valley. Slogans of 'Long live Pakistan' were carved with red-hot irons on the thighs of our Hindu daughters."[62] Hindu nationalists have ridden to

The Rape of the Sabine Women *by Giovanni da Bologna represents an episode in the legendary history of Rome in which the first generation of Roman men acquired wives for themselves from the neighboring Sabine families. (In this context, rape means abduction—raptio—rather than its prevalent modern meaning of sexual violation.) This sculpture, carved from a single block of marble, depicts three figures (a man lifting a woman into the air while a second man crouches) and is considered Bologna's masterpiece.*

power through politicizing the communal divisions between Muslims and Hindus by staging ritual confrontations over sacred space.[63] The Muslim as a rapist of Indian woman is integral to the Hindu nationalist imaginary and was indeed integral to the formation of the women's organization of the RSS. Stories of gang rape circulate

widely during these communal confrontation, as do stories of decapitation and the poisoning of food.[64] In the Hindu nationalist imaginary, one of the things that makes Muslims a national threat is, in fact, their food habits, most importantly that they eat beef. Not only is the consumption of beef believed to be polluting, but, since the late nineteenth century, the cow, the *gau mata* or "mother cow," has been understood as a symbol of the nation. The Muslim, then, literally eats mother India.

Sumathi Ramaswamy shows how the struggle between India and the would-be Tamil nation has been played out as battle of two virginal mothers, one, Bharata Mata, originating in Bengal, representing India, and the other, Tamilttay, "Tamil mother," representing the non-Brahmanical Tamil nation.[65] Tamil patriots experience an erotic longing for this virginal mother. In a typical expression, Mudiyarason, a popular Dravidian poet, declares: "If you reject me, how can I endure this life? Is it not your sweet passion that drives me crazy?" As Ramaswamy points out, the virgin quality of these fecund female collective representations is meant to stand for the inviolability of the language and the land.[66] And, indeed, violent struggles between the Tamil- and Hindi-speaking communities coincided with images of the body of Tamilttay on the verge of being disrobed, dishonored. The unfulfilled and unfulfillable eroticization of the relation between male nationalist and the national figure is thus displaced into actual Tamil women, who are understood to be embodiments of this untouchable nation.

Sexual desire for the nation's territorial body courses through the symbolism of Hindu nationalism as well. Uma Barati was one of the few, and certainly the most prominent, women leaders of Hindu nationalism, a movement that abhors India's partition and fears any further dismemberment of India. In 1992, Uma Barati led masses of men in the movement to destroy the Babri Masjid mosque where, they believe, Ram was born. In one of her speeches, as that struggle moved to its violent climax, Uma Barati declared, "In this country for forty-four years we have been robbed, beaten. . . . People who think that Hindus were weak, impotent, always a slave, this is an illusion. . . . Just to maintain the spirit of brotherhood we cut the organs of our own mother. You have divided the country yet you are not sitting in peace. You could not understand with talk—now you will understand with kicks. So let the bloodshed take place."[67]

As Katherine Komenda has shown, Uma Barati, a low-caste woman, the child of a landed widow, works the semiotics of the land, identifying her body with the body of the nation, with a river, the Narmada, a goddess who fell in love with another river, the Sombhadra, who refused to marry her. Uma Barati claims that her mother, well on in years, realized that she was pregnant when she was making the ritual circumambulation of Narmada. Uma Barati remembers her mother's realization: "Now I am pregnant with Narmada in my womb. She is coming now. I am pregnant with the Narmada River. She is coming as my daughter." Komenda analyzes the Uma Barati's narrative like this:

> By ascribing to herself goddess status, she informs us that this memory, this telling of her life has a sacred dimension and that it is connected to the stories associated with a sacred river that are enshrined in the memories of the devotees of Narmada as a river goddess. She wants the listeners to know that from the very start of her life she stands not for herself but for a collectivity; she is not identified with her body alone but with the body of a nation, a nation which coalesces through the threads of sacred narratives spun out through the memories of its people.

But Uma Barati is an erotic figure. There is an exquisite sexual tension in the stories that she tells her followers. The river of which she is an embodiment is a goddess who loses in love and becomes celibate. Uma Barati herself will hover on the brink of marriage. But, like the river after which she is named, on the eve of the massing of men to take back Ayodhya, the birthplace of the king, who had been exiled from his wife Sita, Uma Barati also takes the vows of renunciation. Perhaps a semiotic logic joins these two acts—Ram has not yet returned. One must wait.

For this woman, who, as a girl, fashioned Siva linga, or phalluses, out of mud and worshiped them, a woman whose destiny was revealed and put in motion at the moment of a wedding procession passing through Dunda, where as a six-year-old girl she corrected a Brahmin who could not remember a verse in the *Ramcharitmanas*, in the way she talks of India, she is penetrated by Ram. "Everywhere there is Ram. So just grab him. Grab his name. Fill yourself with him." Uma Barati, as she seeks to represent the body of India, reerotizes that body as a woman who must be husbanded and loved properly by strong men. Millions of men hang on her every word. Women, however, largely ignore her.

This same ancient identification of female body with national territory in the ancient world, in this case of the Israelites moving under the guidance of Moses from Egypt into the promised land, provided the warrant for contemporary Jewish nationalist violence. If the flesh of its women represents the territoriality of a nation, in this case the flesh of foreign women is a figure for a foreign country, for the dangers of exile, for the prospect of perfidious dispossession. In our day, this identification provided the theological basis for the first assassination of an Israeli Prime Minister. In November 1995, a devout Jewish nationalist, Yigal Amir, pumped two high-velocity, hollow-point bullets through the chest of Prime Minister Yitzhak Rabin. In 1993, Rabin had signed the Oslo Accords with PLO chief, Yasser Arafat, accords that led to the ceding of territory and ultimately sovereignty over a huge chunk of the lands that God had covenanted to the Jewish people.[68]

In 1994, after Dr. Baruch Goldstein, a devout doctor from Kiryat Arba, had murdered scores of Muslims as they prayed in Hebron, the Labor government seriously broached the idea of removing Jewish settlers from the center of Hebron. It was from this city that King David, two thousand years ago, had launched his drive to unify the twelve tribes under his leadership, the city in which the originary patriarchs and matriarchs of Israel are buried. This prospect pushed Amir into action. Seeking to defend Israel's territorial body, to prevent it being passed to foreigners, Yigal Amir killed the Jewish prime minister out of love for God.

Amir found the biblical rationale for his assassination in the book of Numbers, specifically the twenty-fifth chapter, in which the text explains that Moabite women were sexually luring the men of Israel into idolatrous rites, into the worship of Ba'al, the Canaanite god of storm and fertility.

> While Israel dwelt in Shittim the people began to play the harlot with the daughters of Moab. These invited the people to the sacrifices of their gods, and the people ate, and bowed down to their gods. So Israel yoked himself to Ba'al of Pe'or. And the anger of the Lord was kindled against Israel. (Num. 25:1-3)

God instructs Moses to have the judges slay those men who have "yoked themselves to Ba'al." While this was transpiring, an Israelite man, a certain Zimri, brought one of the foreign women, a Midianite named Cozbi, to his family in the sight of Moses and the community. Whether or not he actually made love with her

in plain view, the prospect of intermarriage was evident.

Pinchas (Phin'ehas), without obtaining legal authorization, took up a spear and killed both the Israelite man and the Midianite woman. To kill a Jew without authorization by a judicial process violates the Torah. Yet here, God stops the plague with which he is punishing the people and makes of Pinchas's line a "perpetual priesthood." The Talmud records that, even though the elders condemned Pinchas's act, God not only forgave the act but also rewarded it, for Pinchas "was zealous for my sake among them."[69] It is significant, I think, that it is immediately after this moment, this punished penetration of a foreign woman, that God directs Moses to take a census of the "congregation" to divide the covenanted lands.

Just before assassinating the prime minister, a man who would give the land of Israel to foreigners, Yigal Amir read precisely this passage.[70] In Amir's view, one is obligated to kill a Jew who would give up his country in the same way that Pinchas killed a Jew who, moving homeward, chose to enter the body of a foreign woman.

The import for religious nationalists of women's bodies as symbolic figures for the property over which the state, and the patriarchs who represent it, claim sovereignty is apparent in the Shah Bano case, which exploded in India in 1985. This contest, a conflict over the primacy of Islamic personal law as opposed to Indian civil law, was a site of intense emotional and political interest in India. In 1975, Shah Bano, the Muslim daughter of an Indian police constable, was divorced by her husband of forty years, who, by uttering the performative ("I divorce you") three times, repaid her dowry and ejected her from her home without sufficient monetary means or skill to survive.[71] Shah Bano appealed to unified Indian criminal law, as opposed to particularistic Muslim personal law, and, in 1985, the

Indian Supreme Court finally confirmed her right to alimony—over the Indian Islamic community's outrage that this violated the force of Islamic family law, which also operated under the authority of the Indian state.

This legal contest between Indian civil law and Islamic personal law polarized India, creating a huge rift between Hindus and Muslims, a rift politicized by the Hindu nationalists. The Shah Bano case, which generated unprecedented press coverage, coincided with a material threat to "Mother India," Indira Gandhi having just been assassinated by Sikh separatists. This struggle over the right of a Muslim man to control Muslim women in defiance of the Indian state set the stage for the Hindu nationalist drive, which began immediately thereafter, to eject the Muslims from Ayodhya.[72]

The political, as opposed to legal, consequences of the Shah Bano case were equally important to the mobilization of Hindu nationalism. In the wake of the court's finding in favor of Shah Bano, the congress government of Rajiv Gandhi, to secure electoral support from India's enormous Islamic community, introduced legislation that exempted Muslim women from Indian law regarding their rights to support in the event of divorce. The Hindu nationalists saw, among other things, that political pressure by a mobilized religious community could force the Indian government to retreat from its secular universalist commitments. The very next year, in 1987, the Hindu nationalist movement mobilized around the defense of the *sati*, the immolation of a widow on her husband's funeral pyre, in this case, an eighteen-year-old bride, Roop Kanwar.[73] Although this traditional practice is illegal, Hindu nationalists sprang to its defense as something that represented classical Hindu practice, to be cherished and preserved. In their individuality and their contrapuntal association, we again see the way in which the control of

women is joined symbolically to the control of territory. Through nationalist control of women's bodies, territory is configured as the nation's other natural material body.[74]

The Turkish case is also illustrative. Throughout the 1990s, the Turkish state, the first Islamic state to create a secular constitution, has faced both a growing Islamic political challenge and a territorial challenge from the Kurds, concentrated in southeastern Turkey, bordering Iraq and Iran. The Islamic offensive has been fought over the bodies of women, with the government forbidding young women from wearing headscarves to school, a normative sign of modesty, given the erotic associations of female hair. With some measure of state complicity, and with Iranian backing, the violent wing of an Islamic militant group, naming itself Hizbullah, whose goal is to create an Islamic republic in Turkey, unleashed a reign of terror against the followers of the Kurdistan Workers' Party (PKK). The Hizbullah are believed responsible for up to two thousand unsolved murders over this period, particularly those of Kurdish businessmen who were kidnapped and tortured to death. The violent Islamists not only targeted Kurds and separatists, in particular, but they also directed their violence against Muslim women who challenged the gender divisions that they believe are inscribed in the Qur'an. In January 2000, among the graves of the tortured Kurdish bodies, the police discovered the body of Konca Kuris, one of those rare feminist Islamists who had argued that the Qur'an neither requires that women cover their heads nor that men and women need be separated physically in schools.[75]

The case of Egypt illustrates the way in which Islamists joined women's entry into the public sphere with the limited territorial powers of the state. President Anwar Sadat was vilified by, and ultimately assassinated for, his empowerment of women and his willingness to make peace with Israel, thereby relinquishing the territorially ambitions of Nasser's Arab nationalism. Two events occurred in 1978–1979, one legal and domestic, the other diplomatic. Students of Sadat's assassination tend to center their attention on the second, not the first event. It is their coincidence that interests us here. The year 1979 saw the passage of the "Personal Status Laws," providing women with various legal protections in their conjugal relations, including the right to initiate divorce, as well as a law guaranteeing women thirty seats in parliament. This was the same period when Sadat secured the passage of the Camp David accords with Israel, in which the Egyptians abdicated their responsibility to press Palestinian claims, becoming the first Arab nation to make peace with Israel, and this while Israel asserted its unique sovereignty over Jerusalem. In the eyes of Sadat's opponents, these two were of a piece. The Islamists, who shortly thereafter assassinated him, fought both to reverse women's legal and political advance and to reverse the peace, cold as it was, with Israel.[76]

And finally, US fundamentalist hostility to abortion can be read in terms of this same coupling of female flesh and national territory.[77] Jane De Hart shows the discursive parallels between two efforts to criminalize abortion in the United States, one between 1840 and 1880 and the other after 1973, and the historic *Roe v. Wade* decision of that year. In both, abortion was targeted as a threat to the family and to the nation.[78] In both, the woman was linguistically reduced to a "container," not a person with civil rights enabling her to control her body as her property, but an incubator, nurturant ground in which grows a separate living being. Although the agents attacking abortion were divergent—professional doctors in the first case, Christian fundamentalists in the second—it is striking that, in both, the boundaries of the nation-state, its territorial integrity, and its racial purity were at risk, for the first time, as

a result of the Civil War, and, for the second, as a result of unprecedented immigration, and perhaps, one could argue, as a result of the defeat of the US military in Vietnam. (Eric Rudolph, the reputed abortion bomber, who also hit the 1996 Atlantic Olympics for having refused to allow its torch to pass through a North Carolina county that had passed an ordinance against "sodomy," was also motivated by a hatred of what he called "atheistic internationalism."[79]) I venture that it is their appropriation of the body as a collective representation that accounts for the fact that Protestant opponents of abortion, who defend their stance by "the right to life" also support the right to bear arms and oppose gun control.[80] It also makes sense of the fact that abortion was not a fundamentalist issue until the late 1970s.[81]

Control over the bodies of women easily assimilates to nationalist discourse. The word *nation* derives etymologically from *natio* and *natus,* birth and born, respectively. Nations are living creatures, collective subjects. They are drawn out of female flesh, flesh that must be controlled and cordoned off by men.[82] To be a man is to be able to protect one's woman from unwanted penetration. Possession and property are marked by the ability to monopolize that sexualized sacred space.

THE SUBJECT OF SEX

That religious nationalists celebrate patriarchal authority and sequester and subordinate the feminine is more than a reactionary reassertion of male privileges in a world that has been newly flooded by female participation in the labor force and the political stage, although it is that as well. In their struggle to restore the family, hierarchical gender divisions should also be understood as part of a sexualized semiotic code, one that seeks to regulate both the formation of self and society, individual and collective subjects.

The struggle to reassert the institutional division between masculine and feminine spheres, between man and woman, is also a medium to refigure the self.

It is the father—who wields that first life-and-death power—to whose authority we must first submit. His is the originary model of sovereignty. The father-centered family is the primordial ethical monist world to which religious nationalists would have us return. In that the father is the first authority, the sovereign of a total state, the one whose rule relied overwhelmingly on his voice, the celebration of patriarchy cannot be understood simply as a sexist backwash but also as an effort to construct authority, to combat a situation in which powers abound—without the words that would make them make sense, and desperate and longing words proliferate without any power at all. Capital acts without speaking and social solidarities cannot find voice. The obedience granted by children and wives and the solidarity of which it is a part offer an alternative model of social order to marketplace competition or democratic conflict.

Men and women both learn the sense of subjectivity and of authority through their production and orchestration in the family. This involves, as Pierre Bourdieu and Sigmund Freud have both insisted, a process of embodiment, a forgotten history of corporeal mimesis, leaving in its wake an unconscious habitus. Habitus is produced in a gendered habitat, a sexualized corporeal scene. In the prototypical family, mother love is body talk through the nurturant medium of the mothers' bodies working on the bodies of their children, whereas fathers choreograph their children primarily through words, signs that are often backed by the threat of violence. The family is constituted by the mother's body and the father's word.

The celebration of the male and the expulsion of the female from the public body is a way not simply to reconstitute the collectivity but also a way for men to reconstitute the subject itself. Religious nationalism flourishes in a world where not only do the father's words increasingly fail to signify, where economic transformation undercuts paternal authority, but also where agency itself is at stake. Mark Juergensmeyer traces the rise of fundamentalism to a situation where "male-gendered roles in general are challenged by a public order that denies agency to individuals" leading to "a defense of what are perceived to be traditional male roles."[83]

Individuality has a sexual constitution. In a mothered world, boys and girls, Nancy Chodorow has taught us, learn to individuate differently.[84] Whereas boys must reject the feminine to arrive at their gendered selves, girls need not. If religious nationalism is understood as a social movement seeking to reestablish agency for men, and not simply as a movement to reestablish male hegemony, the struggle to fortify the binary of gender and to cleanse the public sphere sexually takes on a supplemental meaning, an effort to create a world where men can be subjects, a subjectivity to which a distinctive masculinity is essential. So, too, are other men.

Collective representation, a making of symbols, originates outside of the realm of individual body-making, the domain of sexual reproduction, of wombs and breast milk, of women and children. Collective representation, the fabrication of collective bodies, has historically been conducted exclusively and then dominated by men. Although they are no less materially consequential, men populate the world with their symbols; women do so with their living bodies. Certainly the sexuality of the female body is relevant to their production of humans. Is the sex of male body relevant to their production of symbols? We shall see.

THE HOMOSOCIAL COMPACT

Collective representation is the translation of society into a symbol. Complex societies have been most commonly symbolized as a body politic. Not only do men speak in the name of the collectivity, but the collectivity is also typically located in and symbolized as a male body— kings, emperors, sultans.[85] Men represent the collectivity. Is this, as feminists claim, a matter of relations between men and women, of protecting arbitrary male powers and privileges against the claims of women? Or is there something between men that animates the logic of collective representation?

It is striking that religious nationalists counter the feminine heterosexual "other" with male homosociality, the lures of sexualized women with the solidarities of men. Religious nationalism is typically centered on energetic, diffuse, indeed, erotic forms of male bonding. Juergensmeyer points to the male-bonded center of the Christian militia in the United States, Hamas in Palestine, Sheik Omar Abdul Rahman's Islamic Party in Egypt, the Afghani Taliban, the Sikh Khalistani movement in the Punjab, and the Hindu Nationalist Rashtriya Swyamsevak Sangh (RSS) in India.[86] The RSS was organized around refashioned *akhara*, wrestling pits for young men, called *shakha*, where its cadre of boys and young men are daily trained, physically disciplined, and develop lifelong male solidarities.[87] Sikh militants speak of being joined together in a "bond of love."[88] Religious nationalism is a homosocial affair. The homoerotic hovers in the homosocial world as a dangerous and unacknowledged desire.

In *Ego and the Id*, Freud argues that the self, the ego, is first constructed as a bodily form, through the surface of an imagined human morphology, the image of a sexed body.[89] Judith Butler contends that the accomplishment of the gendered self depends on a disavowed, yet internalized, object, namely the body of the same-sex parent. A boy's identification with his father, she writes, "contains within it both the prohibition and the desire, and so embodies the grieved loss of the homosexual cathexis."[90] In this logic, men want the femininity they can never be and want to be the masculinity they can never have. Becoming a man, learning heterosexual desire, requires that one prohibit the feminine within. The constitution of the self involves both a constructed gender and sexuality, exclusively male or female, exclusively heterosexual.

Masculine, as well as feminine, identification and desire are both haunted by homosexual desire. "In a man," Butler writes, "the terror of homosexual desire may lead to a terror of being construed as feminine, feminized, of no longer being properly a man, of being a 'failed' man, or being in some sense a figure of monstrosity or abjection."[91] But perhaps it also operates the other way around, that the sense of masculine failure leads both to homoerotic terror and desire. If the self is under assault, endangered, decomposing within this structure, it would not be surprising for homosexuality to emerge both as problem and solution, a solution that must be ultimately disavowed, discharged, expelled from both the social and the individual body.[92] In other words, homosociality, and the erotic energies that make it pulse, stands as a well out of which to reconstruct manhood, to place women apart, to reenact Freud's mythic primal scene.[93] One returns to men for the energy to be a man, to be a self, which is the same thing; each helps fabricate a male collective representation, a collection of male bodies, in order to be represented as a man. In the company of brothers, one has and is a man. Religious nationalism reeroticizes the public sphere as a masculine space, restores the male as the body language of agency.

These sexual politics were there at the birth of the modern demos. The religious nationalists recapitulate the original republican imaginary. Jean-Jacques Rousseau, the foundational fabricator of the "general will," likewise stripped the public sphere of women, made citizenship into a masculine performance. For Rousseau, men's political relation to the state is founded not on reason, but on love. "The authority the populace accords to those it loves and by it is loved," he wrote in *Discourse on Political Economy*, "is a hundred times more absolute than all the tyranny of usurpers." Rousseau made it clear that homosocial love had to be purged of the homosexual.[94] In his unpublished *Le Levite d'Ephraim*, Rousseau took Ephraim's story from Judges that takes place before Israelite kingship as a parable for his own republican drama. In the story, it is the lust of the men of the tribe of Benjamin for Ephraim and then their subsequent rape and murder of his concubine that sets in motion a murderous civil war. The homoerotic threatens the homosocial logic of friendship, centralized political authority being a solution to politically divisive homoerotic forces.

And indeed the French Revolution begins in 1789 with bourgeois men massed on a tennis court, each with one arm grasping the man next to him and the other raised in ritual oath, breaking away from the Estates General, an institution for the collective representation of the dominant strata of French society, to speak for a new France, a new democratic body politic, a demos. European democracy is launched in a touching male scene.

THE STATE OF LOVE

Religious nationalists are preoccupied with the erotic. This preoccupation is also driven, I suspect, by the affinity between love and divinity. One's faith, for which one is willing to die, is grounded in a fierce, unshakable love of God, a submission in which the believer's self-sufficient sovereignty dissolves and one is reborn through a relation to a supreme Other. These movements are modern in that they put primacy on the individual, on his or her relationship to God, a relationship that has the capacity to transcend class and ethnic division, that even supersedes the demands of kinship.[95] They promote an intimate faith, a faith beyond creed, faith in a God who is present in the members' lives and who makes that life sacred. Although there is considerable historical variation in the primacy of politics in these movements, the premise is that one can win and build a new polis from individuals such as these.

Erotic love is the originary experience of an intimate relationship with another, who gives you to yourself only on condition that you risk yourself, that you cede your ego, at first not knowing whom you love or who you will be as you love and are loved. As Jean-Luc Marion has pointed out, one only knows oneself in allowing oneself to be vulnerable to the other, not through bodies observed and penetrated, but through the giving of a flesh that allows itself to be affected.[96] Flesh individualizes me in relation, not as a sovereign ego. Through the flesh—beyond language and reason—love requires one's passivity, one's lack, one's vulnerability. Love depends on a faith without reason in the presence of the other, the other to whom one is given and who gives herself. It depends on the gap between a me and a you that can never be crossed, transcended, fused. One might even argue that the divine is a figure for the phenomenology of this love, for an excess without which we would find life not worth living, one, indeed, for which we are willing to give our lives. Perhaps I have gone too far, but the parallels suggest that we should expect that those who seek to radicalize an individualized, intimate relationship with God would likewise seek to set their erotic lives apart, to make their love sacred, to ground it in a relation to divinity. And we should not be surprised that they sometimes are willing to die and indeed to murder to defend that love, that exceptional force. Rethinking religious violence pushes us to think of love as a political force, to explore and critique the sex of our states.

FOR FURTHER READING

Becker, Penny Edgell. *Congregations in Conflict: Cultural Models of Local Religious Life.* New York: Cambridge University Press, 1999.

Calhoun, Craig. *Nationalism.* Minneapolis: University of Minnesota Press, 1997.

Hansen, Thomas Blom. *The Saffron Wave: Democracy and Hindu Nationalism in Modern India.* Princeton: Princeton University Press, 1999.

Hawley, John Stratton, ed. *Fundamentalism and Gender.* New York: Oxford University Press, 1994.

Juergensmeyer, Mark. *Terror in the Mind of God: The Global Rise of Religious Violence.* Berkeley: University of California Press, 1999.

Lawrence, Bruce B. *Shattering the Myth: Islam Beyond Violence.* Princeton: Princeton University Press, 1998.

Riesebrodt, Martin. *Pious Passion: The Emergence of Modern Fundamentalism in the United States and Iran.* Berkeley: University of California Press, 1993.

Sprinzak, Ehud. *Brother against Brother.* New York: Free Press, 1999.

RELIGION AND CULTURE IN THE SPACE OF ETHICS

INTRODUCTION

In nation-states influenced by Enlightenment philosophy, citizens are free to choose their own religious identity. The concept of "religion," as an identity chosen freely from among others, is often an alien idea in traditional rural villages. There, only one option is known, and individuals are born into this tradition. Religion is not usually considered to be a category that is separate from culture, and it is often described by locals as "just the way things are." In these circumstances, distinctions between religion, culture, and politics seldom arise. A hundred years ago, for instance, we might assume that someone with an Italian or Spanish surname, such as Valentino or Lopez, was Catholic. Since then a greater access to transportation, forms of media, and legal protections against religious discrimination has increased the likelihood that an individual will discover their Jewish roots, or convert to Pentecostalism, Mormonism, Islam, Scientology, or Wicca. Conversion decisions can have positive or negative outcomes culturally. Imperfectly, individuals undertake decision-making according to the best tools available.

Individuals have a variety of learning styles. In addition to the models provided by parents and peers, individuals are also influenced by the social institutions around them, including cultural and religious influences. Parents are interested in increasing the opportunities available to their children and may adjust ancient traditions with this in mind. For example, in central California, a Palestinian Muslim community leader who is looked upon by his fellow Muslims as a role model sends his children to the local Jewish school because of its high educational quality, its dietary and gender rules, and its nonproselytizing teachers. In southern Wales, a Pakistani Muslim lawyer sends his children to a Welsh-language-only school with the similar motive of optimizing opportunities for success while sacrificing as few core beliefs as possible. Interfaith marriages also change religious demographics gradually over time, making questions of religious identity more perplexing and more complicated, and the category of "secular" can be misleading. In a Rosh Hashanah service, the rabbi calls the non-Jewish spouses of his congregation's members to join him in front of the ark containing the scrolls of the Torah to offer a blessing for their contributions to the Jewish community. To the chagrin of some in the congregation, the rabbi values their commitments to Jewish values and their Jewish identities without formal conversion to the Jewish tradition. In everyday life, formal boundaries may become transparent and permeable. Much like Edward Evans-Pritchard learned while living in rural Sudan during the 1920s, local villagers were completely uninterested in his Victorian distinctions between magic, religion, and science. The members of the communities in which he lived saw boundaries between them as more fluid, so as to provide a religious "toolbox" to find meaning and survive life's obstacles.

In this second part of *Religion and Culture: Contemporary Practices and Perspectives*, we focus on those spaces where religion and culture produce, reproduce, and structure ethics. In chapter 7, Vincent Biondo examines the influences of Jewish, Christian, and Muslim ethics on global capitalism. Even in societies that claim to be secular, ancient revelations about the creation and circulation of wealth continue to influence contemporary debates about human rights, economic imperialism, entrepreneurship, lending rates, credit card fees, sovereign debt forgiveness, industrial pollution, tax rates, and inheritance laws. Economic transactions are socially constructed and influenced by both religious history and culture. Here, there is a faith that self-interested individuals will maximize production. This, however, involves an internal struggle between short-term profit decisions and long-term well-being. Capitalism contains an internal motivation to maximize production in the near term. This means a company has motivation to pollute as much as possible since costs are deferred and future clean-up jobs are created. Religious ethics of sustainability and stewardship, however, help the captains of industry smooth a boom and bust cycle by emphasizing long-term success and quality of life improvements. Indeed, Biondo's chapter shows just how omnipresent religion and culture are to economy. Evan Berry in chapter 8 shows how religion and culture shape our ambivalent relationships with nature. He takes up how the rituals of production and consumption influence our understandings and connections to food and agriculture, how landscapes are structured by religious cosmologies and ultimately push us toward the religious cultures of environmentalism. Alex Norman takes up tourism and demonstrates in chapter 9 that the religious practice has long been connected to travel and movement. He shows us how tourism can resemble religious travel such as pilgrimage. In the same way as there is a social bond between pilgrims, in the contemporary world, where religious institutions have lost some power, individuals forge meaningful relationships with strangers and with their conceptions of the divine through travel. In chapter 10, Colleen Windham-Hughes describes how education and a national curriculum can use symbols, myths, and rituals to create a sense of national unity. As modern nation-states become ever more diverse through the forces of globalization, the religious power of education becomes increasingly important. State-funded schools teach citizens how to celebrate ritualized reenactments of a nation's creation, its wars, and its national heroes. Sarah W. Whedon's second contribution to our collection, chapter 11, explores children's participation in religious communities and their rites of passage. But she is also interested in the ways that power and authority flow between adults and children. When are children expected to follow the narratives that are provided by the adult members of a religious tradition? When do they resist those narratives, and under what circumstances do children create their own narratives and their own religious lives? Finally, in chapter 12, Stephen Hunt examines the religious meanings surrounding death and dying. He shows us how death also has a cultural significance. Death is not just about the afterlife but also belongs to a culture and religion of dying, which includes methods for the moment of death, funerals, and grief and mourning.

Often, the rich examples in these chapters are ritualized moments, which become strict norms of behavior, and therefore ethics, even though they can occur outside formal religious institutions. Each chapter describes the ways that religious and cultural ethics shape modern individuals.

7

THE RELIGIOUS ETHICS OF CAPITALISM

Vincent F. Biondo III

INTRODUCTION

Jews, Christians, and Muslims share traditions of prophecy in which religious ethics about economic life are revealed as divine law. This chapter examines shared economic teachings about equality, charity, sustainability, stewardship, quality of life, and reciprocity. A primary tension is the degree of Hellenization, or how to compromise between revealed law and Greek philosophical teachings regarding honor, liberty, and warfare. In particular, Western religious ritual practices, such as the Sabbath, festival calendar, funerals, and communal worship, reinforce ethical limits on creating wealth through slavery and usury, or excessive lending rates. In modern cities, Western religions promote the circulation of wealth, as opposed to wealth stagnation, through more equitable inheritance rules and sustainable taxation limits that allow for philanthropy. As an overarching theme, the economic teachings of Western religions encourage long-term sustainable success over short-term temporary profit.

Since the publication of Adam Smith's *Wealth of Nations* (1776) and John Mill's *Utilitarianism* (1861), capitalism has come to mean short-term utilitarian calculations for self-interested individuals in a cycle of creation and destruction. Although creative destruction encourages innovation, it also contributes to corruption and greed. For example, bankers who compete to maximize individual self-interest in the near term are motivated to make loans that customers cannot repay. Or a father may leave all of his wealth to a favorite son while disregarding his other children and local charities. After a temporary gain, ten years later, the success of the bank, favorite son, or local community is diminished. Instead of a focus on individual profit in the near term, religious rituals invoke the debt that individuals owe to their society over the longer term. More specifically, religious practices ask us to look past annual financial statements and election results for ways to improve quality of life over a lifetime. Reducing the costs of wages, taxes, or raw materials always helps the bottom line in the short term, but, for long-term success, the reduction must be sustainable. A religion too out of touch with economic realities will cease to exist, which is why religions only provide recommendations or reminders in the face of hard economic realities. Despite divinely revealed truths, every individual makes ethical calculations that compromise or blend religious ideals with practical realities.

A key obstacle to understanding how religions influence economics is an overreliance on a stark public-private distinction in which faith is a private, individual concern that does not influence public life. The dominant interpretation of Matthew 22:21, for instance, "render unto Caesar what is Caesar's," assumes an impermeable boundary between the public realm of political economy and the private realm of individual spiritual concerns. Following the Protestant Reformation, this distinction resulted in increased power for democratic nation-states by lessening the authority of the church over temporal matters. An important component of modernity, a stark public-private distinction ignores the religious roots of political economy and the ways that religions encourage individuals to consider the long-term effects of short-term decision-making.

The second obstacle to understanding how religions influence economics is the misconception that religions only influence individuals who are openly pious or attend public worship regularly. Because every individual is influenced by their peers and by history, people who do not proudly proclaim a particular institutional affiliation nevertheless live immersed in a sea of religious influences. As Ninian Smart elegantly professed, each of us inhabits a world of mythic narratives, ritual practices, philosophical doctrines, emotional experiences, ethical laws, social institutions, and material culture. No human individual lives untouched by one or more religious traditions.

As we navigate religious and economic waters simultaneously, the waves overlap to promote sustainable wealth creation, by providing consistent limits on slavery and usury. In terms of creating wealth, how much to profit from conquering, enslaving, or exploiting a neighbor through illegal physical slavery or state-sanctioned debt bondage is an area of ongoing concern. In addition, the circulation of wealth requires ideal levels of inheritance and taxation. Religious ethics encourages parents and children to support each other throughout the life cycle and to pay taxes and give to charity in exchange for the benefits of communal natural resources and social services.

Patria Potestas *and Primogeniture: War and Honor in Classical Athens*

Ideas and traditions from Greek philosophy have influenced Judaism, Christianity, and Islam in diverse ways. For instance, in the classical world of Athens and Rome, a male property owner passed his title and estate on to his *primogeniture*, or firstborn son. The *pater*, or father, exercised complete dominion over his estate, including the right to punish and, in rare instances, execute his slaves, women, and children, which were his property and responsibility. Instead of paying taxes or serving in the military, the lords of these cities created wealth by funding wars of conquest and competing for philanthropic honor.

Classical Athens did not tax its citizens but instead relied upon a system of philanthropy, by which the wealthy competed for the honor of providing social services.[3] The most vivid description comes from Xenophon's *Oeconomicus*, an ancient economics textbook, where Socrates tells Critobulus,

First of all, I see that you need to offer many large sacrifices, or, I suppose, neither gods nor men would put up with you. Then you are expected to entertain many foreign guests, and generously at that. Thirdly, you must give feasts for the citizens and be a benefactor to them, or else you won't have anyone on your side. Furthermore, I perceive that the state even now orders you to make large payments for keeping horses, and for training choruses for the festivals, and for athletic competitions and presidencies.[4]

The slave economy of classical Athens was based on a father's ability to wage war and give honorably, and it provides the secular foundation to Western economics, which is counterbalanced by the revelations of Western religions. To this day, status-conscious elites compete to enslave or exploit their neighbors. Although sharing a mutual respect for God's equal creation of all humankind in Genesis, Western religions, surprisingly, never condemn slavery outright. Instead, tribal patriarchy is incorporated along with the universal aspiration to more humane relations between peoples. Although outlawed by urban elites in the American and French Revolutions, the twin Hellenistic ideals of *patria potestas* and *primogeniture* continue to influence rural aristocrats, for whom household management is a microcosm of the state. Following in the tradition of Saint Augustine, who used Greek philosophy to create a logical system of Christian theology in *City of God*, James Dobson, in *Dare to Discipline*, also described a direct connection between obedience to one's biological father and obedience to God. This patriarchal argument places minorities and women in subservient roles.

The status of women in the economic teachings of Western religions remains controversial. Although the Torah, Gospels, and Qur'an document improved rights for women in the historical context of their revelation, these sacred Scriptures were also interpreted, over time, by male leaders to decrease rights for women. Whether women's equality requires a religious justification or secular context, there remains a tension with the ancient tribal practices of *patria potestas* and primogeniture, especially in agricultural societies, where physical labor can be more valued and estates are difficult to divide among progeny. Whereas Plato and Aristotle argued that slavery is a natural human institution because of differing intellectual and physical abilities, Western religions discourage slavery, as was the case for Theodora in 523, Bartolomé de las Casas in 1550, and Tom Harkin in 2001.

Theodora from Slave to Empress

In 523, slavery was first outlawed in Christendom by Empress Theodora, herself a former slave. After Theodora was born, in Syria around 500 CE, her father was killed by the bears he trained for the circus at the Hippodrome in Constantinople. By the age of sixteen, Theodora had become the most famous exotic dancer in the Western world.[5] Seven years later, following a religious rebirth, she married the emperor's nephew and made slavery and prostitution illegal before preventing the religious persecution of Monophysite heretics.[6]

Before the reforms of Theodora and Justinian, the greatest philosophers of classical Athens, Plato (in *The Republic*) and Aristotle (in *Politics*) agreed that slavery is a natural part of human life, because people have differing abilities to moderate their animal instincts and bodily impulses. Differing skills and predilections facilitate a division of labor that increases the efficiency of specialized tasks by freeing elites to study, preach, boss, and lead. Rather than condemn slavery outright, Western

The Slave Market is a painting by nineteenth-century artist Gustave Boulanger. It depicts a Roman slave auction and appears to be intended to show the horror, and perhaps the erotic aspects, of the idea of human beings being sold. The auctioneer adds to the sense of horror with his very casual attitude.

religions help to regulate and maintain everyday economic interactions. For instance, the Talmud contains a section describing how employers should strive to be more considerate toward their workers.[7] In their day-to-day operations, Western businesses negotiate compromises between the revealed ethics of human equality and reasoned ethics of human inequality. For instance, should a low-level employee be compensated for an idea that increases company profits? Human beings are naturally unequal according to Aristotle, but we should aspire to treat people better, according to the Mishnah, the Gospels, and the Qur'an.

Aristotle's description of human inequality provides a secular foundation for capitalism that discourages unions and cooperatives and encourages one nation to enslave another. Certainly some citizens of a nation have a more developed sense of self-control that helps them manage the more impulsive, but why should any citizen perform the most menial tasks when noncitizens can perform them? For example, after gaining control of Texas in 1848, the US government began hiring Mexican workers at below minimum wage. This arrangement was formalized in the H-2 Guestworker Program in 1942, which Congressman Charles Rangel called "the closest thing I've ever seen to slavery."[8] Ernesto Galarza described the negative paychecks he received when his employers charged him more in room and board than they paid in wages.[9]

If secular capitalism encourages the slavery of noncitizens and the poor through physical slavery or debt bondage, then prophetic religions recommend sustainable economic relationships across class lines and national borders, to prevent violent revolutions by discouraging slavery, including the debt bondage of usury. Indeed, some conversions by non-Europeans to Christianity and non-Arabs to Islam involved a promise of increased economic opportunity.

As for the circulation of wealth, Western religions recommend fair inheritance rules and taxation limits that allow for philanthropy in the forms of tithing or alms. A millionaire is free to choose between building a private orchid collection or public park. Even a worker must decide between a larger car or television and volunteering at the local soup kitchen. On a day-to-day basis, as individuals, we each have a limited amount of energy that we choose to expend in ways that either help or hurt our neighbors. Regular ritual practices, including the Sabbath, holidays, funerals, and communal worship encourage us to remain mindful of our equality in death and the benefits of social living.

PHYSICAL SLAVERY

Those whose task is to perform manual work, which is the best that can be expected of them, are by nature slaves and it is better for them to be ruled as slaves.
—Aristotle, *Politics* 1254–55

Wealth can be created through innovation or exploitation. When imagination is unreliable or difficult to quantify in the homeland, a successful military expedition abroad is easier to plan

and measure. In short, warfare involves a more rational utilitarian calculation than innovation or entrepreneurship, which waits for revelation or divine inspiration. According to the classical philosophical tradition of ancient Greece and Rome, a primary purpose of government is to supervise a constant state of offensive warfare for economic gain. In Athens, Plato and Aristotle encouraged their elite students to master their passions in order to lord over those unable to control their lesser animal instincts and impulses. Philosophy and science teach that individuals have different mental capacities and are inherently unequal. According to this logic, some people are superior to others, and thus slavery is a natural human institution. In ancient Greece, Xenophon's original *Oeconomicus* textbook was a manual for household management. In the patriarchal era, before the modern rise of bureaucratic nation-states, economists and theologians operated as though the state were a large and complex household, with the paterfamilias (king, pope, caliph, or emperor) at its head.

The God of Abraham, as portrayed in the Torah, the Gospels, and the Qur'an, challenges the logic of the philosophers. Despite inherent inequalities, individual human beings are equal in death before God and thus should aspire to treat one another more humanely in this life. In his *Defense of the Indians*, Bartolomé de Las Casas quoted John Chrysostom: "Just as there is no natural difference in the creation of men, so there is no difference in the call to salvation of all of them, whether they are barbarous or wise, since God's grace can correct the minds of barbarians so that they have a reasonable understanding."[10]

Despite the appearance of rigid doctrines, practiced religion thrives according to pragmatic compromise, and so the three major monotheistic faith traditions did not outlaw slavery altogether but encouraged slave owners to treat their human property more as members of the family than as beasts of burden. Policies protecting slaves were especially likely in the context of co-religionists. Although what defines an outsider varies according to time and place, in Western religions, God prefers that you enslave someone from outside your own religion. A neighbor of a different race, ethnicity, or language with less economic or military power can be more easily enslaved.

Bartolomé de Las Casas Debates Juan Ginés de Sepúlveda

As a young man, Bartolomé de Las Casas departed from Spain for the Caribbean on February 13, 1502, ten years after his father had accompanied Columbus during his first voyage. This visit transformed him into the leading historian of the conquest and an advocate for more humane treatment of the natives, especially while serving as the bishop of the Mayan peoples in Chiapas. In 1543, the emperor's official chronicler and personal chaplain, Juan Ginés de Sepúlveda, authored a book called *Democrates Secundus,* which promoted the use of military force to "civilize" the natives. De Las Casas convinced Spain's religious leaders to prevent its publication, and the controversy caused Emperor Charles V to suspend military operations until God's law could be clarified. At Valladolid in Spain in August 1550, the state-priest and scholar-priest debated whether the indigenous people of the Americas should be treated as beasts of burden without rights or as human souls awaiting conversion. Although no transcript has been found, Lewis Hanke has recreated the debate using their writings. In his defense statement, De Las Casas drew from his fifty years of direct experience with the natives to conclude that the indigenous peoples had culture, religion, and politics and should be treated as human beings. Sepúlveda, who had just finished translating Aristotle's

Politics, trusted for his evidence the accounts of the conquistador Gonzalo Fernández de Oviedo y Valdés, who had burned families alive to steal their gold before calling them sexually perverse cannibals.[11] Sepúlveda suggested that the natives of the Americas "are as inferior to the Spaniards as children to adults, women to men, as the wild and cruel to the most meek, [and] as monkeys to men."[12] In response, De Las Casas wrote: "They are not ignorant, inhuman, or bestial. Rather, long before they had heard the word Spaniard, they had properly organized states, wisely ordered by excellent laws, religion and custom."[13]

Though physical slavery is widely illegal today, human trafficking may soon surpass drugs and weapons as the largest illegal economy according to the US State Department. In addition, Kevin Bales has argued that debt bondage (workers whose debt to their employer surpasses their incomes and who are unable to change employers because of threats of physical violence) makes slavery more widespread today than at the height of the Atlantic slave trade in colonial America.[14] The US government has also recognized the problem. In 2001, Congress asked the State Department to begin documenting the global spread of human trafficking in annual reports.[15] In a speech before the UN General Assembly on September 23, 2003, President George W. Bush referred to 900,000 humans trafficked across international borders annually. According to Kevin Bales, the price of West African slaves has dropped from $60,000 in 1850 (adjusted for inflation) to $600 today.[16] When the price of a human being drops below the price of a doctor visit or sanitation repair, suffering increases.

The consensus definition of a slave (as an individual who cannot change employers out of fear of physical violence) includes a range of interpretations—from being chained like an animal to working eighty hours per week without pay. Certainly chaining workers is widely condemned, yet there are also gray areas of abuse that are open to interpretation, including exposure to toxic substances. The most common form of slavery today is debt bondage, in which wages are less than debts owed to an employer. Another technique is to hire illegal immigrants with the promise of a paycheck at the end of the harvest, only to call immigration authorities the day before payday. Or a part-time worker without health insurance may be injured and turn to credit cards or payday lenders to cover medical costs. Within months, interest payments can exceed the principal, which results in debt bondage. Although Jews, Christians, and Muslims today universally condemn slavery in theory, in practice people tend to privilege coreligionists.[17] In the following examples, people are more comfortable exploiting a neighboring people than their own people.

Why Modern Slavery Tastes Sweet

To be middle class in the Northern Hemisphere means to enjoy small luxuries, such as sugar, coffee, tea, and chocolate, that are harvested by manual laborers in the Southern Hemisphere. In his book *Sweetness and Power* in 1985, Sidney Mintz wrote that "the first sweetened cup of hot tea to be drunk by an English worker . . . prefigured the transformation of an entire society," and he could have added that it transformed the entire planet, because sugar was later added to coffee and cocoa.

Whereas human trafficking for child prostitution is illegal and universally condemned by Western religions today, worker exploitation that borders on slavery plays a larger role in the practices of our daily lives. Before his arrest in 2001, Ramiro Ramos's Mayan slaves in Immokalee were harvesting Florida orange juice. In a darker side of the "Cola Wars," Cargill, Pepsi,

and Coca-Cola compete for the cheapest, sweetest oranges.[18] In West Africa, 40 percent of the world's chocolate comes from the Ivory Coast, where fifteen thousand slaves from Mali and Burkina Faso have yet to be freed by the 2001 Harkin-Engel protocol.[19] Christian Parenti has described in *Fortune* magazine how child workers continue to be trapped there in order to sell more Hershey's Kisses and M&Ms. The harvesters of sugarcane in Brazil,[20] bananas in Ecuador, and asparagus in California have each been prosecuted in recent years for illegal tactics. In critical theory, the term "commodity fetishism" from Karl Marx's *Capital* describes how the suffering involved in obtaining exotic crops from distant lands increases their sweetness on the palette and the social status of the consumer. On a more positive note, children's soccer balls for sale in the United States and Britain have printed on them "not produced by child labor."

USURY AND DEBT BONDAGE

Bad money drives out good money.[21]
—Gresham's Law

Although Thomas Gresham was explaining to Queen Elizabeth why copper coins drive silver coins from circulation, Gresham's Law speaks to an ethical flaw in the utilitarian calculation of free enterprise. Given the choice of earning $100 for building a wall or from the interest on a loan to the bricklayer, most would choose the latter, despite the end result being the same. Today Gresham's Law describes a human tendency to prefer to earn money without work. Initially, Jews, Christians, and Muslims tried to avoid lending money, at interest, to coreligionists altogether. Today, usury means charging excessive rates of interest and is a form of worker exploitation that can lead to debt bondage when a lender deliberately designs a loan that cannot be paid back.

Because interest is another way of saying rate of return, or profit, it represents the cornerstone of the capitalist marketplace. As a result, various mechanisms of compromise have developed to reconcile ethical ideals with earthly practice. Predominant among these is one that occurred when Christians banned Jews from owning land or farms so that Jews had no choice but to become urban traders or middlemen, such as merchants, manufacturers, or financiers. Whereas usury originally referred to a ban on all interest, as Judaism, Christianity, and Islam incorporated Aristotle's natural theory of slavery, usury today generally refers to excessive compound interest, resulting in slavery beyond a sustainable 12 percent limit that takes into account inflation and hassle.

Shakespeare's Shylock Father

Usury is an especially tense topic in Western religions because it is condemned by God yet is essential to capitalism. Whereas military expeditions to capture workers and natural resources openly pit nations against one another, usury dehumanizes on local levels in less obvious ways. For many Western readers, the term *usury* invokes the oppressed role of Jews in medieval European banking, which contributed to massive modern anti-Semitism and the Holocaust. The most famous individual usurer in European history is the fictional character Shylock, in William Shakespeare's 1595 play *The Merchant of Venice*, which depicts some of the resentment directed toward Jews during the time that the original ghetto was established in Venice in 1516. In depicting this character, Shakespeare had firsthand experience. According to the Public Record Office in London, Shakespeare's father, John Shakespeare, had been arrested for usury several times. On October 25, 1568, John Shakespeare lent eighty pounds to John Musshem, with

a promise of one hundred pounds a year later, for a return of 25 percent. Because this violated the 10 percent limit on usury of 1545 and the total ban of 1552, Shakespeare's father was forced to pay a fine to avoid imprisonment. As a Jewish moneylender in the play, when prevented from working outside banking but then condemned for his career choice, Shylock responds with one of the most well-known lines of the play.

> Hath not a Jew eyes? Hath not a Jew hands, organs, dimensions, senses, affections, passions; fed with the same food, hurt with the same weapons, subject to the same diseases, healed by the same means, warmed and cooled by the same winter and summer as a Christian is? If you prick us do we not bleed? (Act 3, Scene 1)

This quote speaks to religious prejudice against Jews in particular, as well as to the larger ethical conundrum of dehumanization when reasoned capitalism triumphs over revealed law. Although we are equal before God, according to religious ideals, we remain unequal economically and philosophically.

Riba is Arabic for Usury

> God hath permitted trade and forbidden usury.
> —al-Qur'an, "al-Baqara," ayah 275

Following the European transition from military imperialism to economic imperialism after World War II, modern Muslims became especially concerned with usury as a barrier to social justice. Although Muslims are Aristotelian capitalists, as are Jews and Christians, newly formed Muslim governments remain uncertain about whether religion inhibits or creates greater financial independence. The Islamic financial ideal is called *mudaraba*, or profit and loss sharing, whereby venture capitalists finance a project without a guaranteed rate of return and then serve as advisors on the project. Muslims prefer debit cards to credit cards and believe that insurance would be more ethical as a cooperative in which a percentage of unused deposits (also called profits) was returned to contributors.

Credit Cards and Payday Loans

The two most common forms of debt bondage in the United States today come from credit card and payday loan companies. When an individual accrues credit card debt, the lenders are free to adjust the interest rate to charge as much as they believe the person can willingly pay before defaulting into bankruptcy. This means that the ideal cardholder lives on the brink of economic collapse, with expenses slightly exceeding income, and the interest compounding into perpetuity. Credit card, payday, and mortgage lenders compete to identify customers who reliably spend slightly more than they earn.

For most of its history, the United States had usury laws to prevent the debt bondage of its citizens.[22] Then, on December 18, 1978, the US Supreme Court invented the credit card industry when it decided, in *Marquette v. Omaha*, that national credit card companies could circumvent state usury laws. Almost immediately, the people of South Dakota and Delaware voted to repeal their state usury laws in order to recruit tens of thousands of jobs from Citibank and Chase, respectively. In the United States from 1993 to 2003, high credit card lending rates increased from 20 to 40 percent compounding.[23] Late-payment, over-limit, and foreign-currency fees also doubled.

Making 39-percent credit card rates seem paltry in comparison, payday lenders who charge 390 percent entered into the national spotlight as a result of the attacks of September 11, 2001, and the resulting "war on terror." Because of the length of the Iraq War and the all-volunteer military force, soldiers became unable to serve—because of debt bondage to payday lenders who intentionally locate their businesses near entrances to military bases. In October 2006, the Department of Defense convinced the Senate to pass, as a matter of national security, a 36-percent usury limit on payday loans for soldiers. In May 2008, Advance America closed its operations in Pennsylvania, after the state Supreme Court ruled its 370 percent interest rate (including fees) usurious and illegal. On June 2, 2008, Ohio became another state to reinstate usury laws, when Governor Ted Strickland signed House Bill 545, limiting the "interest rate for payday loans at 28 percent, reduced from the current annual interest rate of 391 percent."[24]

The libertarian free-market argument is that smart people already know not to use credit cards, payday loans, or adjustable rate mortgages, so it is only the ignorant who suffer. According to certain Christian theological interpretations, ignorance is a product of sin, and sinners must sink low in order to find God and change themselves. In this case, the state should not regulate or interfere with wealthy companies seeking to profit from people's ignorance. In contrast to religious endorsements of Aristotle's natural theory of slavery, Western religions have also inspired some economists to design alternative financial instruments.

Muhammad Yunus Invents Microlending

In Bangladesh in 1976, a professor of economics at Chittagong University named Muhammad Yunus visited the nearby village of Jobra during a time of famine and found forty-two bamboo stool makers in debt bondage to usurers for a total of twenty-seven dollars. Dumbfounded by this unproductive arrangement, he paid off their debts out of his own pocket. This inspired him to invent microlending and to establish the Grameen Bank, which would go on to make successful small business loans to 6.7 million female entrepreneurs before earning Yunus the Nobel Peace Prize in 2006.[25]

College Students Create Jubilee 2000

Whereas Professor Yunus does not explicitly mention religious values in his writings, in 1990, the students of politics professor Martin Dent at Keele University were openly inspired by Leviticus 25:10, which reads, "You shall hallow the fiftieth year and you shall proclaim liberty throughout the land to all its inhabitants. It shall be a jubilee for you." According to this ancient Jewish commandment, slaves should be freed and debts should be canceled every fifty years. Historians are skeptical as to how this can actually be practiced, yet, like the weekly day of rest and leaving the fields fallow every seven years, it is possible that some Jews heeded this commandment. When Martin Dent and his students recognized that European governments had arranged loans to African countries that made it impossible for hard work to be rewarded with economic growth, they invoked the Torah in creating the Jubilee 2000 campaign. Although "chains and whips" slavery has been illegal for over a century, the world's fifty poorest nations, many of them in Africa, continue to be enslaved economically. The Jubilee 2000 campaign brought attention to the world's fifty poorest nations—for which debt payments exceed 80 percent of gross national product. The interest payments of these Heavily Indebted Poor Countries (HIPCs) to the World Bank, International Monetary Fund, Paris Club, and US government make domestic improvements financially impossible. The efforts of a small group of university students may have inspired the United Nations, Pope John Paul II, and U2's Bono to follow their lead.

Jeffrey Sachs and Debt Reduction

Another individual working to improve the lives of millions is Jeffrey Sachs, who was an economic advisor to developing nations before being named the chief architect of the UN Millennium Development Goals to eradicate global poverty, AIDS, and malaria, between 2000 and 2015.[26] The world's poorest earn less than one dollar per day and cannot earn more through hard work or education because of their debt bondage to the World Bank and European nations. Rather than distributing foreign aid as charity, Dr. Sachs promotes sustainable economies through training in farming methods and public health.

Teshuvah: Contemplate and Atone

In everyday life, the most effective way that religion influences wealth creation is through the festival calendar that organizes time. The first economic teaching of the Abrahamic monotheistic Western religions is based on judgment, or the afterlife reward of heaven or punishment in hell. This motivates individuals to follow revealed laws such as the commandment to "observe the Sabbath day" (Deut. 5:12). Abraham Joshua Heschel, who marched with Martin Luther King Jr., has written about the many benefits that a day of rest brings us.[27] At the secular level, a day off work benefits our physical health, improves our family life, and increases worker productivity during the remainder of the week. In religious terms, a day of rest involves contemplation of our pending mortality, place in the universe, role in society, and relationship with God. Jews, Christians, and Muslims each recognize the seventh day of creation in the book of Genesis as the day of rest, although they each have selected a different time on what we now call "the weekend," which illustrates the competitive nature of these sibling traditions. Communal worship at synagogue, church, or mosque successfully promotes group feeling and serves as a focusing lens on the afterlife and therefore this life as well. The Sabbath is an economic teaching as a break in the cycle of work and shopping and also as a time for contemplating human equality in death at judgment before God. God's commandment to rest unifies rich and poor and master and slave, as in Deuteronomy 5:14, which reads:

> The seventh day is a sabbath to the Lord your God; you shall not do any work—you or your son or your daughter, or your male or female slave.

Despite Aristotle's ruthless and fatalistic realism about varying human potentials, the Sabbath frequently reminds us of our equal propensity for death and for increasing good instead of evil.

In addition to the weekly Sabbath reminder, Jews, Christians, and Muslims each recognize annual rebirth-renewal festival cycles that encourage meditations on our position as social beings that are dependent on one another during our short lifetimes.[28] Jews identify with the enslaved and the exploited every spring during the Passover Seder, when guests are invited to dinner to hear a retelling of the exodus from Egypt. As the Talmud says, "In every generation let each man look on himself as if he came forth out of Egypt." Four months later, Jews have the opportunity to forgive debts, apologize for mistreatment, and atone for broken commandments during the ten high holy days, from Rosh Hashanah (New Year's) to Yom Kippur (the Day of Atonement).[29] During this sacred time, Jews are encouraged to perform Teshuvah, or to heal the future through forgiveness and remembrance of the past. Christians feel great equality

and charity during Christmas, celebrating the birth of Jesus to a homeless couple in a manger. Four months later, during the holy week, witnessing reenactments of the crucifixion and resurrection of the savior brings the opportunity for annual renewal and rebirth. Muslims experience great feelings of equality and charity during the unifying fast of the Ramadan month, culminating in the festival of Eid al-Fitr. Four months later, pious Muslims who perform the rituals of the Hajj week are reborn, cleansed, and purified before God. This culminates in the Eid al-Adha charity celebration, during which every Muslim receives a nutritious meal in honor of the sacrifice of Abraham. Each religion has an annual holy week of rebirth as the most sacred ritual in its calendar. On a weekly and annual basis, Western religions provide opportunities to contemplate economic interactions and to atone for profits from slavery or usury.

Great empires create wealth by innovation and entrepreneurship and by conquering and exploiting neighbors. Religious festivals and laws help civilizations to develop a successful balance between enslaving and exploiting the poor while also encouraging philanthropic aid. Philanthropy takes the form of inheritance, taxation, and alms, which encourage a healthy circulation of wealth.

INHERITANCE: FROM RURAL PATRIMONY TO URBAN MERITOCRACY

Within a religion, local interpretations of religious teachings about family and community relations are heavily influenced by cultural and historical contexts. In a boom-and-bust cyclical economy, when times are difficult, family members rely more heavily upon one another and donations to charities diminish dramatically. The foundation of a market economy is the circulation of goods and services, for which money is exchanged so that wealth circulates. Religious values influence the circulation of wealth in two key ways, through tax laws and laws about inheritance.

The consensus rulings of Western religions on inheritance law are not to disown a child unless he or she is convicted of murder, to provide for women and children in addition to the firstborn son, and to give to charity to avoid spoiling children. Each of these three teachings prioritizes modern urban equality over lordly rural freedom. Yet these revealed teachings remain in tension with classical traditions, as in *The Republic* (circa 380 BCE), where Socrates tells the firstborn sons of Athens' wealthiest families that they alone must shoulder the responsibility to determine what is right for their estate and hence the nation as a whole. In contrast to the patrimony of Greek philosophy, Western religious traditions place a greater emphasis on human equality. A famous scriptural example of this more egalitarian ethos comes from the Golden Rule of Rabbi Hillel and Jesus of Nazareth.

> *What is hateful to you, do not to your neighbor: that is the whole Torah, while the rest is the commentary thereof; go and learn it.[30]*
> —Shabbat 31a:13

> *Love thy neighbor as thyself.*
> —Mark 12:31

Since Western religious ethics have incorporated Aristotle's natural theory of slavery, the message of the Golden Rule, regarding when to help another man's women and children in a capitalist society can be divisive.

The difficulty of applying the Golden Rule in practice emerges from an ethical tension between tribal patriarchy and the human rights of natural law. Societies in which the military and agriculture play greater roles are more likely to maintain the feudalistic practice of primogeniture and to oppose the modern legal reforms of the French Revolution. In rural areas, it is not desirable to break up large farms or estates, and so a father was encouraged to leave everything to his firstborn son. Meanwhile, in cities, Western religions are more likely to promote equal opportunity.

The Daughters of Zelophehad (586 BCE Babylon)

Eighteenth-century principles of equality before the rule of law and separation of church and state originate in the Babylonian exile of 586 BCE, during which time rabbinic Judaism based on Torah study replaced biblical Judaism based on temple sacrifice. At this time, Judaism became a portable world religion that could be practiced outside the land of Israel. Among the many important developments was the Jewish overturning of primogeniture and paterfamilias practices, which predominated in the ancient Near East and eastern Mediterranean. Whereas the primogeniture described in Deuteronomy 21:17 was the norm before 1000 BCE, in Numbers 27, God advises that Zelophehad's five daughters should inherit instead of the tribal chief. This innovation strengthens the family and women's rights. According to Zafrira Ben-Barak, the destruction of the temple contributes to greater inheritance rights for daughters in exile.[31] Maimonides has explained that the doctrine of primogeniture in Deuteronomy 21:17 ensures lineage for a minority community undergoing external threats. A successful compromise for Maimonides (also used by Muslims and Christians) was for the firstborn son to receive a double portion of the inheritance, but Maimonides goes on to say that dowries for daughters are also important. These range from one year's worth of maintenance to

10 percent of the family estate. Besides the double portion reserved for the eldest, Maimonides advises that a father should strive not to "make any distinction between his sons."[32]

Inheritance laws in farming areas centered on the almost exclusive power of the father and firstborn son and excluded women. In agricultural societies, it is not possible to divide up large farms or estates, and so the eldest male ruled. This was especially important among minority communities. Developments of diasporic Judaism in exile after 570 BCE were promoted a millennium later by Justinian, in 529 in Constantinople, and by Muhammad in 622 in Medina. As Western religions became urbanized, Christians in Rome and Muslims in Arabia encouraged fathers to treat their children more equitably.

Polygamy was gradually replaced by the private law of the family, which was extended to the public law of the city. Practicing Jews, Christians, and Muslims aspired to a natural law of equality, as in Hillel's negative Golden Rule, because all are equal in death and before God as Adam's children. This aspiration to egalitarianism was further emphasized in the political writings of Rousseau, and egalitarianism inspired democratic revolutions in France and the United States. For example, a Mirabeau-written speech delivered by Talleyrand on April 5, 1791, states, "There are no longer eldest sons, no longer privileged persons in the great national family." The idea that children are born equal is tempered, however, by the teachings of Greek philosophy— that people with different abilities to reason should be free to create hierarchies, including a division of labor from which we benefit. Thus equality and freedom, although both cited as important modern values, are in tension. Religious inheritance laws encourage us to treat our children equally and to reciprocate to the social fabric that makes family wealth possible.

Muhammad in 622 CE Medina

A review of Muslim inheritance laws shows overlaps with Jewish and Christian sources, including the *Jus Gentium* of Justinian.[33] First, God commands fathers not to disinherit their sons, especially late in life when judgment can be impaired. Second, fathers should try to support their wives and daughters and aspire to treat children equitably. Firstborn sons can still be given special consideration, according to the principle of primogeniture, but, over time, younger sons, daughters, and wives should also be taken into account. A son should only be disowned if he is convicted of murder.

According to the Qur'an commentary of Ibn Kathir, for the nomadic Arab tribes before 610 CE, when someone died, his wealth went to the senior male tribal leader. The revelations to Muhammad from 610 to 632 shifted inheritance laws dramatically.[34] Islam also prohibits female infanticide, which Muhammad may have singled out as the most despicable practice of the pre-Islamic period. According to Islamic Law, a parent should strive to love his or her children equally and leave a maximum of one-third of the wealth to public charity.

Two events in Muhammad's life help to clarify the significance of the inheritance verse 4:11, which commands fathers not to disinherit daughters or younger sons, and to include mothers.

> God (thus) directs you as regards your Children's (Inheritance): to the male, a portion equal to that of two females: if only daughters, two or more, their share is two-thirds of the inheritance; if only one, her share is a half. For parents, a sixth share of the inheritance to each, if the deceased left children; if no children, and the parents are the (only) heirs, the mother has a third; if the deceased Left brothers (or sisters) the mother has a sixth. (The distribution in all cases ('s) after the payment of

legacies and debts. Ye know not whether your parents or your children are nearest to you in benefit. These are settled portions ordained by God; and God is All-knowing, Al- wise. (Yusuf Ali trans.)

As an example of the application of this revelation, the historian al-Tabari reports that Muhammad expressed concern when Aws b. Thabit al-Ansari failed to provide for his daughters in his will. Daughters receive 50 percent less than sons, but 50 percent more than previously in a contextual compromise.[35] Later, in 630 CE, Bukhari 2:383 and 4:5 reports that when S'ad b. Abi Waqqas wanted to leave his entire estate to charity, Muhammad said, "A bequest may not exceed one-third of the estate." Although favoritism occurs, in the Risala of the founding jurisconsult Shafi'i (around 820 CE), it becomes even clearer that a father should not privilege one particular heir with an advance bequest. In cases where there is no will, the inheritance laws of 4:11 are employed to divide up the estate among primary and secondary heirs. A bequest is a pre-inheritance gift to a family member, religious institution, or civic charity. In the Qur'an, charity and taxation are both included under the term *sadaqa*. Later scholars distinguished between the charity laws of bequest (*waqf*) and alms (*zakat*).

The Waqf of Abu Bakr al-Khassaf

The law of *waqf*, or charitable trust, is not mentioned in the Qur'an, but charitable trust became a common practice by the end of Umayyad Caliphate in 750 CE. A *waqf* can be a public or familial endowment. It can be used for piety, social services, or to avoid the algebraic formulations of the inheritance verse. Timur Kuran has argued that the *waqf* developed to protect private property from despots. He and David Powers have suggested that some parents used

waqfs to show favoritism or to bypass 4:11.[36] Still, there is some evidence that Muhammad recommended charity as a path to heaven. He donated all of his wealth to charity, and Umar may have established a *waqf* for social services during his reign, as well as an inheritance for his daughter Hafsa.

As described in one of the oldest surviving *waqf* documents, Abu Bakr al-Khassaf was a cobbler and *qadi* (judge), who died in Baghdad in 874 CE. The British Museum holds a fourteenth-century copy of this document. There are two kinds of *waqf*, public and private, although private family *waqfs* were outlawed across the Muslim world during the 1940s.[37] Public *waqfs* have been established for mosques, schools, hospitals, pilgrim hostels, orphanages, and homeless shelters and have been an important source for social services. Rashid al-Din Fadl Allah (died in 1318) left a 250-page *waqf* document that describes his dedication of an entire new quarter to the city of Tabriz, Iran, including housing for 400 scholars, 1,000 students, 50 medical professors, 200 *hafiz* (Qur'an memorizers), 220 service workers, 13 police officers, 24 hostels, and 30,000 families, in addition to shops and factories.[38] *Waqf* philanthropy makes up a civil society. According to Timur Kuran, most of the mosques and all of the soup kitchens built during the Middle Ages were *waqfs*.[39]

Waqfs are not mentioned in the Qur'an but developed after the succession of Muhammad as a means to avoid political tyranny and preserve a separation between church and state. This form of civil society has to be tempered or reigned in, however, by capitalist governments interested in securing efficient markets. In studying *waqfs* in Ottoman Turkey, Timur Kuran has concluded that an excess of philanthropy, resulting from suspicion of a strong federal government, crippled the modern industrial economy and contributed to the decline of Muslim civilization and rise of northern Europe. There is some speculation that the European concept of charitable trust, which was key to the development of the modern university, was an Islamic concept imported by the Crusaders. As shown by Goitein's analysis of the Cairo Geniza documents, Jews, Christians, and Muslims intermarried and traveled freely in the Muslim world during the eleventh century. There is some evidence that the founders of the first law schools in England were familiar with law schools in Muslim Spain.

J. Seward Johnson and J. Howard Marshall

In the weeks before his death in 1983, J. Seward Johnson revised his will to exclude his five children. Instead, he left the bulk of his wealth to his current wife and former immigrant servant, Barbara Piasecka. He was seventy-six and she was thirty-four when they married in 1971. In another case, eighty-nine-year-old oil billionaire J. Howard Marshall married twenty-six-year-old exotic dancer Anna Nicole Smith in 1994, but, in his will, he left all of his wealth to his second son, Everett, ignoring his wife and firstborn son, James III. In both cases, the heirs not named in the legal wills won multimillion dollar lawsuits in court. In inheritance lawsuits, secular courts can invoke religious ethics in overruling the decision of the deceased to disinherit a wife or child.

The Estate Tax

Religious teachings about inheritance also influence debates about the estate tax in an attempt to balance freedom and equality and to guarantee the continued circulation of wealth. In US history, James Kent debated Thomas Jefferson, and George W. Bush criticized Teddy Roosevelt using different interpretations of the Gospels. For the agriculturally minded Kent and Bush,

a father should be free to choose his financial legacy. For the more urban-minded Jefferson and Roosevelt, wealth handed to firstborn sons reduces motivation and skill and causes wealth to stagnate.[40] Furthermore, upon reaching a certain limit, income inequality results in violent revolution. As capitalists, both sides are interested in wealth circulation and a sustainable level of wealth disparity; however, they disagree about these levels and about how much to incorporate Aristotelian freedom into a monotheism-inspired equality of opportunity.

TAXATION AND ALMS: THE FREE-RIDER OBSTACLE TO SUSTAINABLE STEWARDSHIP

> The pocketbook is prayer.[41]
> —Arthur Waskow

In the area of tax law, religious ethics support efforts to overcome the free-rider problem, which is the fear that our neighbor will take advantage of our kindness without offering help in return. This free-rider problem creates a short-term bias in capitalism with environmental consequences. In short-term capitalism, individuals and nations compete to exploit their neighbors and, in the process, destroy the environment. Whereas economists seek short-term maximization, religions can recommend lower profit margins to better serve our neighbors and to preserve the environment for longer term financial success. Debates about tax rates often take the form of raising or lowering them. The reason these debates are so emotional, however, is because taxation is actually a zero-sum game. The historical record reveals a long-term ideally sustainable tax rate that cannot be changed. As a result, short-term allocation decisions become highly competitive. For instance, a 1-percent increase for children means a 1-percent decrease for seniors. A 1-percent increase for logging means a 1-percent decrease for tourism. The zero-sum nature of taxation amplifies the free-rider problem. When should a senior be concerned about a neighbor's child-care or a logger about a neighbor's rafting business? The political economy of taxation involves shifting tax burdens and allocations. More money for schools means less money for pensioners. More money for orphanages means less for addiction counselors. More money for rural farmers means less for urban merchants. More money for timber collection means less for ecotourism. Over the long-term, a 20-percent tax rate is sustainable because individuals are willing to pay it without directing efforts at evading it. From year to year, however, every tax decision helps someone by hurting someone else.

Although the greatest source of philanthropy is from inheritance, a government can compel its citizens to pay a certain tax rate at a sustainable 20-percent level that leaves room for charitable giving, tithing, or alms, called *zakat* in Arabic or *tzedakah* in Hebrew.[42] Because the level of optimal sustainable state tax revenues can never be changed, distribution decisions are moral choices. Individuals prefer not to pay taxes to the state that benefit nonpayers. As a result, if one company releases pollutants to cut costs, it is in the rational interest of all other companies to do likewise. This free-rider problem can only be addressed through voluntary, religion-influenced alms or tithing. Religions can encourage stewardship and sustainability through longer-term thinking. Furthermore, tithing competitions between religious institutions can have a positive impact on the quality of life by encouraging such thinking. Jews, Christians, and Muslims share strategies toward the ethics of taxation that are capable of improving access to health care, education, human rights, the environment, and the arts.

Health care, education, and the environment are historically the recipients of philanthropic

institutions, so their funding involves a combination of state and voluntary taxation. A better understanding of the influence of the history of religions upon economic decision making can improve quality of life. Because the goal of both technology and utilitarian capitalism is to minimize pain in the near term, we constantly make rational calculations that perversely lower quality of life. For example, pollution is classified as an asset in near-term GDP calculations, because its cleanup creates jobs, even though it could be considered as a liability for long-term quality of life. Western religions promote a sustainable combination of state taxation and the giving of alms, in an attempt to overcome the free-rider problem. Recent statements from the Vatican and Southern Baptist Convention lend support to such a conclusion. Through official and unofficial taxation, including *maaser*, tithing, and *zakat*, Jews, Christians, and Muslims share strategies toward the ethics of taxation, which are capable of promoting environmental stewardship.

Taxation takes three forms. First is a flat fee, such as a poll tax or head tax, by which every citizen pays a fixed amount—for example, the fee to get a government identification card. Second is a percentage on property or income. This raises the ethical question of progressive rates, or whether wealthy individuals should pay a higher percentage. Scholars agree this is ethical because wealth begins from social infrastructure resources and is protected later by criminal justice resources. Third is an excise tax, which often means an extra tax on luxury items, such as alcohol or tobacco. Excise taxes have become the most popular recently because of the ease by which a majority group can tax a minority group.[43] Alms compete with excise taxes as the easiest way to increase revenues. A subset of excise taxes is taxes for particular industries. For example, if a port needs repair, each ship that lands can be charged a usage fee to raise the necessary funds, rather than forcing all citizens to contribute equally.

Despite political rhetoric to the contrary, overall tax revenues can never be raised or lowered. Instead, there is an optimal rate, between 15 and 20 percent, that most people are willing to pay in a timely manner. Above this rate, citizens start to evade taxes and revenues decline. Official state taxation below 25 percent allows for voluntary philanthropic offerings or religious community charity. For example, a midrash in the Talmud (*Sifra Emor* 10) tells Jews to continue to tithe in addition to meeting Caesar's top-end 25-percent state tax rate.

King Hammurabi (died in 1750 BCE) of Babylon may have helped ensure a sense of unity and peace in ancient Mesopotamia during his reign through periodic cancellations of tax debt. When poor farmers sold off family members as slaves to meet 33-percent tax rates, the kings of Babylon often canceled these debts at their inaugurations in exercises of sovereignty.[44] Hammurabi built agricultural canals in dry lands to assist with production. City wall and temple maintenance were also acceptable uses of tax revenues.[45]

In ancient Egypt, the pharaoh was god incarnate, as the son of the sky-god, and had control over the rain and Nile flood. All land belonged to the pharaoh, and farmers paid a portion of their yield to tax collectors, who were sometimes cordial and other times cruel.[46] Joseph's 20-percent tax rate on the Jews of Egypt (in Gen. 47:24) may represent a symbolic upper limit for legitimate state taxation. Rates from 20 to 30 percent may be sustainable if state and voluntary religious taxation is combined, although the upper level requires a benevolent philosopher-king with the power to issue periodic reprieves, as described in Plato's *Republic*.

A sustainable 15- to 20-percent government tax rate allows for competitions in tithing and stewardship. The last non-Christian Roman emperor, Julian, complained in 362 about how Christianity gained adherents by extending charity to non-Christians.[47] Another example is that of the editor of the Latin Vulgate, Saint Jerome, telling Christians to "at least imitate the Jews by giving tithes" in his commentary on Malachi 3:10.[48] Last, George Makdisi has written about the Crusader encounter with Muslim institutions of higher learning as the motivation behind the origin of universities in Europe.[49] The quality of a nation's universities, or museums, or hospitals is evidence of economic and religious competitions.

Philanthropic Competitions

Plato described philanthropy as when "daemons took charge of men in order to establish peace and justice among them and to free men from feuds and wars."[50] Another example is the *theorikon*. This was "theater money," whereby the wealthy bought tickets for the poor to participate in the moment of national pride offered by the dramatic festival, which was a state religious occasion preceded by a military parade, much like the Olympics or a royal wedding.[51] Medicine may have begun with Hippocrates as an example of philanthropy. In addition to justice, arts, and health care, philanthropic competitions intend to strengthen society permanently, whereas charity has near-term benefits for particular individuals.

Dominium *or* Imitatio Dei

Philanthropic competitions can also encourage stewardship of the environment. The debate about stewardship in Western religions refers to whether *imitatio Dei* (imitate the kind and righteous mercy of God) should be used to interpret the term *dominium* in Genesis 1:28. The story of Abraham's hospitality to strangers (Gen. 18–19) or the story about destroying the fruit trees of your enemy in war (Deut 20:19—*bal taschchit*—"do not destroy") seem to support the statement of Abraham ibn Ezra in the twelfth century:

> The ignorant have compared man's rule over the earth with God's rule over the heavens. This is not right, for God rules over everything. The meaning of "he gave it to the people" is that man is God's steward (*paqid*) over the earth, and must do everything according to God's word.

The Qur'an also contains a concept of vice regency, or stewardship, called *khalifah* in Arabic (6:165): "He made you his viceregent on earth." *Khalifah* is also mentioned in al-Baqarah (2:23 or 2:30), in accordance with the verse that all creation pleases God (17:44 or 20:53). There is also a qur'anic verse, 2:205, and *tafsir* by al-Tabari similar to the *bal taschchit*. Instead of the language of dominion, animals and birds in 6:38 "are peoples (or communities) like unto you." A *hadith* from Muslim ibn al-Hajjaj reads: "The world is green and beautiful and God has appointed you as his stewards over it." Abu al-Faraj agreed centuries later that "people do not in fact own things, for the real owner is their Creator; they only enjoy the usufruct of things, subject to the Divine Law." Or, as Thomas Jefferson wrote to James Madison in 1789, "The earth belongs in usufruct to the living." If we benefit from natural resources or infrastructure created by others, 1-percent philanthropic competitions for environmental, education, health, or legal protections seem to be a divine minimum.

Gross Domestic Product or Quality of Life Index

A study of sustainable taxation and religious stewardship reveals some attempt to remedy our increased demands upon Earth's natural resources. First, tithing competitions can improve our quality of life. Second, religious stewardship based on judgment and *imitatio Dei* can overcome premillennial dispensationalism and utilitarian capitalism, which privilege quarterly profits over long-term success. Although minimizing pain in this life as a sign of God's grace is an intoxicating mix for disciples of the industrial marketplace, God's gift of free will made it possible for Abraham to extend hospitality to angels. The free-rider obstacle to environmental stewardship, including pollution for example, cannot be solved solely by democratically enforced utilitarian calculation.[52]

Quality of life is unaffected by the raising or lowering of taxes because sustainable taxation is a zero-sum game. There is an optimal rate, and minute allocation decisions only shift the free-rider problem, because special interests defend perverse subsidies. A favorite example of environmental watchdog groups is the US Forest Service building logging roads in the Tongass National Forest, which barely makes it profitable for logging companies to destroy long-term sustainable tourism in the name of a small, one-time gain.[53] Huge dams in India and Canada have been cited for creating expensive cleanups of water supplies poisoned by lead, which are costlier than the electricity profits that they generate. In Brazil, native tribes compete to clear-cut the Amazon rainforest to produce ethanol for American consumers.

Tax reforms can help but are insufficient without a religious rerooting of our relationship with nature—as one of stewardship rather than dominion—because prophecy demands a short-term sacrifice for long-term success. In quantitative terms, we could stop counting pollution, prisons, illness, war, obesity, and debt as positive economic indicators by replacing the popular GDP calculation with a quality of life index, as Robert Kennedy recommended in a speech at the University of Kansas on March 18, 1968.

The gross national product does not allow for the health of our children, the quality of their education, or the joy of their play. It does not include the beauty of our poetry or the strength of our marriages; the intelligence of our public debate or the integrity of our public officials. It measures neither our wit nor our courage; neither our wisdom nor our learning; neither our compassion nor our devotion to our country; it measures everything, in short, except that which makes life worthwhile.

For instance, the Social Science Research Council has developed a human development index based upon three factors: life expectancy, adult literacy, and percentage of citizens earning a living wage.[54] In choosing where to live, access to jobs, education, and health care or low levels of pollution and crime could represent additional considerations. The Redefining Progress think tank has also issued a genuine progress indicator based on thirty factors.[55] Instead of competing to see who can produce pollution and deplete natural resources the fastest, perhaps our religious teachings encourage long joyous lives, not short painful ones, by looking past quarterly earnings reports toward long-term growth.

Jeffrey Sachs of the Columbia Earth Institute won UN support after demonstrating how 1 percent of income can eradicate global poverty and preventable disease.[56] Arthur Waskow recommends that we form 2 percent *tzedakah* collectives to improve the quality of life in our communities.[57] At an optimal level of government taxation, individuals are free to engage in stewardship competitions and to give alms that improve quality of life.

The ways that religious ethics are interpreted within a culture can influence economic life greatly. Judaism, Christianity, and Islam have been Hellenized to varying degrees in different places. In consequence, religions provide practical recommendations that counteract the short-term and egocentric limitations of human reason. Socially speaking, people are dependent on one another as individuals and also across generations. The rational economic inclination to create wealth through military might or economic occupation is tempered by a common humanity and increased social interdependence about which the festival calendar provides weekly and annual reminders. Legal debates about inheritance and taxation are naturally self-interested, yet religious ethics encourages longer-term sustainable success over short-term temporary profit.

FOR FURTHER READING

Agnon, Samuel Y. *Days of Awe.* Edited by N. Glatzer. New York: Schocken, 1948.

Bales, Kevin. *Disposable People.* Rev. ed. Berkeley: University of California Press, 2004.

Burd-Sharps, Sarah, Kristen Lewis, and Eduardo Borges Martins. *The Measure of America.* New York: Columbia University Press, 2008.

Casas, Bartolomé de las. *In Defense of the Indians.* DeKalb: Northern Illinois University Press, 1974.

Finley, Moses I. *Studies in Ancient Society.* London: Routledge, 1974.

Hanke, Lewis. *All Mankind Is One.* DeKalb: Northern Illinois University Press, 1974.

Heschel, Abraham J. *The Sabbath.* New York: Farrar, Straus and Giroux, 1951.

Ilchman, Warren, Stanley Katz, and Edward Queen, eds. *Philanthropy in the World's Religions.* Bloomington: Indiana University Press, 1998.

Khadduri, Majid, ed. *Law in the Middle East.* Washington, DC: Middle East Institute, 1955.

Powers, David. *Studies in Qur'an and Hadith: The Formation of the Islamic Law of Inheritance.* Berkeley: University of California Press, 1986.

Sachs, Jeffrey. *The End of Poverty.* New York: Penguin, 2005.

Tamari, Meir. *With All Your Possessions.* New York: Free Press, 1987.

Waskow, Arthur. *Down-to-Earth Judaism.* New York: Morrow, 1995.

Yunus, Muhammad. *Banker to the Poor.* New York: Public Affairs, 1999.

WEB SITE

PBS Frontline "Secret History of the Credit Card," www.pbs.org/wgbh/pages/frontline/shows/credit/.

8

NATURE

Evan Berry

The term *nature* carries so broad a meaning that it is almost impossible to discuss either "religion" or "daily life" apart from it. In many modern cultures, humans are widely said to be alienated from nature; society is understood as separate from nature in ways that distance people from their environments. There is an abiding notion that the secular flavor and powerful place of scientific authority in our postindustrial, globalized culture renders nature "disenchanted." Within the academic study of religion, there has also been a worry that the cultural legacy of Christianity has been a radical separation of humanity and nature—a socially enacted theology of human dominion over nature. In the late 1960s, a medieval historian named Lynn White expressed this concern in a groundbreaking article titled "The Historical Roots of our Ecologic Crisis."[1] The absolute separation of nature and society imagined by White and others, however, is a conceptual abstraction: the most basic human activities (e.g., eating, farming, or looking outside to see what the weather is before dressing in the morning) indicate that nature plays an important role in the everyday lives of modern

peoples. The decades since White's essay have seen an increasing interest in the way that religions think about, ascribe value to, and engage with (nonhuman) nature. This chapter surveys some of the basic contributions of this area of study, examining, in particular, the implications of knowledge about religion and nature for those interested in the rhythms and rituals of daily life.

These same kinds of practices—ones that emerge from the basic links between peoples and their environments—find expression in all cultures. The weather changes, the seasons turn, food sources come and go, and basic forces of nature—such as disease, drought, and disaster—shape human lives, both personally and collectively. Whether in the present or the past, religious traditions universally grapple with such forces, struggling to understand the place of the human in the broader natural world and working to ensure their proper situation in that world. This chapter explores the tremendous variety of ways that human cultures have conceptualized and responded to nature in the patterns daily life. Humans are always "in" nature—it is manifest in most aspects of human life—so it

THE ACADEMIC STUDY OF RELIGION AND NATURE

Did you know that, during the last several decades, a significant interest in ecological questions has developed within the academic study of religion? In the 1980s and 1990s, in response to Lynn White's critique and to new questions being asked by ethicists, scholars of religion devoted increasing attention to the role of religions in environmental problems and their potential contributions to environmental solutions. Much of this scholarship was carried out by participants in a research group called the Forum on Religion and Ecology, whose founders, Mary Evelyn Tucker and John Grim, argued that,

> as key repositories of enduring civilizational values and as indispensible motivators in moral transformation, religions have an important role to play in projecting persuasive visions of a more sustainable future. This is especially true because our attitudes towards nature have been consciously and unconsciously conditioned by our religious worldviews.[2]

In recent years, scholars have raised important new questions about the relationship between religion and ecology. For example, Bron Taylor, founder of the Society for the Study of Religion, Nature, and Culture, has contributed to scholarly knowledge about beliefs and institutions outside the confines of the conventional understandings of religion. Research in this area examines whether organizations like EarthFirst! need to be understood as spiritual phenomena. Others in religious and ecological studies have pointed to the gap between beliefs and practices shared by industrialized societies of all religious persuasions, questioning the degree to which institutionalized worldviews actually generate environmentally positive behaviors. Questions like these animate an important and growing field of scholarship treated throughout this chapter. The chapter also demonstrates the critical ways that religions comport themselves with respect to the environment and discusses some of the ways that they are contributing to efforts to solve ecological crises.

is helpful to think about how societies engage with and ritualize nature within specific natural domains, such as agriculture and cosmology. This chapter offers a comparative survey of the conceptual resources and ritual practices that animate religious engagements with the natural world. Before any such exploration is feasible, a careful consideration of what is at stake in discussions about nature is necessary.

During the past two centuries, as scholars and writers have become increasingly interested in the relationship between religion and their cultural contexts, there has been an ongoing debate about how to best understand the interplay between societies and their environments. This debate concerns whether environments shape societies or societies shape environments, a question with roots deep in Western history.

As Clarence Glacken, a prominent geographical historian, puts it, "Although the idea of environmental influences and that of man as a geographic agent may not be contradictory . . . the adoption by thinkers of one of these ideas to the exclusion of the other has been characteristic of both ancient and modern times."[3] In other words, most persons thinking and writing about the relationship between nature and culture argue that one or the other is the stronger force. Does nature make culture or does culture make nature? This choice is itself rooted in a religious question: do human beings transcend nature and thus have the capacity to rule over and control it? Conversely, do human beings live primarily at the mercy of nature, seeking only fleeting comforts? Or are human beings part of a natural order, participating in a "community of all things"? Answers to these questions draw heavily on theological history; only by asking fundamental religious questions (e.g., what is human?) can they be fully addressed.

The school of thought that emphasizes the power of nature is called environmental determinism, and it argues that environments shape cultures in fundamental ways.[4] This view rests on two claims: first, that societies necessarily draw their symbols, ideas, and practices from the natural world around them, and, second, that such symbols, ideas, and practices are finite resources that functionally limit the possibilities for social or cultural change. From the perspective of environmental determinism, there are distinct differences between desert cultures and forest cultures, or between island cultures and mountain cultures. This is because, in those various environments, certain symbols are more or less available and certain needs are more or less important. For example, in a desert culture, the scarcity of water furnishes water with sacred value: its collection and consumption would, theoretically, be more intensely ritualized than in cultures where water was more abundant. From this perspective, the powers to which water is attributed in desert cultures (e.g., rain gods, thunder gods, etc.) supposedly serve as the most chief gods. In exploring the tremendous variety of ways that nature has been treated in daily life, we revisit the question of how much environments determine the shape of the societies that inhabit them. However, it is necessary to note that the power of environmental determinism as a way to explain variation between societies is limited in today's globalized world. In an era when most cultures were small-scale societies, with an enduring connection to single place, determinism offered a more persuasive account of cultural difference. The geographic mobility of the modern era, that is, the ability of modern people to move easily from one place to another, coupled with the exchange of cultural resources across vast distances, has opened a new chapter in human history, one that greatly complicates the relationship of culture and nature.

The school of thought that emphasizes the power of humanity over nature is harder to define because it includes a variety of different ideas. Scholars write about the "social construction of nature," which means that they subscribe to the view that nature comprises metaphors, images, and ideas that are socially and historically contingent. This view is an important part of social scientific scholarship in environmental studies, where environmental historians such as William Cronon and Carolyn Merchant have articulated how theological and mythological ideas (e.g., Eden, Israel's sojourn in the wilderness, etc.) have colored Western perspectives about the natural world. Theorists arguing in favor of this approach suggest that the relationship between religious symbols and nature is not an exclusively Western phenomenon. From an anthropological perspective, all cultures employ "cognized models" of their environments, and all discourse about those environments is conditioned by the linguistic and imaginative limits of particular cultures. Many environmentalists have expressed their displeasure with the social constructivist viewpoint. For instance, Gary Snyder has been openly hostile about Cronon's argument that wilderness is a social, rather than an ecological, concept. Snyder's concern, and the potential danger of constructivism, is that, in working to better understand how societies conceptualize nature, attention to concepts of nature will reduce the real environment to a fiction of the (collective) imagination.

In between these two extremes—determinism and constructivism—there is a variety of middle paths that can help us understand the relationship of cultures and their environments. One such idea is cultural ecology, an approach characterized chiefly by the work of Roy Rappaport, an influential anthropologist. Cultural ecology seeks to understand "how culture is affected by its adaptation to its environment,"[5] a view that yields to both culture and nature as having some form of agency. For cultural ecologists, environments establish basic limits on human cultures (e.g., maximum sustainable populations, the presence of certain minerals or lack thereof, etc.), but these limits form only loose boundaries within which cultures can develop variously. In fact, Rappaport and others argue that ritual—performative expressions of fundamental social structures—often functions as an ecological regulatory mechanism. Many rituals have outcomes that, either intended or unintended, are of profound consequence for the ecosystem in which the ritual actors live and breath (see the following sidebar). There are a number of other ways to frame the relationship between cultures and nature that attempt to describe the mutual cocreation of human and ecological systems (e.g., complexity theory, human ecology, sociobiology, and place-based ethnographies), each of

which are important in that they do not suggest that either human agency or natural processes are the lone forces in history.[6]

IDEAS OF NATURE: MYTHOLOGY, COSMOLOGY, AND SACRED SYMBOLS

As the central focus of religious studies, religion offers scholars considerable conceptual flexibility. Although the term *religion* is not native to languages other than Latin or English, scholars use it to designate a variety of cultural phenomena that resemble those called religion in Anglophone cultures. The application of this term to a radical diversity of phenomena is the topic of much debate among scholars of religion, but such argumentation only works to underscore the disciplinary identity of religious studies. A similar conceptual challenge faces scholars interested in nature, which is also an English word of Latinate derivation. The word *nature* comes from the Roman *nascitura*, a verb meaning "to give birth." The invocation of birth signals the importance of origins and origination in the concept of nature: to speak of something as natural is to say that it is given. The status of natural things, to borrow a phrase from Heidegger, is that they have "always-already been there."

In this essay, the term *nature* is used as a broad catchall to indicate those things (and systems of things) that are taken by various cultures as self-evident or given. The term *environment* is used interchangeably with *nature*. Although *environment* is a much more modern word than nature and thus even further removed from ancient and non-Western cultures, it conveys, at least in part, a sense of the totality of things that collectively constitute the world that humans find themselves inhabiting. Although many cultures do not talk about the world they inhabit either as nature or environment, their perspectives are not necessarily unrelated to the biophysical model employed by contemporary scientists. In fact, in much the same way that myths shape how religious persons understand the world around them, so too does the scientific quest for empirical knowledge shape the way that many modern peoples come to know nature. What is self-evident about the world varies tremendously across cultures. Without embracing a hard version of social constructionism, in this section we survey how religious worldviews shape cultural understandings of nature. In some cases, sacred narratives, or myths, act as the primary symbols for thinking about and engaging with the environment. Different societies hold to different concepts of nature, using different metaphors and practices to engage with "self-evident things." Scholars of religion and nature can identify some broad patterns.

The idea of nature in so-called primitive cultures can be generally described as being spatial rather than temporal. Human beings move across the face of the Earth attentive to the cyclical patterns that demonstrate the fundamental and regular order of things. The preponderance of cultures in human history understand nature as sacred: "Despite great differences in their myths and practices, [tribal] religions present a remarkable morphological resemblance as far as their relation to nature."[7] One element of this "remarkable resemblance" is a tendency toward panpsychism, or the interpenetration of consciousness through the whole phenomenal world. This is especially important in cultures with shamanistic traditions, where religious experience is organized around (spiritual) movement outside the confines of everyday human being. Shamanism is grounded on a view of nature in which spirit travel is both possible and necessary. Such cultures, moreover, are typically structured around an image of nature as double: nature comprises both a cosmic and an earthly world. Often connected by what Mircea

Eliade famously calls the *axis mundi*, these two worlds are not separate; rather, they are intimately conjoined, mutually necessary, and often overlapping. Religious ritual in such societies is often designed to facilitate proper exchange between the two worlds, and, as such, the very purpose of religious activity is to maintain the order of nature, thereby guaranteeing human vitality and flourishing. This notion of nature, although voiced in a rich variety of ways, is regnant in many Native American traditions, African societies, and Oceanic cultures.

A twofold concept of nature as a metaphysical order underlying the often chaotic and unpredictable phenomenal world is widely shared by other religious systems. In Chinese tradition, for example, a series of interlocking binaries frames an understanding of the natural world. Everything in nature can be characterized as either yin (feminine, passive, dark, earth) or yang (masculine, active, light, heaven); this system renders visible a cyclical order in nature, an exchange and dynamism among all things. Coupled with this dualism is the concept of *qi* and *li*, which are fundamental premises of neo-Confucianism. *Qi* is the vital force that runs throughout nature, and *li* is the principle of order that holds the world in a coherent form. These pairings also provide the context for ritual praxis. Healing the body (or, perhaps, in the contemporary world, healing the environment) is a matter of establishing proper balance between yin and yang.[8] In contrast to yin and yang, *qi* and *li* do not function in a zero-sum relationship. *Li*, as the basis for order itself, requires that human beings adhere to what is proper for them, and, in so doing, they ensure that the movement of *qi* through the cosmos flows as it should.

The cyclical nature of the cosmos is a prominent feature of southern Asian cosmologies as well. The different traditions of this region—Hinduism, Jainism, Buddhism, Sikhism—share a diversity of common sources, textual and vernacular myths that establish a common framework for thinking about nature. Indian epics, such as the *Mahabharata*, recount the countless cycles of the creation and destruction of the world; within these cycles, human beings strive to uphold the dharma, or teachings. These teachings, an infinitely multiplex reflection of the many faces of divinity, exhort human beings to a variety of virtues, including nonviolence toward other creatures and respect for the sanctity of life. Buddhist cosmology, too, is grounded in a "shared common condition of all sentient life. . . . Every form of sentient life participates in a karmic continuum."[9] The cycle of karma binds all living things together in a system of death and rebirth.

In the ancient Mediterranean world, especially in Greek culture, the term *cosmos* encompassed the world, covering that which later, under the influence of Rome, came to be called nature. Because of the relationship between these two words, it should come as no surprise that cosmology (the symbolic representation of a universal order) is crucial for understanding culturally specific views of nature (a system of relations between things that is taken as self-evident).

This precedent foregrounds the shifting perspectives about nature and its meaning in Abrahamic traditions—Judaism, Christianity, and Islam. Contemporary understandings about how "people(s) of the book" thought about nature are rapidly changing. Before launching into an exploration of how mythologies and cosmologies shape Abrahamic concepts of nature, it is important to acknowledge the diversity of perspectives within each religious tradition. Although some religious communities may hold to theologically rigid notions of the separation of divinity and nature, others strive to connect the two in their sacred narratives and in their practices. Rather than succumbing to the seductive simplicity of White's idea about the anthropocentric (human-centered) character of Judeo-Christian theology, it is helpful to remember that nature has a "both/and relation" to Abrahamic notions of the sacred. Nature, for many Jews and Christians, is both sacred and profane. Taking the book of Genesis as a foundational text, nature can be said to be sacred because God made it and called it "good." At the same time, however, Genesis also recounts God's condemnation of the ground as punishment for Adam and Eve's disobedience, which suggests the view that the natural world is fallen and profane. The createdness of nature is fundamental in Islam as well. Islamic philosophy understands nature as evidencing God's will, a symbol of his power that is legible to human eyes: "Because nature cannot explain its own being, it stands as a sign of something beyond itself, pointing to some transcendental entity that bestows the principle of being upon the world and its objects. Nature, then, is an emblem of God."[10] From this perspective, much as described in Lynn White's critique, nature is understood as existing "for" human beings.

Such traditional religious views are not the only sacred stories about nature that condition the way modern societies think about nature. For instance, physicists have constructed a narrative of the big bang that orients the way many contemporary people understand history: as the gradual, entropic heat death of a primordial explosion. This secular, scientific view undergirds much of the discourse about environmental issues, especially in the sense that biological evolution moves from simplicity to complexity. In fact, there are a number of scientists who call this "the universe story," arguing that it provides an appropriate frame for the quest to understand the proper place of humans in the natural order.

THE GREAT CHAIN OF BEING

One of the most important ideas in Western thinking about nature is the concept of the "great chain of being." The great chain of being is a philosophical concept that arranges all existing things in a hierarchy of forms, ranked from the simplest to the most complex. The great chain of being has its origins in Plato's *Timaeus*. The subsequent Christian theologians, who for centuries sought to synthesize Plato with scriptural sources (a project called neo-Platonism), envisioned the world as a mere derivative of perfect form. A dimension of the great chain of being called the principle of plentitude states that in between the simplest and most complex things is a gradient of forms, each one ever so slightly more complex than the last. In other words, the principle of plentitude imagines that in between the worm and the snake are a variety of slithering creatures of increasing complexity. In the modern era, these ideas—the great chain of being and the principle of plentitude—provided fertile ground for the birth and growth of the naturalistic sciences. As an important basis for speculation about nature, theoretical consistency with the great chain of being suggested a humble anthropology: human beings were but one link in a great chain between the simplest beings (bacteria, perhaps) and the most complex (God). The great chain of being had direct currency for the popularization of Darwinian evolution and ecosystems science. Specifically, the great chain of being operated as the conceptual basis for the idea of the "niche": all living organisms inhabit a unique place in the scale of being, thus a key labor for natural scientists was to devise logically ordered systems that described the place appropriate to each creature. The taxonomic enterprise formalized by Linnaeus is premised on the morphological continuum presupposed in the great chain of being.

RITUALS OF PRODUCTION AND CONSUMPTION: FOOD AND AGRICULTURE

With the possible exceptions of sleeping and working, there is perhaps no more basic activity in daily life than eating. Although foodways vary tremendously across cultures, all peoples eat, and they do so ceremoniously. Meals are important markers of ritual cycles, both daily and yearly, as is fasting. Food is an important dimension of culture that links religion and nature in several ways. To begin with, the necessity of food for human sustenance is a reminder of our animal natures—like any other living creature, humans are biological beings with metabolic needs. Not only do humans need food, they enjoy consuming it, choosing and preparing dishes, and sharing food with others of the same group. Although this fact often remains obscure in modern industrial societies, food comes from natural sources. Until quite recently, agriculture, husbandry, hunting, fishing, and gathering served as the sole sources of foodstuffs. It is not only that human beings are natural creatures; they rely on nature—the seasons, the soil, the forests, the seas—for nourishment. Food has a mythological context too. Many cultures associate the emergence of agriculture and cooking with the advent of civilization itself.

Before Prometheus stole fire from Zeus, he craftily took for himself a superior cut from a slaughtered ox; and, in retaliation, Zeus condemned humankind to a life of labor in the fields. Hesiod's account of the Promethean myth stakes two important claims on this series of immemorial events: first, because of this prideful conspiracy against the gods, humans are agricultural creatures; and, second, it is in remembrance of Prometheus's actions that "the tribes of men upon earth burn white bones to the deathless gods upon fragrant altar" (*Theogony* §545). A similar worldview is expressed in the Genesis account. Not only is the first man, Adam, made from the earth, he is made from "arable land," the Hebrew for which is *adama*.[11] In the biblical account, as with Hesiod's narrative of Prometheus's trickery, the advent of sin condemns humankind to a life of agricultural toil. In each of these myths, being human involves coming to terms with the laborious task of food production, and, in this sense, the question of food is a religious one. The consumption of food is a rich element of religious cultures and serves as a powerful way to situate human beings with respect to one another and to the natural world. Because it is not within the capacity of this chapter to offer a comprehensive view of what and how all of the world's cultures have eaten, a short survey of food-related rituals explores the relationships among nature, food, and religion.

Even where it evokes the link between people and nature, food also serves as a key signal of important moments of everyday life and as a means of reflecting and justifying the social order. The central place of food in ritual culture is readily evident in ancient Greece and Rome, where food guaranteed (or not) the biological survival of all, and in a social sense marked the life cycle of nearly all, the rituals of birth, marriage and death. Foods also marked the religious year and the calendar in public and private feasting which often included all citizens, and sometimes slaves. . . . [Such] meals revealed status or the lack of it, and were rarely if ever occasions where a person simply refueled in a socially neutral way.[12]

The foodstuffs consumed in ritualized meals, as well as the spatial arrangement of the act of eating itself, are directly associated with social hierarchy. Farmers and other laborers need more calories to meet the rigorous demands of their work, but they lack the social and economic capital necessary for the production of elaborately prepared dishes, especially meats. In the Hellenistic world, grains, especially barley and wheat, constituted the bulk of the peasant diet. For the large class of people who were neither farmers nor landed aristocracy, who had kitchens built into their living spaces, food was procured through purchase at street stalls and marketplaces. Thus the consumptive patterns of individual craftsmen, artisans, or merchants actively demonstrated their purchasing power, their place in the social hierarchy.

Most meals take place in private spaces, reflecting the order within the home and the class status of its various residents (masters, hired cooks, slaves, etc.), but some meals, especially religious feasts, take place in public spaces. The public consumption of food can carry powerful religious and symbolic messages. For instance, the infamous practice of "bread and circuses" ritually demonstrated the sovereignty of the emperor. Likewise, the feast purchased and prepared for a wedding served to locate the nuptial families amid the complex strata of society. The breakfast feast of a prominent Macedonian marriage in 300 BCE included "chickens, ducks, pigeons, a goose and a vast amount of such things all heaped up" served on gold plates, "after which followed a second silver plate on which again there was a great loaf, geese, hares, young goats, other elaborate breads, woodpigeons, doves, partridges, and a great number of other fowls."[13] Such a sumptuous meal made tangible the power and wealth of the newly joined families.

In ancient Rome, marriage rituals were so closely associated with food and eating that the term for the form of marriage practiced by Roman nobility, *confarreatio*, literally means "sharing of spelt cake." The significant role of food and eating in weddings is widely shared across cultures. In early American culture, much as today, the formal ceremony of marriage is typically followed by "an elegant supper, a cheerful glass, and a convivial song to close the entertainment."[14] In Mesoamerica, Aztec weddings included a rich feast of "tamales, corn, cacao (chocolate), sauces, pulque, turkeys, [and] tobacco" that was ceremoniously arranged around the hearth, the place "where Xiuhtecuhtli (the fire god) lived, ensuring warmth, cooked food, and the vital force of tonally, which emanated throughout the building."[15] The link between food, fertility, and the kitchen is an important symbolic dimension in rituals of consumption. Culinary traditions, especially the shared experience of eating intricately prepared dishes together in groups, are ritually and mythically associated with the order and meaning of social life.

In fact, rituals of eating—sharing the bounties of the harvest and the hunt—are important conduits for social cohesion: "Ancient eating was . . . not mere refueling, it was an affirmation of family, kinship or civic and religious bonds. The spectre of the man who failed to eat with others . . . was a grim reminder of social deviance."[16] The conviviality of the table is but one of the ways that food and agriculture serve as vehicles for social interaction. Food has always been among the most important of traded goods and, at harvest times, serves as a conduit for contact between people of neighboring regions. In ancient Mesopotamia, "various cities had their own calendar of seasonal feasts. . . . There were special calendar days for the delivery of first fruits and the offering of the first dairy products of the year. [These were] recognized both as a religious celebration and as an exchange of products."[17] Slight geographic and ecological differences (e.g., elevation, soil composition, etc.) between proximate cultures often translate into different crops, diets, and foodstuffs. In such situations, food serves as both a means of cultural exchange and as a marker of identity differences.

Food is a visceral and tactile part of daily life, an important marker of identity. In fact, "the experience of eating and smelling the same dishes and aromas which would have been part of life at another stage of history may be the nearest one can come to understanding the texture and pattern of daily life."[18] This is no less true in the modern era. In his study of an Italian-American Catholic festival, Robert Orsi emphasizes the importance of food as a basis for ritual practice; it works to invoke memories and to rekindle community. Orsi argues that the smell, taste, and availability of traditional Italian foods in an Italian-American diaspora community makes possible the observance of a traditional ritual: "A man . . . would be resituated in the moral world of his culture by the smell of sausage sizzling in a pan or tomato sauce simmering."[19] Food, as much as architecture or language, locates ritual practice in its proper place.

The locative power of food is suggestive of another way in which ritual meals link religion and nature. Food-based rituals locate communities in time. For instance, the Jewish Sabbath meal provides a ritual context in which to reflect on God's creation. As a performative enactment, the Sabbath "places the Creator himself in the rhythm of his work. While labors simply end . . . production is eventually concluded, completed, and ceremoniously interrupted. Interruption and completion join together in the biblical Shabbat and structure of everyday life about the Sabbath commandment."[20] In contemporary religious culture, the relationship between food and the natural environment has become the explicit focus of some ritual activities. In Sarah McFarland Taylor's study of monastic women with strong ecological commitments,

food as symbol, metaphor, and literal life-sustaining substance serves as an entryway into the matrix of issues to which the green sisters have become attentive: the health of ecosystems and the effects of toxins on the well-being of creation, world hunger, ecoracism, environmental justice, spiritual renewal, "simple living," reinterpretations of religious tradition, cultural transformation, and new ways of defining religious community.[21]

The green sisters' ritualization of eating focuses attention on—and provides a religious context for—engagements with the environmental

CULTURAL ECOLOGY, RITUAL, AND AGRICULTURE

Roy Rappaport's work on the ritual economy of the Tsembaga in New Guinea is one of the most well-known scholarly works on the relationship of food rituals to religion and nature. Rappaport's methodological approach, called cultural ecology, attempts to understand ritual practices as part of an ecological system. In other words, Rappaport (in works such as *Pigs for the Ancestors* and *Religion, Meaning and Ecology*) describes the environmental contexts and impacts of religious activities. This perspective is not designed to reduce rituals to their ecological functions; rather, cultural ecology understands human practices, both intentional and unintentional, as but another animal behavior within an ecosystem. Rappaport's central argument—the thesis for which he is well known—concerns the way that religious rituals sometimes serve as ecological regulatory mechanisms. This insight is based on decades of research on Polynesian and Oceanic tribes inhabiting isolated island environments. Rappaport describes these as

terrestrial ecosystems . . . which may be designated as "anthropocentric." In such communities, both the presence of the main biotic elements, particularly the primary producers, and the decisive relationships among them depended upon the ecological niches that human beings had arranged for themselves according to their criteria of self-interest.[22]

Human beings are among the most powerful participants in their ecosystems. Even though their ability to control their environment is not absolute, humans labor to affect and ethical dimensions of food and agriculture. A variety of practices, including fasting in solidarity with the hungry, establishing dietary guidelines for religious orders, growing and preparing important foods, such as the Eucharist or sacramental wine, all serve as ritual evocations of the fundamental link between food and nature.

ENVIRONMENTS OF DAILY LIFE: COSMOS, CLIMATE, AND ECOSYSTEM

In contemporary parlance, nature and environment have become virtually synonymous: they are both frequently used to indicate the materials and creatures, patterns and processes, among which human beings find themselves. Nature or environment establishes the contexts for daily life, in that certain given phenomena—such as climate, vegetation, or landscape—provide a background against which the orderliness of human life takes place. For instance, the cycle of the seasons, the variation of the weather from day to day, and the presence of geographic features such as mountains or deserts play integral roles in the way that different cultures think about and comport themselves toward the world

nature in ways that are beneficial to them. When ecosystems become less conducive to human flourishing, people attempt corrective action. Rappaport focuses on "the ritual cycles of the Tsembaga, and of other local territorial groups of Maring speakers living in the New Guinea interior, [which] play an important role in regulating the relationships of these groups with . . . the nonhuman components of their immediate environments."[23] A chief example of this ritual environmental regulation concerns the Tsembaga science of pig husbandry. There is a definite limit to how many pigs a given tribal territory can support, as well as a limit to how many pigs an individual family can feed (in Tsembaga society, each married woman cares for as many as four pigs). Pigs are allowed to forage for food, and thus overpopulation makes it increasingly difficult to prevent pigs from damaging the taro and cassava gardens that comprise the staple source of food for the Tsembaga. Rappaport describes how

> the *kaiko* or pig festival . . . is thus triggered by either the additional work attendant upon feeding pigs or the destructive capacity of the pigs themselves. It may be said, then, that there are sufficient pigs to stage the *kaiko* when the relationship of pigs to people changes from one of mutualism to one of parasitism or competition.[24]

In the *kaiko* festival, we have a particularly lucid example about how the production and consumption of food take shape ritually within a particular environmental context. The ecological function of the festival is implicit; for the Tsembaga, the festival is chiefly about building alliances with neighboring tribes. However, Rappaport's analysis demonstrates how human societies ritualize their relationship with the natural world in the context of agriculture and husbandry.

around them. This relationship between nature and religious life should be obvious to the astute cultural observer: religions are often, if not always, predicated on a cosmological system, the attribution and explanation of the order evident in the world system as a whole. The quest to find order in nature is the foundation of cosmology, and thus religion is a key conduit for social and cultural ideas about nature. As Yi-Fu Tuan puts it, "In nontechnological societies the physical setting is the canopy of nature and its myriad contents. Like the means of livelihood, worldview reflects the rhythms and constraints of the natural environment."[25] Although they do not entirely presume the cosmological order, natural features as readily apparent as the monsoon season or a horizon dominated by snow-capped mountains necessarily play important symbolic and material roles across cultures. This section considers a variety of ways that daily life has been structured around religious responses to elemental natural phenomena such as climate and ecosystem.

Perhaps no one natural force has as profound an effect on human livelihoods as climate. The annual cycle of the seasons, although it takes very different forms at different latitudes, requires social collectivities to prepare and adjust to changing weather patterns and adapt to climatic contingencies. Around the globe, agricultural societies are replete with tactics to sow seeds and harvest crops at the most opportune time. Both lunar and solar calendars, often administered by religious officials, are used to coordinate and ritualize agricultural practices.

It is worth noting that the division of the year into four seasons is particular to the temperate northern latitudes. Tropical and subtropical cultures often conceptualize the seasonal cycle as having either two or three phases. Moreover, the social modalities for experiencing the seasons do not necessarily correspond with the chronological and meteorological emphases that dominate contemporary Western culture. For example,

> The Nuer, a cattle-herding people of southern Sudan . . . divide the year into two seasons corresponding only approximately to a season of rain, during which they live in villages, and a dry season, spent in camps by streams and lakes . . . The Nuer do not refer to these divisions as periods of time but rather as predominant social activities.[26]

This is a clear example of how environmental patterns—in this case, seasons—shape the practices that constitute daily life. The force exerted by the natural rhythm of the seasons, however, ought not be taken to suggest that meteorological forces dictate social behaviors. Instead, different climates present human collectivities with adaptive challenges, and, in turn, social responses to these challenges often ritualize the natural environment.

The ritualization of weather patterns—that is, the incorporation of climate into the fabric of daily life—is readily evident in religious practices that have been designed to encourage particular kinds of weather, especially rain. Popular culture is laden with images of rain dances practiced by non-Western peoples, and, in fact, many cultures attempt to influence the timing and amount of seasonal rainfalls through a variety of ritual techniques, including dance. Such rituals are of great importance for societies that are dependent on agriculture, husbandry, or seasonally variable gathering. This means that rituals aimed at influencing the weather are practiced around the globe—by the ancient Greeks, modern Romanians, the Zuni of New Mexico, and many other Native American cultures. It is not unreasonable to suggest that Groundhog Day is a pop-culture instantiation of a weather-related ritual, in which Punxsutawney Phil is charged with providing critical climatic information to the public.

For societies that are more immediately dependent on propitious rains, weather-related rituals are crucial to public life, giving voice to the fundamental link between the order of nature and the collective well-being. For the Nuba of Sudan, near neighbors of the Nuer, the rainmaker is a publicly elected official who is entrusted by the community to execute his religious duties faithfully: "Though the rain ceremonial is executed in the privacy of the priest's house and by him and his kin alone, the whole community takes cognizance of it and may even have to take steps to insure an adequate performance."[27] In this example, the ritual obligations necessary to ensure the necessary rainfall are given over to one family, perhaps so that, if the rains should fail, blame can be placed on an individual.[28]

The idea that interruptions in the ordinary patterns of nature—the failure of the rains,

An abandoned village in the Nuba Mountains of Sudan. Long-standing land disputes between Arabs and native farmers in the western region of Darfur have forced the Nuba people into the hilltops, away from the fertile land at the base of the hills. Ethnic conflict, which has defined Sudan since its independence in 1956, erupted into full-scale violence in 2003.

LANDSCAPE AND WORLDVIEW

A classic example of the impact of landscapes on religious systems is evident in the comparison of ancient Egyptian and Mesopotamian worldviews. At opposite ends of the Fertile Crescent, both cultures flourished in desert environments and developed successful agricultural economies and complex cosmological systems. Although both Egypt and Mesopotamia were built on riverine ecosystems, the "dissimilar experiences of nature" of the two cultures help account for their divergent religious perspectives.[29]

The Nile River is the lifeblood of Egypt. Its predictable annual cycle of flooding brings with it both fresh topsoil and ample opportunities for irrigated farming. Egyptian civilization emerged from an ecological context that was dominated by the relentless heat of the desert sun and the fecundity of the yearly floods. In fact, these two forces are personified in Egyptian mythology as *Ra*, the Sun god, and *Hapi*, the god of the river and fertility. The rhythms of ancient Egyptian cosmology were based on the daily cycles of the movement of the Sun and the yearly cycles of the Nile; the pantheon of Egyptian deities was, in effect, a sacred bureaucracy. The northward flow of the Nile grounded Egyptian spatiality. "South" was associated with the source of life and "north" with the downstream flow toward death; moreover, the shape of the cosmos resembled the Nile Valley, an elongated platter, with rims along its edges and overarched by a domed sky.

Strikingly, the Nile ecosystem also structured the political order of ancient Egypt. In the political conquests between the Lower and Upper Egyptian kingdoms, Lower Egypt was associated with the Sun and Upper Egypt with the flooding river. In both regions, the social and economic coordination necessary for an expansive system of irrigation gave rise to a strictly hierarchical political order. The structure of the pyramids makes clear how closely political unity and cosmological order were fused for the ancient Egyptians. Pharaohs were divine kings, gods on Earth, who, supported by the base of farmers and laborers, maintained a theologically centralized system of governance. This earthly order was reflective of a technocratic cosmology; gods, like the pharaoh's administrators, were allotted specific offices over which they had sole authority.

In contrast to Egypt, ancient Mesopotamian civilization emerged in an ecological context quite different than that of the Nile River valley—one where

> the climate of Egypt is truly arid; that of Mesopotamia is less stringent from the viewpoint of the farmer. . . . In the upper portion [of the Mesopotamian plain], rain suffices for agriculture without irrigation. The special blessing of the Nile is its

dependability. The Tigris and the Euphrates, by contrast, have far less predictable regimes.[30]

From the unpredictability of rainfall and flood events, residents of the Mesopotamian plain extrapolated a much more chaotic cosmic order. Internecine strife among the gods was common, and the results of their divine power struggles were reflected in the unruliness of the natural world—floods, storms, droughts, and so on.

Mesopotamian cosmology describes the world as emerging from a confusion of waters—fresh waters, seas, and mist. From a marriage of the fresh waters (*Apsu*) and the sea (*Ti'amat*) was born silt, the first land, which slowly grew up and formed the Earth. Three gods ruled over this primordial world: *An*, the god of heaven; *Enlil*, the god of air; and *Ninhursag*, the Earth goddess. Gradually, *Enlil* consolidated power and became chief among the Mesopotamian gods, carrying out their collective will. *Enlil* was known to lash out in anger against human beings. Endowed with the authority of a divine magistrate, human wickedness was punishable by storms and earthquakes; charged with overseeing the growth of civilization, *Enlil* was also a beneficent creator figure. Mesopotamian myth is rich with political intrigue and gods both kind and cruel, reflecting an unstable social, political, and natural environment. Mesopotamian society was not as centralized or rigidly hierarchical as Egypt; rather, it was more a federation of competing and cooperating city-states than a unified empire. Ecological geography is an important factor in accounting for this difference.

The navigability, linear orientation, and regularity of the Nile River—not to mention the wide buffer of extreme desert on either bank—are environmental features that were amenable to political centralization. The meandering courses, variegated landscapes, and unpredictability of the Tigris and Euphrates Rivers made such centralization difficult. Such basic differences in climate and landscape had profound impacts on the development of the two civilizations and account for some of the differences between the two cultures with respect to agriculture, cosmology, ritual activity, and political order. In short, the ecological differences between ancient Egypt and Mesopotamia exerted a strong influence on the daily lives of their inhabitants. It would be too deterministic, however, to assert that Egyptian and Mesopotamian ideas about nature and cosmology directly produced the political structures of these cultures. It is more reasonable to assert that these "political system[s] evolved *pari passu* with the ideas on the governing of the cosmos."[31]

earthquakes, unseasonable frosts, and so on—can be blamed on particular parties is common. Many cultures have developed a sense of "moral meteorology," the view that dramatic weather events or other natural disasters are direct responses to societal patterns of behavior. For instance, among the tribal cultures of Southeast Asia, there is a widespread belief that "violent perturbations in the realm of nature reflect weaknesses of state rulers and portend their downfall."[32] Blame is often also accorded to behavioral tendencies of whole peoples; the Hebrew Scriptures are rife with meteorological enactments of God's judgment. For instance, the book of Hosea prophesies an "east wind" of drought and ruination as punishment for Israel's idolatrous behavior (Hosea 13:15). Speculation about the causes of environmental calamities, however, is hardly limited to ancient times and premodern cultures. Internet chat rooms hosted intense debates about the moral causes of the 2005 Indian Ocean tsunami: because it occurred the day after Christmas, some Christians surmised that the tsunami was retribution for the ungodly behaviors of Western tourists on holiday; because it occurred in a region of considerable political fragility and complexity, many southern Asians wondered about the relationship between religion and state authority in nations such as Sri Lanka and Indonesia. A similar kind of "moral meteorology" developed around Hurricane Katrina, with the prominent televangelist John Hagee claiming that the hurricane was God's power come to bear against homosexuality in the United States. In these and other religious contexts, the social and ecological landscapes are often understood as interpenetrating one another: weather is caused by social behaviors, and likewise, weather also prompts particular cultural practices.

Conclusion: Religion and Environmentalism

To this point, this chapter has explored the environmental contexts for religious traditions across a selection of the world's many cultures. The analytical focus of this exploration has looked to social practices that respond to natural phenomena such as the bodily necessity of food and the influence of climate and landscape on human communities. In each case where religious life and the natural world come to bear on each other, there has been a careful analysis of "deterministic" and "constructivist" modes of description. The result is a wide range of examples of how different cultures negotiate their natural contexts, actively responding to their environments through the practice of everyday life. For many historical cultures and small-scale societies, religious and ritual responses to nature are "only natural"; that is, such practices would have been conceptualized as everyday, commonplace, and in response to a natural world that always had and always would be there. Increasing concerns about the impacts of industrial civilization on the health of ecosystems worldwide during the past half century have prompted a new kind of ritual engagement with the natural world: religious environmental activism.

Aware that religious practices are both responses to and actions toward the world around them, practitioners and adherents from numerous traditions have called for rituals that are more directly aimed at addressing environmental issues. Although religious responses to the environmental problems facing human communities are too numerous to describe in detail here, a brief account of the greening of religious traditions adds to our understanding of the relationship between religion and nature. At least since the 1980s, religious institutions have taken an active role in shaping national and international conversations about and policies toward environmental issues. Participants in the 1993 Parliament of World Religions jointly issued a statement on "Global Ethics on Cooperation of Religions on Human and Environmental Issues," a document that articulates the common resolve of religious organizations to take initiative on solving environmental problems.[33] For many faith communities, this declaration signals the promise of religion in tackling environmental issues, "because religions help to shape our attitudes towards nature in both conscious and unconscious ways."[34] The depth and breadth of religious traditions offer profound resources for reshaping environmental values.

Beyond the scriptural and theological possibilities that religions portend for newer, more popular directions in environmental ethics lie a variety of practical matters. As a basic constituent of daily life, religion sets the context for everyday practices. The implications of religious praxis for ecology are evident in the dietary practices of "green nuns" or the agricultural practices of New Guinea's Tsembaga people. And, in recent years, green ritual practices have become much more common. Many churches, synagogues, and mosques across the United States have taken substantial measures to reduce their energy consumption and employ environmentally friendly technologies. Many of these congregations also regularly hold services focused on environmental issues.

For example, in the United States, a group in the Pacific Northwest, called Earth Ministry, has organized hundreds of ecologically themed worship services in dozens of communities. Earth Ministry's worship typically resembles traditional Sunday morning services, but with a liturgical focus that calls participants to be thoughtful about creation and their role in it. Earth Ministry, like many other groups of religious environmental activists in the United States, also regularly holds retreats, vigils, and seminars—all structured loosely around ritual—aimed at raising environmental awareness. Such practices can also be found in US Judaism. On April 8, 2009, Jewish communities in the United States and around the world worshiped in celebration of *Birkat Hachama*, a day when the Sun returns to its original position from the moment of creation. Conjoining recognition of the completion of the full cycle of the Jewish solar calendar with a celebration of God's creation, *Birkat Hachama* exemplifies how religious communities are coupling their ritual traditions with ecological awareness. Similarly, many Christian churches are attentive to the relationship between the liturgical calendar and the changing of the seasons; in both its ecological and theological significance, Easter service most clearly presents worship communities with an opportunity to reflect on renewal.

There are differences between religious and more secular forms of environmentalism; the interpretive frameworks and ethical underpinnings can be so different that many religious groups refuse to call their practices environmentalism, preferring instead the terms "creation care" or "stewardship." Nonetheless, the rich resources available to religious persons and communities have given rise to a host of green beliefs and practices. The close connection between religious traditions and the natural world—in domains such as agriculture, food, climate, and landscape—grounds a burgeoning interest in using religion as a way to tackle the world's environmental challenges.

FOR FURTHER READING

Bottero, Jean. "The Most Ancient Recipes of All." In *Patterns of Daily Life*, edited by David Waines. London: Ashgate, 2002.

Brumlik, Micha. "Humankind's Relationship with Nature and Participation in the Process of Creation through Technology in the view of Judaism." In *Nature and Technology in World Religions*, edited by Peter Kozlowski. New York: Springer, 2001.

Carrasco, David, and Scott Sessions. *Daily Life of the Aztecs.* Westport, CT: Greenwood, 1998.

Dove, Michael R., and Carol Carpenter. "Introduction: Major Historical Currents in Environmental Anthropology." In *Environmental Anthropology: A Historical Reader*, edited by Michael R. Dove and Carol Carpenter. Oxford: Blackwell, 2008.

Elkin, A. P. "The Nature of Australian Totemism." In *Gods and Rituals*, edited by John Middleton. New York: Natural History Press, 1967.

Formigari, Lia. "Great Chain of Being." In *The History of Ideas*, edited by Philip P. Wiener. Vol. 1. New York: Charles Scribner's Sons, 1974.

Freilich, Morris. "Ecology and Culture: Environmental Determinism and the Ecological Approach in Anthropology." *Anthropological Quarterly* 40, no. 1 (January 1967): 26–43.

Gill, Sam D. *Beyond the Primitive: The Religions of Nonliterate Peoples.* Englewood Cliffs, NJ: Prentice-Hall, 1982.

Glacken, Clarence J. *Traces on the Rhodian Shore: Nature and Culture in Western Thought from Ancient Times to the End of the Eighteenth Century.* Berkeley: University of California Press, 1967.

Haq, S. Nomanul. "Islam and Ecology: Toward Retrieval and Reconstruction." *Daedalus* 130, no. 4 (Fall 2001): 141–78.

Hiebert, Theodore. *The Yahwist's Landscape: Nature and Religion in Early Israel.* Oxford: Oxford University Press, 1996.

Lovejoy, Arthur. *The Great Chain of Being.* Cambridge, MA: Harvard University Press, 1982.

Miller, James. "Daoism and Ecology." *Earth Ethics* 10, no. 1 (Fall 1998).

Nadel, S. F. "Two Nuba Religions: An Essay in Comparison." *The American Anthropologist* 57, no. 4 (December 1955): 661–79.

Nash, Linda. "The Agency of Nature or the Nature of Agency." *Environmental History* 10, no. 1 (January 2005): 67–69.

Nasr, Seyyed Hossein. *Religion and the Order of Nature.* Oxford: Oxford University Press, 1996.

Nemet-Nejat, Karen Rhea. *Daily Life in Ancient Mesopotamia.* Westport, CT: Greenwood, 1998.

Orsi, Robert. *The Madonna of 115th Street: Faith and Community in Italian Harlem, 1880–1950.* New Haven, CT: Yale University Press, 1985.

Rappaport, Roy A. *Ecology, Meaning, and Religion.* Berkeley, CA: North Atlantic Books, 1979.

Steward, Julian. *Theory of Culture Change: The Methodology of Multilinear Evolution.* Urbana: University of Illinois Press, 1955.

Taylor, Bron. *Dark Green Religion: Nature Spirituality and the Planetary Future.* Berkeley: University of California Press, 2009.

Taylor, Sarah McFarland. *Green Sisters: A Spiritual Ecology.* Cambridge, MA: Harvard University Press, 2007.

Tuan, Yi-Fu. *Topophilia: A Study of Environmental Perception, Attitudes, and Values.* Englewood Cliffs, NJ: Prentice-Hall, 1974.

Tucker, Mary Evelyn, and John Grim. "The Emerging Alliance of World Religions and Ecology." *Daedalus* 130, no. 4 (Fall 2001).

———. "Series Forward," *Christianity and Ecology.* Cambridge, MA: Harvard University Press, 2000.

White, Lynn, Jr. "The Historical Roots of Our Ecologic Crisis." *Science* 155 (10 March 1967).

Wilkins, John M., and Shaun Hill. *Food in the Ancient World.* Oxford: Blackwell, 2006.

Worster, Donald. *Nature's Economy.* Cambridge: Cambridge University Press, 1994.

9

TOURISM

Alex Norman

The practice of religion has a long association with travel. From small-scale rites of passage that involve some sort of physical journey to pilgrimages involving the movement of millions of people, the idea that long distance or long-term travel away from home can transform permeates many cultures. However, advances in travel technologies and changes to class and cultural systems have resulted in the experience of travel being available to many more people than ever before. Many locations previously visited chiefly by travelers participating within the religious traditions they supported now see tourists from all around the world. Not all of these tourists travel for religious reasons, even if they are informed by cultural notions that favor travel as an opportunity for change. Nonetheless, religious tourism has been one of the least studied areas in research on tourism. How these tourists conceive of their journeys and how they place them in their lives reveals the extent to which travel can be seen as a metaphor, and sometimes a surrogate, for religious practice.

OVERVIEW

When people travel today, it may be for a variety of reasons. One may travel for business, to see relatives, to relax, to get away from work, to go and see a particular city or region, or simply to travel for travel's sake. It is also worth noting that people may travel for war, for political gain, or for religious reasons, whether they are foundational to their beliefs or not. In most cases, people travel for a combination of these motives. That travel can function so diversely as a human behavior should begin to suggest to us what a rich and varied field it can be. The shelves of the world's libraries are packed with accounts of discovery, conquest, and self-transformation, not to mention imperialism, destruction, and exploitation, which take place within the context of travel to foreign lands. However, for the purposes of this chapter, we concentrate on the intersection of tourism and religion today, which requires some clarification.

Tourism is defined as voluntary, leisured travel.[1] Tourists are thus people who travel temporarily away from their home, typically for longer than twenty-four hours, for purposes other than work. It is thus distinguished from business travel (and war) by the extent to which it occurs as a leisure activity or during nonwork time. In general, tourism is associated with holidays or vacation time, when people have large blocks of free days during which a journey can be undertaken. Often the word *tourism* (and *tourist*) is used in a pejorative sense—to refer to a lesser type of traveler. These types of definitions see tourism simply as "mindless sightseeing and shopping" or an association that may have come about through the type of travel championed by early industrial tourist agents, such as Thomas Cook.[2] Some theorists, such as Dean MacCannell, have argued that tourism is indeed simply a mode of sightseeing, although he associates it also with a search for "experience."[3] Others have taken a dimmer view, describing tourists as "the barbarians of our Age of Leisure."[4] However, both these interpretations miss the crucial point of tourism and the reason for its astounding prevalence throughout the world—the reasons people choose to travel are many and complex and are woven into individual journeys as they fit.

It is also worth noting here that if tourism is leisured travel, this must also mean that pilgrimage is a form of tourism, because it too tends to occur outside work life. Pilgrimage was initially understood as travel that took place within the institutional bounds of a religious tradition. However, scholars have recently abandoned this empirically problematic position in favor of one that understands pilgrimage and tourism to be closely related, even indistinguishable.[5] Indeed, one of the most-often cited pronouncements on this topic is Victor and Edith Turner's statement that "a tourist is half a pilgrim, if a pilgrim is half a tourist."[6] To further confuse things, recent studies have shown that people also make pilgrimages for nonreligious reasons.[7] Thus the boundaries between pilgrimage and forms of tourism cannot always be distinguished. Preston argued that the key to understanding pilgrimage is the "circulation of people, ideas, symbols, experiences, and cash"[8] that should be our primary focus in documentation. However, tourists often have similar patterns of circulation as pilgrims—and for comparable reasons. Given this, journeys toward some form of ideal that are labeled "pilgrimage," often without specifically religious motivations on the part of the traveler, look decreasingly like necessarily religious activity. As a result, we must question whether some forms of modern tourism and pilgrimage are not simply the same behavior under different labels. A possible avenue forward may be concentrating on reflexive use of the words by travelers—understanding pilgrims as those who identify themselves as such and attempting to work out what that means.

As a result, we may assume that tourism is able to be religiously significant; pilgrimage is simply a form of it, although equally without the necessary involvement of religious traditions. Tourism could be said to be a quasi-religious practice that enables the tourist to gain experiences not offered at home, and we are forced to ask whether it is an equivalent to religious practice. However, this neglects the experiences of tourists who simply want to laze on a beach for a week—not an activity usually associated with religious practice. Holiday brochures sell locations where "nothing" is the most appealing aspect. Here one can relax and let the worries of life wash away in the briny sea. But even this begins to sound quasi-religious. The transformation from stressed to relaxed sounds very much like a ritual transformation from unclean to clean, from profane to sacred. Indeed, it is this multidimensional capability of tourism as recreation and re-creation that tourists fill with their own systems of meaning, which is of interest in the study of religious practice.

Tourism can also be a consumptive and a pleasurable activity, both of which are driving forces in the Western cultural milieu. It is also a sign of wealth and is associated with an abundance of free time. By participating in touristic activities, people are embodying those ideals. In addition, sociocultural currents emerging from the Reformation, such as secularization and an emphasis on individual personal authority, have brought about changes to the ways people in the West construct their personal lives in terms of meaning and identity. These trends have resulted in a reduction in the influence of institutional religious traditions upon people's daily lives and an increased emphasis on individualized construction of religio-spiritual practices. Combined with the notion of tourism as a mode of re-creation and as a search for meaning and experience, this means we can assume that tourism is used by some people as part of their own personal religious practice. How and why this is done is the purpose of this chapter. Further, how people are incorporating such travel into their everyday lives presents an opportunity to look at how religious ideas and practices are conceived in Western society. Insofar as tourism is a mode of consumption and a means of self-exploration, it is logical to assume that it reflects the everyday in some way. In the case of tourism and religion, where tourists view and participate in religious practices, it implies that religious practice can be a commodity.

Returning to the issue of definitions, because the term "tourism" is understood to refer to such a complex subject, it attracts varying definitions, depending on the perspective it is being viewed from. The term *tour* originates from a Greek word describing a tool to make a circle.[9] Many scholars disagree, arguing that the words *tourist* and *tourism*, as we know them now, originated with the Grand Tour, to indicate travel for pleasure or education.[10] Piers Brendon states that the word *tourism* was coined in 1811 to convey the idea of a circular journey, because it had gentler connotations than the word *travel*, which stems from *travail*—meaning "to work."[11] Whatever the case, *tourism* entered the English language in the early nineteenth century, to mean the act of making a tour for pleasure. By looking at a history of leisure travel, we can get an idea of what tourism has evolved into.

HISTORY

The history of tourism has suffered from a lack of critical and multidisciplinary examinations. However, conceiving of tourism as new is mistaken. The word has taken on a negative connotation in popular culture, yet the notion of an earlier age of "perfected" travelers who considered art rather than gazed at it, who were cultural representatives rather than cultural consumers, is not new. William Wordsworth expressed his

---

TRAVEL AND LEARNING

Travel has long been considered a unique and focused practice for learning. In his book *Voyage of Italy*, Richard Lassels writes, "For the first, towit the Profit of Travelling, its certain, that if this world be a great booke, as St. Augustin calls it, none studdy this great Booke so much as the Traveller" (1670, a iij). However, there was a paradox, as Pliny noted in the first century CE, "We travel long roads and cross the water to see what we disregard when it is under our own eyes."

annoyance with the "admiring hordes" visiting him in the 1830s. Similarly, Edward Gibbon remarked on the overcrowding of Switzerland in 1784.[12] Indeed, tourism is older than is popularly realized. Richardson suggests that Herodotus, the "father of history," may also be considered the father of tourism. From 464 to 447 BCE, he visited many of the Greek islands, Persia, the Black Sea, and Egypt, writing accounts of his travels, detailing the land and customs of the places he visited, including what we can interpret as a thriving tourist industry. Likewise, in the writings of Strabo and Plutarch, we see evidence of such obvious tourist indicators as tour guides and even evidence in the form of shows put on for tourists—a type of social activity that Dean MacCannell would describe as "staged authenticity"—some two thousand years later.[13]

We could consider the *Epic of Gilgamesh* the first work of Western travel literature;[14] however, the travails of poor Gilgamesh do not a tourist make. As evidenced by writings of Strabo and Plutarch, there is very good proof of a thriving tourist industry in the ancient Mediterranean. During the reign of the Roman emperor Augustus, travel and tourism became important cultural features of Roman society. As Augustan Rome became more and more oriented toward leisure, tourism became a more social and cultural feature.[15] So developed was this industry that there is even evidence of an Augustan "Grand Tour," of sorts that typically included Delphi, Athens, Corinth, Olympia, Sparta, Rhodes, and "Troy" or "Homer's country." Tourists to this latter site were assisted by professional guides, who showed them various "locations" featured in the Iliad. After soaking up the literary and visual delights of Asia Minor, these peregrinators[16] then moved on to Egypt, where many of the sites that they visited still feature on contemporary tourist itineraries. At all of these locations, souvenirs were available, and

artists were ready at hand to sketch a portrait of the happy tourist in front of some important monument.[17] Rome itself was a tourist destination for non-Romans, with such attractions as the Coliseum, the Roman baths, and the legendary sites associated with the founders of the city—Romulus and Remus. Tourists were also interested in "new Rome" and its impressive monuments.[18] Indeed, Maxine Feifer argues that imperial Rome was the first culture to produce mass tourism.[19] During the Pax Romana, tourism flourished around the Mediterranean, although tourist numbers would surely be but a trickle by today's standards.

Despite good evidence to suggest otherwise, most scholars agree that tourism as it is conceived today originates with what has come to be called the Grand Tour. Taking place roughly from the late sixteenth to the early nineteenth century, with its heyday in the eighteenth century, the Grand Tour can be thought of as a "finishing school," an essential part of a gentleman's education, giving invaluable experience of the world. For the traveler, it was a rite of passage, but also a way to escape parents, studies, and the inevitable duties of life. The term itself was first used in this context by Richard Lassels in *Voyage to Italy*.[20] Most Grand Tourism was a search of high culture, and many Grand Tourists sought out prominent figures, particularly philosophers, to engage in conversation and debate. James Boswell, for example, managed to meet with both Rousseau and Voltaire on a number of occasions.[21] However, such travel was also an occasion to become accustomed to the etiquette and politics of court life, and many were sent by their families specifically to attend a European royal court and acquire social skills.

Rome was the most important destination for most Grand Tourists. Education beyond the rudimentary meant the classics, and educated men were expected to know Latin and Greek.

Rome was therefore considered the source of Western civilization. However, Jeremy Black notes that locations such as Hannover, Dresden, Prague, and Vienna were popular with aristocratic tourists and those seeking patronage.[22] Further, the influence of Italy's lure for the senses should not be forgotten. The land, climate, and cultures of the Mediterranean featured large for northern Europeans (and still do) looking for respite from both cold winters and social conventions.[23] Indeed, the young James Boswell's mentor, Samuel Johnson, remarked that "a man who has not been in Italy is always conscious of an inferiority, from his not having seen what it is expected a man should see."[24]

Despite the natural world being feared and despised by most Grand Tourists, in favor of the order and symmetry of cities, by 1800, the natural assets of countries such as Switzerland were being extolled by Romantic writers, and appreciation of nature began to become a pastime. However, there was a problem. In the ever-growing cities, the pursuit of this pastime required long journeys in order to be done properly; something that was simply out of reach of most people. Prior to the advent of steam power, travel was slow, expensive, and often quite dangerous. The eighteenth and nineteenth centuries saw marked improvements in travel technology and infrastructure. Roads, stagecoach routes, and regular sailing ship services were all expanded. However, steam power brought the greatest change. Prior to its advent, horse and wind power were the main means of long-distance transport. In this mode, people were essentially traveling at the same speeds as the likes of Herodotus and Marco Polo. In 1839, when railways reached Rugby, Thomas Arnold rejoiced that "feudality is gone forever."[25] The journey from London to Edinburgh, a trip of two weeks in 1800, now took only a day. By 1872, the railway from London to Rome went through Paris, Munich, Innsbruck, and the Brenner Pass, taking over three days—a journey that had previously taken weeks by coach.

Despite the rapid technological advances of the early nineteenth century, it was not until Thomas Cook saw in railways the potential for tourism as it is recognized today that they were fully realized. A printer by trade with a passion for the temperance movement, Cook believed that alcohol was the root of most of the evils afflicting Victorian society. His vision was to promote temperance through more "wholesome" recreation than the alehouse, and, after happening upon the idea to conduct a day excursion to this end, Cook began what can arguably be described as the modern tourism industry. The first excursion organized by Cook, for which he drew no personal income, was made on behalf of the Leicester Temperance Society.[26] Cook's first commercial tour was to Liverpool, with a side trip to Snowdon and Caernarvon, in 1845. Like his previous ventures with the temperance societies, this was a success—with both first and second class selling out and even being resold on the black market.[27] Over the next sixteen years, Cook took thousands of tourists to Scotland, and by 1872, Cook was conducting round-the-world tours. More than a political and social force, railways were, as Cook realized, an opportunity for novelty and excitement on a scale and level of accessibility not seen or even envisaged before. They became a fashion of the time—a frenzy even. Thus Cook's real achievement was to capture the technology and spirit of the day. Out of this, he created a global empire of travel that became so popular that "Cook's tours" became a byword for any loosely organized sightseeing trip.

Technological development continued into the new century with the development of the internal combustion engine. The industrial bourgeoisie created by steam power not only wanted to see what had previously been the reserve of aristocracy, but the incredible productive powers that they had harnessed also meant they needed to travel to broaden their markets and establish new ones. The motorcar industry boomed, particularly after World War I, with a massive increase in demand for motorized passenger transport systems. After World War I, industries catering for war tourists begin to emerge.[28] However, the major tourism development of the interwar years was the emergence of the airplane as a form of mass transport. In 1933, the Boeing 247, the first commercial airliner, entered service, and in 1936, American Airlines introduced the DC-3, an aircraft that was to solidify the place of aviation as a viable form of mass transportation. The 1930s also saw Europeans, in particular, begin to understand paid vacations as a right that was bound up with the notion of living standards, a sentiment that accelerated after World War II.[29] Further, World War II spelled the end for the crumbling aristocracies and indifferent plutocracies of Europe. The increased stability and prosperity that came after World War II, especially in the United States, was accompanied by increases in leisure time. A growing desire to see the places that new technologies were making it easy to get to also increased tourist numbers. Rapid expansion of tourist wholesalers, in the style of Thomas Cook Ltd., and the mass marketing of the package tour came alongside the development of the hotel chain. These provided first-time travelers with safe, predictable facilities from which to explore these new worlds.

TRAVEL AND RELIGION AND DAILY LIFE

The history of tourism shows that, in the West, the practice of traveling has become synonymous with change, discovery, and learning, as well as with pleasure and relaxation. It can also be a medium for economic, intellectual, linguistic, scientific, and religious exchange between host and guest. Indeed, these ideas permeate through explicitly religious forms of travel that can be found in pilgrimage traditions, because they too are simply other modes of travel. During the Middle Ages in Europe, a number of instances of mass human movement for religious reasons demonstrated not only the political effectiveness of pilgrimage but the spiritual also. Although locations such as Glastonbury and Rome had drawn travelers for some time, the Crusades—large-scale religio-military expeditions to "the Holy Land" (modern Israel and Palestine)—and, especially, the pilgrimage to Santiago de Compostela introduced the notion that common people could take time out from their everyday lives to travel great distances with the support of the Christian church. Travel to religious sites became a common practice, and, from the end of the fifteenth century onward, it was apparently done as much for the diversion that it offered people as for the religious benefits.[30]

Today, many of the pilgrimages that began in the Middle Ages throughout Europe continue to be significant. Around the world, it is estimated that over 240 million people make pilgrimages every year.[31] For example, the pilgrimage to Santiago de Compostela, usually done on foot and known as the Camino, attracted over 100,000 pilgrims in 2007.[32] Meanwhile, other more recently developed locations, such as Fatima and Lourdes, to which Christian pilgrims go seeking healing from various ailments, see up to 5 million pilgrims and tourists arrive every year.[33] This trend continues throughout the world. In the Middle East, the Hajj—the Muslim pilgrimage to Mecca—attracted over 2.5 million pilgrims in 2008.[34] Similarly, the Maha Kumbh Mela, which occurs every twelve years in India, attracts over 60 million pilgrims, and in Japan the island of Shikoku continues to attract pilgrims to its eighty-eight main temples. It is clear that these pilgrimage sites, along with many more, remain significant drawing cards for millions of travelers around the world.

However, early anthropologists avoided the study of pilgrimage, and it is only in the past forty years that any dedicated examinations of pilgrimage have emerged. Victor Turner was one of the first anthropologists to engage with the topic seriously, and pilgrimage theory continues to be influenced by his work. For Turner, pilgrimage was a ritual process, defined by its spatial liminality in regard to the pilgrim's normal life.[35] That is, the contrast to the pilgrim's everyday experience made it a powerful mode of transformation. Pilgrims are removed from their normal social rules and constraints, "betwixt and between the positions assigned and arrayed by law, custom, convention, and ceremonial."[36] In pilgrimage, this liminal state often forces a "rearrangement" of thoughts and conceptions about the world, precisely because of the contrast it presents.[37] Turner also saw pilgrimage as a rite of passage that replaces rites of puberty in modern societies, especially where it was obligatory rather than voluntary.[38]

In China, mountains have long been places of pilgrimage. Daoist seekers of immortality often chose the high, remote places of China, to be nearer the immortals and to meditate alone.[39] Sacred sites were historically identified as places that were considered *ling* (numinous, efficacious),[40] and, in an originally animistic society, the intrinsic numinosity of the natural world was emphasized on mountaintops—clouds gathered, snow fell, winds blew. Some peaks gained reputations as the homes of certain exalted and powerful deities (*shen*). The objective of going on a pilgrimage to such a place was to get close to and gain from their power.[41] However, no matter the actual reason or complex of reasons,

when pilgrims are asked, the usual explanation given for going on pilgrimage is "to obtain blessings and avert calamities."[42] One pilgrim to the mountain of Tai Shan in 1558 CE wrote of his amazement at what "looked like a large collection of fireflies flickering light from hundreds of boxes. When I asked about it, I was told that what I saw was the train of men and women on their way to pay homage to Yuan-chün."[43] For pilgrims, the journey is understood to be effectual in their daily life, rather than for metaphysical reasons. Pilgrims pray to Yuan-chün for health and prosperity or for more children. Even the merit-making of Buddhist pilgrims, which is nominally to help achieve a better rebirth, also has an element of immanent pragmatism to it. Mountains in particular were chosen as destinations for pilgrimage, specifically because they, and the deities associated with them, are believed to be particularly effective at bringing about change in this world.

In the Indian subcontinent, we see similar motivations at play. In the Sikh tradition, pilgrimage has no institutional purpose but is rather a form of physically embodied prayer. Sikh Scriptures make clear that any form of devotion or asceticism is worthless without meditating on God and working on one's inner self. Nonetheless, many Sikhs still make pilgrimages. Despite normative mandates that essentially speak against pilgrimage, the sheer number of Sikh pilgrims at shrines such as the Golden Temple in Amritsar suggest that more operative issues are at play. Despite institutional arguments against pilgrimage, Sikhs go on pilgrimage to visit their gurus' temples, give thanks for God's blessings, and to pray for continued happiness and health.[44] However, in Hindu traditions, pilgrimage sites are recognized as particularly sacred spaces—because of their connection with particular gurus, the spiritual efficacy of their water, or their location in history.[45] Pilgrimage sites in

Pilgrims climbing the Stairway to Heaven, leading to the Gateway to Heaven Temple atop Mount Tai Shan in Shandong, China. Standing at 1,545 meters above sea level, Tai Shan is the most venerated of China's five sacred Taoist mountains.

Hinduism are thus places of power, and journeying to them is understood to give pilgrims a certain access to that power. Indeed, tourism and religion have a long and unique history in India, with religious motivations being behind up to 95 percent of domestic travel.[46] A visit to bathe in the Ganges River at Varanasi is seen, in particular, as a way to purify the soul. However, as much as these pilgrims look for spiritual renewal when on pilgrimage, they also undertake sightseeing and other leisure activities.

In Europe, we see many of the same ideas of disconnection with one's own world and connection to another. Since the early Middle Ages, pilgrims have walked the routes to Santiago de Compostela, in northwestern Spain, to

gain remission from sins and to visit the tomb of St. James the Apostle, one of the followers of Jesus. However, in addition to this access, Christian pilgrimage in the Middle Ages often had an element of asceticism, allowing pilgrims to imitate, for a time, the life of suffering idealized in Christian culture. It was also a chance to see the world outside the confines of one's local area. Further, for many of these pilgrims, the journey from home to Santiago and back may have taken many months. However, like any pilgrimage, it was a route filled with contesting meanings and discourses, in which religious piety and prayer were contrasted with issues of sightseeing and rowdy behavior.[47] More recently, at Lourdes in southern France, where a Christian pilgrimage tradition has grown since visions of the Mother of Christ by Bernadette Soubirous in 1858, pilgrims journey to a spring to seek healing for various maladies and to pray. Pilgrims also fill water bottles from the grotto spring to take home with them, as a memory of the place and as a link between themselves, the perceived extraordinary holiness of the shrine, and the Virgin. Interestingly, John Eade has demonstrated significant problems with Turner's notion of *communitas*, the sense of equality generated by the shared experience of pilgrimage, in his study of Lourdes pilgrims. In particular, he notes the social and political differences of wider society that are maintained during the journey.[48]

A significant role that such institutionalized pilgrimages can play is that of identity reinforcer, both during and after their journey. Turner argued that, while on pilgrimage, participants form a bond, known as *communitas*, deconstructing preexisting ideas of social status and obligation and uniting them as a unit of equals throughout their journey. However, more recent studies have questioned whether such *communitas* is even an essential dimension of pilgrimage at all. Turner's model idealized *communitas* as a necessary aspect of pilgrimage rather than identifying it as a potential social dimension.[49] Similarly, Turner's *communitas* model itself can be misleading: subsequent research has not found such homogeneity among pilgrims.[50] After their journey, returned pilgrims join the ranks of those in their group who have also participated in the pilgrimage. Within some traditions, this is of critical importance. For example, in Islam, the pilgrimage to Mecca is designated as one of the five pillars of the faith. Returned pilgrims are called "Hajjis" and are entitled to add the appellation to their name. Further, studies have demonstrated that participation in the Hajj leads to an increased sense of unity with fellow Muslims and to a greater level of acceptance of other ways

of life.[51] Similarly, Richard Rymarz found that participation by young Catholics in the World Youth Day pilgrimage led to an increased sense of belonging to their church community and a greater personal commitment to their faith.[52]

However, religion need not be the sole or central reason for going on a pilgrimage. Both Turner and Clifford Geertz understood ritual as a means by which social ties could be reinforced.[53] In addition, they also understood its potential as a mode of transforming the experiential base of the everyday. People's normal daily life may be filled with chores, work, family commitments, social engagements, and so on, each of which demands attention. In contrast, when traveling, they are typically removed from the majority of these distractions. The passage of time changes as a result, and the amount of time for thought, personal reflection, and exploration is vastly increased. However, in conflict with Turner's theory, which understands these liminal entities as being "stripped" of all forms of identity and social status, this author argues that this does not happen in the context of travel. Rather, when modern people travel, they carry with them all of their normal conceptions of identity and status, although they may "play" with them or indeed alter them fundamentally when traveling. Further, even though pilgrimage is often associated with religious traditions, by no means are all pilgrimages explicitly religious. For example, Ian Reader argued that the term *pilgrimage* is applicable to many activities that are not limited in motivation or function to the religious.[54] Pilgrimage sites themselves need not necessarily be religious for a pilgrimage tradition to arise. Indeed, the secular world often creates its own sacred places, such as national shrines, war graves, and sporting venues.

Examples of so-called secular pilgrimages provide a useful insight as to how problematic is the notion of pilgrimage as necessarily religious. At Graceland, in Memphis, Tennessee, in the southern United States, the constant stream of visitors to the former home of rock and roll star Elvis Presley exemplifies "nonreligious" pilgrimage. The site currently attracts over 700,000 visitors per year. Madeleine Rigby links the development of Graceland as a pilgrimage site to the model presented by Victor and Edith Turner.[55] For many Elvis fans, the journey to Graceland is a journey toward a sacred center, even though many deny the status of Elvis as a religious figure.[56] In particular, it is the way that the pilgrimage fulfills a need in pilgrims for a type of religious practice that institutional religions fail to.[57] Similarly, for many Australians and New Zealanders, a journey to Gallipoli, in Turkey, is considered a pilgrimage that is deeply connected to national identity and cultural ideals. The battles fought at Gallipoli in World War I are considered formative moments of Australian and New Zealand national identity. As such, Bruce Scates provides numerous accounts of pilgrims' journeys to Gallipoli, arguing that the trips function as pilgrimages in terms of the extent to which participants seek the site out and the level of meaning, both personal and cultural, that is attached to it.[58] Indeed, the land at Gallipoli has become the "holy land" for the two secular nations, stained with the blood of soldiers who are considered "founding fathers."[59] Pilgrims go to Gallipoli to be at the place where these events occurred and to find some connection with these soldiers.

Further, the growing body of research on film tourism suggests that there may be more to movie-inspired journeys than a simple desire to "see the set." Film-induced tourism is loosely defined as travel, following the viewing of a film, to the locations or settings depicted therein.[60] Examples are numerous and, at least until recently, have probably been more prolifically covered in news and popular media than they have in academic publications.[61] In reference to broader tourism theories, John Urry argued that tourists seek places for which an anticipation of something "other" or noncustomary has been built.[62] Viewing films can bring these pictures to the viewer in high definition, allowing them to "get a taste" before deciding where to go.[63] The critical point is that a film can increase the viewer's familiarity with a place. However, a further step is needed to complete the allure of the destination image. Tourism attractions require markers of meaning to situate them in tourists' minds. Films in particular can be major conduits in the transmission and construction of cultural or social meaning, often for places with which viewers have no prior experience. Such film-induced tourists could be said to be on pilgrimage—they seek out specific locations in order to connect with certain streams of meaning or identity and to taste, as it were, a thing sacred to them, before returning home.

Each of these examples challenges the notion that religion is the central aspect of pilgrimage. Nonetheless, the evidence indicates that the journeys that these people make can be seen as equally significant in terms of life practice, compared with the journeys of explicitly religiously motivated pilgrims. The critical point is that these pilgrims are seeking out locations at which they perceive sources of cultural or personal identity, in much the same way as explicitly religious pilgrims do. Indeed, for Turner, pilgrimage was simply a ritual process. Some contemporary scholars understand all forms of leisured travel (whether tourism or pilgrimage) to be a part of the greater individual project of the search for the sacred, or for authenticity.[64] Within this framework, the ritual dimension of travel is ever present. By its very nature, the act of travel is understood to, at least, create a physical liminality, to remove travelers from their everyday surroundings and give them an opportunity to transform their conception of everyday life, away from its constraints and influences. It is with this understanding that we approach forms of leisured travel, such as pilgrimage or spiritual tourism, but also more "secular" holidays, and see them as being as much concerned with re-creation as they are with recreation.

Although the function of the pilgrimage site is to be a "religious void, a ritual space capable of accommodating diverse meanings and practices" into which individual pilgrims or groups of pilgrims works their own meanings,[65] the notion that pilgrimage is necessarily religious must be contested. It cannot be assumed that, for any given instance of "pilgrimage," all pilgrims are there for devout reasons. Some may be there for aesthetic reasons, filial reasons, or gastronomic reasons, to name but a few.[66] This has given rise to new fields studying instances of pilgrimage without institutional religious involvement.[67] Similarly, participation in a religious pilgrimage in no way necessitates adherence to the tradition concerned. Nancy Frey's seminal work on the pilgrimages to Santiago de Compostela[68] demonstrated the extent to which that tradition is becoming absorbed into popular touristic culture. Further, as Coleman and Eade argue, Turner and many who followed used "place-centered" methodologies to approach pilgrimage.[69] Rather, what are also required are "process-centered" approaches that look to systems of meaning creation and location with pilgrims themselves. As such, Turner's theories become most useful when taken as variable and situational but not as inherent features of all instances of pilgrimage. As Digance noted, pilgrimages in the contemporary world have moved away from being explicitly associated with religion and become spoken of more as journeys that are rich in meaning.[70]

TOURISM THEORY AND RELIGIOUS PRACTICE

Victor Turner's application of ritual theory onto pilgrimage analysis has meant that those forms of travel are often understood as being meaningful to the subject in part because of their contrast to the everyday, their liminality. The logical progression is to apply this methodology to tourism to determine whether it functions similarly. The study of tourism as an anthropological or sociological subject began as late as 1963.[71] However, it was not until 1973, when MacCannell[72] wrote of the links between social structure, belief, and action in tourism, that any serious theories began to take shape. In his later defining work, MacCannell sought a theory of modern social structure and saw tourists as ethnographers of modernity.[73] Similarly, the symbolic and functional aspects of tourism were equivalent to other institutions that were concerned with a search for meaning, particularly pilgrimage resulting from the shared context of travel. Tourism can be defined as voluntary travel that is "re-creation"—leisure practice geared toward renewing individuals for their "normal" working life.[74]

However, not all tourists are alike, and it would certainly be stretching the truth to say that all tourists are on journeys of discovery or transformation. Nonetheless, it seems that tourists tend to seek out contrast with the everyday, both in terms of surroundings and routines. The very notion of "going away" entails a physical contrast to one's normal life. Tourism is symbolically equivalent with many other human institutions involved with creating or embellishing meaning, such as sports events, holy days, and calendrical festivals. That is, tourism manufactures, or has given rise to, sets of symbols that perform and are used in ways that are equivalent with religious practice. Our passports identify us as being from one country or another; a visit to museums indicates that we are learning about the culture we are visiting; and so on. In this sense, tourism ought to be understood as a form of ritual. The "special" elements of leisure and travel are understood as being in opposition to the "mundane" work and home.[75] Here we encounter the metaphor of tourism as a journey. Quite apart from the literal journey that tourists take, often their experience involves a deeper inner journey—whether through forms of regression (playing, lack of responsibility, etc.) or a rite of passage (traveling at the point of entering adulthood, upon retirement, following a death or divorce, as a time of life change). If one of the functions of tourism is to "ease" through change or provide a context for thought and introspection, not only are there clearly some religious notes to be found there, but also the "slotting in" of religious practices in these modes appears to be easy, even natural.

Despite these arguments, some scholars maintain that tourism and pilgrimage are founded in different social conceptions of space and, in particular, in converse notions of the kinds of spaces worth journeying to. The destination may be the same, but it is approached for different reasons. Both socially and physically, in pilgrimage, individuals travel from the periphery toward the cultural center, whereas, in tourism, they move away from their cultural center into the periphery. Erik Cohen sought to account differences in tourist experiences by examining the roles and significance of tourism within the context of individuals' lives, arguing that these are principally derived from their worldview, especially whether they adhere to a "center" or not. He distinguished five main modes of touristic experience, sorted by the extent to which the journey was a "quest for the center" for the tourist—with the pleasure-seeking tourist at the "recreational" end and the modern pilgrim at the "existential" end.[76]

MacCannell, although not discussing pilgrimage at length, argued that the term *tourist* should be read both as "sightseer in search of experience" and as a metasociological example of modern people. In particular, it was the search for authentic experience that identified tourism as an equivalent of pilgrimage; both were oriented toward sources of authentic experiences and identity. However, although pilgrims journey to places of religious importance, tourists also journey to places of social, cultural, and historical importance.[77] Many scholars, such as Vukonić, Turner, Turner and Turner, and Singh,[78] have echoed Cohen and argued that, even though tourists and pilgrims may go to the same places and do the same things, they are distinguished by their motivations. Yet, as shall be discussed in the following, evidence from some tourists belies this notion, often indicating almost identical functional motivations, despite the participants clearly not being on a pilgrimage. In many cases, the only distinguishing factor is adherence to the tradition in question, although even that is a problematic point for a field researcher—a religiously identifying traveler may be on pilgrimage for reasons other than those prescribed institutionally.

It is critical to keep in mind that tourists encounter religion in nearly every place they visit. Wherever there is religion, there is the potential for tourism (if it is not already established). Religious sites express local identity, which is a significantly motivating factor for many tourists (cultural curiosity/voyeurism, the "other").[79] Vukonić notes that religious belief makes up a significant part of tourists' motivation to see religious sites.[80] Yet specific data on the religious makeup of tourists visiting particular holy sites seem to be lacking from his argument. It would seem intuitive that most tourists visiting religious sites have either an interest in religious buildings as tourist sites or in the other cultures in general, for whatever reasons. Nolan and Nolan, in their study of religious tourism sites in Europe, argued that religious attractions could be grouped into three overlapping categories: shrines, buildings, and festivals.[81] Significantly, they found that, for the latter two categories, religious belief was not a significant motivating factor for most tourists, sometimes resulting in a conflict in visitor interests.[82] However, they were not able to comment on the specific role of religion in that context for those nonreligious tourists. There is a large gap in scholarly material about tourists' motivations for visiting religious sites in terms of their own spirituality. Such examples as secular participation in religious pilgrimages or other religious activities by tourists who are otherwise unconnected with the relevant traditions have only recently been touched upon.

Attempting to define pilgrimage in opposition to tourism is a problematic issue. Pilgrimage is certainly understood in popular culture to be journeys that are redolent with meaning, often physically or emotionally difficult, rich in tradition, and often ascetic. However, there are pilgrimages occurring, often defined by the travelers themselves, that are not bound by tradition, not necessarily physically difficult, and often hedonistic. Further, demonstrably, there are instances of tourism that are nonetheless deeply significant for those travelers who do not self-refer as pilgrims. This is the key—the practice of tourism in these cases is meaningful. If these people do not think of themselves as tourists, we should not either. All leisured travelers are tourists, no matter what term is used to describe them. The reflexive definition is, of course, different. Some tourists call themselves pilgrims, and this is important for us, because it signals their intentions. They may mean to venerate a tradition, person, or object, look for sacred healing, or connect with a site known to

them as special. However, some tourists engaged in nearly identical practice do not call themselves pilgrims (e.g., see the following section on India). It might be useful for the study of these phenomena to think of these particular travelers as "spiritual tourists." In the practice of daily life, travel, whether referred to as pilgrimage or tourism, may be used and may function as part of religious practice.

The word *pilgrimage* must therefore be considered as a label applied by social actors to refer to a journey that they see as having purpose, meaning, and significance. Pilgrimage is a performance, but it begins with the referral to the self as "pilgrim." It is an attempt to separate the performer from notions of frivolity, hedonism, and selfishness that come with the often maligned label of "tourist." This is not to say that tourism is the opposite, far from it. Rather, pilgrimage is an umbrella term for a kind of travel behavior that may also be labeled tourism (or any number of other labels, such as backpacking, traveling, "finding one's self," "losing one's self," etc.). *Tourist* is simply a descriptive term for any person traveling for leisure. What is done with that leisured travel and how the traveler articulates it is another matter, and this is where we find the term *pilgrimage* becoming useful.

This may mean that explicitly religious pilgrimages are having some of their religious significance attenuated. That is, even though pilgrim numbers at a particular site may be the same, what we find is that fewer and fewer of them are making the pilgrimage for explicitly religious reasons. Instead, we find a variety of reasons more concerned with recreation, pleasure, and individual spiritual practice. This is indeed what is found on the Camino de Santiago in northern Spain. Despite being a long-established Catholic pilgrimage, with well-stated institutional links and soteriological outcomes, thousands of non-Christian pilgrims walk and cycle the various

THE CAMINO DE SANTIAGO

The Camino de Santiago (usually referred to as the Camino) is a Catholic pilgrimage, usually done on foot, in northern Spain. The eight-hundred-kilometer route from Roncesvalles in northeastern Spain is the most popular; however, there are networks of routes that wind their way toward Santiago from all over Europe, even from as far away as Poland, Norway, and Scotland. Journeys along the Camino have been the subject of numerous travel books over the past twenty years. Actor Shirley MacLaine wrote an account of her time walking one of the routes, as did Brazilian author Paulo Coelho, but there are hundreds more, in a variety of languages. These books, it seems, act as self-generated marketing for the Camino; most walkers cite at least one of them as a source of inspiration for making the physically challenging journey.

routes, sometimes for up to a month or more, every year. Their reasons for walking may be varied, but among them are dominant themes of self-reflection and life change. The author's own fieldwork found that the length of pilgrimage undertaken by those in the sample group varied from three weeks to three months. Some of those interviewed had undertaken the pilgrimage previously or were taking up the path from where they had formerly finished.

For many pilgrims, walking the Camino functioned as a period of thought and contemplation over the direction that their life was to take. For some, this was a source of great tension: the Camino walked alone being seen as the only way that the question could be resolved to their satisfaction. Often, the choice to be faced had to do with career change. Others faced more visceral changes. One, for example, was using the time to consider whether he was ready to have a baby with his partner. However, there is a strong sense among pilgrims that all pilgrims bring with them problems, questions, or life issues and that a part of their desire for undertaking the pilgrimage is to work through them. The commonly heard saying, at all points along the Way, is "everyone has their own Camino," referring to this notion that each pilgrim has their own issues to work through. However, it also refers to the understanding that each has his or her own ways of dealing or working through these issues and that each pilgrim has his or her own way of walking the Camino itself.

Whatever the central purpose of a pilgrim's Camino experience, the walking aspect of the journey is seen as the method by which it is exercised. One pilgrim expressed this eloquently: after a day's walking, toward the end of her journey, she stated, "It's not a holiday. You get up and you work all day." She said she felt people walked through the problems that they brought to the pilgrimage. The process of walking features in many meditative practices. Indeed, Slavin argues that walking allows an unusually deep connection between body and mind that encourages the exploration of the "nexus between the body, self and the world" and "helps to produce experiences that are profoundly spiritual."[83] In a similar vein, for pilgrims to Santiago, the breakdown of normal daily rhythms and their replacement with simple and very (physically) directional ones provided, for many, a sense of guidance and purpose that they had rarely experienced in their normal lives.[84] However, this is not a religiously oriented sense, but a self-oriented one—that understands individual agency as the root of personal happiness. Further, many pilgrims stated that one of the reasons the Camino appealed as a touristic activity was that it involved a level of reenactment. Numerous pilgrims said the thought that they were walking, quite literally, in the footsteps of millions of former pilgrims was of great comfort and motivation.

Belief or adherence to a religious tradition or position is now largely a matter of personal preference in Western cities. Inclination to believe is now a more significant factor than a sense of family or community duty. The result has been a decline in the numerical dominance of Christian traditions and a rise of smaller, diverse religious movements that are drawn from a range of traditions and ideas. The practice of religion has become, to a much greater extent than has been observable previously, a matter of choice, often referred to as "spirituality." Ibrahim and Cordes argue that "spiritual" refers to "a personal belief in, or a search for a reason of one's existence; a greater or ultimate reality, or a sense of connection with God, nature, or other living beings."[85] This prompts Timothy and Olsen to state that it is thus entirely possible for nonreligious, hedonistic tourists to experience moments of spiritual intensity in an otherwise pleasure-seeking day.[86] The "religious tourist"/"spiritual tourist" terminology debate is ongoing. Its solution may lie in the way that the two terms have become separated in popular culture—"religion" referring to organized, dogmatic, institutionalized groups; "spirituality" referring to personal belief and practice of matters of ultimate truth, identity, and psychological growth.

In India, locations such as Goa, Dharamsala, and Rishikesh are host to numerous meditation centers, yoga teachers, ashrams, and gurus. Although thousands of Western tourists come from around the world specifically to study there, there are also many Westerners who decide to try practices such as meditation simply because it is seen as part of the local tradition. The author's own fieldwork suggests that over 90 percent of Western tourists attending practicing or learning yoga, meditation, or the like in Rishikesh do not consider themselves part of a religious tradition. Rather, most express a combined desire to learn spiritual practices that they hope will help them "become better people." Rishikesh sprang to popular Western attention in the late 1960s, after the Beatles spent time at the ashram of Maharishi Mahesh Yogi. It became known as a center for spiritual learning among Western travelers. Nowadays, it is known as the "Yoga Capital of the World" and has a host of other spiritual activities for tourists to practice. Numerous ashrams dot the town, offering anything from casual yoga classes to long-term programs and retreats, as well as courses on meditation and breathing techniques (*pranayama*). There are also plenty of *satsangs*, or teachings, by various gurus to attend, along with other more general New Age activities, such as Reiki courses, crystal healing, astral travel classes, and tarot readings. One can also find Ayurvedic treatments or, for the less spiritually inclined, sitar or tabla courses, elephant rides, or indeed rafting trips down the Ganges. However, the dominant motivation for most Western tourists to go to Rishikesh seems to be the desire to work on or learn a spiritual practice.

The length of time spent in Rishikesh, as well as in other parts of India, among the sample group interviewed varied between one and seven months. Some tourists elected to spend their entire trip to India in Rishikesh; others included it as part of a broader journey through the subcontinent and stayed only for a few weeks in the town. Unlike in the study by Sharpley and Sundaram,[87] who looked at Western tourists at Auroville in southern India, no permanent tourists were found in the sample group. Many, particularly among those who were spending the majority of their stay in India in Rishikesh, were returning visitors. The spiritual activities done while there varied widely within the group. All respondents attended at least one *satsang* while staying in Rishikesh, and most incorporated a number of sessions over the duration of their stay; and over half indicated that they practiced yoga as part of their spiritual activities while in India. The same number indicated meditation as being undertaken. However, it should be noted that the two activities (yoga and meditation) often occurred as part of the same session in a yoga class or retreat.

Whether for reasons of heart, the mind, curiosity, or even simply by chance, spiritual tourists in India tend to have one thing in common—their journey is made for themselves. The emphasis is on finding a workable solution to whatever problems or questions they are confronting in their lives. Indeed, for many, these spiritual practices are seen as fitting into the broader context of what might be called "the science of living" or "health and well-being." For this grouping, notions of spiritual health are seen as just as important and, in fact, on a similar plane as physical health. The ways that spiritual tourists see the practices that they choose as being efficacious thus reveal a great deal—not only about the "use" of spirituality at an individual level but also about its place within the broader social context. However, there is an important point of distinction here, in terms of what it is understood as being sought. For the most part, spiritual tourists do not come to Rishikesh looking for things that they might like. Rather, they come because they are trying to solve the things that they do not like in their lives. Rishikesh, at least in the eyes of some spiritual tourists, can be thought of as a place where one can come to find the medicine with which to heal the wounds of everyday life. Although Nunez states that "tourists are less likely to borrow from their hosts than their hosts are from them,"[88] this rubric seems to be reversed in the ashrams and meditation halls of India, where tourists come specifically to learn new ways of being and alternate techniques for life. Most do not expect to be healed while there; instead, they treat their time as a period of learning or skills acquisition, the lessons/techniques of which can be taken home and applied in everyday life.

There may be some use in conceiving of these two examples in particular, but also all forms of

RISHIKESH

The Beatles' visit to Rishikesh in 1968 to study with Maharishi Mahesh Yogi launched the town into the international spiritual spotlight. Since then, it has continued to attract Western tourists looking for instruction in Indian philosophies and beliefs, as well as in practices such as yoga and meditation. The town now regards itself as the yoga capital of the world and hosts the annual International Yoga Festival, which itself attracts over four hundred visitors. Another option for yoga practitioners is to stay at an ashram and have an intensive period of study, often involving hours of meditation, philosophy lectures, and yoga practice each day. The monastic setting is desired by Western tourists who want to get the most out of their limited vacation time, as well as being seen as a more "authentic" Indian spiritual experience.

holiday time, as a type of sensory deprivation. On holiday, individuals are deprived of most of the normal experiences of their daily lives. In the case of spiritual tourism examined here, the tourists typically remove themselves dramatically from normal life and from much external distraction. Attending meditation courses or yoga retreats or walking everyday for a month or more represents, and is described as, a very simple way of being in comparison to normal life. Referring to the psychopathology model of cult formation, Bainbridge and Stark note that self-initiated periods of sensory deprivation "can produce very extreme psychotic symptoms even in previously normal persons."[89] Although psychopathology may not be at the heart of tourism, what can be observed in such spiritual tourism is analogous. The time spent traveling deprives travelers of their accustomed surroundings and, in particular, the markers with which they orient themselves in moral and social space. They are forced to recast themselves without these markers. The outcome is often spoken of as a rediscovery of the self or normality, albeit somewhat changed.

However, even though these forces certainly may be at play to varying extents, they are more indicative of the trend of deconstruction and dedifferentiation that has been underway within Western society during the last century. Travel has become seen as an effective way to address the needs and shortcomings of normal, everyday life. Holidays are seen by many travelers as holy days, in more ways than one. Supposedly nonreligious travel practices become imbued with religious ideas and meanings. The example of film tourism provides one example, but perhaps a more succinct one can be found in retail shopping trips. The combined forces of secularization, individualism, and consumerism have brought about a change in the way Western people conceive of and experience the

world. In particular, this has led to the shopping mall becoming a space that is dedicated to the insatiable human desire for transformation, in this case through consumption.[90] Where prevailing culture and attitudes of a society are seen to change, we can also expect its leisure pursuits to do so, and, in turn, the study of these leisure pursuits provides an increased understanding of these changes.[91] Campbell has argued that the desire to consume has become the spirit of the modern West. Insatiable daydreaming of products yet to be acquired is, he argues, the defining character of the modern consumer.[92] In this light, travel to particularly revered shopping malls can become equivalent to pilgrimages—the temples of modern consumption. It is the liminal nature of the experience of traveling to such "temples" and the level of "sanctity" with which it is approached that highlight such tours as being pilgrimage-like.[93]

In 1973, Clifford Geertz asserted that worldview and lifestyle were closely related.[94] In the West, one of the worldviews promoted in popular culture since the 1960s has been one directed toward self-discovery, self-realization, and acceptance of other lifestyles. In the same period, accounts of travel and self-discovery have become a small industry of their own. Such books as Sarah MacDonald's *Holy Cow*, Elizabeth Gilbert's *Eat, Pray, Love*, and Tim Moore's *Spanish Steps: One Man and His Ass on the Pilgrim Way to Santiago* are just three examples among hundreds that exemplify the way that religious practice and travel intersect as a part of this quest for the self in the West. Charles Taylor, in *Sources of the Self*, wrote that "to know who you are is to be oriented in moral space, a space in which questions arise about what is good or bad, what is worth doing and what is not, what has meaning for you and what is trivial and secondary."[95] This search for the self is at the heart of spiritual tourism, and it resonates with the accounts of travelers both from the field and in travel writing. With regard to tourists traveling to places such as India or the Camino to search for answers to their life problems, Campbell's thesis opens the theoretical possibility that this desire for answers could be insatiable. However, books such as the ones mentioned previously indicate that, at least as far as a good story is concerned, an end of searching must be reached at the end of the journey. The journey then begins its operation in memory.

The ideals of Romanticism also seem to have had a great influence on the development of tourism in the West. Wordsworth's poems helped Romanticism gain prominence. Critical to this argument is Wordsworth's notion of "spots of time."

> There are in our existence spots of time,
> That with distinct pre-eminence retain
> A renovating virtue, whence—depressed
> By false opinion and contentious thought,
> Or aught of heavier or more deadly weight,
> In trivial occupations, and the round
> Of ordinary intercourse—our minds
> Are nourished and invisibly repaired;
> A virtue, by which pleasure is enhanced,
> That penetrates, enables us to mount,
> When high, more high, and lifts us up when
>   fallen.[96]

Wordsworth's ideas have permeated popular culture to the point that they are built into touristic practice as it is commonly found. Travel, by its liminal nature, is a rich breeding ground for such spots of time—moments etched in memory that people may call on for a sense of happiness, confidence, reassurance, or learning. They may be reminders of identity and ability, reinforcers of status and wealth, or sources of relief and relaxation. They also encourage more travel, acting subtly as their own advertisements. If we have experienced a relaxing holiday on a beautiful beach, from which we returned home renewed and ready to face our normal lives again, we are much more likely to want to go on a holiday again in the future. Alain de Botton, in *The Art of Travel*, argued that Wordsworth's notion was correct and that such "spots of time" could be drawn upon when pensive, vacant, or depressed by the mundane city life.[97]

Also critical is Johnathan Z. Smith's notion that religion is "map making." Religion, and religiosity, Smith argues, is the attempt that we make to map the social and physical universe. Maps are guides that give us an indication of the shape of what we find before us, although the picture that they present is far from the reality. This apparently insatiable project of spirituality and religiosity is thus an attempt to pick out a suitable path according to the terrain at hand.[98] Such a topographical model resonates with Taylor's notion of spirituality as being orientation in moral space. It implies both knowledge of present circumstances (one's location) and the possibilities for the future (the terrain ahead). Tourism, where it is used by the traveler as a mode of personal exploration, becomes just such an exercise in personal map making. The time spent on holiday is used as time to orient one's self in the social and moral universe. It also serves to shore up conceptions of personal identity and continues to act as such in memory, long after the return home. It can be, in these cases, a practice that is deeply religious in significance, despite it being commonly removed from any institutional influence. Tourism here is an exercise in map making and, as such, must be considered part of the practice of religion in daily life.

CONCLUSIONS

Thinking of travel as liminal, or different from the everyday, does not necessarily mean that it is discrete. This chapter is not arguing a Turnerian model of travel as a discrete social phenomenon. Rather, it argues that modes of tourism have been woven into the processes of everyday life and now gain and are given meaning by their contrast to those aspects of it that dominate, such as work, home life, and routine. As well as being able to operate as ritual, rite of passage, and identity reinforcer, tourism can also operate as a mode of re-creation, or a format for self-discovery. Although theories of travel and the fieldwork largely indicate that tourism can be a meaningful and purposeful activity in a person's life, they do not imply success. Far from being an argument for travelers as the enlightened philosopher-kings of the modern age, this chapter states that what we find in particular cases are groupings of individuals who are asking questions or seeking answers in ways that are analogous to religious practice. Indeed, debates continue to rage over whether travel really is as transformative as it is sold to be in holiday brochures. However, the focus of this chapter is the practice of traveling, not subjective analysis of the qualities of travelers' lives upon return.

Where we find explicitly religious pilgrimages, we see some of their religious significance being attenuated, at least in so far as they now attract significant numbers of pilgrims who are not affiliated with the native tradition. Similarly, some supposedly nonreligious touristic practices are becoming imbued with religious ideas and meaning, such as in the cases of film tourism and shopping tours. Further, Victor Turner's application of ritual theory onto pilgrimage analysis has meant that those forms of travel are often understood as being meaningful to the subject, in part because of their contrast to the everyday. The logical progression is to apply this methodology to tourism to determine whether it functions similarly. Many scholars have done

so and found that, in many circumstances, it does indeed.

When people travel, they are expressing, in various ways, aspects of their idealized visions of themselves and their world. Whether it is by relaxing on a beach, trekking over a mountain, shopping in a famous city, or volunteering in an impoverished village, they make their mark on the world around them. Despite its relative ease and cheapness today, any journey requires investments of money and time and a removal of the travelers from their familiar surroundings and, especially, from their family and friends. Tourists' choices of destination or route, their travel style, and the type of things that they choose to do during their travels tell us much about what they idealize in their lives or what they desire. In particular, it is the ability of travel to function as a learning practice and/or space that can make it such a powerful contributor to religious traditions and to personal systems of meaning and identity.

This is not to say that all forms of tourism are equivalent to religious practices. Rather, in some cases, we can see the use of travel and holiday time as a means of exploring issues that are often at the heart of the personal dimension of religious practice. Most often, these journeys appear to be directed inward, with journeys typically spoken of as very self-oriented. This may lead some to argue that tourism is therefore an example of "self-religion" or evidence of the ways in which individualism comes at the expense of society. However, a fundamental part of the ritual process is the return. For the tourists in Rishikesh or along the Camino de Santiago, how they fitted with and were meaningful to their family and society were questions asked as often and with as much weight as deeply individual ones. The majority of such tourists actively recognize that, at their core, human beings are social creatures, who find meaning, purpose, and comfort in the social sphere. For these tourists, traveling is a mode of reconnecting with that notion and is, as such, a distinctly social activity that operates in the practice of their daily life, whether in fantasy, memory, or reality.

GLOSSARY

Communitas: Generally refers to a sense of an unstructured community in which social equality and solidarity are created. A sense of *communitas* is often experienced by people sharing an event. *Communitas* is often associated with liminal events (see entry) and rites of passage.

Liminal: Liminal states and experiences are characterized by being perceived as thresholds between one state and another. Liminal experiences are thus often understood as ambiguous and transitional—they lead to something other than the starting point.

Pilgrimage: Journeys typically made for religious reasons, but also often for nonreligious reasons, that are considered deeply meaningful to the pilgrim. Such journeys may include veneration of a saint, prayer for healing, or a plea for remission from sins in religious contexts. In secular contexts, it may include journeys to war graves, to sporting events, to the homes of celebrities, or indeed to any place of cultural or personal significance to the pilgrim.

Spiritual Tourism: Spiritual tourism is the practice of holiday traveling to undertake a religious or spiritual practice. It may include such activities as meditation, yoga, chanting, a pilgrimage, or healing practices. Spiritual tourism typically suggests a desire in the tourist to effect some kind of change in her or his everyday life.

Tourism: The practice of leisured or recreational travel and its surrounding industry. Tourists travel for short periods before returning home. Among people who travel for leisure and recreation, tourism sometimes comes to occupy a pejorative meaning in the articulation of states of travel—one is either an unthinking tourist or a thinking traveler.

FOR FURTHER READING

Botton, Alain de. *The Art of Travel*. London: Penguin, 2003.

Feifer, Maxine. *Tourism in History: From Imperial Rome to the Present*. New York: Stein and Day, 1986.

Frey, Nancy Louise. *Pilgrim Stories: On and Off the Road to Santiago*. Berkeley: University of California Press, 1998.

Graburn, Nelson H. H. "The Ethnographic Tourist." In *The Tourist as a Metaphor of the Social World*, edited by G. M. S. Dann. Wallingford, UK: CABI, 2002.

MacCannell, Dean. *The Tourist: A New Theory of the Leisure Class*. 1976. Berkeley: University of California Press, 1999.

Morinis, E. Alan. "Introduction: The Territory of the Anthropology of Pilgrimage." In *Sacred Journeys: The Anthropology of Pilgrimage*, edited by A. Morinis. Westport, CT: Greenwood, 1992.

Reader, Ian. "Introduction." In *Pilgrimage in Popular Culture,* edited by Ian Reader and Tony Walter. Basingstoke: Macmillan, 1993.

Swinglehurst, Edmund. *Cook's Tours: The Story of Popular Travel*. New York: Blandford, 1982.

Timothy, Dallen J., and Daniel H. Olsen. "Conclusion: Whither Religious Tourism." In *Tourism, Religion and Spiritual Journeys*, edited by Dallen J. Timothy and Daniel H. Olsen. London: Routledge, 2006.

Turner, Victor, and Edith Turner. *Image and Pilgrimage in Christian Culture: Anthropological Perspectives.* New York: Columbia University Press, 1978.

Urry, John. *The Tourist Gaze: Leisure and Travel in Contemporary Societies.* London: Sage, 1990.

EDUCATION

Colleen Windham-Hughes

Religion is the name of Latin derivation for beliefs and practices that make manifest the ties between people and between humanity and transcendent aims. In this regard, according to educational theorist John Dewey, education can be considered a religious activity. In its most literal sense, of "leading out" or "bringing up," education is not about content, because content requirements fluctuate, but about navigating life and forming character. These two goals are also critical to religion. To a large extent, both education and religion function as tradition—ways of life that are handed down from one generation to the next. Religion and education offer ways of being in the world. By organizing time, disciplining the body, offering direction, and evaluating progress, religion and education help orient participants to a world of meaning. In society, both serve the important function of passing down ways of living, acting, and thinking, as well as content deemed important or essential. Viewed functionally, religion and education overlap in the desires of adults to raise up children in a particular way. Viewed institutionally, religion and education are parallel, and often mutually exclusive, paths to organize society. An institutional approach is often assumed in the invocation of Thomas Jefferson's famous phrase about the "wall of separation between church and state." As institutions, religion and education are distinct and separate, just as church and state are. One is not beholden to the other; each can and must flourish in its own domain. It is, perhaps, no surprise that the pairing of religion and education often provokes passionate debate from all sides. After all, a large part of the remit of both education and religion involves the fervent desire and duty to prepare the next generation for life's challenges. Years of debate have shown that the topic "religion and education" cannot be considered from institutional perspectives alone.

Each of the four sections of this article begins with quotations from various figures engaged in the work of religion and education. These passages are intended to help raise themes for discussion in the article and to provide insight into perspectives that consider the social weight and importance of religion and education. Although they are not reproduced in detail here, each voice quoted offers one point of view from a particular debate within US history. Endnotes provide the details for locating the debates from which quotations are extracted.

RELIGION AND EDUCATION AS TRADITION

A practical unbelief as to the power of education—the power of physical, intellectual and moral training—exists amongst us. As a people, we do not believe that these fleshly tabernacles—which we call tabernacles of clay—may, by a proper course of training, become as it were tabernacles of iron; or, by an improper course of training, may become tabernacles of glass. . . . We manifest no living, impulsive faith in the scriptural declaration, "Train up a child in the way he should go, and when he is old he will not depart from it."

—Horace Mann[1]

Religious worldviews often inform assumptions about human nature and capacity and thus how history itself is understood and interpreted. . . . Religious worldviews also often consciously affected how the subjects of historical inquiry themselves understood and interpreted their own circumstances and the decisions they made in response to them. For example, some religious individuals and/ or communities may have interpreted positive experiences as a sign of divine favor and negative ones as a sign of disfavor. Their reactions to these experiences would have been profoundly affected by these sensibilities and thus difficult to understand from our contemporary lens without knowing this larger context. Finally, religious worldviews are also imbedded in cultural norms and assumptions in ways that are unconscious and which shape the parameters of what emerges as acceptable and unacceptable beliefs and behaviors for

both the subjects and the interpreters of contemporary and historical events.

—Diane Moore[2]

Religion and education are both concerned with "training up" children in the ways that they should go, as Horace Mann suggests. The task of passing on ways of thinking and acting in the world and handing over precious items and ideas is what is meant by the word *tradition* (from the Latin *tradere*, "to pass on," "to hand over"). In this regard, both religion and education are forms of social organization that maintain tradition and cultivate tradition in younger generations. Some aspects of tradition are passed on conscientiously and reflectively; others are passed on without much explanation, as just being part of "our culture" or "the way it is done." One of my teachers defined the work of transmitting tradition in this way: "You have been given gold; be sure it is gold you pass on." With few words, she communicated the both delicate and serious work of tradition. It can be tempting to think of tradition only in institutional terms—as organizations that survive and decay over time, books that are published, and laws that are set down. Taken in its etymological sense, tradition is the proverbial gold that one generation passes down to the next. Given the enormity and fragility of the task of passing on and handing over tradition, it is, perhaps, a small wonder that grand institutions have been established to buttress forces that threaten to interrupt its transmission.

The work of tradition is often described in today's language as "worldview," although users of the term frequently mean much more than a view of the world. Taking only the elements previously highlighted by Diane Moore, worldview can be said to involve ideas about human capacity, historical inquiry and interpretation, decision making, relations with divinity, unconscious cultural norms, and acceptable or unacceptable beliefs. In short, worldview encompasses everything about belonging to, navigating through, and shaping the world in which we live. In his classic book *The Sacred Canopy*, Peter Berger discusses what we now call worldview as "world-building." According to Berger, the effort of world-building has three main components: externalization, by which humans express themselves in ideas and institutions; objectivation, in which ideas and institutions attain a thinglike quality that humans take as reality; and internalization, by which humans absorb ideas and practices from institutions that humans have created as the way the world is.[3] All three components come together very nicely in a consideration of religion and education as tradition, where adults seek to express ideas and practices in such a way and through such institutions that children will be able to internalize the ideas and practices of their society, religion, and culture. Religion and education help humans build and inhabit the world. At their best, religious and educational institutions offer ways into the world and respond to the new energies and challenges of each generation. At their worst, institutions dictate all the terms for participation in the world, closing off possibilities in response to an unknown future and limiting the ability of new generations to cope with changing circumstances.

At the level of etymology, *religion* and *education* refer to slightly different aspects of world-building: *religion* means "to tie" or "to bind"; *education* means "to lead out, to bring up." Religion fosters connections among people and also between humanity and divinity or transcendent goals. Education shows a way—via relationships of leading, following, and mentoring—to approach the world. When religion and education are described by their practices, which have both liberating and oppressing dimensions, it is less easy to distinguish them. Institutions called

religious or educational usually involve both sets of previously listed practices, that is, both practices that foster connections among people and practices that emphasize following in a well-established way. Educational institutions foster connections among students and teachers and encourage connections with transcendent goals, such as civility, tolerance, and good society. Religious institutions often make use of mentoring relationships to cultivate piety and personhood. Broadly, both kinds of institutions make use of a range of practices to help raise children who feel a sense of belonging to and ownership for their world. To this end, both religion and education are concerned with the moral development of children.

Passing on tradition to children requires some attention to the children in care. Repetition and memorization work to embed some aspects of tradition so that it becomes like second nature for children. Both the alphabet and sacred Scripture can be learned effectively through repetition. Patterns and methods of thinking, acting, and relating embed other aspects of tradition, such as formulations of social or ethical problems and pathways of religious guidance. Children learn to recognize patters of suffering and compassion and are taught methods of learning and speaking to negotiate different points of view. Different methods of passing on tradition are employed for children of different ages. Age five is commonly touted as the right time to begin—at school, in the monastery, reciting the Qu'ran, learning Bible stories, and attending rituals. Care is, of course, given at earlier ages. Educational and religious experts agree that children much younger than five can understand, repeat, and relate stories; some even claim that the foundation for all learning is the mother's speech and activity during the child's gestation! Adolescence marks another significant turning point, during which children are deemed ready to articulate ideas for themselves, exercise critical thinking, undergo initiation into deeper mysteries, and engage in serious quests, unaided or with aid at a distance. In these religious and educational moments, adults hope to hear that children have internalized the tradition they have been working to pass on and to see that children's thought and action grows out of the worldview they have tried to hand over. Children are in themselves the future of the tradition and represent to elders future of ways of living.

RELIGION AND EDUCATION FOR A DEMOCRATIC WAY OF LIFE

If "all men are by nature equally free and independent," all men are to be considered as entering into Society on equal conditions; as relinquishing no more, and therefore retaining no less, one than another, of their natural rights. Above all are they to be considered as retaining an "equal title to the free exercise of Religion according to the dictates of Conscience." Whilst we assert for ourselves a freedom to embrace, to profess and to observe the Religion which we believe to be of divine origin, we cannot deny an equal freedom to those whose minds have not yet yielded to the evidence which has convinced us. If this freedom be abused, it is an offence against God, not against man: To God, therefore, not to man, must an account of it be rendered.

—James Madison[4]

Education, then, beyond all other devices of human origin, is the great equalizer of the conditions of men—the balance-wheel of the social machinery.

—Horace Mann[5]

Religious liberty was not created by the Founding Fathers in one generation. Instead,

there was a considerable movement toward religious liberty over the course of the seventeenth and eighteenth centuries. Much of the movement came from dissenting religious denominations, from new ways of thinking about conscience and conversion, as well as from political battles fought to overcome the oppression of established churches. And much of the pressure for religious liberty came from Enlightenment thinkers who believed that natural reason, operating in a free culture, was the way to truth.

—Warren A. Nord[6]

When the colonists joined together to form a new country called the United States of America, they rejected the form of government that had been dominant in Europe for several centuries: monarchy linked to an established church. Political theorists had long claimed that social order depended upon the monarch's authority in both civil and religious affairs. In place of an authoritative figure, founders of the new republic instituted an authoritative creed: "All Men are created equal."[7] Politically, the concept that all rightly qualified citizens are equal translates into the doctrine of one person, one vote. For religion and education, the concept that all are equal carries with it important practical effects. In order that citizens do not, with their votes, drive the new country to ruin, religion and education must be employed to ensure right conduct and proper exchange of information. In short, the success or failure of the experiment in representative democracy is to be found in the merits and achievements of the nation's religious and educational institutions.

Thomas Jefferson is credited with dogged insistence that democracy would not survive absent universal[8] education. He believed that education was necessary for the teaching of rights, duties, and privileges, as well as for the identification of good leaders. In Jefferson's day, several states with significant religious majorities drafted educational plans that entrusted care of the young to the institutions and officials of various Protestant churches. Jefferson's own state of Virginia planned to assess a tax to support the salaries of Christian educators from multiple churches. Although Jefferson was serving his country abroad as minister to France, his good friend and colleague James Madison undertook the argument against the proposed tax. In "Memorial and Remonstrance against Religious Assessments," which subsequently became one of the most influential documents regarding the relationships between church, state, and education, Madison argued against state support for Christian teachers on fifteen grounds, the first two of which relate to the quotation at the beginning of this section: (1) religion belongs in the realm of conscience, which is subject to the free and equal choice of all; and (2) restriction of religious freedom is an offense against God. Circulated as a petition of sorts among Virginians, "Memorial and Remonstrance" eventually garnered two thousand signatures against the proposed assessments. The resulting Act for Establishing Religious Freedom, in 1786, was a pivotal document for provisions against religious establishment in the Constitution.

Early documents, such as the Act for Establishing Religious Freedom and the Constitution, refused institutional interference between religion and the state, but they did not eliminate religious influences. Seldom included in these accolades is Jefferson's conviction that nonsectarian religion should undergird teaching about morality and ethics. Jefferson's fear of sectarian division often led him to urge that Christian ministers not be eligible for teaching positions. He sometimes made an exception in the case of Unitarians, whose deist belief was closest to his own. Here are the elements of religion that

Jefferson believed could be proved by scientific inquiry—a fact that placed them beyond sectarian passion: the existence of a supreme being who is governor of the universe, the freedom of the will, and the eternal significance of punishment and reward. Jefferson accepted Jesus' moral teaching as evidence of true religion, plain to reason and common sense, but he did not accept his divinity. Accordingly, Jefferson believed that Jesus' moral teaching could be included without controversy in public education. As shown in his letter to Peter Carr, he believed that all religious claims and doctrines should be subjected to the light of reason: "Question with boldness even the existence of a god; because, if there be one, he must more approve the homage of reason, than that of blindfolded fear."[9] All such questioning should be undertaken in utmost sincerity, with the desire to live a morally upright life.

Jefferson long advocated universal education as the only path to transform the motley crew of individual states into a unified nation. Using Benedict Anderson's concept of "imagined communities," we can say that Jefferson believed that education was the primary way to foster the imagined community of the United States, that universal education should provide avenues for identity and membership in the new nation.[10] In the nineteenth century, the goal of universal education found a tireless advocate in Horace Mann. Appointed to the position of secretary of education in Massachusetts in 1837, Mann worked for twelve years on a project he called the "common school." His vision was that students of all social classes and religious affiliations would attend the same school together in their neighborhood. Each school would be dedicated to raising morally upright, conscientious, and practical citizens. The educational experience was intended to equalize the distinctions of home, class, and religion so that each child had an equal chance to learn and participate in school. Mann believed that equality achieved in the schools would go a great distance in helping achieve equality in the wider society.[11] He likewise hoped it would limit criminal behavior.

Like Jefferson, Mann advocated the incorporation of nonsectarian elements of religion into the school day. Moral instruction in the classroom often included Bible reading, recitation of the Ten Commandments and the Lord's Prayer, and the singing of hymns. As far as Mann was concerned, the centerpiece of moral instruction

In 1837, Horace Mann abandoned a successful law practice and promising political career to become the first secretary of Massachusetts's new state board of education. He then set out to reform the public school system in Massachusetts until it became a model for the rest of the United States.

was the reading, without comment, of ten verses from the Bible. At the time, Mann was accused of being godless; reading from the Bible without comment seemed a miniscule attempt to discipline and hold at bay the massive forces of wickedness and vice. In the coming years, the practice was attacked for another reason, no less religious. Catholic parents complained that reading from the Bible without comment was a Protestant practice; the Catholic practice of Bible reading required interpretation from a priest. Some Catholic parents were appeased by the substitution of the King James Version of the Bible by the Douay Bible, but others insisted that the practice of reading from the Bible without comment privileged Protestant forms of Christianity, a de facto establishment of a particular form of religion that abridged their children's rights to free exercise of religion.

Catholic resistance to the common school, or "the one best system," was especially strong in Philadelphia, New York, and Boston, where there were public clashes between Catholics and Protestants that became known as the "Bible Riots." Even in 1829, it was clear to Catholics at the First Plenary Council of Baltimore that the goal of universal, free, public education was not adequately serving all of the nation's children. Many at this meeting initiated the argument for a system of parish schools to instruct Catholic children. Although families in other religious traditions may have objected to these practices, only Catholics had sufficient numbers, organization, and money to establish a separate school system. Catholics argued against public schools from two related yet distinct positions: (1) so-called American schools were, in fact, Protestant; and (2) education of children belonged properly to the church. Catholics argued that common schools or American schools were de facto Protestant schools. Not only were Protestant versions of the Bible, Ten Commandments,

Lord's Prayer, and hymnody employed in moral instruction, textbooks related lessons of history and literature from distinctly anti-Catholic perspectives.[12] In short, education in the common schools subverted the religious instruction and formation of Catholic children. In establishing a network of parish schools, the Catholic Church in the United States intended to reclaim what it considered to be the right and responsibility of the church to educate its children. Common schools would be reserved for children from the various Protestant churches, whose "fissiparous" nature had so proliferated the churches and reduced the populations affiliated with each church so as to require joint effort at the behest of the state.[13] With the leadership of Archbishop John Hughes of New York, the Catholic Church went a long way toward achieving the goal of one school for each parish. To date, the Catholic parish school system is the largest system of non-public religiously affiliated schools. Networks of day schools, as well as scattered independent schools, also exist within Judaism, Islam, and various non-Catholic forms of Christianity.

Creating a system of day schools requires an enormous amount of time, energy, and money. In the nineteenth century, each Catholic parish was expected to develop and support a day school for its children. This grand vision required a huge financial commitment, often from populations working low-paying jobs. Very quickly, Catholic schools began to ask for government money to support parish schools. Catholics argued that refusal of government funds contradicted the commitment to universal education and condemned Catholic citizens to a "double tax" situation: as citizens, Catholics were obligated to pay taxes to support public education; as Catholics, they were obligated to support parish schools. Could the commitment to universal education be sustained outside of "the one best system" of the common school?

RELIGION AND EDUCATION GO TO COURT

Congress shall make no law respecting an establishment of religion, or prohibiting the free exercise thereof; or abridging the freedom of speech, or of the press; or the right of the people peaceably to assemble, and to petition the government for a redress of grievances.

—First Amendment to the Constitution of the United States of America

We are dealing with an interest inferior to none in the hierarchy of legal values. National unity is the basis of national security. . . . The ultimate foundation of a free society is the binding tie of cohesive sentiment. Such a sentiment is fostered by all those agencies of the mind and spirit which may serve to gather up the traditions of a people, transmit them from generation to generation, and thereby create that continuity of a treasured common life which constitutes a civilization. "We live by symbols." The flag is the symbol of our national unity, transcending all internal differences, however large, within the framework of the Constitution.

—Justice Frankfurter, *Minersville School District v. Gobitis*[14]

It might well be said that one's education is not complete without a study of comparative religion or the history of religion and its relationship to the advancement of civilization. It certainly may be said that the Bible is worthy of study for its literary and historic qualities. Nothing we have said here indicates that such study of the Bible or of religion, when presented objectively as part of a secular program of education, may not be effected consistently with the First Amendment.

—Justice Clark, *Abington School District v. Schempp*[15]

Religious liberty in the United States of America rests on the first two clauses of the First Amendment to the US Constitution. The two clauses are known as the "Establishment Clause" and the "Free Exercise Clause," and together they undergird most of the case law that pertains to the practice of religion. Government sponsorship of any particular religion or religious activity is prohibited by the Establishment Clause, whereas individual and corporate rights to religious practices and beliefs are guaranteed by the Free Exercise Clause. When courts weigh a claim for free exercise of religion, they must be careful not to accommodate religious practice to the extent that the government may be seen to sponsor religious activity.

Debates about the place of religion in public education, raised through issues such as evolution and sex education, are well-publicized and hard to miss. Most frequently, such debates spring from arguments and decisions in court cases, which lend themselves to polemical arguments. In each case, the foundational commitment to religious liberty in the United States is set against one of two colloquial narratives that flirt with the boundaries of established religion: (1) the United States is a "religious" or even a "Christian" nation,[16] whose history is intimately intertwined with the religious passions of its founders; and/or (2) love of country or patriotism is a legitimate aim of education that cannot be equated with religious commitment. Also at stake in each case is the fundamental commitment to universal education.[17] To what extent can religious liberty be accommodated, given the compelling interest of the state to educate all of its children?

Money and Benefits for Nonpublic Schools

Approximately 10 percent of the nation's children attend nonpublic schools.[18] Nonpublic schools provide education that is parallel to public education, through institutions that are owned and administered by organizations other than state governments. Such nonpublic schools are appealing for various reasons, not all of them religious: families may be attracted to an educational context that is consistent with and supported by a religious worldview, but they may also be attracted to small class sizes, project-based learning, attentiveness to moral development, separate instruction for girls and boys, or dual-immersion language programs.[19] Regardless of religious affiliation, parents tend to want their children to enjoy as many advantages as possible under the banner of universal education, which includes drawing on federal funds to cover expenses when possible. In cases involving secular textbooks for nonpublic schools[20] and transportation to and from nonpublic schools,[21] the Supreme Court has ruled that the state has a compelling interest in providing for the education of all children. Because textbooks and transportation serve secular ends, states may provide them to nonpublic schools. To refuse such help to nonpublic schools would be to show hostility to one religion over others.

Released Time for Religious Instruction

When parallel systems of nonpublic education are not feasible or desirable, some religious groups band together to lobby a local school district for released time for religious instruction. Released time for religious instruction offers time for supplementary religious instruction from within the schedule of the normal school day. Released time has been challenged on several grounds: use of public facilities, use of public servants to promote released time, and peer pressure of fellow students. In 1945, Vashti

McCollum challenged the released time program in her son's school in Champaign, Illinois. Five years prior, religious leaders had established a program of released time, with the cooperation, sponsorship, and supervision of the local school and superintendent. Although the program was labeled voluntary, McCollum claimed that her son was ostracized for not attending. The Supreme Court decided that the program was unconstitutional because the close cooperation of the school authorities in the religious program loaned an air of legal compulsion to the religious classes.

The court's decision in McCollum condemned the Champaign program with strong language about government assistance of religious programs, but it did not end all released time programs. Four years after McCollum, in *Zorach v. Clauson* (1952), the court ruled that released time is allowable if religious institutions host the supplemental instruction and make their own provisions for transportation of students. When released time for religious instruction is employed, it must be granted equally to all religious groups. Schools cannot sponsor released time through advocacy, advertisement, staffing, or facilities. Although proponents of released time remain today, it has been mostly discredited on the grounds that mandatory public education does not prevent the free exercise of religion in hours or on days outside of school. An important challenge to released time is Jum'ah, the Friday prayer that is mandatory for Muslims. Islam is the only major religious tradition for which the most important day of weekly worship falls within the school week. Courts in California and Texas have put an end to school practices that allowed Muslim students to miss class in order to attend Jum'ah in an unused classroom, because students from other school organizations were not granted the same privilege.

The Pledge of Allegiance

The most recent case related to religion and education to go to the Supreme Court involves the Pledge of Allegiance to the United States of America. In 2000 Michael Newdow, a minister in the Universal Life Church and non-custodial parent of a school-aged daughter, challenged the phrase "under God" in the Pledge of Allegiance, which was added in 1954 by President Eisenhower during the Communist threat. Newdow's argument is that these two words make the pledge a religious exercise. Though the case was decided against Newdow on the premise that his daughter could simply opt out of the pledge, the Ninth Circuit Court of Appeals ruled that the pledge as practiced violated the Establishment Clause of the First Amendment. In its 2004 review, the Supreme Court argued that Newdow did not have standing to bring the case before the court because participation in the pledge is not federally mandated. Joined by other parents in 2005, Newdow again brought suit to challenge the wording of the pledge. The second time, the suit was judged in the plaintiffs' favor. On appeal, the decision was reversed. Judge Bea, writing the majority decision for the Ninth Circuit Court of Appeals, argued: "Not every mention of God or religion by our government or at the government's direction is a violation of the Establishment Clause." Bea further explained that the phrase "one nation under God" must be set within the context of the entire pledge. "Because California Education Code § 52720 as implemented by the School District's Policy requires the recitation of the Pledge as a whole, we must examine the Pledge as a whole, not just the two words the Plaintiffs find offensive. In doing so, we find the Pledge is one of allegiance to our Republic, not of allegiance to the God or to any religion. Furthermore, Congress' ostensible and pre- dominant purpose when it enacted and amended the Pledge over time was patriotic, not religious."[22] Newdow's daughter may still exercise her right to opt out of saying the pledge.

Newdow's twenty-first-century challenge to the pledge was not the first. In 1940 and 1943, the Supreme Court heard arguments from Jehovah's Witnesses, who asked for exemption from reciting the pledge on the grounds that it constituted a religious exercise. Both cases had occurred before the words "under God" were inserted into the pledge. In *Gobitis* (1940), the court argued that daily recitation of the pledge promoted national unity, a compelling interest of the government. The flag was extolled as an important symbol that invited Americans to transcend their own narrow needs and self-interest for the purposes of national unity and security. Requiring recitation of the pledge did not violate due process; parents were welcome to engage in the democratic process to change the requirement or to enroll their children in private schools. Three years later, the court issued an opinion that had exactly the opposite result, in *West Virginia State Board of Ed. v. Barnette*, 319 U.S. 624 (1943). Children of Jehovah's Witnesses could be exempt from reciting the pledge on the grounds that the government cannot compel speech. By relying on the Free Speech Clause of the First Amendment, instead of either of the religious clauses, the court sidestepped two possible minefields: it remained silent on whether the pledge constituted a religious exercise—and therefore an establishment of religion—and it refrained from extending protection for the free exercise of religion.

Evolution and Creation

Perhaps the most controversial topic to challenge the Establishment Clause is evolution. The issue captivated the nation in the highly publicized Scopes Trial of 1925, which was later dramatized, first as a stage play and then as a film, under the title *Inherit the Wind*. Although the teaching of evolution was, at that time, a minority practice among teachers, it was prohibited by state law in Tennessee. Even though the jury agreed that John Scopes had violated the law in teaching evolution, they refused to fine him. Despite the technical conviction in the "Scopes monkey trial," as, according to H. L. Mencken's influential account, it was commonly called, the trial came to symbolize the triumph of modernity over ostensibly backward religious belief. Clarence Darrow, an atheist, was a gifted orator and a shrewd interrogator, who put William Jennings Bryan in the position of defending the scientific integrity of his religious belief. Religious belief about the creation of the world and universe was made to look contradictory and childish, whereas evolution was lauded as science's gift to a modern understanding of reality.

However, the 1925 decision did not settle the matter. The origin of the universe continues to be a controversial topic; some school districts persist in attempts to outlaw the teaching of evolution, and others require teachers to deliver disclaimers about the status of evolutionary theory or spend equal instruction time on creationism or intelligent design. In *Epperson v. Arkansas* (1968), Susan Epperson challenged an Arkansas law that prohibited, as an establishment of religion, the teaching of evolutionary theory. The Supreme Court had a chance to weigh in on the practice of "balanced" teaching of evolutionary theory and creationism with its decision in *Edwards v. Aguillard* (1987), in which the court found that the purpose behind the practice was to advance religious explanations for the origins of life. Efforts to incorporate "intelligent design" into science curriculum have met much the same fate as earlier efforts to include teaching time for creationism. *Kitzmiller v. Dover Area School District* (2005) challenged the school district's policy stipulating that science teachers should read a disclaimer—that highlighted evolution as a theory with gaps—and introduced the alternative theory of intelligent design. Judge John E. Jones delivered a lengthy opinion that challenged the scientific features of intelligent design and condemned the disclaimer as an unabashed promotion of religion. Because intelligent design is a theory about how to view and interpret development in the natural world, its proper home in a public school is as sociology or philosophy.

Prayer

Second to the evolution-creation debate, in terms of emotional volatility, is the issue of prayer in schools. In the early days of universal education, it was common practice for the teacher to offer a short prayer at the conclusion of the daily reading from the Bible. In some cases, the prayer was the same every day, approved by the school district for use in each classroom. Just such a universal, nonsectarian prayer was the issue at stake in *Engel v. Vitale* (1962). Here is the text of the prayer: "Almighty God, we acknowledge our dependence upon Thee, and we beg Thy blessings upon us, our parents, our teachers and our Country."[23] The Court's decision revisits the history of religious freedom, as pursued first by the colonists and then by citizens of the new republic. Citing in particular the "Virginia Bill for Religious Liberty," Justice Black condemned, as an establishment of religion, every prescribed prayer in a public setting.

Engel v. Vitale holds a unique place in a certain religious imaginary of the United States as the moment that the nation began to decline in moral values. In the years following the elimination of school-sponsored prayer, the court,

along with the Department of Education, has worked to clarify the situations in which prayer is deemed appropriate at school. *Lee v. Weisman* (1992) tested the constitutionality of prayer at graduation and subsequently outlawed the practice. The US Department of Education is responsible for issuing *Guidance on Constitutionally Protected Prayer in Public Elementary and Secondary Schools*. Based upon consensus readings of Supreme Court decisions, the document advises against school-sanctioned prayer activities and yet upholds the rights of individuals to initiate or participate in such activities outside instructional time in nondisruptive ways. Private prayer is protected, both in the exercise of religious freedom and in the exercise of free speech.[24]

Bible Reading

When Horace Mann argued for the inclusion of religion in education, daily reading from the Bible was his idea of a nonsectarian religious contribution to the moral development of children. The practice of daily reading from the Bible was first challenged in Edgerton, Wisconsin, in 1886, when Catholic parents brought suit against the school district over the practice of reading without commentary from the King James Version of the Bible. Such a practice necessarily excluded Catholics, because they believe that the King James Version of the Bible contains errors and hold that Bible reading must be accompanied by the interpretation of a priest. The school board and lower court argued that Catholic children could sit in the cloakroom during the practice, but the Wisconsin Supreme Court overturned the ruling and banned the practice as sectarian establishment of religion.[25] The "Edgerton Bible case," as it came to be known, enjoyed notoriety again seventy-three years later, when the US Supreme Court banned outright the practice of reading from the Bible in *Abington v. Schempp* (1963).

The decision in *Schempp* is significant not only because it outlawed reading from the Bible as a devotional practice but also because it opened the door for academic study of religion. Writing for the majority, Justice Clark opined, "One's education is not complete without a study of comparative religion or the history of religion and its relationship to the advancement of civilization."[26] Although many interpreted the decision in *Schempp* as sealing the turn away from religion and moral values that had begun with *Engel v. Vitale*, others greeted the decision with energy and determination, to make the study of religion a viable area of education. In the wake of the *Schempp* decision, many colleges and universities opened departments of religious studies, and high school teachers considered how to incorporate study about religion into literature and the social sciences.

"Neutrality" became the court's watchword for study about religion. Government was not supposed to advance—nor was it supposed to inhibit—religion. Subsequently, many have used the language of government neutrality to argue for the academic study of religion. Academic study about religion also satisfies the court's concern that the study of religion be undertaken for a secular purpose—in this case, understood as more informed, conscientious, and tolerant citizens. Secular purpose and neutrality, that is, neither advancement nor inhibition of religion, became the ways to test the constitutionality of the appearance of religion in public venues. In 1971, the court added one more test to the two previously set forth in *Schempp*: excessive entanglement of the government in matters of religion was to be avoided. These three principles together are referred to as the Lemon test; they have been applied in many subsequent cases dealing with religion and education.

Facilities

With the Lemon test operative, the court has been able to determine the right of assembly and use of school facilities for religious groups. Public school facilities may be used by religious organizations, such as student clubs and outside groups, as long as time and space are granted equally to all groups.

One practice that has not survived the Lemon test is the posting the Ten Commandments in public schools and other public places. In *Stone v. Graham* (1980), the court decided that the Kentucky practice of posting a copy of the Ten Commandments in every classroom served no clear secular purpose. Kentucky educators argued that the practice served a secular purpose—to educate students about an important source of law in the United States, but the court decided that the practice crossed over the secular purpose of education into the realm of endorsement or establishment of religion.

RELIGION IN EDUCATION IN THE TWENTY-FIRST CENTURY

Seldom has so much been expected from one institution as Americans expect from their public school. Is there a national crisis? Send the school to the rescue. Is our democratic faith in jeopardy? The school must instill that faith and elicit whole-hearted commitment to it. Is the very survival of the country at stake? The school must save it. Two generations ago the school was called upon to Americanize the immigrant; today it is expected to bridge the widening chasm between white and black Americans. During the 1930's the school helped ease the pains of the great depression; today it must gird our loins for the continuing global struggle with communism while coping with burgeoning numbers of teen-agers who have no other socially acceptable place to go. In American society the school has taken over many of the functions of the family, the church, and the job. It must look to the child's personal development and keep the youth occupied with meaningful tasks. It must be concerned with value commitments as well as with skills. And the magnitude of the school's task has grown with the lengthening of expected years in school and the enrollment explosion.

—Robert Michaelsen[27]

Of necessity the state in its public-education system is and always has been teaching religion. It does so because the well-being of the nation and the state demands this foundation of shared beliefs. . . . In this sense the public-school system of the United States is its established church.

—Sidney Mead[28]

The inclusion of religion in education is perhaps the most hotly debated dimension of our topic. Arguments for the inclusion of religion in education range from the necessity of moral instruction and example, to the importance of religion in the development of history and creation of literature, to the imperative of understanding multiple religions in today's global society. Although one must be hesitant to accept arguments for the study of religion on the basis that such study will "save" the United States from its current condition of ignorance or religious illiteracy, there is no doubt that, in the early years of the twenty-first century, there is new motivation and interest in the study of religion in public schools. Because the decision in *Abington School District v. Schempp* inspired a flurry of courses and departments of religious studies, scholars such as Charles Haynes, of the First Amendment Center, have worked with religious leaders

and scholars of religion to develop guidelines for the inclusion of religion in the public school curriculum. The following are the guidelines from the First Amendment Center.

- The school's approach to religion is academic, not devotional.
- The school strives for student awareness of religions, but it does not press for student acceptance of any one religion.
- The school sponsors study about religion, not the practice of religion.
- The school exposes students to a diversity of religious views; it does not impose any particular view.
- The school educates about all religions; it does not promote or denigrate any religion.
- The school informs students about various beliefs; it does not seek to conform students to any particular belief.[29]

It is now commonplace to distinguish between two main approaches to religion: devotional and academic. Devotional approaches are said to be concerned with adherence to religious visions of reality and are aimed at cultivating religious commitments in students. By contrast, academic approaches emphasize the contributions of religions to the development of society and are aimed at helping students understand forces that shape the contemporary national and global contexts and/or assist students in the development of tolerant attitudes toward religious difference. In academic study about religion, religion is analyzed as a factor in accounts of human motivation for a range of activities. Consider, for example, the wording of this California state standard for seventh-grade social studies: "Students analyze the geographic, political, economic, religious, and social structures of the civilizations of Islam in the Middle Ages."[30] In this case, religion is interpreted adjectivally, as a source of structure within civilization. A devotional approach is appropriate for religiously affiliated schools, which educate children within the context of a religious tradition. However, devotional approaches are not appropriate for public schools. Indeed, many in public education worry that pitfalls of the devotional approach remain in the academic study of religion. Just mentioning religion may seem to recommend it, and mentioning multiple religions may convey the idea that all religions are ultimately the same or equally valid. The latter concern gives voice to the chief pitfall of a strictly academic approach to religion: relativism. When the study of religion is reduced to a set of facts that can be studied from a distance—founders, date and place of origin, global spread, central tenets, notable architecture—religious visions, commitments, and actions can become trivial or generic.

Some educators advocate a third approach, sometimes referred to as transformational. In this approach, academic study is the point of entry, but students and teachers allow some space to discuss religious approaches to big questions of life. In this exercise, students are encouraged to reflect on their own ways of thinking and patterns of commitment. The goal is not proselytism, but self-reflection and meaningful interaction with religious worlds. In such an interaction, students are encouraged to examine and articulate their own views while learning to listen to the views of others. Unsurprisingly, advocates of this third approach make the connection between thoughtful consideration of religious beliefs and practices and meaningful participation in democracy. Engaging in serious and potentially conflictual conversations about religion is seen as good preparation for democratic participation. Opponents argue that transformational approaches, in fact, advocate cultural relativism and fail to take disagreement about religious and democratic values seriously.

The call to take religion seriously is often accompanied by the charge that the exclusion of religion from educational curriculum amounts to a non-neutral position on religion. Warren Nord argues that the practice of outlawing all mention of religion is an extremist secular viewpoint that communicates the idea that religion is erroneous. In some cases, secular education seems to establish its own religion—secular humanism, which advances either the idea that all religions are basically the same or the idea that civilization can cope without religion and will eventually abolish it. To practice fully the court-mandated neutrality in matters of religion, Nord argues, the study of religion must be included. Nord and like-minded educators advocate two main approaches: mandatory classes about religion and/or the incorporation of study about religion across the curriculum. Stephen Prothero's 2007 book, *Religious Literacy: What Every American Needs to Know—and Doesn't*, and its accompanying quiz garnered major media attention.[31] Prothero's claim is that there are certain items of religious content, relevant to the history and current context of the United States, that all citizens need to know as a matter of responsible citizenship. To this end, Prothero argues that classes about religion should be mandatory in public education, from middle school through college. Prothero contests universalistic approaches to the teaching of religion that claim a common essential core of human compassion lies within all religious traditions and wants students to learn that religions have offered different solutions to different sets of problems. Also wishing to take religion seriously, Nel Noddings advocates incorporating elements of the study of religion into all subjects within the curriculum, including her own discipline of mathematics. Noddings's goal for education is for teachers to practice and to cultivate an ethic of care within their students. According to Noddings, instead of carving out discrete subject areas and time blocks devoted to moral instruction or study of religion, moral and religious concerns should be welcome aspects within traditional school subjects. This goal can be accomplished partly through biographical anecdotes and investigations of canonical figures, such as René Descartes, and partly through taking students' existential questions seriously. Teachers need not be experts in religion or moral issues to adopt this strategy, according to Noddings, although teacher training needs to be adjusted to take one or two steps back from specialization in favor of broad training in liberal arts.

At the beginning of the proliferation of departments of religious studies, and for the next few decades, Ninian Smart authored the widely used *Dimensions of the Sacred,* to give some shape and differentiation to discussion of religious traditions. His approach admits matters of belief and doctrine up front but goes on to describe seven other dimensions of religious practice that are appropriate for study. The final edition of *Dimensions of the Sacred* lists eight dimensions of religious traditions: Doctrine-Philosophy, Ritual, Mythic-Narrative, Experiential-Emotional, Ethical-Legal, Social, Material, and Political.[32] In this way, Smart sought to introduce students to religion phenomenologically, that is, the way in which religion shows up in the lives of its adherents.

CONCLUSION

Any activity pursued in behalf of an ideal end against obstacles and in spite of threats of personal loss because of conviction of its general and enduring value is religious in quality.

—John Dewey[33]

Education, even if it does not treat religion explicitly, always endangers blind faith, but it does not necessarily destroy belief; it may indeed deepen it.

—Nel Noddings[34]

We take for granted much of our movement through daily practices, interactions, and institutions. The ways we do things, the ways we spend our time, and the ways we think become second nature to us. Sociologist Pierre Bourdieu calls this orientation to life and world *habitus.*[35] By habitus, Bourdieu means much more than individual habits that can be labeled "good" or "bad." Instead, the word is meant to cover a collection of beliefs and practices that are common to a given group or society. Habitus covers the core commitments and idiosyncrasies of culture, nation, neighborhood, religious affiliation, or educational institution. It names the internalized aspect of world-building discussed by Peter Berger in *The Sacred Canopy.* Students today likely participate in multiple and overlapping forms of habitus. Because each religious and educational institution advances a worldview, there is, indeed, great potential for conflict, as the history of the United States shows.

It has become fashionable to talk about the pluralism of religions that were present at the beginning of the history of the United States. Such description is meant to illustrate the uniqueness of the US commitment to religious liberty, in the context of its founding in the eighteenth century. Critical to this story is the role of the Puritans, who took up residence in the Northeast in the face of religious persecution, with a firm sense of missionary enterprise. In addition to Puritans, the original colonies were home to native traditions, Anglicans, Catholics, Jews, freethinkers of various types, and those with no affiliation at all. Several of the original colonies had established churches—Congregational, Anglican, and Catholic. Other colonies, such as Rhode Island and Pennsylvania, were founded with liberty of conscience and freedom of religion in mind. A latent stronghold for the establishment of religion was, until the middle to late twentieth century, the public school system. Conflation of Christianity with moral rectitude, even with Americanness, caused de facto exclusion of alternative religious beliefs, as well as nonreligious beliefs, in many schools across the nation. According to educational theorist David Tyack, the "search for the one best system has ill-served the pluralistic character of American society."[36] The dawning realization of Protestant hegemony resulted in landmark Supreme Court cases that eliminated public school practices of prayer and reading from the Bible.

Frequently, the end of devotional approaches to religion in schools is accompanied by the end of all discussion of religion. As a result, students are often ill-equipped to understand religious points of view and may even be deprived of instruction about moral reasoning and reflection that sounds too much like religion. At the beginning of the twenty-first century, the United States is poised to incorporate study about religion as a critical component of understanding the pluralistic character of the nation and the world. To teach about religion in terms of inquiry and critical thinking, rather than indoctrination, an adjustment in educational goals and methods may be in order. The current climate of content delivery, standards, and testing stands as an obstacle to the teaching of religion and the preparation for democratic citizenship. Evaluated in terms of content to be delivered and measured, what can education be, apart from lists of facts that have been deemed essential? Taken to an extreme, this method of education can only be indoctrination for every subject. Indoctrination of any kind closes down debate

and critical thinking. If, however, the climate of education shifts—so that classrooms offer some experiences in and debates about democracy[37]—students might be encouraged more often to learn how to follow a path of inquiry, engage in experimentation, and assimilate various thought processes rather than adopt dogmatic positions. The academic study of religion could help foster as well as greatly benefit from such a climate change in education.

FOR FURTHER READING

Berger, Peter. *The Sacred Canopy: Elements of a Sociological Theory of Religion*. Garden City, NY: Doubleday, 1967.

Coles, Robert. *The Spiritual Life of Children*. Boston: Houghton Mifflin, 1990.

Dewey, John. *Democracy and Education: An Introduction to the Philosophy of Education*. New York: Macmillan, 1952.

Marty, Martin E. *Education, Religion, and the Common Good: Advancing a Distinctly American Conversation about Religion's Role in Our Shared Life*. San Francisco: Jossey Bass, 2000.

Michaelsen, Robert. *Piety in the Public School: Trends and Issues in the Relationship between Religion and the Public School in the United States*. New York: Macmillan, 1970.

Moore, Diane L. *Overcoming Religious Illiteracy: A Cultural Studies Approach to the Study of Religion in Secondary Education*. New York: Palgrave Macmillan, 2007.

Noddings, Nel. *Educating Moral People: A Caring Alternative to Character Education*. New York: Teachers College Press, 2002.

Nord, Warren A. *Religion and American Education: Rethinking a National Dilemma.* Chapel Hill: University of North Carolina Press, 1995.

Smart, Ninian. *Dimensions of the Sacred: An Anatomy of the World's Beliefs.* Berkeley: University of California Press, 1996.

WEB SITES

www.aarweb.org: The official website for the American Academy of Religion contains a brief statement, "Religion in the Schools," under the heading for Public Affairs. This webpage provides links to several additional resources for religion and education.

www.ed.gov: The official website of the United States Department of Education. It offers statistics, discussions of many aspects related to religion and education, and guidance on constitutionally protected prayer.

www.firstamendmentcenter.org: An organization for awareness and ongoing research about the First Amendment, sponsored by the Freedom Forum. This is an excellent resource for the study of religion as well as the rights and limits of religious expression in schools.

www.natre.org.uk: The official website for the National Association of Teachers of Religious Education in the United Kingdom. Because religious education has long been an established subject in the national curriculum, there are several good websites related to the teaching of religion in state schools. See and hear, especially, the NATRE project, "Listening to Children and Young People Talking," which is available through a link from the homepage.

www.studyreligion.org: A website sponsored by the American Academy of Religion that summarizes the benefits of the academic study of religion.

11

CHILDREN

Sarah W. Whedon

INTRODUCTION

The 2008 film *The Fall* explores the vivid imagination of a five-year-old girl named Alexandria who is living out an extended hospital stay for a broken arm. In one troubling scene, she has just stolen a Communion wafer from the Catholic Church and carried it with her as she climbed onto the hospital bed of her adult friend Roy, a man much in need of healing, both of the body and the heart. Alexandria takes a bite of the Communion wafer and feeds the rest to Roy, who asks if she is trying to save his soul. But she doesn't seem to understand the question. What are we to make of this scene?[1]

At minimum, we can say that by sharing and partaking of the host, Alexandria is participating in the ritual of Communion. Or can we? Is it really Communion if it is performed outside the boundaries of the church's authority, with a five-year-old girl acting in the role of the eucharistic minister? We don't even know whether Alexandria understands that the stolen object has spiritual significance.

Can we say that, in this moment, Alexandria is a wicked child who has stolen the host and transgressed the holy rite? Or is she an angelic child who can deliver salvation to a desperate adult, even outside the bounds of the formal church? Perhaps she is an innocent child who is entirely ignorant of the meanings layered onto this action? The US film-watching audience might slot her into any of these childhood tropes.

Studying childhood religion is often as troubling as interpreting this brief scene. We can try to pick apart externally observable ritual actions, adult imaginings of the state of children's souls, and children's own interpretations of their religious experiences. These layers often contradict each other and confound explanation. Differences between adult and child perception, language, and culture can make translation of experience and understanding difficult. This is the challenge of child religious studies.

This article takes up that challenge of perspective and interpretation by looking at children's participation in religious communities

RELIGION AND CHILDREN AT THE MOVIES

The Fall is just one of many films that deals with themes of childhood religion. In this film, the story of Alexandria's stay at the hospital is interwoven with colorfully imagined stories told to her by Roy. *Tideland* is another film in which a little girl's imagination is vividly displayed on the big screen.

The Dangerous Lives of Altar Boys depicts Catholic school children and their own religiously informed imaginations. Meanwhile, horror films such as *The Exorcist* link childhood and Catholic religion in terrifying ways.

Little Buddha is a story about the quest to find the child who is the reincarnation of a recently deceased Buddhist lama (teacher). The road movie *Indigo* centers on the New Age notion of Indigo children, young people with indigo-colored auras and extrasensory perceptions. The documentary *Jesus Camp* depicts the religious education of conservative Protestant children.

Watching films, both fictional and documentary, can reveal a great deal about children's religious experiences, although probably more often they directly reveal the adult writer's, producer's, and director's imaginations of children's religious experiences.

and rites from several perspectives and by examining the different directions in which power and authority flow in relationship to children. It considers religious circumstances when children are expected to follow adult scripts, when they resist those scripts, and when they write their own scripts. It begins with a brief consideration of who or what should be included in the category of analysis that is "religion and children."

THE HISTORY OF CHILDHOOD

Historians and anthropologists in the last several decades have contributed to a new understanding of childhood as socially and historically constructed. Historian Phillipe Ariés is notable for drawing attention to childhood as a historical category, with a study of the European shift from treating children as little adults to understanding

them as different sort of people from adults.[2] His work opened a subfield of historians demonstrating that expectations on children, and even understandings of when childhood ends, have changed over time. Following this insight, a lively production of children's histories has emerged, although religion remains largely ignored by this subfield.

Meanwhile, sociologists such as Allison James, Chris Jenks, and Alan Prout have noticed that childhood changes not only across time but also across cultures.[3] They argue that scholars should focus on childhood as a significant phase of life in and of itself, not simply as a stage in development toward the "real life" of adulthood. And they suggest that we think about children as a minority group, thus allowing us to consider children's social position and relationship to power. This subfield, too, has largely ignored religion.

Beyond the halls of academia, in the political realm, the General Assembly of the United Nations ratified the Convention on the Rights of the Child on November 20, 1989. The document is notable for treating children as persons deserving of human rights and capable of participating in decisions affecting them. However, it is remarkable that it took until 1989 for the United Nations to formalize such a document—and that the United States has refused to sign it—given that children are always and everywhere significant members of society, although rarely given credit for this.

Among the rights granted children by this document is "the right of the child to freedom of thought, conscience and religion." The Convention on the Rights of the Child defines children as those persons under the age of eighteen, unless majority is conferred by a government at an earlier age. However, this is only one possible way of determining who is a child and who is an adult. This neat division between childhood and adulthood neglects the historically relatively new life phase of adolescence. In the United States, eighteen years of age is old enough to drive a car or be drafted into the military, but it is still not old enough to consume alcohol or run for certain political offices, and age of consent to marry differs across state lines. So it is not immediately obvious whether childhood includes infancy and the teen years or only the ages in between.

A great deal of the religious treatment of children is rooted in a religion's definition of or conception of the child and childhood. This includes ideas about the time when childhood begins and when it ends. It also includes ideas about what children are made of, capable of, and in need of. Buddhists, for example, see the child as containing the Buddha nature, a kind of fundamental goodness, at the same time as they are also unique individuals because of karma (the law of cause and effect through action).

Some Christians see children as basically sinful and in need of redemption, whereas others see them as pure and in need of protection. Central to this conversation about the condition of children's souls is Saint Augustine's idea of original sin, that is, infants' sinfulness as a direct result of Adam's transgression in the Garden of Eden, redeemable by baptism, which should be performed as early in life as possible. Pessimism about infant sinfulness reached a low point in Protestant Reformer John Calvin's vision of childhood. Meanwhile, Anabaptists like Menno Simons rejected infant baptism, choosing to wait to baptize until children reached an age when they could choose consciously. Nineteenth-century theologian Horace Bushnell saw faith development as a gradual process rather than a sudden change through baptism. Many decried his positive view of children as abandoning the notion of childhood sin, although ultimately his ideas proved popular. Throughout the history of the theology of childhood, Christian theologians have struggled with reconciling Augustine's doctrine of original sin with a belief in a just and merciful God.

If we primarily wanted to know what religions have to say about adults imagining children, we would have abundant data. We could look more closely at theological debates over original sin. We could look at questions of whether children are born essentially pure and clean or essentially sinful and in need of correction. There is much evidence of children imagined as little devils, or else as little angels. For example, the narrative of the bad boys of Bethel in the biblical story of 2 Kings 2 has had continuing power over the centuries.[4] The notion of childhood innocence and special spirituality occurs frequently in major religious mythology. This childhood specialness is epitomized by prankster stories of the young Hindu deity Krishna, or by well-known Christmas carols that extol the infant Christ child's serenity and divinity. These images of extraordinary or especially spiritual children may or may not correlate with understandings and treatment of actual ordinary children within a religious culture.

It can be difficult to stretch our imaginations past these polarized narratives, past seeing the little filmic Alexandria as an unwitting saint (or a willful little devil). After all, it can be delightful to pass on stories about the amusingly innocent utterances of small children, those funny things that children say about adults or about God. Out of the mouths of babes may come great wisdom, but we may not, in fact, be well equipped to hear it. James Kincaid has observed a pattern of cultural imagination in which children are seen as innocent and vacant, as empty vessels ready to be filled with adults' desires and expectations, a pattern that challenges our ability to see real children truly.[5] Can we move beyond what we hope or fear to see when we turn our gazes upon children? How do children actually behave in religious communities? How does their presence affect the shape of a religious community? How do religions influence them, and how do they influence religions? These are the kinds of questions that the study of children and religion must address. Although the research on these topics is sparse, this article provides the contours of the ways in which scholars can provide answers to these questions.

CHILDREN IN RITUALS

Children participate in rituals in many different ways. In several cultures, childhood is ritualized beginning during pregnancy or at birth. Many rites of passage take place during the course of a child's life. Children also participate in the adult-centered rituals of a religious community. Both of these types of rituals are circumstances in which adults control the ritual script and

children are expected to play their prescribed roles. Finally, children may ritualize and mythologize their lives in ways that are independent from adults' control.

Births

During pregnancy and birth, both fetuses, what might be considered future children, and actually birthed children can be ritualized. Many of these rituals are more about the experiences and transitions of the parents, especially the mother, but none of them have purpose or meaning without the children. This is a critical point: children's presence can make a significant difference for adult religious practice, experience, and identity.

Jewish women, both religious and secular, who gave birth in an Israeli hospital reported that most of their childbirth rituals were aimed at averting the threat of disaster for mother and baby. These rituals include wearing a charm, such as a ribbon blessed by a rabbi, or eating particular foods, such as radishes. These women reported that birthing and getting to care for a new, individual child felt to them like a miracle.[6]

In the United States, birth is ritualized even in secular hospitals. Anthropologist Robbie E. Davis-Floyd has argued that US hospital births are organized around rituals that represent and transmit core cultural valuing of science, technology, and medical institutions. She sees these birth systems as rites of passage for the women who give birth.[7]

Very shortly following birth, children are often ritually welcomed into religious communities. Often, names for children are carefully chosen and have familial or formal religious significance. Muhammad, the name of the final prophet of Islam, is one of the most popular names in the world for boys. On the eighth day after birth, Jewish boys are circumcised, as a sign of the covenant between God and the Jewish community, in a ceremony called a bris. Christians of certain denominations are baptized, a ritual that uses immersion or washing in water to bring a person into membership in the church. Wiccan babies are blessed, welcomed into the community, and sometimes formally given their names in a ritual called a Wiccaning. And when secular or interreligious parents have to make often-difficult decisions about naming or ceremonies for a new infant, they make choices that have power to shape the child's religious experience.

Rites of Passage

Rites of passage are ceremonies that mark transitions from one stage of life to another. Once a child is born, he or she may be given certain rites of passage that are chosen and performed by adults, reflecting adult desires and expectations for children. In many cultures, feeding a child the first solid food is ritualized. In certain Christian churches, baptism, first Communion, and confirmation all mark passages through childhood. Even the secular US celebration of birthday parties represents ritualized celebrations of children's development. Candles and cake, gift giving, and the birthday song make up the ritual objects and actions of the child's birthday party. In some cultures, such as Catholic Poland, children do not celebrate on the date of their own birth but on their "name day," that is, the birthday of the saint after which they were named.

Many rites of passage for children mark their formal movement into religious childhood, or beyond into religious majority. For example, in medieval Europe, a rite of passage for Ashkenazi Jewish boys marked their readiness to take on the important task of formal education as young as age five or six. Early on the morning of the spring festival of Shavuot, someone would carry the boy from his house to his teacher. There the teacher would show him Hebrew letters, read them out loud, and require the child to repeat the letters in various patterns. The teacher would then smear honey on the alphabet and ask the boy to lick it off. Specially prepared foods with biblical verses written on them would be eaten, and the teacher would also teach the child an incantation to ward off forgetfulness and show the boy how to sway and chant when studying his lessons. Thus the Jewish boy was initiated into his religious studies. By the late Middle Ages, this ritual was replaced by the bar mitzvah ritual, which is performed for boys at the age of thirteen, thus pushing initiation into religious adulthood later and lengthening the time of childhood.[8]

In the Roman Catholic Church, children of age seven or eight participate in the first Communion rite, in which, for the first time, they partake of the sacrament of the Eucharist, which they continue to do throughout their lives in the church. Susan Ridgley Bales has done innovative work with childhood anthropology to understand children's experiences and interpretations of this rite. She discovered that children's interpretations differ from those of adults. Their interpretations are rooted much more in their bodily experiences, meaning from what they take in with all five of their senses, rather than from formal teaching that they receive about the rite. It is probable that future research will reveal that children in many religions have this sensory orientation, marking their experiences as different from adult narratives of the same rituals.[9]

Participation in Adult Community Rites

Many rituals that are adult-oriented or are intended for an entire community include children. Sometimes children are expected to participate exactly as adults do, and sometimes there are special roles for the children. Robert A. Orsi's examination of Catholic children observes a persistent concern over children's bodies, which were disciplined through behavior at Mass, memorization of prayer, and the cult of the guardian angel. He writes about a preoccupation with children's bodily control at Mass and a persistent problem of the behavior of altar boys. Orsi argues that this role of the altar boy reflected the ambivalence toward children in the history of Western Christianity, seeing in them both innocence and evil. The altar boys in the churches were seen by parishioners both as miniature saints and as constant misbehavers. Children were encouraged to memorize prayers but also to speak those prayers with passion. They were taught that their guardian angel prayed alongside them.[10]

The Puritan preacher Jonathan Edwards gave sermons directed toward children that mixed logical biblical content with appeals to emotion. Children responded to these sermons in a variety of ways. According to Edwards's own reports, some children were convinced by him to give up play in favor of prayer meetings, and a few even used the emphasis on religious affect to justify public speaking themselves. Some children apparently found his jeremiads cathartic. Others struggled with a mixture of anxiety and despair at his Calvinist message of sinfulness. Contemporary scholar Philip Greven sees Edwards's treatment of children as nothing short of psychological and physical abuse.[11]

A young boy participates in his bar mitzvah ceremony at the Wailing Wall in Jerusalem.

In the late nineteenth century, the family altar grew as a middle-class Protestant home institution that included children in whole family activity. Performed in the morning and the evening, family altar included Bible reading and often a hymn or adult-led meditation. In these rituals, children as well as adults had active roles to play. Still, for some children, family altar could be as much a burden as a source of comfort or positive feeling.[12] Whether at church or at home, community rituals with roles for children have the capacity to stifle children, as well as to empower them, sometimes.

Just for Children

Very different from adult rituals that make space for children, some rituals are developed by children and meant only for child participants. Some of this folklore is less obviously religious, such as the playground song "Ring around the Rosey," which some have thought memorialized plague, an interpretation that is not historically substantiated. Iona and Peter Opie's enormous collection of children's folklore from England, Scotland, and Wales includes a chapter on what might be called "superstition" and what they prefer to call "half-belief." These are beliefs often associated with small rituals engaged in primarily by children. For example, according to children's lore, upon spotting an ambulance, a child should perform self-protection by following regionally variant but specific instructions—usually involving touching his or her collar and waiting to see a four-footed animal. These "half-beliefs" are passed among children rather than being taught by adults.[13]

In the homeless shelters of Miami and other cities across the United States, white, black, and Latino children have developed their own ritual of sharing folktales—"secret stories" that they never reveal to parents or older siblings. These stories feature God fleeing from demons, angels feeding on neon light, or the Blue Lady, who can keep children safe from bullets if they know her secret name. In these stories, folklorists can find traces of older stories from Santería or Mexican traditions. The ritual leaders are the most articulate children, who are the ones who tell the stories to new shelter arrivals. Some children even report having had visions of one of these supernatural beings. But, by about age twelve, children lose their sense of belief in and inspiration from these stories—or perhaps they decide they are too old to admit to believing. These are stories of violence and salvation meant to be told by children to children, away from adult ears.[14]

As individuals, children may also carve out their own secret spaces away from adult observations. They may create mythology, lore, or rituals only for themselves. One woman recalls that, after prayers and formal conversation over the parsonage dinner table, when nobody was paying attention to her, she would slip her small body under the table. There, under the tablecloth, she imagined herself to have gone away on what she called a "Moonie," a time apart in her own private space, away from the prayers and expectations of the family. She writes, "I was in a private and magical spot. No eyes. No prayers, challenges, or decisions."[15] This kind of autobiographical reflection on childhood activity may be a profitable source of rich material for future research on children's religious lives.

Another set of experiences that belongs entirely to the world of children is that of imaginary friends. In the secular Western context, children often speak of experiences with companions seen only by them, often referred to as imaginary friends. Experience of or belief in such unseen beings may relate directly to children's developing religious beliefs in the unseen. When asked if they have imaginary friends, children raised in Christian families sometimes answer that they have Jesus. This kind of slippage in understanding the meanings of beings unseen is one reason why fundamentalist Christians tend to dislike imaginary friends as much as they dislike teaching their children to believe in Santa Claus, which they see as deceitful on the part of children and possibly representing the dangers of Satan. Mennonites see play as a waste of time, and Mennonite teachers are not positive about what they see as pretenses, such as Santa Claus, yet they do approve of private fantasy, such as imaginary companions. These kinds of companions can be compared to experiences that Hindu children report that are related to remembering past lives, something that parents take seriously up until about age seven, at which time they expect children to focus on this current life.[16] So there are many ways in which children can develop religious lives outside of adult religious boundaries or with limited support from adults. These religious lives are contained in the realm of childhood.

MATERIAL CULTURE

Material culture is the physical stuff of culture. A great deal of it can be found in children's religious worlds. Illustrated children's Bibles, toys, teaching manuals, videos, jewelry, clothes, holiday gifts, and so on make up children's experience of religion and are often crafted specifically for children's use.

Chinese children traditionally wore a number of special items for their protection, especially to ward off illness. Amulets of jade or coins were believed to ward off evil. Children were also dressed in bright colors, in hats with animal ears, or in clothes with special protective symbols, all for supernatural protection.[17]

CHILDREN AND PLAY

Many observers see play as one of the major defining characteristics of childhood. Some even consider play to be the work of childhood. Protectors of childhood innocence hope to preserve time and space in which children may play. Although Jonathan Edwards urged sinning children to set aside their play to attend to their religious lives, play is not necessarily distinct from religiousness. It can be intimately linked to morality and spiritual experience.

Dr. Stuart Brown of the National Institute for Play believes that playing can help humans develop moral virtues such as compassion and trust. He describes children's immersion in play as a spiritual experience, saying, "And I think seeing a young child just immersed in play and watching them closely is a spiritual experience. And there is spirit emerging in play. Something nonmaterial that's a part of it that at least it's hard for me to define in this as just ions zipping around in a nervous system."

Dr. Brown's research builds on research on wild animal play, in a quest to understand how play benefits humans at all stages of life. Learn more about Dr. Brown's perspective on play from the radio program "Play, Spirit, and Character" on *Speaking of Faith*, July 24, 2008, accessible at http://speakingoffaith.publicradio.org/programs/play/.

In the present-day United States, *Veggie Tales* is an example of religious media produced specifically for children. It began as animated films, featuring anthropomorphic vegetables that teach morality based on Christian religion and Bible stories, and then expanded to include books and other children's products. These are religious teaching tools designed specifically for children and with a sense of children's playfulness and imagination in mind.

Children may also experience the religious material culture of a community quite differently from the adults in their community, who also interact with it. The built environment is generally organized around the needs of adult bodies. Doors, pews, books, and dishes designed for adults may be enormous, awe-inspiring, unwieldy, or frustrating to children. The best explanation for the Bible from a child's perspective could be "It's a big book and it's got small print," or "It's what the Vicar reads from," rather than an adult perspective that it is the word of God or sacred Scripture.[18] More research is needed to better understand children's interaction with religious material culture.

HARM TO CHILDREN

Although most religions that we can discover have something to say about children's right and good roles and treatment within religion, it would be foolish to ignore the ways in which many children's daily religious lives are painful and dangerous. Religion sometimes becomes a context or provides justification for abuse of children. Public hysteria around child abuse can make it difficult to determine when abuse is actually occurring. Catholic priests have been accused of widespread abuse of children in their parishes and church schools. New religious movements, which often experiment with uncommon structures for family, property ownership, and sexuality, are often accused of abusing children. For example, the federal raid on the Branch Davidians in Waco, Texas, was in part justified by accusations of child abuse in the religious community. More recently, the raid on the Fundamentalist Church of Latter Day Saints in El Derado, Texas, was precipitated by a phone call indicating that an adolescent girl had been abused by a much older man to whom she had been married against her will. These kinds of accusations often seem to be as much about anxiety over religious and sexual difference as about real harm, but they do give cause for careful consideration.

In less hysterical tones, conservative Protestants have been identified as supporters of corporal punishment and believers in a theology that aligns with this practice. James Dobson's Focus on the Family is famously visible for preaching this perspective on childrearing to conservative Christians in the United States. Whether this amounts to or even can lead to child abuse is a matter of debate.[19] Nevertheless, it is clear that religion, for some children, is neither comforting nor even simply boring, but rather stifling or even violent.

Children, of course, live where adults live, and one thing adults do is wage war, often for religious reasons or, at least, in religious terms. So children's daily religious lives can be lives of holy war and jihad as much as lives of peace and growth, and children are sometimes made soldiers in these wars. The widely read diary of Anne Frank records a Jewish girl's experience of hiding from Nazi soldiers during World War II. For some children, daily religious life may be more a matter of survival than of innocence or grace.

AUTHORITY

Questions of authority are hugely significant in the study of religion and children. Adults in religious communities have often been deeply engaged in questions about how to develop right authority over children, teaching them how to be humans, how to be religious people, and, eventually, how to be adults. At the same time, children often have creative ways of claiming authority within their communities. Often, they resist adult's expectations for them. Their reinterpretations of adults' stories, rituals, and material culture allow them to subvert authority. Children rarely are afforded a choice of whether to be a part of a religious community or event, whereas, in many contexts, adults have a choice, but the presence of children is almost certain to have an impact on the adults in the community.

Teaching Children to Be Religious

Adults socialize children into religion in both formal and informal contexts, teaching them about beliefs, practices, and ethical conduct. For example, in general it is considered to be the responsibility of every Muslim adult to help in the raising of a new generation of Muslims who will uphold religious responsibilities and values. The Qur'an and Islamic religious law emphasize parents' responsibility to protect children, although they also create a reciprocal relationship in which children have responsibilities to parents.[20]

Nineteenth-century theologian Horace Bushnell, who wrote *Christian Nurture*, a book that profoundly influenced US Protestant thinking about childhood, wrote, "We can never come into the true mode of living that God has appointed for us until we regard each generation as hovering over the next, acting itself into the next, and casting thus a type of character in the next, before it comes to act for itself."[21] Here Bushnell argues for a complete religious shaping of the young by the previous generation. Many religious communities have also established more specific formal structures for religious instruction.

In the United States, Sunday schools, primarily created by philanthropists with the intention of providing basic education for working children, began opening their doors in the 1790s. However, by 1830, a new sort of Sunday school was flourishing in the United States, one in which volunteer teachers provided an evangelical Protestant religious education for children. These schools grew on a foundation of a growing belief that children were easier to reach with a religious message than adults were. It was hoped both that teaching Protestant doctrine to children would enable them to grow up religious and that they would educate their parents. The development of Sunday schools is intertwined with the history of public schools in the United States.[22]

African Americans have a history of emphasizing education for the betterment of their young people. A contemporary African American Baptist church in Utah is a site where children are taught beliefs that aid them in resisting oppression, and the church is a haven from racism for children. Sunday school teaches children the content and application of biblical stories through various narrative techniques in the classroom. This explicitly religious training, as well as other practical skills such as computer training, helps black Baptist children to be more resilient.[23]

Similarly, in Detroit, the Pan African Orthodox Christian Church's community for children, called Mtoto House, focuses on bettering young black children through faith and education. The daily schedule there supports school attendance and after-school studying, with prayer and religious observance throughout. Each day holds three main religious observances for the children, made up of affirmations and prayers, combining Christian faith with racial empowerment, as in the opening of the first affirmation of the morning: "Like every child growing up in the Black Nation Israel, Jesus was taught The Covenant, the Law, and the Prophets."[24] Thus adults explicitly link race, religious history, and theology for the benefit of the children.

Many Old Order Amish communities run their own schools for their children because they prefer to protect the children from what they see as the malevolent forces of the modern world. These schools' goals are to teach religious values, as well as reading, writing, and arithmetic, leaving aside much of the curriculum of public schools, which aims to teach information and skills that are only useful if the children live in the mainstream world. Amish children are taught humility, obedience to God, and harmony with their community, lessons that are well integrated between school and home. One study has shown that Amish children who attend public schools are more likely to identify with the outside culture than those who are educated by the Amish community.[25]

In many communities, storytelling is a major vehicle for children's religious education. This has been true in Hindu families, where, in the home, parents and grandparents told stories of the Hindu gods to children starting as young as two years old. These stories instruct youngsters in Hindu beliefs, and simply hearing the stories is thought to convey merit to the children. In more recent years, this mythology has been conveyed to children via the modern media of comic books and television series.[26]

Fairy tales are another sort of storytelling for children. In the mid-nineteenth century, some observers were concerned that fairy tales' lack of Christian content was problematic for audiences of children. The Brothers Grimm and other writers of fairy tales modified their narratives to assuage these concerns for child protection and necessary instructive moral content for

children. This concern is apparent in the case of "Hansel and Gretel," a well-known fairy tale in which children who come from a family that cannot provide sufficient food are abandoned in the woods, where they encounter a wicked witch and, when they triumph over her, gain the resources that the family needs. Over the course of multiple revisions of "Hansel and Gretel," changes included the addition of the children calling on God three times for help. This change transforms them into moral and faithful Christian children, and it is these qualities that enable them to overcome the evil witch and return to the morally appropriate authority of their father's house. Through oral, literary, and filmic narration, the latter largely through Disney, children continue to be socialized by fairy tales.[27]

In many children's lives, the question of whether or in what religion to raise and teach a child is significant. Mixed-religion families must choose either explicitly or implicitly whether to raise children in one or the other of the family's religions, both, or neither. This is particularly a concern for Jewish communities following the Holocaust, because of the dramatically reduced Jewish population, the Jewish law asserting that, formally, only children of a Jewish mother are Jewish themselves (a Jewish father does not make a child Jewish), and a high incidence of Jewish intermarriage. Thus, many Jewish communities are concerned with encouraging the Jewish rearing of any Jewish children. In a related domain, parents and policymakers alike have been concerned with the question of whether orphans should be religiously matched for adoption and what this means for individuals and communities.[28]

Whether to raise children with a particular religion is a concern, for different reasons, for members of new religious movements, who may have chosen a religious tradition for themselves and value that opportunity for free choice in matters of belief. Contemporary Pagans, practitioners of a contemporary nature-based religious movement that draws on resources from ancient pagan traditions, debate whether to raise their children with the stories and practices of their tradition or to separate these religious components of their lives from their children unless or until the children ask for them. Some Pagans even argue that the magical and esoteric rites of their own lives are meant only for adults, and they refuse to teach or include their children as long as they remain children.

Children as Active Meaning-Makers

Although adults may wish to have complete power over the religious development of the children in their charge, children are not necessarily passively socialized by parents, teachers, or religious leaders. Rather, they have many ways to subvert authority and reinterpret beliefs and rituals passed to them by older generations.

Drawing on interviews, observations, and mother's field diaries, Cindy Dell Clark demonstrates that US children are active participants in shaping the meanings for the childhood experiences of celebrating Christmas, Easter, and visits form the tooth fairy. Clark finds that, even though mothers talk about rituals around childhood visits from the tooth fairy as demonstrations of children's innocent capacity for belief, thus maintaining their childishness, children see this time as an important step in growing up—when their bodies change and they are rewarded through the adult medium of money.

Christmas is a holiday that Clark sees as largely about how adults situate themselves in relationship to children. Power is given to children in the celebration, because adults plan such activities as gift giving according to expected child responses. At Christmas, adults consider both the developmental and historical past with

a nostalgic lens, projecting innocence into both. However, popular celebration of Easter is really a more child-centered holiday than Christmas is. Rather than crying when forced to sit on the lap of a shopping mall Santa Claus to fulfill adult fantasies of children, children run to visit and pet an Easter bunny at the mall. Also, mothers often report that they would prefer not to engage in the seasonal craft of dyeing Easter eggs but that they do it because their children demand it of them.[29]

Attention to children's understandings of God or the divine also reveals children's ability to be active meaning-makers. A study of Catholic, Jewish, Baptist, and Hindu children's conceptions of God revealed that children are hungry for direct interactions with deity, although often seeing formal ritual as dry obligation. These children frequently used maternal and paternal imagery for God, reflecting their daily lived experiences, but they also had a sense of God's more-than-human power, ubiquity, and capacity for intimacy.[30]

Similarly, Robert Coles saw children's daily experiences present in their religious imagination, arguing that children's representations of God matched their own features, although privileged children think less about the anthropomorphic particularities of God than those who struggle with their own appearance. Coles found that notions of God were highly adaptable to children's particular psychological needs, especially in times of crisis, something Coles observed not in the formal religious institutions of churches or temples but working as a pediatrician at a Boston hospital.[31]

When Children Change Adult Communities

Children's perception and thinking not only shifts the meanings of existing religious traditions, but also children's presence in a religious community can change the community itself. In new religious movements, the birth of a new generation—and thus the entry of children into a community previously made up entirely of adult converts—can change the structure of the community and the content and style of rituals. A generation of children with Pagan parents presents a number of problems to the communities. Adults debate whether to include children in ritual practice or wait until they reach majority. Some adults argue that the religion is meant specifically for adults, and others argue for the value of allowing children to find their own religious paths rather than indoctrinating children into a religion chosen by the parents, as the parents wish their parents had done for them.

Routinization of Paganism is occurring partly as a result of this new generation. Many parents want standard traditions to pass on to their children, and they no longer have the time to create new rituals on a regular basis because of the demands of parenting. This routinization manifests in debates over questions such as whether to pay full-time clergy or whether to purchase land, issues that have wide-ranging affects on the adult community, even when children are not present.[32]

Pagans have experienced an increase in births of children in their communities in the late twentieth and early twenty-first centuries, but, at the other end of the spectrum, religions can also be affected by choices not to have children. At its height, the American Shaker movement helped increase its numbers by taking in orphans. Because the community embraced celibacy, its adherents bore no children of their own, so it became a community that would not have younger biological generations to contend with. Twenty-first-century numbers of Shakers have dwindled to those that can be counted on the fingers of a single hand.

When Children Change Adults

Just as the presence of children can change the shape or activity of a religious community, they can also have an impact on the identities, behaviors, and attitudes of adults. In other words, adults can become, or are expected to become, different sorts of people when they have children in their religious lives.

An example of this phenomenon can be found in the alternative education movement of Waldorf schools. Based on the esoteric teachings of nineteenth-century Austrian Rudolf Steiner, around the world these schools use a curriculum based on an understanding of children as unfolding and developing threefold beings—made up of hands, heads, and hearts. In this system, teachers have the responsibility of supporting children not only in their intellectual growth but also in their physical, emotional, and spiritual growth. As such, Waldorf teaching is, ideally, not just a job but a calling—involving a whole life commitment to the work, including a commitment to stay with a class through eight grades and a commitment to tasks such as daily meditation on the children in their care. Teachers become like mothers, doing intense emotional labor.

Meanwhile, in concert with the school environment, parents are also expected to transform their homes and parenting styles to become ideal nurturers. This includes limiting or entirely forbidding television watching at home, filling the home with children's toys and other objects made from natural materials such as silk or wood, and modeling joyful homemaking for young children. In this context, the well-being and healthy development of the child is thought to depend on the model of self and home that parents and teachers present. Thus, in the Waldorf context, the right teaching of spiritual children also means the creation of particular kinds of spiritual adults.[33]

Sometimes, religious adults are expected not only to teach children but also to learn from children. In the New Testament, the Gospel of Matthew records that Jesus said, "Unless you change and become like little children, you will never enter the kingdom of heaven." Christians who follow this Scripture consider how to observe children in order to discover how to change and become like them.

"BECOME LIKE LITTLE CHILDREN"

The following verse from Matthew 18:1-6 of the New International Version translation of the Bible records teachings by Jesus on children and childishness:

¹At that time the disciples came to Jesus and asked, "Who is the greatest in the kingdom of heaven?"

²He called a little child and had him stand among them. ³And he said: "I tell you the truth, unless you change and become like little children, you will never enter the kingdom of heaven. ⁴Therefore, whoever humbles himself like this child is the greatest in the kingdom of heaven.

⁵And whoever welcomes a little child like this in my name welcomes me. ⁶But if anyone causes one of these little ones who believe in me to sin, it would be better for him to have a large millstone hung around his neck and to be drowned in the depths of the sea."

There are other contexts in which adults turn to children for spiritual insight, sometimes believing that they have sensory abilities beyond the ordinary and therefore something to teach adults. The story of the Cottingley fairies is that, in 1920, Arthur Conan Doyle published photographs that he believed showed real fairies. The photographs had been taken by a pair of cousins, aged ten and sixteen, behind the house where they were living in Cottingley, England.

The Fox sisters, whose experiences are acknowledged as the beginning of modern Spiritualism, were about the same age as the girls who supposedly saw the fairies when the sisters first heard the rappings of a spirit in their home in New York State. These young sisters were so eagerly listened to that their story marks the birth of what became, in the nineteenth century, a popular religious movement, many participants in which were adults who could gain comfort through a medium's communication with their deceased children.

The difficulty with the ways in which children transform adults is that, because of this process, discussion of childhood quickly becomes discussion of adulthood, and, before we know it, real children have slipped from our view. In public debates about children, "rallying for children's welfare becomes the front for other agendas, whether that of upholding a pristine vision of marriage, polishing a tarnished memory of stay-at-home mothers, or defending family diversity regardless of the costs."[34] Because beliefs about and morals surrounding children give adults something to do and be, it is easy for conversations that are ostensibly about children to become, in reality, conversations about adults. This is the trap that this article has continually tried to avoid throughout the consideration here of children and religion.

CONCLUSION

So what childhood trope describes little Alexandria of the big screen? All of the ones considered here can fit. Or, if she were nonfictional, we would have to say that none of them fit. A child is best understood as a person, not a cipher into which we may pour our adult hopes, fears, and faith—a person shaped by the specificity of his or her religious location and also constantly interpreting and shaping that situation. Were Alexandria a real child, we would need to discover her as an agent of her own religious experience as well as someone who changes religious life for adults around her, such as her friend Roy. We cannot assume that we know what it means for her to be a child.

Another fictional character, Leah Price, the daughter of a US missionary to Africa in Barbara Kingsolver's novel *The Poisonwood Bible*, is stunned by this realization about her own childhood when she compares herself to her African friend Pascal.

It struck me what a wide world of difference there was between our sort of games—"Mother May I?," "Hide and Seek"—and his: "Find Food," "Recognize Poisonwood," "Build a House." And here he was a boy no older than eight or nine. He had a younger sister who carried the family's baby everywhere she went and hacked weeds with her mother in the manioc field. I could see that the whole idea and business of Childhood was nothing guaranteed. It seemed to me, in fact, like something more or less invented by white people and stuck onto the front end of grown-up life like a frill on a dress. For the first time ever I felt a stirring of anger against my father for making me a white preacher's child from Georgia. This wasn't my fault. I bit my lip and labored on my own small house under the guava tree, but beside the perfect talents of Pascal, my own hands lumbered like pale flippers on a walrus out of its element. My embarrassment ran scarlet and deep, hidden under my clothes.[35]

Leah recognizes that her conception of childhood, filled with amusements that accomplish no work, looks very unlike a childhood that requires labor for survival and care for younger siblings. She also realizes that there is nothing natural or obvious about the age at which one emerges from childhood. Compared to her, her African friends do not seem to be children at all. So the description of childhood for her time and place does not hold in another culture, and the chronological age of childhood is not fixed.

It is tempting to view childhood as a step on the way to adulthood. Although it is interesting and important to think about how children's religious lives are but a part of a life course that also includes adolescence, adulthood, and old age, we must not reduce childhood to a mere means to an end. Children "are in fact already somewhere, not just on their way to an adult destination."[36] We can learn a great deal about religion and about religious people by focusing on the "somewhere" where children live. Indeed, because children in religion have only rarely been carefully studied, there is still a great deal more to be learned about them, making the field of religion and children an exciting arena in which to work.

GLOSSARY

Child Abuse: Physically or emotionally harmful treatment of children. Religious communities have often been accused of fostering child abuse.

Childhood: A socially and historically constructed period of the human life course, during which the person is considered a child. It usually starts somewhere between birth and a couple of years old and ends somewhere between puberty and age twenty-one.

Material Culture: Physical artifacts of a culture. Examples of children's religious material culture include Bibles, teaching videos, amulets, and ritual clothing.

Rite of Passage: A ritual marking transition from one stage of life or social status to another. Examples of rites of passage in childhood are bris, Wiccaning, first Communion, and bar or bat mitzvah.

Socialization: Sociological term for the process by which children learn to behave within a particular society through the implicit and explicit teachings of parents, schools, religious communities, and others.

FOR FURTHER READING

Bales, Susan Ridgley. *When I Was a Child: Children's Interpretations of First Communion.* Chapel Hill: University of North Carolina Press, 2006.

Boylan, Anne M. *Sunday School: The Formation of an American Institution, 1790-1880.* New Haven, CT: Yale University Press, 1988.

Bunge, Marcia J., ed. *The Child in Christian Thought.* Grand Rapids: Eerdmans, 2001.

Clark, Cindy Dell. *Flights of Fancy, Leaps of Faith: Children's Myths in Contemporary America.* Chicago: University of Chicago Press, 1995.

Kincaid, James R. *Erotic Innocence: The Culture of Child Molesting.* Durham, NC: Duke University Press, 1998.

Marcus, Ivan G. *Rituals of Childhood: Jewish Acculturation in Medieval Europe.* New Haven, CT: Yale University Press, 1996.

Ziolkowski, Eric. *Evil Children in Religion, Literature, and Art.* New York: Palgrave, 2001.

Zipes, Jack. *Happily Ever After: Fairy Tales, Children, and the Culture Industry.* New York: Routledge, 1997.

12

DEATH AND DYING

Stephen Hunt

There is no contradiction in stating that death is a part of life. Nor is it a contradiction to say that death is a "lived experience" for those about to depart this world and their "significant others"—relatives, friends and loved ones—left behind after they die. Whatever the cause of death and at whatever age it occurs, the way in which individuals and entire societies perceive and come to terms with the final episode of life varies as much as it differs with other major life events. In short, there are countless variations by which death has been attributed meaning and coped with throughout history, and those difference still diverge considerably between cultures. Nevertheless, cultural commonalities have also existed and continue to exist, indicating that human beings display the similar psychological and social need to adjust to a very human event, the inevitability of the end of life. Whether expressing cultural similarities or divergence, religion has, as this chapter attempts to show, a central and erstwhile role to play in aiding individuals and communities in coming to terms with the natural process of death.

Max Weber (1854–1920), the renowned sociologist, regarded religion, whatever its expressions, as a "theodicy of suffering," by which he meant a belief system addressing many of the negative experiences of the human condition.[1] Weber speculated that suffering may be at the very root of religious belief and practice or, at the very least, an integral part of it. Suffering includes death not only for those who are at the end of life but also for those left to mourn and adjust to their loss. Death may be a painful experience for the dying, yet it is generally a negative event for those associated with the process. So often death seems unfair, often untimely, and leaves the human mind asking the question as to why it should occur at all. It is not surprising that, as with all aspects of suffering, death has a deeply religious dimension for the social collective. The natural phenomenon of death sets the mind to think profoundly of the meaning of life, matters that perhaps only religion can address. For example, it is no coincidence that the highest philosophy in Indian Hinduism commences with the subject of death and is a common theme in the important scriptures of Bhagavad Gita, Kathopanishad, and Chandogya Upanishad. In this respect, however, Hinduism is not unique. Other major religions also make the topic of death central to their holy writings.

Religion has, throughout the millennia of human history, both forged and reflected perception of death and how it is dealt with in a multitude of societies. Across a wide variety of cultures, whatever the precise belief system, religion can explain the causes of death and embellish it with meaning and significance. Religion can provide the backdrop to funeral and mourning processes and, perhaps most obviously, give expression to faith in the afterlife; shaping the worldview accompanying the final rites of passage from earthly life to the "hereafter" (however that is perceived) with the hope that existence continues in another realm and another form. Despite the infinite variety of belief systems that can be found and that deal with the subject of death, there remains, to reiterate, considerable commonality.

This chapter embraces a comparative approach to the subject of death and dimensions of religiosity that call upon anthropology, history, psychology, sociology, and other disciplines to tease out both variation and common concerns. In this regard, the chapter includes the following interrelated themes. First, cultural perception of death: its understood nature, "causes," and the relevance of accompanying afterlife beliefs. Second, the chapter explores death rituals and mourning processes that help individuals and social collectives express grief and come to terms with death. In that sense, such rituals are richly engraved with symbolic relevance: giving expression to community sentiments and desires. Third, this chapter overviews the social significance of death, which entails probing the everyday experience of death—not just for the dying, but for those left behind, the bereaved.

As part of the cross-cultural themes embraced by this chapter, we explore changing attitudes to death in Western societies and how the experience of death has been affected by such factors as distinctive cultural perceptions, processes associated with medicalization, and the institutionalization of the later stages of life and death itself. Adding to the rich variety of the ways in which death is perceived and dealt with are the cultural changes evident in Western societies that give distinct expressions to death-related procedures and rituals, including mourning and funeral arrangements. Perhaps, above all, the cultural prism through which the contemporary West views death, as well as the social processes around it, is, in many respects, quite unique compared to previous historical cultures, as well as those in the majority world today, where death remains an everyday familiarity and, in short, is a part of the stark reality of life. In the majority world, where life expectancy is low and infant mortality is high, death is a common aspect of routine existence, especially when resources are scarce and poverty rife. By contrast, in Western societies, death is typically given a very different meaning; it is related to long life expectancy and associated with old age as a result of relatively high levels of health and economic prosperity and where death tends to be hidden from public view.

THE SOCIAL SIGNIFICANCE OF DEATH

Human beings, by nature or necessity, are social animals. Their experiences of life are shared, literally from the cradle to the grave. Death, of course, is a profoundly personal experience: it is the final life event that comes to all. The thought of death may increase in a person's later years as he or she grows older and experiences inevitable physical decline. It may well be, however, that the matter of death preoccupies the individual subconsciously throughout life. This was certainly the conclusion reached by the psychoanalyst Sigmund Freud. Freud believed that humans are driven by two conflicting central desires, a theme that was explored most cogently in his work *Beyond the Pleasure Principle*. These desires are the life drive, or "libido" (such as survival, hunger, thirst, reproduction, and sex), and the death drive, or what Freud referred to as "Thanatos." His description of "cathexis," the energy of which constitutes the libido, includes all creative, life-producing drives. The death drive (or death instinct), whose energy Freud designated as "anticathexis," represents an urge that is inherent in all living things—to return to a state of calm without danger: in other words, an inorganic or dead state—a place of safety as protective as the womb from which life originally emerged.

In a sense, Freud was aware of the social implications of death. In one of his most controversial conjectures associated with his death-instinct theory, he postulated that all living creatures are involved in an ongoing struggle between competing impulses for activity and survival, on the one hand, and withdrawal and death, on the other. From this theory, Freud contentiously argued that it was human destructive impulses that could eventually annihilate civilization itself, unless they were rechanneled by improved child rearing, psychoanalysis, and more effective societal patterns. Freud also identified these "immature" impulses as the source of what he saw as the delusion of religious belief.

The subject of the social significance of death has also been addressed more directly by anthropologists. A good number have explored the relationship between death and aspects of religiosity in the social context. For example, Malinowski, in his seminal account of the tribal people of the Trobriand Islands, indicated that religion was particularly significant during certain times: situations of individual emotional stress that threatened collective solidarity and sentiment that was necessary for the effective functioning of the social order.[2] Contexts that produced these emotions included "crises," such as birth, puberty, marriage, and death, with all the uncertainties that they generate. Malinowski noticed that, in all preindustrial societies, life crises are surrounded with religious ritual. Death was the most disruptive of these events because it severed strong personal attachments and thwarted human designs—often occurring in a seemingly arbitrary and unpredictable way.

From this observation, Malinowski concluded that the ability to deal with the problems associated with death is probably the main source of religious belief and rituals. Thus, through funeral ceremonies, mourning is expressed and belief in immortality articulated—in a sense denying the finality of death itself and subsequently comforting the bereaved. Indeed, the significance of religiosity in the bereavement process signifies a particular type of discontinuity. Death means the cessation of someone's life and the end of the relationship that the deceased shared with others. Moreover, it brings a unique form of psychological challenge because death is final. From his study of the Trobrianders, Malinowski was able to deduce that the high level of religious activity surrounding death was a common feature of all societies and performed many of the same functions.

Death, in Malinowski's account, is not just a personal experience: it is a social and shared event. This was a theme also developed by Halbwachs,[3] a student of one of the so-called founding fathers of sociology, Émile Durkheim (1858–1917). For Durkheim, individuals are undoubtedly affected by biological and psychological drives, but human life is overwhelmingly shaped by social phenomena. And, according to Durkheim, social phenomena can be regarded as "social facts" that display distinctive social characteristics and determinants that are not amenable to explanations on the biological or psychological level.[4] Social facts are external to the individual as a biological entity. They endure over time, despite the fact that particular individuals die and are replaced by others.

If, for Durkheim, social characteristics and determinants shaped individual experiences of life in the human collective, Halbwachs insisted that the same went for the social implications of death. Death is a biological process, but the way that it is culturally understood is, in a sense, external to the individual who shares its social significance, and it was its social significance that shaped psychological needs. Irrespective of the considerable cultural variations of how death is perceived and understood, it has a profound social relevance. Halbwachs stressed the fact that death must be comprehended and appraised within the environment of wider community relationships. This was certainly so in traditional, preindustrial societies, where the broader social context and extended kinship networks are so evidently relevant to the everyday life of the individual.

To illustrate the importance of the social collective at the time of death, Halbwachs distinguished between "physical death" and "social death." The former refers to what is now understood as the medical definition of death: simply, the human body ceases to function biologically. The latter denotes the social consequences of death. The "live" person may have gone, but his or her social significance remains, and the implications are immeasurable, including those of a religious nature. This is starkly seen in the example of traditional culture in Malaysia, where death is a "process"—a series of religious ceremonies marking the slow transition from the "living world" to the afterlife as it is understood. Because it is a very hot climate, the deceased is

buried as soon as possible. This represents physical death. A few days later, the body is exhumed and a funeral ceremony takes place, in which friends and relatives say a final goodbye—rich in its religious significance—to the dead person who was once integral to their lives. Moreover, in a profound way, the deceased is still part of continuing social relations for an appreciable period after death. This is why most cultures have elaborate funeral ceremonies and an accompanying period of mourning that symbolizes the fact that society slowly withdraws from the dead over a time of transition, until the memory of that person diminishes and the implications of his or her loss gradually recedes.

In all cultures, the social significance of the deceased is exemplified by the eulogy often spoken at a funeral—an oration given in tribute to a person or people who have recently died. In traditional cultures, the eulogy is of particular importance in highlighting past social relationships. Here, religion plays its erstwhile role. For instance, the eulogy (*Hesped*) in Orthodox Judaism is a brief and simple yet vital part of the funeral service and intended primarily for the honor and dignity of the deceased (*yekara d'schichba*). The worthy values that the deceased lived by, the good deeds they performed, the noble aspects of their character, how they performed their social and religious duties and partook of communal relationships are eulogized.

The principal function of the eulogy, however, is not to comfort the bereaved, although by highlighting the good and the beneficial in the life of the departed it affords an implicit consolation for the mourners. Because the eulogy not only praises the deceased but also confronts all who attend with the fact of their own mortality—to take stock and live their lives to the full, fulfill their obligations, and live the correct way, according to the Judaic faith. Moreover, for Orthodox Judaism, and many other faiths for that matter, death also brings a leveling process. This is recognized in the Jewish tradition, where it is stressed that, wealthy or poor, all are equal before God. Judaism therefore demands that all Jews be buried in the same type of garment. Death shrouds have no pockets. The deceased, therefore, can carry no material wealth into the next world. Because it is not a person's possessions but his or her soul that is of ultimate relevance, the clothes to be worn should be appropriate for one who is shortly to stand in judgment before God.

A universal cultural fact is that the dead are not immediately forgotten, despite the funeral rite and accompanying eulogy; they remain, for a short period at least, a primary element of the lives of those significant others who have been left behind. At the same time, wider society has lost one of its members—an individual who may have once performed important social roles. In this way, the death of an individual constitutes a societal loss. Frequently, this means that relatives and, in the case of small-scale preindustrial societies, entire communities have to deal with psychological and emotional challenges, as well as new practical arrangements, arising in the wake of the death of a social member.

In some cultural systems, the dead are seen as profoundly involved in earthly matters. Although this may be expressed in a diversity of religious systems, it is perhaps most obvious in ancestral worship. Ancestor worship is a practice based on the belief that deceased family members have a continued existence, take an interest in the affairs of the world, and/or possess the ability to influence the fortune of the living. The goal of ancestor veneration is to ensure the ancestors' continued well-being and positive disposition toward the living; sometimes they are asked for special favors or assistance. The social or nonreligious function of ancestor veneration is to enhance kinship values, family loyalty,

and continuity of the family lineage. Veneration implies a continuation of filial piety—to be good to one's parents, to take care of them, and to engage in good conduct—not just toward parents but also outside the home—so as to bring a good name to one's parents and ancestors.

Ancestor worship is, by way of example, one of the most unifying aspects of Vietnamese culture: practically all Vietnamese, regardless of religious expression (Buddhist or Christian), have an ancestor altar set up in their home or workplace. In Vietnam, people do not traditionally celebrate birthdays; instead, the death anniversary of a loved one is always an important social occasion. The event constitutes an essential gathering of family members for a banquet in memory of the deceased: incense sticks are burned and great platters of fruit and food are made as offerings on the ancestor altar, which usually displays pictures of the deceased. These offerings and practices are conducted frequently during important traditional or religious celebrations, the starting of a new business, or even when a family member needs guidance or counsel, and they are a hallmark of the emphasis that Vietnamese culture places on filial duty.

Whatever the precise belief system, religious beliefs often dictate that the deceased should leave this world on good terms with those left behind. In Judaism, it is hoped that the dying will depart this life forgiven and having forgiven others: ensuring that social relations are left sound and that life continues with a measure of peace, once old wounds are healed. If there is anyone the person feels they have wronged, the dying should seek the forgiveness of the offended party. The Talmud, the record pertaining to Jewish law, ethics, and customs, relates that God can forgive trespasses against others only after they have forgiven. *Teshuvah* means, according to Jewish tradition, that the faithful can repair, enhance, and put to rights any aspect of life, as long as they still live. Through deep regret and firm resolve, the dying have the power, literally, to return in time to past iniquities and failings. In a single moment of *teshuvah*, they can repair the damage and fill the spiritual inadequacies of their lives.

Other religious systems also seek to ensure that the dying leave the social world in good terms with those left behind. A particular feature of the Hindu funeral ritual is the preparation of rice balls (*pinda*) that are offered to the spirit of the dead person during memorial services. In part, these ceremonies are seen as contributing to the merit of the deceased, but they also pacify the departed soul so that it will not linger in this world as a ghost but will pass through the realm of Yama, the god of death. Hindus who perceive what they witness as a "bad" death may be very anxious about the ghost of the deceased. This is especially so with the premature death of an infant. Hindu belief dictates that if an infant leaves the "earthly" realm, it departs into an intermediate zone in readiness for its journey to the "divine realm." Thus, it has not quite departed this world nor yet reached the next. An elaborate funeral, which nonetheless has many of the elements provided to adults, is therefore necessary to ensure that the transition takes place. As a baby approaches death, the family chants *Ram Ramor Om* and recites from the Bhagavad Gita. A thread with a religious significance may be tied around the wrist or neck of the baby. A leaf from a tulsi shrub (basil leaf) is placed in the baby's mouth, occasionally with a gold coin. After a ritual wash, new clothes are put on the infant, who is subsequently wrapped in a white shroud.

Death almost certainly changes existing social obligations and roles and generates new ones. This is particularly so in preindustrial societies, where such roles and obligations are unchanging across the generations and the pressure to perform them are strong. This may vary from one culture to another. For example, as part of the traditional Chinese funeral arrangement, on the passing away of the father, the eldest son becomes the head of the family, reflecting the deeply embedded patriarchal structures. If the eldest son passes away, his second brother does not assume leadership of the family. Leadership passes to the eldest son or the grandson of the father. He must assume the responsibilities and duties, including religious ones, to the ancestors on behalf of the family.

The loss of a close relative in many cultures may also include a change of life that entails social exclusion: the nonsocial. This may most obviously be expressed, as explored in the following, by retreating from wider society during the immediate period of bereavement and sometimes for much longer. Social exclusion may also have more dire consequences. For example, according to Hindu mythology, Sati, the wife of the god Dakhsha, was so overcome at the demise of her husband that she immolated herself on his funeral pyre and burned herself to ashes. Since then, the name Sati has come to be symptomatic of self-immolation by a widow, even to the point of throwing herself on her husband's funeral pyre. Today the practice of *sati* is illegal in India, although it is believed to continue in the remote rural corners of the country.

Despite the mythological origins of *sati*, it is not entirely clear why the practice initially came into being. One explanation sees it as connected to the origins of the dowry: the money, goods, or estate that a woman brings to her husband in marriage in traditional India. Immolation was always more prevalent among the higher martial caste. Among the lower castes, it is nearly absent. Among the higher castes, a bride was looked upon as a burden, because she represented a drain on the family's income, while not contributing anything toward it. She thus became an ill omen to all those around her. If this was her status as a bride, it is not surprising that, if she had the misfortune to become a widow, her presence in the family was despised. Other reasons for the practice have also been offered: the near impossibility of widow remarriage—arising from the taboos and prejudices that sanctified virginity of a bride within the Hindu tradition—or the nonrecognition of the individuality of a woman, who was considered part and parcel of her husband, without whom her life became irrelevant.

Death in Western Societies

The function of religion at the time of death in many societies ranges further than dealing with the matter of social roles. Another dimension is religion's utility in offering consolation. In pre-modern societies, the acceptance of the inevitability of death as a natural cosmic process, informed by religious belief systems, often shapes the consolation of the dying (as well as that of those closely associated by blood or friendship), preparing them for the next world. In the more secular West, this has become more problematic. The picture, however, remains complex, given that it is something of an underresearched area, even in the United States, where religious attitudes to life appear to be more prevalent than in many Western European countries. Nonetheless, in Western societies in general, the social significance of death has observably declined in the sense previously discussed. This is partly as a result of the fact that, in such nations, extended family and community relations have become less significant, where individualism has become a prime cultural idiom, and where religious belief has observably experienced a decline. There are numerous implications for all of these developments that can now be detailed.

In the Western setting, the dying person is typically segregated from one of the foremost social supports that provide meaning—the family. Moreover, the death of the individual is of less and less social significance, in the sense that it is institutionalized and largely anonymous. Death, as the last rites of passage, is not a public event; hence its social relevance declines. Rather, it is a private experience and is likely to take place within the institutional context of the hospital, hospice, or home for the elderly. In that sense, society begins to isolate the dying, withdrawing from them even before they depart this world. Neither is death central to everyday life, and there are few reminders of the departed. In many parts of Europe, the church and its surrounding graveyard were physically located at the center of village life. Graves typically declare the names of the departed and the years in which they lived. Today, the common disposal of the dead is by way of cremation, taking place in crematoriums that are largely located on the remote outskirts of towns and cities—rendering death "out of sight and out of mind." Although the cremation may include a short religious service, for many of the bereaved attending, they may be impersonal and inadequate ways of marking the departure of a loved one.

Perceptions of death in Western cultures, by contrast to premodern societies, profoundly reflect social change—not least of all as a result of increasing secularity: religious belief is reduced, and there is declining communal context in which religiosity is embedded.[5] At the same time, Western culture is age- and death-denying. Where there is an emphasis on prolonging life, of consuming strategies to retain youth, there is an inability to tolerate death in a culture that is orientated toward perpetual life.[6] In short, it becomes a subject of profound taboo, perhaps even more so than for preindustrial societies. As a result, the Western mind finds it difficult to come to terms with death, particularly the death of a child, in a society where infant mortality is low and life expectancy is high. The reality of death is particularly hidden from children, who are generally protected from death as a reality of life. Whereas in traditional societies, such as rural Hindu India most funeral rites are fulfilled by the family, all of whom participate, including the children, who need not be shielded from the reality of death.

There exists, moreover, a contradiction and dilemma generated by the death-denying culture of Western societies—one that displays profound difficulty in accepting the reality of death, on the one hand, while sustaining a familiarity with real death through media images and the "celluloid death" of fictional literature, films and television, and video games, on the other. Whereas, in the majority world, where there is a familiarity of death and where death is truly part of life, death in Western societies becomes distant, remote, and unreal. These cultural distortions of real death have had an impact in ways that change the meaning of death, the social significance of death, and even mourning processes and beliefs in the afterlife. These matters are now considered by way of a comparative analysis.

AFTERLIFE BELIEFS

If Weber was correct and religion is a "theodicy of suffering," this can be affirmed in the evidence provided by many cultures as death approaches and eventually occurs. In a psychological vein, a comparative study by von Franz,[7] developing the psychoanalytic theories of Carl Jung (1875–1961), a student of Freud, stressed that the unconscious beliefs in a life after death become more significant from middle age onward but are especially important as death approaches. Unconscious religious impulses, especially expressed as dreams, prepare individuals for the hereafter—often pointing to imbalances in attitudes that need to be corrected and

that constitute something approaching a review of the person's life. Such a review allows older people to come to terms with the past. In this way, religion, once again, may enhance psychological and social well-being. There is evidence that this function of religion is observable even in the more secular West. Consistent with the previously described observations with respect to Orthodox Judaism, the findings of nationwide research in the United States by Krause and Ellison[8] disclosed the tendency of older people, coming to a realization of their own mortality, to be concerned with distressing events in earlier life and to see such events in religious terms. Among other considerations, those who forgive others in later life tend to enjoy a greater sense of psychological well-being than older people who are less willing to forgive transgressors for the negative things that they had inflicted upon them.

Perhaps more obviously, religious belief prepares those who are growing older for their own death and includes not only engendering reconciliation with those left behind but also generating conciliation with God (however God is perceived). One of the most common interpretations of the implications of aging for religiosity is premised on the awareness of finitude—that the proximity to death heightens a focus on "making peace with one's maker."[9] For this reason, belief in an afterlife may be especially evident in later stages in the life course, in so far as older people typically display higher levels of belief in a life after death. However, as Finney notes in his survey in the United States, *Finding Faith Today*, bereavement and suffering, often associated with old age, are among the factors reported in finding faith at any time in the life course in Western societies. Moreover, although it may well be that the aging process and bereavement of family and peers are accentuated in old age, they could equally lead to a loss of faith.[10] In that sense, experiences of suffering and loss may convince older people that the seemingly arbitrary nature of life suggests that God and the afterlife do not exist and that "this is all there is."

In the West, where we may not live in fear of death in everyday life, the fear is more likely to stalk us in later years. How we respond and whether we make the decision to take a recourse to religious solace vary in the pluralist context, where the pressures of society to defer to a single religious worldview decline. It follows that differing degrees and types of religious commitment remain strongly evident on the approach of death and that, if they do, they may ease anxieties about its inevitability. For instance, Kalish and Reynolds found that, in the United States, strong religious believers were rated lowest on death anxiety, but those with "confused" religious beliefs were rated higher than agnostics or atheists.[11] In other words, they were not convinced one way or another that God and the afterlife exist. These researchers also found that older people differed from other age groups in the opinions expressed concerning preparation for their own death. When asked to imagine that their deaths would occur within thirty days and to report what changes would be made in their lives as a result, older people were more likely to say that they would not change their lifestyle, but they would, nonetheless, concentrate on aspects of the contemplative "inner life" or spiritual concerns in preparation for the end of their lives.

Without doubt, religious belief systems give succor to the dying and their significant others. The majority of religious systems provide articulation to the nature of life and death—to beliefs in the afterlife that can comfort the dying and those left behind, the bereaved. This may be socially and psychologically beneficial in explaining the "causes" of death. Religious beliefs frequently advance the view that death is in the will and design of God. Throughout the Hindu holy works, for example, death constitutes a time for those left behind to reflect and to seek the goal of "truth" and the nature of God, the eternal Brahman. For the Hindu, death is nothing but the transformation of the body as part of a cosmic process. The eternal soul throws off its physical shroud like a used garment. Human life is purged and perfected to attain the final bliss. This takes place through myriad rebirths; life is one continuous, never-ending process. The soul is immortal. It takes one form after another, on account of its own actions. Death is only a necessary and passing phenomenon. Just as an individual moves from one house to another, the soul passes from one body to another to gain spiritual enlightenment.

Similarly, for Buddhists, although they do not believe in a supreme deity, death is an inevitable part of the cycle of life and the transmigration of souls (reincarnation). Old age and death are merely preparation for the next life. When someone is approaching death in a Buddhist Burmese home, monks come to offer comfort and chant verses such as the following.

> Even the gorgeous royal chariots wear out; and indeed this body too wears out. But the teaching of goodness does not age; and so goodness makes that known to the good ones. (Dhammapada 5.151)

This is a basic teaching of Buddhism that highlights the idea that existence is suffering, whether via birth, daily living, old age, or dying. Such teaching is never more profound than when death itself approaches.

Many religious systems stipulate that death does not have to be viewed negatively. The Islamic understanding of death is, in a very real sense, a positive one. Muslims, on the whole, are encouraged to be ever mindful of the mortality of the self, because death is divinely willed, and, when it arrives, it should be readily accepted.

The Qur'an states: "Everyone shall have to die" (3:185). Although a traumatic time, at death, Muslims are encouraged to remember that Allah is the one who gives life and takes it away. The Prophet Muhammad taught that "to Allah belongs what He took, and to Him belongs what He gave." All human life is recorded with him for the appointed time of death. There should therefore be no reasoning by the bereaved as to why they have lost their loved one. Islam requests the faithful to reflect constantly on the fact that death can arrive at any moment. Only God knows when his servants and unbelievers alike will die: it is not for the faithful to question his wisdom. However, there is a caveat that death should not be wished for, even by the faithful.

Islam, like other world faiths, insists that another life begins after death and, as with other faiths, advances the view of a day of judgment for deeds performed in this life. Indeed, the brief and temporary life is but a preparation for *Akhirah,* which is never-ending. Islam teaches that, after death, at a particular time, there will be a momentous occasion of God's judgment (*Yawmul Akhir* or *Yawmuddln*). God, who makes human beings out of nothing, can raise them again after death. The Qur'an asks: "Does man think that we shall not assemble his bones? Yes, surely, yes, we are able to restore the very shape of his fingers" (75:3, 4). On this great day, all human beings will be brought to life again, and God will present to each of them a record of how they conducted their lives.

The realms of paradise and hell are vividly described throughout the Qur'an, and, as such, these realms are not metaphorical to many Muslims but will become concrete realities, when Allah determines it to be (for instance, Qur'an 7:718; 4:59; 46:40, 55). If the deceased is pious, the angels will treat him or her with exceptional courtesy, and the intermediate realm will be one of peace and blissfulness. The pious Muslim will

be rewarded in heaven (*al-Jannah*), a place of beauty and joy. But there is also hell. One traditional account of what happens in hell (*al-Jahannam*) is given by al-Ghazali, an Islamic scholar, in his book *The Remembrance of Death and the Afterlife.* He presents a graphic description of the tortures and torments that the unbeliever and the sinner are subjected to in hell, the realm of the horrible pit, full of horrors and tortures.

In the West, the nature of afterlife beliefs in mainstream culture, despite secularization processes, appears to be fairly buoyant, but these ideas are observably changing. For many people, this belief is a tentative one, and the content of the afterlife remains vague. Certainly, traditional Christian beliefs are being eroded and are being replaced by a plurality of beliefs. For a sizeable number of young adults, in particular, there may be a refusal to rule out an afterlife, even though they would not go so far as to say that they positively believe one actually exists. This is a generation that finds itself in the culture of relativism that is associated with postmodernity, one that does not trust religion but that also no longer has faith in science. It is a culture where one person's view of the possibility of the afterlife and what it might entail is as good as another's. In short, it is an age group of individuals who keep an open mind on the subject of life after death.[12]

The precise range of beliefs regarding the afterlife, held by the populations of Western societies, has proved to have been of considerable interest to sociologists of religion over several decades. Recent surveys suggest that orthodox Christian beliefs remain evident, but they are supplemented by a range of alternatives. In his research in Britain, Douglas Davies identified five options of a possible afterlife between which respondents discerned fairly easily.[13] In his sample of 1,603 individuals, Davies found that 29 percent believed that nothing happens after death; 43 percent that the soul passes on to another world; 8 percent that the body awaits resurrection; 12 percent that reincarnation as something or someone else exists; and 22 per cent that what precisely occurs after death "is in God's hands." The striking figure relates to reincarnation beliefs, a notion that had traditionally been alien to Western culture. Earlier research in the United States, by a Gallup opinion poll, had established such belief as high as 20 percent when respondents answered yes to the question "Do you believe in reincarnation?" In this research, the pollsters presented those asked with the option of replying "yes", "no", or "don't know" to the possibility of reincarnation.[14]

Walter and Waterhouse discovered in their survey that those in Britain who answered yes to whether they believed in reincarnation far outnumbered those who belonged to minority group religions such as Hinduism, Sikhism, and Buddhism, which formally teach reincarnation or rebirth. Reincarnation is not part of a well-established and communally held folk-religion in most Western societies.[15] This means that belief in reincarnation is not something that has been formally codified by the culture and conventional religion of the indigenous population. Indeed, the notions involved are underdeveloped and rarely seem to originate distinctly in any particular world religion. Walter and Waterhouse also argue that afterlife beliefs are becoming semidetached from other religious beliefs and almost entirely detached from morality; hence there is no overriding fear of future retribution for actions in this life.

A number of Walter and Waterhouse's findings were reflected in the European Values Surveys (EVS) of 1981 and 1990. The surveys asked respondents whether they believed in life after death and found that those answering yes constituted around 40 percent of the sample. This figure had changed little over the decades. Moreover, the EVS data indicated that those

who believed in an afterlife tended to be religious, according to other measurements. However, these surveys also contained more specific questions about what the afterlife was actually supposed to entail. For instance, it showed that, whereas belief in heaven remained fairly buoyant (at around 30–50 percent across Western European countries), belief in hell had definitely gone out of fashion. Lambert, interpreting the 1999 EVS data, nonetheless suggests an increasing belief in the afterlife in terms of death, heaven, and reincarnation among young people.[16]

THE MOMENT OF DEATH

In many cultures, religion has great significance at the very moment of death. According to Buddhist tradition, when a person is dying, every effort should be made to fix the mind upon the scriptures or to ask the individual to repeat one of the names of Buddha, such as *Phra Arahant* (Enlightened One). The name may be whispered in his or her ear if the person is far advanced in the dying process. Sometimes, four syllables that are considered to be the heart of the *Abhidharma*—third-century-BCE and later Buddhist works; that is, *ci, ce, ru,* and *ni,* representing the heart, mental concepts, form, and nirvana (the state of being free from both suffering and the cycle of rebirth)—are written on a piece of paper and put in the mouth of the dying person. It is hoped that, if the last thoughts of the dying are directed to Buddha and the precepts, the fruit of this meritorious act will bring good to the deceased in their new existence.

Ideally, the Hindu devotee dies at home, knowing the merits of dying among loved ones. When death is imminent, kindred are notified. The person is placed in his or her room or in the entryway of the house, with the head facing east. A lamp is lit near the head of the dying, who is urged to concentrate on a mantra. Kindred keep vigil until the great departure, singing hymns, praying, and reading Scripture. If the dying person is unconscious at the time of death, a family member chants the mantra softly in the right ear. If none is known, the mantras of *Aum Namo Narayana* or *Aum Nama Sivaya* are intoned (this is also conducted for sudden-death victims). Holy ash or sandal paste is applied to the forehead, Vedic verses are chanted, and a few drops of milk, Ganga (water from the holy Ganges River), or other liquids of religious importance may be offered to the dying person.

A widespread practice throughout the Islamic world is to adjust the position of the dying person so that the head is at the east and the feet at the west, enabling the face to turn to toward the *Qiblah* (the Kabaa in Mecca). In all Islamic traditions, when a Muslim is near death, those around him or her are called upon to give comfort and reminders of God's mercy and forgiveness. They typically recite verses from the Qur'an, give physical comfort, and encourage the dying one to recite words of remembrance and prayer. As death draws closer, someone near to him or her gently recites the *shahada,* to ensure that the last thing a person hears is the declaration of faith (*nyebut*) (and other affirmations of faith): "There is no god but God and Muhammad is the Messenger of God" (*'Laa ilaaha illa-Allah'*). Hence, the last words that a Muslim hears are ideally those heard on entering the world on birth. It is hoped that Allah will be in the last mortal thoughts of the dying, and thus, upon awakening in the grave, God will be first and foremost in the mind of the deceased.

Orthodox Judaism similarly prescribes observances and customs for life's closing moments. As death nears, the faithful, along with all who are present at the time, should recite the Shema and other verses affirming

> Soul of Christ, sanctify me.
> Body of Christ, save me.
> Blood of Christ, refresh me.
> Water from the side of Christ, wash me.
> Passion of Christ, strengthen me.
> O good Jesus, hear me.
> Within your wounds hide me.
> Let me never be separated from you.
> From the power of darkness defend me.
> In the hour of my death, call me
> and bid me come to you,
> that with your saints I may praise you for ever and ever.
> Amen.
>
> *The Anglican Prayers for the Death and the Dying*

belief and faith in God and his oneness. If there is a single sentence that encapsulates the faith and life mission of the Jew, it is the words *Shema yisrael, Ado-nai E-loheinu, Ado-nai echad*— "Hear O Israel, the Lord is our God, the Lord is one." Ideally, Jews say these words every morning and evening and thus depart life as they lived it, with the words of the Shema on their lips. These are the words that the Jew proclaims at life's culmination. If the dying person is unconscious, those present should recite those verses for him or her. In the closing moments of life, a person should repent, with all his or her heart, for all wrongdoing committed in the course of life.

Religious belief systems articulate the afterlife, particularly for those who subscribe to them. This is true in the case of the Christian tradition as much as it is for other major faiths. In the Christian Anglican formula, the funeral is held about a week after death. It can take place either in a church or at a crematorium. Typically, the Anglican priest opens the service with the reading from the scriptures:

> "I am the resurrection and the life," saith the Lord; "he that believeth in me, though he were dead, yet shall he live: and whosoever liveth and believeth in me shall never die."

In the medicalized setting of death in Western societies, the religious significance of death is minimal. The specialized roles of those tending the dying seldom include the provision of the meaning of death and dying, religious or otherwise. Unlike traditional meaning systems, modern medical systems do not consider as part of the role of staff that of helping the patient assign meaning to illness and death, especially a religious meaning. In the institutional setting of the hospital, as Ariès points out, the priest has been replaced by the doctor at the closing moments of life.[17] The problem of the social meaning of death, from which religious significance is at least partially derived, becomes especially acute, because the value system assigns comparatively great worth to individual lives. Moreover, in Western societies, dying and death have become particularly vulnerable to loss of meaning. This partly results from the undermining of the traditional theodicies that Weber spoke of, the belief systems that forge explanations of death and that help individuals come to terms with it. In the West, this may leave the dying and those close to them culturally confused. This has, by way of illustration, given rise to suggestions that the funeral event has less meaning and that the mourning process has been rendered psychologically inadequate. It is to these themes that we now turn.

FUNERALS

When death occurs, precisely how the dead are disposed of is of great social significance. Many of the major religions prescribe procedures in disposing of the body on death, and they often display some remarkable similarities. Several examples may be given. With respect to Islam, death and funeral ceremonies show, in their essence, the most consistent features throughout the Muslim world, more so than for any other rites of passage. This is evident in the preparations of the body for burial and constitutes a *Fard Kifaayah*—a communal obligation for Muslims that follows a fairly universal set of rituals and share some comparable aspects with other major faiths. There are, however, some localized variations.

Muhaimin shows how, in Moslem Cirebon, in West Java, preparing the dead for the funeral is very much a communal event.[18] Women bring bowls or containers, covered with handkerchiefs, to the home of the deceased. The bowls are filled with rice, and some money is conveyed to the dead person's family as a contribution for the funeral. This visit (called the *nglayat*) entails people working together to care for and bury the corpse. A divan for bathing the body is put near a well, where a tank full of water containing herbs and flowers is ready. The corpse is then laid on the divan, pillowed on three sections of a banana tree trunk at the nape, waist, and legs. The bathing is led by a specialist, or *lebe*, and involves the dead person's close relatives, especially older children. After the bathing is finished, the corpse is taken and put on mats in the front room of the house, with the head at north and the feet at south. All bodily orifices are closed with cotton, and the whole body is perfumed, embalmed with herbs, and wrapped in seamless clothes of white sheets tied around its feet, waist, and top of the head. The next procedure after washing is the obligatory act of shrouding the entire body in clean, ideally white cloth (*kafan*), wrapped with one or two sheets. The preferable number is generally considered to be three, given that the Prophet was shrouded in three at his death.

Hindu death rituals in all their expressions follow a fairly uniform pattern that is drawn from the Vedas, with variations according to sect, region, caste, and family tradition. Certain rites are traditionally performed by a priest but may also be performed by the family if no priest is available. After the death of a family member, the relatives become involved in ceremonies for preparation of the body and a procession to the burning or burial ground. Typically, after death, in the Hindu convention, the body is laid in the home's entryway, with the head facing south, on a cot or on the ground—reflecting a return to the lap of Mother Earth. (Hindus often prefer to die lying on the ground.) The lamp is kept lit near the head, and incense is burned. A cloth is tied under the chin and over the top of the head. The thumbs are tied together, as are the big toes. Religious pictures are turned to the wall, and, in some traditions, mirrors are covered. Relatives are beckoned to bid farewell and sing sacred songs at the side of the body.

Depending on the gender of the deceased, relatives carry the body to the back porch, remove the clothes, and drape it with a white cloth. (If there is no porch, the body can be sponge-bathed and prepared where it is.) The body of the departed is bathed with water from the nine water pots (*kumbhas*) and dressed in fresh clothes. Each relative applies sesame oil to the head before placing the deceased in a coffin (or on a palanquin) and carrying it to the *homa* shelter. Fragrant sandalwood paste is applied to the corpse, which is then decorated with flowers and garlands, followed by a small amount of gold dust sprinkled on different parts of the head

and face. In the Hindu tradition, individuals are cremated, although many groups practice burial instead; infants are buried and special rites conducted to ensure a good afterlife. At the funeral site, in the presence of the male mourners, the closest relative of the deceased (usually the eldest son; the youngest son in the case of the mother's death) takes charge of the final rite and, if it is cremation, lights the funeral pyre. The chief mourner then performs *arati*, passing an oil lamp over the remains, before flowers are offered. After a cremation, ashes and fragments of bone are collected and eventually immersed in a holy river.

In many religious traditions, the funeral process may span a long period, as in the time-honored Chinese funeral arrangement. The funeral ceremony conventionally lasts over forty-nine days, the first seven days being the most important. Prayers are said every seven of these forty-nine days if the family can afford it. If the family is in poor circumstances, the period may be shortened to three to seven days. Usually, it is the responsibility of the daughters to bear the funeral expenses. The head of the family should ideally be present for, at least, the first and possibly the second prayer ceremony. The number of ceremonies conducted depends on the financial situation of the family. The head of the family should also be present for the burial or the cremation. In an alternative tradition, the prayer ceremony is held every ten days. The initial ceremony is held, followed by three succeeding periods of ten days, until the final burial or cremation. After one hundred days, a final prayer ceremony is conducted, but such a ceremony is optional and not as important as the initial ceremonies.

GRIEF AND MOURNING

Although few people may take seriously all the theories of Freud on the subject of death, one of

A Hindu funeral pyre on the Ganges River in India. Rich Hindus can afford a cremation on the shore of the holy river; otherwise, the body is thrown into the water to be eaten by scavengers. For Indian Hindus, the body is an empty shell after the soul departs.

the more impressive aspects of his writings was the view of the repercussions of loss and grief. This was borne out of his own experiences. At the time that he wrote, mass death had occurred as a result of the catastrophe of World War I. Affecting Freud more directly was his observation that his own family members and friends were suffering from depression, agitation, physical ailments, and suicidal thoughts and behavior. This he attributed to the fact that many people lived in grief for deaths that were not related to the conflict and that these losses might account for the various emotional and physical problems from which they suffered. Freud's grief-work theory suggested the importance of expressing

grief and detaching emotionally from the deceased in order to recover full personal function. Many of the major religions deal with grief and mourning and, once more, display remarkable similarities, suggesting practical, time-honored rites that deal adequately with the social and psychological problems that frequently arise at the time of death.

Anger is one of the essential components of mourning. Comparing Western societies to others, Geoffrey Gorer notes that, although our culture gives no symbolic expression to anger, a considerable number of others have done so.[19] This is seen in such rituals as the destruction of the dead person's property or possessions or, more indirectly, by the various mutilations that mourners feel compelled to inflict upon themselves as a sign of the pain of experiencing bereavement brought upon them by the dead. According to some psychoanalysts, this anger is a component of all mourning, and one of the main functions of the mourning process is to work through and dissipate this anger in a symbolic and, to a great extent, unconscious fashion. The emotion of anger is intimately tied up with that of grief.

Mourning processes in Orthodox Judaism are extensive. Ritualized mourning has several purposes: it shows respect for the dead, comforts those left behind, helps prevent excessive lament, and eventually helps the bereaved return to normal life. There are five stages to the mourning process that correspond with the stages of the soul's "ascent," as it gradually disengages from the material world and assumes a less palpable, although no less real, presence in the lives of those led behind. First, there is *aninut*, pre-burial mourning. Upon initially hearing of the death of a close relative (parent, child, sibling, or spouse), grief is traditionally expressed by tearing (*keriyah*) one's clothing. The Torah records many instances of rending the clothes after the news of death. The tearing of garments allows the mourner to give vent to pent-up anguish by means of a controlled, religiously sanctioned act of destruction. The bereaved wears the torn clothing through the first seven days of mourning. The relative then recites a blessing, describing God as the true Judge. During the period between death and burial, the primary responsibility of mourners is to care for the dead and prepare the body for burial. This duty takes precedence over all other commandments. The family is left alone to grieve during *aninut*; calls or visits are not to be made during this time.

The second and third stages, the *shivah*, constitute a seven-day period following the burial. The world was created with humanity as its focus. This took a full cycle of time: six days for God to create the world and rest from his work on the final day. When creation is reversed and the human soul returns to its source, that too is marked with a week's cycle: the *shivah*, seven days when the closest relatives devote exclusively to mourning the soul's departure and when the extended family, friends, and community comfort them with their presence, their empathy, and their words of consolation. Within the *shivah*, the first three days are characterized by a more intense degree of mourning. After the burial, a relative or friend prepares the "meal of condolence," which traditionally consists of eggs (symbolizing life) and bread. This meal is for family only, although visitors may come to offer condolences afterward. The family then enters a seven-day period of intense mourning. Mourners sit on low stools or the floor instead of on chairs; they do not wear leather shoes, shave or cut their hair, wear cosmetics, work, bathe, engage in sex, put on fresh clothing, or study the Torah (except parts of the Torah related to mourning and grief). They wear the clothes that they tore when they learned of the death or at the funeral. Mirrors in the house are covered. Prayer services are held with friends, neighbors, and relatives making up the *minyan*.

Next, there is a thirty-day mourning period (*shloshim*). The laws of mourning are incumbent upon seven first-degree relatives of the deceased: son or daughter, brother or sister, father or mother, and spouse. The other relatives and friends form the more outer circle of mourning, and they offer support and comfort to the primary mourners. During this period, the bereaved do not attend parties or celebrations, do not shave or cut their hair, and do not listen to music. This isolation from others constitutes the nonsocial element of bereavement, in short, withdrawing from social engagement as those close to the deceased become themselves a subject of taboo and undertake their own rites of passage. In this void, or what van Gennep called "liminality," those close to the dead go through a period of exclusion, before returning to normal social life and its duties.[20]

In Judaism, regular remembrances are performed in the years following the death. The fifth period of mourning (*avelut*) takes place in the first year after death and is observed only by the children of the deceased. During *avelut*, mourners do not go to parties, the theater, or concerts. The son of the deceased recites the Kaddish prayer every day for eleven months. Traditionally, the soul must purify itself before going to the world to come, which takes up to twelve months for the most evil. After the first year, the anniversary of death (*yahrzeit*) is remembered annually at the synagogue. The son recites the Mourner's Kaddish and performs the *aliyah*, and a candle is lit that burns for twenty-four hours.

In Islam, loved ones and relatives of the deceased are to observe a three-day mourning period. Mourning (*hidaad*) for more than three days is not permitted, except in the case of a widow on the occasion of her husband's death. Mourning is observed by increased devotion, receiving visitors and condolences, as well as avoiding decorative clothing and ostentatious jewelry. A widow observes an extended mourning period (*iddah*), four months and ten days long, in accordance with the Qur'an 2:234. During this time, she observes the "waiting" period (*'Iddah*), in which she is prohibited from remarrying. She is not to wear jewelry, *kohl* (eye makeup), silk, perfume, or henna dye on her hands and feet. During her *'iddah*, she is not to move from her home; she is only permitted to leave in order to fulfill her economic and social needs. If, for example, she works to sustain her family, she may continue to leave her home daily for the period of work. Apart from leaving the house for necessities and social visits to relatives and friends, a widow during her *'iddah* should pass the night in her own home until her term lapses; that is, she is not to sleep outside of her house.

Offering condolences to the relatives and friends of the deceased is an important act of kindness, which was displayed by the Prophet Muhammad. It is not uncommon in the evening after burial for people gather at the dead person's family's house (*ta'ziyah*) to cheer the surviving family and pray for them and for the deceased's well-being, reciting the Qur'an, especially sura 36 (*Yasin*) and then *tahlil*. When consoling a fellow Muslim, it is important in the faith to remind the bereaved of the triviality of this life: that everything belongs to Allah and that one should submit patiently to his decrees. It is also deemed beneficent to make them hopeful of Allah's mercy toward the beloved one that is lost and that, by the will of Allah, he or she will be united with the deceased on a day after which there is no parting. Offering condolences is not limited to three days and can be extended for as long as it is required. A very common practice is gathering to offer condolences to the deceased's family and relatives in the graveyard, house, or mosque. Although the sharia specifies that mourning of the dead be limited to three days, the practice of extending memorial feasts for the dead is known across the Muslim world. Some Muslims also commemorate the first, third, seventh, twentieth, or fortieth day following someone's death, although there is no basis for it from the Qur'an or Sunnah. Memorial feasts in most Muslim societies are on the seventh, fortieth, and sometimes the hundredth day after the death of a family member.

It is recommended in the Islamic tradition to visit the graves for the purpose of admonishment and remembering the hereafter. It is, however, forbidden to associate the visit with anything that would anger Allah, such as supplicating to the dead, invoking their assistance, wailing, or other types of sinful actions. Difference of opinion exists among Muslim scholars concerning the permissibility of women visiting graves. Although it is allowed for women to visit graves, it is not recommended that they visit frequently. Muslims are allowed to visit the graves of disbelievers for reflection; however, they are not permitted to participate in the funeral rites of non-Muslims.

For Hindus, after returning home after a funeral, family members bathe and share in cleaning the house. A lamp and water pot are set near where the body earlier lay at rest. The water is changed daily, and pictures remain turned to the wall. The shrine room is closed, with white cloth draping all icons. During these days of ritual impurity, family and close relatives do not visit the homes of others, although neighbors and relatives bring daily meals to relieve the burdens of preparing food during mourning. Neither do they attend festivals and temples, nor take part in marriage arrangements. Some Hindus observe this period up to one year. For the death of friends, neighbors, or associates observances are optional. Although mourning is never suppressed or denied, Scriptures admonish against excessive lamentation and encourage joyous release. The departed soul is acutely conscious of emotional forces directed at him or her. Prolonged grieving can hold him or her in earthly consciousness, inhibiting full transition to the heaven worlds. In Hindu Bali, it is shameful to cry for the dead.

In Buddhist northern Thailand, it is not unusual for the bodies of prominent or wealthy persons to be kept for a year or more in a special building at a temple. Cremations are deferred this long to show love and respect for the deceased and to perform religious rites that benefit the departed. In such cases, a series of memorial services are held on the seventh, fiftieth, and hundredth days after the death. As long as the body is present, the spirit can benefit from the gifts presented, the sermons preached, and the chants uttered before it.

All these religious traditions—Judaic, Islamic, Hindu, and Buddhist—attempt to deal adequately with the human need for mourning. The secular West offers a different picture. Let us return to Gorer's prior statement that, in comparison with other cultures, funerals and mourning processes of Western cultures are inadequate. Recent studies have tended to emphasize the failure of traditional funerals, stressing that orthodox Christian beliefs of the afterlife are not always congruent with those of the general population in increasingly secular

In Sikhism, death is considered a natural process and God's will. Any public displays of grief at the funeral, such as wailing or crying out loud, are discouraged. Cremation is the preferred method of disposal. The body is usually bathed and clothed by family members and taken to the cremation grounds. There, hymns that induce feelings of detachment are recited by the congregation. As the body is being cremated, *Kirtan Sohila*, the nighttime prayer, is recited, and *Ardas* is offered. The ashes are disposed of by immersing them in the nearest river. A noncontinuous reading of the entire *Sri Guru Granth Sahib* is undertaken and timed to conclude on the tenth day. This marks the end of the mourning period.

societies. In short, they fail to provide the funeral and mourning functions that are associated with preindustrial societies. At the same time, contemporary culture is often identified as void of religious meaning and deals with the mourning process insufficiently because it is unable to provide sufficient guidelines in these areas. This plausibly explains the rise of "alternative" funerals that are underscored by the value of "choice." Increasingly, the "alternative" means little or no religious element, apart from that concocted by relatives of the deceased from a pick 'n' mix spirituality.[21]

Enduring perceptions of death and processes of mourning, alongside prescribed forms of funeral arrangements, are nevertheless evident among ethnic minorities in the Western setting. For various faith communities, ways of disposing of the dead provide a means for rooting their identity in Western soil, and these have frequently become part of legal and political controversies.[22] Furthermore, in pluralist Western societies, there are numerous difficulties facing ethnic communities in observing preparations regarding funerals.[23] The only acceptable way of disposing of a body in the eyes of the majority of Muslims is through burial underground with the head facing Mecca. Religious doctrine also dictates that, ideally, a person is to be buried within a day of his or her death. In practice, in the Western context, burials are often delayed by several days. There are other limitations. Joining in a funeral procession is considered a collective duty: if there are sufficient people accompanying the body to the cemetery, individual Muslims are duty-bound to join in. In the streets of modern cities, the observance of this rule is increasingly rare.

By contrast, cremation is the ideal disposal of the corpse for Hindus. At death, as explored previously, the family prepares the body of the deceased, carries it in a procession to the cremation grounds, and recites specific prayers while the body is cremated. The god of death is called upon to give the deceased an honored place among the ancestors, and other deities are also invoked to intercede on behalf of the departed. Once the body has been cremated, the ashes and bones of the deceased are either committed to a holy river or buried. After the funeral, the family members, being in a state of ritual impurity, proceed to a brook or river to purify themselves with ritual baths. Because of the difficulties in performing many such rituals associated with the traditional Hindu funeral, modifications may be observable within the Western context.[24]

SUMMARY

This chapter has presented a comparative overview of death in everyday life. It has necessarily been brief, and, as a result, the vast complexities of death and dying and the various expressions of religiosity that surround it have scarcely been given justice. However, certain core themes have presented themselves. We began our overview of the subject of religion and death by observing that death is a part of life. Yet to what extent death is an integral part of everyday life in terms of lived experiences in the social setting varies considerably. It remains true that death is a "lived experience" for those about to depart this world and for their significant others, those close to them by family ties or friendship, who are left behind. Here, as we have seen, religion plays its erstwhile role in articulating afterlife beliefs and in shaping funeral and mourning processes and the moment of death itself. However, in Western societies, death is compartmentalized and marginalized. Its religious significance has become less important. In a rationalized and secularized context, however, it adds to the rich variety of meaning given to death throughout history.

While acknowledging the variety of ways that different cultures deal with death, commonalities also exist, indicating that human beings display the similar psychological and social need to deal with a very human event. Whether expressing cultural similarities or divergence, religion has a central role to play in the natural process of death. Death is a communal as well as individual experience and affects wider circles of social life, even in the West. It is the community that is left to deal with the implications of losing one of its members before the wounds can eventually be healed. At the same time, the taboo surrounding death ensures that those associated with it withdraw from society, at least for a period.

We concluded our comparative survey by noticing the difficulties that minority-faith communities have in disposing of their dead in Western societies, as well as the mourning processes involved. It would be too simplistic to see this problematic area as a result of cultural disparities of living in a "host" culture that often fails to give solace to those who mourn and where funeral processes are often found wanting. However, the matter is really that of the disjuncture between religious communities and a secular context in which the final life event is, in many respects, dealt with inadequately. It is a context in which the business and busyness of everyday life leave little room to deal adequately with the declining social significance of death and to ponder the religious significance of life's closing event, the "final frontier" of a very real human experience.

GLOSSARY

Afterlife: A conception, common to most religious systems, to articulate belief in the continuation of the spirit or soul after death.

Aging: A physical process, generally describing deterioration of the mind and body. In many cultures, but by no means all, it is a negative term.

Ceremonies: An annual, seasonal, or recurring occasion, celebrated by individuals, groups, or entire societies.

Death: A natural physical event that marks the end of a living organism. In human societies, it is often given a social and religious significance.

Dying: A term denoting the process of death of a living organism, resulting from natural or unnatural causes.

Funerals: A ceremony in the form of rites of passage, marking the death of an individual and possible transition to an afterlife (see entry).

Mourning: A term often connected with grief, expressing emotions on the death of someone loved or admired.

Rites of Passage: A set of rituals that mark the transition of one stage of life to another, in either a social or a biological sense.

FOR FURTHER READING

Brooks-Gordon, Belinda. *Death Rites and Rights.* New York: Hart, 2007.

Davies, John. *Death, Burial and Rebirth in the Religions of Antiquity.* London: Routledge, 1999.

Freud, Sigmund. *Beyond the Pleasure Principle.* 1913. New York: Norton, 1960.

Howarth, Glynnys. *Death and Dying: A Sociological Introduction.* London: Polity, 2006.

Howarth, Glynnys, and Oliver Leaman, eds. *Encyclopedia of Death and Dying.* London: Routledge, 2001.

Jupp, Peter, and Glynnys Howarth, eds. *The Changing Face of Death: Historical Accounts of Death and Disposal.* Basingstoke, UK: Macmillan, 1997.

Kastenbaum, Robert. *Encyclopedia of Death and Dying.* Phoenix: Oryx, 1989.

Walter, Tony. *Funerals: And How to Improve Them.* London: Hodder, 1990.

———."Modern Death: Taboo or not Taboo?" *Sociology* 25, no. 2 (1991): 293–310.

———. *The Eclipse of Eternity: A Sociology of the Afterlife.* London: Macmillan, 1996.

Part

3

RELIGION AND CULTURE IN THE SPACE OF AESTHETICS

INTRODUCTION

The final part of *Religion and Culture: Contemporary
Practices and Perspectives describes a third space, with aesthetics at its center. In contrast
to politics and ethics, the religious and cultural production in this space involves greater
creative freedom. The aesthetic, third space is a highly synthetic one, where disparate ideas,
emotions, and innovations are reconstituted and reshaped with seemingly few rules governing them. Michel de Certeau observed in his *The Practice of Everyday Life*, how beliefs,
practices, and symbols, located between the spaces of politics and ethics, are pieced together
in makeshift fashion, according to what he called in French *bricolés,* or bricolage. In the third
space, the elements that constitute religion and culture are held in tension so that one does
not subordinate the other. For instance, what gives one work of contemporary art or music a
more powerful resonance than another? A significant part of the answer is located in this creative tension. Sometimes, performances of religion and culture legitimate the existing order,
or status quo, but in other instances they can be highly critical. Some sociologists of religion
might describe social criticism as a "prophetic" function of religion, as in the Hebrew Bible,
when the ancient Hebrew prophets were critical of the excesses and immoralities of their
age. Today, when religion and culture join together in an effective aesthetic performance,
the result can destabilize what was taken for granted in the first and second spaces to erode a
seemingly unassailable authority and ultimately to visualize new alternatives.

We thus begin this part of our study with Elizabeth Adan's essay on contemporary visual
arts. The very first sentence in chapter 13 reads, "Religion, and especially ritual, is central
to the field of contemporary art." She writes that this bold statement seems counterintuitive
because many artists would deny their work as having much to do with religion. Adan takes
us through a number of art controversies where religion was at the center. She explores a

wide variety of contemporary artists like Amalia Mesa-Bains, Shirin Neshat, Bill Viola, Mark Rothko, and many others where it is impossible to deny the religious content of their work. Adan argues that the visual arts and their makers are continuing the ancient tradition of art in the service of religion. But in contemporary visual arts, the sacred is explored through the secular or profane. It is in the arts that ritual performances challenge existing norms and values, as in a political satire or hunger strike. In chapter 14, Masen Uliss begins his examination of contemporary music with a Grateful Dead concert and the "deadheads." He pursues, among other matters, various tensions that are a part of this aesthetic space of religion and culture, including the tension between individual and group identification. Similar tensions are expressed in the consummate symbol of the counterculture, Bob Dylan, who at midcareer allowed his songs to appear in television advertisements. This brought immediate disapproval from his fans, who accused him of "selling out" his political values in an act of self-contradiction. Uliss surveys a broad range of contemporary music, from punk to some varieties of jazz. Carole M. Cusack, in chapter 15, examines sport and begins with the centrality of ritual to both religion and sport, which she traces to the ancient Olympics, where rituals intended to honor the ancient gods of Greece. In this chapter, the reader will follow Cusack's interpretations of sumo wrestling in Japan and cricket in Australia, sports that are not well-known in the United States but that display highly ritualized events.

A fan of the local concert hall, sports stadium, or art museum experiences the same event format in a similar audience, repetitively. The fans of music, sports, and art are engaged in a ritual activity outside the walls of traditional religious institutions. A baseball game always has pitchers and batters, balls and strikes, innings and outs, and is played on a diamond, and though each individual game is unique, the infinite randomness conforms to a preexisting pattern. Keeping box scores is almost as old as baseball itself, and a young boy or girl who begins marking their cards may keep them throughout their lives in order to return to the ritual in their memories. Sports can contain life lessons of victory and defeat, teamwork, and overcoming obstacles and accepting limitations in ways that unify family members who may have difficulty discussing these topics directly. Every performance is unique aesthetically, yet symbolic archetypes mirror the various life challenges facing audience members. The hotshot rookie, the hard-working veteran, or the over-the-hill performer who channels nostalgia mirror our own life experiences as we grow older and age.

In chapter 16, David J. Cooper begins his study of humor by recalling two very different experiences—the Episcopal church in which he grew up, where control of the body was intended to instill in children the necessity for quiet respectfulness and his experience in a Tibetan Buddhist monastery, where young monks fired spitballs at parishioners before ducking out of sight. While religion is always a weighty matter, humor is critical to it, and Cooper shows us how humor functions as a teaching tool, marker of transcendence, release valve, and weapon. In chapter 17, S. Brent Plate describes a series of parallels between religion and film as both creating alternative worlds by reinterpreting or remaking the raw and abstract material of time and space. But this remaking is, in both religion and film, a performance. In discussing these parallels, Plate uses a number of films, including Woody Allen's *Purple Rose of Cairo*, David Lynch's *Blue Velvet*, and James Cameron's *Avatar*. Stephanie Stillman-Spisak, in chapter 18, provides an account of how a government can strengthen national unity by controlling memorialization rituals. She examines the commemorations of Muhammad during Ramadan in Saudi Arabia, the martyrdom of Husayn during Ashura in Iraq, and of Jesus during Easter in Jerusalem. Of course, all three are primordial events in the history of Islam and Christianity, and she demonstrates how these premodern rituals continue to influence national and local politics during the annual reenactment performances. In these reenactments, past, present, and future are seamlessly compressed together, which aids in the comprehension of contemporary conflicts and generates authority and energy for change. We conclude this volume with chapter 19, and Gary Laderman's "The Disney Way of Death." While Laderman's focus here is on how Walt Disney's religious imagination continues to shape American culture, it also is a fitting conclusion for this volume. In this essay, Laderman shows how each of the three spaces—politics, ethics, and aesthetics—are integrated in the phenomena of life, especially in how Disney provided a series of mythic worlds, which not only provide escapes but also new ways of interpreting American life in the twentieth century.

13

CONTEMPORARY VISUAL ART

Elizabeth Adan

Religion, and especially ritual, is central to the field of contemporary art. In the face of many commonly held notions about both religion and contemporary art, this statement may appear to be counterintuitive, even incorrect. In particular, for many authors and observers, general notions of religion—as deeply moral, profoundly spiritual, and inherently sacred—suggest that it has no place or role to play in what is often taken to be the rigorously secular, frequently political, and unapologetically profane field of contemporary art. In this vein, some of the most vocal and thus most familiar and public debates about contemporary art have been not so much debates as outcries against contemporary art, in which religion stands as the antithesis, and often the victim, of the outrageous, immoral, and blasphemous content and practices present in visual art made from the 1960s to the present.

In many cases, these outcries come from conservative politicians, pundits, and religious figures who are especially virulent in their complaints against contemporary art. However, less antagonistic and censorial, but by no means

unrelated, claims that religion and contemporary art are antithetical or irrelevant to each other have also been circulated by some art historians and critics.[1] Indeed, although art historians and critics generally argue for a more complex and nuanced understanding of what can admittedly appear to be challenging and, at times, intentionally confrontational examples of visual art, on the question of religion, even these experts can adopt attitudes similar to those expressed by conservative politicians and critics.

In recent years, these approaches by art historians and critics have begun to shift, and some scholars, critics, and curators have paid more serious attention to the relationships between religion and contemporary art.[2] However, even the more conservative outcries that pit the two fields against each other belie the claim that religion plays no role in contemporary art, if for no other reason than that discussions of (purported) antagonisms between religion and contemporary art themselves establish a definite, although not necessarily easy or seamless, connection between the two fields of cultural endeavor. In particular, from certain vantage points, such claims make religion an important component of contemporary art as its "other," against which contemporary art constitutes itself. That is to say, in even the most virulent and censorious attacks on contemporary art as antireligion, religion and contemporary art in fact become yoked together and play a central role in defining each other, the one being everything that the other is not.

RELIGION AND CONTEMPORARY ART: CONTROVERSIES, CHALLENGES, AND RESIGNIFICATIONS

The more common notions about the opposition between religion and recent visual art are founded in part upon several heated controversies that have developed around certain contemporary artworks from the 1980s and 1990s, perhaps none more infamous than Andres Serrano's *Piss Christ*. A 1987 Cibachrome photograph that depicts a slightly soft-focus image of a crucifixion in red and yellow tones, *Piss Christ* has what appear to be pointillist areas of light or texture, randomly arranged across the surface of the artwork. However, these scattered dots are air bubbles that formed within a container of the artist's urine, in which Serrano submerged a small, inexpensive, mass-produced plastic crucifix that he then photographed to create this artwork.

These details of Serrano's work, referenced in its title, incited a series of outraged protests, accusing both the artist and his photograph of blasphemy and sacrilege; conservative politicians such as US Senator Alfonse D'Amato denounced *Piss Christ* as "a deplorable, despicable display of vulgarity" that desecrates a holy Christian symbol.[3] Such views of Serrano's work are, however, based upon assumptions that do not necessarily hold up under close scrutiny, assumptions not only about the artist's intent and the artwork's significance but also about the role of desecration and profanity in the larger context of religious activity and practice.

For example, Serrano himself has indicated that, although the artwork was intended as a form of critique, it was not an attack on Christian faith or doctrine. Indeed, many accusations of contemporary art as antireligious often assume that any critique or interrogation of religion is synonymous with antagonism toward, if not outright destruction of, faith and belief. Instead, however, Serrano has affirmed his own artistic interest in Christian symbols and has asserted that he takes his work to be "religious, not sacrilegious."[4] Serrano has also commented, "Rather than destroy icons, I make new ones."[5] And in the particular case of *Piss Christ*, the artist has noted that the artwork is meant in part as "a protest against the commercialization of sacred imagery"[6] and thus could itself be understood as an indictment against sacrilege or blasphemy, though in different forms from the sacrilege and blasphemy that conservative commentators frequently take contemporary art to be.

In addition, Serrano's juxtaposition of bodily fluids such as urine (as well as blood and milk in other examples of his work) with Christian imagery and symbolism could be seen as an investigation into the relationships between the human body and the Christian faith.[7] In particular, even though the body is considered "base," "unclean," or "sinful" in some Christian contexts, Serrano's work provides an alternative understanding of the body as a source of illumination, given the luminous yellow and red tones of *Piss Christ* that derive in part from the artist's use of urine and that simultaneously seem to radiate from the crucifixion itself. In Serrano's case, it is not simply the body, but the body at its most (supposedly) "base"—its waste products—through which a glowing quality of light, perhaps even divine illumination or inspiration, emanates. In this sense, Serrano's work further demonstrates the ways in which religious faith and practice combine sacred and profane objects, activities, and properties. As Serrano himself has also remarked, "You can't have the sacred without the profane."[8]

In Serrano's case, the relationships between religion and contemporary art are thus much more complex than assumptions of indifference or antagonism suggest. Even in the various highly fraught controversies that have surrounded Serrano's work, controversy itself does not preclude religious, sacred, or perhaps even holy significance in contemporary art, as even a brief visual analysis of Serrano's photograph demonstrates. In another similarly notorious example of an artwork attacked as antireligious and, specifically, as anti-Catholic—Chris Ofili's 1996 painting *The Holy Virgin Mary*—what conservative commentators took to be the blasphemous elements of the artwork are materials that in fact involve religious significance of their own.

Composed of oil paint, glitter, resin, collaged paper elements, map pins, and elephant dung on linen, Ofili's work garnered especially harsh attacks from religious and political figures in the United States for its use of dung in its depiction of the Virgin Mary. However, these attacks ignore the sacred importance of the elephant in a range of religious traditions around the world (perhaps most prominently in the form of the Hindu god Ganesha) and the additional significance of animal dung as an "extremely potent" material in a number of "traditional sub-Saharan societies."[9] In addition, animal dung serves as an important artistic material in many such societies, whose artists use it to strengthen the "spiritual powers" of various artworks and artifacts.[10] The attacks on Ofili's artwork also ignore the artist's use of a glimmering gold background, which recalls the long history of holy religious icons in Byzantine art.[11] A British artist of Nigerian descent and Catholic upbringing, whose years as an art student included a trip to Zimbabwe, where he reportedly began to incorporate elephant dung into his work,[12] Ofili thus juxtaposes African religious traditions with Western Christianity in *The Holy Virgin Mary*. Indeed, with its references to multiple religious traditions, Ofili's painting is striking for what could be interpreted as the connections it draws between religious symbolism and significance across cultures rather than any antireligious antagonism supposedly manifest by the work.[13]

Serrano and Ofili are only two examples of contemporary artists who foreground religious imagery in their work. And although interrogation and critique may be the most common, or at least the most commonly interpreted, function of this religious content in contemporary visual art, these critiques are not always or exclusively focused on religion in terms of faith or doctrine. For example, in Renee Cox's *Flipping the Script* series of photographs (1992–1996), in which the artist restages Christian scenes such as the Pietà and the Last Supper with African American figures in the central roles, Cox comments on Western ideologies of race and gender in addition to Christian content and belief.[14] Another example of an artist whose work has been attacked as blasphemous and antireligious, Cox, like many of her colleagues, can also be understood to use such contemporary artistic practices as appropriation and resignification to refashion a series of religious images with meanings and content that might have greater relevance for contemporary audiences and congregations in both secular and religious contexts.

In addition, a combination of appropriation and resignification is at work in the recurrent use of the image of the Virgin of Guadalupe and related female religious figures in works by a number of Chicana artists since the 1970s. In two early examples—Ester Hernandez's *La Virgen de Guadalupe Defendiendo los Derechos de los Xicanos* (*The Virgin of Guadalupe Defending the Rights of Xicanos)* (1975) and Yolanda M. López's *Portrait of the Artist as the Virgin of Guadalupe* (1978)—both artists have fashioned images of the religious figure as a powerful force who conquers rather than is conquered by Western patriarchies. In particular, both Hernandez and López depict the Virgin of Guadalupe as a woman with everyday features, such as the karate outfit worn by Hernandez's Virgin and the contemporary dress and running shoes worn by López's, who is also surrounded by, and simultaneously a source of, divine or spiritual power, in the form of the mandorla, with rays of light that frame the figure in both artworks.[15]

As several authors have demonstrated, in these artworks that make use of the Virgin of Guadalupe, Hernandez and López remake the female religious figure, altering her traditional image of feminine grace and submission to become instead an icon of female and, specifically, Chicana feminist empowerment.[16] And although some accounts have suggested that these images effectively remove religious meaning in favor of Chicana feminist resignification, more recent analyses propose that at least certain aspects of religious content, and especially the references to spiritual or sacred power, do inform these Chicana feminist

APPROPRIATION AND RESIGNIFICATION

While there are many examples of visual artists who borrow ideas, imagery, and/or materials from existing sources in the field of art history and other arenas, *appropriation* is a term used in particular to describe the work of a number of artists in the 1970s and 1980s who did not simply draw inspiration from earlier models or ideas but addressed the very question of authenticity, artistic origins, and related concerns. Contemporary artists closely associated with the rise of appropriation include Sherrie Levine, Richard Prince, and Cindy Sherman. For example, Levine is especially known, in her early work, for rephotographing the work of prior twentieth-century artists such as Walker Evans and Edward Weston. However, in her act of rephotographing the work of Evans and Weston, Levine did not restage any of their artworks and then photograph the images herself from scratch, so to speak. Instead, Levine photographed Evans's and Weston's artworks from existing reproductions, such as books and posters, thus calling viewers to consider, among other issues, the ever-increasing distance of viewers from anything like an "authentic" source or an "original" artwork and to question the authenticity of any photographic project, including that of Evans or Weston, two especially hallowed figures in histories of photography. In a similar vein, Prince and Sherman both appropriated imagery from popular culture in their early work. For example, similar to Levine, Prince also rephotographed existing imagery, including advertisements for Marlboro cigarettes, and Sherman borrowed images from cinema in her series of *Untitled Film Stills* photographs (1977–1980). However, in the latter case, although Sherman appropriated general image structures and visual vocabularies from movies, she created the reconstitutions of the Virgin of Guadalupe in important ways.[17]

What is more, these Chicana appropriations of an iconic religious figure have also generated controversies and conservative attacks against the artworks and artists, similar to works by Serrano, Ofili, Cox, and other artists. Indeed, in the case of the Chicana artists' works, these attacks have ranged from negative critiques to the bombing of a magazine headquarters in Mexico City after the magazine in question, *fem*, used one of López's Virgin of Guadalupe artworks as a cover image.[18] More recently, another artist who has also recast the Virgin of Guadalupe as a Chicana feminist icon and source of empowerment, Alma Lopez, faced calls to have her 1999 artwork *Our Lady* removed from an exhibition in Santa Fe.[19] In this latter instance, Lopez depicted the Virgin as a seminude woman and, even though there are numerous, highly sanctioned images of female nudes throughout museums and across Western art history, in Lopez's case, the image of a partially naked female body in the form of the Virgin of Guadalupe generated accusations of sacrilege.[20] Yet, in spite of these accusations and controversies, artworks by Hernandez, López, Lopez, and related Chicana artists serve as important examples of the ways in

various scenes that she photographed (using herself as the model in each image), unlike Levine and Prince.

In many instances, appropriation also involves the further tactic of resignification—the process of creating new, critical, and politically resistant meanings for existing images and vocabularies. Resignification frequently occurs in the face of stereotypic or otherwise potentially hurtful, damaging imagery, which is invested with alternative meanings through additional tactics such as irony and recontextualization. As such, Cindy Sherman's *Untitled Film Stills* might be understood as an example of resignification, in the ways that the artist creates alternative meanings for what appear to be familiar images borrowed from well-known film directors and movie genres (such as film noir, Hitchcock, and European new wave cinema, all of which are appropriated in Sherman's project). In addition, Sherman's work has also been widely regarded as an important example of new approaches and attitudes toward gender and identity, given the ways in which it is impossible to locate any singular sense of "femininity" or female identity in the wide range of images of women that proliferate across the sixty-nine photographs that constitute the series. Perhaps an even stronger example of resignification is Betye Saar's 1972 mixed media sculpture *The Liberation of Aunt Jemima*, in which Saar appropriates the stereotypically racist and sexist image of the mammy. However, Saar provides the figure with a pistol under one arm (next to her broom, an object present in many conventional images of mammy figures) and a shotgun in the other, and positions Aunt Jemima behind a fist shaped into the Black Power salute, which thus invests the figure with a new set of meanings, particularly a highly charged, deeply resistant sense of political agency and self-determination.

Yolanda Lopez, Portrait of the Artist as the Virgin of Guadalupe, *1978. Lopez depicts an energetic young woman to convey her own deep appreciation of the everyday hardworking woman. The image evokes a superhero in motion, with her blue cape swirling around, her right hand firmly grasping the serpent. All rights reserved. Used by permission of the artist. Image courtesy of The Chicano Studies Research Center, UCLA.*

which religious imagery and content play a significant role in contemporary art.

RELIGION AS CONTENT IN CONTEMPORARY ART: INTERROGATION AND CRITIQUE

These various examples of contemporary art that appear to transgress (at least according to some standards) religious doctrine and beliefs give shape to one category or type of the various

relationships between religion and contemporary art: art that is about religion, even in the form of interrogation and critique. In addition to photographs and paintings that employ religious imagery and content, there are important examples of contemporary art about religion in mixed media sculpture and installation artworks as well.

For example, another Chicana artist, Amalia Mesa-Bains, has created what she terms "altar installations" since 1975, artworks that adapt altar forms and other religious constructions. In *An Ofrenda for Dolores del Rio* (originally constructed in 1984), for instance, Mesa-Bains uses materials and construction techniques related to *altares*, personal devotional structures that are especially important in Chicana cultural traditions. Usually built in the home to record and honor family histories and events, *altares* are frequently composed of objects and images drawn from domestic life, often in the form of personal photographs and special keepsakes, carefully arranged on a piece of furniture in the corner of a living room or bedroom.[21] Mesa-Bains follows these traditions quite closely in *An Ofrenda for Dolores del Rio*, perhaps above all with her use of numerous photographs of del Rio, along with the lace, tulle, and satin fabrics that recall curtains and other window treatments as well as fancy costumes and dresses befitting an actress.[22]

However, Mesa-Bains's artwork also draws upon Day of the Dead traditions, especially the *ofrendas,* commemorative shrines devoted to spirit figures and forces.[23] In its references to spiritual practices and its dedication to an important actress who worked in both the US and Mexican film industries and who became "a successful crosser of national borders," as well as "an icon of binational/bilingual representation in mainstream popular culture,"[24] Mesa-Bains's installation thus jointly invokes political and religious meanings. That is to say, as "offerings to those women [such as del Rio] whose lives and work struggle against the power and domination of a masculine world," Mesa-Bains's altar installations invoke spirits and related religious forces at the same time that they commemorate important Chicanas and their achievements, and together these elements of Mesa-Bains's work make Chicana women and their accomplishments more visible.[25] Mesa-Bains's altar artworks thus foreground memory and visibility—two extremely important and popular themes of contemporary art—as political issues that also take shape as religious and spiritual phenomena.[26] What is more, Mesa-Bains articulates political content and significance in a "spiritual art for[m]" that "echo[es] and transform[s] established forms of religious art"[27] and that also incorporates religious content, meanings, and cultural forms into gallery and museum contexts, as well as the larger field of contemporary art.

In a related vein, Helène Aylon has created a series of installations in which she investigates and, like so many other contemporary artists, critiques traditional religious doctrine and theology, specifically that of Judaism. In particular, Aylon, who was raised in an Orthodox Jewish family and married an Orthodox rabbi as a very young woman, challenges gender hierarchies and inequalities that are evident in Orthodox Jewish doctrine and texts.[28] For example, in her large-scale project *The Liberation of G-d* (1990–1998), Aylon, working with multiple copies of the Torah in both Hebrew and English, identifies passages that communicate and promote gender inequalities and oppression by highlighting the passages in question (and to be questioned) with a pink marker, applied to sheets of vellum laid over the pages of the Torah volumes. In *The Liberation of G-d*, Aylon embarks upon a project that can be understood as "an extended midrash, or Biblical commentary," in which she "battle[s] with iniquities sanctified by Judaism's holiest scriptures."[29] As Aylon herself asserts, "I LOOK INTO THE PASSAGES/ WHERE PATRIARCHAL ATTITUDES/ HAVE BEEN PROJECTED ONTO/ G-D/ AS THOUGH MAN/ HAS THE RIGHT TO HAVE/ DOMINION/ EVEN OVER/ G-D."[30]

In subsequent projects—*The Women's Section* (1997), *My Notebooks* (1998), and *Epilogue: Alone with My Mother* (1998)—Aylon invokes her family history and experience in the figures of her grandmothers, to whom she addresses *The Women's Section*, as well as her mother, with whom she discusses her work in the audiotape component of *Epilogue: Alone with My Mother*. In all these works, Aylon engages in a "critique . . . from within" that is also, according to Robert Berlind, an attempt at "a *tikkun*, a repair or healing, a reestablishment of harmony, where serious damage has been done to our relation to God."[31]

As both midrash and *tikkun*, Aylon's project is thus a devotional one, and a devotional project that is as much an act as it is an object. For example, as Berlind observes, "The carefully ritualistic activity documented by *The Liberation [of G-d]* brings to mind the devotion and workmanship of scribes copying a Torah scroll."[32] Indeed, although she stands in serious disagreement with sections of the Torah, at the same time, Aylon demonstrates a careful attention to and respect for the sacred texts, perhaps above all in her use of the sheets of vellum upon which she makes the pink highlighter marks, rather than making these marks directly on the Torah. What is more, in the act of highlighting, continued repeatedly over a span of eight years and through numerous Torah volumes, along with the highly involved components of her other projects—such as the row upon row of unused journals with pages unfurled and rolled into fluted, columnlike forms in *My Notebooks*—Aylon works with a level of dedication and devotion that recalls, even instantiates, religious faith and practice, side by side with interrogation and critique, within the field of contemporary art.

The photography, video, and film projects of Shirin Neshat also examine the highly complex gender roles and relationships involved in religious doctrine and practice, specifically Islam, especially in the aftermath of the 1979 Islamic Revolution in Iran.[33] For instance, in the black-and-white photographs that constitute her early *Women of Allah* series (1993–1997), Neshat employs one of the most provocative, controversial, and stereotyped symbols of Islam in her repeated depiction of women clothed in the veil.[34] However, in photographs such as *Rebellious Silence* (1994), *Seeking Martyrdom #2* (1995), and *Speechless* (1996), the veiled women (often the artist herself) also hold guns, further referencing another highly controversial and stereotyped figure often associated with Islam, that of the so-called extremist or fundamentalist, armed for combat and, in some cases, preparing for religious martyrdom.[35]

In addition to bringing these two stereotypes of Islam together in her early photographs, Neshat juxtaposes her images of armed and veiled women with calligraphic markings, especially, in some instances, those of Farsi text. These calligraphy elements emphasize the lengthy history of Islamic artistic practices that often privilege script over iconic or figurative imagery, even though the texts themselves are seldom taken from the Qur'an or related religious sources.[36] Instead, many of these inscriptions are taken from Iranian literature, such as the work of Forough Farrokhzad, one of the most significant twentieth-century women poets in Iran, whose writings explore women's personal, daily, and, in some cases, sexual experiences.[37]

For example, in *Offered Eyes* (1993), Neshat has inscribed an excerpt from Farrokhzad's poem "I Feel Sorry for the Garden" onto the surface of the photograph, in the triangular areas of the whites of the eye in a woman's face, seen in extreme close-up.[38] The lines of the poem acknowledge and express empathy for a neglected and dying

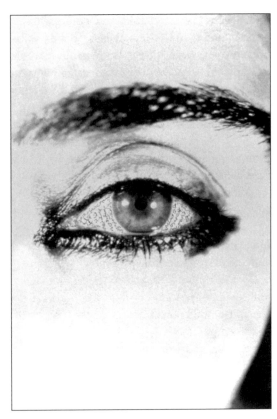

Shirin Neshat, Offered Eyes, 1993. *RC print & ink, 11 x 14 inches. Copyright Shirin Neshat. Courtesy Gladstone Gallery, New York.*

garden, which, in the context of Neshat's work, could be interpreted as the woman in the photograph.[39] Indeed, given these visual and textual components—the combination of the Farsi text of the work of a major, controversial Iranian woman poet with the extreme close-up of a woman's wide-open and alert eye, a combination further juxtaposed to additional images in the series, of women wearing the chador and in some cases carrying guns—Neshat's photograph radically complicates many perceptions of the role and status of women in Islam.

More specifically, Neshat creates images of women who can be understood as simultaneously, perhaps even paradoxically, subordinate to and yet soldiers of certain elements or interpretations of Islam. That is to say, while Neshat's use of the veil in her *Women of Allah* photographs calls to mind what Western audiences often perceive as the oppression of Muslim women, her visual evocation of the militant stance of certain types of Islamic practice complicates both the general image and the Western stereotype of the veiled Muslim woman. Although the image of an armed Muslim individual has itself become another common Western stereotype of Islam, at the same time, when this second stereotype is extended to or invoked by women, as it is in a number of Neshat's photographs, it can be understood to contradict the first.[40]

By foregrounding these stereotypes, Neshat challenges them, through their gender-based complexities and contradictions as well as through the calligraphy and text elements of her photographs, which describe another set of Muslim women's roles and experiences, in and from the voices of individual Muslim women.[41] However, these text elements of the *Women of Allah* series do not simply provide a more "liberated" or a more "authentic" alternative to the more common, Western-derived stereotypes. Instead, these text elements further foreground and underscore the many tensions and potential paradoxes across different elements and forms of Islam, from within Muslim contexts as well as from without. And even though Neshat's work interrogates these paradoxes, ultimately it neither judges nor resolves them.[42]

RELIGION AS CONTENT IN CONTEMPORARY ART: ARTICULATING MEANING AND EXPERIENCE

However, not all examples of contemporary art that are linked to religion via their imagery and content interrogate and critique religious doctrine and belief. In the work of Bill Viola, for instance, articulating religious meaning and experience seems to be one of the primary goals of his videotapes and video installations—that is to say, more a point of destination than departure. Indeed, this is especially important because, even though many accounts assert that religion holds at best an "'outsider' status" in the fields of modern and contemporary art,[43] it is quite central to much of Viola's work, and Viola is an artist who has achieved considerable professional success in both critical and commercial contexts. The degree of his success, combined with the religious themes and overtones that pervade much of his work, further belies prevailing accounts of religion and contemporary art as counterintuitive or counterproductive to one another.[44]

In Viola's case, many critical accounts of his work note its religious overtones, although critics often account for religion in Viola's work in conjunction with the philosophical notion of the sublime. For example, David Ross has written that Viola is "associat[ed] . . . with historical artists working within sacred traditions" and that the artist has a particular "concern with the representation of the sublime and the evocation of transcendent states."[45] Similarly, Lisa Jaye Young contends that Viola's projects, which "provoke boundless questions about the relationships of the filmic or video image to traditional notions of beauty and the sublime," are projects that also "encourag[e] a meditative response from the viewer" and thus "transfor[m] the art museum into both public viewing space and private meditational space."[46] However, while the sublime is the larger critical framework through which a number of authors interpret Viola's work, religious issues and themes—including the transcendentalism noted by Ross, the meditative properties noted by Young, and religious concerns such as baptism, noted by the artist himself—operate in tandem with and perhaps generate the sublime properties of the artist's video-based projects.[47]

Religious content and concerns are particularly prevalent in a series of projects that Viola has created since 2000, together known as *The Passions*. Within this larger group of artworks, Viola has drawn inspiration from a range of religious sources, especially mystical texts from Hindu, Buddhist, and Judeo-Christian traditions.[48] And although these sources are not brand-new to Viola's work—indeed, Viola has used mysticism, especially from Hindu and Buddhist faiths, as sources of inspiration throughout his career—in *The Passions* these sources are combined with imagery that borrows from additional religious themes and contexts.

For example, in his 2001 artwork *Unspoken (Silver and Gold)*, Viola creates a diptych using video projections in which the images are projected onto surfaces covered with silver and gold leaf, recalling Western European and Byzantine traditions of religious painting. And in artworks such as *The Greeting* (1995), which predates *The Passions* series but is taken by some authors as a precursor to the later works, along with *Emergence* (2002) and other projects, Viola borrows imagery from European Medieval and Renaissance paintings, such as Masolino's fifteenth-century *Pietà* and Pontormo's sixteenth-century *Visitation*.[49] Although the artist asserts that his intent is not simply to reproduce the earlier paintings,[50] it is nonetheless difficult not to see these meticulously staged and produced

THE SUBLIME

A central tenet of aesthetic theory, the notion of the sublime dates back to antiquity, especially in the work of the philosopher Longinus, and was taken up in the Enlightenment era by thinkers such as the British philosopher Edmund Burke (*A Philosophical Inquiry into the Origin of Our Ideas of the Sublime and Beautiful*, 1756) and the German philosopher Immanuel Kant (*Critique of Judgment*, 1790). In a general sense, the sublime is an aesthetic category that stands in contrast to the beautiful; while the category of the beautiful encompasses sensations that are harmonious and pleasing and that do not incite any extremes of experience, the sublime is defined by intensity and is linked to great awe, horror, or other overwhelming experiences. However, although the sublime is overwhelming and awe-inspiring, it remains an aesthetic sensation and does not include experiences that might overpower one to the point of extreme fear, danger, or death. Instead, the sublime is a sensation of awe or horror to which one is nevertheless drawn, as it elevates and expands one's experience in ways that ultimately allow one to acknowledge (though often not to fully comprehend or assimilate) the boundless scope of life, nature, and the like. Especially popular examples of sublime experiences are often found in nature—a thunderstorm, a windswept sea, a dark forest—all of which can incite in their observers sensations of awe and greatness akin to religious feelings of a divine creator or other spiritual force.

videos as referencing and perhaps updating religious, and in these cases specifically Judeo-Christian, imagery and content for contemporary audiences.

However, Viola's work invokes religion in something of a more experiential sense as well. For example, in *Catherine's Room* (2001)—another example of Viola's work that borrows its form and elements of its imagery from Italian Renaissance art, specifically from a fourteenth-century predella of Saint Catherine by Andrea di Bartolo—Viola depicts a figure engaged in a range of activities, including some with direct connections to religious practice, such as yoga exercises and lighting row upon row of candles. In addition, even in the more everyday tasks of sewing, writing, and preparing for bed also depicted in the artwork, the central figure of Catherine "moves about mindfully," writes John Walsh, "in the Buddhist sense, her attention entirely focused on the ordinary tasks she is performing, thereby making of them a spiritual practice."[51]

What is more, in Viola's large-scale installation *Five Angels for the Millennium* (2001), the artist transfers some of this spiritual or religious experience to his viewers. Composed of five different video projections, each of which depicts a fully clothed figure "plunging into a pool of water," the project depicts "a luminous void of unknown dimensions where the laws of physics seem suspended and the borders between the infinite cosmos and the finite human body merge."[52] "Shining bubbles," the artist continues, "float like stars in the night sky as the human form traverses the gap between heaven and earth, suspended between light and darkness, time and eternity, life and death."[53] And something of this cosmic, transcendent content translates into the exhibition space as well; the darkened interior in which the five images, or angels, are projected gives rise to "an enveloping

emotional experience" for viewers, transfiguring the exhibition space into, in Viola's words, "that of a church."[54]

With these elements of Viola's work in mind, the artist may be heir not only (or not so much) to medieval and Renaissance religious painting but also (or instead) to more recent developments in modern and contemporary art, especially certain developments in abstract painting that similarly invoke something of religious meaning and experience. Beginning with some of its initial manifestations in early twentieth-century modern art (in both Europe and the United States), the rise of abstract painting was articulated by a handful of artists in terms of a search for and engagement with deeper or higher meanings linked to, in Wassily Kandinsky's words, "the spiritual life."[55] For a later generation of artists, the Abstract Expressionists working in the United States in the 1940s and 1950s, abstraction similarly served not only to meet some compendium of aesthetic or formal goals but also to explore and express what one of these artists, Barnett Newman, termed "metaphysical secrets" of the world at large.[56]

While many critical and historical accounts of Abstract Expressionism emphasize formal and aesthetic significance, artists such as Newman have asserted a more multilayered series of motives and interpretations at work in mid-twentieth-century abstract painting in the United States, motives and interpretations that include religious content and meanings. For instance, with painting titles that make explicit references to religious themes—*The Slaying of Osiris* (1944), *Covenant* (1949), *Abraham* (1949), *Dionysius* (1949), *Eve* (1950), *Cathedra* (1951), and *The Stations of the Cross: Lema Sabachthani* (1958–1966), to name some prominent examples—Newman foregrounds religion as a significant component of his work. What is more, Newman himself described Abstract

Expressionism as "a religious art which through symbols will catch the basic truth of life."[57] Several commentators have also noted a range of religious concerns in his work, including Thomas Hess, who has suggested that the signature elements of Newman's work, the linear stripes or "zips" of color that bisect and orient the artist's paintings, may have their source in the artist's "readings in Jewish mysticism . . . especially as they were given form by the great Kabbalists."[58] Similarly, Robert Rosenblum has written that Newman's paintings suggest "the intrusion of a divine, shaping force."[59]

Of the painters who are generally classified as Abstract Expressionists, Mark Rothko is the artist whose work has arguably been put to the most tangible religious use, in the Rothko Chapel, located in Houston, Texas. The nondenominational religious space, commissioned by the de Menil family in 1964 and dedicated in 1971, is a large-scale manifestation of what many observers and authors have experienced as the sublime, mystical, religious qualities of Rothko's larger body of work, in which, as Rosenblum describes it, "luminous fields of dense, quietly lambent color . . . seem to generate the primal energies of natural light."[60] Indeed, Rothko's paintings are often taken to be emblematic of a quest to express and communicate spiritual content and religious meaning in the modern world, as seen, for example, in Dore Ashton's discussion of Rothko's work.[61] And, like his colleague Newman, Rothko himself claimed religious properties for his work, asserting, "The people who weep before my pictures are having the same religious experience I had when I painted them."[62]

Rothko's comment is especially significant because it suggests not simply that his paintings involve important, if abstract and nondenominational, religious content but also that the artist's works evoke, in his own words, "religious experience." Although Rothko does not specify a particular type of religious experience, one of the more common assumptions, especially in light of the chapel project, is that his paintings inspire observation and contemplation of a meditative, religious sort.[63] And with this emphasis on religious experience in his work, Rothko thus suggests that his paintings not only depict religious doctrine or theological content but also invoke religious practice.

Religious Activities in—and as—Contemporary Art

This shift toward experience and practice signaled by Rothko's comment about his work calls to mind a larger shift that began to take shape in mid-twentieth-century art, a shift away from formal and object-based concerns to an emphasis on artistic activities, along with their experiential qualities. In part, the shift that Rothko's remark articulates is not limited to religious elements or properties in his paintings, and it could be understood as indicative of a much broader series of developments in the visual arts, beginning in the 1950s and 1960s, in which a number of artists deemphasized the object form and status of artworks in favor of artistic actions and their experiences and effects.[64] What is more, with this growing emphasis on art as action and experience, contemporary art becomes a field that is increasingly understood and, in some instances, defined by its practices, similar to critical and cultural frameworks that identify ritual, with its emphasis on practice, as the central characteristic of religious engagements.

This shared emphasis on practice invokes a second category or type of relationship between religion and art: art that engages in and/or activates behaviors related to religious practices and, in particular, art that has affinities to ritual. While this shared emphasis on practice may seem excessively broad—and indeed, although it may be possible for almost any artwork to be interpreted as being defined and constituted by its practices and perhaps thus as being linked to ritual activities in at least a vague sense—there are certain developments in contemporary art that are particularly intentional in their emphasis on practice, especially artworks that fall under the category of performance art. As authors such as RoseLee Goldberg and Kristine Stiles have demonstrated, the term or classification of "performance art" encompasses artistic activities across a range of styles, movements, and locations, including happenings, Fluxus, and Actionism, to name a few examples.[65] And although performance art can itself seem to be a proliferating, open-ended field, many examples of performance art often share at least one goal, to bring artistic endeavors and practices together with behaviors and engagements from everyday life.

As such, performance art bears an important general or structural connection to ritual practice, for ritual also often involves a commingling of objects and activities from both religious and secular arenas, as well as a crossover between sacred and profane contexts and events. Indeed, although ritual is often commonly understood as a sacred or spiritual practice evident in a vast range of religious faiths, ritual is, according to many authors, an activity in which objects, behaviors, and participants themselves transition between two states of being or categories of meaning, usually between sacred (or otherwise extraordinary) and profane (or otherwise mundane). In particular, the transformation between sacred and profane is often taken to demarcate these categories and to set them distinctly, even distantly, apart from one another.[66]

However, in enacting these transformations, many rituals involve a period or phase in which the distinctions between these two categories dissolve, even disappear altogether. For example, in their study of sacrifice as a specific type of ritual practice, Henri Hubert and Marcel Mauss assert that, during the inner or middle phase of a ritual, the sacrificial object or victim "draw[s] together the sacred and the profane."[67] This produces, Hubert and Mauss write, "a mingling of the two substances [sacred and profane, or extraordinary and everyday] which become absorbed in each other *to the point of becoming indistinguishable* . . . all the forces . . . are blended together."[68] Victor Turner observes a similar phenomenon in what he terms the margin or "limen" phase of ritual, which, according to Turner, does not create any "distinction," as he puts it, "between 'secular' and 'sacred.'"[69] Rather, Turner continues, the central, liminal stage of ritual is a "limbo" state,[70] in which otherwise oppositional states or categories such as sacred and profane become integrally bound together such that their opposition to one another itself dissolves.[71]

In this blurring of boundaries between sacred and profane, or in more general terms between extraordinary and mundane, ritual thus parallels performance-based developments in the field of contemporary art that themselves blur boundaries, in the latter case between art and daily life. In addition, such developments in contemporary art, like ritual practices, often take shape as physical engagements in which the work of art is constituted by a live enactment of some sort. And, with this emphasis on the performance of the endeavors in question, both sets of practices—ritual on the one hand, contemporary art on the other—routinely center their behaviors and energies on the body of a participant or participants, without whom ritual, as well as many examples of contemporary art, effectively ceases to exist.[72]

In the field of contemporary art, performance-based artworks are rooted in part in the somewhat earlier development of Abstract Expressionism. At first glance, Abstract Expressionist paintings by artists such as Newman and Rothko appear to have little if any relevance or significance as activities and instead seem to be more important for their recourse to what is often assumed to be a higher-order, esoteric spiritual property or experience, divorced from the exigencies of day-to-day life. However, in Harold Rosenberg's discussion of much of this work, these artists, also known as "action painters" (the primary example being Jackson Pollock), became involved not simply in creating "a picture" but also in acting out, in Rosenberg's words, "an event."[73] For pioneers of performance art such as Allan Kaprow and Carolee Schneemann, Pollock's work and related modes of mid-twentieth-century painting—in which the artist's physical process and his or her body were as much a part of the artistic medium as canvas, brush, and paint—became an important precedent for the emphasis on art as action and practice in subsequent work.

HAPPENINGS AND EARLY PERFORMANCE ART

For example, writing in a slightly later article, Kaprow notes, similarly to Rosenberg, that Pollock's works function as "acts" that give rise to a "new concrete art."[74] In this concrete art, Kaprow continues, contemporary artists, "Not satisfied with the suggestion through paint of our other senses . . . shall utilize the specific substances of sight, sound, movements, people, odors, [and] touch" to make art.[75] Furthermore, Kaprow observes, "Objects of every sort are materials for the new art," objects that include activities, as well as materials, taken from daily life.[76] In Kaprow's 1964 happening *Household*, for instance, a range of everyday activities—such as hanging clothes on a clothesline, spreading jam,

taking off clothing, and eating—are enacted by a group of participants who together create the work of art. And, in each case, the everyday activities take shape in their everyday forms; the outline of the happening indicates that there are no major adjustments or alterations to the activities themselves.[77] However, these everyday activities are staged in locations and combined with objects and additional behaviors that render their familiar, everyday status less straightforward and mundane.

In one stage of *Household*, for instance, participants engage in the completely routine activity of spreading jam, but they spread it onto a wrecked car. In later stages of the happening, participants also lick at the jam on the surface of the car, and, later again, participants eat jam sandwiches while seated around the car.[78] In the latter case, eating while seated outdoors is an especially mundane component of *Household*, but in conjunction with the additional actions that constitute the happening, especially those that incorporate jam, the familiar act of picnicking, even eating in general, takes on new, if perhaps somewhat perplexing, significance. *Household* thus activates everyday activities precisely in their everyday forms, but in ways that give rise to a modified, often heightened or new experience of the otherwise routine actions put into practice. Such heightened experience closely parallels the raised awareness and intensity that frequently characterize ritual actions; indeed, as Kaprow himself has observed, happenings, as well as related practices, "pla[y] with the materials of the tangible world" in ways that give rise to "conscious ceremonies acted out" in the form, in the artist's words, of "quasi-rituals."[79]

While Kaprow's happenings foreground connections between ritual and contemporary art in their activities that overlap art and life, Carolee Schneemann's performance-based artworks call to mind ritual practices perhaps above all in their integral focus, and frequently transformative impact, on the human body. For example, in one of her early performances, *Eye Body* (1963), Schneemann incorporated her naked body into a large-scale art environment that she was building at the time. In *Eye Body*, Schneemann "Covered" her naked body "in paint, grease, chalk, ropes, [and] plastic," in a series of actions that made her body into both an "integral material" and a "visual territory" within the work of art.[80] Schneemann's actions thus conjoin the physical, active, fleshy properties of her body with the optical, formal properties that have often been taken to be the more traditional province of visual art. In particular, Schneemann, like Kaprow, draws upon the dual issues that inform Abstract Expressionism—action and painting—to embrace a multitude of media and meanings that are no longer understood as strictly separate or oppositional engagements.[81]

What is more, Schneemann's use of her own naked body in *Eye Body* also changes the status and meaning of the female nude. Traditionally an objectified image in Western art history, the female nude takes on an additional role, in Schneemann's project, as a moving, animate element of *Eye Body* and even as a dynamic agent of the "stroke and gesture" that constitute the work of art.[82] That is to say, although Schneemann does not do away with the female nude or its traditional meanings altogether, at the same time, the female nude in *Eye Body* also becomes an "image maker," and the nude is an artist as much as she is an image. In its expansion of possibilities and meanings of the unclothed female body, this body further becomes, as Schneemann puts it, a "votive" force that hones "the coherence, necessity, and personal integrity" of the artist's insistently visual and corporeal practice.[83]

With these artistic practices that overlap and transform image and flesh, Schneemann's *Eye Body* can thus be understood as a series of actions that shares something of its intent and effects with ritual, if perhaps in a somewhat general sense. However, in a subsequent project, Schneemann's 1964 performance *Meat Joy*, these connections between the artist's work and ritual practices become more direct and intense. In *Meat Joy*, which the artist describes as having "the character of an erotic rite," nine performers enact a series of carefully ordered and staged, loosely choreographed encounters with one another.[84] The performance initially develops with the performers strewing crumpled paper around the performance area, moving and pulling one another's bodies through the masses of paper. In subsequent stages of the performance, which has an overall duration of sixty to eighty minutes, the performers apply paint to each other's seminaked bodies, and *Meat Joy* finally culminates with one performer tossing large quantities of raw chicken, fish, and hot dogs onto the bodies of the rest of the group, who improvise a range of movements and behaviors as they become covered in raw flesh and more paint and finally submerge one another once again in the piles of crumpled paper.[85]

In *Meat Joy*, Schneemann continues her "celebration of flesh as material," taking it in ever more "ecstatic" directions.[86] And even though the ecstasy of *Meat Joy* might be understood as sexual, in the bodies writhing together across the performance space, it can also be understood as a religious ecstasy—one that, rather than foregoing bodily sensation in favor of a spiritual state, instead heightens one's experience of the body, extending and transferring bodily sensation across space.[87] Indeed, as Schneemann herself describes it, this is precisely what occurs in *Meat Joy*, a performance that "enacted" a series of "physical equivalences" that take shape "as a psychic and imagistic stream in which the layered elements mesh and gain intensity by the energy complement of the audience."[88] That is to say, *Meat Joy* gives rise to a range of energies—simultaneously physical, psychological, and visual—that extend from the performers to the viewers, who "were seated on the floor as close to the performance as possible."[89] In particular, with this physical proximity between viewers and performers in *Meat Joy*, the "physical equivalences" of the artwork in turn "heightened the sense of community" between these bodies, ultimately, Schneemann continues, "transgressing the polarity between performers and audience."[90]

Thus, although Schneemann seldom integrates viewers into her artworks as fully active participants, the artist's insistent use of and intensive focus on the body nevertheless forges important physical connections with her audience, connections that also blur boundaries between artwork and audience and, by association, between art and life. What is more, in the artist's references to physical, psychic, and visual energies that establish equivalencies and implicate viewers in the rigorous and what might even seem extreme or excessive actions of *Meat Joy*, not only does Schneemann articulate an important crossover or transfer of experience between performers and viewers, but she also describes, like Kaprow, something of a profound or heightened quality of experience operating in her work, a quality of experience that has often been associated with religious practice and, especially, ritual. As Kristine Stiles has similarly

Carolee Schneemann, Meat Joy, *1964. Performance: raw fish, chickens, sausages, wet paint, plastic, rope, paper scrap. Photo: Al Giese. Courtesy of the artist.*

observed, one of the artist's "larger . . . concerns" is her "research into the heightening of psychical awareness through the intensification of physical experience," a concern that, Stiles continues, draws important connections between spirituality and sensuality and that is central to *Meat Joy*, as well as to many other examples of the artist's work.[91]

In *Meat Joy*, the crossover or transition between performers and viewers effected by Schneemann is experienced above all on and through the body, in the extension and transference of bodily experiences and energies between performers and viewers. As such, *Meat Joy*, along with *Eye Body* and other examples of Schneemann's work, makes the body into the medium or material of the practice-based field of contemporary art, just as ritual routinely makes the body the medium of its own practices. And although Schneemann's work clearly seems to foreground the body as a site of "spiritual conditions,"[92] just as ritual also routinely does, the specific components of Schneemann's practices seem to be rather unique to her own work. However, in a number of additional examples of performance art, artists borrow and adapt activities that have been associated with more familiar ritual practices that are frequently drawn from the field of religion.

RELIGIOUS PRACTICE AND RITUAL ACTIVITIES IN BODY AND PERFORMANCE ART

For example, Hermann Nitsch, one of the artists constituting the Viennese Actionist group, staged a series of performances in the 1960s and 1970s in which the artist's actions closely resemble sacrifice and related religious practices. Beginning with one of his earliest performance projects, his *First Action* (1962), Nitsch made use of blood, a material with strong sacrificial

overtones, which he had splashed over his body while he was tied into a crucifixion-like pose. In subsequent performances, especially his *Orgies Mysteries (OM) Theatre* (begun in the 1960s), Nitsch has continued to use blood, along with animal carcasses—and often lamb carcasses, providing another especially potent connection to religious sacrifice—that participants tear apart in a series of physical and, for some observers, quite violent behaviors with strong references and connections to Dionysian rites, among other rituals.[93]

A number of the additional artists in the Viennese Actionist group, specifically Otto Mühl, Günter Brus, and Rudolf Schwarzkogler, have also created performance artworks that involve extreme physical activities, often with cutting, bruising, or other elements of self-mutilation. While these activities may also be excessive if not downright disturbing to some viewers, at the same time, they are practices that are not uncommon in religious rituals. Although such work has been extremely controversial—for example, a number of the Viennese Actionists' performances were shut down by the police, and several of the artists spent time in jail as a result of their work[94]—similar experiments with destructive, violent, often self-mutilating practices have been made by a range of artists, including Stelarc, Paul McCarthy, Karen Finley, and Bob Flanagan.

Additionally, in some of his early works, Chris Burden has engaged in physically dangerous activities with especially direct links to mythology and religion. For example, Burden's 1973 performance *Icarus* explores and enacts themes drawn from the Greek myth of Icarus; in the performance, Burden had two large sheets of plate glass balanced upon his bare shoulders. Assistants poured gasoline over the sheets of glass and lit them on fire, at which point Burden flung his naked body into the air, and the blazing glass also went flying and shattered as it hit the floor. Furthermore, in a particularly explicit reference to religion, Burden had himself crucified to the rear bumper and roof of a Volkswagen in his 1974 performance *Trans-Fixed*.[95]

As Thomas McEvilley has noted, many of these performances, with their extreme behaviors enacted upon artists' bodies, also have what are often described as shamanic overtones. McEvilley writes, for example, that in works such as Nitsch's actions, "the artist is seen [from certain vantage points] as a kind of extramural initiation priest, a healer or guide."[96] And in the work of Joseph Beuys, references to shamanism are especially pronounced, especially in two of the artist's best-known performances, *How to Explain Pictures to a Dead Hare* (1965) and *I Like America and America Likes Me* (1974). For example, in *How to Explain Pictures to a Dead Hare*, Beuys isolated himself in a gallery space, and, head covered in honey and gold leaf, he toured the gallery with a dead rabbit in his arms. As he approached various paintings on display, he quietly discussed the artworks with the rabbit carcass. Beuys's efforts to communicate with and through an animal mark a particularly strong connection to certain aspects of shamanic ritual activities in a number of religious traditions.[97]

In a related vein, Beuys also incorporated an animal into *I Like America and America Likes Me*. For this performance, Beuys traveled to New York City, where, as soon as he disembarked from his plane, he was transported to the René Block Gallery by an ambulance. Cloaked in felt and carrying a shepherd's staff, the artist was met in the gallery by a live coyote, with whom he lived, on and off, for five days. Although the coyote initially kept its distance from Beuys, as it grew more familiar with the artist's presence, Beuys was increasingly able to interact with it. Beuys also had fifty copies of the *Wall Street Journal* delivered to the gallery on a daily basis,

and his performance has been interpreted by some critics as an attempt to negotiate two poles of US history and culture—its ties to nature, landscape, and the so-called frontier tradition, on the one hand, and the ever-growing force of capitalism, on the other.[98] In more general terms, Beuys has been understood to draw upon the figure and role of the shaman as part of an effort to heal the modern world, an effort in which his artworks serve as "the instrument of resurrection, for the unification of [humanity]."[99]

From their almost messianic overtones to their more down-to-earth if occasionally perplexing everyday activities, these diverse examples of performance art exhibit a range of concerns and activities that constitute this category of art that engages in and/or activates behaviors related to religious practices. Additional artists give shape to this range of activities in their work as well. For example, in performance projects such as her *Hartford Wash* actions (1973) and *Touch Sanitation* (1978–1980), Mierle Laderman Ukeles has employed the extremely mundane, often ignored activities of cleaning and related forms of maintenance work to foreground and heighten awareness about the importance of these activities.

In her *Hartford Wash* projects, for instance, Ukeles performs the usually afterhours work of cleaning the public spaces of a museum (the Wadsworth Athenaeum in Hartford, Connecticut) during regular business hours, confronting viewers with the typically hidden but crucial maintenance labor without which museums, along with other public institutions and spaces, would cease to function.[100] Similarly, in *Touch Sanitation*, Ukeles uses the very simple, familiar gesture of the handshake to mark and acknowledge the often unseen, undervalued labor of sanitation workers in New York City. In particular, *Touch Sanitation* involved the artist shaking hands with and personally

Mierle Laderman Ukeles, Touch Sanitation Performance, *1979-80. "Handshake Ritual" with workers of New York City Department of Sanitation. Courtesy Ronald Feldman Fine Arts, New York. Artist Mierle Laderman Ukeles shakes the hand of one of the 8,500 New York Department of Sanitation workers she met with over this eleven-month performance project.*

thanking more than 8,500 workers employed by the Department of Sanitation in New York City. Completed over eleven months, Ukeles's performance displays a degree of commitment that makes the routine and repeated gesture of the handshake, accompanied by Ukeles's greeting, "thank you for keeping New York City alive," into a mark of gratitude, perhaps even something of a secular prayer. With *Touch Sanitation*, Ukeles thus honors maintenance labor itself with a quality of attention and care that not only sheds more light on but also assigns greater value and meaning to sanitation and maintenance work.[101]

In a related vein, Linda Montano has also engaged in numerous performance projects in which she makes everyday activities into art. In artworks such as her 1973 performance, with

Tom Marioni, *Handcuff: Linda Montano and Tom Marioni,* and the 1983–1984 artwork *A Year Spent Tied Together at the Waist,* created in collaboration with Tehching Hsieh, every possible activity that constitutes the artist's daily life becomes an element of the work of art. Due to the necessities of behaving more consciously in order to perform even the most routine of actions, necessities that themselves result from the demands of being physically bound to another individual, the meanings of otherwise banal activities become altered in these artworks.[102] Similarly, in her solo projects *Seven Years as Living Art* and *Another Seven Years of Living Art* (1984–1998), Montano takes the work of integrating art and life to an extreme. Predicated upon principles of careful discipline as a means of generating heightened awareness, these projects draw on religious sources such as the Hindu chakras, through which the artist institutes a series of self-imposed limits, in order to structure and focus more attention upon her daily life and transform it into a work of art.[103]

This emphasis on heightened awareness and a more intentional state of being and action also derives from Montano's religious training and experience, including her Catholic upbringing, her early studies to become a nun (she left before becoming ordained), and her practice of Zen meditation. This training and experience informs additional examples of Montano's work as well, including her 1975 performances *The Screaming Nun* and *Three Days Blindfold/How to Become a Guru*. What is more, Montano's interest in religious figures such as nuns and gurus can also be seen in her various early chicken performances from 1971 and 1972, in which the artist donned a feathered costume and assumed various poses and activities in galleries and other public spaces.[104] Although it is very different from that of Beuys, Montano's incorporation of an animal figure might constitute a reference to shamanic figures and practices as well.

Some authors have also hinted at shamanic properties in the work of Ana Mendieta, especially several of the artist's early performances, such as *Untitled (Death of a Chicken)* (1972) and *Bird Transformation* (1972). In *Untitled (Death of a Chicken)*, for example, Mendieta beheaded a chicken in front of an audience, in an artwork that appears to enact a sacrificial gesture. Standing before her viewers, Mendieta holds the chicken by its legs, and blood flows out of the chicken's neck, some of which sprays across the artist's naked body. In a somewhat different though not entirely unrelated vein, Mendieta merges a human body with bodily materials associated with a chicken (or with birds more generally) in *Bird Transformation*, in which the

artist covers a model's body with white feathers. The end result is a figure that has what might be understood as totemic or shamanic significance.[105] In a similar vein, Mendieta's two projects *Untitled (Blood and Feathers)* and *Untitled (Blood and Feathers #2)*, both 1974 (and repeated in 1976), involve performances in which the artist applies a layer of white feathers to her own naked body; in these two cases, Mendieta further charges the artworks with religious and ritual significance through her use of blood, which she rubs onto her body as part of the process of affixing the feathers to her own skin.[106]

Mendieta also made a number of artworks dedicated to various sacred female figures during her career, including the Mayan goddess Ix-Chell in *Untitled (Ix-Chell)* and *El Ix-Chell Negro*, both 1977, as well as a number of goddesses associated with the Taíno peoples, an indigenous Cuban society that was decimated by the arrival of European colonists in the fifteenth and sixteenth centuries. In particular, Mendieta devoted her *Rupestrian Sculptures* (1981), carved in situ in a number of caves in Jaruco, Cuba, to Taíno goddesses Guabancex (Goddess of the Wind), Atabey (Mother of the Water), and Itiba Cahubaba (Old Mother Blood), among others.[107] Throughout her career, the artist also drew upon ideas central to the Afro-Caribbean, hybrid Catholic religion of Santería, especially its central principle of *ashé*.[108]

What is more, Mendieta created several artworks in important sacred, holy, and otherwise religious sites. For example, in 1976, Mendieta installed an *Untitled* artwork in the Cuilapán monastery and church in Mexico; composed of a white sheet imprinted with the shape of her body traced in blood, the artwork is not only located in a religious compound but also references religious practices such as sacrifice, along with earthen forces and forms—the latter through the pile of branches positioned below the hanging sheet. In a subsequent project, *Ceiba Fetish* (1981), Mendieta made an artwork at the site of a tree sacred to Santería practitioners in Miami. And in her 1973 project *Imagen de Yagul (Image from Yagul)*, Mendieta placed her naked body in an ancient Zapotec tomb in Mexico and had her body covered in white flowers, to create the artwork that is generally considered to be the precursor or first example of her best-known project, the *Silueta* series.[109]

In the *Silueta* series, made between roughly 1976 and 1982, Mendieta used her body to fashion a female silhouette out of a range of materials (dirt, sand, grass, flowers, fire, and the like) in various outdoor landscapes located primarily in the United States and Mexico. Seen by many authors as an attempt on the part of the artist to reclaim some sense of connection to land and place in the wake of her highly dislocating experience of exile from Cuba as a teenager,[110] the *Siluetas* can also be understood to evoke a religious or spiritual force. In particular, with the form that each of the *Siluetas* takes—a female figure that simultaneously emerges from and submerges into different landscape settings—Mendieta's artworks seem to demarcate their locations and terrains as characterized, perhaps even inhabited, by some kind of otherwise invisible force.

Finally, in the work of Marina Abramović there is an especially wide range of practices that both reference and are more actively linked to religion and ritual. For example, Abramović's early solo performances often involve bodily risk and, in some cases, self-mutilation; in one of the artist's best-known projects, *Rhythm 0* (1974), Abramović positioned herself in front of a table covered with seventy-two different implements, including a gun and a bullet, matches, a candle, scissors, paint in various colors, flowers, food items, yarn, a comb, lipstick, and perfume. The audience was invited to pick up any of the implements and use them on Abramović's body, for

which the artist bore complete responsibility.[111] And in *Lips of Thomas* (1975), over the course of a two-hour performance, the artist physically abused and mutilated her body, cutting a star shape into her stomach with a razor blade and whipping herself until her abdomen and thighs bled, in an act of self-flagellation through which Abramović explores, as she herself has put it, "the *limits* of the body . . . us[ing] performance to push my mental and physical limits beyond consciousness."[112] In this vein, *Lips of Thomas*, like so many of Abramović's projects, recalls religious practices in both its form (that is to say, in the activities that the artist uses, often adapted from various religious traditions) and in its aims, experiences, and effects, particularly its achievement of a heightened, extrarational or otherwise altered state of being.

In these early performances, Abramović initiates a particular focus on the physical experience and spiritual capacities of the body that continues throughout her career. The subsequent artworks she made in collaboration with Ulay (Uwe Laysiepen; their collaboration began in 1976 and ended in 1988), for instance, are especially noteworthy for their qualities of bodily endurance, engaged and explored via familiar, even mundane physical behaviors such as running, standing, and sitting. For example, in *Relation in Space* (1976), the two artists repeatedly move past one another in an exhibition space, speeding up their pace over the course of nearly an hour and increasingly slamming their naked bodies into one another. Or, in *Imponderabilia* (1977), the two artists, again naked, stand facing each other across a hallway. The simple act of standing constitutes the artists' performance, which is designed to force viewers, who must pass through the hallway to access the exhibition space, to choose whether to turn and face the naked female or the naked male body as they squeeze through the narrow space.[113] Thus,

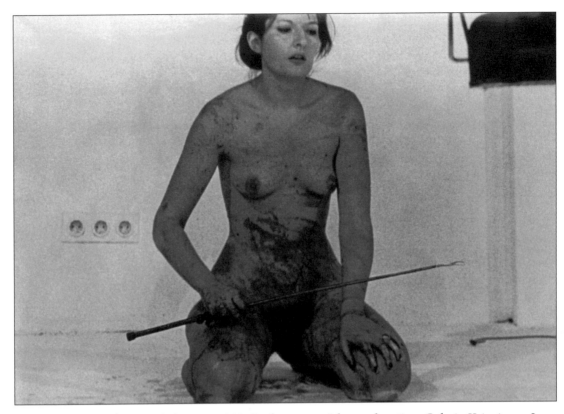

Marina Abramović, Lips of Thomas, *1975. Performance, 2 hours duration. Galerie Krinzinger, Innsbruck. Courtesy of Marina Abramović Archives and Sean Kelly Gallery, NY.*

using practices that are so familiar and mundane as to be unremarkable in other forms or venues, Abramović and Ulay make these practices into an intense meditation on and exploration of the relationships between bodies, and, in the process, the artists insistently heighten viewers' awareness of their own bodies and their physical movements in space.[114]

This issue of heightened awareness especially comes to the fore in Abramović and Ulay's artwork *Nightsea Crossing*, performed in a number of forms and locations between 1981 and 1987. In *Nightsea Crossing*, Abramović and Ulay sit across a table from one another for seven hours a day, doing so for at least one day and as many as sixteen consecutive days. Different versions of the performance incorporate different additional elements—various objects placed on the table, different colors of clothing, more performers involved in the event—but in each instance, the artists do not speak or eat for the duration of the performance.[115] Instead, they sit incredibly still and channel their attention into being present to one another in the performance, charging the exhibition space with what the artist has termed a "live energy" that can subtly but not insignificantly alter and again heighten experience of space.[116]

In later solo artworks, Abramović further explores and expands these qualities of energy and presence. For example, in her series *Transitory Objects for Human Use* (begun in 1989), Abramović creates objects meant for audience interaction that are designed to hone "potential energy," serving, according to Germano Celant, as "an invitation to transcend the limits of one's own sensory and spiritual capability."[117] In one project from the series, *Shoes for Departure* (1991), the artist has carved openings into large, extremely heavy chunks of amethyst. Positioned in pairs in the exhibition space, the objects are accompanied by directions for viewers, who are instructed to take off their shoes, place their feet in the openings, and "depart."[118] However, given the physical mass and weight of the amethyst forms, these shoes are not meant to facilitate a physical departure, but a psychic or spiritual one, transporting viewers to a level of consciousness, perception, and sensation "which lie[s] outside of rational conventions."[119]

This invocation of a heightened mode of attention or a higher level of consciousness recurs throughout Abramović's work, and in most cases these experiences are meant to spark and expand energies that are best understood as religious or spiritual. Indeed, as Thomas McEvilley has written, Abramović's accounts of the "experiences of enfolding energy, energy fields surrounding her and the audience" and of the "trance-like state of attention and energy vibrations" that develop during her performances frequently "overlap with yogic descriptions" from "many of the world's religious traditions" and also involve a quality of "shamanic practice."[120] Especially important, McEvilley notes, is the artist's "intensity of commitment," which is especially tangible in the extremes to which the artist takes the body, particularly her own body, throughout her work.[121]

For example, in addition to the self-mutilation and flagellation of her earlier performances, Abramović has also subjected her body to risk, danger, and endurance in some of her more recent works. In *Dragon Heads*, for instance, performed on several occasions between 1990 and 1994, Abramović is covered with five live pythons while seated on a chair, perfectly still, for sixty or more minutes in an exhibition space partially enclosed or otherwise marked off by blocks of ice. In addition, in her 1997 artwork *Balkan Baroque*, Abramović stages an extremely demanding performance: surrounded by three video projections and three sink- and bathtub-like containers filled with water, the artist laboriously scrapes and cleans flesh and fat from fifteen hundred cattle bones while singing folk songs that she learned as a child in Yugoslavia.[122] Seated atop the pile of bones while performing over the course of four days, Abramović becomes hoarse, and her clothes become soaked in animal blood, as she enacts the artwork, with its activities that, although mundane, nevertheless require intense physical stamina and mental concentration—not unlike various cleansing and healing rituals found in many religious traditions. What is more, Abramović compounds these cleansing and healing elements with animistic and sacrificial overtones, in her constant and bloodied contact with the huge pile of cattle bones, along with the continuous ritual chant of her singing voice.

Abramović's work is thus an especially sustained example of artistic practices with strong connections to religion, which, together with the additional examples of performance and related practice-based modes of art explored in this section, constitute an important arena in contemporary art: namely, artworks with integral affinities to ritual.[123] And while these examples of performance-based artworks, with their emphasis on practice, demonstrate an important, if at times undertheorized, connection to ritual activities, in addition, this latter set of connections between religion and contemporary art also necessitates at least a partial reassessment of artworks about religion as well. Indeed, even though photographs, paintings, sculptures, and similar artworks do not have links to ritual that are as direct or explicit as the connections between ritual and performance art, photography, painting, sculpture, and related artistic media can nevertheless evoke or incite some type of religious practice and experience as well, perhaps especially for their viewers.

For example, the icon-like imagery of Serrano's photograph *Piss Christ* and Ofili's painting *The Holy Virgin Mary* might call forth a meditative or prayer-like state from viewers, just as the altar forms and configurations of Mesa-Bains's and Aylon's installation projects can recast the museum as a site of devotion or worship. However, the prayer and devotion that these artists stage is perhaps more in the mode of political and cultural activism than in that of orthodox theology, and the mode of worship is as much transgressive as it is unquestioningly faithful or committed to any traditional notion of belief.[124] In a somewhat related vein, Kristine Stiles suggests that a nontraditional mode of belief also develops in performance and practice-based artworks, precisely through, in her terminology, their status as actions. Stiles asserts, for example, that "action artists . . . operate as commisures entrusted with the idea of communicating the value and image of *anyone doing something*."[125] The value of the "doing" of action art is, Stiles continues, the very act of doing itself, because, in this doing, something happens—something "rather than nothing"—and this something constitutes activity "without which," Stiles writes, "it is practically impossible to live" and through which "one survives."[126]

However, for Stiles, action art calls forth more than basic survival; "beyond mere survival," she adds, "*belief* may emerge from making things happen."[127] According to Stiles, the belief that emerges in the actions of performance art and related work "is not the belief so frequently associated with faith or organized religion, or even with notions of God."[128] It is, instead, "the intentional causal essence of an empowered political act," in which "individuals act with belief and with a sense of responsibility toward others with whom one commits to acting together."[129] As such, what Stiles proposes is a utopian and activist understanding of action, emphasizing social bonds and political communities, and not religious in any theological or denominational way. And yet, rather than jettisoning religion altogether, perhaps Stiles's recourse to belief in her assessment of action and practice-based art further suggests an alternative notion or mode of religion, a religion that is founded, precisely, in practices, experiences, and effects that constitute not doctrine or theology so much as social connections, political formations, and cultural meanings.[130] In this sense, Stiles's remarks, and the many examples of contemporary art discussed throughout this chapter, not only spark a reexamination of the relationships between religion and contemporary art but might also involve an ongoing reconsideration of our very notion of religion itself.

Glossary

Abstract Expressionism: An artistic style or movement that took shape in the United States, specifically in New York City, in the late 1940s and 1950s; also known as the New York School. Informed by earlier developments in various modes of expressionism and abstraction, as well

Helène Aylon. The Liberation of G-d, *1990-96. Altered versions of the Five Books of Moses, velvet panels, velvet-covered pedestals, lamps, magnifying lenses, video monitors. Dimensions variable. Collection of the Jewish Museum of New York. Art © Helène Aylon/Licensed by VAGA, New York, NY.*

as Surrealism, Abstract Expressionism is often grouped into two subcategories: action or gesture paintings, on the one hand, in which paint is used in such a way that it seems to emphasize the artist's actions, often with a sense of handed or otherwise performed gestures (e.g., Jackson Pollock, Willem deKooning, Franz Kline), and color field painting, on the other hand, in which paint is applied in broad planes or fields of color, often in an attempt to depict or evoke spiritual, transcendental, or related experiences (e.g., Mark Rothko, Barnett Newman).

Happenings: A live-action form of artistic production developed in the late 1950s and 1960s in which boundaries between art and life were intentionally blurred; everyday activities and practices often became the means and media of art, and audience members frequently became active participants in the creation and staging of art, especially in the work of Allan Kaprow.

Performance Art: A live-action form of artistic production developed in the 1960s and 1970s in which artists engaged in performance practices, often with an emphasis on the body as a primary mode of or medium for art. Performance art often overlaps with developments in experimental theater and dance that also took shape in the 1960s and 1970s, and it continues in various forms into the present day.

Site-Specific Art: Artistic projects that are made for or are otherwise linked to a particular place or location, often in the form of practices that are now called installation. In some cases, site-specific art is bound and shaped by the physical parameters of its location (e.g., Richard Serra, Robert Smithson); in other instances, site-specific art responds to the historical, social, and/or political contexts and meanings that are associated with a particular site (e.g., Ann Hamilton, Mark Dion), and some site-specific artworks overlap these two approaches to site-bound practices.

FOR FURTHER READING

Elkins, James. *On the Strange Place of Religion in Contemporary Art*. New York: Routledge, 2004.

Heartney, Eleanor. *Postmodern Heretics: The Catholic Imagination in Contemporary Art*. New York: Midmarch, 2004.

Kaprow, Allan. *Essays on the Blurring of Art and Life*. Edited by Jeff Kelley. Berkeley: University of California Press, 1993.

Out of Actions: Between Performance and the Object, 1949-1979. Los Angeles: Museum of Contemporary Art; New York: Thames and Hudson, 1998.

Schneemann, Carolee. *More Than Meat Joy: Performance Works and Selected Writings*. Edited by Bruce McPherson. New York: McPherson and Company, 1997 (1979).

The Spiritual in Art: Abstract Painting 1890-1985. Los Angeles: Los Angeles County Museum of Art; New York: Abbeville, 1986.

Warr, Tracey, and Amelia Jones. *The Artist's Body*. New York: Phaidon, 2000.

14

CONTEMPORARY MUSIC

Masen Uliss

INTRODUCTION

There is nothing like a Grateful Dead concert," or so the saying goes among followers of the US rock band and stalwart of the countercultural music scene. This aphorism, common among fans, known as "deadheads," since "the Dead's" early years, became canonized by its inclusion in the liner notes to its album *Europe '72*. It expressed the belief that the experience of attending a performance by the Grateful Dead was special—uniquely removed from ordinary life. As explained in the general introduction to this collection of essays, scholars of religion since Rudolf Otto have defined the sacred in terms of this status of exception from the ordinary world. When Grateful Dead guitarist Jerry Garcia died in 1995, it was difficult to find a news article covering the story that did not cite a deadhead's explanation of the band's importance to their life in terms of an experience of the sacred or a description of the concerts as "like our church." Similar language of ritual and family provided context for media coverage of the remaining members' return to the road in

2009 after a five-year hiatus. In a video posted on the band's website at the outset of that tour, two deadheads explained that "because the Dead are being resurrected on Easter Sunday, we couldn't miss it for the world."[1]

An outside observer to one of the band's thousands of concerts between 1965 and 1995, or of its related later offshoots through the present day, might indeed have found considerable truth in the saying if they compared the form or content of the experience to that of other rock concerts. However, they would also have found a great deal that was familiar—the same stadium that was filled with deadheads on a Saturday might be filled with football fans on a Sunday, all thoroughly engrossed and enrapt in their sweaty experiences of those rather worldly rituals, all finding commonality among other individuals united by their distinction from other sorts of fans. The sense in which Dead shows were unique—even sacred—to deadheads was rooted as much in their relatedness to the ordinary world and their occurrence in it.

Certainly, Grateful Dead concerts were like many other things, in that music has come to

Appreciative fans waiting for a performance of the Grateful Dead at a concert at Red Rocks Amphitheatre, Morrison, Colorado.

occupy a complex place in the daily ritual lives of individuals in contemporary society and in the ways that they find meaning and experience the world. Although it takes a broad view, this chapter necessarily examines the complex relationships between music and religion from a limited point of view—to present them in the context of contemporary daily life. In particular, it tends to focus upon Western cultures, especially that of the United States and in its presentation of details is based upon choices that are illustrative but neither wholly representative nor arbitrary.

Rather, the goal in these pages is to argue that the interrelations of those aspects of culture commonly thought to be "religious" and those thought not to be are, in fact, rather complicated and interwoven—especially where the creative, artistic realm of music is concerned. This is particularly the case in the everyday lives of people living in modern cultures, which are replete with conflicting sources of authority over both ordinary and extraordinary daily practices and their meanings. Thus the author's purposes will be served if, after considering this argument and its illustrations, the reader is inspired to think of different examples or illustrations that better capture the intricate giving and taking that goes on as individuals meaningfully experience the world through their musical practices.

The many roles occupied and functions served by music in contemporary daily life are very often connected to questions of identity. The choice of what music to enjoy and have as "one's own" is thought to say a great deal about people, both to themselves and to others. As young people begin to develop a sense of who they are on their own and apart from their families, and what their lives mean in their own terms apart from what they have been told, musical tastes and associations are among the readily available means for asserting their new identities as individuals. Although the trend has a longer history, at least since the mid-twentieth century, popular music has been connected in the public imagination with a "youth culture" that represents a break with the prior generation and with established, received tastes. However, identity in modern societies is formed in the tension between individuals and groups. The concept of a rebellious "youth culture" itself is by now a tradition, and it is one that bears significant resemblances to the "rites of passage" noted cross-culturally by scholars of religion and anthropologists. Each formation of individual identity, no matter how iconoclastic in intention, takes place within the context of group identities and is assembled with found and given cultural tools and materials.

Exploring the religious dimensions of music in contemporary culture brings into view more than one powerful tension; that between individual and group identification is but one. This sort of tension, unlike a simple argument or disagreement, is not solely a destructive or disunifying phenomenon. As in the first example, these tensions in culture are also remarkably generative and creative forces; they are able to bring together seemingly different forces and hold them together so that society can continue to function. Closely tied, for example, to the tensions between individual and group identity formation are the opposing forces of innovation and change, on one hand, and the impulse toward conservation and reassertion of tradition, on the other. Through these tremendous opposites, cultures are able to find new ways of doing familiar things, to adapt existing needs and materials to new circumstances, to accommodate the drive to innovate and deviate, while maintaining continuity with the past. Individual people are similarly able to scratch the itch for change and newness and find culturally sanctioned forms of individuality, rebellion from the norm, and departure from expectations, without actually threatening the bonds of social cohesion. This phenomenon has been true of many religious traditions throughout the worlds' cultures and is equally useful in understanding the role of music in the lives of those cultures' people.

One of the aspects of religious life that has demanded this sort of flexibility has been the differentiation between the spheres of the sacred and profane in the lives of participants. Otto's interpretation of the biblical burning bush described in the general introduction accounts not only for the obvious and absolute distinctness of the sacred as manifest in God's communication through the bush but also for the necessity of its emergence into the ordinary or profane world. The logic of this explanation seems to follow common sense by dictating that there must always be a worldly (profane) context for the appearance of the otherworldly and exceptional (sacred) in a person's actual life. This meeting of the sacred and profane need not be as unusual or exceptional as Moses's encounter with the burning bush; in fact, most of the time, it is more routine, as in the demarcation of sacred time and space in a religious prayer service. Nevertheless, anyone who has attended regular services at a church, synagogue, mosque, temple, gurdwara, or other place of worship knows that such "ordinary" encounters with the sacred are taken just as seriously. Of course, the experience of individuals at such services varies widely, and, for some, the mundane rules the day, but for others an encounter with the sacred during an everyday service is on a par with those described in sacred texts, such as the Judeo-Christian Bibles. In the instance of a Grateful Dead concert, mundane concert venues are temporarily transformed from theaters and sports arenas into spaces where, through the efficacy of the appropriate rituals of preparation, an encounter with the sacred during the musical performance becomes possible.

The boundaries between sacred and profane are continually monitored, patrolled, and maintained by participants. In the Christian New Testament, a story of Jesus Christ's rejection of profane "money changers" inside the boundaries of the sacred temple is told as a model for the proper separation between these spheres. Other interpreters note that these money changers were not in violation of the sacred space at all and were actually essential for the proper daily operation of the temple's sacrificial worship; pilgrims were biblically required to make material offerings that required the official coinage of Jerusalem. Regardless of which version of the story one subscribes to, they are both about the maintenance of proper separation and boundaries between what is understood to be sacred or profane. Scholars of religion have continued to explore Otto's notion of the sacred, and some have described the sacred as that which is capable of being desecrated.[2]

These factors imply yet another important part of the equation: there are both proper and improper actions and intentions for religious participants. Proper actions or intentions respect or maintain the proper boundaries between sacred and profane, whereas improper ones transgress those boundaries. Transgression, sin, profanation, and desecration are all terms that describe these improper boundary crossings or confusions. All of these are subject to interpretation, just as was the role of the biblical money changers. Although some transgressions are more widely agreed upon, others are vigorously contested. The tendencies toward innovation and change lead some practitioners to actions or intentions that they understand as appropriate but that are seen by traditionalists as sins or desecrations. In some cases, disagreements of this nature lead to permanent breaks and divisions—new religions, sects, or groups are formed. In the case of the biblical money changers, the followers of Jesus decided that their Jewish contemporaries had wandered so far from the path that God had ordained for them that "true" adherence to tradition required transgression against the prevailing order. Thus, although they probably had difficulty seeing it from the other's perspective, both sides in this instance claimed to be upholding the correct path to the sacred, as distinct from the other's deviance from it.

CULTURAL BRIDGES AND DIVIDES

Surprising as it may seem for those accustomed to thinking of music, especially popular music, as secular, these patterns and tensions play out in this realm of culture as well. Groups and individuals who proudly wear the badge of transgression and departure from tradition, such as punk musicians and fans, do so by making claims of purity and integrity from the profane compromises understood to be required by conventional, mainstream popular music. Nevertheless, punks and others—who pride themselves on a forceful rejection of what they see as the banality of the mainstream, in favor of values such as originality, individuality, and thoughtful nonconformity—are themselves following in a long tradition of dissent. Like Jesus' rejection of his contemporaries in ancient Israel and Martin Luther's later invocation of Jesus in his rejection of then-contemporary Christianity, what is seen as transgressive and deviant from one perspective is considered an answer to the prophetic call from another. Examples abound outside of Christianity as well, but it should come as no surprise that among today's nondenominational Christian churches and movements are iconoclastic preachers who are building younger congregations, in which the dress, attitudes, and musical aesthetics of punk rock are joined with yet another attempt to return to the "true" or "original" message of Christian tradition. Alternatively, members of the "straight edge" movement reject drugs and alcohol, commercialization, and, often, meat eating in an austere, ascetic manner.

As is clear from what we have already reviewed, performance of rituals is a central part of how the religious dimensions of music are experienced in daily life. Later in this essay, we examine more specific examples, but the central phenomenon of concertgoing for the Grateful Dead mentioned previously is a form of ritual practice that enables members of that community to have meaningful experiences that stand apart from their mundane drudgery. The performance of a wide variety of ritual activities can be observed in individual practices related to music; furthermore, those individual acts are meaningful in connecting that person to one or more larger collectivities or communities.

Membership in cultural subgroups is not necessarily exclusive—more than one can overlap. For example, deadheads might understand their experience of freedom in the ritual space of a concert as connected to their sense of national identity and patriotism. Punk musicians might understand their critique and rejection of mainstream popular culture in terms of a rugged individualism that is more truly "American" than the life lived by their suburban, cubicle-dwelling contemporaries. Political and personal meanings and beliefs—those involving what Paul Tillich termed "ultimate concerns"—find voice in the choices of expression and association made through the daily rituals surrounding music. The separate or unique qualities of these rituals for participants connect them to one another—not only in terms of meanings or beliefs but also in terms of emotional, bodily, tactile, and even ecstatic access to the sacred. This experiential component of music in contemporary culture can fluidly connect such differing spheres as institutional religions (as through a church choir or other group), commercial music (as through radio, commercial recordings, concert performances), and personal expression (as through the practice of playing or composing music).

In addition to providing occasion for uniting individuals in communal groups and settings, music and its cultures in contemporary life can also serve as points of departure for the expression of cultural divides and disagreements. Both the Grateful Dead and punk communities previously examined are examples of what are sometimes called "subcultures" or "countercultures." As those terms imply, such groupings represent smaller sections of the larger collective, set apart by differences that are usually expressed as critiques or disagreements with that larger collective. These differences can be marked in rather specific ways that are not always meant to be obvious to the uninitiated. For example, Dick Hebdige has written that, in 1970s London, young rockers with shaved heads and bomber jackets might be either neo-Nazi skinheads or antiracism skinheads, depending on subtle dress codes, such as suspenders, pegged pants, or the color of shoelaces.

But distinctions between countercultural groups and a perceived "mainstream" are not the only divisions of this kind. Earlier distinctions between "high" and "low" forms of culture, usually based upon parallel class and power distinctions, have persisted in the era of modern mass media popular culture. The most obvious example of this sort of perspective can be observed in the role of Western classical traditions, often simply called "the arts." This grouping includes orchestral music and opera, the "high" art of museums and galleries, and is thought by many to stand in contrast to "folk" or other "common" and "low" traditions. Although these divisions are often understood in terms of the amount of training required, this is also often a false perception and refers only to the type of training or to whom it is made affordable or available—again, a distinction primarily of class. Although these lines are not as clearly marked as at some other times in the past, they still inform our understanding of classical traditions. Folk music in its many contemporary commercial forms has moved out of its outsider status and come to occupy places in society across class lines.

A still more complicated example is jazz, a relatively new musical form that was originally produced by people living outside of the elite and powerful classes—primarily African Americans in the southern United States. At the time of those origins, it was seen from the outside as a dangerous subculture, connected with all manner of sin, crime, and vice—especially those involving sexuality or drug use. Because jazz also emerged, in large part, from the unique multiracial environment of New Orleans, it was even less comprehensible to mainstream culture elsewhere, black or white. During the course of the twentieth century, jazz gradually gained wide popularity and mainstream acceptance—until it

was not only appropriate for the white middle class, but also, in many instances, the province of the elite upper class, who now buy expensive tickets to see famous jazz musicians in posh clubs and refined concert halls. Race, insinuated as it is into the core of identities in the United States, informs many other forms of music in the daily lives of contemporary individuals. This will become apparent as we later examine some aspects of the development of rock and roll and, later, of hip-hop, as well as the role of folk and rock music in relationship to the civil rights movement of the mid-twentieth century.

Another form of social division and conflict in which the cultures of popular music play a role can be found in the so-called culture wars, identified by social conservatives and those on the political right in efforts to advance their vision of the United States. Although this interpretation of social change starts with a narrative of the 1960s counterculture, it emerged in this form during the 1980s as a revitalized conservatism rode into public awareness on the popularity of Ronald Reagan's presidency. According to subscribers of the "culture war" theory, the nation was increasingly polarized between right and left, liberal and conservative, in a way that crossed the lines of geography and religious affiliation. The left, so the story went, threatened the established social order and its moral values—and a great deal of this threat was seen to lie in a "liberal" mass media and its movies, television, and music. In response, many social progressives and members of the political left explained their version of the story: social change is a constant, and the stable "past" that the conservatives claim to protect is no more "traditional" than any other. Furthermore, they claimed, the actual past was filled with things far better left behind rather than preserved or protected, such as slavery, sexism, exploitive child labor, and other forms of inequality.

Many others, including some musicians associated with the counterculture, saw the whole culture war debate as a made-up distraction and instead chose to continue expressing their versions of the individual and national good. In the case of 1960s musicians and fans, their role as a countercultural youth culture became more complex as they aged and came to occupy the positions of social and political leadership once occupied by those they had protested against. Thus one can find touring acts today, including the surviving members of the Grateful Dead, whose concerts are simultaneously attended by younger fans who are attracted to the counterculture and older deadheads who are now members of Congress or powerful figures in business. In the 1990s, members of the Grateful Dead were received by President Clinton and Vice President Gore in the Oval Office. This scene was repeated with President Obama in 2009, after the band had reunited to play benefit concerts for his campaign.

These continually evolving, complex, and sometimes nonintuitive forms of cultural blending have always been connected, throughout the age of mass media, to the world of business: capitalism, commerce, consumption, and, increasingly, globalization. With the advent of modern recording and broadcasting technologies, what had previously been relegated more to local communities and economies jumped onto the national stage. When it did so, for the most part, there was a charge for admission: hence, the birth of the "music business," now taken for granted but still relatively new in the history of music. Along with these changes came revolutions in the array of ritual practices of individuals.

Public versus Private Life

As noted in the general introduction, the distinction between public and private life has been made for organizational convenience and not theoretical reasons. This is especially relevant for the topic of this chapter, which involves both spheres in more or less equal dosage. There, the editors cite Henri Lefebvre's assertion that every private decision has public implications. The famous feminist adage expresses this basic point in another way: "The personal is political and the political is personal." Feminist thinkers, in the process of rediscovering the previously untold history of women, pointed out that women's political power had often been stifled by their exclusion from the public sphere—a woman's domain was often limited to the home or other private space. In this light, the assertion that the personal is political and vice versa makes the point that, even when it is left out of the official version, history is in fact influenced not only by the powerful elites but also by the sometimes small and often ignored daily acts and practices of ordinary people. Conversely, this adage points out that what the powerful elites do has real, although often ignored, effects on the lives of others. Because we are most interested in "religion on the ground," we always keep one eye on the complex relationships between the broad public world of the music business and the numerous smaller private worlds of individual daily life. Any examination of the contemporary cultures of popular music and their religious dimensions must take into account the permeable boundaries of and fluid dynamics between these two spheres or realms.

Inside and Outside of Religious Institutions

Another way in which we must always have each foot in different realms concerns the relationships between music inside as well as outside of religious institutions. Although this article devotes much of its space to popular culture outside of religious institutions, because of the very nature of the subject, the complicated give and take between popular culture and official religion is key to understanding the religious dimensions of what is often dismissed as secular. In doing so, we neither ignore the institutions nor focus on any one particular religious tradition.

Music has long been deeply involved in the lives of many religious traditions throughout the world. In Judaism, for example, early sacrificial worship included a special class of professional musicians (found among the Levites) without whom the daily activities of the central temple, led by its priests (the Cohanim), would not have been possible. A lyrical sensibility informs many of the biblical texts, some of which were composed with the intention of vocal performance or musical accompaniment. Later Jewish diaspora cultures, not only in the more-often-studied Ashkenazi context but also in the Sephardic and near Eastern ones, developed rich music traditions. Some of these, such as the cantorial methods of chanting prayer or Scripture during regular or holiday services, played a direct role in the sacred life of a community. Others, such as the Klezmer folk music tradition of Eastern European Jews, existed outside of formal synagogue life but occupied privileged positions in essential community and life-cycle events such as marriages, births, and other celebrations.

Still later, as the Jewish Reform movement began to separate from traditional communities in light of the intellectual developments of the Jewish Enlightenment (or *Haskalah*) and the new political opportunities of Emancipation, music played a critical role. Reformers sought to adopt aesthetic and material practices that were more in keeping with the norms of their former oppressors and now neighbors and fellow citizens, not only to "fit in" practically but also to accord with and mark as different what they

understood to be a more modern and evolved form of their own religious tradition. Thus formal choirs and even the traditionally forbidden organ, both inspired by their use in churches, were adapted for use in Reform services. These musical changes were powerful, both as symbolic markers of the changes that Reformers advocated as well as features that strongly shaped individuals' everyday experiences of religious ritual.

One can also look to Christian traditions for many examples of the historical roles of music in religious life. In the earlier periods of church history, its music was dominated by formal traditions of sacred music, including the chanting and liturgical forms that have had recent popular revivals. Local folk traditions quickly emerged throughout the areas of the world in which Christianity took hold and, along with other cultural localizations, contributed to the ability of Christian communities to develop continuity with local and national cultures, even while adopting a "foreign" religious tradition. Because these local musical cultures were woven into the daily ritual life of practitioners—often alongside formal church traditions—they made otherwise jarring religious changes more coherent and digestible. A later example from the US context is the Appalachian "shape-note singing" tradition, a distinctive harmonic form that developed a style of notation in which the shape of the written notes, as well as the notes themselves, directed singers. Whereas some other Christian churches forbid music, in the fast-growing Pentecostal movement, music is a major focus of worship. Because most in the United States celebrate Christmas, Christmas music contributes to the maintenance and spread of Christianity among those who do not attend church.

A form of Christian music that has emerged from African American communities is gospel music. African American churches, having emerged from the unique experience of slave religiosity that eventually adopted, integrated, and reappropriated the religion of their oppressors, have made numerous unique contributions to Christianity more generally. Forcibly separated from the religious cultures of their African origins, slaves deftly wove new forms of religious life from the materials at hand. In so doing, they gained power through a Christianity that threatened the slaveholding population with its troubling appearance as a combination of acceptance of and compliance with slave-owner religion, alongside reinterpretations with revolutionary potential. In the generations after Emancipation, African American churches navigated between hopes for full integration and new forms of continued repression—and the expressive traditions of gospel music developed right alongside their modern churches, drawing in part from the singing traditions of the former slaves. During the twentieth century, gospel adopted and innovated instrumentation (including the electric organ) and vocal harmonies that proved to be an important influence on forms of popular music outside of the churches. As we examine more closely in the following, gospel provided one of the central influences and inspirations to rock and roll, the most pervasive form of popular music in the second half of the twentieth century. In turn, recent decades have seen the adoption by contemporary Christian churches of rock music with suitably modified lyric content. In some cases, even the form of rock concerts themselves have been adopted by "megachurches," which hold services in huge stadiumlike auditoriums that are designed so that individuals who grew up going to rock concerts are more likely to feel at home than those who are used to more conventional Protestant churches.

Although our focus remains on the Western context, further illustrations of the significance and centrality of music to religious institutions abound throughout history and around the world. In the Muslim world, music has had a particularly complex history. Many understand music per se to be forbidden by Islam, as a vain form of aesthetic indulgence that distracts one from the proper submission to Allah and that mocks divine perfection in a manner that borders on the idolatrous. Of course, this form of orthodoxy does not mean that the many Muslim cultures have not developed rich artistic traditions that include many forms of what, to outsiders, is clearly music but, to insiders, is something else entirely. These distinctions are anything but mere trifles; in fact, many of the destructive patterns caused by initial contact between Muslim cultures and Western scholars came from just such reductions. However, when made respectfully, the comparisons bear merit.

Perhaps the primary example is the widespread and extraordinarily developed tradition of qur'anic recitation. This beautiful manner of engaging the scriptural texts is centered on the official religious institutions, but it has a vibrant life outside of those walls as well. Recordings of such recitations are widely distributed and quite popular, lending pop-star status to some of the genre's leading figures.[3] Another set of musical forms that emerged from the religious life of Islam are those surrounding Sufi practice, also clearly tied to official institutional religion but broadly practiced and experienced outside of its confines. Sufi ecstatic singing and instrumentation, best known in the West through the importation of Qawwali, is connected to its mystical interpretation of Islam; whether performed by well-known masters or in less formal settings, this is a ritual path that is accessible to the wide population.

The Western success of the Sufi musician Nusrat Fateh Ali Khan presents a useful point of departure linking our examination of music in religious institutions with global commerce and the realm of music outside of religious institutions, so often dismissed as secular. The success of his recordings is a prime example of the burgeoning genre known as "world music." This emerged, for both better and worse, from the scholarly field of anthropology and the legacies of imperialism and colonialism and found an eager market for the consumption and celebration of "exotic" music from other parts of the world. A great deal of the modern West's knowledge of the musical traditions of non-Western cultures has arrived via this route. Thus religious traditions and national cultures with a rich and ancient heritage, including numerous Buddhist, Hindu, Chinese, and African traditions, and far too many others to list, have entered the modern realm of commercial music, already packaged as products and abstractions and less as parts of living traditions—even when these living traditions continue to exist. Although most of these entered Western awareness through scholarly and commercial routes, simultaneous movements and exchanges have also taken place. Intriguingly, increased immigration to Europe and the United States since the mid-twentieth century has placed import and export versions of these religions and their artistic traditions in proximity with one another, even as they tend to operate independently or even unaware of one another.

Often, music outside of a particular tradition has been the target of derision and fear; sometimes labeled as "pagan" or some other similar term, the competing meanings and experiences found in the expressive nature of music cultures have seemed ominous and threatening to those seeking to maintain order and stability within traditions. This has been no less true in the modern period as mass media has emerged at the center of cultural production. As we briefly explore some of the recent history of music in contemporary popular culture, pay attention to the dimensions that might be seen as religious and why the authorities of religious institutions might wish to lend credence to the notion that these areas of culture are firmly secular and thus not worthy of serious consideration.

POPULAR MUSIC AND CULTURE OUTSIDE OF RELIGIOUS INSTITUTIONS: RECENT DEVELOPMENTS AND BACKGROUND

As mentioned at the outset of this article, attention is here focused upon contemporary life in US culture—partly out of convenience to keep the scope reasonable but also in part as a result of the uniquely formative role that US culture has played in the expanding global popular culture marketplace. Although the history and continuing development of globalization is a large subject unto itself, it is sufficient for our purposes to say that the exchange has been primarily one of export from the United States rather than the reverse. Valid exceptions and counterarguments can and elsewhere should be provided, but related daily ritual life around the world is very often formed in conversation with what has taken place in the United States—whether in imitation of it or by contrast or opposition to it. Furthermore, the globalization of mass media and popular culture throughout the world, however far-reaching, is far from being complete or the "only story in town." Many traditions and rituals involving music that do not fit these criteria are beyond our scope and are thus not observed from the vantage point taken here. However, those represent excellent starting points for those interested in pursuing future research and exploration, and what is provided here should provide sufficient context and general narrative to begin that journey.

The relevance to the discussion of religion of musical genres and traditions that have been commonly dismissed as secular becomes clear when viewed in light of the powerful cultural tensions introduced earlier in this essay. These include the tensions between individual and community in the formation of identity, between the opposing impulses toward change, on one hand, and toward the preservation of tradition, on the other, and between the realms of sacred and profane. The religious dimensions of contemporary culture that surface in connection with music are also found in the maintenance and patrolling of boundaries between these realms, in debates about proper and improper conduct with regard to them, and in struggles for authority over such debates and questions. Finally, ample evidence is also found in the following brief musical history supportive of the emphasis throughout these essays upon ritual practice and daily life.

In surveying, however briefly, the modern history of music in US culture, we begin with the origins of what has become known as folk music. The term *folk* is situated in the perception of a "high/low" cultural divide and has been understood as the low or common culture associated with common, everyday people. As argued previously, this kind of distinction is dubious at best and, for our purposes, is not taken as true. Nevertheless, it has been an important perception and used in both a positive and a negative light. Many kinds of folk music traditions have existed and continue to exist in the United States; they have roots in all of the many cultures that make up the ancestry of the nation's populace. The various European folk traditions that came along with those who settled the continent continued, much as did the religious traditions brought by the same individuals and communities: they were adapted to new circumstances through the ever-present tension between innovation and conservation. However, in the US context, folk traditions from the various parts of Europe were geographically mixed in with one another and also with the forms of folk music and instruments played by Native Americans and brought by slaves from Africa. These blended locally to produce many individual strains of tradition throughout the nation in the period before mass media, and, at the dawn of the recording era, some of these kinds of folk music were recorded and documented in a manner parallel to the work being done outside of the West by anthropologists in colonized lands. For some, these archival recordings and transcriptions form an opus distinct to the United States—to be preserved and studied as a unique cultural heritage.

By the mid-twentieth century, the modern genre of folk music began in the form of "cleaned up" versions of folk singing, in which songs were more formally arranged and performed or recorded by conventionally trained musicians who utilized precise vocal harmonies and instrumental flourishes that were not found in the originals. Aimed at commercial audiences for popular consumption, these groups were also groomed in a manner befitting the budding celebrity culture: surnames were changed to conceal ethnicity, and matching tailored clothing accompanied carefully cut hairstyles. Known as the "folk revival" or, in jest, as the "folk scare," this wave of public interest brought secondary attention to many of the older musicians who had been featured in the archival recordings of earlier decades. Novel forms of these traditions began to proliferate, especially in the work of topical singer/songwriters and, later, in their contributions to what became known as "folk-rock." In addition to touring acts, the folk revival helped popularize the music festival format, later adopted by many across genres, in which numerous acts were assembled at a single site for a multiday event.

What is now known as "country music" has origins parallel to those of folk. Some of the innovations and combinations of various ballad and instrumental traditions that came together in rural and small-town America inspired new forms of commercial music around the same time as the folk revival. A form of early country music was bluegrass, a more tightly arranged twist on old-time country tunes and song that was made more suitable to showmanship. Also contributing to the new blend was the genre of "western music," which brought to country various stories (often idealized) of the nation's frontier. The brand of slickly produced "mainstream" country music, targeted at a largely white, conservative audience, that dominates today's market bears only superficial similarity to the work of the new genre's early innovators, many of whom expressed unpopular and countercultural themes or who represented the struggles of those with little social power and access. Other smaller strains of country music, including those that originally contributed to the commercial form, continue to exist and evolve as contemporary subgenres.

"The blues," in its many variations, came from relatively straightforward origins that addressed the miserable conditions of daily life for those on the margins of society—usually for reasons of racism, poverty, or both. Overlapping at times with both folk and country genres, some types of the blues were played on acoustic instruments—in groups, as in the country blues, and by individuals, as in the delta blues guitar. Blues music was transformed into an electric format and continues in both forms to the present. Movement into the mainstream took place through more than one route for the blues. Its melodic components, styles of arrangement, and instrumentation had significant impact on the later development of rock music. But the blues, like folk and country, also became a more formally mainstream commercial genre itself. In an ironic twist, today it is marketed for

consumption by those social elites that are actually causing the conditions among poor people that were originally decried in the blues.

The genres of "rhythm and blues" (R&B) and "soul" also arose primarily from African American communities and combined some of the elements of the genres already mentioned. Featuring similar electric instrumentation and arrangements as the simultaneously developing blues genre, R&B and soul came at the meeting place between these secular forms and the explicit and institutional religiosity of gospel. Sometimes the meeting was seen to be a natural one, joining meaningful life concerns that transcended the boundaries of institutions, but in some instances the combination caused controversy. This was true of several "crossover" artists, including Ray Charles and Sam Cooke, who began as gospel musicians but crossed over into R&B and soul. Without changing the sound of their music, such artists departed in subject matter from clearly biblical themes to those of secular, profane, or mundane life—relationships, work, and other aspects of daily life, sanctifying them anew. Fans and religious authorities alike were of split opinion on such departures, and musicians like Charles and Cooke both lost and gained fans and supporters as a result of the move.

Probably the most significant development in twentieth-century popular music was the birth of rock and roll music, or simply rock. What started out as revolutionary but fairly simple electric arrangements that drew widely from across the spectrum of popular music— folk, blues, country, R&B/soul—soon splintered anew into as diverse an array of subgenres and styles as those of its origins. More than any of its constituent parts, however, rock music brought about a cultural context in which its participants—musicians as well as fans—found alternative forms of identity. Often understood by both enthusiasts and detractors as a youth culture, rock music provided pathways back and forth between the cultural mainstream and countercultures and, through the mass media, brought participants from across the United States to that critical juncture. This came at a price, at least initially: early rock was able to gain a foothold in white, middle-class America only once it was dominated by white musicians, having "borrowed" heavily from African American innovators and contemporaries. However, this later paved the way for rock music's role in complicating racial boundaries in society. It contributed to the context of the civil rights movement—both by adding to the general sense that rapid social changes were possible and by providing some early settings of racially mixed, middle-class recreation, both on- and offstage, at concerts. By the 1960s, the cultures surrounding rock music were a central part of the countercultural protest movements that, for many observers, felt like a full-fledged revolutionary crisis.

The very possibility of a musical movement or genre being simultaneously revolutionary or countercultural and yet popular in the terms of the contemporary mass media marketplace is counterintuitive. It is helpful to make comparison with the ability of institutional religions to balance the maintenance of tradition with the impulse for radical change. We address this from the perspective of ritual practices as follows, but, in our exploration of the historical development of contemporary popular music traditions, it is useful to note these countermovements contained within musical cultures.

Punk rock, a subgenre identified first and foremost with its break from the mainstream, illustrates this multilayered aspect of form and content. It originated in the 1970s, after the role of popular music as an agent of cultural change and critique was already well established. Punk music expressed its critique with a disruptive and sometimes intentionally rude, dramatic aesthetic that mirrored the frustration and anger felt by its artists and fans. Although punk musicians sometimes took up specific political positions, more often they expressed a general sense of disgust with the prospect of conformity within a social system perceived to be corrupt and grounded in outdated falsehoods. Some scholars of punk music, however, have located much of the movement's power in its distinctive visual as well as musical styles, which managed to convey a kind of unity in otherwise anarchic dissent. Paradoxically, once punk became popular, it demanded its own kind of conformity, sparking debates about its continuing relevance or "death" that persist through the present. However, like other forms of musical protest, punk contributed to a vocabulary of dissent that continues to be referenced and adapted by later musicians who may or may not identify outwardly with that ancestry.

Hip-hop is another of the principal musical movements of the late twentieth century that illustrates the internal complexity, and contradiction, critical to understanding music's relevance to the beliefs and practices of daily life. It started in New York City's African American neighborhoods and, soon thereafter, grew in other urban centers and, not unlike punk, embraced a wider culture. The umbrella of this larger hop-hop "lifestyle" included clothing, dance, linguistic dialect, and graffiti art, along with its music, which grew around the twin poles of rapping and DJing. Although both drew from existing traditions, their playful and competitive fusion of word and rhythm with dance and style tapped the materials of modern urban life for new purpose. Rappers deftly rewrote lyrical and grammatical rules, and DJs tapped into public electrical lines to power their use of record turntables themselves as new instruments. These occasions became popular, widely attended events and came to feature "battles" between rival groups. This nonviolent version of urban turf wars was a refreshing change for many who saw cultural renewal in hip-hop.

However, the relatively innocent illegality of subway graffiti and hijacked power lines at local parks that characterized the earlier, smaller hip-hop scene was replaced by far more injurious and dangerous forms, as the new cultural form headed for the mainstream. By the time "gangsta rap" had become a household term in the United States, the boasts of violence—that were often mixed with a pervasive misogyny in popular hip-hop—were all too frequently reflective of a real culture of violence. Intense debates within hip-hop communities took place about the meaning of its culture's adoption and adaptation by the cultural mainstream, and many saw its young stars as unwittingly used by the music industry. According to this interpretation, what started as a powerful local cultural form—that had great potential for positive change in marginalized communities—was co-opted for profit by the dominant culture. Supporters of hip-hop thus found themselves caught in between their own criticism of mainstream artists who glamorized violence or sexism and external critics who were all too eager to write off the entire genre.

CONVERGENCE IN DAILY LIFE

The examples explored in the preceding pages were presented to illustrate the variety of religious dimensions of contemporary culture that are associated with religion, both inside and outside of religious institutions. In this next section, that set of varied threads are woven together around the central theme of the volume—the practices of daily life.

Music is both a subtle and an obvious part of daily life in contemporary society. The patterns of everyday practice and ritual that are familiar

to modern observers, of course, bare traces of their roots in longer-standing traditions. The concept of "rites of passage," advanced by scholars, including Van Gennep and Turner, and reviewed in the general introduction is useful for understanding these connections between past and present. In these rituals, an individual moves from one stage of life to another according to the community-sanctioned method. Music has often been associated with rites of passage in traditional institutional settings of both Western and non-Western cultures. Examples include the indigenous cultures initially studied by Van Gennep, Turner, and other prominent anthropologists; many of these included some form of singing, chanting, or use of instruments. Western examples include the chanting, singing, or instrumental accompaniment used in such rituals as the Jewish bar mitzvah, a coming-of-age ceremony in which a young man takes on the formal responsibilities of adulthood through public chanting of Scripture.

The presence of music at these particularly significant ritual events underscores its presence throughout the more everyday forms of ritual life. In the bar mitzvah example, the forms of scriptural chanting, as well as the melodic recitation of prayers and blessings, are those used daily or weekly; it is only the context of their use by the person on the threshold between childhood and adulthood that makes the ritual an exception to the everyday. Such uses of music within religious institutions continue to be practiced widely by both religious specialists or professionals and laypeople. Whether it is through chanting in a monastic setting or volunteer involvement in a local church choir, many individuals express their membership in a religious group through the performance of music. Those practices, in turn, enter the daily lives of an even wider circle of people, who experience such performances as congregants.

Although these experiences of music in ritual context have great meaning for those involved, others outside of or alienated from religious institutions may not find them meaningful and may see them simply as "empty" formalities. Mircea Eliade observed that the sacred, sometimes hidden from view, persists through its "eruption" into modern culture through mass media arts, such as music and cinema. For those who do not participate in religious institutions or find meaning in those forms of ritual life, the comparatively recent modern emergence of music and other forms of cultural production outside of ceremonial life has provided an alternative means to similar ends. Perhaps because of this iconoclasm, the place of popular music in daily life has been strongly connected to a sense of individualism.

In particular, that aspect of individualism that is about developing one's own unique tastes and identity represents a break with authority, whether parental or social, and functions as a rite of passage. The Grateful Dead's Jerry Garcia once described the allure of going on tour with the band for deadheads as a manifestation of the same impulse toward individuality and against authority that had earlier led young people to "run away to the circus." This formation of individual identity through one's choice of music might take the form of a bold step, such as leaving home to join the musical version of a traveling circus, but it also might be as uncontroversial as the development of a different "brand preference" than that of one's family or peers. In either case, the experience is common to many in contemporary culture and functions as a coming-of-age ritual.

We have already seen that the mass media and communications technologies characteristic of the modern period helped propel popular music to the center of daily life. The effects of this change grew exponentially: the nationwide availability of music via radio broadcast was at first revolutionary, but, before much time had passed, yet another revolution took place. The widespread ability of home stereo equipment allowed individuals to purchase recordings for the home and further customize their listening experience according to taste. The invention of portable devices, such as the Sony Walkman cassette tape player, soon moved this ability beyond the household level and more deeply into the individual, personal realm.

The more recent technological advances of the so-called information age have continued this trend and added multiple new avenues for the intertwining of individual personal identity with everyday musical practices. In the closing decade of the twentieth century, the dominant technology through which individuals related to music switched from the home stereo to the home or personal computer. Digital recording and distribution of music had been common since the arrival of compact discs, in the 1980s, at around the same time that computers started to become more commonly found in homes. Those two phenomena collided in the 1990s, when consumers began to store music on portable digital audio (MP3) players.

These tiny devices detached music from the physical confines of home in two significant ways. First, they extended the portability of the Walkman—to allow even smaller players to carry one's entire collection of music instead of only one recording at a time, connecting that collection more closely to one's very person. Music devices had, until this point, functioned like furniture but now became more like clothing—and thus understood more and more as a finely tuned expression of an individual's identity. Furthermore, digital music files entered consumers' lives as detached from any one particular physical device—they could be easily moved back and forth between computers and portable players.

Because this phenomenon arrived in conjunction with the newly popular Internet, individuals suddenly had not only exposure to greatly increased amounts of information about an increasingly large variety of music but also easy access to communication with others who had similar likes and dislikes. This served both to extend the role of music as a defining element of personal identity and to strengthen its awkward conjunction with the formation of community.

The increasingly vast and portable libraries of music that ordinary people could now acquire and enjoy brought with them new behaviors and practices that have sparked a set of contentious legal and moral debates. The sheer ease with which the new technologies expanded the ability to collect, organize, and transfer music turned many previously casual fans into ardent collectors. This new tendency to become a collector combined in powerful synergism with two other developments: the revolutionary advances in networks of communication between collectors, brought about by the Internet, and the ability of computers to duplicate flawlessly exact copies of digital music files. Collectors quickly became traders as well; through an array of online forums and networks, they began the practice of sharing and downloading digital music files—a practice that is now as much a part of the everyday ritual of music as the production of singles on 45 rpm vinyl was a half century earlier. The music industry, however, has viewed this activity as an illegal and immoral encroachment on its territory. The industry advanced its case through legal actions against downloaders, especially on college and university campuses, and eventually by adopting downloading and sharing—as paid services—in its own business models.

During the same period, a different type of technological change helped further attach music to individualism and to the development of personal identity. New computer software promised to popularize the production of music itself, bringing to home users a range of electronic tools. Some of these brought the basic tools of a recording studio, previously only available to professionals, within the range of everyday musicians. Still others brought about new capabilities altogether and lowered the cost and complexity of creating, orchestrating, and recording music to professionals and amateurs alike. The wide distribution of these tools appealed to those who looked forward to the democratization of formerly professional resources as a means to bring music more fully into the daily life and practice of average individuals.

According to some music professionals, however, this sort of democratization has the negative side effect of standardizing individual expression rather than supporting or enhancing creativity. They argue that the widespread availability of these new tools distributes an advanced but overly standardized set of resources. These critics of the new tools are, however, in agreement with their supporters about the nature of musical creativity. Figures at both ends of this argument believe that the formation or evolution of new musical traditions, especially for those social classes with less access to formal education and resources—often identified as "folk"—usually takes place through the innovative use and reuse of whatever materials are available. Supporters of the new electric, electronic, and digital technological tools point to continued creativity and innovation of this kind that simply draw these new tools into the process as new raw materials that are subject to uses that were not envisioned by their creators.

Although widespread experimentation with many of these technologies is still taking hold in the early twenty-first century, some examples of comparatively early adaptation prove useful illustrations of this point. The phenomenon of "sampling" began as early as the 1960s but, by the 1980s, became firmly entrenched in contemporary music at both the commercial and vernacular levels. The name comes from the use of excerpts, or samples, taken from previous recordings and integrated into new compositions and performances. Although this process was first done in a relatively limited fashion, by hand through the laborious use of tape loops, hip-hop DJs later began to loop portions of vinyl records. They took the existing materials of records, turntables, and simple mixers and created a new set of sounds and styles, as well as new kinds of performance, in which rappers performed solely with a DJ and not a live band. Sampling quickly became even more common with the availability, first, of sampling digital keyboards and, later, of computer editing software. Because of legal controversies surrounding the copyright status of sampled works, sampling kept one foot in the music underground even while the practice became widespread and popular in successful albums. Even though record companies eventually worked out legal arrangements in which artists could pay for permission to use a sample in their recordings, unsanctioned (thus likely illegal) sampling has remained popular among those songwriters and DJs who lack the financial or legal backing of the record industry.

A still-more-recent offshoot from these musical forms is the genre of "mashups." Mashups bring together two (or more) different musical works in a combinative effort of which the results are at once clearly derivative and yet original. Unlike sampling, in which small elements of a prior recording are included in the production of a substantially new work, mashups bring together large elements—often full albums—of each component. A famous example is DJ Dangermouse's 2003 *Grey Album*, which brought together the Beatles' *White Album* and Jay-Z's *Black Album*; the Beatles' work has also been reimagined in combination with Beastie Boys'

recordings in a series of "Beastles" mashups. Because of copyright law, mashups are almost always noncommercial, and they sometimes face online takedown efforts by rights owners. Nevertheless, the genre has thrived and grown in the first decade of the twenty-first century and taken root in a network of Internet sites, forums, and sharing tools, as well as occasional offline gatherings by enthusiasts. Recent refinements in technique have resulted in impressively polished original compositions, made entirely from large numbers of Internet "found art" from video and audio sharing sites such as YouTube, including amateur videos of individuals' home performances (some of quite poor quality), instructional videos, and old "ephemeral" films in the public domain.

One final example of the impact that recent technology has had on the increased role of music in the daily lives of more and more people can be found, surprisingly, in the arena of video games. Like earlier examples, this development has as many detractors as supporters, and, like those mentioned previously, it is one for which the significance as a part of contemporary vernacular musical culture is hard for either side to deny. Throughout most of their prior decades of existence, video games had little direct connection to music; in fact, the simplistic jingles that formed the soundtracks to many computer games were the subject of joke and ridicule, even among avid gamers. The games have, however, usually required skill and manual dexterity. A series of games involving rhythmic movement and even dance appeared in the 1990s, and these were followed by several very successful games that were explicitly about music.

The most popular and profitable titles were *Guitar Hero* and *Rock Band*, in which the player or players use specialized game controllers to "play" instruments on screen. They offer nonmusicians an experience that is rooted in the appeal of being a "rock star," and they have thus attracted many nongamer customers. The wild success of these games caught the attention of the music industry, which has joined with the game makers to allow players to "play" along with pop music hits. Recent incarnations of the games have been retooled as additional distribution platforms for mainstream record labels that are seeking to adapt to a changing marketplace. Other games in this new genre include the ability to adapt to each user's computer music library, creating different "levels" of game play, based on that individual's taste and listening habits. All of these phenomena demonstrate both the ability of recent technological innovations and socioeconomic developments to advance the intricate involvement of music in the everyday practices of individuals, as well as the impressive adaptability of existing music traditions to new circumstances.

COMMUNITY LIFE

As much as music is associated with the individual in terms of everyday life and ritual practice, it is simultaneously associated with community life and the individual's role in it. This chapter began with an account of the uniqueness, in the lives of deadheads at least, of Grateful Dead concerts. What is not unique about Grateful Dead concerts, however, is that other concerts of all sorts also provide participants with an experience of the sacred in their everyday lives. Concerts, here broadly defined to include any form of musical performance with an audience, are an important means of expression and ritual practice in the vernacular lives of many people. At the same time, they contribute to a set of shared experiences from which members of a community can draw. Because so much music, through concerts, takes place in the setting of community, concerts help build community

and foster the sense of belonging to one among individuals.

Music festivals are something of an extension of the concert form—they take place over the course of one or more days and feature multiple performances, usually by several different artists. Festival participants experience an even greater sense of separation from the mundane, because the special arrangements in both time and space that make regular concerts an exception from the rest of the world are more pronounced for festivals. Many festivals take place on large sites, such as parks or fairgrounds, that allow for the inclusion of activities that are not part of ordinary concerts, including elaborate concessions for food and other goods. In some cases, festivalgoers actually live on the site or in nearby campgrounds for the duration of the event. All of these components help create a separate world in time and space that is set off from the mundane.

Smaller festivals, organized locally around a single musical genre, usually a type of folk music, have a longer history in the United States, and these contributed to the rise of the larger phenomenon that is more common in contemporary culture. A famous example that helped bridge the gap between these was the Newport Folk Festival, which is notable as the site where Bob Dylan "went electric." His controversial embrace of rock styles and electric instruments alienated many of his fans, who understood his earlier acoustic work through the lens of a particular folk tradition. This sort of genre-crossing has come to dominate contemporary festival life.

The most famous popular music festival of the twentieth century, and the first of its size, took place near Woodstock, New York, in 1969. Advertised as "three days of peace and music," Woodstock grew out of and later came in hindsight to symbolize the entire 1960s counterculture. That event, however, was almost as famous for its lack of food, water, and basic facilities as it was for music. Woodstock, and similar later festivals, served as a significant rite of passage for many young people in attendance.

Over the next few decades, the organizing process was streamlined and improved, as festivals became a part of regular musical life. Numerous annual multigenre festivals have, over the course of several decades, provided pilgrimage sites for thousands of devotees who attend year after year. Depending on circumstances, these sometimes function as rites of passage for some participants, but they have also become regular parts of the cyclical ritual calendars of others. The Telluride Bluegrass Festival, in the Colorado Rocky Mountains, has long grown beyond its original confines of bluegrass and attracts diversity both on- and offstage. Doc Watson's Merlefest has filled a comparable niche in the southeastern United States. Similarly, the New Orleans Jazz and Heritage Festival, or simply Jazzfest, over its years has incorporated a wide array of genres and a national audience. Rock festivals underwent something of a renaissance in the 1990s, with the alternative/punk Lollapalooza and neopsychedelic H.O.R.D.E. and furthur festivals. In the early twenty-first century, several comparatively huge festivals brought together even more sets of artists and genres; the most successful example is Tennessee's annual Bonnaroo.

SACRED TIME, SACRED SPACE, AND THE SYMBOLIC

Stepping back from these details to place them in some perspective, it may appear that holding together the seemingly opposing poles of individual and group described so far would result in a paradox; indeed, this view is not without merit. Given our focus on the experience of practices in everyday life, it may also seem out of place to

emphasize so strongly a conception of the sacred as that which is apart from the regular world. These discontinuities are not an indication, however, that we have veered off course from our goals. The tension between these opposites is, in fact, precisely what gives them symbolic power. The religious dimensions of music in the practice of daily life are structured around these dual symbols of the individual and the community. In turn, experiences of the sacred—when the ordinary, mundane flow of time or continuity of space is interrupted—serve to explain the relationship between individual and community. Although conceived as distinct ideals, individual and community are mutually dependent and serve as horizons against which daily life/everyday ritual takes place. By connecting some of the ideas presented, we can illustrate this symbolic arrangement.

We have seen several roles that music plays in religious life, both in traditional religious institutions or outside of them in the fulfillment of religious functions. One of the examples that we examined—the rite of passage—demonstrates the ability of ritual to structure the passage of time. Although a rite of passage is an exception to the ordinary flow of time (and usually involves some form of exceptional ritual space as well), it is an exception that fits into larger patterns and cycles. Everyday musical practices also fit into the cycles of ritual life, in both public and private spheres, lending them structure and comprehensibility.

In this light, the example of teenagers whose development of their own musical tastes and affiliations serve as rites of passage marking their arrival to distinct selfhood and individuality helps us see the private sphere not as private in the sense of isolated from others but rather as a location within the public sphere. The phenomena of musical subcultures, "scenes," "cult followings," and other intense fan cultures serve to distinguish individuals as individuals as well as locate them within the larger culture as members of smaller communities. This means for organizing culture—into "lifestyles" and "lifestyle enclaves"—was brought into wide public view in the mid-1980s by the popular sociological work *Habits of the Heart*.[4] In the early part of the twenty-first century, online social networking websites provided further evidence for this interpretation of contemporary cultural organization.

If we view the private as a location within the public, the reverse is also true: the public sphere serves as the setting of and context for the private, as the backdrop against which the private must be structured. This might seem to imply that there actually is a single, universal, agreed-upon public culture, of which individuals and subcultures are a part; however, even a cursory test of such a hypothesis shows that it is far from true. There is great contestation over the national (or international) meanings of public life and culture. Remember, however, that the public sphere, or community, is but one component of a symbolic ideal. It more neatly represents something in a way that is not found in the actual, messy patterns of real history. Of those vying for a place in the public sphere, those voices that lay claim to official status (sometimes as universal) via connection to government or nation are very prominent.

These so-called official voices fit nicely into the model of "civil religion" that was summarized in the general introduction. Well-known manifestations of music in this aspect of culture include the use of formal bands in the various branches of the armed forces and in ceremonial pieces of music, such as national anthems, that are typically adopted by Western nations. The rituals in which these groups play or these anthems are sung are marked by reverential attitudes and behaviors that are analogous to those

accorded to religion. They are also frequently tied ritually to other nonmusical aspects of the civil religion, including the handling of national flags or recognition of national holidays and remembrances.

Sometimes, music appears in official public rituals, when ordinary music is brought into extraordinary circumstances. Official ritual can draw upon materials, figures, and styles from the pop-cultural lexicon to powerful effect, as in the 2009 US presidential inauguration, when soul star Aretha Franklin performed a version of "America the Beautiful" on the steps of the Capitol. In that context, the use of a musical style that was first popular among African Americans around the time of the civil rights movement, in the mid-twentieth century, during one of the more potent and solemn ceremonies of state powerfully conveyed a message of social progress and announced the arrival of significant changes at the national level. Other similar, but more ordinary, examples of the overlap between official national culture and popular music can be found in federal funding and other forms of support for the arts generally. This support is symbolized in events such as the annual honors program at the national Kennedy Center for the Arts, which is usually attended by the president.

Joining these official voices, however, are those of protest and dissent. Complex critiques of society, including many based on the presumption that their version is just as legitimate or patriotic as any other, continue to be a part and parcel of the music that is emerging from and shaping the practices of everyday life. This is true in many of the cases that we have examined, as well as in many others that we cannot cover. Although many of these protests occur in the protective context of subcultures and are unlikely to reach the national stage, others rise at times to the level of national discourse and compete with official interpretations.

Prominent among twentieth-century examples is Bob Dylan, crowned by both fans and critics alike (and against his own wishes) as "the voice of a generation." This view was catalyzed by the emergence of his remarkably well-crafted early protest songs, which drew from a combination of lyrical and melodic traditions that had been well established by other, less popular singers, at a time in US history when dissatisfaction with the war in Vietnam and public doubts over ideological consensus raged along generational lines. Fans disillusioned by his subsequent move from folk singer to rock star were only strengthened in their purist approach to those protest materials by what they saw as his betrayal of principles. Neither Dylan's own disavowal of prophetic status at the time nor his later claims to have never been a "protest singer" has dulled this perception of his early work. Its power to speak to a national audience found formal recognition in 1997, when Dylan received the Kennedy Center Honor in the presence of President Clinton.

NATION, AUTHORITY, AND THE MARKETPLACE

Those who interpreted Dylan's protest songs as prophetic were correct in at least one sense: the manner in which many of those songs called the nation to task for losing sight of or failing to live up to its own core values fits neatly with what historians of religions have termed the "prophetic" aspect of religion. This is used in opposition to the "priestly" aspect, which emphasizes maintenance of the social order and the functioning of its systems and leadership. Although the language itself comes from biblical usage, this model has been employed more generally in the interpretation of cultures. Like the symbolic interdependence of individual and community described previously, these two kinds of religious orientation are poles in mutual tension. Both represent a commitment to the achievement of a just, moral, and good society—but one focuses on strengthening the status quo and the other attacks it.

Nationalism itself is a tradition in constant need of maintenance and adaptation, and in this respect, music fits in alongside other cultural practices that take up similar or complementary roles as "priests" or "prophets"; patriotism and protest are often interwoven in very complex ways, in music as elsewhere. In music, they serve as frameworks for integrating hegemonic and counterhegemonic impulses (those in support of or opposing the powers of the status quo). As the case of Dylan illustrates, public perception or critical reception of music can be as significant as (or more than) what the artist actually intends along these lines. In contrast with Bob Dylan, the rock musician Bruce Springsteen has been widely interpreted as a patriotic figure, representing a more priestly approach. These opposing interpretations persist, in spite of evidence of conservatism in Dylan's music and life and counterhegemonic protest in that of Springsteen.

The role of music in national life, as with other forms of cultural production, extends beyond both the specifically political or ideological or the more generally patriotic or nationalist. Because music in the contemporary world is now widely understood as a commodity and is so closely tied with the consumer marketplace and music industry, it has become impossible to understand its relevance apart from the context of capitalism. Although there is no single interpretation of the relationship between capitalism and the modern nation (even in the United States), any account of the religious dimensions of the latter must take into account the former.

Of course, not all music is made by professionals or sold for profit. However, the reach of capitalism's effects extends beyond whether or not this is the case. Perceptions that musical styles or genres are "corporate" or "mainstream," as opposed to "independent" or "alternative," often have little to do with whether the music actually serves as someone's livelihood or not. Status as an insider or outsider to the mainstream has long been important to some musicians and fans, and iconoclasm has been associated with many of the most commercially successful forms of contemporary music—especially rock. This is, once again, a result of the complex ways that the tension between individual and group identities or associations plays out in practice. This can be illustrated by following once again the example of Bob Dylan. By midcareer, Dylan agreed to allow his songs to appear in television advertisements for unrelated commercial products. This move brought vocal disappointment from many of his fans, who accused him of "selling out." These fans were no doubt aware that Dylan has always sought payment for his work and that he, as one of the top-grossing musical acts for over four decades, has been remarkably successful in doing so. Each time that Dylan's music appeared in another high-profile advertisement, this outcry returned as if it hadn't happened before.

What is really at stake is the perception that corporate interests have control over the content or meaning of music, which reflects concern over the role of social authority in music. This underscores the significance of music for scholars of religion in contemporary culture, because it evidences the importance that people place on music beyond mere entertainment. As in matters of ritual practice in religious institutions, there is wide interest in the question of where authority lies: Who does the ritual practices? Who says that they should be done this way? Many, though not all, religious institutions have hierarchies of leaders who are empowered to wield authority over ritual practices and their authorized

meanings. Even when that is the case, however, the historical record is replete with examples in which the everyday practices of ordinary people affect, directly or indirectly, that authority and, in turn, the nature of ritual practices.

In the case of contemporary music, there isn't a formal central locus of authority, but the shared interests and coordinated efforts of the recording industry are quite powerful, even when they are not centralized. Because of the unofficial nature of their authority, however, there is both confusion about where authority truly lies and, as a result, about the distribution of it throughout the networks of musicians, fans, and industry figures. One particularly powerful illustration of how this works can be seen in the question of what is popular. As new forms and genres emerge, they break with established tradition and usually have some mixture of iconoclasm and popularity. Those with staying power undergo a seemingly inevitable rise to increasingly rigid and established authority over their adherents, as was the case when, in many quarters, jazz gave up some of its originally free-form qualities to hold up as a genre that was coherent enough to sell records and concert tickets. Of course, the cycle can always be repeated; some jazz musicians who were not content with the genre's entrance into the establishment broke off and began to identify their music as "free jazz."

As these sort of processes take place, the interests of various parties shift accordingly— for an individual who values music that is "independent," "alternative," "old school," or "cutting edge," a favored band might lose its appeal when it becomes more successful and popular. In such a case, it is in the music industry's interest to promote this band's products as "independent" or "alternative," even though its actual goal is to bring about the group's greatest popularity and success. Struggles of this sort are never fully resolved, and authority of this kind remains a matter of perspective and opinion. The illusion of individual and/or popular tastes is thus of great importance and guarantees their continued manipulation, on one hand, by corporate focus groups and advertising campaigns, or, on the other hand, by musicians or fan communities.

As the example of free jazz illustrates, tensions between the impulses toward innovation and the reaffirmation of tradition that are familiar to historians of religion are replicated throughout the everyday practices related to contemporary music. Self-styled purists, traditionalists, innovators, and iconoclasts continue to influence the struggles over tradition and its authorities. They do so as part of the everyday give-and-take and exchange involved in the practices and rituals through which the powerful meanings connected to music in their lives are expressed and experienced.

FOR FURTHER READING

Chidester, David. *Authentic Fakes: Religion and American Popular Culture*. Berkeley, University of California Press, 2005.

Lott, Eric. *Love and Theft: Blackface Minstrelsy and the American Working Class*. Oxford: Oxford University Press, 1995.

Marcus, Greil. *The Old, Weird America: The World of Bob Dylan's Basement Tapes*. New York: Picador, 2001.

———. *Lipstick Traces: A Secret History of the Twentieth Century*. Cambridge, MA: Harvard University Press, 1990.

McNally, Dennis. *A Long Strange Trip: The Inside History of the Grateful Dead*. New York: Broadway, 2002.

Rose, Tricia. *Black Noise: Rap Music and Black Culture in Contemporary America*. Middletown, CT: Wesleyan University Press, 1994.

Wuthnow, Robert. *All In Sync: How Music and Art Are Revitalizing American Religion*. Berkeley: University of California Press, 2006.

15

SPORT

Carole M. Cusack

INTRODUCTION: THE RELATIONSHIP BETWEEN RELIGION AND SPORT[1]

At first glance, sport and religion appear to have little in common, apart from being perennial human activities. Religion is transcendent, concerned with the divine, and involves sacred things (prayers, rituals, holy objects, and the spiritual realm). Sport is immanent, concerned with the human, and involves profane things (competition, the body, fans, and earthly glory). However, a deeper examination reveals that there are at least five ways in which sport and religion are deeply interrelated: first, it can be demonstrated that, in premodern societies, ritualized sport was very often part of worship of the gods; second, altered states of consciousness attained during sport have frequently been compared to religious or mystical experiences (for example, where a sense of oneness with the universe or a loss of ego-consciousness is felt); third, some modern sporting champions have professed religious faith and attributed their success to divine power; fourth, the devotion of fans to sporting teams and individual "stars"

resembles religious fervor; fifth and final, in the modern West, sport has become a functional equivalent of religion (or an actual religion) for some people.

These connections between religion and sport are undeniable, but not uncontroversial. Scholars and critics who have attempted to articulate them and offer explanations for them have encountered pitfalls. Adherents of traditional religions such as Judaism and Christianity have vigorously objected to the equation of sport with religion and of sporting "peak experiences" with religious experiences or mysticism. Christian commentators have questioned how compatible the modern sporting ethos of bodily perfection and fierce competition is with a religion focused on the suffering savior who was broken on the cross and preached turning the other cheek.[2] The problematic relationship of sport to war in the West is significant here. In the European Middle Ages, valued physical activities were those that could serve as military training, such as archery. The English king Edward III (r. 1327–1377) "prohibited on pain of death all sport except archery."[3] Although Barbara Tuchman has argued that the one-on-one combat of tournaments gained popularity as the actual role of the knight in war declined (which suggests that the actual violence of war was sublimated as a "game"), the medieval church denounced death in tournaments as suicide, and Saint Bernard of Clairvaux condemned all participants to hell.[4]

Yet modern religious believers are themselves disunited over sport; some regard its elevated place in modern Western culture as idolatry and Sunday matches as a profanation of the Sabbath, whereas others are happy to view sport as a means of making spiritual and moral gains, in addition to attaining physical excellence.[5] Secular critics, setting aside all theological considerations, are equally disunited as to whether sport functions as religion or how fandom relates to religious fervor—whether it is directed toward sporting heroes or rock musicians, actors, and other celebrities—and on a host of other questions.

Defining *sport* and *religion* is also complex and problematic. The English word *sport* is a modern term, only distantly related to its Latin root *deportare* (which means "to carry away"), and philosophical consideration of what constitutes sport is surprisingly fraught. Sport is often contrasted with "play," which is unstructured, not geared to winning or losing, and is "engaged in for the intrinsic enjoyment of play itself."[6] Sport, by contrast, has rules and is often viewed as essentially concerned with winning and losing, with competing for an extrinsic prize. Yet there are many games that, although they have rules, are not contests. Allen Guttmann has shrewdly observed that even though "leapfrog and basketball . . . both have rules . . . Leapfrog is not a contest and basketball is."[7] Attempting to define *religion* is even more controversial. The Latin term *religio* (meaning "reverence for the gods") is usually traced to two possible roots. These are *religare* (which means "to rebind")

and *relegere* (which has the sense of to "reread" and suggests immersion in tradition). Simon Robinson concludes that the Latin etymologies indicate that "at the heart of [religion], then, is commitment to something, be it a way of life, an idea, a belief."[8] There is always a public, external "doing" of religion (a way of life) as well as a private, internal "believing" (an idea).

In the contemporary West, that status of religion has been eroded since the eighteenth century, when the Enlightenment, a philosophical movement stressing the authority of human reason, challenged traditional religious (supernaturalist) explanations of the purpose of human life, the nature of the physical universe, ethics, and other received understandings. Secularization, "the process whereby sectors of society and culture are removed from the domination of religious institutions and symbols,"[9] has resulted in reduced church attendance, eclectic spiritualities, the founding of new religions, and a changed social fabric—in which diversity of ethnicity, sexuality, and lifestyle choice predominates. Communication technologies made it possible for millions to view a sporting match, although they were not physically present, and created drive-in churches and online prayer forums. In the twenty-first century, traditional religion is formally identified with institutions such as the Roman Catholic Church and with services held in purpose-built synagogues and temples, whereas eclectic "spirituality" flourishes outside traditional religious contexts, in the activities of everyday life. It is this important shift that makes it possible for sport to function as religion, for Sunday spectator sport to usurp attending church on the Sabbath, and for sporting champions to be the role models and idols of innumerable people, in place of the saints and other exemplars of Christian virtue.

The academic study of sport and religion has focused on the centrality of ritual in both domains for multiple reasons. Ritual is an important human activity, experienced at all levels of life. Anthropologist Victor Turner (1920–1983), building on the insights of Arnold van Gennep, characterized ritual as having three phases: the first is separation from everyday life (the profane, the structured); the second is a period of liminality (from the Latin *limen*, "threshold," indicating a realm of possibility, the sacred and what Turner termed "anti-structure"); and the third is reintegration into everyday life after the experience of transformation.[10] During the liminal phase, those undergoing the ritual (for example, making a pilgrimage or being initiated) experience *communitas*, a spontaneous bonding that is based on shared spiritual conditions. Large-scale communal rituals involve activities that are accorded a particular sequence and significance and are repeated for the purpose of reinforcing group solidarity.

Sociologist Émile Durkheim (1858–1917) argued that religion was, at a fundamental level, concerned with the classification of the world into two categories, the sacred and the profane. Rituals enacted these categories and revealed the deepest concerns of the community. Durkheim rejected theological approaches to religion. Religion is a human cultural product. It is important to realize that whatever was called "sacred" had no intrinsic claim to the title. The categories were negotiated by the society itself, and the dramatic, affective, ceremonial act of ritual "reaffirms the values which unite the community."[11] Thus the ultimate object of worship is society itself. Sociologists building upon Durkheim have argued that contemporary societies are not monolithic and that ritual, the sacred, and the profane may be determined by a myriad subcultures coexisting in a larger society. Further, ritual (both traditional and modern) may involve apparently profane activities from everyday life, such as tea drinking and cleaning.[12] Ritual has also been analyzed at the micro level of the individual, where it can reinforce personal identity and confer meaning upon everyday life.

It is clear that Durkheim's interpretation of religion and the categories of sacred and profane can be applied to domains other than religion. This has led to important scholarship on the synergies between sport and religion, including contributions by Harry Edwards and Allen Guttmann. In 1973, Edwards produced a list of parallels between modern sport and religion that is still relevant and insightful. He argued that sport had saints (deceased players who exemplified the sport's code in their careers), patriarchs (the coaches, managers, and bureaucrats who run sports clubs and other organizations), gods (the "stars" worshiped and emulated by the fans), high councils (bodies that interpret the rules of competition), scribes (sports journalists and other chroniclers of sport history), shrines (museums, trophy rooms, and halls of fame), churches or temples (playing fields and stadia), sacred symbols (personal equipment of sporting heroes), what he called "seekers of the kingdom" (devoted fans), and a number of other striking similarities.[13]

Allen Guttman drew attention to the way that sport, like religion, had been changed by modernity. He argued that modern sport was defined by seven characteristics. Modern sport is secular (that is, it is a formally distinct domain from religion), it offers equality of opportunity for competitors (there is no discrimination on grounds of race or gender), it has specialization of roles (athletes concentrate on one sport or specific position in a team sport and are professionals), it is rationalized (there are rules and training regimes), it is bureaucratized (organizations exist to administer competitions, interpret rules, and the like), it has an emphasis on quantification (technological innovations, such as the stopwatch, have increased the ability to measure performance), and, finally, it keeps records (statistics on performance are diligently noted).[14] The typologies of sport produced by Edwards and Guttmann stem from the changed conditions of modern Western society, conditions that have altered both sport and religion.

In the premodern era, medieval peasants played amateur games in village and festival contexts (including football) rather than professional sport. Aristocratic amusements included tournaments, hawking, and hunting. Because these activities involved violence, they were frequently condemned by the church, although certain churchmen agreed that "knightly sport is justified if it prepares warriors for their military tasks and if it is a *ludus* and not a *bellum*."[15] After the Reformation, the Protestant Christian churches had a negative perception of games and leisure generally, arguing that "idling away the precious time allotted to us by our Saviour"[16] was sinful and that all amusements should be prohibited and strict Sabbath observation mandated by law. In eighteenth- and nineteenth-century Britain, the lineaments of modern sport began to emerge in the framework of an industrializing and secularizing society, and with it a new attitude to physical activity developed among liberal Christians. "Muscular Christianity," a term first associated with the clergyman, social reformer, and novelist Charles Kingsley, rapidly gained popularity. Kingsley, a prodigious hiker, horseman, and rower, advocated a manly and physically robust conception of Jesus and argued that physical activity contributed "not merely to physical, but to moral health."[17] This changed relationship between religion and sport was transmitted to the New World and enthusiastically adopted.

Today, professional sport in the United States has a large number of participants who profess Christianity and whose spiritual needs are met by a diverse range of organizations for Christian athletes. These include the Fellowship for Christian Athletes, Athletes in Action, Pro Sports Outreach, Motor Racing Outreach, Baseball Chapel, Inc, Sports Ambassadors, the Fellowship of Christian Anglers, the Christian Motorcyclists' Association, and the Race Track Chaplaincy of America.[18] Around the world, Christian churches have embraced sport, employing Christian sports celebrities and stars as evangelists and championing the discipline and dedication needed to achieve athletic success as being analogous to (and perhaps part of) the discipline and dedication needed to develop spiritual strength and virtue.[19] Indeed, so closely aligned are sport and religion in the modern West that many critics accuse the churches of cynically adopting the technique of sports media coverage to attract the attention of the unchurched and of promoting religious devotion within the ranks of sports stars to win converts.[20]

Before considering the relationship between sport and religion in two case studies—the ancient Olympic Games and Japanese sumo wrestling—it is necessary to observe that the modern West acknowledges a diversity of "ultimate concerns" among its citizens. In a variegated culture without a unifying religious, civil, or cultural metanarrative, individuals are free to attribute absolute significance to a range of activities, including sport, rock music, film and television, art, family, and politics. Sport is religion for some but not for others. William Baker records a humorous but telling anecdote about sports commentator Max Hellerman discussing the origin of sport spectacles with his brother Sam.

Sam declared sport to be "man's joke on God": "You see," God says to man, "I've created a universe where it seems like everything matters, where you'll have to grapple with life and death and in the end you'll die anyway, and it won't really matter." So man says to God, "Oh yeah? Within your universe we're going to create a sub-universe called sports, one that absolutely doesn't matter, and we'll follow everything that happens in it as if it were life and death." '[21]

This is both a funny joke and a genuine insight into the way the contemporary West approaches the sacred. Durkheim's theory of the social allocation of the sacred and the profane, discussed previously, as applied to the subculture of sport, can result in a world in which traditional religious concerns are ignored (profane) and the minutiae of sport are the "ultimate concern" (sacred).[22]

THE ANCIENT OLYMPICS: SPORT AS RITUAL HONORING THE GODS

The search for the origins of sport in the West is usually focused on ancient Greece, partly because the Greeks contributed substantially to Western culture in politics, philosophy, art, and aesthetics (among other areas), but also because the ancient Greek tradition of games is recognizably the ancestor of modern athletics and of a range of other competitive sports. Greek sport and religion were intimately intertwined in the daily life of the people; at important religious festivals, the gods were honored by contests of musical and dancing talent, poetry and drama presentation, and athletic skill. The origin of the Olympic Games is shrouded in mystery, but the traditional date provided by the writer Hippias is 776 BCE. The games were held in honor of Zeus Olympios, the chief god of the Greeks, at Olympia, a remote site approximately sixty kilometers (by road) from the city of Elis in the northwest of the Peloponnese.[23]

The most sacred place at Olympia was the *Altis* (or *alsos*), a grove dedicated to Zeus, but there were several major temples erected there, as well as altars to more than seventy individual gods. The Olympic Games were held every four years and, by the fifth century BCE, were the most prestigious of a circuit of four Games. The other festivals (Greek *synodai*) were the Pythian Games, in honor of Apollo at Delphi; the Isthmian Games, in honor of Poseidon at Corinth; and the Nemean Games, in honor of Zeus at Nemea.[24] These were *stephanitic*, or "crown games," where the victor's prize was a simple wreath of vegetation. (Ancient Greece also had *chrematic* competitions—"prize games"—where money and valuable objects could be won.) This raises the question of whether Greek athletes could be classified as "amateurs" or "professionals." In the nineteenth century, European scholars professed a romantic view of Greek sport and asserted that the athletes were gentleman amateurs. However, there are some athletes, about whom a fair bit is known, who suggest that sport was a viable profession; the aristocrat "Theagenes of Thasos, who is alleged to have won . . . 1,300 victories in boxing and the *pankration* in just twenty-two years of the early fifth century . . . was a professional, that is a full-time, athlete, who must have devoted his youth and early manhood almost exclusively to the . . . pursuit of athletic success."[25]

The first Olympic competition was a simple footrace, the *stadion*. Over time, more events were added; the final program was three races, the *stadion*, the double race (*daiulos*), and the "long" race (*dolikhos*); two chariot races, the two-horse (*sunoris*) and the four-horse (*tethrippon*) races; the horse race with jockeys (*keles*); boxing (*pux*) and wrestling (*pale*); a brutal combination of boxing and wrestling called *pankration*; the *pentathlon*, which replicated the *stadion* and wrestling, but featured three unique events, the discus (*diskos*), javelin (*akon*), and jump (*halma*); and the *hoplitodromos* (race in armor), which

PAUSANIAS'S DESCRIPTION OF THE TEMPLE OF ZEUS AT OLYMPIA (FROM BOOK 5, *DESCRIPTION OF GREECE*, AVAILABLE AT: WWW.THEOI.COM/TEXT/PAUSANIAS5A.HTML)

[5.11.1] XI. The god sits on a throne, and he is made of gold and ivory. On his head lies a garland which is a copy of olive shoots. In his right hand he carries a Victory, which, like the statue, is of ivory and gold; she wears a ribbon and—on her head—a garland. In the left hand of the god is a scepter, ornamented with every kind of metal, and the bird sitting on the scepter is the eagle. The sandals also of the god are of gold, as is likewise his robe. On the robe are embroidered figures of animals and the flowers of the lily.

[5.11.2] The throne is adorned with gold and with jewels, to say nothing of ebony and ivory. Upon it are painted figures and wrought images. There are four Victories, represented as dancing women, one at each foot of the throne, and two others at the base of each foot. On each of the two front feet are set Theban children ravished by sphinxes, while under the sphinxes Apollo and Artemis are shooting down the children of Niobe.

[5.11.3] Between the feet of the throne are four rods, each one stretching from foot to foot. The rod straight opposite the entrance has on it seven images; how the eighth of them disappeared nobody knows. These must be intended to be copies of obsolete contests, since in the time of Pheidias contests for boys had not yet been introduced. The figure of one binding his own head with a ribbon is said to resemble in appearance Pantarces, a stripling of Elis said to have been the love of Pheidias. Pantarces too won the wrestling-bout for boys at the eighty-sixth Festival.

concluded the games.[26] There were also boys' versions of some of these events. These athletic contests took place within a sequence of religious solemnities and ritual celebrations. Moreover, they were panhellenic (open to all Greeks), and a military truce, the *ekecheiria*, was enforced for a month prior to the games so that competitors and spectators could travel to Olympia in safety.

Much of what we know about the ancient Olympics was recorded by the travel writer Pausanias, who visited Olympia in approximately 160 CE and dedicated books 5 and 6 of his ten-volume *Description of Greece* to the site. Several myths of the origin of Olympia have been preserved, connecting its foundation to the divine hero Herakles (Hercules) and to Pelops, who gives his name to the Peloponnese region. Eligibility to compete in the games was strictly controlled; all athletes had to be "male, belonging to a Greek city-state and tribe, but also be of free birth, legitimate parents, and not guilty of homicide."[27] Olympic victors were highly regarded, and they exemplified the quality of *arete*, which is often translated as "virtue" but which more accurately "referred to the attainments of a warrior and a gentleman among which his body image . . . [being] a strong and skilled warrior, played a dominant part."[28]

The need for the *ekecheiria* (truce) raises the issue of the relationship between the game contests of the ancient Olympics and war in Greek society. The poet Pindar referred to the assembled athletes at Olympia as "the whole fellowship of warriors," and there was a definite warrior ethos pervading Olympia. This was most apparent in the three combat sports: boxing, wrestling, and *pankration*. Norbert Elias noted that "a boy or man killed in one of the Olympic boxing or wrestling matches was often crowned as victor to the glory of his clan and his city and that the survivor—the 'killer'—was neither punished nor stigmatized."[29] Death in the service of the gods (or, at least, in the service of one's clan or city) was recognized as noble and worthy of praise. Although the marathon (which is a highlight of the modern games) was unknown at Olympia, the Greeks held the warrior who first ran that distance in time of war in high esteem: "In 490 BCE a young Athenian named Pheidippides ran twenty-five miles from the plains of Marathon to Athens with news of a Greek military victory over the Persians. 'Rejoice, we conquer,' he announced, and then dropped dead from exertion."[30]

The Olympic environment was aggressively masculine. Further, it was homosocial in orientation and comfortable with bisexuality, rather than exclusive heterosexuality or homosexuality. The beauty of male athletes was celebrated, and Greek vases "with athletic scenes often bear young men's names accompanied with the adjective *kalos* ('he is beautiful')."[31] Women were not permitted at the Olympic Games as competitors or spectators. The only exception was the priestess of Demeter Chamyne, who could watch the events from an altar opposite the seating of the *Hellanodikai* (judges of the games).[32] Athletes competed naked, and—after a woman sneaked in to watch her son compete in the boxing, disguised as a trainer, in 404 BCE—trainers had to be naked too. The story of this mother, Kallipateira (who is also called Pherenike in some

texts), is intriguing. Women who violated the sanctity of Olympia, if discovered, were thrown to their deaths from nearby Mount Typaion. Kallipateira revealed herself when her son was successful; she could not contain her joy at his victory and leaped across the fence to embrace and congratulate him. She was not condemned to death "out of respect for the fact that her father (the well-known Diagoras of Rhodes) and brothers, and now her son, were Olympic victors."[33] This reveals the respect in which Olympic victors were held in ancient Greece.

In a fascinating reconstruction, Stephen Miller has worked out the schedule for the 300 BCE Olympic Games. His research is very important because it situates the ancient Olympics in the context of Greek daily life and foregrounds the religious context of the athletic contests. Miller's reconstruction utilizes information from archaeological excavations and from textual and art historical sources. Miller starts with the preparations for the competition at nearby Elis. In his discussion of Elis, Pausanias mentions three *gymnasia* (literally "naked training place"), the judges' rooms on the *agora*, and the horse racing track. Miller concludes that "Elis was, then, an athletic training town, the ancient predecessor to the modern Olympic village."[34] In Elis, the *Hellanodikai* (ten Olympic judges) were trained before the opening of the Games. The judges' decisions could be appealed to the ninety-member Olympic Council but were otherwise final. Preparations were also made for the announcement of the truce (*ekecheiria*), which began on July 10, 300 BCE. Envoys were sent to all regions of Greece to publicize the truce.

The games proper began August 6, when the judges charged the competitors with the following: "If you have worked so as to be worthy of going to Olympia, if you have done nothing indolent or ignoble, then take heart and march on; but those who have not so trained may leave and go wherever they like."[35] Those who felt confident followed the *Hellanodikai* in a procession from Elis to Olympia, spending the day and night of August 6, 300 BCE walking the road, reaching Olympia on the morning of August 7. The religious nature of the games is immediately recognizable from the fact that, just prior to arriving at Olympia, the party (the ten judges, up to two hundred athletes in a well-attended year, with the spectators and their families) paused at a water source, the Pieria, where the judges were anointed with pig's blood by the priests of Zeus, and the spring water was used for ritual ablution. After being rendered ritually pure by the spring water, they could enter the Altis, the sacred grove of Zeus. This day also saw a contest for trumpet players, the winner of which was Herodorus of Megara, who could play two trumpets simultaneously. His skill won him ten Olympic trumpet contests, and he attained a modest fame for his dietary habits; "He was accustomed . . . to eat five kilograms of bread and eight kilograms of whatever meat he could put his hands on while he drank six litres of wine."[36]

After these preliminaries, the remainder of August 7 was at leisure. People chatted together, organized their accommodation, went sightseeing, and rested. These activities seem profane and everyday, but they contributed to the sense of *communitas* among those at Olympia. The games proper began the next day, on August 8, 300 BCE. A procession set out and made offerings at all the altars. The *Hellanodikai* charged the athletes with the gravity of their task, and they offered oaths at the altar of Zeus Horkios, patron of oath-takers, in the *bouleuterion* ("council house"). Pausanias says the oath involved the vow to "do nothing evil" at the games and that the athletes promised that they had been training for appropriately ten months. The judges also vowed to "judge fairly, accept no gifts, and keep secret any information about the

competitors."[37] The judges, priests of Zeus, competitors, and spectators then went in procession to the sporting area of the sanctuary, which was roped off from the ritual area. Athletes entered the stadium via underground passages, and heralds announced their names, fathers' names, and city-state citizenship. Any challenges to a competitor's right to compete were heard at this time.

The chariot races and horse races were the first contests of the games. These were unusual, in that the owners of the horses rarely ever competed as charioteers or jockeys. Jockeys were often slaves, and, because ancient Greece had neither saddle nor stirrups, they often fell off. This was not an impediment to the horse winning the race. With chariot racing, extremely wealthy aristocrats sometimes entered several teams of horses; Alkibiades the Athenian entered seven *tethrippa* (four-horsed chariots) "in 416 BCE, winning first, second and fourth places."[38] It was also possible for chariot teams belonging to women to compete, and in 396 BCE, Kyniska, the sister of the king of Sparta, entered a team that won. The base of a statue that she erected, commemorating her achievement as the first female victor at Olympia, survives to this day.

The pentathlon took place after the horse races. Miller notes that modern scholars are still uncertain as to how the winner of the pentathlon was determined. However, the final wrestling bout was not held if any one athlete had won three of the previous four competitions, and it seems there was an elimination process, so that those athletes who competed in the wrestling were all potential winners (for example, one bout between two competitors, who had each won two contests, or two bouts featuring four athletes, who had each won one contest). The day, August 8, 300 BCE, ended with a sacrifice to Pelops, one of the divine heroes of Olympia, and attendees celebrated into the night. The religious aspects of the games and the recreational revelry were deeply connected. John Gould has noted that the central ritual of Greek religion was sacrifice, usually animal sacrifice, and that after the gods had received their part of the offerings, the remainder of the cooked meat was eaten by the community in a joyous feast.[39] The applicability of Durkheim's model of religious ritual, which reinforces the sacred and results in a stronger, more unified and cohesive society, is obvious. Feasts and parties celebrating victory or the act of simply being at Olympia were part of everyday life, yet for the Greeks they were sacred activities that strengthened the links between the human realm and the realm of the gods. It is worth commenting that the gods of ancient Greece were anthropomorphic (humanlike), and it has been argued that one reason games and athletic contests may have become integrated into religious ceremonies is that the Greeks assumed that the gods took pleasure in those things that humans took pleasure in.

That night in 300 BCE was the full moon (Greek *panselenos*), and the morning of August 9 bustled with preparations for the sacrifice to Zeus, which was the ritual and spiritual high point of the games. The sacrifice began with a great procession through the Altis, led by the priests. The most impressive participants of the procession were the one hundred oxen that were to be sacrificed. Miller states that the "animals were taken to the great altar and slaughtered. Then their thighs were taken to the top of the altar and burned for the gratification of Zeus, while the remainder of the animals was roasted and distributed to the crowd."[40] Ancient sources are frank concerning the discomforts experienced by the attendees at the Olympic Games; it was very hot, the accommodation was primitive (usually tents), and there was little in the way of food and water.[41] One of the most popular altars for offerings in the sanctuary was the altar of Zeus Apomyios, Zeus the Fly-Averter,

because the site was plagued by flies, which were attracted by the meat of the sacrifices. Yet these discomforts were rendered unimportant by the sacred atmosphere of Olympia and the delight in participation of the athletes and spectators.

The final day of competition in the 300-BCE Olympic Games was August 10, during which the individual track and field events were decided. At the ancient games, records of the athletes' performance were not kept, nor of second or third placings. Only the winners were recorded.[42] The victor in the *stadion*, the original Olympic competition, received the greatest honor in that his name was given to that Olympiad. Thus the 300 BCE Olympics are "the Olympiad when Pythagoras of Magnesia (in Asia Minor) won the *stadion*."[43] Victors were also celebrated in poetry (such as the *Olympian Odes* of Pindar), and statues of them were erected at Olympia itself or in their home city-state. Several well-known statues of athletes have survived from ancient Greece, including Myron's *Discobulos* and the *Charioteer of Delphi*. After the close of events, many stayed at the site for the final day of celebrations, August 11, on which the crowns of wild olive leaves (sacred to Zeus) were presented to the winners and a victory dinner was held by the Elean hosts of the games. The crowns were important symbols: they were not valuable in themselves but withered within a few days' time. The sacredness of the crown came from the fact that it was made of a plant sacred to the god and that it represented the glory of the athlete's achievement. In four years, the rituals of Olympia were celebrated again, creating a cycle of sacred time that structured the lives of the ancient Greeks.

It is difficult if not impossible not to be fascinated by the ancient Olympic Games, with their mixture of athletic excellence, religious extravagance, and holiday travel. Therefore, the revival of the games in the modern world has a certain inevitability. The site of Olympia was rediscovered in 1766 by Richard Chandler, an Englishman traveling in Greece, with Pausanias as his guidebook. Classical Greek culture was fundamental to the European education system of the eighteenth and nineteenth centuries, and the modern era saw the foundation of museums and public art galleries in which the antiquities of Greece, uncovered through the new discipline of archaeology, were displayed.[44] In 1829, the Greek war of independence ended, with Greece freed from the suzerainty of the Ottoman Empire. An Olympic revival was suggested as early as 1835, but it did not happen until 1896, when Pierre de Coubertin, the founder of the modern Olympic movement, succeeded in realizing his vision.

It may initially seem strange that Coubertin had a decidedly religious understanding of the modern games, given that nineteenth-century Europe was a Christian culture, seemingly very distant from the polytheistic paganism of the ancient Greeks. However, the Enlightenment and Romanticism, eighteenth-century aesthetic and philosophical movements, had by this time contributed to an emergent historical narrative that argued for Christianity's negative influence upon Western culture. From this perspective, rather than being the true religion that saved Europe from the darkness of paganism, Christianity was a repressive and puritanical system that had closed down the ancient Olympics in 394 CE (the Christian emperor Theodosius I correctly identified the games as a pagan religious celebration) and that preached a world-denying doctrine that demonized sexuality, alienated humans from their bodies, and, as Louis Ruprecht poetically puts it, "peopled the waters with monsters and fearful chaos, so that western people stopped swimming altogether."[45]

This attitudinal shift was a more radical version of the same impulse that led to the development of muscular Christianity; a desire to recast the body and physical experience as positive and to embrace sexuality and sensuality in a religious context. For the classical enthusiasts, a "pagan revival" seemed necessary to neutralize the malign inheritance of Christianity. It was not, however, driven by the desire to believe in or worship the ancient Greek deities literally, which Christians call idolatry.[46] Rather, Coubertin espoused a paganism that, he argued, "humanity will never shake off, and from which—I will risk this seeming blasphemy—it would not be well for it to free itself completely: and that is the cult of the human being, of the human body, mind, and flesh, feeling and will, instinct and conscience."[47] This paganism advocated the pursuit of bodily perfection as the pursuit of virtue itself. Coubertin's vision extended the panhellenism of the ancient Games to the modern internationalism of the revived Games. Although Coubertin initially opposed women competing in the games—and although the victory in the marathon of 1896 by Spiridon Louys, a Greek shepherd, reinforced the image of the amateur athlete—the eventual form of the modern games fits the seven characteristics of modern sport advanced by Guttmann and discussed earlier in this chapter.

Similarly, the religious elements of the modern Olympic Games also conform closely to the list of parallels between sport and religion proposed by Harry Edwards in 1973. The symbolism of the games was carefully chosen, and the theatricality of the rituals was skillfully orchestrated. The "Oath of the Athletes," intended to recall the vows before the statue of Zeus Horkios, was introduced at the 1920 Olympics in Antwerp. The wording remained constant till 1960: "We swear that we will take part in the Olympic Games in loyal competition, respecting the regulations which govern them and desirous of participating in them in the true spirit of sportsmanship for the honour of our country and for the glory of sport."[48] After the establishment of the ceremony of lighting the cauldron, Coubertin's collaborator, Carl Diem (secretary-general of the organizing committee of Hitler's Olympics), introduced the torch relay to bring the Olympic flame from Olympia to Berlin in 1936.[49] Even though Coubertin had envisaged international peace and harmony being facilitated by the modern Olympics (in an extension of the *ekecheiria*), the World Wars closed the Games in 1916, 1940, and 1944.

The International Olympic Committee (IOC), the guardians of the new tradition, have made politic choices of Olympic host cities, particularly Antwerp (1920), in a Belgium devastated by World War I, and London (1948), struggling to recover after the Blitz. The records set and the medals won are among the highest sporting honors achievable. Great athletic performances, such as that of Jesse Owens (1913–1980) at the Berlin Olympic in 1936, live on in the world's collective memory. Owens won four gold medals in the 100-meter sprint, the 200-meter sprint, the long jump, and as a member of the 4 x 100-meter relay team, a feat not equaled until Carl Lewis's achievements at the 1984 Olympics. Owens's victories are the more poignant because Adolf Hitler's Nazi Party espoused the supremacy of the "Aryan" races, yet Owens was an African American, and because, in 1936, he was a second-class citizen even in his home country, where he lived out the remainder of his life in poverty and relative obscurity.[50] He is nevertheless now cherished as one of sport's "saints." Other Olympic achievers have been disgraced and their medals rescinded as a result of scandals over performance-enhancing drugs. For example, American Marion Jones won five medals at the 2000 Sydney Olympics, but she later admitted to taking anabolic steroids. Her medals were confiscated, and she was sentenced to serve six months in prison for perjury.[51]

Thus it can be seen that the modern Olympic Games are a form of sport that manifests all of the connections with religion with which this chapter opened. The origins lie in the ancient Olympic Games, which were indubitably a religious festival in honor of Zeus Olympios. The revived Olympics were conceived deliberately in a religious fashion, with symbolism to evoke feelings of religious experience. Stars and record holders have achieved a place in the ranks of sport's "saints." Christian athletes have made their mark, including Scottish missionary to China Eric Liddell (1902–1945), the "flying Scotsman," who won the 400-meter event at the 1924 Paris Olympics after refusing to compete in his best event (the 100-meter race) because it would require him to run on the Sabbath.[52] The four-year cycle of the games creates a sense of repeatable ritual time that the whole world (made smaller through globalization) prepares for. And media coverage and affordable international travel have resulted in fans attending and watching the games, which provoke "wild enthusiasm" that translates them into a liminal space where *communitas* is experienced and it is "possible to escape the pressures of everyday life,"[53] that is, to participate in the sacred.

SUMO: JAPAN'S OLDEST SPORT, FROM MYTHOLOGY TO MODERN MEDIA

This chapter now examines a different culture and historical era, with a case study of sumo wrestling in Japan, focusing on medieval and modern sources. To test the theory that sport and religion are intimately connected or to establish the applicability of taxonomies such as those of Edwards and Guttmann, it is necessary to explore more than one culture and historical era. Sumo is credited as Japan's oldest sport, and its popular histories often trace it to a tale in the *Nihon Shoki* ("chronicles of Japan"), which is the second-oldest written text from Japan, dating from 720 CE. In this text, there is a wrestling match in the court of Emperor Suinin, and Nomi no Sukune defeats Taima no Kuyehaya by brutally kicking him to death.[54] There are reasons to doubt that this anecdote refers to sumo at all, because kicking is explicitly prohibited in the rules.

Seeking the origin of the Olympic Games in Greece requires that myths and legends be sifted and facts carefully checked. Similarly, in the case of sumo, mythology is not recorded until relatively late; writing came to Japan from China (along with Buddhism and other cultural imports) during what would be called the

Middle Ages in Europe. Shinto (the way of the gods, or the way of the *kami*—"powers" or "spirit beings") is broadly accepted as the "indigenous" religion of Japan, although scholars document many phases in its development. Shinto has been a folk religion, a religious organization, a state religion, a nationalist ideology, a civil institution, and a personal spirituality.[55] From prehistory to the eighth century, it was an oral tradition. For over a millennium, it was intimately connected to Buddhism, a connection that was only broken with the Meiji Restoration of imperial rule in 1867.[56] The origins of sumo are dated by some scholars to the Tumulus Period of Japanese prehistory (250–525 CE), because terracotta figures

Three sumo wrestlers pose outdoors with spectators in the background (c. 1905). (Photo by Burr McIntosh, 1905. Copyright © Library of Congress. Used by permission.)

THE WRESTLING OF TAIMA AND NOMI, NIHON SHOKI (BOOK 6, "SUININ TENNO") (AVAILABLE AT HTTP://SUNSITE.BERKELEY.EDU)

The Emperor, hearing this, proclaimed to his ministers, saying: "We hear that Kuyehaya of Taima is the champion of the Empire. Might there be any one to compare with him?"

One of the ministers came forward and said: "Thy servant hears that in the Land of Idzumo there is a valiant man named Nomi no Sukune. It is desirable that thou shouldst send for him, by way of trial, and match him with Kuyehaya."

That same day the Emperor sent Nagaochi, the ancestor of the Atahe of Yamato, to summon Nomi no Sukune. Thereupon Nomi no Sukune came from Idzumo, and straightway he and Taima no Kuyehaya were made to wrestle together. The two men stood opposite to one another. Each raised his foot and kicked at the other, when Nomi no Sukune broke with a kick the ribs of Kuyehaya and also kicked and broke his loins and thus killed him. Therefore the land of Taima no Kuyehaya was seized, and was all given to Nomi no Sukune. This was the cause why there is in that village a place called Koshi-oreda, i.e., the field of the broken loins.

found at archaeological sites might be sumo wrestlers; however, this is based only on the fact that "they are wearing loincloths, the typical dress of sumo wrestlers."[57]

The sources reveal that, like Shinto in general, sumo has changed markedly over time. Certain earlier types of wresting with which historians connect sumo in terms of ancestry were very specifically religious; but, like the modern Olympics, modern sumo is a popular cultural form, with extensive media coverage and celebrity wrestlers. In short, it exhibits the seven characteristics of modern sport listed by Guttmann. The original religious context of sumo is obscure. Harold Bolitho argues that it may be traced to *sechie-zumo*, a form of wrestling practiced in the imperial court and based on Chinese models. *Sechie-zumo* was performed in front of a limited audience in a purpose-built pavilion, the Shishinden, and was linked to the emperor's ceremonial responsibility to

ensure good harvests. The religious importance of wrestling was signaled by the accompanying poetry, dancing, and feasting, which included "a procession to the sound of drums, gongs, conch shells and . . . [an] orchestra."[58] These wrestling bouts lasted for one day only and took place in the seventh month, initially on the seventh and later on the sixteenth day. The combatants were the seventeen members of the "left side" and the seventeen members of the "right side" of the imperial guard. The oldest Japanese text, the *Kojiki* ("record of ancient matters," dated 712 CE), deals with the history of the Yamato clan, the clan of the imperial family, who claimed descent from the sun goddess Amaterasu. The *Kojiki* states that the supremacy of the Yamato clan was won through a wrestling match between the divine Takemikazuchi no Kami and Takeminakata no Kami of the Izumo dynasty. Patricia Lee Cuyler deduces from this tale that wrestling matches were "viewed as a means of determining the will of the gods" in early Japan.[59]

This aristocratic sumo was wedded to a more popular wrestling form in the Tokugawa period (named for Tokugawa Ieyasu, b. 1543, d. 1616, shogun, or military ruler, of Japan from 1603). This popular wrestling was religious in the sense that it was a feature of rural festivals or *matsuri* (which means "to entertain the *kami*"), where strong men vied with each other for victory in a number of physical tests (lifting heavy weights, tug of war, and the like). In the late sixteenth century, troupes of wrestlers began to assemble to put on displays, and by the seventeenth century, professional sumo emerged as a spectacle for a paying public. This shift in wrestling practice was linked to the fact that wrestling had formerly been regarded as practice for military action, and in the Tokugawa era, this perception changed. The warrior aristocracy developed a taste for exhibition sumo, and it ceased to be regarded as a martial art. Jujitsu was favored for military preparation, and sumo became a public phenomenon, a part of everyday life.[60]

Formal organizations developed in the mid-eighteenth century. Printed programs for sumo exhibitions were produced. The ranks of wrestlers were fixed according to the row of the program in which they appeared: on the top row were the high-ranked wrestlers, *makuuchi* (named for the fact that they sat behind a curtain, *maku*); the group below were known as *makushita* ("below the curtain"), but they had specific names according to the in row which they featured: *nidamme* (second row), *sandamme* (third row), *jonidan* (the row above the bottom, so designated as the word for four, *shi*, could also mean "death"), and *jonokuchi* (entrance to *jo*).[61] The success of sumo can be seen in the size of the audiences; in the late eighteenth century, crowds of up to three thousand people gathered to watch sumo tournaments, and Edo (later Tokyo) emerged as the dominant city, with the Edo Sumo Association gradually taking control of the sport. In contemporary sumo, the four top titleholder ranks are *yokozuna* ("horizontal rope"), *ozeki* ("champion"), *sekiwake* ("at his side"), and *komusubi* ("the little knot").

All that is needed to conduct a sumo match is a ring (*dohyo*), demarcated by a *shimenawa* (ritual rope), and two wrestlers wearing loincloths.[62] The wrestlers face off and may choose to fight or not to fight. If they fight, victory is won when a combatant forces his opponent out of the ring or forces him to place a part of his body (not the soles of his feet) on the earthen floor. Pushing and shoving are acceptable, but a range of tactics are expressly banned: "kicking, hairpulling, punching with the fists, and shaking, or clutching the part of the loincloth covering the sexual organs."[63] As well as exhibition sumo, contemporary Japan also is home to a range of *shinji-zumo* (*kami*-service sumo), which are rituals that take place at Shinto shrines during religious festivals. One intriguing example is called *nakizumo* ("child crying" sumo) and is held during the winter months at the Ikiko shrine in Tochigi Prefecture in central Honshu, the main island of Japan. This ceremony exemplifies the Japanese proverb "a crying child will thrive." Babies are dressed in loincloths and rocked in a sumo enclosure by wrestlers. The first baby to cry is the winner.[64] This ritual exhibits the connection between the Japanese life cycle and Shinto shrines; when a child is one month old, he or she is brought to the local shrine "to be presented to the *kami*."[65]

Another very interesting ritual is the Crow Sumo Festival of May 9, part of the lead-up to the Kamo Festival, which is one of the three great festivals held in Kyoto. The venue is the Kamigamo Shrine, which is also linked to the mythology of the Yamato clan. The story is that when Jimmu, the first emperor, left the Plain of High Heaven to live on earth, the "grandfather of Kamigamo Shrine's *kami*, Kamo Taketsunomi-no-mikoto, became a strange big crow . . . and led Jimmu to Yamato."[66] The descendents of this crow-*kami* built the Kamigamo Shrine and became powerful in the region. The Crow Sumo ritual is believed to reinforce the collective memory of the locals and to remind them of the crucial role played by the Kamo people in the establishment of the imperial family. The ritual involves two teams of ten boys, representing east and west, that set out from the shrine after being purified with water at ten in the morning on May 9. They follow a procession of priests, community authorities, their team leaders, and a proxy priestess through the street. Upon their return to the shrine gate, a prayer detailing the Crow Sumo is recited, and the *kami* are asked to deliver a good harvest.

At eleven, the boys are assembled in a courtyard south of the shrine building, in front of the dais where the proxy priestess is seated, flanked by the priests. The priests draw magical figures in the ritual enclosure, and spells are recited to harness spiritual forces. The team leaders emerge from their enclosures into the ring and hop like crows, fetching ritual objects (bow, arrows, fan, sword, mat) and making "kaw, kaw, kaw" crow sounds. They return to their enclosures before the combat between the boys begins. Each wrestler gets two turns, and the results of the matches are recorded. The final victor is then knocked to the ground by all the other boys, to dispel any lingering resentment. This is an important ritual in the daily life of the shrine community; the priests announce each phase of the proceedings over a public address system, and, after the wrestling is over, most spectators remain at the shrine for some time, perhaps half an hour, to drink sake in honor of the *kami* and talk with friends and neighbors.[67] In Durkheim's terms, the Crow Sumo Festival is a ritual that takes place in a sacred enclosure and draws the whole community into that enclosure, leaving behind profane concerns. The ritual's narrative concerns the noble history of the shrine community and reinforces its sense of solidarity.

However, the grand tournaments (*honbasho*) of sumo, which are held six times per year, are events that are richly symbolic and involve ceremonial accoutrements and dignified settings. Three events (in January, May, and September) are held in the Sumo Hall (*Ryogoku Kokugikan*) in Tokyo, and one each in Osaka (March), Nagoya (July), and Fukuoka (November). Tournaments begin and end on a Sunday and last for fifteen days. Audiences in excess of a thousand are a regular occurrence. Sumo wrestlers have myriad special elements to their physical presentation and image. They wear their hair long, being the only class of Japanese men permitted to retain long hair after the Meiji Restoration. The high-ranking wrestlers wear a *mawashi* (loincloth) made of silk, whereas others wear cotton, and great champions (*yokozuna*) wear ritual ropes around their waists. Ann Fischer notes that these ropes are of the same "design made by priests and used to shake over people or objects in purification rituals."[68] This draws attention to the fact that the wrestlers are accorded a similar sacred status to the priests. The ring at these large tournaments is very elaborate; there is packed clay strewn with sand, with bales of rice-straw to mark the edge of the clay. There is a roof, similar to that of a shrine, erected above the ring, and at the corners of the clay square are four pillars representing the four seasons (in some modern arenas, these have been removed to aid visibility and are present symbolically in four tassels hanging from the ceiling). The wrestlers themselves all regularly use professional names (*shikona*), although there is a recent trend to compete under one's own name. In the latter part of the twentieth century, more non-Japanese contestants entered the ranks of sumo wrestlers.

It has been noted by scholars that, contrary to expectations, sumo has actually become more religious over time. In the late seventeenth century, it was merely a martial art; once it had broken free of that classification, Shinto elements were added to the ritual of the combat. Greater emphasis was laid on preparing the ring, which was sprinkled with salt to purify it for the sacred contest ahead. The demarcation by ritual rope (*shimenawa*) indicates that the ring is sacred, filled with the power of the *kami*.[69] Wrestlers anointed their tongues with salt to ward off evil spirits, and the "ring-entering ceremony, which first appeared in . . . the early . . . eighteenth century, adopted the Shinto rituals of clapping the hands to attract the attention of the deities and stamping the feet to drive away malignant spirits."[70] Referees took on some of the responsibilities of Shinto priests, although they wore traditional *samurai* war dress. In a striking parallel to the Olympic Council in Greece, at the end of the eighteenth century, "sumo elders" began formally attending tournaments to deal with disputed verdicts of referees. They numbered four and were known as the "four pillars" (*shihom-bashira*).

In conformity with Guttmann's seven characteristics of modern sport, sumo went through a process of codification, which began in earnest in 1789, when the Edo sumo authority Yoshida Oikaze submitted several documents to a magistrate in Edo. These asserted his own status in the sumo world and a history of certain sumo traditions.[71] His documents were accepted, and from that point on, sumo had a respectable history. From a religious perspective, the elements of sumo contest were analyzed and accorded meaning in terms of Shinto, Buddhism, and Confucianism. For example, contemporary sources claimed that the earth of the ring represented the five elements (earth, metal, wood, fire, and water) and the five Confucian virtues, and the left and right entrances to the arena symbolized yin and yang. The overall attempt was to give to sumo "an extremely complex symbolic melange" that would satisfy all.[72]

An actual wrestling bout is governed by strict protocol. The wrestlers in a tournament are divided into two teams, but that does not affect the opponents that they are assigned. Each enters the ring according to a modified version of the eighteenth-century ring-entering ceremony, signifying "a pledge to the deities that the wrestlers will fight fairly and with the proper spirit."[73] The champion wrestlers (*yokozuna*) have a special ring-entering ceremony that dates from 1789, which involves loud clapping, rubbing the hands together, and extending the arms horizontally. This is derived from a ritual purification using grass. Attendants clap blocks together to announce each new bout, and the referee directs proceedings using his war-fan as a signal.[74] Wrestlers have buckets of purifying "water of luck" in their corners (the eastern and western corners), which they use to rinse out their mouths. Wrestlers face off (*shikiri*) for four minutes before actually fighting. Once fighting commences, matches rarely last more than a couple of minutes.[75] Losers bow briefly and depart, and the winners are announced by the referee. The last day of a tournament is the most exciting, because the competition has become more intense. Championships are contested within each division, and prestigious prizes such as the Emperor's Cup are awarded.

In the 1960s, Ann Fischer studied the pattern of career for sumo wrestlers from an anthropological viewpoint. She noted that wrestlers formed familylike troupes, and within these troupes (called a *heya*, "room"), they considered themselves to be "brothers." Most young wrestlers are too poor to marry and dedicate themselves to excellence in sumo; purity and virtue are prerequisites for "success in the harvest and in the fight" and enable those who lose to face disappointment with dignity.[76] The sumo family extends into the wider Japanese society, with millions of Japanese fans of the sport eagerly following the careers of titleholding champions. Those champions who uphold the traditional values of the sport are especially loved and respected. Chiyonofuji Mitsugu (b. 1955), nicknamed "The Wolf," held the rank of *yokozuna* for ten years, between 1981 and 1991. He was a distinctive stylist, with strength and speed, despite weighing approximately 120 kilograms, which is light for a sumo wrestler. His career began in 1970, and he retired with over a thousand career wins. In addition to his success in winning titles, he was the embodiment of restrained Japanese virtue. He maintained stoical dignity, despite frequent injuries and the death of his small daughter, and was fond of solitary pursuits. In 1991, his final year as *yokozuna*, he was the subject of a television documentary,[77] and after his retirement, he became manager of the Kokonoe stable of wrestlers, which has since produced notable champions. His exemplary career made him a respected tournament judge, and in 2008 he became a member of the Japan Sumo Association.

However, sumo also has its scandals, with wrestlers falling from grace. In December 1987, a young *yokozuna* named Futahaguro was expelled from the ranks of sumo. Futahaguro was promoted to *yokozuna* at the age of twenty-three in 1986, despite not having won a title, "because the *Sumo* Association felt that more *yokozuna* were needed to maintain fan interest," and he rapidly crumbled under the pressure.[78] His hot temper and lack of self-control, both severely frowned upon in Japan, saw him beat up his personal attendants (several of whom resigned), and in December 1987, while quarrelling with his stable master, Tatsunami, he kicked an elderly supporter and struck Tatsunami's wife. The Japan Sumo Association denied him a hearing and forced his resignation. What is fascinating from a moral and religious point of view is that, as Haberman noted,

> Tatsunami felt that more was at stake . . . "Even though he may have the highest rank, total selfishness is not allowed. *Sumo* people must live together in a group." To many Japanese . . . any disruptions of group harmony can have broad consequences. Futahaguro was not the only one to pay for the misadventure. The directors of the *Sumo* Association reprimanded the stable master for having been negligent in supervising his young wrestler. And for good measure, they cut their own salaries by 20 percent for three months, to show that they, too, bore responsibility.[79]

The sphere of sumo here manifests troubles that are interpreted to be of national significance. When sumo champions embody exemplary values and conduct themselves with dignity, they engage in a performance of identity for the nation. Futahaguro's misconduct caused particular grief to Japanese people because he was one of them. Globalization has brought foreign wrestlers into sumo, and they have often offended against the code of conduct (for example, smoking marijuana, having inappropriate sexual relationships, and so on). But they are not Japanese; their inability to conduct themselves respectfully is less culpable. Sumo champions are moral and ethical role models for Japan; if they offend, the nation suffers.

Conclusion: Sacred and Profane Ritual in Contemporary Sport

If the West's Christian heritage is taken into account, there is no doubt that sport and religion in the twenty-first century are closer than they have ever been previously. In certain countries, there are "national" sports, distinctive markers of identity, that show this intimate relationship particularly well. US baseball is an obvious example. Although modern baseball is definitely a development of the popular English ball game, rounders, it has developed a distinctive mythology in the United States that is related to national identity. At the start of the twentieth century, A. G. Spalding, a sportswear tycoon, was involved in a dispute over the origins of baseball. Spalding argued that in "1839 in Cooperstown, New York State, the Civil War general Abner Doubleday had established the rules, diamond field, and name" of baseball.[80] Historians of sport have since established that none of this is accurate, but in 1907 the Spalding Baseball Commission ruled that it was true. The origins of baseball could not be English—they had to be found in the United States itself. Further, Doubleday was a revered historical figure, and his military achievements lent luster to the national recreational game. More recently, Ken Burns's 1994 nine-part documentary series, *Baseball*, offers a grittier, more factual history that nevertheless records the spiritual power of the game and its stature as "the metaphorical successor to the Civil War," a prism through which to view US history.[81]

David Chidester has advanced the idea that baseball, as an institution, constitutes a "church" for many Americans. He argues that the match season creates a sense of sacred time (it has been noted that the baseball season begins in spring and signals the renewal of the seasons), the rules of baseball are standards that are largely unchanging and create stability in peoples' lives, baseball grounds are sacred places (many pitchers ritually jump over the boundaries of the field out of respect), and the large fanbase gives baseball tens of millions of believers, who are united in "an extended

family."[82] Baseball's folk-religious appeal is endorsed in the films made about it, many of which have a religious flavor (for example, *Angels in the Outfield*, 1994; *Field of Dreams*, 1989; *For Love of the Game*, 1999; *The Natural*, 1984; and hundreds more). In one of the best baseball films, *Bull Durham* (1988), the opening credits show photographs of baseball greats, and, in the voiceover, Annie Savoy, a baseball "groupie" (who in religious terms might be more honorably described as an initiating priestess) speaks a profession of faith.

> I believe in the Church of Baseball. I've tried all of the major religions, and some of the minor ones. I've worshipped Buddha, Allah, Brahma, Vishnu, Siva, trees, mushrooms, and Isadora Duncan. . . . And the only church that truly feeds the soul day in and day out is the Church of Baseball."[83]

What Annie is advocating here is baseball as a legitimate and spiritually satisfying religion, which renders traditional religions unnecessary. Many scholars agree with her that sport and religion are completely identified for a sizeable percentage of Americans. The Super Bowl, the championship game of the National Football League (NFL), is played on a Sunday in late January and is watched by more than half the US population and by a significant percentage of the world. Over twenty years ago, in 1985, it was necessary to delay the presidential inauguration of Ronald Reagan because the constitutionally mandated date, January 20, was also the date of the Super Bowl. Academic commentators have noted that Super Bowl Sunday is a de facto national holiday and that being at the Super Bowl physically has taken on the quality of a religious pilgrimage to a sacred place, where attendance is participation in a sacred ritual. Joseph L. Price has noted that Americans spend more money on the Super Bowl than they "spend on traditional religious practices and institutions throughout the entire month."[84] The television sets of the nation take on the quality of shrines, or perhaps visions (for what else is an image electronically communicated to a majority of the homes of the nation?).

Other countries have other sports that generate similar passion in the people. Cricket in England has a noble tradition, originating in the Middle Ages; revered deceased players, such as W. G. Grace (1848–1915); a formal code, called "The Laws of Cricket," the custodian of which is the Marylebone Cricket Club; heroic contests, including the Ashes (against rivals Australia); and sacred grounds, including Lord's and the Oval.[85] Australia shares England's passion for cricket, along with other former British colonies such as India and Sri Lanka, and has particular heroes in Victor Trumper (1877–1915) and Sir Donald Bradman (1908–2001). However, its de facto national holiday is Melbourne Cup day, the first Tuesday in November. The Melbourne Cup is a horse race for three-year-olds, established in 1861, and more than any other holiday (including Australia Day, celebrating the birth of the nation, and Anzac Day, honoring the war dead), it is a day for the performance of Australian national identity. This is acknowledged by federal politicians: the Liberal Party's Andrew Robb nominated "the first Tuesday in November as one of the Australian cultural values that aspiring migrants might have to know to become citizens";[86] and his fellow Liberal Don Randall suggested that the public holiday in June for the Queen's birthday should be dropped and a "truly national day . . . observed on the first Tuesday in November each year" should replace it.[87]

This essay has argued that sport and religion are closely related human domains that enjoyed a particularly harmonious connection in polytheistic ancient Greece. The rise of Christianity brought with it a different, less exuberant attitude to embodiment and physical achievement (and a savior who advocated turning the other cheek rather than agonistic combat), which resulted in a separation of sport and religion in the Christian West from the late fourth century (when Emperor Theodosius I banned the Olympic Games) to the nineteenth century, when the ethos of "muscular Christianity" was first promulgated. This separation of sport and religion is not present in medieval and modern Japan, where sumo wrestling had religious antecedents and took on further religious qualities as it developed, meeting community spiritual needs. Sport and religion were reunited with the emergence of global modernity, which is characterized by a degree of secularization, increased communication technologies, the emergence of personal spiritualities, and the transformation of sport (including traditional exhibitions, such as sumo contests; revived ancient traditions, such as the Olympic Games; and increasingly bureaucratized and rationalized sports, such as baseball, cricket, football, and horse racing) into mass entertainment and stunning spectacular rituals that, increasingly, have come to function as and "feel like" religion for many people.

GLOSSARY

Profane: Profane refers to those things that a community views as diametrically opposed to the sacred (see entry). It is important to note that these distinctions are context-dependent. An activity or object may be profane in one set of circumstances and sacred in another.

Religion: Religion is a system of beliefs and practices relevant to sacred things, which acts to focus a community or group upon those values and actions that it holds to be transcendent.

Religion has public and private dimensions but must involve adherence to a community and a tradition, unlike spirituality, which may be entirely individual.

Ritual: Ritual is any activity that externalizes meaningful beliefs as actions. Rituals are repetitive, in that even if an individual might only undergo a ritual such as initiation once, the community or tradition into which he or she is welcomed has performed that initiation over time upon many such individuals. Rituals create social bonds and facilitate group identity.

Sacred: Sacred refers to that which a community views as transcendent and opposed to the mundanity of the everyday. Sacredness may be encountered in nature, in the figures of priests and priestesses, and in apparently mundane activities that are contextualized in particular ways (e.g., sex, dance, music, eating and drinking, and washing).

Sport: Sport is any physical activity that involves rules and contest and that, successfully completed, results in a victor. It stands in direct contrast to play, which is unstructured, has no rules, and does not involve the elements of contest or victory.

For Further Reading

Baker, William J. *Playing with God: Religion and Modern Sport*. Cambridge, MA: Harvard University Press, 2007.

Cuyler, P. L. *Sumo: From Rite to Sport*. New York: Weatherhill, 1979.

Harvey, Graham, ed. *Ritual and Religious Belief: A Reader*. London, Equinox, 2005.

Higgs, Robert J. *God in the Stadium: Sport and Religion in America*. Lexington: University Press of Kentucky, 1995.

Kasulis, Thomas P. *Shinto: The Way Home*. Honolulu: University of Hawai'i Press, 2004.

Sinn, Ulrich. *Olympia: Cult, Sport, and Ancient Festival*. Princeton: Markus Wiener, 2000.

Young, David C. *A Brief History of the Olympic Games*. Oxford: Blackwell, 2004.

16

HUMOR

David J. Cooper

A priest, a rabbi, and an imam walk into a bar. And the bartender says, "What is this? A joke?"

There is something about religion that invites humor—something about the sacred that beckons the profane, something about order that tempts chaos. As children growing up in the Episcopal Church, my brothers and I reveled in bringing a bit of chaos to an otherwise very orderly hour. From a child's perspective, weekly services required an impossible degree of bodily control—kneeling, sitting, standing, praying, singing—all with little chance for free emotional expression or movement. Church was a place to be quiet and respectful. Our hyperactive minds and bodies resisted every minute of it. We would strategically wait until the congregation (and, most important, our parents) had closed their eyes in prayer before launching spitballs from our balcony seats onto the heads of parishioners below and then ducking back out of sight. To us, this was endlessly amusing. If we wanted to increase the humor quotient, we tried even more daring things, such as aiming for the heads of bald men.

Fifteen years later, I was surprised to witness a very similar occurrence while attending a prayer service (*puja*) at a Tibetan Buddhist monastery nestled in the Himalayan foothills of northeastern India. During the service, I watched, with somewhat embarrassed delight, as a few of the young monks entertained themselves by throwing spitballs at the unsuspecting monks sitting in front of them (waiting, incidentally, until their teacher had closed his eyes in prayer). These young monks, ranging in age from nine to twelve, were every bit as amused by their antics as my brothers and I had been by ours. The fact that they were not allowed to laugh made their laughter that much harder to stifle. Their laughter finally stopped only when the disciplinarian (a twenty-something monk who had once been the rowdiest monk at the monastery) walked by and threatened to hit them with his oversized prayer beads, designed specifically to inflict pain on disobedient young monks!

The rules of decorum that shape both of these disruptive acts are similar—bodily control, silence, and respect for the sacred. Laughter is out of place, incongruous. In fact, important figures in both the Christian and Buddhist traditions have said so explicitly. Saint John Chrysostom (c. 347–407) warned, "This world is not a theater in which we can laugh; and we are not assembled . . . in order to burst into peals of laughter, but to weep for our sins."[1] The Buddha sounded a similarly dour note: "How can anyone laugh who knows of old age, disease, and death?"[2]

Religion, we gather, is about weighty matters. Humor seems, at best, a frivolous distraction from the serious import of the religious message or from engaging in righteous activity. At worst, humor is an assault on reverence, morality, and perhaps the sacred itself. The notion that humor disrupts something rather fundamental about religion lies behind its prohibition and discouragement in a variety of cultural contexts. The notable absence of humor in certain religious contexts even helps mark the sacredness of a time, place, or event by distinguishing it from "ordinary" life.

But although our species has been described as "the religious animal," it is also "the laughing animal."[3] Wherever there are humans, there is humor. And, in fact, humor exercised in religious contexts is not always greeted with horrified gasps or dirty looks. Religious people use humor for a wide variety of religiously appropriate purposes. If we are paying attention, we find manifestations of religious humor everywhere, from the ubiquitous corny joke in a preacher's sermon to the Dalai Lama's infectious and often self-effacing laughter. Even the orthodox Confucian tradition, which otherwise deemed humor inappropriate, explicitly promoted one kind of humor: satirical criticism of those who deviated from the Confucian moral order.

So, in practice, the outright prohibition of humor among religious communities has been extremely rare (and has generally been limited to small groups of ascetics). Much more frequently, religious communities have sought to contain humor's "chaotic" potential by emphasizing the need for appropriateness (of time, place, and content), thereby bringing it into the service of religious "order."

Successful humor requires a receptive audience, and people are likely to be receptive to things that conform to what they already value. In religious contexts, where maintaining particular values is essential, the same principles apply. Religious humor succeeds, in a broad sense, to the extent that it falls within a community's norms. It may even be deemed useful when it promotes or supports those norms. When humor "crosses the line" and threatens a community's standards or worldview, however, it may not simply be regarded as "not funny" but also as offensive or even blasphemous. But religious communities are neither static nor monolithic; norms evolve, interpretations conflict, and boundaries shift. For this reason, when humor is used to push the boundaries, it may also get some laughs, perhaps resonating with a countercurrent or expressing as "just a joke" what is difficult to say directly. This laughter response, both to boundary-pushing and norm-upholding religious humor, thus offers a useful window into the enduring and emerging values of a group, as well as its tensions and strains.

At play between the sacred and the profane, order and chaos, social control and subversion, and continuity and change, humor is used to negotiate religious boundaries in a variety of ways. Returning frequently to these themes, this chapter explores four distinct ways in which religious people and communities have used humor for religious purposes:

- **As a teaching tool:** to instruct adherents in the ideas, norms, or values of the tradition.
- **As a sign of transcendence:** to indicate the presence of sacred or extraordinary qualities in divine beings or holy people.

- **As a release valve:** to relieve pent-up tension through the regulated expression of otherwise prohibited ideas, images, or behaviors.
- **As a weapon:** to both defend and attack one's own religious tradition and to negotiate the place of religious traditions in broader social contexts.

HUMOR AS A TEACHING TOOL

People like to laugh. We find amusement in incongruity—things that "don't quite fit," the playful juxtaposition of opposites or unlike things. Humor allows a brief departure from the ordinary that can be exhilarating and enjoyable. The pleasure of sharing laughter with a group can bond a community together and affirm a common way of looking at things. As the rapid spread of jokes suggests, a "good one" begs to be shared; it is not just memorable, but compulsively so. Thus humor can be a very effective means for a religious community to transmit its values and norms, communicating a well-established message in a way that demands attention and even prompts renewed reflection and affirmation. Such didactic religious humor has come in a wide variety of packages, ranging from informal and ambiguous formats, such as jokes, to traditional sources of authority, such as sacred texts or stories.

The Abrahamic traditions of Judaism, Christianity, and Islam and their respective sacred texts (the Tanakh, the Christian Bible, and the Qur'an) provide an interesting starting place to examine the use of humor in traditional sources of authority. Not only do these traditions share a number of stories, but each also places special emphasis on a single text (unlike, for example, most of the traditions originating in southern and eastern Asia). In comparison with the textual traditions of southern and eastern Asia, the Abrahamic texts contain less obvious humor. One philosopher noted that "the total absence of humour from the Bible is one of the most singular things in all of literature."[4] In these traditions, and especially in the Christian and Islamic traditions, there has been a reluctance to find humor in sacred texts, a notion that acknowledging such humor is akin to not taking the texts seriously. Saint John Chrysostom made much of this perceived absence of humor in the Bible. He argued that a Christian should not laugh, precisely because Jesus is not explicitly depicted as laughing in the Bible! (Of course, the Bible is also silent on the question of whether or not Jesus ever defecated.)

Nevertheless, a number of interpreters (theologians as well as secular scholars) believe that humor is found in the Scriptures of the Jewish, Christian, and Islamic traditions. The barriers of time, culture, and language, however, can make it difficult or even impossible to understand, much less appreciate, the humor that may be present in the texts.

In the Tanakh, laughter plays a pivotal role in the story of Sarah, who, when very old, laughs when she overhears an angel telling Abraham, her husband, that she will have a son. It is a play on incongruities: How can a barren woman become pregnant? It contradicts ordinary human experience. That Sarah did, in fact, become pregnant can be seen as God's "joke" on her and Abraham, but it is a joke that teaches the folly of doubting God's promises and God's transcendent power. Appropriately, they name their son Isaac, which means, "He laughs."[5]

Some scholars argue that several of the most memorable teaching images used by Jesus in the Christian New Testament would have been perceived as clever or witty by his audience. For example, Jesus said, "It is easier for a camel to go through the eye of a needle than for someone who is rich to enter the kingdom of God." He also used clever imagery to remind people not to judge one another: "Why do you see the speck in your neighbor's eye, but do not notice the log in your own eye?"[6]

A humorous story in the Qur'an involves the prophet Yusuf, who has been sold into slavery, and his owner's wife. The woman has attempted to seduce the irresistibly handsome Yusuf and is being chided by her friends. As the women are gathered together, cutting fruit in preparation for a party, Yusuf unexpectedly arrives. The woman's friends are so awestruck by his appearance that they accidentally begin cutting their hands instead—revealing their own susceptibility to the very passions that they had criticized in their friend.

The presence of humor in the textual traditions of southern and eastern Asia is much more palpable than that in the Abrahamic traditions. One of the most venerated texts in philosophical Daoism is the *Zhuangzi*. It is also, arguably, the most deeply humorous text in all of religious literature. One famous story from the collection involves a man who dreams he is a butterfly, flying around happily, and completely unaware he is a man. After he awakens, he isn't sure whether he is a man who has dreamed he was a butterfly or a butterfly now dreaming he is a man. The story joins a memorable image with a lighthearted tone in order to pose an important question about how we know what we know. This humorous tone pervades the *Zhuangzi* and is not only a useful tool to convey a serious message but also a fundamental part of the message itself.

Among the most important Indian Buddhist literary works is the *Jataka*, a collection of tales about the past lives of Siddhartha Gautama, the Buddha.

These stories, many of which feature the Buddha's previous incarnations as various animals, often have a jovial quality and always have a clear moral. As is appropriate to their original

Mischievous "baby Buddha" figurines, popular in eastern Asia, from the Mu Ryang Sa Korean Buddhist Temple in Honolulu, Hawai'i. (Photo by David J. Cooper)

oral format, the stories communicate Buddhist ideas and values in a simple and memorable way that is designed to reach a broad audience. Although most of the stories would not offend the sensibilities of the modern reader, some contain what might be called "dirty" humor—humor with sexual or scatological themes, which is not uncommon in the religious literatures of southern and eastern Asia.

For example, in a story that takes place during the lifetime before the one in which he became enlightened, the Buddha was born as a brahmin who was very devoted to the practice of austerities. Every day, as he sat on the banks of the Ganges in contemplation, mastering the perfection of patience, a rambunctious monkey came along, stuck his prick in the ear of the Buddha-to-be and fucked away as the consummately detached Buddha-to-be remained calm and tranquil. One day a tortoise, crawling out of the river to have a nap in the sun, fell asleep with its mouth open. The randy chimp, seeing the open mouth of the tortoise, promptly jumped off the head of the Buddha-to-be and quickly treated himself to some fellatio. Thus rudely awakened, the tortoise bit down on the monkey's prick. Screaming with pain, holding the tortoise that refused to loosen its grip on his penis, the monkey hopped about, howling for help. The Buddha-to-be emerged from his deep meditation and laughed at the monkey. "Who is this wandering around holding a begging bowl? Is it a brahmin seeking offerings of food or a monk collecting alms?" The monkey cried out, "Help! I'm a fool! Please! Release me!"

As the translator of this passage explains, this is not simply a dirty joke. Rather, it is a parable, an illustration of the truths that desire, especially sexual desire, is the fundamental cause of suffering and that beings seek refuge and release from suffering. The story continues, with a rare joke by the Buddha.

"The tortoise is a member of the Kassapa clan, and the monkey is a member of the Koṇḍañña clan. Between the two clans intermarriage is permissible. Now that the marriage has been consummated, you, Mr. Tortoise, can let him go." The monkey freed his prick as soon as the tortoise laughed.[7]

While illustrating the predicament of beings trapped in the cycle of suffering, the story also shows the Buddha, even in his not-yet-enlightened state, to be alarmingly imperturbable, as well as forgiving and selfless. Most important, he is one to whom beings can go to end their suffering.

Popular literary forms can effectively transmit a message to an otherwise uninterested audience. This is the point of a humorous Jain story that addresses an apparent contradiction within the tradition: that despite an ascetic ideal in which romantic love is viewed as a hindrance, there exists a profusion of love stories. In the story, a merchant, concerned about the company his son is keeping, entrusts him to a Jain monk.

While pretending to listen to the monk's sermons the son instead counts the monk's Adam's apple as it goes in and out 108 times. The disappointed father sends him to another monk. This time the son counts a train of 108 ants entering their dwelling hole. . . . Then the son is entrusted to the care of a third monk. This monk begins his sermons with fascinating stories about women. The young man is entranced and begins visiting this monk regularly; in the course of time he comes to accept religious vows. The desired effect was thus created in the young mind.[8]

Through humor, an incongruity is both acknowledged and resolved, subsumed in and contained by the language of the authoritative Jain tradition.

Jokes can also be an effective, if less stable, means of conveying values and norms. The Jewish tradition has a rich history of joke-telling. Jewish jokes express a range of experiences and points of view befitting a group whose members are not only and not always religious in identification but ethnic and cultural as well. Sometimes these jokes are ambiguous enough that the message is evident only in the precise context of their telling. Consider the following joke.

Yossel stops in at Rabinovitch's shop and orders a pair of pants from him. "But it's on one condition: that you deliver the pants to me tomorrow evening. I need them; I'm about to set out on a trip. Otherwise I'll go to Hirschberg."

"Count on me. I give you my word of honor that you will have them tomorrow evening."

But Rabinovitch is lazy and forgets his customer's order. Two years later, he remembers, hurriedly makes the pants and rushes off to deliver them. Yossel looks very displeased:

"Rabinovitch, you're some tailor! It takes you two years to make a pair of pants, while God needed only six days to create the world!"

"Yossel, please, don't compare me to God: take a look at the world, and just look at these pants!"[9]

The ambiguity of this joke is such that, depending on its interpretation, it can be as seen as reflecting the values of two deeply divergent streams of Jewish thought. According to one set of values, the appropriate attitude of humans toward God is one of submission and "worshipful reverence."[10] This is put forward, in particular, in the book of Job. From this perspective, one laughs at the tailor, taking his statement in the punch line as "outrageously arrogant" in its "lack of respect for God, just as it is a clever move in a purely tactical sense."[11] From another perspective, however, the tailor's statement has a resonance (despite its self-serving purpose); it fits into what one scholar calls "the more radical current of Judaism," allowing or approving complaint against God.[12] This reflects a tradition that traces its beginnings to Abraham's righteous argument with God over his plans to destroy Sodom. Such complaints center on the difficulty of reconciling the prevalence of injustice in the world with the idea that God punishes evil and rewards good. This stream of Jewish tradition affirms the value of holding God to the standards of justice that he has decreed for human beings and asserts the people's right to maintain independent judgment, even against God. Thus, people within either stream of thought can understand the joke as

affirming values that they believe are central to the Jewish tradition.

Another joke about God is even more malleable and can be found in both Jewish and Christian versions. A Christian version of the joke follows.

A flood was on its way, forcing everyone to evacuate. The police rowed up to the most pious woman in town and said, "Ma'am, you have to leave this house! People are dying out here!" The woman replied, "No, I'm not leaving. God has always helped me before, and he will do it again." As the water started to rise, she went to the second story of her house. Another boat came by, and the captain yelled, "Ma'am, you have to get on this boat or you're going to drown!" The woman replied again, "No, God helped me before, and he will do it again." The water rose even higher. This time she went to the top of the roof, where a helicopter came and hovered overhead. The pilot called into his loudspeaker, "Please climb aboard, ma'am. You are going to drown!" The woman sniffed and again replied, "God is going to save me!" But the water rose higher, and soon she drowned. She went to heaven, and there she asked God, "Why didn't you save me, O Lord?" God replied, "I *did* help—I sent you two boats and a helicopter!"[13]

Another version of the same joke is framed in a Jewish context: the woman is replaced by a rabbi; the rabbi argues with God, asking him how he could have let this happen to him when he kept his *mitzvot*; and God throws in some Yiddish: "You *shmuck*! I sent three boats!"[14] The joke's easy adaptability to both Christian and Jewish traditions reflects overlapping values on the subject of God's intervention in the world.

Humor not originally intended to convey a religious message—even humor that criticizes a religious message—can sometimes be used by religious teachers for their own purposes. A curious example is *The Brick Testament*, a website featuring elaborate re-creations of select biblical stories made entirely out of Legos®. Created by a self-described "atheist on a mission from God," *The Brick Testament* focuses, in particular, on the most violent biblical stories. In these scenes, the contrast between the cuteness of the children's toys and the graphic violence that they are used to show creates an ironic dissonance that calls into question, among other things, the notion that children learn good lessons from the Bible. Introducing "God Wreaks Havoc," a depiction of scenes from 1 Kings, the website's creator writes,

> In our latest set of five new illustrated stories, we find God regularly and repeatedly stepping into the course of human events. Is it to cure diseases, alleviate needless suffering, and bring peace to Earth? Heavens, no. God only meddles in human affairs for the important stuff, like doling out punishments of the most brutal sort when people choose to worship other gods or simply worship him in the wrong manner.[15]

And yet, even though some Christian groups regard these creations as blasphemous, a number of others have actually used *The Brick Testament* to get young people interested in learning biblical stories (echoing the tale of the Jain monk).

HUMOR AS A SIGN OF TRANSCENDENCE

Besides being a tool useful for teaching the principles and values of religion, humor also functions as a sign of transcendence, indicating the presence of sacred or extraordinary qualities in the founders, prophets, divine beings, and saints of different religious traditions.[16]

Notwithstanding the typically sober personalities of most religious founding figures or prophets, instances of humor or laughter among such figures can provide insight into a tradition. The uniqueness of Zarathustra (c. thirteenth century BCE), founder of the Zoroastrian religion, was demonstrated at his birth: he was said to have been the only child ever born laughing instead of crying. Appropriately, he would one day teach that "laughter and joy belong to God, and tears and grief to the Devil."[17]

Similarly, anecdotes about the laughter of Muhammad (570–632) illustrate the warmth of his personality, an admirable trait befitting a prophet of Allah. In one story, he laughs so hard that his molars are visible. In another, Muhammad and his wife laugh joyfully, entertained by a little girl who visits and plays children's games in their presence. When the girl unexpectedly becomes ill and dies, Muhammad leads her funeral prayer, praying to Allah to "make her laugh heartily" as she used to make him and his wife laugh.[18]

Humorous depictions of the gods in religious traditions are varied. The laughter of God in the monotheistic traditions of Judaism, Christianity, and Islam, where the chasm between the human and divine is vast, seems to be almost exclusively the scornful laughter of a clearly superior being, aimed at foolishly arrogant and disobedient children. Polytheistic traditions seem to have an easier time with jovial or even trickster gods, perhaps because a pluralistic conception of the divine allows for distinct and varied personalities—a broader range of godly behavior.

For example, the Greek cult and mythology of Dionysus, the god of laughter, was naturally full of an ecstatic, celebratory kind of humor. In the Daoist tradition, the eccentricity and unconventional behavior of the Eight Immortals serve as markers of their divinity. In the Hindu pantheon, the juxtaposition of divinity and humor is common and multidimensional. The mischievous humor of Krishna as a baby, for example, becomes an endearing focal point for his devotees' affectionate worship. In one story, Krishna, who has a reputation as a butter thief, is suspected of having eaten dirt, though he denies it. His mother goes to check his mouth, preparing to scold him. He responds by laughing. While his mouth is open, his mother sees that the dirt in his mouth has become the Earth, the butter he stole has become the sacred Mount Kailash, and the milk he sneaked has become the cosmic Ocean of Milk. The entire universe is contained inside the mouth of a mischievous child. The story relates the paradox of incarnation: transcendence that is both contained within and yet beyond our world and its structures.[19]

A similar paradox, and a tension between order and chaos, emerges in the lives and stories of many of the most notably humorous saints. If the standard saints are marked by otherworldliness and heroic moral virtue, humorous saints are often marked by an otherworldliness that is disguised as worldliness, eccentricity, or even madness. Their humor can be seen as a sign of their transcendence—their embodiment of the chaos of the divine in the midst of our mundane world and conventional religiosity. The humorous saint often plays between these two worlds, the conventional and the ultimate.

Saints are frequently associated with mystical experiences; in some cases, these experiences are punctuated by laughter. Often in a flash, the saint sees beyond the superficial (such as language, norms, and worldly distinctions) and grasps the essential (which is often beyond words). When this happens, the "ah-ha" moment becomes a "ha-ha" moment. The saint gets the cosmic joke.

The Zen Buddhist tradition abounds with such stories.

There is the story of the enlightenment of Shuilao . . . at the hands or rather the feet of his master Matsu. . . . He asked, "What is the meaning of Daruma's coming from the West?" Matsu immediately gave him a kick in the chest and knocked him down. Shuilao became enlightened, got up, and clapping his hands, laughed aloud. Taihui tells us that when Shuilao was asked what his enlightenment was, he answered, "Since the master kicked me, I have not been able to stop laughing."[20]

As the Japanese Zen master Hakuin Ekaku (c. 1685–1768) said, "Those who understand jokes are many; those who understand true laughter are few"; the deeper the enlightenment, the deeper and more overflowing the laughter.[21] In the same vein, the great Sufi poet Jalal al-Din Rumi (1207–1273) wrote of a God-intoxicated, ego-dissolving laughter.

> I laugh like a flower
> not just a mouth-laughter.
> From non-being I burst forth
> with gaiety and mirth
> but Love taught me
> another way of laughter.
> The neophyte laughs
> According to profit and gain.
> Like a shell, I laugh when broken.[22]

The often radical reorientation resulting from mystical experience may show itself in unconventional behavior. In the Zen tradition, the eccentric master is so common as to be almost conventional. The Zen master's dramatic, iconoclastic actions are intentionally shocking—paradoxical punch lines that are designed to jolt a student into awakening, beyond attachment to words and concepts. One master burned a Buddha statue to keep warm, another is depicted tearing up the sacred Scriptures, and still another, when asked by a disciple, "What is the Buddha?" responded, "A dried shit-stick!"[23]

Great Zen masters also frequently mock themselves, lest students become attached to the idea of their teacher as a "Great Zen Master." Hakuin painted an odd-looking self-portrait, accompanied by the following poem.

Loathed by a thousand buddhas in the realm
   of a thousand buddhas,
hated by demons among the troops of demons,
this foul-smelling blind bald-head
appears again on someone's piece of paper.

Damn![24]

We find an analogous lack of concern with worldly convention and status among the *zaddik* of the Hasidic Jewish tradition. The Baal Shem Tov (Israel ben Eliezer [1700–1760]), the tradition's founder, was considered something of a "holy fool" for his radical rejection of formality and elitism in favor of a relationship with God marked by simple joy.

One Yom Kippur, an illiterate shepherd boy entered the synagogue where Israel Ba'al Shem Tov . . . was praying. The boy was deeply moved by the service, but frustrated that he could not read the prayers. He started to whistle, the one thing he knew he could do beautifully, as an offering to God. The congregation was horrified at the desecration of their service. Some people yelled at the boy, and others wanted to throw him out. The Ba'al Shem Tov immediately stopped them. "Until now," he said, "I could feel our prayers being blocked as they tried to reach the heavenly court. The young shepherd's whistling was so pure, however, that it broke through the blockage and brought all our prayers straight up to God."[25]

The Daoist sage Zhuangzi (c. 370–286 BCE) likewise joyfully rejected the norms of his own time and place. His refusal to get ahead in Confucian society is one of the fundamental themes running through his work. His playful "obsolescence" carries both spiritual and political messages and inspired the nonconformity of drunken poets such as Ruan Ji (210–263), one of the Seven Sages of the Bamboo Grove. The Hindu saint Chaitanya (c. 1485–1533) also rejected social norms. In states of ecstatic devotion to Krishna, he mimicked his god, playing children's games and crawling around like a baby.

In some instances, saints' actions defy not only social norms but also the conventional ethical standards of their traditions. This is particularly true of the so-called crazy saints of the Tibetan and Zen Buddhist traditions.

The Japanese Zen master Ikkyu Sojun (1394–1481) referred to himself as "Crazy Cloud." Yet, "in the paradoxical reasoning of Zen, opposites often trade places"; by calling himself crazy, he "asserted his sanity in a world gone mad."[26] His poems allude to masturbation and, frequently, to sex, often with prostitutes. He also employed scatological imagery: "The scriptures from the start have been toilet paper" and, "The dog pisses on the sandalwood old Buddha Hall,"[27] in order to question "the conventional distinction between the sacred and the profane."[28] In one story, he is invited to perform an "eye-opening" ceremony for a statue of the *bodhisattva* Jizo.

Without further ado, Ikkyū climbed right up the ladder, and from the level of Jizō's head he began to piss all over the place. It was like the waterfall of Mount Lu Shan. Soon all the offerings were thoroughly soaked, and as this veritable flood ceased Ikkyū told them, "So much for an eye-opening," and set off rapidly toward the east. The locals, mad at him, ran after him, while some lay-nuns started washing the image. They worked themselves into a strange frenzy, and went after Ikkyū to ask him to repeat the ceremony. Instead, he gave them his loincloth and told them to tie it around Jizō's head, because it would cure ills instantly. And so they did.[29]

The Tibetan Buddhist tradition also includes stories of transgressive saints with a penchant for bizarre but effective displays of miraculous powers. Among the Tibetan Buddhist *nyönpa* ("mad") lamas, the "misbehavior" of the saints reaches a radical extreme. This is particularly true of Drukpa Kunley (1455–1529), whose tales of sexual and drunken exploits are enjoyed throughout the Tibetan Buddhist world. As he journeys from town to town, Drukpa Kunley sings spontaneously composed, bawdy songs that mock all aspects of religious life and culture and, in particular, monks and scholars. He seduces countless virgins and "subdues" demons with his "flaming thunderbolt of wisdom," that is, his enormous, magical penis.[30] Even the most extreme taboos are not off limits. In one story, he seduces his own mother. However, his "crazy" actions are always shown to be wise and usually result in the spiritual awakening of his "victims." For example, women who sleep with him invariably become enlightened. In one tale, startlingly reminiscent of Ikkyu's "eye-opening" ceremony, Drukpa Kunley "blesses" a precious religious scroll painting for a woman by defecating on it. Outraged, she nevertheless discovers later that the feces have turned to gold and that he has conferred not only a blessing but also a miracle.

Perhaps to contain any potentially anarchic ethical or social implications, traditional stories of such saints often include a "do not try this at home" caveat. In the stories previously described, the miracles of the saints make it clear that they are not ordinary people committing immoral actions. Further, the saints themselves explicitly discourage others—even other religious aspirants—from mimicking their behavior. In one story, one of Ikkyu's disciples

tried to follow in his iconoclastic footsteps and began using pages of Scripture for toilet paper. Ikkyu questioned him,

"Do you think that you are a Buddha?"

"Yes," the disciple replied. "We are all Buddhas—you said so yourself."

"If you are a Buddha, then why use something filthy such as a sutra page for toilet paper? Doesn't a Buddha deserve something better like clean, white paper?"[31]

Ikkyu then asked the disciple to compose a poem that demonstrated his level of enlightenment. However, the disciple's verse showed that he still had far to go on the road to awakening. Ikkyu then provided a verse demonstrating a true understanding, and the disciple stopped imitating his ways.

In other traditions, we find stories of "crazy" saints for whom transgression is a means toward, not strictly an outgrowth of, saintliness. The Christian "holy fools" are an interesting example. Following St. Paul's suggestion that Christians should become "fools for Christ's sake," these holy fools feigned madness, flouting social norms and courting abuse in order to reduce their own pride and teach others through their provocations.[32] Saint Symeon of Emesa (sixth century) left his life as a monk in the desert and entered the city, where he scandalized others by dragging a dead dog through town, walking around naked, relieving himself in public, visiting women's baths, and disrupting a church service by throwing nuts at the churchgoers and extinguishing the lamps. Like Ikkyu and Drukpa Kunley, Symeon's true status as a saint is revealed through the miracles that he performs (although, in his case, they are hidden from the people of his time). Symeon's apparent inability to live up to the ethical demands even of ordinary Christians, much less clergy or saints, is in reality the complete renunciation of the superficial, programmatic piety of both layperson and cleric. Thus he "preserves his sanctity on some higher level."[33]

The full flourishing of the Christian holy fool occurred with the Russian Orthodox *yurodivy*, in particular between the fifteenth and eighteenth centuries, during which time a number of holy fools were canonized as saints. The pursuit of the *yurodivy* path eventually lost official sanction, largely because of the prevalence of "imposters," who apparently disrupted the lives of Russian Christians to an unacceptable degree. Even so, the type has continued into modern times—a powerful symbol in Russian culture, as seen, for example, in the novels of Fyodor Dostoevsky (1821–1881), especially *The Idiot* and *The Brothers Karamazov*.

In various religions, mystical or ascetic orders have prescribed certain kinds of social transgression for the purpose of spiritual development. For example, in some Sufi orders, "renunciation of society through outrageous social deviance" is a fundamental part of the path to sanctity.[34] The Malamatiyah pursued, as a group, a "path of blame" similar to that of some of the Christian holy fools. Concealing their spiritual identity to avoid pride and self-complacency, they intentionally transgressed "the limits of social and legal acceptability" while staying within the limits defined by their order.[35] Echoing Symeon, the *muwallah* ("fool of God"), Ali al-Kurdi (thirteenth century), once threw apples at the mosques in Damascus.

The Pashupatas, a Hindu ascetic sect devoted to Shiva, likewise provoked aggression by acting insane, making lewd gestures toward women, and so forth. Their purpose, however, was neither to instruct nor to hide their sanctity in order to avoid pride. Rather, they believed that, in provoking aggression and suffering the inevitable counterattacks, they could transfer their own bad karma to their "unsuspecting revilers" and receive their revilers' good karma in return.[36]

In their own time and place, the previously mentioned saints' transgressive acts (to the extent that they have a basis in historical fact) certainly would have been unsettling and even caused pain and harm. Surely, it is easier for traditions to incorporate such stories when time has provided a safe distance from the actual, disruptive events.

Over the past half century, individuals have continued to view themselves and be viewed by their followers as "holy madmen." Three recent holy madmen, Jung Kwang, Chögyam Trungpa, and Bhagwan Shree Rajneesh, have not been so easily incorporated into their respective traditions. Some people have heralded them as masters of authentic traditions of "crazy wisdom," uncompromised by the platitudes of conventional religion; others have derided them as heretics, charlatans, hypocrites, and hedonists.

Jung Kwang (1935–2002) was a Korean Son (Zen) monk and artist who described himself as a "Buddhist mop," which "gets dirty itself but makes everything it touches clean."[37] One finds echoes of Ikkyu in Jung Kwang's claim to have slept with a thousand women, in his reputation for drunkenness, and in his eccentric approach to the arts. One printed collection of Jung Kwang's work includes art that looks as though it could have been done by a child and photographs of the artist "in action" that reveal someone at play. In one case, he wears a clown nose and a bra; in another, he executes a painting while squatting over a large piece of paper, having tied the brush onto his penis.[38] His claims to the practice of "unlimited action," as an outgrowth of his enlightenment experience, are entirely consistent with his tradition's logic.[39]

Like Ikkyu, Jung Kwang discouraged others from copying him, saying that—although he believed there should always be a few like himself, "to remind people of their habits and patterns"—one who is "not ready" to undertake these practices will find them "draining" and will "fade and grow ill within a few weeks." He said, "I have practiced 'unlimited action' for years and I am always rested. Had I pretended, I would have died long ago."[40]

Is Jung Kwang's "unlimited action" the equivalent of Ikkyu's urinating on a statue of Jizo, or of Ikkyu's disciple's use of pages of Scripture for toilet paper? Although these acts may seem interchangeable, within the context of the tradition's ethical framework, the chasm between them is vast. Some embraced Jung Kwang as a living Buddha, an authentic exponent of "wild Zen," maintaining the vitality of a tradition in danger of becoming stale; others regarded him as profligate. His actions resulted in his expulsion from the Chogye Order; and yet other Zen saints have been expelled from their monasteries—and sometimes their very expulsion has been taken as a sign of their authenticity.

The Tibetan Buddhist lama Chögyam Trungpa (1939–1987) and the Indian Tantric guru Bhagwan Shree Rajneesh (1931–1990) were two prominent and controversial twentieth-century exponents of the "crazy wisdom" traditions of Asia in the West. Both made conscious use of humor by telling jokes and by using humor as a theme and a tool to help bring about awakening. More than simply using humor for pedagogical ends, however, like many of the holy fools discussed previously, they "lived out" their jokes, publicly flouting accepted codes of behavior. They presented these apparent transgressions as crazy wisdom in action—evidence of their being "beyond morality." In general, their followers accepted their actions as just this, but, in both cases, concerns with the ethical behavior of these teachers eventually caused rifts within these communities. In Trungpa's case, concerns

centered on his abuse of alcohol and humiliation of and violence against students; in Rajneesh's case, the concerns were an opulent lifestyle, the sexual abuse of students, and his implication in an assortment of crimes. Critics of Trungpa and Rajneesh argued that their behavior had crossed the line, even for that of a crazy wisdom master, and that it was harmful rather than helpful. Their defenders, however, insisted that ordinary, unenlightened people are not in a position to judge an enlightened master, because what appears to be harmful may eventually be seen to be helpful. The paradox is summed up as follows.

> For his adherents, Bhagwan's habit of saying one thing one day, and something completely different the next, revealed the relativity of truth and their master's superior outlook. . . . His critics saw it differently: "Rather than be caught out by any criticism, he [Bhagwan] calls his behavior deliberate, a joke or a test or a trick. How can he lose? Simply by allowing himself to be called God, he inspires the double-edged perception that, while God would never do such a thing, who but God would have the gall?"[41]

In these recent cases, we do not yet know how these figures will be regarded by their traditions in the future—whether they will be seen as figures who enlivened their traditions with an authentic and holy chaos, fitting into the crazy saint model, or as imposters, or self-deluded men, who do not fit within their tradition's moral framework. In these and other cases, the profane humor and outrageous behavior of the holy fools confront religious communities with this conundrum: When they cross the line, is it comic or tragic?

HUMOR AS A RELEASE VALVE

In the previous section, we examined the sacred disguised as the profane. Here we investigate how religious traditions incorporate the truly profane into their sacred structures. The "release-valve" theory of humor is helpful for understanding why religions might sanction the ludic "violation of taboos," "reversals of language and action," and "ubiquitous obscenity."[42] According to this theory, on both personal and social levels, humor is cathartic, providing the release of pent-up aggressive or sexual energies and permitting the restoration and reinforcement of order. Humor's cathartic effects may be particularly necessary in the religious context, where, generally, much is repressed. Here we explore how religious traditions have used the "carefully circumscribed expression of prohibited impulses" to prevent the serious disruption of the sacred and social order.[43] In particular, we focus on three common religious phenomena that follow this pattern: the trickster tale, the ritual of reversal, and the ludic festival. We also discuss a historical circumstance in which such humor failed to fulfill its release-valve social function and became a legitimate threat to social order.

Trickster is a term that has been applied to a wide variety of figures who appear in the oral (and sometimes written) lore of many cultures: some are mythical, some historical; some human, some animal, some shape-shifting; some associated with the sacred, and some seen as opposing the sacred. They are consistent only in that they are almost always hard to pin down. The general trickster type is a socially marginal character who, motivated by selfish impulses, breaks social taboos and uses wit and deception in pursuit of his dubious goals. One scholar describes the trickster's social function in this way.

> By breaking the patterns of a culture the trickster helps define those patterns. By acting irresponsibly he helps define responsibility. He threatens, yet he teaches, too. He throws doubt on realities but helps concentrate attention on realities. He crosses supposedly unbreak-

able boundaries between culture and nature, life and death, and thereby draws attention to those boundaries. Not only do societies "tolerate" trickster tales, but they also "create and re-create" them . . . because they serve the vital purpose of questioning and affirming, casting doubt and building faith upon the most important social concepts.[44]

Ananse the spider, the Akan (West African) trickster, follows this pattern. He is related to the supreme being, Nyame, but undermines Nyame's authority and frequently attempts to imitate him or "usurp his prerogatives" (occasionally succeeding).[45] He is also relentlessly antagonistic toward the rules of Akan society. Generally, he demonstrates his antagonism by hatching deceptive schemes to further his own greedy self-interest—at the expense of others and the proper functioning of the community. He even breaks the trust of others during a famine: while others starve, he hoards food. When he finds a magic pot that produces food, he refuses to share, even with his own family. His actions, however, play out against the backdrop of a fairly well-functioning society. "While Ananse is stealing, his neighbors are cooperating; while Ananse is scheming, his neighbors are planting their crops; while Ananse is violating rules, his neighbors are obeying them."

> Ananse threatens societal order . . . the other characters in the stories maintain order. Ananse creates doubt about the permanence and power of Akan institutions; the other characters reaffirm faith in them. Ananse breaks the people's rules, but the rules still stand. In regard to the Akan people as in regard to Nyame, Ananse is the exception who probes and proves the rules.[46]

In addition to their frequent appearance in the traditional mythology of many African societies, trickster figures have been integral to the mythology of many Native North and South American communities. For example, in North America, trickster stories involving Coyote are told among communities in much of the western United States; tales of Raven are found on the northwestern coast. Tricksterlike figures have also featured variously—and often precariously—as either integrated with, or antagonistic to, the religious and social worlds in other broad cultural spheres. Examples include Nasruddin/Juha in the Islamic world, Sun Wukong (Monkey) in eastern Asia, Narada in the Hindu world, and Maui in the Pacific.

Human characters similar to tricksters also appear within the context of ritual or religious performance; these performers behave in ways that comically reverse or mock the sacred proceedings. For example, in the southwestern United States, the Hopi *paiyakyamu* are ceremonial clowns, known for their "pranks, jokes, wild behavior, and indecent acts."[47] Wearing horns and painted with black-and-white stripes, their reversed behavior and speech "direct social attention and action," placing them "in the position of keepers of Hopi tradition."[48] While sacred *kachinas* perform proper religious ceremonies, the *paiyakyamu* stand alongside, making fun of them and burlesquing the rituals themselves. To demonstrate the absurdity of gluttony, they wildly gobble watermelon, throwing it everywhere and never sharing. Theirs is an upside-down, disordered world: they descend ladders headfirst; they "arrange themselves in two facing lines and tie their penises together, engaging in a tug of war."[49] By showing "life as it should *not* be lived," they amuse and affirm the need for tradition.[50]

A similar phenomenon occurs in a variety of cultural contexts, from the street masquerades of the *kaka* ("shit-devils") of Sierra Leone, to the theatrical performances of the *komali* of Tamil Nadu, in southern India.[51] Contrasted with performers who demonstrate the "heroic" mode, these figures use grotesque and humorous exaggeration to embody all that their communities reject.

In the ludic festival, we find a similar dynamic, but with a much more wide-ranging level of participation. Often, ludic festivals mark periods in the religious calendar that, although not unimportant, are not the most sacred of days. In contrast to the specialized performance of the ritual clown or the individual telling of a trickster tale, ludic festivals feature periods of license among a large number of people and are fraught with tension between chaos and order. The potential for social disruption is not always just a joke. Such festivals have been the scenes of sexual transgression (orgies, transvestism, etc.), scatological profanation and blasphemy, drunkenness, and the like.

Ludic festivals can be found even among communities described as fundamentalist (highly controlled, "totalizing" communities that monitor every aspect of life). One striking example is the celebration of Purim among Jewish "fundamentalists" in Israel. Purim commemorates the deliverance of the Jewish community in ancient Persia from a plot to destroy it. The festival is celebrated with masquerades, the performance of humorous plays, and drinking to intoxication. During Purim, there is license "not only for raucousness, but for challenging that which is sanctified." So, even though the "injunction to joy" is taken seriously, it is strictly supervised. The "outburst" is institutionalized.[52] For example, among some ultra-Orthodox communities, men may not masquerade as women. In other contexts, certain subjects are deemed off-limits for parody: students may not mimic their rabbis at the pulpit, nor may anyone mock "ludicrous halakhic decisions."[53] One member of a group of fundamentalist Israeli settlers used the occasion to mock an opposing Israeli group.

N., one of their leaders, came to synagogue on Purim wearing jeans, John Lennon glasses, and a T-shirt emblazoned with the symbol of Peace Now, the left-wing group diametrically opposed to Jewish fundamentalism. True to his masquerade, N. appeared for prayers without a skullcap on his head. After the initial shock at his daring, it turned out that he was wearing a wig, so that he could appear to be bare-headed and yet be head-covered at the same time.[54]

Festivals that license otherwise unorthodox and even outrageous behavior, or allow status reversals in which those of lower and higher status temporarily switch places, occur in a wide range of religious traditions. The Hindu festival of Holi features temporary status reversals. For example, subordinate people are given license to "attack" their superiors with colored water. The Islamic festival of Mawlid, marking the birth of Muhammad, is sometimes celebrated in a carnival atmosphere, particularly in Cairo. Losar, the festival celebrating the Tibetan Buddhist new year, was at one time a period of extreme public transgression, reportedly including monks fornicating in the streets. All of these festivals have, to varying degrees and for different reasons, been subject to criticism and control.

As mentioned previously, humor as a release valve always involves what would be transgressive behavior under normal circumstances, so it is particularly susceptible to crossing the line and bursting out of the ordering frame. Criticism of such behavior, often made on the grounds that the ethical or sacred has been truly violated and/or that the humor has become too pointed or politically provocative, sometimes results in attempts to curtail excesses, or in outright bans. In such cases, the humor may be seen not as letting off steam but as blasphemy or even as a catalyst for revolutionary activity.

This was sometimes an issue with the medieval Christian Carnival, a festive season of excess and transgression that immediately preceded the Lenten season of repentance and prohibitions. As with many such festivals, Carnival allowed for the inversion of social and religious norms: the powerful and holy were satirized by the lower classes; scatological aggression, sexual debauchery, and drunkenness were common. At the conclusion of this period of inversion and chaos, which was intended both to give vent to aggression and remind one of the need for structure, order was reestablished. The Feast of Fools, held in churches at the beginning of the Carnival season, is a particularly vivid example of the precarious balance between being "social criticism in disguise and being an instrument for social control."[55] Led by lower-level clergy, the feast's antirites were described as follows by an outraged Theological Faculty of Paris in 1445.

> Priests and clerks may be seen wearing masks and monstrous visages at the hours of office. They dance in the choir dressed as women, panders or minstrels. They sing wanton songs. They eat black puddings at the horn of the altar while the celebrant is saying mass. They play dice there. They cense with stinking smoke from the soles of old shoes. They run and leap through the church, without a blush at their own shame. Finally they drive about the town and its theatres in shabby traps and carts; and rouse the laughter of their fellows and the bystanders in infamous performances with indecent gestures and verses scurrilous and unchaste.[56]

The Roman Catholic Church attempted to control or ban the Feast of Fools for centuries, with little success. On a variety of levels, the threat to the authority of the church and to the broader social order was a concern; chaos always seemed in danger of spilling over. In fact, between 1500 and 1800, there were a number of instances in which what began as Carnival ended in bloody revolt.

The minor clergy, however, defended the order-preserving function of such festivals, offering an explicitly release-valve theory of humor, using their own distinctive metaphor. Such festivals were necessary, they argued, "so that foolishness, which is our second nature and seems to be inherent in man might freely spend itself at least once a year. Wine barrels burst if from time to time we do not open them and let in some air."[57]

HUMOR AS A WEAPON

The use of humor as a weapon—that is, the use of humor to express criticism—is frequently just below the surface of each of the other types of humor (and especially the transcendent and release-valve types). Humor used within religious communities to attack or criticize has appeared in a wide range of forms, from scholastic polemics to informal jokes. With such humor, boundaries are sharply drawn between those who get it and those who don't. Whether boundaries are being defended or challenged, they are engaged in a way that is relatively straightforward; the position of the joker is more clear and purposeful, perhaps, than in any of the former humor types. In response to pointed humor, one is compelled to choose sides—by laughing or remaining serious—so one is often in the position of being included or excluded, of judging or being judged. To justify what might otherwise be considered malicious or, at least, distasteful, satirical humor often assumes a moral high ground, by presuming to attack vice, corruption, and ignorance rather than individuals or groups themselves. Here, we examine the use of such humor directed at those of one's own religion (internally directed); directed toward elements outside one's own religion (externally directed); and as a mediating force with respect to religion in a broader social context.

We begin with internally directed religious humor. First, we discuss mocking criticism of coreligionists, whose deviations threaten the tradition. Second, and with an opposite effect on religious boundaries, we explore satirical critiques of the tradition's authoritative elements.

Humor used to punish deviance is an old and widespread feature of religious communities. Its effectiveness as a means of social control hinges on the dynamics of social superiority and inferiority. As one scholar argues, "We all dislike—even fear—being laughed at, precisely because we associate this with being in a position of inferiority. Laughter can therefore act as a very powerful 'social corrective': a weapon society can use to restrain those insufficiently flexible to adapt to whatever it demands of them."[58]

An example of such derisive humor can be seen in Western religious traditions. In parts of the pre-Christian Mediterranean and Europe, as in pre-Islamic Arabia, there was a link between satire and magic. Satire was thought to be a powerful force, closely related to the curse and capable of destroying the well-being and even the lives of the satirist's victims. In the Jewish, Christian, and Islamic traditions, in which God is seen as intervening in history, the prophet's role as a conveyor of God's message has been crucial. Frequently, the prophets convey God's angry judgment against his people, who have deviated from his commandments or his will in specific ways. The prophets often express such messages through derisive criticism, laughter, and ironic mockery. Most of the examples of laughter in the Abrahamic Scriptures are of this sort.

In the Hebrew Bible, shared by the Jewish and Christian traditions, both God and "the righteous" laugh at the unrighteous: "the LORD laughs at the wicked, for he sees that their day is coming" and "the righteous . . . will laugh at the evildoer." Contemptuous laughter is deemed an appropriate response to the unrighteous, who ignore the counsel of the prophets. Lest the unrighteous get any ideas about laughing at the righteous, the story of the prophet Elisha serves as a useful warning. As the prophet enters the city of Bethel, he is greeted with jeers from a group of children, who yell, "Go away, baldhead! Go away, baldhead!" Not to be mocked, Elisha curses them "in the name of the Lord," and two she-bears immediately come out of the woods and maul forty-two of them.[59]

In today's Abrahamic communities, the threat of bears may not be needed—a critical joke may be enough to make one's point. One Orthodox synagogue in Brooklyn, concerned about congregants talking during its long prayer services, sent out the following questionnaire to its members.

Please check off your own areas of interest so that we can seat you during services with people who have shared interests. Do you prefer to sit near people who

- Talk about the stock market?
- Share neighborhood gossip?
- Sit quietly and actually pray?
- Talk about sports?[60]

Satirical humor has also been an important way for religious people to criticize the official practices and institutions of their own traditions. The important role of satirical humor during the Protestant Reformation in Europe is a historically significant example. At that time, the previously discussed Carnival culture, with its coarse forms of satire against the official Roman Catholic Church, was still influential. Into this atmosphere, one of the greatest minds of his day, the theologian Desiderius Erasmus (c. 1466–1536) released *The Praise of Folly* (1509), in which he

satirized current ecclesiastical abuses. To his surprise, the book became very popular, producing strong reactions; it laid important groundwork for the Reformation—which, in fact, Erasmus did not support. Martin Luther (1483–1546), who is credited with starting the Reformation, used satirical humor, much as Erasmus had, but more explicitly in the service of reform. Luther used scatological and coarse language and imagery to attack what he viewed as the church's abuses. As his split with the church became more pronounced, his satirical attacks became more pointed. When, in 1542, a cardinal offered indulgences to those who viewed his large collection of relics, Luther responded with an unsigned pamphlet advertising a mock exhibition. The pamphlet, which was widely circulated, promised the opportunity to view newly discovered relics and receive "a special indulgence offered by Pope Paul II." Among the relics:

- A nice section from Moses's left horn.
- Three flames from the burning bush on Mount Sinai.
- Two feathers and an egg from the Holy Spirit.
- A remnant of the flag with which Christ opened hell.
- A large lock of Beelzebub's beard, stuck on the same flag.
- One-half of the archangel Gabriel's wing.
- A whole pound of the wind that roared by Elijah in the cave of Mount Horeb.
- Two ells [about ninety inches] of sound from the trumpets on Mount Sinai.
- Thirty blasts from the trumpets on Mount Sinai.
- A large heavy piece of the shout with which the children of Israel tumbled the walls of Jericho.
- Five nice strings from the harp of David.[61]

Unlike Erasmus's criticism, Luther's criticism of "us" became a criticism of "them." The Protestant tradition that followed has included a number of important satirists who critiqued elements of their own tradition from a religious perspective. For example, Søren Kierkegaard (1813–1855) humorously mocked the complacency of his Danish Lutheran Church. A contemporary example of self-critical Protestant humor is the popular *Wittenburg Door*, a magazine founded in 1971 by an evangelical Protestant in the United States who was "hoping to provoke reform—or at least self-awareness . . . (by) poking fun at the hypocrisy and failings of the Christian church from the inside."[62]

In contrast to internally directed critical humor, externally directed critical humor aims its barbs at other religious groups, their institutions, or their individual members. Such attacks on other traditions are extremely common in the history of religion and seem to be found wherever distinct religious traditions or sects come into contact with one another. Externally directed critical humor is found in a wide range of contexts and genres, and its effects are twofold. Internally, satirically attacking "them" serves to solidify group identity and cohesion, using exaggeration and stereotyping to assert "our" superiority and "their" inferiority. Because the reference is external, the internal effect is social control—one's tradition is defended against a perceived threat. In defining "us" versus "them," a group also defines the central and superior elements that make "us" "us" and "them" "them." In some cases, "our" opposition to "them" is itself an essential part of a group's identity. In this sharply drawn model of "us," an internal deviant runs the risk of being mocked as one of "them." Externally, rhetorical battles of this type attract adherents, political influence, or patronage; they may also assert power over or defame another group; or defend a group that is "under attack."

Such critical humor seems to surface wherever there are boundaries to be drawn. In geographical regions where multiple religions or sects coexist, there are long traditions of critical humor between groups. The Catholic-Protestant polarity has provided countless critical jokes through the centuries. The Chinese cultural mix of Confucianism, Daoism, and Buddhism has likewise produced many centuries of satiric humor from all sides. Also, the trio of dominant religions in early India (Hindu, Buddhist, and Jain) produced an enormous amount of satire.

In one story, an apparently austere Indian Buddhist monk reveals his true colors to an innocent questioner.

"Why are your robes so long and loose?"
"Because I use them as a net for the catching of fish."
"You eat fish?"
"Yes, for fish with my liquor is a most savory dish."
"You drink booze?"
"Yes, but just when I'm out with whores pursuing my pleasure."
"You go to whores?"
"Yes, after thrashing my enemies, just for good measure."
"You have enemies?"
"Yes, but only those whose homes I have robbed of their treasure."
"You steal?"
"Yes, to pay off the debts I've incurred with my gambling itch."
"You gamble?"
"Yes, yes, yes! I am, as you see, a real son of a bitch."[63]

Unsurprisingly, humor of this type seems to increase and intensify in politically charged climates that feature religion as a source of conflict. For example, several scholars have noted the prevalence of politically charged, religiously embedded humor on both sides of the long-standing conflict between Israelis and Palestinians.

Where deep disparities in numbers, power, or influence exist between religious groups, the social and political effects of critical humor can be significant—for example, in cases where the use of humor by a majority religious group against a minority one cements prejudice or otherwise reinforces the minority community's marginal status. The persecuted early Christians in the Roman Empire were mocked as gullible fools with ludicrous beliefs. In predominantly Christian Europe, Jewish people have been denigrated by anti-Semitic jokes, which have played a role in normalizing or even promoting the oppression of Jews by Christians. The viciously anti-Semitic cartoons of the Nazis illustrate both the propagandistic effectiveness of such humor and the brutal uses to which it can be put. In contemporary India, the popularity among majority Hindus of "Sardarji" jokes about the Sikh community has been analyzed as reflecting anxiety about both the Sikhs' economic success and the recent history of Sikh groups seeking an independent Sikh nation.[64]

Critical humor has also been used, however, by less powerful religious groups—in self-defense and for cultural survival against a dominant or imposing community. Sikhs have developed Sardarji counterjokes, and the list of Jewish jokes satirizing Christians is long and funny. Jewish jokes of this type often involve clergy.

Catholic priest: "When will you get rid of your silly and ridiculous dietary laws?"
Rabbi: "At your wedding."

Catholic priest: "Tell me, rabbi, did you ever cheat and try eating ham?"
Rabbi: "Well, to tell you the truth, I did break down once, just out of curiosity.
"Since I've confessed my experiment to you, let me ask, have you ever had a woman?"
Catholic priest: "Yes, though I hate to admit it, earlier in my career I just had to find out what it was like."
Rabbi: "A lot better than ham, no?"[65]

FEEDING FRENZY

In the Western world, satire has long been a weapon in conflicts between the religious and the antireligious. The culture wars in the United States have featured particularly heated exchanges in this regard, with conservatives, often Christian, on one side and progressives, often secular, on the other. Countless Americans have proclaimed their positions on these issues by using bumper stickers to mock the other side. One widespread example is the "Jesus fish" decal. In the 1970s, some Christians began affixing to their bumpers decals of a stick figure fish, a symbol that began as a secret identity marker used by the persecuted early Christian community in Rome. Beginning in the 1980s, the "Darwin fish" emerged, sporting legs—a symbol of evolution and a satiric critique of creationist Christians. More recently, a bigger, stronger Jesus fish has appeared—eating the Darwin fish. Not to be outdone, some Jewish motorists have entered the fray with bumpers bearing fish of the gefilte variety!

The satirical humor of the European colonial period was not limited to the proverbial colonialist scoffing at the absurd superstitions of "the natives" but also involved humor aimed in the other direction. A missionary to South Africa in the 1830s recalled with frustration that, although a group of Mfengu refugees listened patiently to his lecture on Christian beliefs about

God, immortality, the resurrection, and the last judgment, "an audible laugh instantly proceeded from all who were present" when he told them that God "had declared in his Word that man's heart was full of sin.' "[66] Another missionary in the region observed, "People in one Bechuana town laugh at Livingstone telling them about God, mimic him preaching and singing, and the chief and his councilors fill the air with shouts and yells." Another reported, in a different context, "The chief, after we left his presence, proceeded, amid the merriment of his attendants, to draw a ludicrous picture of the state of Matabele [Ndebele] society were the Christian views adopted."[67]

Christian missionaries also feature in the joke lore of Native Americans, as in the following story.

> [A missionary] was traveling from Gallup to Albuquerque in the early days. Along the way he offered a ride to an Indian who was walking to town. Feeling he had a captive audience, he began cautiously to promote his message, using a soft-sell approach.
> "Do you realize," he said, "that you are going to a place where sinners abound?"
> The Indian nodded his head in assent.
> "And the wicked dwell in the depths of their iniquities?"
> Again a nod.
> "And sinful women who have lived a bad life go?"
> A smile and another nod.
> "And no one who lives a good life goes there?"
> A possible conversion, thought the missionary, and so he pulled out his punch line: "And do you know what we call that place?"
> The Indian turned, looked the missionary in the eye, and said, "Albuquerque."[68]

Beyond the internal and external dynamics of particular religious traditions, satirical humor

relating to religion also plays an important role in broader social contexts. For example, our globalized contemporary "jokescape," increasingly connected by the Internet and mass media, includes people of all religions and none, the fanatically religious as well as the antireligious. In this sphere, satirical humor has played an important role in the negotiation of religious identities. This has been dramatically illustrated in the United States in the years since the attacks of September 11, 2001; satirical humor has been used to define "Islam" and "the West" in ways that have fostered both hatred and reconciliation.

The September 11 attacks were perpetrated by religious absolutists who viewed themselves as engaged in a violent, cosmic struggle between good and evil. In response, the Bush administration also made use of absolutist rhetoric: the United States was in a "war on terror" against "evildoers." Iraq, Iran, and North Korea constituted an "axis of evil," and the people of the world were either "with us" or "against us." This language of binary opposition, adopted by the US media, cemented caricatures on both sides.

As political events unfolded, hostile humor in the United States reflected and perpetuated this chasm between "us" (the West, Christians, Jews, freedom-loving, righteous) and "them" (Muslims, freedom-hating, terrorists). US political cartoons in the mainstream media reinforced these associations—Muslim men were frequently depicted as some combination of irrationally violent, religiously fanatical, misogynistic, and duplicitous; Muslim women were oppressed, invisible, or exotic. In 2005, the Danish newspaper *Jyllands-Posten* published twelve incendiary cartoons that not only intentionally violated the Muslim taboo against depicting Muhammad, but also portrayed him as a terrorist. This sparked outrage and violent protest by some Muslims in various parts of the world. In response to the publication of the Muhammad cartoons, the state-run Iranian newspaper, *Hamshahri*, held an "International Holocaust Cartoon Competition," highlighting what they viewed as Western hypocrisy for allowing and justifying as "free speech" blasphemy against Islam but restricting denial of the Holocaust. "Cartoon wars" had become a global phenomenon.

Sadistic humor was on display in the infamous photographs capturing laughing, joking US guards as they tortured and humiliated prisoners at Abu Ghraib in Baghdad. Although many Americans were outraged, hostile jokers such as Rush Limbaugh defended the torturers as having a "good time," calling the abuse a "brilliant maneuver."[69] In response to reports of investigations into similar stories of abuse the following year at Guantánamo Bay, Limbaugh created an elaborate parody on his website asserting that the prisoners were, if anything, being treated too well. He portrayed "Club G'itmo" as a "one-of-a-kind Muslim resort paradise," where "every check-in gets a brand new Koran and prayer rug" and is treated to "in-room dining" and "ethnically sensitive snacks."[70]

Although satirical humor has often been used as a wedge to broaden this divide between Islam and the West, it has also been used as a bridge. Caught between these two supposedly irreconcilable worlds, American Muslims found themselves on the receiving end of suspicion, hatred, and harassment, often being seen as alien and humorless, at best, or terrorists, at worst. Finding no platform from which to counter the caricatures, some turned to stand-up comedy. In 2005, four American comics with Middle Eastern backgrounds formed the Axis of Evil Comedy Tour. They achieved a good deal of success and interest among both Muslims and non-Muslims, with humor that deconstructs the us-versus-them narrative and redirects criticism at voices of distortion and division on both sides. In his performance, the Iranian-American comic Maz Jobrani expressed his frustration about one-sided news reports, asking why it is only the "crazy guys" who ever make it onto television, burning American flags and chanting "Death to America!" "Just once," he said, "I want them to be like, 'Okay, now we're gonna go to Muhammad in Iran.' And then they show some guy who's like, 'Hello, I'm Muhammad, and I'm just baking a cookie! I swear to God! No bombs, no flags, nothing. Back to you, Bob!'"[71] By voicing concerns of Muslim Americans and also painting a picture that is complex and human, these comics challenge a hard us-versus-them dichotomy. By laughing with "them," "they" become "us"; "us" is redefined and expanded.

Conclusion

The relationship between humor and religion is complex. Humor does more than just cross the line, disrupting boundaries and structures set by religious traditions; it plays among those boundaries in manifold ways—defending and attacking, defining and upholding, explaining and transforming, transgressing and transcending—a lively form of discourse engaged with living traditions. Time and again, we find humor and religion intertwined, an odd couple, always in some amusingly contorted embrace.

Glossary

Incongruity: The conjunction of dissimilar or mismatched things.

Ludic: Playful; marked by spontaneity and frivolity.

Paradox: Something apparently self-contradictory or absurd that, upon deeper investigation, may be resolved or shown as true in some way.

Satire: Humor used to criticize or ridicule; frequently makes use of exaggeration.

Transcendence: The state of going beyond or above ordinary human experience or material limitations.

Transgression: The violation of codes of behavior or recognized boundaries (commandments, laws, religious precepts, etc.). Crossing the line.

FOR FURTHER READING

Apte, Mahadev L. *Humor and Laughter: An Anthropological Approach*. Ithaca, NY: Cornell University Press, 1985.

Berger, Peter L. *Redeeming Laughter: The Comic Dimension of Human Experience*. New York: Walter de Gruyter, 1997.

Blyth, Reginald Horace. *Oriental Humour*. Tokyo: Hokuseido, 1959.

Gilhus, Ingvild Sælid. *Laughing Gods, Weeping Virgins: Laughter in the History of Religion*. London: Routledge, 1997.

Hyers, M. Conrad. *The Laughing Buddha: Zen and the Comic Spirit*. Wolfeboro, NH: Longwood Academic, 1989.

Morreall, John, ed. *The Philosophy of Laughter and Humor*. Albany: State University of New York Press, 1987.

Morreall, John. *Comedy, Tragedy, and Religion*. Albany: State University of New York Press, 1999.

Raskin, Victor, ed. *The Primer of Humor Research*. New York: Walter de Gruyter, 2008.

Rosenthal, Franz. *Humor in Early Islam*. Leiden: E. J. Brill, 1956.

Siegel, Lee. *Laughing Matters: Comic Tradition in India*. Chicago: University of Chicago Press, 1987.

Ziv, Avner, ed. *Jewish Humor*. New Brunswick, NJ: Transaction, 1998.

RELIGION AND FILM

Making Movies, Making Worlds

S. Brent Plate

O n September 1, 2008, Don LaFontaine, the disembodied, narrating voice of film trailers across the English-speaking world, died. He had an unmistakable intonation and catchphrase that filmgoers recognized without even knowing his name. In a deep voice, while images of cosmic importance lit up the theater, we heard the words: "In a world where . . ." He discussed this strategy of introducing films in an interview, not long before he died.

> "We have to very rapidly establish the world we are transporting them to," he said of his viewers. "That's very easily done by saying, 'In a world where . . . violence rules.' 'In a world where . . . men are slaves and women are the conquerors.'—you very rapidly set the scene."[1]

LaFontaine knew the secret that binds religion and cinema: *films create worlds.* The cinematic experience of watching them brings viewers into another, previously unknown, unimagined world. Films do not passively mimic or directly display what is "out there" but actively reshape elements of the lived world and twist them in new ways that are projected on-screen and given over to an audience. Which is not unlike the activities of religion.

Religions and films each create alternate worlds utilizing the raw, abstract material of space and time, bending them each in new ways and forcing them to fit particular standards and desires. Film does this through camera angles and movements, framing devices, lighting, costuming, acting, editing, and other aspects of production. Religions achieve this through setting apart particular objects and periods of time and deeming them "sacred," through attention to specially charged objects (symbols), through the telling of stories (myths), and by gathering people together to focus on some particular event (ritual). The result of both religion and film is a re-created world: a world of recreation, a world of fantasy, a world of ideology, a world we may long to live in or a world we wish to avoid at all costs. The world presented at the altar and on the screen connects a projected world to the world of the everyday. In this way, religion and film are akin. This is not to say they are equated but rather to say there are analogies that can be productively drawn between them.

My approach in this chapter is to relate the world "out there" to the re-created world on-screen and at the altar, and how these worlds mutually influence one another. The impact, furthermore, is often so great that participants do not see differences in the worlds but view them as a seamless whole. Religious worlds are so encompassing that devotees cannot understand their personal worlds any other way; filmic worlds are so influential that personal relationships can only be seen through what has already been seen on-screen. *My hypothesis is that by paying attention to the ways films are constructed, we can shed light on the ways religions are constructed, and vice versa.* Film production borrows millennia-old aesthetic tactics from religions—at the dawn of the twentieth century, filmmakers were more self-conscious about this then they are at the start of the twenty-first century—but contemporary religious practices are likewise modified by the pervasive influence film has had on modern society. This is not about "spotting the Christ figure" in the film, or finding choice sayings that could have been the words of the Buddha, or finding ethical parables that parallel ancient Jewish teachings. Instead, religion and film are sutured on a much more primal level.

To create this relationship, I play the role of editor, or perhaps of *bricoleur*, juxtaposing film theory and religious theory in order to highlight the ways both religion and film are engaged in the practice of world-*making*, and even world-*creating*. The avant-garde filmmaker Maya Deren intimates as much when she claims, "All invention and creation consist primarily of a new relationship between known parts."[2] Invention and creation do not operate by bringing something into being "out of nothing" (a troubling myth of creativity perpetuated by Christian theology and a romantic view of the modern artist alike), but of taking what is already known and creating a new relationship. There is nothing new under the sun, but there are new relationships between old substances. Along these lines, I adopt the language of the great Soviet filmmaker Sergei Eisenstein, who once wrote of the social value of "intellectual montage," in which new and revolutionary ideas might spring from the juxtaposition of previously separate images. On the other side of the disciplinary divide, I juxtapose Eisenstein with the words of religionist Wendy Doniger, who suggests of the comparative study of religion: "The comparatist, like the surrealist, selects pieces of *objets trouvés*; the comparatist is not a painter but a collagist, indeed a bricolagist (or a *bricoleur*), just like the mythmakers themselves."[3] Worlds, religious and filmic, are made up of borrowed fragments and pasted together in ever-new ways; myths are updated and transmediated, rituals reinvented, symbols morphed. By lighting up religious studies and film studies side by side, I hope to re-create the understanding of the relation between religion and film.

In the remainder of this essay, I examine the concept of world-making and re-creation from a religious studies and a film studies standpoint. Along the way, I suggest that both activities can be seen in light of the other and can offer examples of how religious myths and rituals correspond to the formal structures of filmmaking. I interject the theoretical approaches with specific examples from specific, though quite varied, films, in hopes that this will provide some grounding to the theory, and also a model for how a religious-studies-oriented approach to film might be achieved.

Cinematic-Religious World Crossings

Take One: Woody Allen's Purple Rose of Cairo and the Two-Worlds View

The attraction and promise of cinema is the way films offer glimpses into other worlds, even if only for ninety minutes at a time. We watch,

Film poster, *The Purple Rose of Cairo*

hoping to escape the world we live in, to find utopian projections for improving our world, or to heed prophetic warnings for what our world might look like if we don't change our ways and get it right. In the theater we live in one world while viewing another, catching a glimpse of "what if?"

Yet, in the practice of film viewing, these two worlds begin to collide, leaking ideas and images across the semipermeable boundaries between the world-on-screen and the world-on-the-streets. Such world-colliding activity is entertainingly exemplified in Woody Allen's 1985 film *Purple Rose of Cairo*. Here, the fluidity between the worlds is enacted when the actor named Tom Baxter (played by Jeff Daniels) steps down off the screen and enters the "real world"

in which Cecilia (Mia Farrow) sits, seeking relief from her otherwise troubled life. In Allen's film, two worlds cross and both characters are altered because of their shared desires that transcend the boundaries of the screen. Nonetheless, *The Purple Rose of Cairo* does not let go of the fact that there *is* a screen in place between Tom and Cecilia. The screen is a border that is crossable, yet there are distinctions between the two sides, for example when Tom enters Cecilia's world and takes her out for a night on the town and tries to pay for dinner with the fake prop money he has in his pocket. They eventually come to realize they live in two worlds, and a permanent connection is impossible. Of course, all this takes place *on*-screen and not in the real world per se.

Woody Allen's film, while delightfully self-referential about the experience of cinema, also tells us much about the experience of religion. Religions function like films, and vice versa. Among the myths, rituals, symbols, doctrines, sacred times and places, and ethical components of religions, the faithful are presented with alternate worlds, prescriptions for a better life, and imaginative tools for re-viewing the world as it is. Religions provide promises, warnings, and compelling narratives for behaving in particular, and often peculiar, ways. In each, there is an initial world lived in and then a secondary, projected, idealized world. In the midst of this, communities of religious adherents work out their lives betwixt and between the two worlds. Powerful stories in the form of myths keep religious imaginations inspired, while aesthetic performances in the form of rituals keep human bodies moving to a rhythm. Even so, when the story is over, when the chanter has finished and/or the lights go up, when the feast has been eaten and/or the credits run, we return to our everyday world, as Cecilia has to do. The two worlds seem to remain in a state of separation, yet there are many avenues for connection between them and transformation, however small or large scale, can occur in the oscillation between the one and the other.

II. Religious World-making

In the background of my argument are the world-making and world-maintaining processes of religion brought out in Peter Berger's now-canonic work, *The Sacred Canopy*. In this section, I provide an overview of "world-making" with regard religion and film, and later I will explore "world maintenance."

We humans, the sociologist of religion suggests, collectively create ordered worlds around us to provide us with a sense of stability and security, "in the never completed enterprise of building a humanly meaningful world."[4] Reality, like religion and like cinema, is socially constructed, allowing its members to engage with it on deeply felt, personal levels. Cultural products such as film offer conduits of significance between the individual and the cosmic order of the universe. And if culture staves off meaninglessness at the societal level, religion does so at a cosmic level by constructing a "sacred canopy" that keeps the threatening forces of chaos at bay.

Ever important is the grounding of human laws and regulations in cosmic structures. The *nomos* must be in synch with the *cosmos*. There is a dialectical, ongoing process between the human and divine realms, and it is religion that supplies the link: "Religion implies the farthest reach of man's self-externalization, of his infusion of reality with his own meanings. Religion implies that human order is projected into the totality of being. Put differently, religion is the audacious attempt to conceive of the entire universe as being humanly significant."[5] Indeed, Berger himself states that while most of history has seen religion as key to creating such

a meaningful totality, in modern times "there have been thoroughly secular attempts at cosmization."[6] Science has most importantly made the attempt, but here I am suggesting that we think about cinema as another audacious attempt. Cinema may be part of the symbol creating apparatus of culture, yet it can also aspire to more, to world-encompassing visions of the nomos and cosmos.

The philosopher Nelson Goodman similarly understands the culturally/socially constructed nature of the world, particularly as found in his book *Ways of Worldmaking*. Approaching the topic from an epistemological standpoint rather than Berger's sociological one, Goodman draws an analogy between philosophy and the arts to understand how we humans go about creating worlds around us. Goodman suggests, "Much but by no means all worldmaking consists of taking apart and putting together, often conjointly: on the one hand, of dividing wholes into parts and partitioning kinds into subspecies, analyzing complexes into component features, drawing distinctions; on the other hand, of composing wholes and kinds out of parts and members and subclasses, combining features into complexes, and making connections."[7] The activity of world creation is a process of taking things apart and putting them back together, of reassembling the raw materials available, of dissection and analysis, and of mending fragments. Such philosophical/religious activity is easily translatable in terms of filmmaking, through the framing of space through cinematography and reprojecting it on-screen, or with its partitioning of time through cuts and recombination done in the editing room.

I borrow the language of world-making from Berger and Goodman, but in the background is the work of Immanuel Kant, Émile Durkheim, and others. Meanwhile, scholar of comparative religion William Paden has synthesized many of these studies, offering evocative and accessible ways to approach both religion and film. On Paden's view, religions posit and construct their own version of "the" world through various organizing categories made up of the activities, behaviors, beliefs, language, and symbol usages of persons and communities. By looking at religious systems as "worlds," as opposed to the disembodied examination of texts and doctrines, the student of religion can come to understand the broader environmental constructions of religious practices and traditions within particular places and times.

Paden says, "Religions do not all inhabit the same world, but actually posit, structure, and dwell within a universe that is their own. . . . All living things select and sense 'the way things are' through their own organs and modes of activity."[8] "Any world," Paden states elsewhere, "is an open-ended, interactive process, filled with various and complex sensory and cognitive domains, encompassing both representation and practice, both imaginal objects and bodies-in-performance."[9] Central here are the processes of selection and organization, of an active, performative, ongoing creation of the world. Such language runs uncannily parallel to the language of film production, as each film (and, indeed, the film industry as a whole) offers specific geographies, times, languages, and personas; and is filled with many sensory details (though, unlike religion, must remain limited to sight and sound, and arguably, touch), intellectual suggestions, imaginary and "real" objects, and performing bodies.

World-making is an active engagement with the raw materials that make up what is in the strictest sense called the "earth" and with the universe. Religions and films, as two varieties of world-making enterprises, both achieve this. On the broadest and most abstract level, world-making makes use of the spaces and times that are available in the physical world, significantly incorporating common elements such as earth, air, fire, metal, wood, and water. *World-making is a performative drama in which humans are the costume designers and liturgists, scriptwriters and sermon givers, saints and cinematographers, priests and projectionists. All the world's a stage, and all worlds are stages.* The dramatic activity is what humans partake in when we attempt to make meaning of the spaces, times, and people that constitute our lives. And it is what filmmakers, artists, and religious figures offer to this human drama.

When we get to analytical descriptions of mythic and ritualistic operations, we begin to see the dramatic nature of world-making unfold. Myths and rituals assist in the creation of worlds through activities that frame, exclude, focus, organize, and re-present elements of the known world. Anthropologist Mary Douglas speaks to the function of rituals, indirectly noting the power of mythic story: "A ritual provides a frame. The marked off time or place alerts a special kind of expectancy, just as the oft-repeated 'Once upon a time' creates a mood receptive to fantastic tales. . . . Framing and boxing limit experience, shut in desired themes or shut out intruding ones."[10] Meanwhile, Paden offers this definition for the function of ritual: "The basic feature of ritual is its power of focus. . . . In ritual, what is out of focus is brought into focus. What is implicit is made explicit. All ritual behavior gains its basic effectiveness by virtue of such undivided, intensified concentration and by bracketing off distraction and interference."[11] These are not quotes from scholars directly engaged with film, but the metaphorical dimensions of framing, telling tales, creating moods, focusing, and the intensification of concentration provide fertile grounds for investigations across religion and film.

Similarly, for myth, Paden claims that it is "a definitive voice that names the ultimate powers that create, maintain, and re-create one's life," and that it works by "organizing and presenting reality in a way that makes humans not just conceivers but respondents and partakers."[12] I am not suggesting these brief examples are comprehensive definitions of these terms but am rather introducing the ways myth and ritual participate in the larger process of world-making. As should be somewhat apparent, myths and rituals operate like films: they utilize techniques of framing, thus including some themes, objects, and events while excluding others; and they serve to focus the participants' attention in ways that invite humans into its world to become participants.

III. Cinematic-Religious World Crossings

Take Two: David Lynch's Blue Velvet and the Cinematic Making of a World

The opening shots of filmmaker David Lynch's *Blue Velvet* (1986) introduce an orderly world created through vertical and horizontal spatial dimensions and primary colors. Shot One begins in the sky, blue with scattered clouds, as the camera tilts down to the vertical array of a white picket fence. Eventually red tulips appear against the white fence with blue sky in the background. The larger themes of the film could have fit anywhere, and yet Lynch makes clear that this is the United States, as the red, white, and blue composition of the first shot is extended by the proverbial white picket fences of US residential life. The next several shots are edited so as to alternate between horizontal and vertical spatial orientations: vertical tilts are followed by horizontal pans, and back again. Meanwhile, red, white, blue, and yellow colors dominate, as mundane, neighborly images of fire trucks and crosswalks appear.

The viewer is eventually brought inside, to a living room where a woman sits sipping coffee while watching daytime television. It is a beautiful day in the neighborhood until we see what the woman is watching: a black-and-white close-up image of a man's hand holding a revolver. This is the first subtle disturbance in the so-far cosmically ordered world—not much, but enough to knock the neat and tidy perspective off-kilter. The next images bring us back outside to a man watering his garden (later revealed to be the protagonist's father, Mr. Beaumont), just as strange noises begin to emerge from the water spigot. A kink in the hose halts the water flow, and while the man attempts to untangle it, he suffers a stroke. The camera then resumes its downward tilt, this time passing below Mr. Beaumont—who is now lying on the grass with water still spurting out of the now-phallic hose and a dog attempts to drink the water—delving into the earth below. Here the creepy-crawly domain of bugs and insects are revealed to be scampering over each other, all of which is reinforced by an eerie soundtrack, making the viewer feel as if they are truly in that very underworld. The next 118 minutes of *Blue Velvet* continues with such premonitions, surrealistically disturbing as they are.

Lynch's film imagistically begins by revealing a world similar to what a great many films' opening shots reveal: Cosmos above, chaos below; begin far away and high up, and then zoom in, down to earth, down and up-close to a particular face/apartment/event. In this way, films present worlds both radically new and entirely ancient, connecting macrocosmos and microcosmos. In this most modern of visual media, we find filmmakers relying on primeval cosmologies where peace and harmony exist *above*, and chaos subsists *below*. Rather than leaving us in the mythically distant "long time ago and far, far away," *Blue Velvet* brings the cosmos down to earth, to our neighborhood, connecting up with the mundane tasks of watering the lawn, going

Film graphic, *Blue Velvet*

to school, and watching television. And then it unveils the chaos that lies under the very ground on which we walk. The macrocosm is transplanted into the microcosm, the world out there is remade into the here and now.

Blue Velvet shows, at least in one sense, what rituals are capable of doing: bringing the cosmos into the present space and time, allowing people to interact with the alternative, religiously-constructed world and often to re-enact the myths that help establish those world structures. I am not suggesting that the cinematography and mise-en-scène of *Blue Velvet* is itself a ritual but that its formal structures are

akin to the formal structures of ritual, a powerful force in the maintenance of religious worlds.

IV. WORLD MAINTENANCE AND RE-CREATION

Worlds are not merely created once and for all, but they also must be kept going, maintained. From time to time, people will see through the constructed nature of the world and ask questions, poking holes in the sacred canopy. So sociocultural systems like religion have to continually legitimate the world that has been created. World-making, in other words, is deeply bound to what Berger calls "world-maintenance." Because there is a dialectical process between the projected societal views of the cosmos and individual inquiry and creativity, the world must be maintained on a perpetual basis. I transpose world-maintenance as "re-creation" in order to get at the dynamic dialectics that Berger, Goodman, and Paden highlight. The world is not simply built but is constantly being maintained through rebuilding, reconstruction, recombining and retelling.

The hyphen is injected into re-creation to remind us how to pronounce this word in a way that resonates with its deeper meaning. Modern English has transformed the term into "recreation"—as in "recreational vehicle," or departments of "parks and recreation"—it is something we do to *get away from* the world. Yet at the heart of the idea, even if we forget it, is the activity of creation. Recreation is a way to re-create the world, which often means taking a step back from the world to see how it is put together, if only to figure out how it can be rearranged. On those days of re-creation, the world looks different. We see what we should have seen all along. We remember what is truly important.

That recreation, including moviegoing, most often occurs on the weekends in the modern world is not accidental. These two days coincide with the Jewish and Christian holy days, when the good folk of the world attend religious services, participate in their "true" communities, and take time to be in touch with their Creator. At least, that's the idea. As the Western world has grown restless with its religiosity, new forms of re-creation have emerged, one of which is of course the world of cinema. Indeed, what preacher's sermon can compete with multi-million dollar special effects? What Sabbath meal can steer us away from the possibilities that such beautiful people as Julia Roberts and Javier Bardem, Jennifer Aniston and Jason Bateman, Cameron

Diaz and Justin Timberlake might fall in love?[13] Indeed, many priests and pastors are now incorporating film clips into their very sermons, creating a multimediated spectacle of the Sunday morning worship service.

The Jewish tradition of the Sabbath is particularly insightful as a way to approach the re-creation of the world as it relates to film. "On the seventh day, God rested," we are told in the mythical language at the beginning of Genesis. But in the next chapter, we read that the Creator was not so passive at this time. If religions, in contemporary religious studies language, are centered on that which is "sacred," then the Jewish and Christian traditions would be first and foremost centered on the Sabbath day, for that is the first thing that God blesses and makes holy (Hebrew *kadosh*) according to the Scriptures: "God blessed the seventh day and made it holy" (Gen. 2:3).

As Abraham Heschel puts it in his classic little book on the Sabbath, "It is a day on which we are called upon to share in what is eternal in time, to turn from the results of creation to the mystery of creation; from the world of creation to the creation of the world."[14] Contrary to public opinion, the idea of the Sabbath is not one hollowed out by a list of rules and regulations leaving a community in a state of passivity but rather is an active, vital time. Judaism has a strong tradition of understanding the Sabbath as the *completion* of creation; on the seventh day, God did not refrain from creating as much as God created the Sabbath. The Sabbath, on this view, is the "real world," the rest of the week a necessary other world. "The Sabbath is not for the sake of the weekdays; the weekdays are for the sake of the Sabbath."[15] Indeed, Judith Shulevitz has more recently written on the topic and used precisely the language for which I am arguing. The title of her book is *The Sabbath World: Glimpses of a Different Order of Time.*[16] The Sabbath is its own world, an alternative way of seeing so-called reality.

If the Sabbath is the day we turn "to the mystery of creation" and "from the world of creation to the creation of the world," then film mimics this very process. Film makes us wonder about the world again, makes us say "Wow!" Film offers images that allow us to see things in a new way. This is not to say all film accomplishes this, for there seems to be somewhat of an inverse relation between the spectacular images of film and the capacity for the viewer's imagination—the more dazzling the image, the more depressed the imagination—but then again, the challah bread, the candles, the recitation of prayers, are not foolproof ways to stir our minds and bodies either. At its best, the Sabbath puts people in touch with their Creator, with their family, and with the created world. Bobby Alexander defines the aims of religious rituals in general: "Traditional religious rituals open up ordinary life to ultimate reality or some transcendent being or force in order to tap its transformative power."[17] At its best, film puts people in touch with the world again in new ways. In both of these, one is connected with their world only by experiencing another world.

To be active consumers, adherents, and participants in front of the film screen, altar, or Sabbath table—in order to maintain the hyphen in re-creation—it is necessary at times to dissect and analyze, to take things apart and then recombine them, as Goodman suggests. As students of religion and film, we must see, hear, feel, and think through the ways these worlds are made and re-created.

V. Cinematic-Religious World Crossings

Take Three: James Cameron's Avatar and Modern Mythologizing[18]

You lay on your back in a cool summer's grass, staring at the clouds. Familiar shapes begin to emerge, depending on your perspective and imagination: a rabbit here, a human figure there, a turtle further on. Or perhaps you sit in a comfortable seat and wear odd glasses and stare into the luminescent world of Pandora. Familiar stories begin to emerge, depending on your perspective and imagination: a tale of American colonization, a cheap rip off of *Pocahantas* or *Dances with Wolves*, or an allegory for the Chinese industrialization process. Writing in the *New York Times*, Dave Itzkoff outlined the many ways in which James Cameron's *Avatar* has been praised and/or condemned, the ways viewers have interpreted the movie as an allegory for this or that, the way it might even serve as a "Rorschach test for your personal interests and anxieties."[19] Indeed, it is a curious phenomenon. Not unlike staring at the clouds. But how and why does *Avatar* evoke such a variety of responses?

Like many a great piece of art, literature, music, or film, *Avatar* does the same things traditional mythologies do: it begs, borrows, and steals from a variety of long-standing human stories, sights, sounds, and interests, puts them through the grinder, and comes up with something new, even as the observers still, however hazily, find familiar elements.

In modern parlance, art, movies, and myths are "mashups," achieving their goals through the same processes that promoted the iPod to international sales: rip. mix. burn. All great artworks, all lasting mythologies, even new technologies, operate in the same way: a dash of this, a cup of that, a pinch here and there. There is nothing new under the sun. And yet there are endless varieties of the same ole. Meanwhile, it is up to the viewers to respond, to make meaning of the reconfigured setting, time, and characters, in a new time and place.

The process of reappropriation does not make any of it lesser art or myth, for it is precisely the mixing and merging of influences that interfaces with a larger tradition, knows where it comes from, where it is, and where it is going. The writers of Genesis 1 and 2 borrowed from Babylonian and other ancient Near Eastern stories of the creation of the cosmos and reused it for their own emerging monotheistic society. Over a millennium later the writer of the Gospel of John proclaimed, "In the beginning was the *logos*/Word," a phrase appropriated from the ancient Hebrew tradition ("In the beginning God created . . ."), mixed it with a Greek philosophical understanding of the *logos* that was crucial for Heraclitus and Plato as it became identified across the Hellenized world, and interlaced the older stories with the newly arisen notion of Jesus of Nazareth as the Christ/Messiah. Such results are always something borrowed, something blue, something old, something new.

Before Cameron's film are a range of examples of mythological borrowings: *The Matrix* (a pastiche of Christian, Buddhist, and "Hollywood" mythologies), *Star Wars* ("The Force" is the "Tao," Obi-Wan Kenobi is a Bodhisattva), *The Legend of Bagger Vance* (a retelling of Krishna and "R. Juna" from the Bhagavad Gita), and nearly every recent Disney and Pixar animated film from *Little Mermaid* to *Shrek*, to *Cars,* to *Finding Nemo* are all, to the tee, Hero stories. The birth of the Disney Corporation itself began with the success of the 1928 *Steamboat Willie,* and its introduction to a little big-eared mouse later to be called Mickey. Meanwhile, that film borrowed wholeheartedly from the great Buster Keaton film *Steamboat Bill* from earlier in that year. Likewise, Shakespeare's *King Lear* is a retelling of an older Celtic legend, which is then re-created on film in a Japanese setting in Akira Kurosawa's *Ran* and Ang Lee's Chinese setting of *Eat Drink Man Woman.* In a further turn, Lee's film is rearranged into the Latino-oriented *Tortilla Soup,* and the African American-centered *Soul Food.*[20]

Avatar is unoriginal, but it is regenerative and re-creative for many. It reaffirms age-old narrative structures of "heroes" who must come from elsewhere to achieve the task of salvation; of power structures based on race, class, gender, and disability; of the colonized and the colonizers; and of the inspirations that come from glimpses into other worlds. These ongoing products are not only regenerative, re-creative, and imaginative, but they also have the added advantage of using tried and tested stories. Moreover, it's not simply the tale, it's the telling, and retelling. The task of the teller of the renewed tales is to demonstrate how relevant these stories continue to be in contemporary settings.

VI. Re-Creating the World Through Film

The re-creation of the world is perhaps so obvious in the cinema that we tend to overlook it. In the beginning, every film begins with the production studio's logo. Many of these self-consciously demonstrate the ways in which the world is not simply being reflected on-screen but also the way the world is being actively reimagined, and the way cinema functions to relate the nomos and cosmos. These moving logos continually portray a predominant theme through their scenarios: the heavens and earth are connected through the productions of cinema. The logo for Universal Studios depicts a spinning earth, with a thousand points of light appearing across the continents (presumably movie theaters) as the view zooms out to show the whole globe, and the name "Universal" spins into place as a belt spanning the planet. Dreamworks' logo begins with an image of still water, into which a fishing line is dropped, then the camera moves up to find a boy cradled in the curve of the "D" of "Dreamworks" as the name hangs, suspended in midair and surrounded by clouds, evoking a lunar look on the world below.

Lionsgate is especially intriguing, as it has the viewer looking at machinery that then closes to a door as we continue to peer through the door's keyhole—in a nice voyeuristic-implying twist. The door then reopens on to the light-infused cloudy heavens. Elsewhere, Warner Brothers displays the "WB" shield floating among the clouds; the now-defunct Orion showed its eponymous star sign; and Paramount and Columbia both set their icons so high up on a pedestal that only the clouds and a few other mountain peaks can join them in their pantheon of world-imagining.

Through such examples, it is clear that film-production companies are fully cognizant of the other worlds and ethereal perspectives they provide for their viewers, and they gleefully promote these perspectives as they reaffirm a cosmology that evokes a "looking up" to where the wondrous things are. In this way, cinema offers a glimpse of the heavens, of other worlds above and beyond earthly existence, even as these other worlds must be relatable to the visible worlds on earth.

Such posturing is not far from the need for religious worlds to legitimate their world-making activity. As Berger suggests, "Religion legitimates social institutions by bestowing upon them an ultimately valid ontological status, that is, by *locating* them within a sacred and cosmic frame of reference." Further, "Probably the most ancient form of this legitimation is the conception of the relationship between society and cosmos as one between microcosm

and macrocosm. Everything 'here below' has its analogue 'up above.' By participating in the institutional order men, *ipso facto*, participate in the divine cosmos."[21] Likewise, cinema "projects" a particular human order onto a screen, promoting its productions as a link between the "here below" and "up above"—on mountaintops, in the clouds, encircling the earth. At the same time, the screen is literally created to be *larger than life*. Transcendent of this-worldly concerns, rules, or behaviors, the cinema enables a god's-eye view of things, even if we have long ago given up the "heaven above/earth below" cosmic separation.

Filmmakers and theorists, alongside production companies, realize the re-creative activity of film production as well, and they tend to understand world-making in terms of *space* and *time*. Siegfried Kracauer, in his *Theory of Film*, suggests the spatial significance of the larger-than-life images and the ways in which worlds are remade when projected on screen: "Any huge close-up reveals new and unsuspected formations of matter; skin textures are reminiscent of aerial photographs, eyes turn into lakes or volcanic craters. Such images blow up our environment in a double sense: they enlarge it literally; and in doing so, they blast the prison of conventional reality, opening up expanses which we have explored at best in dreams before."[22] And editor Paul Hirsch connects world-making to the temporal dimensions of filmmaking when he claims, "Film is truth, but it's all an illusion.

It's fake. Film is deceptive truth! . . . Editing is very interesting and absorbing work because of the illusions you can create. You can span thirty years within an hour and a half. You can stretch a moment in slow motion. You can play with time in extraordinary ways."[23]

Through the very technology of film, a new world is assembled—through the camera lens and in the editing room—and then projected on-screen. Viewers see the world but see it in entirely new ways because everyday perceptions of space and time are altered. Such time and space travel are not foreign to the procedures of religious world-making. In fact, if one were to substitute the word "myth" for "film" in Hirsch's comment, we would come across a popular definition of myth: "Telling lies to tell the truth." And through the re-creation of time and space, we have a world, created anew.

VII. CONCLUSION: LAYERING REALITY

In the 1950s, the aesthetician-cum-film theorist Etienne Souriau made a scientific stab at distinguishing several layers of "reality" when dealing with film and inadvertently offers some suggestions to religious studies scholars interested in film. These are his levels.

1. afilmic reality (the reality that exists independently of filmic reality)
2. profilmic reality (the reality photographed by the camera)
3. filmographic reality (the film as physical object, structured by techniques such as editing)
4. screenic (or filmophanic) reality (the film as projected on a screen)
5. diegetic reality (the fictional story world created by the film; the type of reality "supposed" by the signification of film.)
6. spectatorial reality (the spectator's perception and comprehension of a film)
7. creational reality (the filmmaker's intentions)[24]

I note these here to further evidence the multiple layers of reality that one must engage when dealing with film. It is not enough to encapsulate the narrative arc and suggest some religious implications from a literary perspective; rather, the edited, cinematographic, and projected layers of film's re-creation of the world must be taken into account.

And while these seven layers are each of individual interest, the full implications complicate the more general analogous relations I am attempting here. One could, I suppose, discuss each of these layers in ways that relate to Clifford Geertz's extensive definition of religion, defined as "(1) a system of symbols which acts to (2) establish powerful, pervasive, and long-lasting moods and motivations in men by (3) formulating conceptions of a general order of existence and (4) clothing these conceptions with such an aura of factuality that (5) the moods and motivations seem uniquely realistic."[25] Souriau's level 2 could relate to Geertz's point 3, Souriau's level 4 could relate to Geertz's point 4, Souriau's level 6 could relate to Geertz's point 5, and so forth. Such systematizing may be of interest to a scholar somewhere but ultimately detracts from the broader analogous dimensions I am recording here. The key point I take from Souriau is the general distinction between the profilmic and afilmic realities, the world "on-screen," and the world "out there," but also of their mutual implication.

Finally, to bring this theoretical filmic and religious re-creating of the world down to a more concrete level, consider the following brief note on the production of Terry Gilliam's film *Tideland* (2005):

Terry Gilliam filmed his newest movie, *Tideland*, in Saskatchewan last fall, racing to complete the location shots before winter set in. The Mitch Cullin novel on which the film is based is mostly set in West Texas, but Mr. Gilliam had substituted the Canadian prairie instead. The evening after he wrapped, it started to snow, and the cast, crew and director all saw this as an omen. . . .

Most of *Tideland* takes place inside a long-abandoned farmhouse, and the set was a miracle of grunginess and dilapidation in which cobwebs had been applied, brand new walls had been distressed to look old and water-stained, and ancient household implements had been knocked around until they looked even older. But as the camera tracked around and the crew moved props in and out, they accidentally created little pathways of relative orderliness, and Mr. Gilliam several times called for more dust.[26]

This vignette tells much about the relation of the world-making activities of film and religion. In the making of film—which is not far from the making of religion—through symbolic representational images, scenarios can be substituted, just as afilmic weather encroaches on profilmic realities, and even entropy can be created on-screen. On the flip side, viewers end up seeing this re-created world on-screen, believing in the fiction, because such belief is how we humans survive our everyday life. We go to the cinema and to the temple for recreation, to escape, but we also crave the re-creative aspects, maintaining the canopy of meaning over our individual and social lives as we imagine how the world could be. *What if?*

18

MEMORIALIZATION

Stephanie J. Stillman-Spisak

In his 1849 publication *The Seven Lamps of Architecture*, John Ruskin argued that "of all the pulpits from which the human voice is ever sent forth, there is none from which it reaches so far as from the grave." The dead inform the daily life, religious and otherwise, of all of us. They are the foundations upon which our histories, personal and social, have been built. They are the humic ground from which it is possible for us to be human. Religions and religious practitioners have long placed great emphasis on their relationships with the dead, because the deads' sermons from the pulpit of their graves inform our todays and our tomorrows. Robert Pogue Harrison notes as follows:

> The dead depend on the living to preserve their authority, heed their concerns, and keep them going in their afterlives. In return they help us to know ourselves, give form to our lives, organize our social relations, and restrain our destructive impulses. They provide us with the counsel needed to maintain the institutional order, of which they remain the authors, and prevent it from degenerating into a bestial barbarism. The dead are our

guardians. We give them a future so that they may give us a past. We help them live on so that they may help us go forward.[1]

This is the human contract with the dead. How humans choose to memorialize the dead, to give them a future, and to give ourselves a past through physical structures and rituals has immense implications for the moods, motivations, and textures of daily life.

The act of memorialization is a creative and physical aspect of all human life. Some philosophers and scholars insist that the foundation of being human is being in relationship with the dead. The definition of Homo sapiens as a species is often collapsed with the definition of the human. Harrison points to the important difference between the two: "Humanity is not a species (*Homo sapiens* is a species); it is a way of being mortal and relating to the dead." He adds, "As human beings we are born of the dead—of the regional ground they occupy, of the languages they inhabited, of the worlds they brought into being, of the many institutional, legal, cultural, and psychological legacies that, through us, connect them to the unborn."[2] Harrison draws upon the work of Giambattista Vico's *New Science,* in which Vico notes that "*humanitas* in Latin comes first and properly from *humando,* burying." Harrison contends, "To be human means above all to bury."[3]

As humans, we are constituted by loss; as humans, we are constituted as mourners. At some juncture in the human life, an individual is charged with the task of burying someone or something that he or she loves. All humans participate in this sepulchering act, but there exists the ethical task of examining this act, of questioning whether our relationship with the dead through our acts of memorialization are done recklessly, unintentionally, or with great care and consideration. The present chapter explores the ways that individuals, groups, and institutions have engaged in the act of memorialization. The first section begins with a theoretical grounding in Daniele Hervieu-Léger's contention that "religion is a chain of memory." The second section focuses on acts of memorialization that take place in physical space. The third section examines acts of memorialization that take place in ritual. The final section raises questions and critiques of acts of memorialization, with the hope that such inquiries might spur dialogue regarding the contemporary ethics of memorialization.

The examples included here focus on acts of memorialization in Judaism, Islam, Christianity, and US civil religion. These are certainly not the only traditions in which memory and memorialization play a significant role. For instance, the foundation of Buddhism rests in the narrative of the life of Buddha and the Scriptures that guide Buddhist practices. Various Hinduisms would not be what they are without the festivals that memorialize various Hindu gods and goddesses. Nor would African diaspora traditions exist as they do without the memorialization

of the various events that led to dispersion. For the purposes of consolidation, I have chosen to focus on the four areas previously noted, although I encourage the reader to consider and to question the roles of memory and memorialization in other traditions.

Religion as a Chain of Memory

Before examining particular locations and rituals of memorialization, it is important to ground such an exploration in the question of how scholars understand the role of memory and memorialization as a significant aspect of religious life. Harrison and Vico provide some indication of why the human relationship with the dead is so significant, but what does the act of memorialization have to do with daily religious practice in particular?

French sociologist Émile Durkheim was haunted by the legacy of the French Revolution. His earliest examinations of religion stemmed from his questions regarding how societies could hold themselves together in the midst of and in the aftermath of violence. In his landmark work *The Elementary Forms of Religious Life,* Durkheim argues that it is religion, and particularly religious ritual, that plays a significant role in uniting communities through acts that generate unity and sustain solidarity. The religious ritual worked especially well in reinforcing social mores in the face of collapse, through a curbing of undesirable fragmentations in society. What religion and religious ritual give to communities—especially in the aftermath of violence that renders profound anxieties about the world and about the self—is a secure understanding of the cosmos, a secure location within the cosmos, and the means to generate and sustain moral order.

Maurice Halbwachs, a student of Durkheim's, agreed that religion and religious ritual were capable of uniting communities, but he argued that it was the formation and role of collected memory in particular that held societies together. Throughout his examination of memory formation in families, religious communities, and among social classes, he noted that memory and acts of memorialization are always social. Halbwachs claimed, "No memory is possible outside frameworks used by people living in society to determine and retrieve their recollections."[4] He also found that memory is both recollected and reconstructed, given the present circumstances of a society; the needs and desires of individuals and communities therefore determine which dead are called forth from the grave to be recognized, to speak, and to be heard through the process of memorialization. Through acts of memorialization, people who have lived or events that have occurred are named significant if they are considered to be part of a "usable past."[5] Although the more private aspects of memorialization may not have political undertones, there is no public act of memorialization that does not seek to educate or speak to its contemporary community.

Halbwachs saw that, in the process of retrieving and remembering the past, there was a "natural distortion" that occurred, and this distortion was understood to serve the community well, because it served to eliminate memories that threatened social cohesion. Halbwachs understood that the memories that were most often distorted were those of violence. The memory of violence was transformed through the process of memorialization into a narrative of redemption. This is evident in the forthcoming examination of battlegrounds and historical events. But it is important to note that, even though Halbwachs saw the memory of violence transformed in such a way that the pain that threatened a community was alleviated, later scholars of Judaism

and of religion in the United States, such Peter Novick, Edward Linenthal, and Kenneth Foote, argue that the painful aspects of memories of violence are kept open for retrieval and utilization. Instead of eliminating violence from the memory, through the transformation of violence into redemption, the painful memory is kept painful: the self, community, and nation are "remembered," that is, brought together once more, in that pain (e.g., the evocation of memories of 9/11, the Holocaust, the suffering of Christ, and the Civil War).

Although Halbwachs focused on the role of collected memory in uniting a particular community in a particular situation, later French sociologist Daniele Hervieu-Léger was more interested in the question of memory's role in uniting religious communities over a long period of time. Hervieu-Léger argues that religion is "a chain of memory," connecting believers to a lineage that gathers together the experiences of the past and the hopes of the future into the present moment. A collapse in the chain of memory, a failure of individuals to memorialize the dead, indicates a threat to the social cohesion of a community.

Hervieu-Léger also argues that the processes of secularization—particularly the dismantling of a singular institution that functioned as the body that decided who and what should be memorialized and how memorialization should occur—has led to an immense fragmentation of memory and of the acts of memorialization and, therein, of society. She asserts that one of the chief characteristics of modern societies is that "they are no longer collective depositories—custodians—of memory."[6]

Although the notion that memory was once completely unified under a single canopy certainly deserves some questioning, Hervieu-Léger points to an important shift in memory politics. In the rubble of the collapsed canopy of collective memory and clearly stipulated regulations and practices of memorialization, smaller institutions arose, such as libraries, media franchises, museums, and education centers that labored to frame, store, and teach those memories that were deemed usable. The practices and ethics of memorialization became increasingly divergent and diverse, thanks in great part to both globalization of opportunity and localization of memorialization. What has been created in modernity is a network, not a canopy, of collected memory.

Given that contemporary memory is dispersed through a network of smaller institutions, or communities of memory, there is often a leader, a memorialization expert, at the center of these memory institutions. These experts, or memory technicians (such as memorial builders, religious leaders, government officials, and journalists), dictate what should be publicly memorialized. These individuals are charged, or take upon themselves the charge, with stabilizing, securing, and giving meaning to memory. Hervieu-Léger argues that the memory technician has immense power in these smaller memory communities and institutions. She notes that "it is the recognized ability to expound the true memory of the group that constitutes the core of religious power."[7]

The individual charged with the regulation of memory through the act of memorialization often has great control over the normative claims of a community. If the survivability of religious communities depends upon connection to and through a chain of memory, that individual charged with the task of welding the links of memory holds the power to direct and make moral claims for the community. What is stipulated as the grievable death, the significant meaning of death, or the special truth found in a particular death becomes the link in the chain of memory that binds a community.

Finally, within this network are billions of people whose daily acts of memorialization form the ongoing relationships that individuals and communities have with the dead. Within this network are thousands of grave markers that are visited daily by mourners. Within this network are hundreds of tokens of memory that are ritually prayed over, prayed to, or held in prayer. The Internet also plays a significant role in the network of memory, by allowing virtual space for individuals to memorialize the dead in websites, such as www.mydeathspace.com and various others devoted to particular people or tragedies, such as www.fallenheroesmemorial .com, dedicated to those who have been killed in the war in Iraq, and www.sept11thmemorial .com, dedicated to those who lost their lives in the various hijacking attacks that took place in New York, Washington, DC, and Shanksville, Pennsylvania, on September 11, 2001.

There is undoubtedly a complex relationship that exists between the memory technicians and institutions of memory and those individuals who seek to memorialize the dead in their own ways, just as there is a complex relationship between public acts of memorialization and those that take place in private. Whether institutional or individual, public or private, it is the creative act of memorialization that is central to the religious lives of many, because it is in conversation with the dead that the future is given life.

Memorialization in Space

The creative act of memorialization is often directed toward or rooted in particular places in which significant historical events occurred (often violent events) and in which monuments have been built to honor a particular group of people or a particular individual. For instance, every year, hundreds of people visit places such as the battlefields at Gettysburg or Napoleon's tomb in order to forge links to the events or the people in the past who have lived, struggled, and died in such places. In these cases, memorialization has an intense quality of spatial orientation— where a particular location serves as a portal for remembrance, recognition, and reorientation of individuals and communities. These locations of acts of memorialization often serve as teaching centers, in which the physicality of the monument, gravesite, or historical event serves as the ground upon which events from the past and the significances of their meanings are remembered in order that they may be passed to future generations. The locations and the physical memorials that stand in these locations serve not only as sacred spaces for rituals of mourning but also as centers of protest against the possibility of forgetting. Historian Edward Linenthal writes, "It is a protest, a way of saying, 'We will not let these dead become faceless and forgotten. This memorial exists to keep their names, faces, stories in our memories.' Increasingly, memorial expression has become an immediate language of engagement, not just a language of commemoration."[8]

MEMORIALIZATION OF HISTORICAL EVENTS

This and the following section focus on two types of memorialization, including the memorialization of historical events and the memorialization of particular people.

Day of Ashura

The Day of Ashura occurs on the tenth day of the month of Muharram (the first month of the Islamic calendar). It is a day that marks the tenth day of the mourning of Muharram (or Remembrance of Muharram)—in memory of Imam Husayn ibn Ali, who was killed in the Battle of Karbala in 680 CE by the forces of the second Umayad caliph Yazid I. The Battle of Karbala was fought between two branches of Muslims, the Shia and the Sunni, over who was to be the rightful leader of Islam following the death of the Prophet Muhammed. Husayn ibn Ali, the grandson of the Prophet Muhammed, was the leader of the Shia Muslims, and his slaying on the battlefield is remembered each year on the Day of Ashura. This day marks the martyrdom not only of Husayn ibn Ali but also of the others who fought and died in the Battle of Karbala.

Each year, on the Day of Ashura, thousands of mourners, the majority of which are Shia Muslims, travel to Karbala to participate in rituals that reflect both remembering and mourning. Masses of individuals journey through the streets of Karbala to participate in *dasta-gardani* (mourning processions), where they demonstrate their grief through practices such as *zangir-zani* (beating oneself with metal chains), *sine-zani* (beating of the chest), and *gamazani* (slashing oneself with swords or knives). During the Day of Ashura, mourners also participate in gatherings in which religious leaders retell the deeds of the martyrs of Karbala and incite the mourners through cursing the enemy. During the Day of Ashura, some individuals participate in reenactments of the Battle of Karbala (known as *taziya*) in an attempt not only to connect the present to the past but also to participate in a past that is understood to be foundational for the present and for the future.

In Karbala stands the Shrine of Husayn ibn Ali, which is built on top of the graves of the Battle of Karbala martyrs. Thousands of mourners travel each year in pilgrimage to this shrine, with the highest attendance days being those during the first ten days of the Remembrance of Muharram. At the center of the shrine is the grave of Husayn ibn Ali, and to the right of this grave is the tomb of Habib ibn Madahir al-Asadi, a close companion of Husayn ibn Ali, who was also killed in the Battle of Karbala. At the foot of

Husayn ibn Ali's grave is a mass grave that marks the burial of all seventy-two martyrs of Karbala. Also buried next to Husayn ibn Ali are his two young sons, Ali al-Akbar and Ali al-Asghar. Finally, the shrine also serves as the burial site for Ibrahim Musa al-Kadhim, who had dedicated his life to telling the story of Husayn ibn Ali's martyrdom and the Battle of Karbala.

The shrine serves as a focal point for the memorialization of the martyrs of the Battle of Karbala. It is a place to which mourners travel so that they may remember, where they may show their respect and honor, and where they may gather as a community in remembrance of the past that grounds their present and their future. This is the location through which mourners orient their histories, through the recitation and reenactment of the Battle of Karbala, and this is the location in which memorialization is marked on the body through outward signs of grief. Each of these acts of memorialization serves to link the individual in the present to those who have come before in a chain of memory. The act of memorializing Husayn ibn Ali and the other martyrs of the Battle of Karbala works to make possible the past, present, and the future of the Shia tradition and community.

Civil Rights Memorial

The United States is founded upon a set of historical events that have been narrated from one generation to the next. These narratives provide the texts, oral and written, that frame what some scholars have called US civil religion. US civil religion comprises a set of sacred narratives, spaces, believes, rituals, and traditions that have similarities to the textures, moods, and motivations of many more traditional religions, including Judaism, Christianity, and Islam. One of the founding narratives of recent US civil religion is the story of the civil rights movement of the 1950s and 1960s, which has been made concrete in memorials such as the Civil Rights Memorial in Montgomery, Alabama.

The Civil Rights Memorial is a memorialization of forty individuals who died in the struggle for integrated and equal opportunities for individuals with African descent in the United States. The memorial was built in 1989 by the Southern Poverty Law Center. The architect, Maya Lin, who also designed the Vietnam Memorial in Washington, DC, conceived the memorial in such a way that it would serve not only as a location of memorialization for those who died in the movement but also as a place for education and reflection. The memorial includes a black granite table inscribed with the names of those who died during the civil rights movement—such as Martin Luther King Jr. (preacher and civil rights leader), Virgil Lamar War (a youth killed in Birmingham, Alabama), and Addie Mae Collins, Denise McNair, Carole Robertson, and Cynthia Wesley (schoolgirls who were killed in a bombing of 16th Baptist Church in Birmingham, Alabama). A thin layer of water constantly flows over the granite table, representing renewal, rebirth, and the mighty waters of change of which Martin Luther King Jr. spoke in several of his speeches. King's words, "until justice rolls down like waters and righteousness like a mighty stream" are engraved on a round black granite stone that stands beside the engraved table.

The physical aspects of the memorial allow visitors the space to remember the events and the people who have made possible the increased integration and opportunity for those of African descent in the United States. The text on the stone table provides a timeline, a chain of memory, which links the visitor to a narrative of struggle and liberation. At the same time, the flow of water serves to mark this act of memorialization as temporally unstable, meaning that the waters continue to flow over these names, reminding visitors that the struggle for civil rights is unfinished and that the story continues, just as the waters continue to flow.

The memorial includes a "contemplative area" that Lin describes as "a cool tranquil place rich in the history of struggle and transformation." It is, in the words of Lin, "a place to remember the civil rights movement, to honor those killed during the struggle, to appreciate how far the country has come in its quest for equality, and to consider how far it has to go." This aspect of a contemplative space that is intended for reflection and education is a common feature of many memorials throughout the United States. Such memorials, including the US Holocaust Museum

and the Memorial Center in Oklahoma City, are sites of both civic renewal and civic education. They are memorials that are intended to evoke acts of memorialization with a pedagogical purpose. Historian Edward Linenthal writes, "Visitors, ideally, do not come merely to consume them [memorials] as cultural commodities but to enter them as civic pilgrims, to be transformed by the lessons that emerge from imaginative narrative engagement." He adds that institutions such as these "offer the civic equivalent of being 'born again'—the movement from passive unaware inhabitant of the nation state to active vigilant citizen empowered with the agency of a coherent moral public narrative."[9] The Civil Rights

Located on the site of the former Alfred P. Murrah Federal Building, the Oklahoma City National Bombing Memorial commemorates the victims of the bombing of April 19, 1995. The memorial's main components are two "Gates of Time" inscribed with the moments before and after the blast, a reflecting pool, an arrangement of 168 empty chairs, the "Survivor Tree," and a children's area.

Museum, in Montgomery, Alabama, serves as such a place—in which the act of memorialization is an act of civic renewal and engagement in a civic education. The questions, consequences, and tensions over who decides the nature of the civic and religious lessons is a topic discussed in a later section on the politics of memorialization.

Memorial to the Murdered Jews of Europe

Across the world, hundreds of physical memorials have been built as memorializations of the approximately six million Jews, political dissenters, homosexuals, and individuals with disabilities who were systematically murdered as part of a program of deliberate extermination designed and executed by Nazi Germans under the guidance of Adolf Hitler during World War II. Some of these memorial sites are statues, lists of names, educational museums, or markers that signify the violence of the Holocaust. Each of these sites serves as a place of remembrance that protests forgetting and as a place of education that links individuals in the present to individuals in the past in a chain of memory.

In 2005, the Memorial to the Murdered Jews of Europe was opened in Berlin, Germany. The memorial was designed by architect Peter Eisenman and engineer Buro Happold. The memorial covers a 4.7-acre site that is covered with 2,711 stone boxes that are each 7.8 feet long, 3 feet and 1.5 inches wide, and that vary in height from 8 feet to almost 16 feet. These boxes, or stelae, are arranged in a grid pattern that covers a sloping field. Eisenman designed the memorial so that the stelae produced an uneasy and somewhat confusing landscape that represents a seemingly ordered system that still seems out of place with the standards of human reason and understanding. Underneath the memorial is a museum that holds the names of all of the known Jewish victims of the Holocaust.

Whether intentional or not, the Memorial to the Murdered Jews of Europe has an eerie resemblance to a cemetery, although the varied and random heights of the stones provide a sense of disorientation that is difficult to articulate. If one were to walk among the stones, it would be difficult to see anything outside of the memorial, perhaps serving to indicate the overwhelming magnitude of loss of Jews during the Holocaust. What is also striking about the memorial is that, above ground, it is absent of text, quite unlike the Civil Rights Museum in Montgomery, Alabama. Instead, the connection to the past is a connection to the enormity of violence that cannot be calculated, spoken, or written. No one sentiment dominates the memorial, thus highlighting the ways in which the Holocaust has not only many narratives, but also many silences that betray efforts of consolidation into the written or the spoken word. A visit to the Memorial to the Murdered Jews of Europe is an act of memorialization that builds a link in the chain of memory to an event for which the magnitude and atrocity baffle the imagination and silence all efforts of explanation. Still, this is a place of renewal and education. It is a place that protests a particular kind of death rather than protesting particular persons who have died.

Holocaust memorials throughout the world—in whatever shape, texture, or tone—have become centers for memorialization on the Jewish Day of Remembrance. On this day, Jews gather to remember those who were murdered in the Holocaust and also those who fought for Jewish liberation and were killed in their struggles. On this day, thousands of mourners gather to grieve together. They gather to remember and honor the past and to bind themselves as a community of collected memory that refuses to forget—in order to give a foundation to those who will come in the future. Many Jews believe that such remembering is in fact one of the commandments. The fourth of the Ten Commandments is to "Remember the Sabbath day, to keep it holy." The word that is translated "to remember" is *zah-khor*, which implies more than just a recollection of the past but rather suggests actively focusing the mind on the relationship between the past and the present. For many Jews, remembering the Holocaust and memorializing the dead mean coming into relationship with a past that must inform the future lest such an atrocity occur again. (It has always struck me to witness the twenty-four-hour reading of the names in a public place.)

MEMORIALS TO PARTICULAR PEOPLE

Landscapes across the world are marked by memorials that have been built for particular individuals. These memorials can, but do not necessarily need to, house the body of the memorialized individual. Consider for a moment the landscape of the United States: within the Washington, DC, area, there are memorials dedicated not only to groups of individuals who have died in World War II, the Korean War, and the Vietnam War, but there are also monuments dedicated to particular individuals, such as Thomas Jefferson, Abraham Lincoln, George Washington, Martin Luther King, and Franklin Delano Roosevelt. These memorials serve as a guide to the significant figures that shaped the history of the United States, and they set the tone for US values of honor, sacrifice, and loyalty. Although none of the aforementioned memorials house the body of the deceased individual that is memorialized, Grant's Tomb in New York City houses the body of the Civil War general and eighteenth president of the United States, Ulysses S. Grant. These memorials stand as physical reminders, locations of memorialization, which serve as the foundation of US civic religion.

But US civic religion is certainly not the only system or tradition that memorializes particular individuals. In 2570 BCE, the Great Pyramid of Giza was constructed as a tomb for Pharaoh Khufu (also known as Cheops), who lived during the fourth Egyptian dynasty. Saint Francis of Assisi (an Italian monk, missionary, saint, and founder of the Franciscan order) is buried in the Basilica of St. Francis in Assisi, Italy. This site has served as a location of pilgrimage, where Catholics have come to memorialize one of the most significant religious figures in Catholic history. Martin Luther, the father of the Reformation, has two central sites of memorialization, including Castle Church in Wittenberg, Germany, which holds his tomb, and Luther's Sterbehaus, where visitors come to see Luther's death mask and the home in which he spent his last few days. These sites, along with such others as King David's Tomb in Jerusalem and the Prophet's Mosque in Medina, serve as locations to which millions of people travel each year to memorialize the dead that link them to a past history and to past traditions.

It is important to note that not all acts of memorialization of particular individuals take place on the grand scales of monuments, pyramids, and tombs. Every day, many of us pass by one of the most common locations where acts of memorialization occur—a cemetery. Within cemeteries, whether they are Jewish, Christian, or Islamic, there often stand before the visitor hundreds of memorializations to the dead. Each gravestone, each engraving, and each marker, of whatever form, signifies that the dead is the product of someone's or some group's conscious engagement in the act of memorialization. Thousands of people across the world visit cemeteries every day in order to lay flowers at a gravesite, to leave prayers or tokens of memory, and, perhaps most important, to communicate with the dead. There are also thousands of people who may not go to a particular site to perform rituals, to give prayers, or to be in relationship with the dead but who do these acts of memorialization in their homes—around dinner tables, in the writings of obituaries, and in the privacy of prayer. These acts of memorialization should not be minimized, because they reveal so strikingly the ways that each of us chooses to stand in relationship to the dead. These acts of memorialization demonstrate the ways that the dead are helped to live on so that the living may go forward.

MEMORIALIZATION IN RITUAL

There are many factors—such as time, money, and limited mobility—that make it impossible for all acts of memorialization to occur at the sites of historical events or at the monuments or graves that honor the lives of individuals. So how do religious individuals continue to take part in a chain of memory that links them to those people and events that have laid the foundations for their ritual life? The religious ritual can also serve as an act of memorialization. It can be the way in which the individual remembers and, in some cases, reenacts the past in order to establish a link in the chain of memory. Such rituals often include an engagement with texts of the past that tell particular stories, such as the Last Supper or the exodus from Egypt, which connects believers today to the histories that ground their faith and practice. The memorialization that occurs in these rituals also serves to bind the present community together, as a community of collected memory that labors to secure traditions so that they may be passed to future generations. To illuminate the role of memorialization in ritual, the focus here is on three religious rituals, including the Eucharist, the Passover Seder meal, and Ramadan.

Eucharist

The ritual of the Eucharist is a ritual that memorializes the past, in particular the Lord's Supper, and it is a ritual that reminds participants of their bonds of community and the heavenly future that Christ has made possible. The two ways of remembering that are operative in the ritual of Eucharist are *anamnesis*, the recollection or remembering of the past in a refusal to forget, and *prolepsis*, the remembrance of the ties of the Christian community with the witnesses in heaven and the promises made to that community and to those who are unborn for the second coming of Christ.

In 1 Corinthians, the apostle Paul gives the first account in the Bible of Christ's Last Supper with the apostles. The passage in 1 Corinthians 11:23-33 reads as follows.

> For I received from the Lord what I also handed on to you, that the Lord Jesus on the night when he was betrayed took a loaf of bread, and when he had given thanks, he broke it and said, "This is my body that is for you. Do this in remembrance of me." In the same way he took the cup also, after supper, saying, "This cup is the new covenant in my blood. Do this, as often as you drink it, in remembrance of me." For as you eat this bread and drink the cup, you proclaim the Lord's death until he comes. (NRSV)

In the apostle Paul's account, the Lord's Supper is portrayed as a ritual of remembrance, a memorialization in recognition and honor of the Christ figure, who has given his body and blood so that the believer could be a part of the community to come with Christ's resurrection and return. The ritual of the Eucharist is in part a reenactment of the Last Supper. Believers are called to the ritual to partake of bread, often in the form of a wafer or cracker, and wine, often in the form of juice, in remembrance of the body and the blood that Christ has sacrificed for the present and future communities.

In Catholicism and Eastern Orthodoxy, the bread and wine consumed have gone through a process of transubstantiation, over which a priest has presided. In transubstantiation, the bread or wafer becomes the actual body of Christ, and the wine or juice becomes the actual blood of Christ. Therefore, in the ritual, the believer is not only reenacting the story of the Last Supper but is partaking, quite literally, of the body and the blood of Christ. Many Protestant denominations practice the ritual of Eucharist without transubstantiation and argue instead that the bread and the wine represent symbolically the body and the blood of Christ. In both cases, what is significant is that the Eucharist is an act of memorialization in that it is a remembrance of Christ, who has been sacrificed so that his community may have a future.

The ritual of the Eucharist therefore is an act of memorialization that is both *anamnesis* and *prolepsis*. First, the ritual of the Eucharist reminds the believer of the narrative of the Lord's Supper and the sacrifice of body and blood that Christ made, and it therein forms a chain of memory between the believer and the dead who have come before him or her. Second, the ritual of the Eucharist binds the present community, through a symbolic feast that gathers believers around the communion table in order to partake of the same meal and the same promise. The community is bound together through the act of memorialization, which is commanded by Christ, who insists that the taking of the bread and the drinking of the wine is done in remembrance of him. Last, the ritual of the Eucharist not only makes the past present, but it also reminds the community of the promises made for the future. The ritual of the Eucharist is therefore exemplary of a ritual of memorialization that serves to connect

believers to a past, to bind them together as participants in shared memory, and to remind them of the future that must be built upon those who have come before them.

The Passover Seder

The Passover Seder meal is a Jewish ritual feast that takes place on the first, or first and second, nights of the Jewish holiday of Passover, which takes place on the fifteenth day of the Hebrew month of Nisan. During the meal, friends and families gather together to partake of a meal in which each food eaten and each cup drunk has symbolic ties to the story of the Israelite exodus from Egypt. During the meal, the participants read through one of many versions of the Haggadah, the story of the Israelite exodus. Because the Haggadah is roughly standardized, the ritual of the Passover Seder not only unites the Jewish people to their past but also serves to unite individuals to Jews around the world who are also participating the Passover Seder. As such, the Passover Seder is a central aspect of Jewish life and identity. The Haggadah explains that, if it were not for the exodus from Egypt, the Jews would still be an enslaved people. Therefore, the Passover Seder meal is a memorialization of a founding narrative that made possible the present and the future. It is a time for thanksgiving, praise, and a rededication to the ideals of liberation and community.

The Passover Seder meal is also the vehicle through which Jewish faith and identity are transferred from one generation to the next. One of the founding verses for the Seder meal is Exodus 13:8–10, which reads, "You shall tell your child on that day, 'It is because of what the Lord did for me when I came out of Egypt.' It shall serve for you as a sign on your hand and as a reminder on your forehead, so that the teaching of the Lord may be on your lips; for with a strong hand the Lord brought you out of Egypt. You shall keep this ordinance at its proper time from year to year" (NRSV). Like the ritual of the Eucharist, the Passover Seder meal serves to make the past present, to bind a community of believers, and to remind believers of the promised future that must be striven for through the transference of faith and practice from generation to generation.

The Haggadah, meaning "telling" or "telling your son," establishes the order of the Seder meal. The Haggadah begins with the *Kadeish* (a blessing for the first cup of wine) and then moves to the *Ur'chatz* (washing of the hands). The next step is the *Karpas* (appetizer), in which a vegetable is dipped into salt water, vinegar, charoset, or wine. This ritual is meant to serve as a reminder of the tears that have been shed by the Israelites in their exodus from Egypt. After the *Karpas* is completed, the *matzah* on the Seder plate is broken in half and then begins the *Magid*, the retelling of the story of the Israelites' exodus. This retelling is particularly significant because the language of the Haggadah is all written in a way that participants in the Seder meal are also participants in the exodus. When the Haggadah is read aloud, it is not a story of "they" or "the Israelites" who have left Egypt, but rather it is a story of "when *we* left Egypt." As such, the Seder meal is not only an act of remembering the past, but it is also an act of participation in the past, in order to ground the present community and to give a future to the young and the unborn.

Following the *Magid*, an invitation to the Seder meal is given (*Ha Lachma Anya*), and then the community present moves to the *Mah Nishtanah* (the Four Questions). The four questions are asked by a child, or the youngest adult in the room, and are intended to remind the participants why they have gathered together in remembrance of the exodus narrative. The four questions focus on what makes this night different from all others and includes the following.

- Why is it that on all other nights we do not dip our food even once, but on this night we dip it twice?
- Why is it that on all other nights we eat either leavened bread or *matza*, but on this night we only eat *matza*?
- Why is it that on all other nights we eat all kinds of vegetables, but on this night we eat bitter herbs?
- Why is it that on all other nights we eat sitting upright or reclining, but on this night we recline?

In giving the answers to each of these questions, those gathered for the Passover Seder meal direct their attention toward the memory of the exodus narrative and, in doing so, participate in a recollection of the foundations upon which the broader tradition rests.

Other aspects of the Haggadah that illuminate the memorialization character of the Passover Seder meal are the Four Sons, who also ask questions regarding the meaning of the service, along with the part of the Haggadah that commands participants to "go forth and learn what the Laban and Aramean wanted to do to our father Jacob." In this part of the Seder meal, four verses from Deuteronomy 26:5-8 are read aloud and explored in detail. The verses read as follow.

> You shall make this response before the Lord your God: "A wandering Aramean was my ancestor; he went down into Egypt and lived there as an alien, few in number, and there he became a great nation, mighty and populous. When the Egyptians treated us harshly and afflicted us, by imposing hard labor on us, we cried to the Lord, the God of our ancestors; the Lord brought us out of Egypt with a mighty hand and an outstretched arm, with a terrifying display of power, and with signs and wonders." (NRSV)

The Haggadah expands upon the meaning of these verses and reviews the ten plagues, during which time the participant places a drop of wine from his or her fingertip on the Seder plate and thanks is given to God for each of his actions that led the Israelites from slavery to liberation. Again, this ritual serves to memorialize the past and to render the participant part of the past and part of the present community that is responsible for the transmission of faith and practice to future generations.

The Seder meal continues with the consumption of various foods that remind participants of and allow participation in the exodus narrative. For example, a *Z'roa* (a shank bone) and a *Beitzah* (roasted or boiled egg) are eaten to symbolize sacrifices made at the temple in Jerusalem. The *Chazret* (usually a bitter lettuce) and *Maror* (horseradish) are bitter herbs, eaten to remind participants of the harshness of the experience of enslavement. The charoset is a brown, sweet, pebbly mixture that is eaten to remind participants of the mortar that slaves used to build structures in Egypt. Finally, a *Karpas* (vegetable other than bitter herb) is dipped into a liquid such as salt water during the appetizer portion of the Seder meal in order to remind participants of the bitter tears shed by the Israelites.

There are also four cups of wine consumed during the meal, each of which represents one of the four ways of deliverance promised by God in Exodus 6:6-7, which reads, "Say therefore to the Israelites, 'I am the Lord, and I will free you from the burdens of the Egyptians and deliver you from slavery to them. I will redeem you with an outstretched arm and with mighty acts of judgment. I will take you as my people, and I will be your God. You shall know that I am the Lord your God, who has freed you from the burdens of the Egyptians'" (NRSV). The consumption of the wine serves as yet another ritual in which the participants in the Passover Seder not only remember but also participate in the exodus narrative, thus memorializing the past, with the intent to utilize that past as a foundation for the future. Like the ritual of the Eucharist, the Passover Seder meal exemplifies the ways in which religious rituals can be profound acts of memorialization. It is a way in which the people of the present moment recognize and honor the past and bind themselves as a community of collected memory that is entrusted with the task of remembering so that future generations cannot forget.

Ramadan

Ramadan is an Islamic religious observance that takes place during the ninth month of the Islamic calendar. This is the month in which Muslims believe that the Prophet Muhammed received the Qur'an from the archangel Gabriel. Laylat al-Qadr (also known as The Night of Measures or the Night of Decree), which takes place on an odd-numbered day during the last ten days of Ramadan, is considered one of the most important days in the Islamic calendar. This is the night in which the first verses of the Qur'an were delivered to the Prophet Muhammed. This is also believed to be the night in which the fate of individuals and communities is decided for the following year. Throughout the month of Ramadan, Muslims fast from dawn to dusk in an effort to remind themselves of the sacrifices made by the Prophet and by those who have come before. Fasting also serves to remind the religious individual of the values of humility, patience, and sacrifice.

The month of Ramadan is a month of rituals of memorialization. It is a time in which Muslims remember the gift of the Qur'an. During the month, Muslims are encouraged to read through the entire Qur'an. As with the texts utilized in the ritual of the Eucharist and the Passover Seder meal, the Qur'an serves not only as a reminder of past events but also as an avenue through which believers participate in the past. During the month of Ramadan, many Muslims attend evening services in the mosque, during which special prayers, called *Tarawih*, are recited. The *Tarawih* is a recitation of one-thirtieth (a *juz*) of the Qur'an, which is done every night from the start of Ramadan to the final evening. Participation in the reading of the Qur'an not only serves as a memorialization to the Prophet Muhammed and the narrative of the giving of the Qur'an, but it also serves to bind the community as a group with a shared, collected memory. This is particularly true thanks to the call and answer and the communal, out-loud praying that occurs during the recitation of the *Tarawih*. In these rituals, the community is united physically through their voices and the tempo of the recitation.

The act of fasting and feasts also binds the community together as a group that remembers and that, because it remembers, sacrifices together. During the month of Ramadan, Muslims around the world rise before dawn to eat *Suhroor*, the predawn meal, and perform the *fajr*, the first prayer of the day. They are then required to fast until the fourth call for prayer, the *Maghrib*, at which time they are allowed to eat until the call for the *fajr* the following morning. The ritual of fasting in remembrance of the deliverance of the Qur'an serves as an embodied act of memorialization that not only binds a practitioner to a religious chain of memory but also binds the practitioner to the fellow community of Muslims around the world who are also sacrificing during the month of Ramadan. The end of Ramadan is marked by Eid ul-Fitr, a celebration that marks the end of fasting and the beginning of the new month. During Eid ul-Fitr, communities come together to celebrate, break the fast together, and donate food to the poor (a fulfillment of zakat, one of the five pillars of Islam). This celebration marks the renewal of the Islamic community, which has spent the month of Ramadan remembering its roots, religious ties to one another, and the promises for the future that have been delivered through the Qur'an.

The physicality of the act of remembrance and memorialization has resonances with the ritual of the Eucharist and the Passover Seder meal, in the sense that each of these rituals of memorialization demands a physical engagement that serves to link the practitioner to the past, to the present community, and to the future of the tradition to come. In both the rituals of memorialization and in physical monuments built in order to remember historical events or people, it is clear that the act of memorialization often demands physical engagement. In each of these cases, memory is written onto both the individual body and the social body, in order to make strong the chain of memory that constitutes the respective religious tradition.

THE POLITICS OF MEMORIALIZATION

No one site of memorialization or ritual of memorialization discussed here exists without contestation. Throughout, I have intentionally used the term "collected memory" in contrast to "collective memory." The term "collective memory" suggests that all individuals share the same memory of a particular event or a particular person, but anyone who has had an experience alongside another person and then attempts to share the memory of that event often realizes that memory is greatly influenced by past experiences, context, and position in relationship to that event. I utilize the term "collected memory" to indicate "the many discrete memories that are gathered into common memorial spaces and assigned common meaning." Historian James Young writes, "A society's memory, in this context, might be regarded as an aggregate collection of its members' many, often competing memories. If societies remember, it is only insofar as their institutions and rituals organize, shape, and even inspire their constituents' memories. For a society's memory cannot exist outside of those people who do the remembering—even if such a memory happens to be at the society's bidding, in its name."[10] Despite the seeming stability of memory as it is portrayed in the memorial or ritual of memorialization, memory never exists without contestation.

As such, acts of memorialization are subject to struggles of power over who has the right and responsibility to shape the ways in which an event or person is remembered. Who decides which forty names are to be written on the black granite table at the Civil Rights Memorial in Montgomery, Alabama? Who dictates which expressions of grief are acceptable or not in the Day of Ashura rituals and festivities? Who chooses which version of the Haggadah is to be used for the Passover Seder meal? Such questions are complicated; their answers likely depend upon the context of power, historical moment, and hierarchy within which the questions are asked. It is also likely that there is no one right answer.

Still, an ethics of memory demands attention to these questions. An ethics of memory requires consideration of which lives are considered meaningful and worthy of memorialization. Judith Butler writes on the role of the obituary in public discourse, "The obituary functions as the instrument by which grievability is publicly distributed. It is the means by which a life becomes, or fails to become, a publically grievable life, an icon for national self-recognition, and the means by which a life becomes noteworthy."[11] Attention to stipulated grief, to the lives that are chosen to be publicly significant and to those that are not, has immense potential to illuminate social values and social regulations. Said differently, an examination of the ways in which a community selects who or what to memorialize and how it memorializes a person or event has the potential to provide a window into the hopes, fears, and current status of a given community.

Not only does the choice of whom or what to memorialize indicate the contested and collected character of memory, so too does the timeline with which memorializations occur, particularly in the aftermath of violence. In the past fifty years, there has been a significant decrease in the time between an act of violence and the memorialization of that event. The memorial to World War II in Washington, DC, was opened in 2004, more than fifty years after the conclusion of the war. The Oklahoma City National Memorial that recognizes the victims, survivors, and rescuers of the April 19, 1995, Oklahoma City bombing of the Alfred P. Murrah Federal Building was open just over two years following the bombing. In the United States in particular, there is often a rush to memorialize violent events in the history of the nation. Some scholars have argued that this rush to memorialize may in fact be a flight from the anxiety that grieving evokes. Butler writes, "When grieving is something to be feared, our fears can give rise to the impulse to resolve it quickly, to banish it in the name of an action invested with the power to restore the loss or return the world to a former order, or to reinvigorate a fantasy that the world formerly was orderly."[12] When the messy labor of grieving is feared, there is often a flight into quickly conceived acts of memorialization that promise security, comfort, and closure. But such flights often render the living more painfully haunted by the dead, because engagement through a memorialization constituted by care often requires time even when rush is demanded, patience in the face of anxiety, and silences in the spaces where talkativeness seemingly comforts.

Finally, in considering the politics of memorialization, one must ask the question of why a community chooses to remember rather than forget. Are there instances in which forgetting might be preferable? Are there even religious rituals—in Buddhism and in other traditions—that are intended to release one from the past? The answer to both of these questions is yes, and yet the public demand to remember particular events in particular ways is fueled by media networks, religious leaders, and other experts of memorialization who labor in the networks of memory. Edward Linenthal notes, "As we have become acutely aware of important individuals, groups, and events consigned to oblivion for the sake of maintaining digestible national narratives, acts of 'complicit forgetting' now register as evidence of moral cowardice, while acts of resurrection, excavation, and representation are viewed not only as correctives to a flawed view of the past, but as a sign of moral integrity."[13] Linenthal points to a critical consideration of the interwoven threads of memory and morality in any given community. A lengthy discussion of this topic falls outside of the purview of this chapter, but it remains an important question to consider in the examination of any act of memorialization.

WHY IS MEMORIALIZATION CENTRAL TO A CONSIDERATION OF RELIGIOUS LIFE?

In *Imagining Religion,* Jonathan Z. Smith contends, "I take my point of departure from the observation that each scholar of religion, in his way, is concerned with phenomena that are historical in the simple, grammatical sense of the term, that is to say, with events and expressions from the past, reconceived vividly. The scholar of religion is, therefore, concerned with dimensions of memory and remembrance—whether they be the collective labor of society or the work of the individual historian's craft."[14] The study of religion is always a study entangled in the examination of memory and memorialization. If Daniele Hervieu-Léger is correct in her view that religion is a chain of memory, as I believe she is, the scholar of religion is always already a scholar of memory, intentional or not.

As a scholar of memory, the scholar of religion is also often concerned with the ways that traditions are formed and passed onto new generations. The word *religion* stems from the Latin roots *re-legere* and *re-ligare,* which indicate a binding back upon itself. Jacques Derrida argues, "What is at issue is indeed a persistent bond that bonds itself first and foremost to itself. What is indeed a reunion <*rassemblement*>, a re-assembling, and a re-collecting. A resistance or a reaction to dis-junction."[15] Religion as a re-collection has the character of re-membering. What is at stake in the activity of religion and the activity of memorialization are the ways that we bind ourselves to what has come before. Some of this binding occurs with an understanding of the past as linear and secured—a warehouse of truths placed on standing reserve for our use. In such cases, there is little questioning of the past to which we bind ourselves. Martin Heidegger writes, "Tradition takes what has come down to us and delivers it over to self-evidence; it blocks our access to those primordial 'sources' from which the categories and concepts handed down to us have been in part quite genuinely drawn. Indeed it makes us forget that they have had such an origin, and makes us suppose that the necessity of going back to these sources is something which we need not even understand."[16]

But there are other options for the activity of religion and memorialization. In contrast to accepting the giving over of a secured past without questioning, Robert Pogue Harrison suggests a conversation with the dead that is open. He writes that "our intercourse with the dead must be frank and ongoing: so that we may keep open the possibility of a 'reciprocative rejoinder' that never simply denies but freely avows or disavows the will of the ancestors—and not only of the ancestors but also of those around us who, with sanctimonious piety, seek to make the historical present conform to an 'outstripped' past."[17] In an open conversation with the dead, within an ethics of memory, we keep the future's possibilities possible, not disavowed or blindly embraced. In an open conversation with the dead, we keep open the world and the self.

Because we are constituted by time's trinity of past, present, and future, we are the hounded and the hopeful. The past will not leave us alone, and the future directs our activity in the present. The deads' sermons from the pulpit of their graves inform our todays and our tomorrows. Harrison writes: "Certainly in most world cultures the dead are hounders, harassing the living with guilt, reminding them of their debts to the forefathers, calling on them to meet their obligations." He continues, "They trouble our sleep, colonize our moods, whisper in the dark, insinuate themselves into our imagination, urge us to continue their work on behalf of the unborn."[18]

This is the content of our binding back and bending forward in religion and in the creative act of memorialization. This is the way in which we stand the ligature between those who have passed and those who have yet to arrive. How we act points the way between the horizon of death and the horizon of birth. Whether we choose a binding back that is unquestioning or the embrace of an ethical engagement with memory and memorialization makes all the difference in our relationships with the dead and the future that opens for the unborn.

FOR FURTHER READING

Chidester, David, and Edward T. Linenthal, eds. *American Sacred Space.* Bloomington: Indiana University Press, 1995.

Foote, Kenneth. *Shadowed Ground: America's Landscape of Violence & Tragedy.* Austin: University of Texas Press, 2003.

Gray, Peter O., and Kendrick Oliver, eds. *The Memory of Catastrophe.* Manchester: Manchester University Press, 2004.

Harrison, Robert Pogue. *Dominion of the Dead.* Chicago: University of Chicago Press, 2005.

Hervieu-Léger, Daniele. *Religion as a Chain of Memory.* Translated by Simon Lee. New Brunswick, NJ: Rutgers University Press, 2000.

Stier, Oren Baruch, and J. Shawn Landres, eds. *Religion, Violence, Memory, and Place.* Bloomington: Indiana University Press, 2006.

Yerushalmi, Yosef Hayim. *Zakhor: Jewish History and Jewish Memory.* Seattle: University of Washington Press, 2005.

Young, James E. *The Texture of Memory: Holocaust Memorials and Meaning in Europe, Israel, and America.* New Haven, CT: Yale University Press, 1994.

19

THE DISNEY WAY OF DEATH

Gary Laderman

The man most intimately associated with the imagination of children in twentieth-century America is Walt Disney. His lasting cultural power is a testament to his creative energies, bold innovations, philosophy of entertainment, and identification with dominant American values; the fact that his work continues to shape the fantasy life of generations of children only makes his crucial position in American cultural history more obvious. Disney's life, beginning in Chicago at the turn of the century and ending in a hospital directly across the street from his Burbank studios in 1966, is a paradigmatic American rags-to-riches story. But his achievements were not solely limited to success in the business of entertainment.

Disney's cultural productions, including films, television shows, and theme parks, have left an indelible mark on the life of the nation. In many ways, his work helped usher in the emerging value systems that transformed the United States in the first part of the century. According to recent biographer Steven Watts, "In the broadest sense, Disney smoothed the jagged transition from the values of the Victorian age

to those of the fledgling consumer America. . . . He helped Americans accommodate to a new age by appealing to older traditions while forging a new creed of leisure, self-fulfillment, and mass consumption. More than a mere cartoonist or entertainer, he managed to become, to use his own phrase, a spokesman for the American way of life."[1] Taken as a whole, the mythic worlds animated and brought to life in Disney's work provide Americans with both an escape from reality and effective interpretive tools to make sense of reality—in other words, his cultural legacy has as much to do with religion as it does with mass entertainment.

If Disney was a mouthpiece for an American way of life, the force of his voice depended on a curious obsession with death—not surprising considering the usual connections between the religious imagination and mortality.[2] While recent critical studies have begun to examine the rich cultural material found in his life and work, focusing on gender, sexuality, class, and politics, little has been said about a glaring propensity to focus on death in many of his early films.[3] The present essay will address this lacuna and investigate Disney's cultural productions in relation to cultural history, American religious life, and a burgeoning field of study, the history of death.[4]

DEATH IN AMERICA: TABOO OR NOT TABOO?

Conventional wisdom holds that America is a death-denying culture. From the early 1960s, psychologists, sociologists, nurses, doctors, anthropologists, historians, journalists, and others have supported this cultural diagnosis, which has proven to be a powerful trope in the literature on death in America. Relying in part on the assumption that there is a universal fear of death, many writers have argued that the subject of death in American society is taboo, that the reality of death has disappeared from everyday life, that death itself has become bereft of meaning for most people—particularly over the course of the first half of the twentieth century. An explosion of writings on death began to appear by the end of the 1960s, and the argument about an "age of death denial" has carried the day since.[5]

Those early studies shaped conventional wisdom about the past and convinced a nation that its views on death were determined by out-of-control modernizing social forces, irrational personal anxieties, and culturally pervasive taboos. In the preface to *The Meaning of Death* (1959), one of the first publications to address this topic, Herman Feifel makes an important observation about death in America: it has not attracted much scholarly attention. He writes, "Even after looking hard in the literature, it is surprising how slim is the systematized knowledge about death. Far too little heed has been given to assessing thoroughly the implications of the meaning of death."[6] Feifel, a psychologist who served as editor for this collection of essays,

rightly recognizes the unique status of the book, both as a contribution to the interdisciplinary study of death and as a premier text in a new field of research in America.

Before explaining the organization of the book, which includes sections on theory, psychology, and sociology, Feifel makes the following cultural observation: "In the presence of death, Western culture, by and large, has tended to run, hide, and seek refuge in group norms and actuarial statistics. The individual face of death has become blurred by embarrassed incuriosity [*sic*] and institutionalization. The shadows have begun to dwarf the substance. Concern about death has been relegated to the tabooed territory heretofore occupied by diseases like tuberculosis and cancer and the topic of sex. We have been compelled, in unhealthy measure, to internalize our thoughts and feelings, fears, and even hopes concerning death."[7] Although Feifel refers to "Western culture" in this passage, he is primarily concerned about American society, as he makes clear when he identifies the first "dominant leitmotif" running throughout the book: "Denial and avoidance of the countenance of death characterize much of the American outlook."[8] Similar observations had been made before Feifel's, but in many respects this collection marks a turning point in the published literature on death in America. The principal characteristics associated with the American experience of death—invisibility, silence, dispassion, institutionalization, taboo—can be found in almost every subsequent publication on the topic.

As suggested earlier, the proliferation of literature on death in America was produced by people associated with a number of social settings, including universities, hospitals, therapy sessions, hospices, and funeral homes. Although the focus of these writings varied, most either implicitly maintained or actively supported the notion that America was a death-denying culture. One of the most authoritative voices to shape public opinion was Elisabeth Kübler-Ross, whose *On Death and Dying* popularly linked the vocabulary of denial with the language of death.[9] Kübler-Ross identified denial as the first stage to the ultimate acceptance of death among terminal patients, but she also argued for a much larger social tendency to refuse the reality of death. Kübler-Ross first describes a childhood experience with death she had growing up in Europe that was distinguished by acceptance, communal support, and mature realism. She then states how this compares with America at midcentury: "This is in great contrast to a society in which death is viewed as taboo, discussion of it is regarded as morbid, and children are excluded with the presumption and pretext that it would be 'too much' for them."[10]

Important features of the literature on death are the lack of attention to religion and the often-tacit assumption that the forces of secularization were demystifying the realities of death and expunging them from everyday life. The modern experience of death, as it appears in much of the literature, was generally linked to such recent social developments as the rise of hospitals as places of dying, advancements in scientific and medical knowledge, increased analytic interest in the psychology of grief, and the dramatic economic growth of funeral homes throughout the country. The passage from life to death, and the physical remains after the last breath, became associated with a range of secular values and technological interventions rather than traditional spiritual questions and theological explanations. In the introduction to a collection of primarily social-scientific studies of death published in 1965, Robert Fulton employs imagery from the field of medicine to characterize the shift from a religious to a secular perspective on death overtaking contemporary culture: "In America today we have come to a point in our

history when we are beginning to react to death as we would to a communicable disease. Death no longer is viewed as the price of moral trespass or as the result of theological wrath; rather, in our modern secular world, death is coming to be seen as the consequence of personal neglect or untoward accident. Death is now a temporal matter. Like cancer or syphilis, it is a private disaster that we discuss only reluctantly with our physician. Moreover, as in the manner of many contagious diseases, those who are caught in the throes of death are isolated from their fellow human beings, while those who have succumbed to it are hidden quickly from view."[11] For many writing on the subject in the 1960s, 1970s, and 1980s, the invisibility of death in American culture was produced in an increasingly secular society—in other words, arguments about the disappearance of death went hand-in-hand with arguments about the "desacralization" of death.

One of the most important figures to perpetuate the notion that, in his words, "society has banished death," is French historian Philippe Aries. His monumental study of attitudes toward death in Western society, *The Hour of Our Death* (originally published as *L'homme devant la mort* in 1977; translated in 1981), concludes with an analysis of the twentieth century, tellingly labeled "The Invisible Death." In the chapter, "Death Denied," Aries turns to a discussion of the United States. Rather than push the denial thesis full force, he presents a much more subtle commentary on the contradictory cultural forces at work in the first half of the twentieth century. On the one hand, he writes "is as if one whole part of the culture were pushing America to erase every vestige of death. . . . It is the [trend] that is spreading the taboo about death or the idea of the insignificance of death throughout the modern world." On the other hand, Aries understands the American funeral as a site where a contradictory attitude toward death finds expression, a place where death remains "quite visible" and firmly in the mind of the living.[12]

While Aries is one of the few to suggest that America has more complicated views on death than previously believed, the first trend, related to erasures and taboos, is the one most often reaffirmed by those who refer to his work. It is also the prevailing view found in another relevant source of information: textbooks on death and dying, a growth industry by the end of the 1970s. In a recent example from *Confronting Death: Values, Institutions, and Human Mortality,* David Wendell Moller presents a historical overview of attitudes toward death based on Aries's research on the European context. He then moves "across the ocean" to America and, although briefly commenting on death in Puritan New England and nineteenth-century society, focuses on "the disappearance of death" in the twentieth century. Like Aries, Moller quickly raises the possibility that American attitudes might be more nuanced and complicated than they appear. But he, like so many others, concludes this discussion by falling back on conventional wisdom and historical nostalgia for a bygone era: "The traditional orientation to death with its essential patterns of religion, ritual, and community, has been replaced by the denial, confusion, contradiction, and meaninglessness of the modern styles of death and dying."[13]

Although the weight of these arguments is strong, they either do not tell the whole story about death in American society or only hint at the possibility that American responses do not have to be classified as forms of denial or acceptance. Instead of readily accepting the sweeping generalizations associated with the "taboo" argument, a more intricate cultural analysis must take into account the simultaneous presence of prohibitions and public expressions and make sense of the variety of responses to death—often

distinctly religious responses—that can be found circulating within American society. The material and cultural landscape is too infested with ghosts, personal lives too haunted by the loss of significant others, collective memory too dependent on the blood of martyrs and victims, for death to easily slip away from the sight of living Americans—even in the first half of the twentieth century. In addition to the silence and whispers surrounding death during this period of time, there were telling signs of preoccupation with the end of life and fascination with the unmistakable realities of death.

Numerous case studies from the twentieth century could be explored, including the rise of successful funeral homes across the country, the impact of two world wars on American sensibilities, the growing literature in the psychology of grief, and the variety of representations of death found in popular culture. The rest of this essay will explore a series of popular representations of death in American culture that can be found in films produced by Walt Disney during his life. These texts offer evidence of a set of cultural meanings different from those associated with the taboo arguments. In order to understand these meanings better, it will be necessary to stray from the texts themselves and consider both the audience that flocked to the films and the man who produced them.

"DEATH, DISNEY'S OBSESSION WITH"

Walt Disney is a complex American figure, and the picture that has emerged in numerous studies of his life contains telling contradictions. A creator of beloved cartoon characters like Jiminy Cricket, Bambi, and Dopey, but also an anti-Semite who saw Jewish conspiracy and corruption all around him; a patriotic American who made propaganda films for the US military in World War II, and an FBI informant who ratted on other early Hollywood pioneers; an industrious, self-made man who stands as an icon for ingenuity and creativity, yet for many an industrial tyrant who exploited the labor of others. As suggested earlier, Walt Disney the man is just as attractive to the cultural historian as "Uncle Walt," one of the most significant mythmakers in twentieth-century America.

Rather than begin with the usual celebration of Walt Disney's imaginative and profoundly popular animated films, let us turn to a little-discussed cruel act of brutality that one writer places at the center of his success. Biographical information about Walt Disney has been a well-guarded secret by the Disney corporation until recently, but this illuminating early life experience was reported in a 1938 edition of the *New York Times Magazine*. In the article—one of the few written with Disney's cooperation—Douglas Churchill suggests that Disney's philosophy about entertainment can be tied to a specific experience of death in childhood.

An owl drowning in the cool shade of a tree on a Missouri farm one afternoon thirty years ago influenced the career of a man and helped fashion the fantasy of an era. Blinking in the uncomfortable light, the bird felt hands encircling it. Instinctively it beat its wings and clawed, and just as instinctively a frightened lad of 7 hurled the owl to the ground and, in his terror, stamped on it. That owl is the only thing that Walt Disney ever intentionally killed. The incident has haunted him over the years. Occurring in a formative period, it directed his attention, subconsciously, to the birds and gentle beasts that play such an important part in his craftsmanship, and helped to shape his philosophy.[14]

According to a later biographer, Disney felt such stinging remorse afterward that he decided to bury the dead owl. But even though the owl had been put in the ground, it apparently haunted the dreams of the young boy for some time.[15]

Roughly ten years prior to Churchill's 1938 article, Disney produced the first of the Silly Symphonies, an animated short called "The Skeleton Dance" (1929), which contained haunting, though hilarious, images of death. It was released just before the stock market crash in October and on the heels of Disney's enormously popular short, "Steamboat Willie," which introduced the world to Micky Mouse.[16] The idea of animating skeletons in a graveyard to perform a modern, and playful, dance of death appealed to Disney, who began working on the cartoon with his early associate Ubbe Iwerks. The final product depicts four skeletons dancing in a moonlit graveyard to a musical composition derived from Edvard Grieg's, "March of the Dwarfs."[17] Originally titling the piece "The Spook Dance," Disney expressed his enthusiasm for its commercial prospects in a letter to Iwerks: "I am glad the spook dance is progressing so nicely—give her Hell, Ubbe—make it funny and I am sure we will be able to place it in a good way."[18] He also wrote to his wife, Lilly, that he was convinced of its success: "I feel positive the 'Spook Dance' will make a real hit when shown."[19]

Contrary to a deep-rooted American tradition of popular death imagery in which the afterlife is depicted with domesticated scenes of pious family members reunited in the great beyond, this modern danse macabre relies on the physical return of the dead literally to get in the face of the living—in one sequence, the dancing skeleton's face moves forward and fills the entire frame of the screen.[20] Initially, all the theater managers who previewed it hated the macabre piece, with one purportedly exclaiming to Walt's brother, Roy, "What's he trying to do, ruin us? You go back and tell that brother of yours the renters don't want this gruesome crap. . . . What they want is more Mickey Mouse. You go back and tell Walt. *More mice,* tell him, *More mice!*"[21] According to another account, one exhibitor "visibly shivered after he had seen it and said it would give his customers goose bumps."[22] While many were shocked by Disney's thematic choice, the first Silly Symphony finally had a showing in Los Angeles, where critics and patrons raved about it, turning the "gruesome crap" into the national hit Disney expected.[23]

Two years after the Churchill piece, Disney released *Fantasia* (1940), a full-length feature film that consisted of animated stories and images set to seven classical pieces of music. It was a highly experimental film, and although critics disagreed on its merits, the public response was clear: it was Disney's first major box office flop (although in time, it too became a money-making project for Disney).[24] The final sequence of this series of short segments actually contains two very different pieces: Mussorgsky's "Night on Bald Mountain" and Schubert's "Ave Maria." As a rather simplistic meditation on the battle between good and evil, the entire sequence moves literally from the darkness and destruction of night to the glory and beauty of the rising sun. In spite of the uplifting, spiritually inspiring scenes set to the Schubert piece, the imagery associated with "Night on Bald Mountain" is particularly graphic for a Disney film.

The sequence returns the audience to the space of a haunted graveyard, though this time the mood is less lighthearted and the setting is much more menacing to the living. In this version, the dance of death is a decidedly adult affair, with fantastic visions of monstrous demons, dangerous witches, and a mountaintop transformed into an evil overlord who controls the spirits of death in the tiny village cemetery below. The sexual and highly sadistic energy that animates this segment arises from a curious mixture of images, including resurrection

of the dead, transformative fires from hell, and the seductive lure of malevolent femininity and female body parts. Fortunately for the living, just as the demonic forces are about to invade the village next to the burial ground, daylight strikes and the church bells begin to toll. At this point, the music shifts to Schubert, and a fog-shrouded line of candle-carrying pilgrims emerges on the screen, and daylight overtakes the night.

Disney's fascination with the dance of death, his early childhood experience, and, as we will see, the recurring death-related themes in his films all lead to a question that the title of this section answers: did Disney have an obsession with death? Richard Schickel's biography, *The Disney Vision: The Life, Times, Art and Commerce of Walt Disney*, contains the index entry: "Death, Disney's obsession with."[25] Schickel and other biographers, including Disney's own daughter, Diane, include this personality trait in their reconstruction of Disney's life. Although the Disney corporation tried to keep the personal life of the founder out of the public eye—according to Schickel, because "corporate drive has always been toward the preservation of an easily assimilated image"[26]—this characteristic and other revealing aspects of Disney's personality that have come to light in recent studies provide a more complete picture of the man than the "image" originally managed by his family and the studio.

The first to suggest that Disney was obsessed with death was his daughter, whose account of its origins is a standard feature in the prevailing Disney lore. According to Diane, in the early 1930s, Disney attended a Hollywood party and had an unfortunate session with a fortune-teller, who gave him some particularly bad news: he would die at thirty-five. At this point in his life, Disney had achieved enormous financial success and become a bona-fide celebrity; but, in the words of Schickel, this prediction "plagued"

Disney, and "for the rest of his life he avoided funerals and when forced to attend them, fell into long, brooding depressions. He even avoided would be biographers, commenting to more than one acquaintance that 'biographies are only written about dead people.'"[27] Other biographies note that this prediction remained with Disney into his later years. Leonard Mosley writes that at a party celebrating his thirtieth wedding anniversary, Disney had been drinking quite a bit and at one point "gloomily speculated out loud whether the fortune-teller might have made a mistake. Could she have meant he was going to die at fifty-five and not thirty-five—next year, in fact?"[28] While the psychological effects of this preoccupation are numerous, at least one biographer suggests that Disney was "in a race against time" to finish all of his projects.[29]

One of the projects he did not see to fruition but was passionate about near the end of his life was the creation of a futuristic city, what he described as an "experimental prototype community of tomorrow"—EPCOT. According to Mosley, this vision of a tightly controlled, highly regulated utopian community can also be linked to another expression of Disney's obsession with death: his curiosity about cryogenics, a technologically innovative form of real-life "suspended animation." Cryogenics attracted a great deal of attention in the 1960s as a sophisticated scientific intervention in the dying process—in effect freezing the corpse until a future date, when advances in medical science could allow for the reanimation of life. Mosley argues that in Disney's mind EPCOT had profound implications for the future of humanity and links his enthusiasm for the project to his newfound interest: "Faced by mankind's suicidal impulse to destroy itself by nuclear war or the poison of pollution from toxic wastes, Walt Disney had envisaged EPCOT as the community of the future from which all the blights and blemishes of twentieth-century

civilization had been banished. It would demonstrate that if people would only learn how to live in an enlightened and sanitized environment, they would be able to avoid not just war and disease but indefinitely postpone death and enjoy life, health, and happiness almost everlasting. . . . It was about this time [early 1960s] that Walt Disney became acquainted with the experiments into the process known as cryogenesis."[30]

While some question the truth of Disney's interest in this scientific chimera, it too has found a permanent place in Disney lore. When Disney died of acute circulatory collapse on December 15, 1966, the studio delayed making an announcement for one day for a variety of reasons, including a concern about the financial impact of the news. According to family members who attended a private ceremony, between the death and the public notification, Disney was cremated and deposited in Forest Lawn Cemetery in Los Angeles. Despite this official version of events, rumors that Disney's body had been frozen and secretly stored in an undisclosed location began to circulate almost immediately in popular consciousness. Watts discounts such a "wild rumor," writing that "Walt's supposed interest in cryogenesis prompted speculation that his body had been frozen and stored in a lab somewhere to be revived later. There was no truth to this story."[31] The cultural durability of this "speculation" continues to be strong, however; one of the many persistent rumors about Disney's deep-freeze is that he was cryogenically sealed and placed within the confines of Cinderella's palace.

Another source for evidence of Disney's obsession with death can be found in the stories he depicted in full-length feature animated films, films that left a lasting impression on American culture in general and generations of children in particular. Indeed, the popularity of his films as both mass entertainment and socially significant pedagogical texts in the moral development of children suggests that an investigation of the role and symbolism of death in the films themselves can lead to greater understanding of the larger cultural and religious meanings associated with his work. In this light, films that gave expression to Disney's obsessions and became defining narratives in American mythology provide important material for the examination of twentieth-century society.

FEARS, FAIRY TALES, AND AMERICAN CULTURAL RELIGION

According to many studies, Disney was both pioneer and prophet in American society. For historians, biographers, and cultural critics, his work articulated a range of celebrated American doctrines in a form that any child could understand. The success of his cultural productions mark Disney as a formidable presence in the making of modern culture. In many biographies, the story of his life is the story of twentieth-century America herself. Disney's genius lay in the ability to both express the popular sentiments and values of "the people" and reinforce particular conservative social tendencies in response to the political, economic, and cultural changes of the period. According to Watts, Disney the man and Disney the corporation grasped essential American views about social order, particularly as they relate to work and family, during an era of tremendous historical change. "In a stream of memorable work over several generations, he shaped into a synthetic, compelling form the diverse bundle of images, values, and sensibilities that many twentieth-century Americans struggled with—individualism and community, fantasy and technology, populism and corporate authority, modernism and sentimentalism, consumerism and producerism, progress and nostalgia."[32]

Watts rightly notes the distressing tendencies that emerged in both Disney's life and American society in the early twentieth century—a drift toward authoritarianism, dependence on social conformity, and deeprooted anti-intellectualism, to name a few. But he also acknowledges an unmistakable popular sentiment that remains to this day: "In typical 'American Century' style, [Disney] expressed a mythical, idealized version of the values and aspirations of the modern United States."[33] His films are especially significant cultural productions; they act, in fact, as modern fairy tales, primarily but not exclusively created for the consumption of children and convey distinctive religious messages about life and meaning in the twentieth century. These messages can be characterized as "religious" because they teach about order, meaning, transcendence, and orientation. In addition, like many religious expressions, they acquire social weight because they are so intimately tied to a desire to triumph over death, a point to be discussed shortly.

The audience for Disney's films, as for most fairy tales, includes adults as well as children—indeed, the timeless quality of these stories partially depends on their attracting people from every age. But the association of fairy tales with children, and the assumption that they are integral to the socialization and development of children are recent phenomena. As literary critic Maria Tatar argues in her study of the Grimms' fairy tales: "Originally told at fireside gatherings or in spinning circles by adults to adult audiences, fairy tales joined the canon of children's literature . . . only in the last two or three centuries. Yet the hold these stories have on the imagination of children is so compelling that it becomes difficult to conceive of a childhood without them."[34] She also makes the important observation that, while fairy tales express "our deepest hopes and most ardent desires," they also contain within them darker visions: "Wishes and fantasies may come to life in the fairy tale, but fears and phobias also become full-blooded presences."[35] The fact that the Grimms' tales include instances of "murder, mutilation, cannibalism, infanticide, and incest" makes Tatars arguments even more convincing on this point.[36]

Although many understand fairy tales as tapping into universal structures and predispositions in the human psyche, some cultural historians strive to keep these stories in perspective—that is, they explore the social context in which certain stories appear and thrive, and they chart how these stories change over time.[37] For cultural historian Robert Darnton, such stories "are historical documents. They have evolved over many centuries and have taken different turns in different cultural traditions. Far from expressing the unchanging operations of man's inner being, they suggest that *mentalités* themselves have changed."[38] Some of Disney's films are entirely modern, but many are drawn from the deep well of European folklore (e.g., *Snow White and the Seven Dwarfs* [1937], *Cinderella* [1950], and *Sleeping Beauty* [1959]). Darnton and others argue that the content, tenor, and texture of these tales depend on historical period and national setting.

Regardless of origin and their timeless nature, Disney tales reflect twentieth-century American society and dominant American *mentalités,* or worldviews. They also express certain religious sensibilities on the American landscape that are not contained within the bounds of any particular religious tradition. The study of American religion outside the boundaries of specific traditions—that is, with an anthropological eye squarely on cultural forms of expression and behavior—is a relatively new area of investigation that challenges long-held assumptions about what counts as data. Whether religion is paired with "civil," "popular culture," or

"vernacular," Americanists have slowly begun to realize there is more to religious history than denominations, doctrines, and deliverance.[39]

Historian of religions Catherine Albanese identifies one form of this religion as "American cultural religion" and argues that, though "diffuse and loose," it can be understood as an integral component of American religious history. According to Albanese, American cultural religion is a complex, multilayered religious system, providing people with "additional symbolic centers" that contain distinctive themes, practices, meanings, and value orientations that upset the conventional boundaries between the ordinary and the extraordinary. Along with two other symbolic centers in society that promote identification with core American values, civil religion and public Protestantism, cultural religion "seeks to dissolve differences in American life."[40] Some of the pervasive themes found within it include millennial dominance and millennial innocence, the search for "religious experience and for a community of feeling," the redemptive nature of some forms of violence, perfectionism, and commitment to personal fulfillment.

Another book that explores this kind of religious sensibility in America, *The American Monomyth*, devotes an entire chapter to Disney. The authors, Robert Jewett and John Lawrence, argue that a particularly powerful mythic structure inhabits the American imagination and that one of its dominant tropes is the saving, redemptive actions of one individual in the face of dangerous evil. They examine a range of materials within American popular culture to investigate the "ritually predictable plots in the mythic landscape [that] provide some of the best clues to tensions and hopes within current American consciousness."[41] Jewett and Lawrence highlight the ways in which this monomyth represents a peculiar form of popular religion and suggest that Disney himself "credibly reinstated the sense of the miraculous" with his cultural productions.[42] They also emphasize the acknowledged pedagogic force of his "entertainment": "Disney's efforts to create a sanitary form of happiness were regarded as the finest examples of educational entertainment."[43] The "sanitary form of happiness" that shines through by the end of the narratives depends, in fact, on the triumph over death.

In his stories, the Disney way of death is structured around "ritually predictable plots"— indeed, in addition to articulating crucial aspects of American cultural religion, his films provide Americans young and old alike with templates for understanding death. The presence of death in his films is so significant in this regard because these representations convey moral teachings about so many of the essentials of life, including sex, kinship, transcendence, suffering, and misfortune. During a period that witnessed severe economic turmoil, a second world war, scientific and technological revolutions, and other tumultuous social developments in the 1930s, 1940s, and 1950s, Disney's early animated films simultaneously entertained the masses and inculcated Americans with simplistic notions of right and wrong, virtue and vice, and innocence and corruption. And what is most striking—though not surprising—about these films is that for many stories, death, or the threat of death, is the motor, the driving force that enlivens each narrative. In addition, the preoccupation with the individual encounter with death, the impact of death on family members, and the optimistic view that death can be overcome found in most of these films, offered Americans in the first half of the twentieth century an accessible, generally Christian and broadly American, religious vision that avoided fundamentalist, apocalyptic scenarios, on the one hand, and abstruse, theological reflection, on the other.[44]

The pivotal role of death in these stories is unmistakable: in *Snow White and the Seven Dwarfs* (1937), the queen's desire to kill the young girl sets the story in motion; in *Pinocchio* (1940), the wooden puppet has to die in order to be resurrected as a real boy; in *Bambi* (1942), the small fawn becomes a mature deer in the aftermath of his mother's cruel murder; the *Cinderella* (1950) story begins with the death of her mother, which in turn leads to the introduction of the step-family; and in *Sleeping Beauty* (1959), the mortal curse by the evil fairy Maleficent leads the three good fairies to hide the princess in the woods. Rather than disappearing from sight, death and death-related themes are front and center in these films. Contrary to arguments about denial, these animated cartoons— like many fairy tales and other forms of children literature[45]—demonstrate a fixation on the presence of death in life.

One of the only people to discuss this characteristic in Disney films was an educational psychologist who wrote a piece for the English journal *New Society*. After the rerelease of *Fantasia* (1940) in London in 1968, Nicholas Tucker states in his essay, "Who's Afraid of Walt Disney?": "With his penchant for melodramatic settings, and his preoccupation with grief, death and bereavement, Disney is curiously old-fashioned. In some ways he anticipated the 1950 boom in horror comics, which also tended to have a nineteenth-century air of morbidity about them. Death or near-death abounds."[46] Tucker is correct to insert this morbidity into a much larger history; indeed, in the American context, this persistent fascination with death, and its representational weight in popular culture, must be understood as a critical dimension of American cultural religion.

It is often, though not always, the case that in Disney films the threat of death is framed in millennial terms—that is, powerful forces in the cosmos that bring death and destruction are overcome with virtuous heroic action, unyielding optimism in a better world, or miraculous intervention. For Disney, who grew up under the stern hand of his father, a religious, working-class man who represented a disappearing world based on such Protestant values as hard work, sobriety, self-denial, and frugality, the emerging complex moral order of the universe could be depicted in paint-by-number fashion. In the film *Fantasia,* the association between death and evil is both unequivocal and at times quite surprising. According to Robert Feild, who wrote a tribute to the man in 1942, Disney made the following unpretentious comments about the setting for the "Night on Bald Mountain" sequence: "It sort of symbolizes something. The forces of good on one side and of evil on the other is what I'm trying to see in the thing. What other reason can there be for it?"[47] As Jewett and Lawrence and others point out, this and other early Disney films show no interest in capturing the "moral gradations" in life.[48] His films depict a millennial vision of the universe, where absolute good battles with absolute evil, with death usually imagined as the result of evil intentions, or as a justified fate for the unredeemable.

Jewett and Lawrence also identify a peculiar aspect of the personification of evil in many films—it is often linked with "curvaceous femininity": "The 'curves' of the wicked Queen are played off visually against the pure, straight lines of Snow White. A similar effort to associate curvaceous femininity with evil is made in 'Night on Bald Mountain,' where demonic hags are presented with bare breasts and extended nipples—the only occasion in Disney's film-making career for unveiling these menacing anatomic structures."[49] While Disney films promote obvious stereotypes relating to gender, the phallic symbolism of the demonic figure ruling over all the dark, fiendish activity is equally striking

during this segment. It is clear that the malevolent forces of evil are also associated with masculinity, or perhaps a "penetrating" masculinity.[50] In one of Disney's most popular films, Bambi's mother is killed by merciless hunters whose guns violate the pastoral innocence found in the forest. As one early critic playfully, and derogatorily, summarized the action of *Bambi* (1942): "The hero is a deer named Bambi, whose mother is killed by the villain, Mr Man, whose sweetheart is attacked by Mr Man's dogs, whose terrestrial paradise is destroyed by Mr Man's fire."[51]

Evil comes in many forms in Disney films—man, stepmothers, bad fairies, curvaceous women, menacing whales, and so on—but whatever may cause the death, or insert the threat of death into the lives of the animated characters, the response is pure human pathos. In most cases, this response is depicted in the film itself. But in the special case of *Bambi* (1942), the profound emotional response is erased from the narrative in the fade-to-black after the fawn confronts the reality of his mother's death. What contributes to the astonishing lingering power of this death scene in the lives of many Americans is the way in which the emotional weight is left for the audience to bear.

In his essay on *Bambi,* masculinity, and American hunting culture, David Payne identifies something shared by many Americans who have seen the film: "*Bambi* is often recalled as the most memorable film of people's youth, not only for its charm and natural wonders, but because there children learned about death."[52] Although Bambi's mother is killed off camera, and the young fawn's response is blacked out, many in the audience experience the trauma, are impressed by its filmic reality and its depiction of a common childhood fear of permanent separation from the mother, and remember the moment for the rest of their lives. The community of feeling that usually forms on-screen in the wake of death, or apparent death, is transferred in this film to the audience members watching together.

The experience of death as a profound, unacceptable rupture in the insulated world of the domestic family unit is a deeply rooted cultural script that, according to Aries, came to prominence in the nineteenth century.[53] Aries labels this culturally dominant attitude "the death of the other" and associates it with the emergence of the nuclear family, new forms of memorialization glorifying the irreplaceable individual, and valorization of the affections of the survivors. As the nuclear family came to represent a comforting, secure remedy to the chaos and danger found in the streets of late-nineteenth- and early twentieth-century America, the intrusion of death into homelife brought the religious character of these bonds into sharp relief. Although absent from *Bambi,* the deathbed scene could also convey the sentimentality and holy anguish that erupts as grief at the sight of death. For example, in *Pinocchio* (1940), after Gepetto is saved from the whale by his creation and he places the deanimated puppet on the bed, the scene lingers on the heaving sobs of the gentle puppetmaker and the dispirited countenance of Jimminy Cricket, the surrogate family whose lives have been enchanted—indeed given special meaning—by the presence of Pinocchio.

While Disney may have avoided funerals later in his life, he clearly understood the dramatic and commercial possibilities of the artfully illustrated deathbed scene. Transcripts from story conferences for the first, full-length animated film, *Snow White and the Seven Dwarfs* (1937), capture Disney's awareness of these possibilities, as well as his energies and dominance in the creative process of producing films. Imagining the conclusion of the film, Disney articulates his vision of Snow White's encoffined body and the dwarfs' reactions to it.

Fade in on her in the glass coffin, maybe shaded by a big tree. It's built on sort of a little pedestal, torches are burning, two dwarfs on either side with things like guards would have, others are coming up and putting flowers on the coffin. It's all decked with flowers. The birds fly up and drop flowers. Shots of the birds; show them sad. Snow White is beautiful in the coffin.

Then you hear the Prince. The birds, dwarfs, everyone hear him offscreen. As they turn to look, here he is silhouetted against the hill with his horse. As he walks down the hill singing the song, cut to Snow White in the coffin. As he approaches, everyone sort of steps back as if he had a right there [*sic*]. He goes up to the coffin and finishes the song. As he finishes the song, he lifts the glass lid of the coffin and maybe there's a hesitation, then he kisses her. From the kiss he drops down and buries his head in his hands in a sad position, and all the dwarfs see it and every dwarf drops his head.[54]

The dwarfs foil the queen's plans by not burying the young woman alive. They, like many Americans in the first half of the twentieth century, were fixated on the beautiful body, too entranced by it to say goodbye forever but unencumbered by professional managers whose job is to ensure the final separation between the living and the dead.

The joyful moments following the kiss that brings Snow White out of her "sleeping death" signal another element in the Disney way of death, an element that appears in all the films and contributes to their mythic power in American culture. That element, found in most religious systems as well, is, of course, the happy ending where death is not really the end but is defeated by the commendable main characters who live on in a safer, purified world. By the end of many Disney films, the threat of death is vanquished, and, most importantly, the integrity of the family is reconstituted and made secure. After the death of Bambi's mother, the advice of his father, the strong, dispassionate, wise Stag, is that he must carry on. The mourning and torment of losing a mother are hidden behind the black screen of time so that he can stoically make the transition from innocence to maturity. The rest of the movie follows Bambi's often difficult rite of passage into adulthood, where in the end he gets the girl. Payne remarks that the remainder of the film after the death encodes a certain type of sexual politics that relates to "Bambi's emergent masculinity discovered in combat, heroism, and survival, all of which are inspired, even manipulated by, his desire to win Faline for his mate (from the other deer) and to protect her from the ravages of survival (the evils of the hunters, the forest fire caused by invading 'Man')."[55]

In many Disney films, death is a rite of passage for the individual hero that leads from, in many cases, an alternative, temporary, even broken family to the promise of living in the midst of an eternally loving, transcendent family unit—a model enshrined in various cultural expressions and publicly celebrated by a variety of religious institutions from the 1940s and 1950s on. We can see this commitment to a deep-rooted domestic religious ideology, and something of its millennial flavor, in the curse of the evil Maleficent, in the triumph of love after battling evil, and in the enactment of another death-defying kiss in *Sleeping Beauty* (1959). As in *Snow White,* the threat of death, or eternal sleep, imposed by a vain, powerful witch who does not have quite enough power to thwart the forces of good, inspires the actions of others to make sure the proper order of social life is not destroyed.

In *Pinocchio,* it is clear that the puppet, not fully human and not quite the son Gepetto wishes for, spends most of the film in a dangerous environment where perverse adults are eager to kidnap and exploit the labor of donkey-children. As a result of his sacrificing his own life for the lives of others, the fairy sees that Pinocchio has learned his lesson and is worthy of her magic powers of resurrection. The dead puppetboy is then reborn as a real individual, securely and safely delivered into the hands of his creator and father, Gepetto. In the Disney imaginative universe, death can be overcome and serve as a source of regeneration because there are wondrous, supernatural forces in the universe that help us face our darkest fears: abandonment, disintegration, chaos. The vibrancy of American cultural religion depends in part on the potency of family relations and the desire to perpetuate the ties that bind individuals to a family unit, realities that are stronger and more powerful than the evil forces in the cosmos that conspire to destroy families. The idealized order presented in these fairy tales depicts moral teachings about the centrality of family in terms of gender roles, sexuality, the relation of the individual to the family, and the transition out of childhood.

In most of his films, Disney ends the story with the promise of domestic bliss, a ray of hope in an uncertain, malevolent world. The fact that most of these films were released during a period in which American society as a whole was struggling with both national and international conflicts and relied on a variety of domestic symbols and images is not surprising. As Watts points out, a "Disney Doctrine" is the ideological driving force behind the man's vision, a doctrine that is essentially a recapitulation of dominant American values of the time, including the "notion that the nuclear family, with its attendant rituals of marriage, parenthood, emotional and spiritual instruction, and consumption, was the centerpiece of the American way of life."[56]

In many ways, the Disney way of death is a critical reason the "Disney Doctrine" has so much cultural capital. As modern-day fairy tales, his films both reflect and shape religious sensibilities across the grain of American culture—they are popular meditations that rely on a cultural system of religious meanings to make sense of death. The centrality of death in these films marks them not only as significant cultural artifacts in the history of attitudes toward death in America but also as revealing cultural texts that communicate popular fears about social disorder, common fantasies about family life as a source of transcendence, and idealistic dreams about American values and virtues. Without this preoccupation with death, Disney would not have had the cultural impact he did in twentieth-century America; if Americans in this period did not have similar preoccupations and similar strategies for imagining meaning in the face of death, his films would have held little public interest.

FOR FURTHER READING

Aries, Philippe. *The Hour of Our Death.* Translated by Helen Weaver. New York: Vintage, 1982.

Albanese, Catherine. *America: Religions and Religion.* 3rd ed. Belmont, CA: Wadsworth, 1999.

Bell, Elizabeth, Lynda Haas, and Laura Sells, eds. *From Mouse to Mermaid: The Politics of Film, Gender, and Culture.* Bloomington: Indiana University Press, 1995.

Bellah, Robert. *The Broken Covenant: American Civil Religion in Time of Trial.* New York: Seabury, 1975.

Boyer, Paul. *When Time Shall Be No More: Prophecy Belief in Modern America.* Cambridge, MA: Belknap Press of Harvard University Press, 1992.

Bryman, Alan. *Disney and His Worlds.* London: Routledge, 1995.

Charmaz, Kathy. *The Social Reality of Death: Death in Contemporary America.* New York: Random House, 1980.

Chidester, David. "The Church of Baseball, the Fetish of Coca-Cola, and the Potlatch of Rock 'n' Roll: Theoretical Models for the Study of Religion in American Popular Culture." *Journal of the American Academy of Religion* 64, no. 4 (Winter 1996): 743–65.

Churchill, Douglas W. "Disney's 'Philosophy.'" *New York Times Magazine.* March 6, 1938, 9 and 22.

Culhane, John. *Walt Disney's Fantasia.* New York: Harry N. Abrams, 1983.

Darnton, Robert. *The Great Cat Massacre and Other Stories in French Cultural History.* New York: Vintage, 1985.

DeSpelder, Lynne Ann, and Albert Lee Strickland. *The Last Dance: Encountering Death and Dying.* Mountain View, CA: Mayfield, 1999.

Douglas, Ann. *The Feminization of American Culture.* New York: Anchor, 1988.

Farber, Manny. "Saccharine *Symphony-Bambi!*" In *The American Animated Cartoon: A Critical Anthology,* edited by Danny Peary and Gerald Peary. New York: Dutton, 1980.

Feifel, Herman, ed. *The Meaning of Death.* New York: McGraw Hill, 1959.

Feild, Robert D. *The Art of Walt Disney.* New York: Macmillan, 1942.

Fulton, Robert, ed. *Death and Identity.* New York: Wiley, 1965.

Jackson, Kathy Merlock. *Walt Disney: A Bio-Bibliography.* Westport, CT: Greenwood, 1993.

Jewett, Robert, and John Shelton Lawrence. *The American Monomyth.* 2nd ed. Lanham, MD: University Press of America, 1988.

Kübler-Ross, Elisabeth. *On Death and Dying.* New York: Macmillan, 1969.

McDannell, Colleen. *Material Christianity: Religion and Popular Culture in America.* New Haven, CT: Yale University Press, 1996.

McDannell, Colleen, and Bernhard Lang. *Heaven: A History.* New Haven: Yale University Press, 1988.

Moller, David Wendell. *Confronting Death: Values, Institutions, and Human Mortality.* New York: Oxford University Press, 1996.

Mosley, Leonard. *Disney's World: A Biography.* New York: Arno, 1985.

Payne, David. "*Bambi.*" In *From Mouse to Mermaid: The Politics of Film, Gender, and Culture,* edited by Elizabeth Bell et al. Bloomington: Indiana University Press, 1995.

Primiano, Leonard. "Vernacular Religion and the Search for Method in Religious Folklife." *Western Folklore* 54 (1995): 37–56.

Pyles, Marian S. *Death and Dying in Children's and Young People's Literature: A Survey and Bibliography.* Jefferson: McFarland, 1988.

Schickel, Richard. *The Disney Vision: The Life, Times, Art, and Commerce of Walt Disney.* Rev. ed. New York: Simon and Schuster, 1985.

Sullivan, Lawrence E., ed. *Death, Afterlife, and the Soul.* New York: Macmillan, 1989.

Tartar, Maria. *The Hard Facts of the Grimms' Fairy Tales.* Princeton: Princeton University Press, 1987.

Thomas, Bob. *Walt Disney: An American Original.* New York: Simon and Schuster, 1976.

Tucker, Nicholas. "Who's Afraid of Walt Disney?" *New Society* 288 (1968): 502–3.

Watts, Steven. *The Magic Kingdom: Walt Disney and the American Way of Life.* Boston: Houghton Mifflin, 1997.

Willis, Susan, ed. "The World according to Disney." *South Atlantic Quarterly* 92, no. 1 (1993 Special Issue).

NOTES

CHAPTER 1: CONFLICT AND PEACEBUILDING

1. John Rawls, *Political Liberalism* (New York: Columbia University Press, 1996).

2. See Elizabeth Shakman Hurd, *The Politics of Secularism in International Relation* (Princeton: Princeton University Press, 2008).

3. Benedict Anderson, *Imagined Communities: Reflections on the Origin and Spread of Nationalism* (New York: Verso, 1991).

4. Ernest Gellner, *Nationals and Nationalism* (Ithaca, NY: Cornell University Press, 1983).

5. Anthony Marx, *Faith in Nation: Exclusionary Origins of Nationalism* (Oxford: Oxford University Press, 2003).

6. Anthony D. Smith, *Chosen Peoples: Sacred Sources of National Identity* (Oxford: Oxford University Press, 2003).

7. Scott W. Hibbard, *Religious Politics and Secular States: Egypt, India, and the United States* (Baltimore: The John Hopkins University Press, 2010).

8. Ibid, 19.

9. Ibid, 20.

10. David Little, "A Double-Edged Dilemma," *Harvard Divinity Bulletin* (Autumn 2007). Available at http://www.hds.harvard.edu/news-events/harvard-divinity-bulletin/articles/a-double-edged-dilemma.

11. Ian Buruma, *Murder in Amsterdam: The Death of Theo van Gogh and the Limits of Tolerance* (New York: Penguin, 2006), 2–3.

12. Ibid., 4.

13. Israel Shahak, *The Background and Consequences of the Massacre in Hebron*, 1994. Available at http://www.geocities.com/israel_shahak/1994_2.htm (accessed 2008).

14. Charles Kimball, *When Religion Becomes Evil* (New York: HarperOne, 2008).

15. Samuel Huntington, "The Clash of Civilizations," *Foreign Affairs* (Summer 1993).

16. Christopher Hitchens, *God Is Not Great: How Religion Poisons Everything* (New York: Twelve, 2007).

17. Cited in the *Middle East Times*, September 28, 2001.

18. See http://news.bbc.co.uk/1/hi/world/middle_east/3059365.stm.

19. William T. Cavanaugh, "Does Religion Cause Violence? Behind the Common Question Lies a Morass of Unclear Thinking," *Harvard Divinity Bulletin* (Spring/Summer 2007).

20. Paul Collier, "Economic Causes of Civil Conflict and Their Implications for Policy," in *Turbulent Peace: The Challenges of Managing International Conflict,* ed. Fen Osler Hampson, Pamela Aall, and Chester A. Crocker, (Washington, DC: United States Institute of Peace Press, 2001), pp. 143–62.

21. Michael Sells, "Pilgrimage and 'Ethnic Cleansing'

in Herzegovina," in *Religion and Nationalism in Iraq*, ed. David Little and Donald Swearer (Cambridge, MA: Harvard University Press, 2006), pp. 145–56.

22. Ibid., 145.

23. Ibid., 145–46.

24. Ibid., 146.

25. Ibid., 147.

26. Ibid., 148.

27. Ibid., 150.

28. Ibid., 150–51.

29. Eva Neumaier, "Missed Opportunites: Buddhism and the Ethnic Strife in Sri Lanka and Tibet," in *Religion and Peacebuilding*, ed. Harold Coward and Gordon S. Smith (Albany: State University of New York Press, 2004), p. 75.

30. John Paul Lederach, *The Little Book of Conflict Transformation* (Intercourse, PA: Good Books, 2003).

31. Rajmohan Ghandi, "Hinduism and Peacebuilding," in *Religion and Peacebuilding*, ed. Harold Coward and Gordon S. Smith (Albany: State University of New York Press, 2004).

32. Gabriel Almond, Scott Appleby, and Emmanuel Sivan, *Strong Religion: The Rise of Fundamentalisms around the World* (Chicago: University of Chicago Press, 2003), 23–89.

33. Ibid, 25.

34. Scott Appleby, *Ambivalence of the Sacred: Religion, Violence and Reconciliation* (Lanham, MD: Rowman & Littlefield, 2000).

35. Mohammed Abu Nimer, Amal Khoury, and Emily Welty, *Unity in Diversity: Interfaith Dialogue in the Middle East* (Washington, DC: United States Institute of Peace Press, 2007).

36. Lisa Schirch, *Ritual and Symbol in Peacebuliding* (Sterling, VA: Kumarian, 2005), 2.

37. Ibid., 23.

38. Ibid., 61.

39. Laurie Goodstein, "An Effort to Foster Tolerance in Religion," June 13, 2011, http://www.nytimes.com/2011/06/14/us/14patel.html?emc=eta1.

40. Sunanda Y. Shastri and Yajneshwar S. Shastri, "Ahimsa and the Unity of All Things: A Hindu View of Nonviolence," in *Subverting Hatred: The Challenge of Nonviolence in Religious Traditions*, ed. Daniel L. Smith-Christopher (Maryknoll, NY: Orbis, 2007), 59.

41. Ibid., 62.

42. Ibid.

43. Ghandi, "Hinduism and Peacebuilding," 63.

44. Ibid.

45. Shastri and Shastri, "Ahimsa and the Unity of All Things," 73.

46. David Cortright, *Peace: A History of Movements and Ideas* (Cambridge: Cambridge University Press, 2008), 44.

47. Ibid., 47.

48. Christopher Queen, "The Peace Wheel: Nonviolent Activism in the Buddhist Tradition," in *Subverting Hatred: The Challenge of Nonviolence in Religious Traditions*, ed. Daniel L. Smith-Christopher (Maryknoll, NY: Orbis, 2007), 15.

49. Ibid., 16.

50. Neumaier, "Missed Opportunities," 74.

51. Ibid.

52. Queen, "The Peace Wheel," 29.

53. Thich Nhat Hanh, "Being Peace," in *Approaches to Peace: A Reader in Peace Studies*, ed. David P. Barash (Oxford: Oxford University Press, 1999), 206.

54. Ibid., 207.

55. Marc Gopin, "Judaism and Peacebuilding," in *Religion and Peacebuilding*, ed. Harold Coward and Gordon S. Smith (Albany: State University of New York, 2004), 111–18.

56. Ibid., 118–19.

57. Tanenbaum Center for Interreligious Understanding, "An Open House: Yehezkel Landau," in *Peacemakers in Action: Profiles of Religion in Conflict Resolution*, ed. David Little (Cambridge: Cambridge University Press, 2007), 358.

58. Cited in Gopin, "Judaism and Peacebuilding," 119.

59. Ibid.

60. Ibid., 120.

61. Ibid., 121.

62. Ibid., 121–24.

63. Ibid., 122.

64. Ibid., 123.

65. Cortwright, *Peace*, 201.

66. Ibid., 200–203.

67. Tenenbaum Center for Interreligious Understanding, "Peasant Power: Jose Inocencio Alas, El Salvador," in David Little, ed. *Peacemakers in Action*, 32–49.

68. Ibid., 48.

69. Scott Appleby, "Building Sustainable Peace: The Roles of Local and Transnational Religious Actors," in *Religious Pluralism, Globalization, and World Politics*, ed. Thomas Banchoff (Oxford: Oxford University Press, 2008), 137.

70. Ibid., 137–39.

71. Ibid., 140.

72. Ibid.

73. Ibid., 130–31.

74. Ibid., 134.

75. Ibid., 136.

76. Donald Shriver, *An Ethic for Enemies: Forgiveness in Politics* (New York: Oxford University Press, 1995).

77. Audrey R. Chapman, "Truth Commissions as Instruments of Forgiveness and Reconciliation," in *Forgiveness and Reconciliation: Religion, Public Policy, and Conflict Transformation*, ed. S. J. Helmick and G. Raymond (Radnor, PA: Templeton Foundation Press, 2001), 258.

78. Ashutosh Varshney, *Ethnic Conflict and Civil Life: Hindus and Muslims in India* (New Haven, CT: Yale University Press, 2002).

79. Appleby, "Building Sustainable Peace," 128.

Chapter 2: Civil Religion

1. Michael Mandelbaum, *The Meaning of Sports: Why Americans Watch Baseball, Football, and Basketball and What They See When They Do* (New York: Public Affairs, 2004), ch. 2.

2. Erik Brady, "Continuity of Sports Helped Heal the Times," *USA Today*, cited in Robert S. Brown, "Sport and Healing America," *Society* (November/December 2004): 37–41.

3. David Caldwell, "Canadians Issue Apology for Fans' Booing Anthem," *New York Times*, March 22, 2003.

4. The four months leading up to the 1968 Olympics had witnessed some of the most tumultuous political and social events in U.S. history—the assassinations of Martin Luther King Jr. and Senator Robert Kennedy and widespread rioting in protest of the Vietnam War at the 1968 Democratic National Convention in Chicago. Gary Gerstle, *American Crucible: Race and Nation in the Twentieth Century* (Princeton: Princeton University Press, 2002), pp. 303–5.

5. William Bradford, *History of Plymouth Plantation: Bradfords' History of the Plymouth Settlement, 1608–1650* (San Antonio: The Vision Forum, 2003). For a full account and analysis of the historical and theological significance of Puritan and early settlement of the New World, see Sydney Ahlstrom, *A Religious History of the American People* (New Haven, CT: Yale University Press, 1972), chs. 8–12.

6. John Winthrop's famous reference was to lines from Jesus's Sermon on the Mount: "You are the light of the world. A city set on a hill cannot be hid" (Matt. 5:14-16 NRSV). See Francis J. Bremer, *John Winthrop: America's Forgotten Founding Father* (Oxford: Oxford University Press, 2003).

7. Julian P. Boyd, Charles T. Cullen, John Catanzariti, Barbara B. Oberg, et al., eds., *The Papers of Thomas Jefferson* (Princeton: Princeton University Press, 1950), 1:494–95.

8. For an analysis of myth that helps bring these features of the holiday to light, see Mircea Eliade, *Myth and Reality* (New York: Harper and Row, 1963), pp. 18–19.

9. George Washington, "1789 Thanksgiving Proclamation by George Washington," *George Washington Papers at the Library Congress*. http://lcweb2.loc.gov/ammem/GW/gw004.html.

10. James Hutson, " 'A Wall of Separation': FBI Helps Restore Jefferson Obliterated Draft," *Library of Congress Information Bulletin* 57, no. 6 (June 1998).

11. Robert W. Venables, *American Indian History: Five Centuries of Conflict and Coexistence: Conquest of a Continent, 1492-1783* (Santa Fe, NM: Clear Light, 2004), 90.

12. John Winthrop, *Winthrop Papers* (Boston: Massachusetts Historical Society, 1929–1944), 4:149; cf. Gloria Lund Main, *Peoples of a Spacious Land* (Cambridge, MA: Harvard University Press, 2001), cites Winthrop as invoking a principle of occupation reminiscent of John Locke's limitation upon the natural right to property. Winthrop wrote, "The Indians having only a natural right to so much land as they could and would improve it" (349).

13. Venables, *American Indian History*, 90. For an extensive account of the "doctrine of discovery" and its pivotal role in realizing "manifest destiny," see Robert J. Miller, *Discovered and Conquered: Thomas Jefferson, Lewis & Clark, and Manifest Destiny* (Westport, CT: Greenwood, 2006).

14. Martin Marty, *A Nation of Behavers* (Chicago: Chicago University Press, 1980), 194.

15. Chief Justice Morrison R. Waite, "*Reynolds v. United States*," in John T. Noonan Jr., and Edward McGlynn Gaffney Jr., eds., *Religious Freedom: History, Cases, and Other Materials on the Interaction of Religion and Government* (New York: Foundation Press, 2001), p. 292.

16. Garrett Ward Sheldon, *The Political Philosophy of Thomas Jefferson* (Baltimore: Johns Hopkins University Press, 1991), pp. 41–52, 103–11.

17. "Text of Eisenhower Speech [Monday, December 22, 1952]," *New York Times*, December 23, 1952; cf. Patrick Henry, "'And I Don't Care What It Is': The Tradition-History of a Civil Religion Proof-Text," *Journal of the American Academy of Religion*, 49, no. 1 (1981): 35–49.

18. Richard V. Pierard and Robert D. Linder, *Civil Religion and the Presidency* (Grand Rapids: Zondervan, 1988), Chapter 8.

19. Richard Rorty, "Religion as a Conversation-Stopper," in *Philosophy and Social Hope* (New York: Penguin, 1999), pp. 168–74.

20. Examples are rulings that removed compulsory Bible reading and prayer from public schools (*Murray v. Curlett*, 1963) and legalized abortion (*Roe v. Wade*, 1973), challenges to traditional family models in the form of the Women's Liberation movement, Equal Rights Amendment (1972), increase in divorce rates, decrease in marriage rates, and the sexual revolution of the 1960s.

21. Pierard and Linder, *Civil Religion and the Presidency*, ch. 10.

22. Jerry Falwell, "Revival in America," excerpted from *Falwell, Listen America!* (Garden City, NY: Doubleday, 1980), pp. 243–44, 265–66.

23. William Martin, *With God on Our Side: The Rise of the Religious Right in America* (New York: Broadway, 1996); see also Charles Marsh, *Wayward Christian Soldiers: Freeing the Gospel from Political Captivity* (Oxford: Oxford University Press, 2008).

24. "Excerpts From Federal Court Ruling on the Pledge of Allegiance," *New York Times*, June 27, 2002.

25. Associated Press, "Court Rejects Challenge to Pledge of Allegiance," *New York Times*, August 11, 2005.

26. Ibid.

27. In an address to the Islamic Center in Washington on September 17, 2001, George W. Bush declared that "these acts of violence against innocents violate the fundamental tenets of the Islamic faith. . . . The face of terror is not the true faith of Islam. That's not what Islam is all about. Islam is peace."

28. For a meticulous account of this, see John Kelsay, *Arguing the Just War in Islam* (Cambridge, MA: Harvard University Press, 2007). It is true that some scholars of Islam argue that the sources of Qur'an and Prophetic Tradition (Sunna/Hadith) are basic to Islam, whereas jurisprudential discourses are secondary and provisional—see, for instance, Mohammad Talaat Al Ghunaimi, *The Muslim Conception of International Law and the Western Approach* (The Hague: Martinus Nijhoff, 1968). Sensitivity to the nuances of these scholarly debates, however,

was not the motivating concern of George Bush's appeal to Islam as "a religion of peace."

29. This paragraph follows the analysis conducted in Robert Wuthnow's *America and the Challenge of Religious Diversity* (Princeton: Princeton University Press, 2005), ch. 7. Full results of the "Religion and Diversity Survey" appear at http://www.thearda.com /Archive/Files/Descriptions/DIVERSTY.asp.

30. Ibid., pp. 6–7.

CHAPTER 3: DREAMING IN THE CONTACT ZONE

1. See Fernando Ortiz, *Cuban Counterpoint: Tobacco and Sugar*, trans. Harriet de Onís (New York: Alfred A. Knopf, 1947); Mary Louise Pratt, *Imperial Eyes: Travel Writing and Transculturation* (London: Routledge, 1992); and David Carrasco, "Jaguar Christians in the Contact Zone: Concealed Narratives in the Histories of Religions in the Americas," in *Beyond Primitivism: Indigenous Religious Traditions and Modernity*, ed. Jacob K. Olupona (London: Routledge, 2004), 128–38.

2. Jeff Guy, *The Destruction of the Zulu Kingdom* (London: Longmans, 1979); Timothy Keegan, *Colonial South Africa and the Origins of the Racial Order* (Cape Town: David Philip, 1996); John Lambert, *Betrayed Trust: Africans and the State in Colonial Natal* (Scottsville: University of Natal Press, 1995).

3. Norman Etherington, *Preachers, Peasants, and Politics in Southeast Africa, 1835–1880: African Christianity in Natal, Pondoland and Zululand* (London: Royal Historical Society, 1978); "Kingdoms of This World and the Next: Christian Beginnings among Zulu and Swazi," in *Christianity in South Africa: A Political, Social, and Cultural History*, ed. Richard Elphick and Rodney Davenport (Berkeley: University of California Press, 1997), 89–106; "Outward and Visible Signs of Conversion in Nineteenth-Century KwaZulu-Natal," *Journal of Religion in Africa* 32 (2002): 422–39.

4. C. G. Jung, *Collected Works*, trans. R. F. C. Hull (London: Routledge & Kegan Paul, 1964), 10:63–64.

5. Frank McLynn, *Carl Gustav Jung: A Biography* (New York: St. Martin's, 1997), 282. See also Blake Burleson, *Jung in Africa* (New York: Continuum, 2005).

6. Henry Callaway, *The Religious System of the Amazulu* (Springvale: Springvale Mission, 1860–1870; repr., Cape Town: Struik, 1970), 228; see Callaway, "On Divination and Analogous Phenomena among the Natives of Natal," *Proceedings of the Anthropological Institute* 1

(1872): 163–83. See also Norman Etherington, "Missionary Doctors and African Healers in Mid-Victorian South Africa," *South African Historical Journal* 19 (1987): 77–91; and David Chidester, *Savage Systems: Colonialism and Comparative Religion in Southern Africa* (Charlottesville: University of Virginia Press, 1996), 152–71.

7. E. B. Tylor, *Primitive Culture* (London: John Murray, 1871), 1:380.

8. E. B. Tylor was impressed by the apparently unmediated access to "savage" religion afforded by Callaway's *Religious System of the Amazulu*. In September 1871, Tylor tried to raise funds, by making an appeal through the *Colonial Church Chronicle*, to subsidize the completion and publication of Callaway's work, declaring that "no savage race has ever had its mental, moral, and religious condition displayed to the scientific student with anything approaching to the minute accuracy which characterizes" the *Religious System* (Marian S. Benham, *Henry Callaway, First Bishop of Kaffraria: His Life History and Work: A Memoir* [London: Macmillan, 1896], 247). For discussions of British imperial comparative religion and southern Africa, see David Chidester, "Colonialism," in *Guide to the Study of Religion*, ed. Willi Braun and Russell T. McCutcheon (London: Cassell, 2000), 423–37; "'Classify and Conquer': Friedrich Max Müller, Indigenous Religious Traditions, and Imperial Comparative Religion," in *Beyond Primitivism: Indigenous Religious Traditions and Modernity*, ed. Jacob K. Olupona (New York: Routledge, 2004), 71–88; "Colonialism and Shamanism," in *Shamanism: An Encyclopedia of World Beliefs, Practices, and Culture*, ed. Mariko Namba Walter and Eva Jane Neumann Fridman (Santa Barbara: ABC-Clio, 2004), 1:41–49; and "Real and Imagined: Imperial Inventions of Religion in Colonial Southern Africa," in *Religion and the Secular: Historical and Colonial Formations*, ed. Timothy Fitzgerald (London: Equinox, 2007), 153–76. More broadly, what I am calling imperial comparative religion has been analyzed in relation to Hinduism (Richard King, *Orientalism and Religion: Postcolonial Theory, India, and the "Mystic East"* [London: Routledge, 1999]; and Peter van der Veer, *Imperial Encounters: Religion and Modernity in India and Britain* [Princeton: Princeton University Press, 2001]), Buddhism (ed. Donald Lopez Jr., *Curators of the Buddha: The Study of Buddhism under Colonialism* [Chicago: University of Chicago Press, 1995], Chinese traditions (Norman J. Girardot, *The Victorian Translation of China: James Legge's Oriental Pilgrimage* [Berkeley: University of California Press, 2002], and the European genealogy of "world religions" (Tomoko Masuzawa, *The Invention of World Religions: Or, How European Universalism Was Preserved in the Language of Pluralism* [Chicago: University of Chicago Press, 2005].

9. I have adapted this formulation, "hermeneutics and energetics," with a different purpose from Ricoeur (Paul Ricoeur, *Freud and Philosophy: An Essay on Interpretation*, trans. Denis Savage [New Haven: Yale University Press, 1970]), who used the term "energetics" to refer to dynamic energy flowing between the subconscious and consciousness, while I use the term for dynamic energy flowing between dreaming and acting in the world. A useful overview of the cross-cultural study of dreams can be found in Barbara Tedlock, "Dreams," in *The Encyclopedia of Religion*, ed. Lindsay Jones, 2nd ed. (New York: Macmillan, 2005), 2482–91. The edited collection by Jederej and Shaw (M. C. Jederej and Rosalind Shaw, eds., *Dreaming, Religion, and Society in Africa* [Leiden: Brill, 1992] presents different analytical approaches to dreaming in African religion and culture. Lohmann (Roger Lohmann, ed., *Dream Travelers: Sleep Experiences and Culture in the Western Pacific* [New York: Palgrave Macmillan, 2003] collects important research on dreaming in aboriginal Australia and Melanesia.

10. Callaway, *Religious System of the Amazulu*, 238–39.

11. Ibid., 238, 241.

12. Ibid., 237.

13. Tylor, *Primitive Culture*, 1:110, citing Callaway, *Religious System of the Amazulu*, 241.

14. Andrew Lang, *The Making of Religion*, 3rd ed. (London: Longman, 1909), 106. For an ethnographic survey of interpreting dreams according to the principle of contraries, see Robert K. Dentan, "Ethnographic Considerations in the Cross-Cultural Study of Dreaming," in *Sleep and Dreams: A Sourcebook*, ed. Jayne Gackenbach (New York: Garland, 1986), 317–58.

15. Callaway, *Religious System of the Amazulu*, 238.

16. Ibid., 242.

17. Ibid., 246.

18. Ibid., 6.

19. Ibid., 142.

20. Ibid., 160–61.

21. Ibid., 146–47, 157.

22. Marguerite Poland, David Hammond-Tooke, and Leigh Voigt, *The Abundant Herds: A Celebration of the Nguni Cattle of the Zulu People* (Vlaeberg: Fernwood, 2003).

23. Callaway, *Religious System of the Amazulu*, 172.

24. Ibid., 190n50.

25. Ibid., 212.

26. Theophilus Shepstone was a crucial colonial administrator at the nexus between imperial ambitions and local realities in Natal and Zululand, mediating both structure and history. Structurally, he devised a system of indirect rule through collaborating or appointed "chiefs"—the "Shepstone system"—that became a model for British administration in colonial Africa (Norman Etherington, "The 'Shepstone System' in the Colony of Natal and Beyond the Borders," in *Natal and Zululand From Earliest Times to 1910: A New History*, ed. Andrew Duminy and Bill Guest [Pietermaritzburg: University of Natal Press, 1989], 170–92). Analytically, on the front lines of colonial conflict, conquest, and administrative control, he proposed a three-phase history of the Zulu people that was very different than the vision of evolutionary progress from primitive to civilized that was current among imperial theorists in Britain. In the first phase of Zulu history, according to Shepstone, "we have simple, primitive, unalloyed barbarism . . . peace, prosperity, and plenty." This idyllic barbarism, a "primitive" situation that seemed more like paradise than like the "primordial stupidity" imagined by the British evolutionists, was destroyed by a second phase, in which the original barbarism was mixed with "a dash of civilization" under the kingship of Shaka, who "cut off all that sustains life, turned thousands of square miles into a literally howling wilderness, shed rivers of blood, annihilated whole communities, turned the members of others into cannibals." Finally, in the third phase of Zulu history, according to Shepstone, "we see civilization," in its pure form, driven by direct British influence and control, intervening in the devastation of the Zulu people caused by Shaka by "protecting and ameliorating the remnants of this wreck" (J. R. Sullivan, *The Native Policy of Theophilus Shepstone* [Johannesburg: Walker and Snashall, 1928], 9–10). Historians have pointed to two ironies in this version of Zulu history—the tyranny of Shaka was an invention of British propaganda and the terror of Shaka was eventually claimed by the colonial representative of "pure" civilization, Theophilus Shepstone.

27. Callaway, *Religious System of the Amazulu*, 206–7, 209.

28. Ibid., 185, 260.

29. Ibid., 187–88.

30. Ibid., 190.

31. Ibid., 192.

32. Ibid., 260.

33. C. M. Doke and B. W. Vilakazi, *Zulu-English Dictionary*, 2nd ed. (Johannesburg: Witwatersrand University Press, 1958), 175.

34. David Chidester, *Religions of South Africa* (London: Routledge, 1992), 3–6.

35. Callaway, *Religious System of the Amazulu*, 188–89.

36. Ibid., 246.

37. Ibid., 250.

38. Ibid., 249–50.

39. Ibid., 300.

40. Ibid., 303–4.

41. Tylor, *Primitive Culture*, 1:399–400, citing Callaway *Religious System of the Amazulu*, 260, and "On Divination and Analogous Phenomena," 170; see David Chidester, "Animism," in *Encyclopedia of Religion and Nature*, ed. Bron Taylor and Jeffrey Kaplan (New York: Continuum, 2005), 78–81.

42. Callaway, "On Divination and Analogous Phenomena," 166–67.

43. Ibid., 184.

44. E. B. Tylor, "On the Limits of Savage Religion," *The Journal of the Anthropological Institute of Great Britain and Ireland* 21 (1892): 283.

45. Ibid., 298.

46. Tylor, *Primitive Culture*, 2:449.

47. Ibid., 2:451.

48. Ibid., 2:453.

49. The potential for analyzing dreaming under different colonial conditions is enormous. I cannot begin to chart all the possibilities here. Frantz Fanon, as might be expected, provides a good place to start, incorporating a psychoanalytic tradition from Freud to Lacan, but critiquing the psychoanalytically informed analysis of Mannoni (Octave Mannoni, *Prospero and Caliban: The Psychology of Colonization*, trans. Pamela Powesland [Ann Arbor: University of Michigan Press, 1990]) in Madagascar by insisting that "the discoveries of Freud are of no use to us here. What must be done is to restore the dream to its proper time, and this time is the period during which eighty thousand natives were killed" (Frantz Fanon, *Black Skin, White Masks*, trans. Charles Lam Markmann [New York: Grove, 1967]), 104. Accordingly, in this essay I have tried to begin restoring nineteenth-century Zulu dreams to their proper time.

50. See Eileen Jensen Krige, *The Social System of the Zulus* (London: Longmans Green, 1936); Axel-Ivar Berglund, *Zulu Thought-Patterns and Symbolism* (London: C. Hurst, 1976); E. M. Preston-Whyte, "Zulu Religion," in vol. 15 of *Encyclopedia of Religion*, ed. Mircea Eliade (New York: Macmillan, 1987); and David Chidester, Chirevo Kwenda, Robert Petty, Judy Tobler, and Darrel Wratten, *African Traditional Religion in South Africa: An*

Annotated Bibliography (Westport: Greenwood, 1997), 212–75.

51. Chidester, *Savage Systems,* 116–72.

52. Jennifer Weir, "Whose Unkulunkulu?" *Africa* 75, no. 2 (2005): 203–19; and William H. Worger, "Parsing God: Conversations about the Meaning of Words and Metaphors in Nineteenth-Century Southern Africa," *Journal of African History* 42, no. 3 (2001): 417–47.

53. Irving Hexham, ed. *Texts on Zulu Religion: Traditional Zulu Ideas about God* (Lewiston, NY: Edwin Mellen, 1987).

54. Luc De Heusch, *Sacrifice in Africa: A Structuralist Approach*, trans. Linda O'Brien and Alice Morton (Manchester: Manchester University Press, 1985), 38–64; and Michael Lambert, "Ancient Greek and Zulu Sacrificial Ritual: A Comparative Analysis," *Numen* 40, no. 3 (1993): 293–318.

55. Brian M. Du Toit, "The Isangoma: An Adaptive Agent Among Urban Zulu," *Anthropological Quarterly* 44, no. 2 (1971): 51–65; Harriet Ngubane, *Body and Mind in Zulu Medicine: An Ethnography of Health and Disease in Nyuswa-Zulu Thought and Practice* (London: Academic, 1977), and "Aspects of Clinical Practice and Traditional Organization of Indigenous Healers in South Africa," *Social Science and Medicine* 15, no. 2 (1981): 361–65.

56. Max Gluckman, "Social Aspects of First Fruits Ceremonies among the South-Eastern Bantu," *Africa* 11 (1938): 25–41.

57. Jeff Guy, *The Maphumulo Uprising: War, Law, and Ritual in the Zulu Rebellion* (Scottsville: University of KwaZulu-Natal Press, 2005).

58. Carolyn Hamilton, *Terrific Majesty: The Powers of Shaka Zulu and the Limits of Historical Invention* (Cape Town: David Philip, 1998); and Dan Wylie, *Savage Delight: White Myths of Shaka* (Pietermaritzburg: University of Natal Press, 2000).

59. W. Wanger, "The Zulu Notion of God according to the Traditional Zulu God-Names" *Anthropos* 18, no. 19 (1923–1926): 656–87; 20:558–78; 21:351–58.

60. Irving Hexham, "Lord of the Sky—King of the Earth: Zulu Traditional Religion and Belief in the Sky God," *Sciences Religieuses/Studies in Religion* 10 (1981): 273–78.

61. Etherington, "Missionary Doctors and African Healers"; and Chidester, *Savage Systems*, 160–65.

62. Thomas McClendon, "The Man Who Would Be Inkosi: Civilising Missions in Shepstone's Early Career," *Journal of Southern African Studies* 30, no. 2 (2004): 339–58.

63. Jan Platvoet and Henk J. van Rinsum, "Is Africa Incurably Religious? Confessing and Contesting an Invention," *Exchange: Journal of Missiological and Ecumenical Research* 32, no. 2 (2003): 123–53.

64. Tylor, *Primitive Culture*, 2:387.

65. John S. Mbiti, *African Religions and Philosophy* (London: Heinemann, 1969), 1–2. See also *Introduction to African Religion* (London: Heinemann, 1975), 30.

66. On the distinction between "locative" orientations, fixed in place, and "utopian" orientations toward anyplace (or no place), see Jonathan Z. Smith, *Map Is Not Territory: Studies in the History of Religions* (Leiden: Brill, 1978). The utopian portability of Zulu religion, with specific attention to Zulu dreaming, divination, and visions, has recently proliferated in the contemporary global network of neo-shamanism (David Chidester, "Credo Mutwa, Zulu Shaman: The Invention and Appropriation of Indigenous Authenticity in African Folk Religion," *Journal for the Study of Religion* 15, no. 2: (2002) 65–85; and "Zulu Dreamscapes: Senses, Media, and Authentication in Contemporary Neo-Shamanism," *Material Religion* 4, no. 2 (July 2008): 136–58.

67. See David Lewis-Williams, *The Mind in the Cave* (London: Thames & Hudson, 2002).

68. E. Thomas Lawson and Robert N. McCauley, *Rethinking Religion: Connecting Cognition and Culture* (Cambridge: Cambridge University Press, 1990), 35. See also Robin Horton, *Patterns of Thought in Africa and the West: Essays on Magic, Science, and Religion* (Cambridge: Cambridge University Press, 1997).

69. In more recent research on Zulu dreaming, analysts have emphasized persistence and change. Lee (S. G. Lee, "Social Influences in Zulu Dreaming," *Journal of Social Psychology* 47 [1958]: 256–83) introduced the notion of "time-lag" in accounting for the persistence of traditional elements in Zulu dreams, while Thwala et al. (J. D. Thwala, A. L. Pillay, and C. Sargent, "The Influence of Urban/Rural Background, Gender, Age, and Education on the Perception of and Response to Dreams among Zulu South Africans," *South African Journal of Psychology* 30, no. 4 [2000]: 1–5) tracked a range of structural differentials—urbanization, gender, age, and education—to account for the discontinuity of contemporary Zulu dreaming with traditional or ancestral themes. Among Zulu Zionist Christians, Kiernan (James P. Kiernan, "The Social Stuff of Revelation: Pattern and Purpose in Zionist Dreams and Visions," *Africa* 55, no. 3 [1985]: 304–17) found a balance between attributing spiritual visions to the Holy Spirit and significant dreams to ancestral intervention.

70. See Chidester, *Word and Light: Seeing, Hearing, and Religious Discourse* (Urbana: University of Illinois Press, 1992); and Lawrence Sullivan, "Sound and Sense: Towards a Hermeneutics of Performance," *History of Religions* 11 (1986): 1–33.

71. Louis Althusser, "Ideology and Ideological State Apparatuses," in *Lenin and Philosophy and Other Essays* (London: New Left Books, 1989), 170–86.

72. Ladislav Holy, "Berti Dream Interpretation," in *Dreaming, Religion, and Society in Africa*, ed. M. C. Jederej and Rosalind Shaw (Leiden: Brill, 1992), 89.

73. W. J. T. Mitchell, *What Do Pictures Want? The Lives and Loves of Images* (Chicago: University of Chicago Press, 2005).

74. David Morgan, *Visual Piety: A History and Theory of Popular Religious Images* (Berkeley: University of California Press, 1998).

75. Christopher Pinney, *"Photos of the Gods": The Printed Image and Political Struggle in India* (London: Reaktion, 2004).

76. Birgit Meyer, "Religious Sensations: Why Media, Aesthetics, and Power Matter in the Study of Contemporary Religion," Inaugural Lecture at Free University, Amsterdam, 2006.

CHAPTER 4: SCIENCE

1. The Greek version, as opposed to the Hebrew version, reads "evil shall increase."

2. Important authors who have contributed to the notion of "mind uploading" include Frederick Pohl, Roger Zelazny, Greg Egan, Rudy Rucker, Vernor Vinge, and William Gibson.

3. Mitochondria, which are responsible for providing the cell's energy, have a small amount of DNA, which is exclusively passed through the maternal line. Mitochondrial problems can, apparently, be fixed by fertilizing an egg with sperm from the father and removing the nucleus formed through the combination of the mother's and father's DNA to use the donor cell.

4. I owe this term to John Evans, a sociologist of religion and bioethics at University of California–San Diego.

5. Uncited survey numbers come from the author's own survey data.

CHAPTER 5: WOMEN

1. Linda King Newell, "Gifts of the Spirit: Women's Share," in *Sisters in Spirit: Mormon Women in*

Historical and Cultural Perspective, ed. Maureen Ursenbach Beecher and Lavina Fielding Anderson (Chicago: University of Illinois Press, 1992), 111–50.

2. Nancy Auer Falk and Rita M. Gross, eds., *Unspoken Worlds: Women's Religious Lives*, 3rd. ed. (Belmont, CA: Wadsworth, 2001), xv.

CHAPTER 6: SEXUALITY OF RELIGIOUS NATIONALISM

1. I should like to thank Vince Biondo for his helpful commentary and edits, and Richard Hecht and Mark Juergensmeyer, for having made visible a startling world.

2. Even within Europe, Christian Democratic welfare states differ dramatically from those of the social democratic in their greater support for families organized around the single male-earner. Christian Democratic welfare states tend, in fact, to be more egalitarian in their impact than those of the social democrats' centered families, which are targeted to the needy. Walter Korpi and Joakim Palme, "The Strategy of Equality and the Paradox of Redistribution," *American Sociological Review* 63, no. 5 (October 1998): 661–87.

3. Martin Riesebrodt, *Pious Passion: The Emergence of Modern Fundamentalism in the United States and Iran* (Berkeley: University of California Press, 1993), 145.

4. Inferred from R. Stephen Humphreys, *Between Memory and Desire: The Middle East in a Troubled Age* (Berkeley: University of California Press, 1999). Professor Humphreys privately confirmed this inference to me in conversation. The Islamic regulation of family life has, in fact, been the core of Islamic law during this century. "Throughout this century," writes Humphreys, "the sections on women, the family, and personal morality have been the most vital and living elements of the Shari'a, and in the courts of most countries they are the only parts of it still enforced" (212).

5. Indeed, looking across US congregations in the 1990s, the single most important sources of conflict within them was over the role of women, the participation of homosexuals, and the status of traditional heterosexual morality more generally. See Penny Edgell Becker, *Congregations in Conflict: Cultural Models of Local Religious Life* (New York: Cambridge University Press, 1999). See ch. 5, "What Is Right? What Is Caring?"

6. Pat Robertson, *The New World Order* (Dallas: Word, 1991), 237.

7. Paul Apostolidis, *Stations of the Cross: Adorno*

and *Christian Right Radio* (Durham, NC: Duke University Press, 2000).

8. Riesebrodt, *Pious Passion*, 57.

9. "Each individual is understood to derive his or her identity in such direct and basic ways from membership in the nation. This is sharply different from the discourse of kinship and the ideology of honour of the lineage. Their children derive their membership of the whole only through their concrete and specific relationships to parents and kin." Craig Calhoun, *Nationalism* (Minneapolis: University of Minnesota Press, 1997), 46–47.

10. Darrin McMahon, *Enemies of Enlightenment: The French Counterenlightenment and the Making of Modernity* (New York: Oxford University Press, 2002).

11. Suzanne Desan, "'War between Brothers and Sisters': Inheritance Law and Gender Politics in Revolutionary France," *French Historical Studies* 20, no. 4 (1997): 597–634.

12. Lynn Hunt, *The Family Romance of the French Revolution* (Berkeley: University of California Press, 1992). This understanding was not specific to France. In Protestant colonial America, when dissenters broke state laws, they were told that they had broken the Fifth Commandment, to honor one's father and one's mother. William G. McLoughlin, *Revivals, Awakenings, and Reform* (Chicago: University of Chicago Press, 1978), 46.

13. Valentine M. Moghadam, *Modernizing Women: Gender and Social Change in the Middle East* (Boulder, CO: Westview, 1993).

14. There is also, of course, a parallel basis for this argument in secular political theory as well.

15. In her book, *Congregations in Conflict: Cultural Models of Local Religious Life*, a study of congregational life in the United States, Penny Becker finds that, when congregants divide internally over the sexual limits of inclusion, the debates are not organized on a liberal/conservative axis, which members find to be irrelevant, but are organized around what she calls "a moral logic of caring" and a "moral logic of authoritative religious judgment or truth." Becker critiques my and Robert Alford's original position that argues that the institutional logic of religion, like science, is about truth. Becker is correct in her critique, in that, although Abrahamic religions differ in their relationship to the state and the market, they all concern themselves with the regulation of familial relations, with sexuality, and with the organization of a solidaristic community.

16. Janet Afary, "The War Against Feminism in the Name of the Almighty: Making Sense of Gender and Muslim Fundamentalism," *New Left Review* 224 (July/August 1997): 89–110.

17. Bruce B. Lawrence, *Shattering the Myth: Islam Beyond Violence* (Princeton: Princeton University Press, 1998), 112–15; Riesebrodt, *Pious Passion*, 117.

18. Azar Nafisi, "The Veiled Threat," *The New Republic*, February 22, 1999; Freda Hussain and Kamelia Radwan, "The Islamic Revolution and Women: Quest for the Quranic Model," in *Muslim Women*, ed. Freda Hussain (New York: St. Martin's Press, 1984), xx, Lawrence, *Shattering the Myth*.

19. Lawrence, *Shattering the Myth*, 64, 122–24.

20. Margaret Lamberts Bendroth, *Fundamentalism and Gender, 1875 to the Present* (New Haven, CT: Yale University Press, 1993); and "Fundamentalism and the Family: Gender, Culture, and the American Pro-Family Movement," *Journal of Women's History* 10, no. 4 (Winter 1999): 35–53. The remoralization of the family is not the exclusive concern of politically engaged fundamentalists. Charismatic Pentecostalism, which draws from a poorer social base, has a similar preoccupation, not only in the United States but in Latin America as well. Martin Riesebrodt and Kelly H. Chong, "Fundamentalisms and Patriarchal Gender Politics, *Journal of Women's History,* 10, no. 4 (Winter 1999): pp. 55–77.

21. Amrita Basu, "Women's Activism and the Vicissitudes of Hindu Nationalism," *Journal of Women's History* 10, no. 4 (Winter 1999): 104–23. Hansen writes: "Forgetting oneself, discovering the pleasure of giving and serving rather than receiving, cultivating the virtues of forgiveness and compassion, and putting the service of the nation above anything else are some of the themes that in a rather sentimental language and style, assumed to conform with and confirm the likings and self-images of its female audiences, still runs through the contemporary publications from the Veika Samiti." Thomas Blom Hansen, *The Saffron Wave: Democracy and Hindu Nationalism in Modern India* (Princeton: Princeton University Press, 1999), 98.

22. Ibid., 114. The same kind of attitude obtains in the Brahmin-dominated women's movement, *Jan Kalyan*, or "People's Welfare," in Madras, in southern India. Mary Hancock, "Hindu Culture for an Indian Nation: Gender, Politics, and Elite Identity in Urban South India," *American Ethnologist* 22, no. 4 (1995): 907–26.

23. Fatima Mernissi, *Beyond the Veil: Male-Female Dynamics in Modern Muslim Society* (Bloomington: Indiana University Press, 1987); Mernissi, *Islam and Democracy: Fear of the Modern World*, trans. Mary Jo Lakeland (Reading, MA: Addison-Wesley, 1992).

24. Riesebrodt, *Pious Passion,* 57.

25. Pierre Bourdieu has written: "I say that the idea of masculinity is one of the last refuges of the identity of the dominated classes. . . . It's characteristic of people who have little to fall back on except their labour-power and sometimes their fighting strength." Although Bourdieu is correct to point out this association, the case of religious nationalism, which is predominantly a middle-class movement, indicates that public celebration of the masculine is not the exclusive purview of the working class. See Pierre Bourdieu, *Sociology in Question* (London: Sage, 1993).

26. Hegel, for instance, saw India as pure spirit, but a soft, imaginative spirit, unlike the rational, masculine spirit of the West. Hansen, *Saffron Wave,* 68.

27. Ibid., 214.

28. Ibid., 83.

29. Anuradha Kapur, "Deity to Crusader: The Changing Iconography of Ram," in *Hindus and Others,* ed. Gyanendra Pandey (New Delhi: Viking, 1993), 76–77.

30. P. K. Datta, "VHP's Ram: The Hindutva Movement in Ayodhya," in Pandey, *Hindus and Others.*

31. Thomas B. Hansen, "Recuperating Masculinity: Hindu Nationalism, Violence and the Exorcism of the Muslim 'Other,'" *Critique of Anthropology* 16, no. 2 (1996): 137–72. Female divinities are also masculinized. In the case of the Hindu nationalists, the women's organization, the Simiti, worships Ashta Bhuja, an eight-armed goddess fashioned from elements of three pre-existing goddesses—Kali, Saraswati, and Lakshmi. Ashta Bhuja, a new form of Durga, is a warrior armed with a variety of weapons including a lotus, the Bhagavad-Gita, fire, a sword, and a saffron flag. See Paola Bachetta, "All Our Goddesses Are Armed: Religion, Resistance, and Revenge in the Life of a Militant Hindu Nationalist Woman," *Bulletin of Concerned Asian Scholars* 25, no. 4 (October–December 1993): 38–51. I am indebted to Anna Bigelow for this reference and for her insistence that I keep gender always in view. In the Gandhian vision, nonviolence, or *ahimsa,* is understood to be a feminine virtue. See Hancock, "Hindu Culture," 910–11.

32. I am indebted to Serena Vicari for this formulation.

33. Sarah E. Hinlicky, "Subversive Masculinity," *Boundless Webzine,* www.boundless.org/2005/articles/a0000195.cfm.

34. Riesebrodt and Chong, "Fundamentalisms," 64.

35. Margaret Lamberts Bendroth, "The Search for 'Women's Role' in American Evangelicalism, 1830–1980," in *Evangelicalism and Modern America,* ed. George Marsden (Grand Rapids: Eerdmans, 1984); Riesebrodt and Chong, "Fundamentalisms," 62–63. Riesebrodt and Chong interpret the absence of female leadership as a result both of the theological interpretation of woman's moral disability through her identification with Eve and of the importance of abstract interpretation, as opposed to charismatic experience, which is presumed to be a masculine domain.

36. Riesebrodt, *Pious Passion,* 179. This erosion of patriarchal norms, he writes, "takes place primarily in the sphere of the family and sexual morality. The progressive repeal of gender-specific distinctions of legal status and the diminishing need for a gender-based division of labor weakens paternal authority over women" (202). Joseph Paul Franklin, the man to whom William Pierce dedicated his novel about a solitary white warrior, *Hunter,* not only murdered interracial couples and attacked synagogues, but he also seriously wounded Larry Flynt, the publisher of *Hustler* magazine. Defending the racial boundaries of the United States was bound up with the defense of the chaste, decommodified body of the American woman. Jo Thomas, "New Face of Terror Crimes: 'Lone Wolf' Weaned on Hate," *New York Times,* August 16, 1999.

37. Tony Hendra, ed., *Sayings of the Ayatollah Khomeini* (New York: Bantam, 1980).

38. Karen McCarthy Brown, "Fundamentalism and the Control of Women," in *Fundamentalism and Gender,* ed. John Stratton Hawley (New York: Oxford University Press, 1994), 175–202.

39. The de-eroticization of the social is achieved through wants, which are mental, and needs, which are bodily. Desire has an alternative constitution.

40. Take the case of the Sikh nationalists. Mark Juergensmeyer describes listening to the Sikh leader: "Bhindranwale addressed his congregation as if the men (especially the young men) were the only ones listening, encouraging them to let their beards grow in the long Sikh fashion and describing their acts of cowardice as 'emasculation.' One senses in this longing for a recovery of virility expressed by Bhindranwale and other religious activists a strange, composite yearning that is at once sexual, social and political. The marginality of such persons in the modern world is experienced by them as a kind of sexual despair." Mark Juergensmeyer, *The New Cold War* (Berkeley: University of California Press, 1994), 169.

41. Mernissi, *Beyond the Veil,* 45.

42. Binnaz Toprak, "Women and Fundamentalism: The Case of Turkey," in *Identity Politics and Women:*

Cultural Reassertions and Feminisms in International Perspective, ed. Valentine M. Moghadam (Boulder, CO: Westview, 1994).

43. Basu, "Women's Activism," 115.

44. Nikki R. Keddie, "The New Religious Politics and Women Worldwide," *Journal of Women's History* 10, no. 4 (1999): 11–34.

27. Keddie writes: "For women who want to work outside the home . . . religiopolitics offers a badge of traditionalism and respectability to carrying out a new way of life, and, in Iran and other countries, many women can work in fundamentalist dress who could not work outside the home before."

45. See, for instance, Paula Bacchetta, "Militant Hindu Nationalist Women Re-Imagine Themselves: Notes on Mechanisms of Expansion/Adjustment," *Journal of Women's History* 10, no. 4 (1999): 125–47. One of the consequences of the rise of politicized Islam, for instance, is the movement of women into the mosques, something that has enabled them to garner religious legitimacy for pursuit of their claims.

46. Basu, "Women's Activism," 118. Mary Hancock argues, in the case of Hindu women in Tamil Nadu, that the politicized public performance of *puja,* in which ritual offerings are made, typically done in the home, is a way to claim the public space as a sacred home in contradistinction to the secular state. "Hindu Culture."

47. Christian Smith, *American Evangelicalism Embattled and Thriving* (Chicago: University of Chicago Press, 1998), 80.

48. Robin Wright, *The Last Great Revolution: Turmoil and Transformation in Iran* (New York: Vintage, 2000), 151–52.

49. Ibid., 162.

50. Lila Abu-Lughod, "The Marriage of Islamism and Feminism in Egypt: Selective Repudiation as a Dynamic of Postcolonial Cultural Politics," in *Remaking Women: Feminism and Modernity in the Middle East,* ed. Lila Abu-Lughod (Princeton: Princeton University Press, 1998).

51. Cynthia Enloe, *Making Feminist Sense of International Politics: Bananas, Beaches, and Bases* (Berkeley: University of California Press, 1989); Aihwa Ong, "State Versus Islam: Malay Families, Women's Bodies, and the Body Politic in Malaysia," *American Ethnologist* 17, no. 2 (1990): 258–76.

52. Linda Kintz, *Between Jesus and the Market: The Emotions That Matter in Right-Wing America* (Durham, NC: Duke University Press, 1997).

53. Kristin Luker, *Abortion and the Politics of Motherhood* (Berkeley: University of California Press, 1984).

54. Mark Wigley, "Untitled: The House of Gender," in *Sexuality and Space,* ed. Beatriz Colamina (Princeton: Princeton Architectural Press, 1992), 327–89.

55. Sigmund Freud writes: "The almighty and just God, and kindly Nature, appear to us as grand sublimations of father and mother, or rather as revivals and restorations of the young child's ideas of them." *Leonardo da Vinci and a Memory of His Childhood* (New York: W. W. Norton, 1989), 83.

56. It is striking that even Iranian president Mohammed Khatami, a cleric, at the same time both forbade students to bring to class materials bearing the Latin alphabet or other "decadent Western symbols" and from portraying women on magazine covers. Azar Nafisi, "The Veiled Threat," *New Republic,* February 22, 1999. I venture that, in the United States at least, religious nationalism's preoccupation with women's bodies is related to the larger obsession, a consuming interest, with bodily form and functioning, where the body is a substitute for other forms of collective incorporation over which we have lost control.

57. Bourdieu, *Sociology in Question,* 52.

58. See, for example, Joan B. Landes, *Visualizing the Nation: Gender, Representation, and Revolution in Eighteenth-Century France* (Ithaca, NY: Cornell University Press, 2001).

59. Margaret D. Caroll, "The Erotics of Absolutism: Rubens and the Mystification of Sexual Violence," *Representations* (Winter 1989): 3–30.

60. Jawaharlal Nehru, *The Discovery of India* (New Delhi, India; Oxford University Press, 1994), 50, cited in Katherine J. Komenda, "The Narmada Flows Through It: Remembering History" (PhD dissertation, February, 2000, UC Santa Barbara); see also Ashis Nandy, *The Intimate Enemy* (New Delhi, India: Oxford University Press, 1983).

61. Bacchetta, "Militant Hindu Nationalist Women," 129–30. Bachetta shows how the women of the RSS have a distinctive view of mother India as a powerful mother who can protect her children, both female and male.

62. Hansen, *Saffron Wave,* 180.

63. Roger Friedland and Richard Hecht, "The Bodies of Nations: A Comparative Study of Religious Violence in Jerusalem and Ayodhya," *History of Religions* 38, no. 2 (Spring, 1998): 239–59. Thomas Blom Hansen, "The Vernacularisation of Hindutva: BJP and Shiva Sena in Rural Maharashtra," *Contributions to Indian Sociology* 30, no. 2 (1996): 177–214.

64. Hansen, *Saffron Wave*, 204.

65. Sumathi Ramaswamy, *Passions of the Tongue: Language Devotion in Tamil India* (Berkeley: University of California Press, 1997); and Ramaswamy "Virgin Mother, Beloved Other: The Erotics of Tamil Nationalism in Colonial and Post-Colonial India," *Thamyris* 4, no. 1 (Spring 1997): 9–39.

66. Ramaswamy, "Virgin Mother, Beloved Others," 17.

67. "Excerpts from Speeches Given by Sadhvi Uma Shri Barati," Speech on Ramjanmabhumi Struggle in Ayodhya; circa October 30, 1992, translated by Katherine Komenda, personal communication.

68. Roger Friedland, "Religious Terror and the Erotics of Exceptional Violence," *Anthropological Yearbook of European Cultures* 14 (2005): 39–71.

69. Ehud Sprinzak, *Brother against Brother* (New York: The Free Press, 1999), 102.

70. Ibid., 281. It is striking that the residue of the racist order who, operating on their own or in small groups to commit violence against Jews, blacks, homosexuals, or abortion clinics likewise call themselves the Phineas Priesthood. James Sterngold, "Man with a Past of Racial Hate Surrenders in Day Camp Attack," *New York Times*, August 12, 1999. Bufford Furrow, who shot five people at a Jewish community center, was carrying a book by Richard Hoskins, who wrote a manifesto on the Phineas Priesthood. The book in Hoskins's car was in fact a book, named *War Cycles/Peace Cycles*, that Hoskins said dealt with the history of usury and the role of the Jews in banking. As we shall see, there is a semiotic relationship between monetary interest and abortion.

71. On the Shah Bano case, see Ainslie T. Embree, *Utopias in Conflict: Religion and Nationalism in Modern India* (Berkeley: University of California Press, 1990).

72. Lawrence, *Shattering the Myth*, 135.

73. John Stratton Hawley, "Hinduism: *Sati* and Its Defenders," 79–110, in John Hawley Stratton and Wade Proudfoot, eds., *Fundamentalism and Gender* (New York: Oxford University Press, 1994).

74. Jane De Hart writes, "By defining men and women as, respectively, progenitors and womb, nationalist discourse located both sexes in nature. By then linking them to the nation and its destiny, the nation is naturalized as well. The result is to make it easier to think of the nation not as a historical construction but rather as a natural, organic community" (23). "Saving the Fetus, Saving the Nation: Abortion as an Un-American Activity," unpublished essay (Fall 1999), Department of History, University of California, Santa Barbara, 1999.

75. Stephen Kinzer, "Among Turkish Terrorists' Victims, a Muslim Feminist," *International Herald Tribune*, January 26, 2000; Kinzer, "Hizbullah Is Prime Example of State's 'Playing One against the Other' Policy," *Turkish Daily News.com,* January 31, 2000.

76. See Lawrence, *Shattering the Myth*, pp. 122–123.

77. Jane Sherron De Hart, "Abortion Politics and the Politics of National Identity," Lecture for UCSB Interdisciplinary Humanities Center, March 2, 1999. In her account, De Hart stresses the centrality of familial reproduction to the production of a racialized ethnicity necessary to national identity and the ways in which perceived threats to national identity "resonate" with anti-abortion discourse.

78. As a result of these efforts, in the United States, women's access to abortion was significantly curtailed by reducing state funding for abortion, lowering the number of hospitals and clinics offering abortions, and placing restrictions on the conditions under which abortions are legally permissible. See De Hart, "Saving the Fetus."

79. Mark Juergensmeyer, *Terror in the Mind of God: The Global Rise of Religious Violence* (Berkeley: University of California Press, 1999), 54

80. For example, Nikki R. Keddie writes: "The use of murder to stop abortion (by a small minority, but discussed sympathetically by many more) makes doubtful the defense of life explanation, as does the fact that many 'pro-life' people advocate handguns, capital punishment, and reductions in support for those whose lives are at risk for reasons of health, menacing family, or community conditions" (Keddie, "New Religious Politics and Women Worldwide," 22. I have no explanation for this last association.

81. Bendroth, "Fundamentalism and the Family," 48.

82. Italian fascism recapitulated many of the themes of the Italian *risorgimento*, the political movement through which Italy, with its distinctive regional and indeed local languages, was unified. What is striking here is that, in both cases, in which the extent of the territorial body of Italy was at stake, the political discourse sought a masculinization of the public sphere and the expulsion of women from it. I am indebted to Lucia Re for bringing this to my attention.

83. Juergensmeyer, *Terror in the Mind of God.*

84. Nancy J. Chodorow, *The Reproduction of Mothering: Psychoanalysis and the Sociology of Gender* (Berkeley: University of California Press, 1989).

85. The premodern European state was imagined as a king's body. The king had two bodies: one, a fleshy

body that dies, leaving behind a more substantial body, one of greater import, a symbolic body, to be occupied by his successor, the body of kingship outliving the body of the king.

86. Juergensmeyer, "The Ritual Empowerment." He writes with regard to Bhindranwale's Sikh followers: "The intense loyalties of male comrades in these militant groups suggest in some cases a homoerotic element. In India, some of the young men in militant Sikh cadres pair off and are bonded as blood brothers in a quasireligious ceremony." (*New Cold War*, 243).

87. Hansen, *Saffron Wave*, 95. Hansen writes of "one of the fundamental themes of RSS ideology: the creation of a brotherhood held together by affection for peers and superiors, and psychologically based on the sublimation of sexual energy to patriotic devotion and work" (97).

88. Juergensmeyer, *Terror in the Mind of God*, 321–22.

89. Sigmund Freud, *The Ego and the Id* (New York: W. W. Norton, 1962), 16.

90. Judith Butler, *The Psychic Life of Power: Theories in Subjection* (Stanford: Stanford University Press, 1997), 136.

91. Ibid., 136.

92. If the distinction between the meaning of heterosexual and homosexual male bonding is ephemeral, there are compelling motives to expel explicit homoerotics from the male sphere, to export its problematic afficionados, its aberrant doubles. Part of the expulsion is accomplished by joining sexual acts and gendered identities, denying manhood to the company of men who engage in, prefer, or exclusively engage in sex with other men. In a world where desires and acts always have the potential for multiplicity, making a kind of person out of a kind of act not only essentializes sexual identity, but creates a symbolic firewall between an exclusive homosexuality and an exclusive heterosexuality. Man is not to woman as heterosexual is to homosexual. Robert Davidoff, *In My Father's House Are Many Closets*, March 1997, unpublished. "In effect," Davidoff writes, "all the terms we know for same sex love between men— sodomite, homosexual, faggot, queer, cocksucker, gay man—remain captive to the culture's need to marginalize these people because of its need not to accept the implications of these activities."

93. For a discussion of homosociality, see Eve Kosofsky Sedgwick, *Between Men: English Literature and Male Homosocial Desire* (New York: Columbia University Press, 1985).

94. See Elizabeth Wingrove's discussion, "Republican Romance," *Representations* 63 (Summer 1998): 13–38.

95. Olivier Roy, *Globalized Islam: The Search for a New Ummah* (New York: Columbia University Press, 2004), 246, 268.

96. Jean-Luc Marion, *The Erotic Phenomenon* (Chicago: University of Chicago Press, 2007).

Chapter 7: The Religious Ethics of Capitalism

1. The other part of Marx's theory, and a cause of discomfort for people of faith, is that the wealthy interpret religion and deliberately teach it to their employees to distract them from seeking higher wages.

2. Ninian Smart, "The Seven Dimensions of Religions," in *Religions of the West* (Englewood Cliffs, NJ: Prentice Hall, 1994), 11–20.

3. Moses I. Finley, *Studies in Ancient Society* (London: Routledge, 1974), 95–96.

4. Xenophon, *Oeconomicus*, trans. Sarah Pomeroy (Oxford: Clarendon, 1994), 113.

5. Charles Diehl, *Theodora*, trans. S. R. Rosenbaum (1904; New York: Frederick Ungar, 1972), 14. The reign of Theodora from 527 to 548 was documented sensationally by gossip columnist Procopius in a text released by the Vatican in 1623.

6. Diehl, *Theodora*, 146–47.

7. See Meir Tamari, *With All Your Possessions* (New York: Free Press, 1987).

8. United States Representative Charles Rangel on CNN's *Lou Dobbs Tonight*, CNN, January 23, 2007, quoted in Mary Bauer, "Close to Slavery: Guestworker Programs in the United States" (Montgomery: Southern Poverty Law Center, 2007), 1–48.

9. Ernesto Galarza, *Strangers in Our Fields* (Washington, DC: Joint United States-Mexico Trade Union Committee, 1956).

10. Bartolomé de Las Casas, *In Defense of the Indians*, trans. S. Poole (DeKalb: Northern Illinois University Press, 1974), 271.

11. Lewis Hanke, *All Mankind Is One* (DeKalb: Northern Illinois University, 1974), 106–7.

12. Ibid., 84. From Juan Ginés de Sepúlveda, *Democrates Segundo*, A. Losada, trans. (Madrid: Consejo Superior de Investigaciones Cientificas, Instituto Francisco de Vitoria, 1984), 33. The "monkey" comment may have been removed.

13. Hanke, *All Mankind Is One*, 76.

14. Kevin Bales, *Disposable People*, rev ed. (Berkeley: University of California Press, 2004), 8, reports 27 million people living in physical or debt bondage slavery, including at least 15 million in South Asia.

15. U.S. Department of State, "Trafficking in Persons Report," June 2008, 1–292.

16. Bales, *Disposable People*, 16, 86.

17. Social class, nationality, and ethnicity are additional factors.

18. John Bowe, "Nobodies: Does Slavery Exist in America?" *New Yorker*, April 21, 2003, beginning on 106.

19. Christian Parenti, "Chocolate's Bittersweet Economy," *Fortune*, February 4, 2008.

20. Andrew Downie, "The Hunt for Slave Outposts in the Amazon," *Christian Science Monitor*, September 7, 2004.

21. Gresham's Law originally appears in Aristophanes, "The Frogs," 405 BCE, Stanford ed., 183, where silver-plated copper coins drive solid silver coins out of circulation. The satirical quote from Aristophanes is "True as an ancient coin, gold against modern brass. Everyone knows the gold . . . we prefer the brass" (Lines 721–732, D. Fitts, trans., 1955).

22. As explained in section 1, the term *slavery* carries a particular emotional weight, especially in US history, so that many prefer to say "economic exploitation that limits physical mobility."

23. Patrick McGeehan, "The Plastic Trap," *New York Times*, November 21, 2004, a joint report with PBS Frontline, "Secret History of the Credit Card" www.pbs.org/wgbh/pages/frontline/shows/credit/. Compound interest and opportunity cost are powerful economic concepts that are seldom understood even by educated citizens.

24. From a governor's office press release at www.governor.ohio.gov/Default.aspx?tabid=988.

25. Muhammad Yunus, *Banker to the Poor* (New York: Public Affairs, 1999).

26. Jeffrey D. Sachs, *The End of Poverty* (New York: Penguin, 2005).

27. Abraham J. Heschel, *The Sabbath* (New York: Farrar, Straus and Giroux, 1951).

28. Alan Brown, ed., *Festivals in World Religions* (London: Longman, 1986).

29. Schmuel Y. Agnon, *Days of Awe*, ed. Nahum N. Glatzer, trans. Maurice T. Galpert and Sloan (New York: Schocken, 1948).

30. The Negative Golden Rule of Hillel is cited in I. Epstein, ed., *Soncino Babylonian Talmud* (London: Soncino, 1935–1948).

31. Zafrira Ben-Barak, *Inheritance by Daughters in Israel and the Ancient Near East* (Jaffa: Archaeological Center, 2006), 92.

32. Maimonides, *Mishnah Torah*, Book 13, Treatise 5, p. 280.

33. Henry S. Maine, *Ancient Law* (1861; New York: Holt, 1884).

34. David S. Powers, *Studies in Qur'an and Hadith: The Formation of the Islamic Law of Inheritance* (Berkeley: University of California, 1986), 212. Powers calls it not merely a reform but a revolution.

35. This is a basis both for and against religious feminism.

36. Timur Kuran, "The Provision of Public Goods under Islamic Law," *Law & Society Review* 35, no. 4 (2001) 841–98, see esp. 858.

37. Henry Cattan, "The Law of Waqf," in *Law in the Middle East*, ed. Majid Khadduri (Washington: Middle East Institute, 1955), 218–22.

38. Said Amir Arjomand, "Philanthropy, the Law, and Public Policy in the Islamic World before the Modern Era," *Philanthropy in the World's Religions,* ed. Warren Ilchman, Stanley Katz, and Edward Queen II (Bloomington: Indiana University Press, 1998), 109–32, see esp. 124.

39. Kuran, "Provision of Public Goods," 850.

40. In Virginia in 1779, "Jefferson prepared a 'Statute of Descents' to abolish primogeniture and replace it with partible inheritance in equal shares to the children of a descendant," according to Stanley N. Katz, "Republicanism and the Law of Inheritance in the American Revolutionary Era," *Michigan Law Review* 76, no. 1 (November 1977): 1–29, esp. 12.

41. Arthur Waskow, *Down-to-Earth Judaism* (New York: Morrow, 1995), 216.

42. Jewish *tzedakah* is based on *chesed* (lovingkindness) yet is different from *caritas* (charity) in emphasizing just assistance. The Semitic (Hebrew-Arabic) emphasis on social justice implies that development aid is more beneficial than charitable aid. In *Moral Education*, Émile Durkheim argues that individual charity only helps the conscience of the giver but reifies, rather than challenges, existing inequalities. In his *Mishnah Torah*, Maimonides quotes Deut. 15:7–8 and Lev. 25:35 as commandments of charity.

43. In Proposition 13, in 1978, California homeowners voted to amend the state constitution to transfer their property tax payments to future homeowners.

44. Marc Van de Mieroop, *King Hammurabi of Babylon* (Malden, MA: Blackwell, 2005), 10–12.

45. Ibid., 82–83.

46. Cyril Aldred, *The Egyptians* (London: Thames and Hudson, 1961).

47. Wilmer Wright, *The Works of the Emperor Julian* (New York: Macmillan, 1923), 3:69. See Peter Brown, *Poverty and Leadership in the Later Roman Empire* (Hanover, NJ: University Press of New England, 2002).

48. Quoted from Giles Constable, *Monastic Tithes* (Cambridge: Cambridge University Press, 1964), p. 13.

49. George Makdisi, *The Rise of Colleges* (Edinburgh: Edinburgh University Press, 1981).

50. Plato, "Laws," Ioannes Burnet, ed., line iv. 713d.

51. Arthur R. Hands, *Charities and Social Aid in Greece and Rome* (Ithaca: Cornell University, 1968), 98.

52. There is no concept of a common good in the utilitarian structure of secular capitalism except for negative liberty, which does not supplant the religious desire for calling, community, and nature.

53. David Madland, ed., "Green Watchdog" (Washington: Friends of the Earth, 2005), 1–20.

54. Sarah Burd-Sharps, Kristen Lewis, and Eduardo Borges Martins, *The Measure of America* (New York: Columbia University Press, 2008).

55. John Talberth, Clifford Cobb, and Noah Slattery, "The Genuine Progress Indicator 2006" (Oakland, CA: Redefining Progress, 2007), 1–33.

56. His argument is more economic than humanitarian, in that it is cheaper to prevent social unrest than to quell it with military force.

57. Waskow, *Down-to-Earth Judaism*, 218.

CHAPTER 8: NATURE

1. Lynn White Jr., "The Historical Roots of Our Ecologic Crisis," *Science* 155 (10 March 1967).

2. Mary Evelyn Tucker and John Grim, "The Emerging Alliance of World Religions and Ecology," *Daedalus* 130, no. 4 (Fall 2001): 4.

3. Clarence J. Glacken, *Traces on the Rhodian Shore: Nature and Culture in Western Thought from Ancient Times to the End of the Eighteenth Century* (Berkeley: University of California Press, 1967), viii.

4. See Morris Freilich, "Ecology and Culture: Environmental Determinism and the Ecological Approach in Anthropology," *Anthropological Quarterly* 40, no. 1 (January 1967): 26–43.

5. Julian Steward, *Theory of Culture Change: The Methodology of Multilinear Evolution* (Urbana: University of Illinois Press, 1955), 31.

6. Linda Nash, "The Agency of Nature or the Nature of Agency," *Environmental History* 10, no. 1 (January 2005): 67–69.

7. Seyyed Hossein Nasr, *Religion and the Order of Nature* (Oxford: Oxford University Press, 1996), 31.

8. James Miller, "Daoism and Ecology," *Earth Ethics* 10, no. 1 (Fall 1998).

9. Donald K. Swearer, "Principles and Poetry, Places and Stories: The Resources of Buddhist Ecology," *Daedalus* 30, no. 4 (Fall, 2001): 227.

10. S. Nomanul Haq, "Islam and Ecology: Toward Retrieval and Reconstruction," *Daedalus* 130, no. 4 (Fall 2001): 146.

11. Theodore Hiebert, *The Yahwist's Landscape: Nature and Religion in Early Israel* (Oxford: Oxford University Press, 1996), 139.

12. John M. Wilkins and Shaun Hill, *Food in the Ancient World* (Oxford: Blackwell, 2006), 42–43.

13. Ibid., 43.

14. David Freeman Hawke, *Daily Life in Early America* (New York: HarperCollins, 1988), 92.

15. David Carrasco and Scott Sessions, *Daily Life of the Aztecs* (Westport, CT: Greenwood, 1998), 117.

16. Wilkins and Hill, *Food in the Ancient World*, 63.

17. Karen Rhea Nemet-Nejat, *Daily Life in Ancient Mesopotamia* (Westport, CT: Greenwood, 1998), 195.

18. Wilkins and Hill, *Food in the Ancient World*, 1.

19. Robert Orsi, *The Madonna of 115th Street: Faith and Community in Italian Harlem, 1880–1950* (New Haven, CT: Yale University Press, 1985), 173.

20. Micha Brumlik, "Humankind's Relationship with Nature and Participation in the Process of Creation through Technology in the view of Judaism," in *Nature and Technology in World Religions,* ed. Peter Kozlowski (New York: Springer, 2001), 25.

21. Sarah McFarland Taylor, *Green Sisters: A Spiritual Ecology* (Cambridge, MA: Harvard University Press, 2007), 162.

22. Roy A. Rappaport, *Ecology, Meaning, and Religion* (Berkeley, CA: North Atlantic Books, 1979), 13.

23. Ibid., 28.

24. Ibid., 37.

25. Yi-Fu Tuan, *Topophilia: A Study of Environmental Perception, Attitudes, and Values* (Englewood Cliffs, NJ: Prentice-Hall, 1974), 79.

26. Sam D. Gill, *Beyond the Primitive: The Religions of Nonliterate People* (Englewood Cliffs, NJ: Prentice-Hall, 1982), 14.

27. S. F. Nadel, "Two Nuba Religions: An Essay in

Comparison," *The American Anthropologist* 57, no. 4 (December 1955): 670.

28. Ibid., 672.

29. Tuan, *Topophilia,* 85.

30. Ibid., 89.

31. Ibid., 90.

32. Michael R. Dove and Carol Carpenter, "Introduction: Major Historical Currents in Environmental Anthropology," in *Environmental Anthropology: A Historical Reader,* ed. Michael R. Dove and Carol Carpenter (Oxford: Blackwell, 2008), 20.

33. Mary Evelyn Tucker and John Grim, "Series Forward," *Christianity and Ecology* (Cambridge, MA: Harvard University Press, 2000), p. xxviii.

34. Ibid., p. xvi.

CHAPTER 9: TOURISM

1. Nelson H. H. Graburn, "Tourism: The Sacred Journey," in *Hosts and Guests: The Anthropology of Tourism*, ed. Valene L. Smith (Philadelphia: University of Pennsylvania Press, 1989), 17–19.

2. Edmund Swinglehurst, *Cook's Tours: The Story of Popular Travel* (Poole, Dorset; New York: Blandford Press, 1982), 8–12.

3. Dean MacCannell, *The Tourist: A New Theory of the Leisure Class* (1976; Berkeley: University of California Press, 1999), 1.

4. Louis Turner and John Ash, *The Golden Hordes: International Tourism and the Pleasure Periphery* (London: Constable, 1975), 11.

5. Aliza Fleischer, "The Tourist behind the Pilgrim in the Holy Land," *Hospitality Management* 19, no. 3 (2000): 311–26; V. Gupta, "Sustainable Tourism: Learning from Indian Religious Traditions," *International Journal of Contemporary Hospitality Management* 11, no. 2/3 (1999): 91.

6. Victor Turner and Edith Turner, *Image and Pilgrimage in Christian Culture: Anthropological Perspectives* (New York: Columbia University Press 1978), 20.

7. Madeleine Rigby, "Graceland: A Sacred Place in a Secular World?" in *The End of Religions? Religion in an Age of Globalisation*, ed. Carole M. Cusack and Peter Oldmeadow (Sydney: Sydney Studies in Religion, 2001); Bruce Scates, *Return to Gallipoli: Walking the Battlefields of the Great War* (Cambridge: Cambridge University Press, 2006).

8. James J. Preston, "Spiritual Magnetism: An Organizing Principle for the Study of Pilgrimage," in *Sacred Journeys: The Anthropology of Pilgrimage*, ed. A. Morinis (Westport, CT: Greenwood, 1992), 40.

9. Ian Jackson, *An Introduction to Tourism* (Melbourne: Hospitality Press, 1989), 3.

10. John I. Richardson, *A History of Australian Travel and Tourism* (Melbourne: Hospitality Press, 1999), 4; Lynne Withey, *Grand Tours and Cook's Tours: A History of Leisure Travel, 1750 to 1915* (London: Aurum, 1998), x.

11. Piers Brendon, *Thomas Cook: 150 Years of Popular Tourism* (London: Secker & Warburg, 1991), 10–11.

12. Withey, *Grand Tours*, ix.

13. Dean MacCannell, "Staged Authenticity: Arrangements of Social Space in Tourist Settings," *American Journal of Sociology* 79, no. 3 (1973): 589–603.

14. Eric J. Leed, *The Mind of the Traveler: From Gilgamesh to Global Tourism* (New York: Basic, 1991), 6.

15. Loykie Lamine, "Tourism in Augustan Society (44 BC–AD 69)," in *Histories of Tourism: Representation, Identity and Conflict*, ed. John K.Walton (Clevedon, UK: Channel View, 2005), 85–86.

16. According to Feifer, the Latin word for a holiday excursion was *peregrinatio*. Maxine Feifer, *Tourism in History: From Imperial Rome to the Present* (New York: Stein and Day, 1986), 10.

17. Lamine, "Tourism in Augustan Society," 72–74.

18. Ibid., 80.

19. Feifer, *Tourism in History*, 8.

20. Christopher Hibbert, *The Grand Tour* (London: Weidenfeld & Nicolson, 1969), 10.

21. Withey, *Grand Tours,* 17–20.

22. Jeremy Black, *The British and the Grand Tour* (London: Croom Helm, 1985), 9–15.

23. Withey, *Grand Tours*, 8.

24. Hibbert, *The Grand Tour*, 10.

25. Richardson, *A History of Australian Travel*, 7.

26. Edmund Swinglehurst, *Cook's Tours: The Story of Popular Travel* (New York: Blandford, 1982), 7.

27. Swinglehurst, *Cook's Tours*, 15.

28. Scates, *Return to Gallipoli*.

29. Ellen Furlough, "Making Mass Vacations: Tourism and Consumer Culture in France, 1930s to 1970s," *Comparative Studies in Society and History* 40, no. 2 (1998): 249.

30. Jonathan Sumption, *Pilgrimage: An Image of Medieval Religion* (London: Faber and Faber, 1975).

31. Antoni Jackowski, "Religious Tourism: Problems with Terminology," in *Peregrinus Cracoviensis*, ed. A. Jackowski (Krakow: Institute of Geography, 2000).

32. Pilgrims Office of Santiago de Compostela,

"Distribution of Pilgrims: Pilgrims Classification 2006–2007," http://www.archicompostela.org/Peregrinos/Esta disticas/ESTADIST2005INGLÉS.htm (accessed December 31, 2008).

33. Lourdes Tourist Office, http://www.lourdes-infotourisme.com/ (accessed December 31, 2008).

34. Royal Embassy of Saudi Arabia, Washington DC, "Pilgrims Move Smoothly into Mina as the Eid Al-Adha Begins," http://www.saudiembassy.net/2008News /News/HajDetail.asp?cIndex=8284 (accessed December 31, 2008).

35. Victor Turner, *Dramas, Fields, and Metaphors: Symbolic Action in Human Society* (Ithaca, NY: Cornell University Press, 1974), 166; Turner, "The Center Out There," 192.

36. Victor Turner, *The Ritual Process: Structure and Antistructure* (Chicago: Aldine, 1969), 95.

37. Turner, *Dramas, Fields, Metaphors*, 168.

38. Ibid., 173–82.

39. Edward H. Schafer, *Pacing the Void: Tang Approaches to the Stars* (Berkeley: University of California Press, 1977), 227.

40. S. Naquin and C. Yü, "Introduction: Pilgrimage in China," in *Pilgrims and Sacred Sites in China*, ed. S. Naquin and C. Yü (Berkeley: University of California Press, 1992), 11.

41. R. Birnbaum, "The Manifestation of a Monastery: Shen-ying's Experiences on Mount Wu-t'ai in T'ang Context," *Journal of the American Oriental Society* 106, no. 1 (1986): 119.

42. Naquin and Yü, "Introduction," 12.

43. Wang Shih-chen, *Yu T'ai-shan chih* 5:13a, P.Wu (trans). Quoted in P. Wu. "An Ambivalent Pilgrim to T'ai Shan in the Seventeenth Century," in *Pilgrims and Sacred Sites in China*, ed. S. Naquin and C.Yü (Berkeley: University of California Press, 1992), 69.

44. Rajiner S. Jutla, "Pilgrimage in Sikh Tradition," in *Tourism, Religion and Spiritual Journeys*, ed. Dallen J. Timothy and Daniel H. Olsen (London: Routledge, 2006), 210–17.

45. Rana P. B. Singh, "Pilgrimage in Hinduism: Historical Context and Modern Perspectives," in *Tourism, Religion and Spiritual Journeys*, ed. Dallen J. Timothy and Daniel H. Olsen (London: Routledge, 2006), 221.

46. Richard Sharpley and Priya Sundaram, "Tourism: A Sacred Journey? The Case of Ashram Tourism, India," *International Journal of Tourism Research* 7 (2005): 164.

47. John Eade and Michael J. Sallnow, "Introduction," in *Contesting the Sacred: The Anthropology of Christian Pilgrimage*, ed. John Eade and Michael J. Sallnow (London: Routledge, 1991).

48. John Eade, "Pilgrimage and Tourism at Lourdes, France," *Annals of Tourism Research* 19 (1992): 24.

49. Simon Coleman and John Eade, "Introduction: Reframing Pilgrimage," in *Reframing Pilgrimage: Cultures in Motion*, ed. Simon Coleman and John Eade (London: Routledge, 2004).

50. Barbara N. Aziz, "Personal Dimensions of the Sacred Journey: What Pilgrims Say," *Religious Studies* 23 (1987): 247; Eade, "Pilgrimage and Tourism at Lourdes," 24.

51. David Lawrence Clingingsmith, Asim Ijaz Khwaja, and Michael Kremer, "Estimating the Impact of the Hajj: Religion and Tolerance in Islam's Global Gathering," *HKS Working Paper* No. RWP08-022 (April 2008), Available at SSRN: http://ssrn.com/abstract=1124213.

52. Richard Rymarz, "The Impact ofWorld Youth Day: A Twelve Month Follow-up of Under 18 Australian WYD 2005 Participants," *The Australasian Catholic Record* 84, no. 4 (2007): 387–400.

53. Turner, *Dramas, Fields, and Metaphors*; Clifford Geertz, *The Interpretation of Cultures* (New York: Basic, 1973), 142–69.

54. Ian Reader, "Introduction," in *Pilgrimage in Popular Culture*, ed. Ian Reader and Tony Walter (Basingstoke: Macmillan, 1993), 5.

55. Rigby, "Graceland," 158.

56. Christine King, "His Truth Goes Marching On: Elvis Presley and the Pilgrimage to Graceland," in *Pilgrimage in Popular Culture*, ed. Ian Reader and Tony Walter (Basingstoke: Macmillan, 1993).

57. Rigby, "Graceland," 165.

58. Scates, *Return to Gallipoli*.

59. Renee Lockwood, "Sacrifice and the Creation of Group Identity: Case Studies of Gallipoli and Masada," in *On a Panegyrical Note: Studies in Honour of Garry W. Trompf*, ed. V. Barker and F. Di Lauro (Sydney: Sydney Studies in Religion, 2007), 53.

60. Sue Beeton, *Film-Induced Tourism* (Clevedon, UK: Channel View, 2005), 9.

61. Roger Riley, Dwayne Baker, and Carlton S. van Doren, "Movie-Induced Tourism," *Annals of Tourism Research* 25, no. 4 (1998): 920.

62. John Urry, *The Tourist Gaze: Leisure and Travel in Contemporary Societies* (London: Sage, 1990), 3.

63. Beeton, *Film-Induced Tourism*, 5.

64. See MacCannell, *The Tourist*; Erik Cohen, "A Phenomenology of Tourist Experiences," *Sociology* 13 (1979): 179–201.

65. Eade and Sallnow, "Introduction," 15.

66. Ellen Badone and Sharon R. Roseman, "Approaches to the Anthropology of Pilgrimage and Tourism," in *Intersecting Journeys: The Anthropology of Pilgrimage and Tourism*, ed. Ellen Badone and Sharon R. Roseman (Urbana: University of Illinois Press, 2004), 2.

67. Scates, *Return to Gallipoli*; Rigby, "Graceland"; Carole M. Cusack and Justine Digance, "'Shopping for a Self': Pilgrimage, Identity-Formation, and Retail Therapy," in *Victor Turner and Contemporary Cultural Performance*, ed. Graham St. John (New York: Berghahn, 2008); Richard West Sellars and Tony Walter, "You'll Never Walk Alone: The Anfield Pilgrimage," in *Pilgrimage in Popular Culture*, ed. Ian Reader and Tony Walter (Basingstoke: Palgrave Macmillan, 1993).

68. Nancy Louise Frey, *Pilgrim Stories: On and Off the Road to Santiago* (Berkeley: University of California Press, 1998).

69. Coleman and Eade, "Introduction: Reframing Pilgrimage," 2–4.

70. Justine Digance, "Religious and Secular Pilgrimage: Journeys Redolent with Meaning," in *Tourism, Religion and Spiritual Journeys*, ed. Dallen J. Timothy and Daniel H. Olsen (London: Routledge, 2006).

71. Theron A. Nuñez, "Tourism, Tradition and Acculturation: Weekendismo in a Mexican Village," *Ethnology* 2, no. 3 (1963): 347–52.

72. MacCannell, "Staged Authenticity," 589–603.

73. MacCannell, *The Tourist*, 1–4.

74. Graburn, "Tourism: The Sacred Journey," 17–19.

75. Nelson H. H. Graburn, "Secular Ritual: A General Theory of Tourism," in *Hosts and Guests Revisited: Tourism Issues of the 21st Century*, ed. V. L. Smith and M. Brent (New York: Cognizant Communication, 2001), 42.

76. Cohen, "A Phenomenology of Tourist Experiences," 180–90.

77. MacCannell, "Staged Authenticity," 593.

78. Boris Vukonić, *Tourism and Religion*; Turner, "The Center Out There"; Turner and Turner, *Image and Pilgrimage in Christian Culture*; and Singh, "Pilgrimage in Hinduism."

79. Thomas S. Bremer, "Sacred Spaces and Tourist Places," in *Tourism, Religion and Spiritual Journeys*, ed. Dallen J. Timothy and Daniel H. Olsen (London: Routledge, 2006).

80. Vukonić, *Tourism and Religion*, 53–57.

81. Mary Lee Nolan and Sidney Nolan, "Religious Sites as Tourism Attractions in Europe," *Annals of Tourism Research* 19 (1992): 69–70.

82. Ibid., 73–77.

83. Sean Slavin, "Walking as Spiritual Practice: The Pilgrimage to Santiago de Compostela," *Body & Society* 9, no. 3 (2003): 16.

84. Frey, *Pilgrim Stories*, 102.

85. Hilme Ibrahim and Kathleen A. Cordes, *Outdoor Recreation: Enrichment for Lifetime* (Champaign, IL: Sagamore, 2002), 18

86. Dallen J. Timothy and Daniel H. Olsen, "Conclusion: Whither Religious Tourism," in *Tourism, Religion and Spiritual Journeys*, ed. Dallen J. Timothy and Daniel H. Olsen (London: Routledge, 2006), 271.

87. Sharpley and Sundaram, "Tourism," 161–71.

88. Theron Nuñez, "Touristic Studies in Anthropological Perspective," in *Hosts and Guests: The Anthropology of Tourism*, ed. Valene Smith (Oxford: Blackwell, 1978), 208.

89. William Sims Bainbridge and Rodney Stark, "Cult Formation: Three Compatible Models," *Sociological Analysis* 40, no. 4 (1979): 286.

90. Cusack and Digance, "'Shopping for a Self,'" p. 232.

91. P. M. Wadsworth, "Leisure Pursuits in Nineteenth-Century Bath," Unpublished MA thesis, University of Kent, 1975.

92. Colin Campbell, *The Romantic Ethic and the Spirit of Modern Consumerism* (York: Alcuin, 2005 [1987]), pp. 88–89.

93. Cusack and Digance, "'Shopping for a Self,'" 238–39.

94. Geertz, *The Interpretation of Cultures*.

95. Charles Taylor, *Sources of the Self: The Making of Modern Identity* (Cambridge MA: Harvard University Press, 1992), 28.

96. William Wordsworth, *The Prelude*, Book 11, ed. W. J. Harvey and Richard Gravil (London: Macmillan, 1972), II. 258–78.

97. Alain de Botton, *The Art of Travel* (London: Penguin, 2003), 154–56.

98. Jonathan Z. Smith, *Map Is Not Territory: Studies in the History of Religions* (Chicago: University of Chicago Press, 1978), 291.

CHAPTER 10: EDUCATION

1. Horace Mann, "Our Education: Its Dignity and Its Degradation," in *On the Crisis in Education*, ed. Louis Filler (Yellow Springs, OH: Antioch, 1965), 20–21. Mann, progenitor of the "common-school" movement discussed in the following, encountered a great deal

of resistance in his work as secretary for education in Massachusetts.

2. Diane Moore, *Overcoming Religious Illiteracy: A Cultural Studies Approach to the Study of Religion in Secondary Education* (New York: Palgrave Macmillan, 2007), 134–35. Moore argues that the study of religion is important to the understanding of self, history, and culture.

3. Peter Berger, *The Sacred Canopy: Elements of a Sociological Theory of Religion* (Garden City, NY: Doubleday, 1967), 4.

4. James Madison, "Memorial and Remonstrance Against Religious Assessments" (1785), excerpted from section 4, http://religiousfreedom.lib.virginia.edu/sacred/madison_m&r_1785.html. Accessed December 17, 2008.

5. Horace Mann, "Twelfth Annual Report," in *The Republic and the School: Horace Mann on The Education of Free Men*, ed. Lawrence A. Cremin (New York: Teachers College, Columbia University, 1957), 87. Mann picked up the clarion call of Jefferson that universal education was necessary to sustain the democratic republic.

6. Warren A. Nord, *Religion and American Education: Rethinking a National Dilemma* (Chapel Hill: The University of North Carolina Press, 1995), 108.

7. Thomas Jefferson, *Declaration of Independence* (1776). Jefferson's language modified George Mason's original formulation in *The Virginia Declaration of Rights* (1776), which appears in the quotation from James Madison: "All men are by nature equally free and independent."

8. By "universal," Jefferson meant one system for all children who were eligible to attend school, regardless of religious creed or social status; he did not advocate education for all children.

9. Thomas Jefferson, To Peter Carr, Aug. 10, 1787, in *Crusade against Ignorance: Thomas Jefferson on Education*, ed. Gordon C. Lee (New York: Teachers College, Columbia University, 1961), 146.

10. Benedict Anderson, *Imagined Communities: Reflections on the Origin and Spread of Nationalism*, rev. ed. (London: Verso, 1991).

11. The common-school movement gained further steam in the wake of the Civil War, the conclusion of which led to increased interest in reconstructing and promoting the union of the nation. And, as child labor practices were exposed and ended during the Industrial Revolution, schools proliferated, offering relatively safe places for children to go while their parents worked.

12. The anti-Catholic bias of school textbooks in the nineteenth century is demonstrated amply by Ruth Miller Elson in *Guardians of Tradition: American Schoolbooks of the Nineteenth Century* (Lincoln: University of Nebraska Press, 1964).

13. This colorful description of Protestant churches is taken from Francis X. Curran, *The Churches and the Schools: American Protestantism and Popular Elementary Education* (Chicago: Loyola University Press, 1954), 13. Curran argues that the church has always claimed and exercised its right to educate children. His account of Protestant efforts for education in the United States shows, first, that the motivation behind educational institutions was proper moral instruction so that, second, the retreat of Protestant churches from the task of education is unprecedented and morally reprehensible. Protestant churches are described as having abandoned the responsibility to education children, instead relinquishing or surrendering the task to the state, whose consequent activity may be seen as an intrusion upon religious liberty.

14. *Minersville School District v. Gobitis*, 310 U.S. 586 (1940).

15. *Abington School District v. Schempp*, 374 U.S. 203 (1963).

16. In *Holy Trinity Church v U.S.*, 143 U.S. 457 (1892), the United States is defined as a Christian nation: "If we pass beyond these matters to a view of American life, as expressed by its laws, its business, its customs, and its society, we find everywhere a clear recognition of the same truth. Among other matters note the following: The form of oath universally prevailing, concluding with an appeal to the Almighty; the custom of opening sessions of all deliberative bodies and most conventions with prayer; the prefatory words of all wills, 'In the name of God, amen;' the laws respecting the observance of the Sabbath, with the general cessation of all secular business, and the closing of courts, legislatures, and other similar public assemblies on that day; the churches and church organizations which abound in every city, town, and hamlet; the multitude of charitable organizations existing everywhere under Christian auspices; the gigantic missionary associations, with general support, and aiming to establish Christian missions in every quarter of the globe. These and many other matters which might be noticed, add a volume of unofficial declarations to the mass of organic utterances that this is a Christian nation."

17. Today, "universal education" is intended to cover all children, regardless of religious affiliation, social status, race, gender, or ability.

18. National Center for Education Statistics, Institute of Education Science, U.S. Department of Education, http://nces.ed.gov. Accessed September 12, 2008.

19. Many of these same concerns have motivated parents and educators to establish charter schools, or "public schools of choice," in their neighborhoods. In 2007, two public charter schools that emphasize dual-language instruction, Khalil Gibran International Academy in New York (Arabic) and Ben Gamla Charter School in Florida (Hebrew), came under close scrutiny because of religion/state boundaries. Both schools are public, and neither promotes religious instruction. Although many charter schools support instruction in two languages, Khalil Gibran International Academy and Ben Gamla seem to have been targeted because of assumptions that instruction in Arabic and Hebrew is inherently religious. See the commentary (9/2/07) by Charles C. Haynes of the First Amendment Center: "Do Arabic, Hebrew Public Schools Cross Church-State Line?: Inside the First Amendment," September 2, 2007, www.firstamendmentcenter.org/do-arabic-hebrew-public-schools-cross-churchstate-line.

20. *Cochran v. Louisiana State Board of Education*, 281 U.S. 370 (1930); *Board of Education v. Allen*, 392 U.S. 236 (1968); *Lemon v. Kurtzman*, 403 U.S. 602 (1971). The decision in *Lemon v. Kurtzman* established a three-prong test for government establishment of religion that has been applied many times in the past thirty years. The Lemon test is discussed in greater detail at the end of the subsection on Bible Reading.

21. *Everson v. Board of Education*, 330 U.S. 1 (1940).

22. Newdow v. Rio Linda Union School District, 05-17257. The entire decision is available through the following website: http://www.ushistory.org/betsy/images/courtdecision05-17257.pdf.

23. *Engel v. Vitale*, 370 U.S. 421 (1962).

24. "Guidance on Constitutionally Protected Prayer in Public Elementary and Secondary Schools," http://www.ed.gov/policy/gen/guid/religionandschools/prayer_guidance.html. Accessed September 12, 2008. See also "Student Religious Expression in Public Schools: United States Department of Education Guidelines."

25. *State ex rel Weiss v. District Board*, 76 Wis. 177 (1890).

26. *Abington School District v. Schempp*, 374 U.S. 203 (1963).

27. Robert Michaelsen, *Piety in the Public School: Trends and Issues in the Relationship between Religion and the Public School in the United States* (New York: Macmillan, 1970), 254–55.

28. Sidney Mead, *The Lively Experiment: The Shaping of Christianity in America* (New York: Harper & Row, 1963), 68.

29. Guidelines developed by a coalition of religious leaders and scholars in 1988 and listed at http://www.firstamendmentcenter.org/publicschools/madison/wp-content/uploads/2011/03/. Accessed September 12, 2008.

30. California State Standards for Social Studies in Seventh Grade, http://www.cde.ca.gov/be/st/ss/hstgrade7.asp. Accessed September 12, 2008.

31. "Test your Religion IQ" with Prothero's quiz by following a link from his Web site: www.stephenprothero.com.

32. Ninian Smart, *Dimensions of the Sacred: An Anatomy of the World's Beliefs* (Berkeley: University of California Press, 1996).

33. John Dewey, *A Common Faith* (New Haven, CT: Yale University Press, 1934), 27.

34. Nel Noddings, *Educating for Intelligent Belief or Unbelief* (New York: Teachers College Press, 1993), 143.

35. Pierre Bourdieu, *The Logic of Practice*, trans. Richard Nice (Stanford: Stanford University Press, 1990).

36. David Tyack, *The One Best System: A History of American Urban Education* (Cambridge, MA: Harvard University Press, 1974), 11.

37. Shifts of this kind are already underway in many charter schools and nonpublic schools.

Chapter 11: Children

1. I wish to thank Susan Ridgley Bales for insightful comments on an early draft of this article.

2. Phillipé Aries, *Centuries of Childhood: A Social History of Family Life* (New York: Alfred A. Knopf, 1962).

3. Allison James, Chris Jenks, and Alan Prout, *Theorizing Childhood* (New York: Teachers College Press, 1998).

4. Eric Ziolkowski, *Evil Children in Religion, Literature, and Art* (New York: Palgrave, 2001).

5. James R. Kincaid, *Erotic Innocence: The Culture of Child Molesting* (Durham, NC: Duke University Press, 1998).

6. Susan Starr Sered, "Childbirth as a Religious Experience? Voices from an Israeli Hospital," *Journal of Feminist Studies in Religion* 7 (1991): 7–18.

7. Robbie E. Davis-Floyd, *Birth as an American Rite of Passage* (Berkeley: University of California Press, 1992).

8. Marcus, Ivan G. *Rituals of Childhood: Jewish*

Acculturation in Medieval Europe (New Haven, CT: Yale University Press, 1996).

9. Susan Ridgley Bales, *When I Was a Child: Children's Interpretations of First Communion* (Chapel Hill: University of North Carolina Press, 2006).

10. Robert A. Orsi, "Material Children: Making God's Presence Real for Catholic Boys and Girls and for the Adults in Relation to Them," in *Between Heaven and Earth: The Religious Worlds People Make and the Scholars Who Study Them* (Princeton: Princeton University Press, 2005).

11. Catherine A. Brekus, "Children of Wrath, Children of Grace: Jonathan Edwards and the Puritan Culture of Child Rearing," in *The Child in Christian Thought*, ed. Marcia J. Bunge (Grand Rapids: Eerdmans, 2001), 300–329.

12. Margaret Lamberts Bendroth, *Growing Up Protestant: Parents, Children, and Mainline Churches* (New Brunswick, NJ: Rutgers University Press, 2002), 50–55.

13. Iona and Peter Opie, *The Lore and Language of Schoolchildren* (Oxford: Oxford University Press, 1959).

14. Lynda Edwards, "Myths over Miami," *Miami New Times* June 5, 1997, http://www.miaminewtimes.com /news/myths-over-miami/1997-06-05. Accessed November 1, 2001.

15. Noel Riley Fitch, "A Symposium on Secret Spaces," in *Secret Spaces of Childhood,* ed. Elizabeth Goodenough (Ann Arbor: University of Michigan Press, 2003), 31.

16. Marjorie Taylor and Stephanie M. Carlson, "The Influence of Religious Beliefs on Parental Attitudes about Children's Fantasy Behavior," in *Imagining the Impossible: Magical, Scientific, and Religious Thinking in Children,* ed. Karl S. Rosengren, Carl N. Johnson, and Paul L. Harris (Cambridge: Cambridge University Press, 2000).

17. Elizabeth Lominska Johnson, "Child and Family in Chinese Popular Religion," in *Religious Dimensions of Child and Family Life: Reflections on the UN Convention on the Rights of the Child,* ed. Harold Coward and Philip Cook (Waterloo, ON: Wilfrid Laurier University Press, 1996), 135.

18. Ronald Goldman, *Religious Thinking from Childhood to Adolescence* (1964; San Francisco: Harper-SanFrancisco, 1984), 70.

19. Christopher G. Ellison, "Conservative Protestantism and the Corporal Punishment of Children: Clarifying the Issues," *Journal for the Scientific Study of Religion* 35, no. 1 (1996): 1–16.

20. Bahira Sherif-Trask, "Muslim Families in the United States," in *Handbook of Contemporary Families: Considering the Past, Contemplating the Future,* ed. Marilyn Coleman and Lawrence H. Ganong (Thousand Oaks, CA: Sage, 2004), 394–408.

21. Horace Bushnell, *Christian Nurture* (1861; repr., Cleveland: Pilgrim, 1994), 252, quoted in Margaret Lamberts Bendroth, *Growing Up Protestant: Parents, Children, and Mainline Churches* (New Brunswick, NJ: Rutgers University Press, 2002), 27.

22. Anne M. Boylan, *Sunday School: The Formation of an American Institution, 1790–1880* (New Haven, CT: Yale University Press, 1988).

23. Wendy Haight, *African-American Children at Church* (Cambridge: Cambridge University Press, 2002).

24. Shelley McIntosh, *Mtoto House: Vision to Victory: Raising African American Children Communally* (Lanham, MD: Hamilton, 2005), 39.

25. John A. Hostetler and Gertrude Enders Huntington, *Children in Amish Society: Socialization and Community Education* (New York: Holt, Rinehart and Winston, 1971).

26. Vasudha Narayanan, "Child and Family in Hinduism," in *Religious Dimensions of Child and Family Life: Reflections on the UN Convention on the Rights of the Child,* ed. Harold Coward and Philip Cook (Waterloo, ON: Wilfrid Laurier University Press, 1996), 53–77.

27. Jack Zipes, *Happily Ever After: Fairy Tales, Children, and the Culture Industry* (New York: Routledge: 1997).

28. Ellen Herman, "The Difference Difference Makes: Justine Wise Polier and Religious Matching in Twentieth-Century Child Adoption," *Religion in American Culture* 10, no. 1 (2000): 57–98.

29. Cindy Dell Clark, *Flights of Fancy, Leaps of Faith: Children's Myths in Contemporary America* (Chicago: University of Chicago Press, 1995).

30. David Heller, *The Children's God* (Chicago: University of Chicago Press, 1986).

31. Robert Coles, *The Spiritual Life of Children* (Boston: Houghton Mifflin, 1990).

32. Helen Berger, *A Community of Witches: Contemporary Neo-Paganism and Witchcraft in the United States* (Columbia: University of South Carolina Press, 1999).

33. Sarah W. Whedon, *Hands, Hearts, and Heads: Childhood and Esotericism in American Waldorf Education* (PhD diss., University of California, Santa Barbara, 2007).

34. Bonnie J. Miller-McLemore, "Children and Religion in the Public Square: 'Too Dangerous and Too

Safe, Too Difficult and Too Silly,'" *The Journal of Religion* (2006): 389.

35. Barbara Kingsolver, *The Poisonwood Bible* (New York: HarperCollins, 1999), 114–15.

36. Clark, *Flights of Fancy*, 123.

CHAPTER 12: DEATH AND DYING

1. Max Weber, "The Social Psychology of the World Religions," in *From Max Weber: Essay in Sociology,* trans. Hans H. Gerth and C. Wright Mills (New York: Oxford University Press, 1946).

2. Bronislaw Malinowski, *Magic, Science and Religion* (London: Souvenir, 1954).

3. Maurive Halbwacs, *Les Causes de Suicide* (Paris: Alcan, 1930).

4. Émile Durkheim, *The Rules of the Sociological Method*, ed. S. Lukes, trans. W. D. Halls (1938; New York: Free Press, 1982), pp. 50–59.

5. Compare Philippe Ariés, *Western Attitudes Towards Death: From the Middle Ages to the Present* (Baltimore: Johns Hopkins University Press, 1974).

6. Michael Featherstone, "The Body in Consumer Culture," *Theory Culture and Society* 1, no. 2 (1982): 18–31.

7. Marie von Franz, *On Dreams and Dreaming: A Jungian Perspective* (Boston: Shambhala, 1986).

8. Neal Krause and Christopher Ellison, "Forgiveness by God, Forgiveness of Others, and Psychological Well-Being in Late Life," *Journal for the Scientific Study of Religion* 42, no. 1 (2003): 77–93.

9. James Thorson, "Spiritual Well-Being in a Secular Society," *Generations* 8 (1983): 10–11.

10. John Finney, *Finding Faith Today: How Does It Happen?* (Swindon, UK: British Bible Society, 1995), 50.

11. Richard Kalish and David Reynolds, *Death and Ethnicity: A Psychocultural Study* (Los Angeles: University of Southern California Press, 1974).

12. Tony Walter, "Popular Afterlife Beliefs in the Modern West," in *Death and Eternal Life in the World Religions,* ed. P. Badman and C. Becker (London: Paragon, 1999).

13. Douglas Davies, "Contemporary Belief in Life after Death," in *Interpreting Death: Christian Theology and Pastoral Practice,* ed. P. Jupp and T. Rogers (London: Cassell, 1979).

14. George Gallop, *The Spiritual Life of Young Americans: Approaching the Year 2000* (Princeton: George H. Gallop International Institute, 1999).

15. Tony Walter and Helen Waterhouse, "A Very Private Belief: Reincarnation in Contemporary England," *Sociology* 60, no. 2 (1999): 187–97.

16. Yves Lambert, "A Turning Point in Religious Evolution in Europe," *Journal of Contemporary Religion* 19, no. 1 (2004): 204–15.

17. Ariés, *Western Attitudes Towards Death.*

18. Abdul Muhaimin, *The Islamic Traditions of Cirebon: Ibadat and Adat among Javanese Muslims* (Canberra: ANUE Press, The Australian National University, 2006).

19. Geoffrey Gorer, *Death, Grief and Mourning in Contemporary Britain* (London: Cresset, 1967).

20. Arnold van Gennep, *Les Rites de Passage* (1908; London: Routledge, 1960).

21. Tony Walter, *On Bereavement: The Culture of Grief* (Buckingham, UK: Open University Press, 1999).

22. Compare John Harte, "Law after Death, or 'Whose Body Is It?': The Legal Framework for the Disposal of the Dead," in *Ritual Remembrance: Responses to Death in Human Societies,* ed. J. Davies (Sheffield, UK: Sheffield Academic Press, 1994).

23. Compare Yvonne Haddad, *Muslims of America* (New York: Oxford University Press, 1991).

24. Compare Cybelle Shattuck, ed., *Hinduism* (London: Routledge, 1999).

CHAPTER 13: CONTEMPORARY VISUAL ART

I would like to thank the artists and their galleries and various representatives for their generosity in granting permission to reproduce the artworks included with this article. I also thank the project editors for their insightful comments and suggestions.

1. James Elkins raises similar points in his book *On the Strange Place of Religion in Contemporary Art* (New York: Routledge, 2004). One of several recent authors who examines relationships between religion and contemporary art, Elkins notes that one common approach to these topics by art historians is to comment "that religion is simply absent from much contemporary art" (Elkins, *On the Strange Place of Religion in Contemporary Art*, 115). However, as Elkins demonstrates throughout his book, the relationships between religion and contemporary art are far more complex.

2. In addition to Elkins, *On the Strange Place of Religion in Contemporary Art*, see also *The Spiritual in Art: Abstract Painting 1890–1985* (Los Angeles: Los Angeles County Museum of Art; New York: Abbeville, 1986);

Richard Francis, ed., *Negotiating Rapture: The Power of Art to Transform Lives* (Chicago: Museum of Contemporary Art, 1996); Dawn Perlmutter and Debra Koppman, eds., *Reclaiming the Spiritual in Art: Contemporary Cross-Cultural Perspectives* (New York: State University of New York Press, 1999); Christian Eckart, Harry Philbrick, and Osvaldo Romberg, eds., *Faith: The Impact of Judeo-Christian Religion on Art* (Ridgefield, CT: Aldrich Museum of Contemporary Art, 2000); Erika Doss, "Robert Gober's 'Virgin' Installation: Issues of Spirituality in Contemporary American Art," in *The Visual Culture of American Religions*, ed. David Morgan and Sally M. Promey (Berkeley: University of California Press, 2001), 129–45 and 322–24; Eleanor Heartney, *Postmodern Heretics: The Catholic Imagination in Contemporary Art* (New York: Midmarch Arts Press, 2004); Ena Giurescu Heller, ed., *Reluctant Partners: Art and Religion in Dialogue* (New York: The Gallery at the American Bible Society, 2004); and Laura E. Pérez, *Chicana Art: The Politics of Spiritual and Aesthetic Altarities* (Durham: Duke University Press, 2007), to name a few examples.

3. Senator D'Amato's comments appear in *Congressional Record* 135, 64 (May 18, 1989): S 5594, cited in Carole S. Vance, "The War on Culture," in *Art Matters: How the Culture Wars Changed America*, ed. Brian Wallis et al. (New York: New York University Press, 1999), 220–31; 222 and 231n1. For additional sources related to the so-called culture wars of the late 1980s and 1990s, see Richard Bolton, ed., *Culture Wars: Documents from the Recent Controversies in the Arts* (New York: The New Press, 1992).

4. Coco Fusco, "Andres Serrano Shoots the Klan: An Interview," in *English Is Broken Here: Notes on Cultural Fusion in the Americas* (New York City: The New Press, 1995 [1991]), 79–86; 81.

5. Fusco, "Andres Serrano," 81.

6. Serrano's comments included in William H. Honan, "Congressional Anger Threatens Arts Endowment's Budget," *New York Times*, June 20, 1989, Arts Section, C15 and C20; cited in Vance, "War on Culture," 231n24.

7. Eleanor Heartney makes a similar claim about *Piss Christ*, which, she writes, "is part of Serrano's ongoing exploration of the spiritual dimensions of base matter" (Heartney, *Postmodern Heretics*, 112). In addition, Heartney considers a range of topics on the relationships between the human body and Catholicism in various examples of contemporary art throughout her book.

8. Celia McGee, "A Personal Vision of the Sacred and Profane," *New York Times*, January 22, 1995, Arts and Leisure Section, 35, cited in Heartney, *Postmodern Heretics*, 114.

9. Museum label text accompanying display of *boli*, Brooklyn Museum, cited in Donald J. Cosentino, "Hip-Hop Assemblage: The Chris Ofili Affair," *African Arts* 33, no. 1 (Spring 2000): 40–51 and 95–96; 48.

10. Cosentino, "Hip-Hop," 48. In addition, Eleanor Heartney has asserted that animal dung is "venerated in parts of Africa as a symbol of fertility"; see Eleanor Heartney, "A Catholic Controversy?" *Art in America* 87, no. 12 (December 1999): 39–41; 39. However, the question of the religious or spiritual significance of elephant and other animal dung in sub-Saharan and additional cultural traditions is extremely complex. For an especially detailed and insightful discussion of these issues, see Cosentino. And, as Cosentino also observes, the use of dung and bodily waste in contemporary art is not unique to Ofili; there are important precedents for the use of such materials, especially in the work of David Hammons (Cosentino, "Hip-Hop," 47).

11. Linda Nochlin, "Saluting 'Sensation,'" *Art in America* 87, no. 12 (December 1999): 37–39; 39.

12. Lynn MacRitchie, "Ofili's Glittering Icons," *Art in America* 88, no. 1 (January 2000): 96–101; 97. See also David Barrett, "Chris Ofili," in *Sensation: Young British Artists from the Saatchi Collection* (New York: Thames and Hudson; London: Royal Academy of Arts, 1997), 203.

13. Heartney suggests a similar interpretation of Ofili's work; see Heartney, "A Catholic Controversy?" 41.

14. See, for example, Cox's interview with Karen Croft, "Using Her Body," Salon.com, http://archive .salon.come/sex/feature/2001/02/22/renee_cox/print .html. Accessed June 22, 2008.

15. For similar descriptions and discussions of these artworks, see Amalia Mesa-Bains, "El Mundo Femenino: Chicana Artists of the Movement—A Commentary on Development and Production," in *Chicano Art: Resistance and Affirmation, 1965-1985*, ed. Richard Griswold del Castillo et al. (Los Angeles: Wight Gallery, University of California, Los Angeles, 1991), 131–40; 136–37; Alicia Gaspar de Alba, *Chicano Art Inside/Outside the Master's House: Cultural Politics and the CARA Exhibition* (Austin: University of Texas Press, 1998), 19–43; and Pérez, *Chicana Art*, 269–72.

16. Mesa-Bains, "El Mundo Femenino," 131–33; Pérez, *Chicana Art*, 258–60; 267–80.

17. See especially Mesa-Bains, "El Mundo Femenino," 133; Pérez, *Chicana Art*, 267.

18. Pérez, *Chicana Art*, 264.

19. Ibid., 264–67.

20. Ibid., 266.

21. Tomas Ybarra-Frausto, "Cultural Context," in *Ceremony of Memory: New Expressions in Spirituality among Contemporary Hispanic Artists* (New Mexico: Center for Contemporary Arts of Santa Fe, 1988), 9–13; 9–10; Amalia Mesa-Bains, "*Domesticana*: The Sensibility of Chicana *Rasquachismo*," in *Chicana Feminisms: A Critical Reader*, ed. Gabriela F. Arredondo et al. (Durham: Duke University Press, 2003), 298–315; 302–4.

22. On *An Ofrenda for Dolores del Rio*, see also Jennifer González, "Rhetoric of the Object: Material Memory and the Artwork of Amalia Mesa-Bains," *Visual Anthropology Review* 9, no. 1 (Spring 1993): 82–91.

23. Ybarra-Frausto, "Cultural Context," 10–11; Mesa-Bains, "*Domesticana*," 311–12. On the question of memory and spirit figures and forces, see also Anne Barclay Morgan, "Interview: Amalia Mesa-Bains," *Art Papers* 19, no. 2 (March–April 1995): 24–29; 29.

24. Gaspar de Alba, *Chicano Art*, 77.

25. Mesa-Bains, "*Domesticana*," 311.

26. For a more extensive discussion of the joint roles of politics and religion in Mesa-Bains's work, although with a focus on some different issues and a different set of artworks, see Pérez, *Chicana Art*, especially 59–68; 94–101.

27. Ybarra-Frausto, "Cultural Context," 13.

28. Robert Berlind, "Helène Aylon: Deconstructing the Torah," *Art in America* 87, no. 10 (October 1999): 142–47. See also Norman L. Kleeblatt, ed., *Too Jewish: Challenging Traditional Identities* (New York: The Jewish Museum; New Brunswick, NJ: Rutgers University Press, 1996), especially 32–33.

29. Berlind, "Helène Aylon," 142.

30. Exhibition text, cited in Berlind, "Helène Aylon," 147.

31. Berlind, "Helène Aylon," 146 and 142, respectively.

32. Ibid., 146.

33. Neshat was born and grew up in Iran, and, when the revolution began, she was in the United States, working on an undergraduate degree at the University of California at Berkeley. She was prevented from returning to Iran for more than fifteen years, and, when she was finally able to travel back to Iran, in 1990, the trip was, in her words, "probably one of the most shocking experiences that I have ever had. . . . I had never been in a country that was so ideologically based" (Lina Bertucci, "Shirin Neshat: Eastern Values," *Flash Art* 30, no. 197 [November–December 1997]: 84–87; 86). On these

and related points, see also Anne Kirker, "The Politics of Spirituality: Shirin Neshat Interviewed by Anne Kirker," *Photofile* 41 (November 1996): 42–43; Rose Issa, Ruyin Pakbaz, and Daryush Shayegan, *Iranian Contemporary Art* (London: Booth-Clibborn Editions, 2001); and John B. Ravenal, "Shirin Neshat: Double Vision," in *Reclaiming Female Agency: Feminist Art History after Postmodernism*, ed. Norma Broude and Mary D. Garrard (Berkeley: University of California Press, 2005), 446–58.

34. For more on the veil and its use in Neshat's work, see, for example, Carly Butler, "Ambivalence and Iranian Identity—The Work of Shirin Neshat," *Eastern Art Report* 47 (2001–2002): 40–48; *Shirin Neshat* (Milan: Edizioni Charta, 2002); and David A. Bailey and Gilane Tawadros, eds., *Veil: Veiling, Representation, and Contemporary Art* (Cambridge, MA: MIT Press, 2003).

35. On these points, see especially Kirker, "The Politics of Spirituality"; Igor Zabel, "Women in Black," *Art Journal* 60, no. 4 (Winter 2001): 17–25; and *Shirin Neshat*.

36. For more on the role of Arabic script and calligraphy in the history of Islamic art, see Venetia Porter with Isabelle Caussé, *Word into Art: Artists of the Modern Middle East* (London: The British Museum Press, 2006); and Nada M. Shabout, *Modern Arab Art: Formation of Arab Aesthetics* (Gainesville: University Press of Florida, 2007).

37. See especially Kirker, "The Politics of Spirituality," 43; Butler, "Ambivalence," 42–45; Porter, *Word into Art*, 46.

38. See especially Butler, "Ambivalence," 42–45; Porter, *Word into Art*, 46.

39. For an English translation of Farrokhzad's poem in full and a discussion of additional interpretations of the poem and Farrokhzad's work more generally, see Butler, "Ambivalence," 43–45.

40. See, among other authors, Kirker, Zabel, Butler, and Ravenal.

41. In addition to the work of Farrokhzad, Neshat also uses texts taken from poems by Tahereh Saffarzadeh, another important Iranian woman poet; see Kirker, "The Politics of Spirituality," 43; Butler, "Ambivalence," 45–48.

42. On these and related points, see Kirker, "The Politics of Spirituality"; Butler, "Ambivalence"; Babak Ebrahimian, "Passage to Iran: Shirin Neshat Interviewed by Babak Ebrahimian," *PAJ/Performing Arts Journal* 72 (2002): 44–55; and Ravenal. Ebrahimian and Ravenal both take up these issues, with a particular focus on Neshat's later video and film projects; for more on these

projects, see also Bill Horrigan, *Shirin Neshat: Two Installations* (Columbus, OH: Wexner Center for the Arts/The Ohio State University, 2000); *Shirin Neshat*; *Shirin Neshat: 2002-2005* (Milan: Edizioni Charta, 2005); and Wendy Meryem K. Shaw, "Ambiguity and Audience in the Films of Shirin Neshat," *Third Text* 57 (2001/2002): 43–52.

43. Doss, "Robert Gober's 'Virgin' Installation," 134.

44. Again, see 134. And, while Doss's points are made in her discussion of the work of Robert Gober, they also apply to Viola, in addition to artists such as Georgia O'Keeffe, Andy Warhol, Kiki Smith, and Gary Hill, among others.

45. David A. Ross, "Foreword: A Feeling for the Things Themselves," in *Bill Viola* (New York: Whitney Museum of American Art; Paris and New York: Flammarion, 1997), 19–29; 24. See also Lewis Hyde and Bill Viola, "Conversation," in *Bill Viola*, 143–65.

46. Lisa Jaye Young, "The Elemental Sublime," *Performing Arts Journal* 19, no. 3 (1997): 65–71; 65.

47. Viola comments on the theme of baptism evident in his early work *The Reflecting Pool* (1977–1979) in Raymond Bellour, "An Interview with Bill Viola," *October* 34 (Autumn 1985): 91–119; 97.

48. John Walsh, "Emotions in Extreme Time: Bill Viola's *Passions* Project," in *Bill Viola: The Passions*, ed. John Walsh (Los Angeles: J. Paul Getty Museum; London: National Gallery, 2003), 25–63; 25.

49. Walsh, "Emotions," 29–31; 55–57.

50. Hans Belting and Bill Viola, "A Conversation," in *Bill Viola: The Passions*, 189–221; 199.

51. Walsh, "Emotions," 47.

52. Kira Perov and Bill Viola, "Passions and Angels 2000-2002," in *Bill Viola: The Passions*, 65–157; 146.

53. Ibid., 146.

54. Viola cited in Walsh, "Emotions," 48, from artist's personal communication to Walsh.

55. Wassily Kandinsky, *Concerning the Spiritual in Art*, trans. M. T. H. Sadler (1911; New York: Dover, 1977), 4.

56. Newman cited in Thomas B. Hess, *Barnett Newman* (New York: Museum of Modern Art, 1971), 38.

57. Cited in Hess, *Barnett Newman*, 38.

58. Ibid., 52–53. Also noted in Robert Rosenblum, *Modern Painting and the Northern Romantic Tradition: Friedrich to Rothko* (New York: Harper and Row, 1975), 209.

59. Rosenblum, *Modern Painting*, 209.

60. Ibid., 214.

61. Dore Ashton, "Rothko's Passion," *Art International* 22, no. 9 (February 1979): 6–13; see also Robert Rosenblum on this and related points.

62. Mark Rothko, "Notes from a Conversation with Selden Rodman, 1956," in *Writings on Art*, ed. Miguel López-Remiro (1956; New Haven: Yale University Press, 2006), 119–20; also cited in Rosenblum, *Modern Painting*, 215. On this topic of crying in front of Rothko's work in relation to the question of religion, see also James Elkins, *Pictures and Tears: A History of People Who Have Cried in Front of Paintings* (New York: Routledge, 2001).

63. See Ashton and Rosenblum on this point.

64. For various documents and discussions of this issue, especially in relation to the slightly later arena of conceptual art and related developments, see, for example, Lucy Lippard, *Six Years: The Dematerialization of the Art Object from 1966-1972* (Berkeley: University of California Press, 1997 [1973]); Alexander Alberro and Blake Stimson, eds., *Conceptual Art: A Critical Anthology* (Cambridge, MA: MIT Press, 1999); and Ann Goldstein and Anne Rorimer, eds., *Reconsidering the Object of Art: 1965-1975* (Cambridge, MA: MIT Press; Los Angeles: Museum of Contemporary Art, 1995).

65. See, for example, RoseLee Goldberg, *Performance: Live Art 1909 to the Present* (New York: Harry N. Abrams, 1979); Kristine Stiles, "Performance Art," in *Theories and Documents of Contemporary Art: A Sourcebook of Artists' Writings* (Berkeley: University of California Press, 1996), 679–94.

66. For overviews of these and related points, see, for example, Edmund R. Leach, "Ritual," in *International Encyclopedia of the Social Sciences,* ed. David L. Sills (New York: The MacMillan Company and the Free Press, 1968), 13:520–26; Evan M. Zuesse, "Ritual," in *The Encyclopedia of Religion*, ed. Mircea Eliade et al. (New York: MacMillan, 1987), 12:405–22.

67. Henri Hubert and Marcel Mauss, *Sacrifice: Its Nature and Function*, trans. W. D. Halls (1899; Chicago: University of Chicago Press, 1968), 32.

68. Ibid., 43–44; my emphasis.

69. Victor Turner, *The Ritual Process: Structure and Anti-Structure* (1969; New York: Aldine de Gruyter, 1995), 94–96.

70. Ibid., 97.

71. Ibid., 83; 96–97; 126–28. What Turner describes as the breakdown of distinctions themselves in the liminal phase of ritual is noteworthy, among other reasons, for the ways in which, in its utter disintegration of traditional social codes and categories, this middle phase of ritual might be described, especially from some traditional or conservative vantage points, not as a sacred

or sacralizing activity, but instead as deeply profane. I note this not because I think our notions of ritual (or our concepts of sacred and profane) should be guided by traditional or conservative positions—far from it—but because it adds another element of complexity to the otherwise oversimplified conservative assessments of contemporary art as blasphemous and profane, as discussed in previous sections. Indeed, if ritual, even in its most religious instances or contexts, were nonetheless understood as a deeply profane activity, this would make for another intriguing connection, rather than opposition, between the larger field of religion and the "profane" or "blasphemous" practices of contemporary art. For an additional discussion of the intertwined relationships between sacred and profane, including several examples of such relationships in works of recent visual art, see Michael Taussig, *Defacement: Public Secrecy and the Labor of the Negative* (Stanford: Stanford University Press, 1999).

72. For a related and somewhat expanded discussion of the significance of the body in contemporary art and its relationship to ritual, see my chapter "Ritual and Contemporary Body Art," in Elizabeth Adan, *Matter, Presence, Image: The Work of Ritual in Contemporary Feminist Art* (PhD diss., University of California Santa Barbara, 2006), 76–112.

73. Harold Rosenberg, "The American Action Painters," in *The Tradition of the New* (1952; New York: Horizon, 1959), 23–39; 25.

74. Allan Kaprow, "The Legacy of Jackson Pollock," in *Essays on the Blurring of Art and Life*, ed. Jeff Kelley (1958; Berkeley: University of California Press, 1993), 1–9; 4 and 9, respectively.

75. Ibid., 7.

76. Ibid., 9.

77. Allan Kaprow, *Assemblage, Environments, and Happenings* (New York: Harry N. Abrams, 1966), 323–37.

78. Ibid., 323–24.

79. Kaprow, "The Happenings Are Dead: Long Live the Happenings!" in *Essays on the Blurring of Art and Life* (1966), 59–65; 64–65. While Kaprow notes important parallels between happenings and a range of both religious and secular rituals, it is not entirely clear why he calls happenings "*quasi*-rituals" (my emphasis). Although he does not discuss his use of the prefix in explicit terms, it appears to be his way of distinguishing between, on the one hand, more "real," "official," or "sanctioned" forms of ritual practices versus, on the other hand, unconventional, even antitraditional practices such as happenings. Such distinctions can be quite important, but, at the same time, ritual practices have been and remain extremely difficult to classify or categorize. In particular, efforts to determine some ritual practices as more "authentic" or "real" than others, though certainly attempted by a range of scholars, seldom succeed in these goals. For an overview of these issues and the challenges involved in producing a definitive definition, let alone hierarchies, of ritual practices, see my chapter "Defining Ritual," in Adan, "Matter, Presence, Image," 6–43. And, for more detailed discussions of these issues, see, for example, Jack Goody, "Religion and Ritual: The Definitional Problem," *British Journal of Sociology* 12 (1961): 142–64; Sally F. Moore and Barbara Myerhoff, eds., *Secular Ritual* (Amsterdam: Van Gorcum, 1977); Ronald Grimes, *Beginnings in Ritual Studies* (1982; Columbia: University of South Carolina Press, 1995); Jonathan Z. Smith, "The Bare Facts of Ritual," in *Imagining Religion: From Babylon to Jonestown* (Chicago: University of Chicago Press, 1987), 53–65 and 143–45; Jonathan Z. Smith, *To Take Place: Toward Theory in Ritual* (Chicago: University of Chicago Press, 1987); Catherine Bell, *Ritual Theory, Ritual Practice* (New York: Oxford University Press, 1992); and Catherine Bell, *Ritual: Perspectives and Dimensions* (New York: Oxford University Press, 1997).

80. Carolee Schneemann, *More Than Meat Joy: Performance Works and Selected Writings*, ed. Bruce McPherson (1979; New York: McPherson and Company, 1997), 52.

81. On the particular and, at times, overlooked importance of painting in Schneemann's work, see Kristine Stiles, "Schlaget Auf: The Problem with Carolee Schneemann's Painting," in *Carolee Schneemann: Up to and Including Her Limits* (New York: New Museum of Contemporary Art, 1996), 15–25; Kristine Stiles, "Uncorrupted Joy: International Art Actions," in *Out of Actions: Between Performance and the Object, 1949–1979* (Los Angeles: Museum of Contemporary Art; New York: Thames and Hudson, 1998), 227–329.

82. Schneemann, *More Than Meat Joy*, 52.

83. Ibid., 52.

84. Ibid., 63.

85. Ibid., 67–87.

86. Ibid., 63.

87. One of the historical definitions of ecstasy provided by the Oxford English Dictionary reads: "used by mystical writers as the technical name for the state of rapture in which the body was supposed to become incapable of sensation, while the soul was engaged in the

contemplation of divine things." From the Oxford English Dictionary online, Second Edition (July 14, 2008).

88. Schneemann, *More Than Meat Joy*, 63.

89. Ibid., 63.

90. Ibid., 63.

91. Stiles, "Schlaget Auf," 19; see also 18.

92. Ibid., 18.

93. See, for example, Hubert Klocker, ed., *Viennese Aktionism, Vienna 1960–1971: The Shattered Mirror* (Vienna: Ritter Verlag Klagenfurt, 1989); Hubert Klocker, "Gesture and the Object, Liberation as Aktion: A European Component of Performative Art," trans. Nita Tandon, in *Out of Actions: Between Performance and the Object, 1949–1979*, 159–95; and Thomas McEvilley, "Art in the Dark," *Artforum* 21, no. 10 (June 1983): 62–71; 65–66.

94. Klocker, ed., *Viennese Aktionism*, 270; Klocker, "Gesture and the Object," 183.

95. Burden's work has been widely studied and written about, but for general discussions of these and related projects, see, for example, Paul Schimmel, "Leap into the Void: Performance and the Object," in *Out of Actions: Between Performance and the Object, 1949–1979*, 17–119; 94–99; Tracey Warr and Amelia Jones, *The Artist's Body* (New York: Phaidon, 2000), especially 102–3.

96. McEvilley, "Art in the Dark," 65. McEvilley further notes that such artworks reference not only religious figures and practices but also "the residual influence of Romanticism"; for a more in depth discussion of the role of spirituality and religion in Romanticism in the visual arts, see Rosenblum, *Modern Painting*.

97. Whether one sees Beuys as occupying the actual role of a shaman or simply adopting it as an aesthetic trope is open to considerable debate, as are the political implications of Beuys's work, especially in the context of postwar Germany. On the political issues sparked by Beuys's work—including his invocation of shaman figures and practices—see, for example, Benjamin H. D. Buchloh, "Beuys: The Twilight of the Idol, Preliminary Notes for a Critique," *Artforum* 18, no. 5 (January 1980): 35–43; Benjamin H. D. Buchloh, Rosalind Krauss, and Annette Michelson, "Joseph Beuys at the Guggenheim," *October* 12 (Spring 1980): 3–21; Thierry de Duve, "Joseph Beuys, or the Last of the Proletarians," *October* 45 (Summer 1988): 47–62; Stefan Germer, "Haacke, Broodthaers, Beuys," *October* 45 (Summer 1988): 63–75; Eric Michaud, "The Ends of Art According to Beuys," trans. Rosalind Krauss, *October* 45 (Summer 1988): 36–46; and Gene Ray, ed., *Joseph Beuys: Mapping the Legacy* (New York: D. A. P.; Sarasota, FL: Ringling

Museum, 2001). In addition, the question of shamanism is similarly complex; on this complexity and some of the problems with a generic category of shamanism, see, for example Gloria Flaherty, "The Performing Artist as the Shaman of Higher Civilization," *MLN* 103, no. 3 (April 1988): 519–39. And for an especially compelling account of certain specific shamanic practices, see the work of Michael Taussig, including his "Viscerality, Faith, and Skepticism: Another Theory of Magic," in *In Near Ruins: Cultural Theory at the End of the Century*, ed. Nicholas B. Dirks (Minneapolis: University of Minnesota Press, 1998), 221–56.

98. Schimmel, "Leap into the Void," 80–84.

99. Michaud, "The Ends of Art," 36.

100. Ukeles's *Hartford Wash* projects demonstrate in part the points that she makes in her 1969 "Maintenance Art Manifesto: Proposal for an Exhibition, 'CARE,'" reprinted in *Conceptual Art: A Critical Anthology*, 122–25. For an additional discussion of Ukeles's *Hartford Wash* projects, see Helen Molesworth, "House Work and Art Work," *October* 92 (Spring 2000): 71–97.

101. Robert C. Morgan, "*Touch Sanitation*: Mierle Laderman Ukeles," in *The Citizen Artist: 20 Years of Art in the Public Arena: An Anthology from High Performance Magazine, 1978–1998*, ed. Linda Frye Burnham and Steve Durland (New York: Critical, 1998), 55–60.

102. See, for example, Linda Montano, *Art in Everyday Life* (Station Hill: Astro Artz, 1981).

103. Judy Kussoy, "Linda Montano," in *Connecting Conversations: Interviews with 28 Bay Area Women Artists*, ed. Moira Roth (Oakland, CA: Eucalyptus Press Mills College, 1988), 124–30. See also Bonnie Marranca, "Art as Spiritual Practice: Panel Discussion with Alison Knowles, Eleanor Heartney, Meredith Monk, Linda Montano, and Erik Ehn," *PAJ/Performing Arts Journal* 72 (2002): 18–34.

104. Montano, *Art in Everyday Life*; see also Kussoy, "Linda Montano."

105. See, for example, Mary Jane Jacob, "*Ashé* in the Art of Ana Mendieta," in *Santería Aesthetics in Contemporary Latin American Art*, ed. Arturo Lindsay (Washington: Smithsonian Institute Press, 1996), 189–200; Charles Merewether, "From Inscription to Dissolution: An Essay on Expenditure in the Work of Ana Mendieta," in *Ana Mendieta*, ed. Gloria Moure (Barcelona: Ediciones Polígrafa, S. A. and Centro Galego de Arte Contemporánea, 1996), 83–131; and Olga M. Viso, ed., *Ana Mendieta: Earth Body, Sculpture and Performance 1972-1985* (New York: D. A. P.; Germany: Hatje Cantz Verlag, 2004), 49–50; 63–64; 152.

106. On the *Untitled (Blood and Feathers)* projects, see especially Viso, ed., *Ana Mendieta*, 213–16. On related points, also see Jacob, "*Ashé*," 193.

107. On the *Rupestrian Sculptures* and the importance of Taíno religious traditions in Mendieta's work, see Viso, ed., *Ana Mendieta*, 77–90; Bonnie Clearwater, *Ana Mendieta: A Book of Works* (Miami Beach: Grassfield, 1993).

108. Again, see Jacob in particular on this point. Additional authors who have noted the importance of Santería in Mendieta's work include Ann-Sargent Wooster, "Ana Mendieta: Themes of Death and Resurrection," *High Performance* 41–42 (Spring–Summer 1988): 80–83; Miwon Kwon, "Bloody Valentines: Afterimages by Ana Mendieta," in *Inside the Visible: An Elliptical Traverse of 20th Century Art in, of, and from the Feminine*, ed. Catherine de Zegher (Cambridge, MA: MIT Press, 1996), 164–71; Anne Raine, "Embodied Geographies: Subjectivity and Materiality in the Work of Ana Mendieta," in *Generations and Geographies in the Visual Arts: Feminist Readings*, ed. Griselda Pollock, (New York: Routledge, 1996), 228–49; Amelia Jones, *Body Art/Performing the Subject* (Minneapolis: University of Minnesota Press, 1998); Jane Blocker, *Where Is Ana Mendieta? Identity, Performativity, and Exile* (Durham: Duke University Press, 1999); Michael Duncan, "Tracing Mendieta," *Art in America* 87, no. 4 (1999): 110–13 and 154; Irit Rogoff, *Terra Infirma: Geography's Visual Culture* (New York: Routledge, 2000); and Gill Perry, "The Expanding Field: Ana Mendieta's *Silueta* Series," in *Frameworks for Modern Art*, ed. Jason Gaiger (New Haven: Yale University Press, 2003), 153–205.

109. On the Cuilapán artwork, see, for example, Jacob, "*Ashé*," 194; Viso, ed., *Ana Mendieta*, 159–60. On *Ceiba Fetish*, see Jacob, "*Ashé*," 195; Viso, ed., *Ana Mendieta*, 95; 236. And on *Imagen de Yagul*, see Jacob, "*Ashé*," 194; Viso, ed., *Ana Mendieta*, 52; 166.

110. For a range of arguments about the relationships between Mendieta's work and her experience of exile, see, for example, John Perreault, "Earth and Fire: Mendieta's Body of Work," in *Ana Mendieta: A Retrospective* (New York: The New Museum of Contemporary Art, 1987), 10–23; Luis Camnitzer, "Ana Mendieta," *Third Text* 7 (Summer 1989): 47–52; Shifra M. Goldman, "Ana Mendieta: A Return to Natal Earth," in *Dimensions of the Americas: Art and Social Change in Latin America and the United States* (Chicago: University of Chicago Press, 1994), 236–68; Kaira M. Cabañas, "Ana Mendieta: 'Pain of Cuba, Body I am,'" *Woman's Art Journal* (Spring/Summer 1999): 12–17; many of the authors listed in notes 105 and 108; and Elizabeth Adan, "Matter,

Movement, Exile, and Ritual in Ana Mendieta's *Silueta Series*," in *Matter, Presence, Image*, 113–53.

111. For the artist's outline and descriptions of *Rhythm 0*, see *Marina Abramović* (Stuttgart: Edition Cantz, 1993), 68–85; *Marina Abramović: Artist Body, Performances 1969–1998* (Milan: Edizioni Charta, 1998), 80–93; and *Marina Abramović: Public Body, Installations and Objects 1965–2001* (Milan: Edizioni Charta, 2001), 52–55. In addition, these three texts are excellent sources of descriptions and documentation of Abramović's work throughout her career.

112. Abramović interviewed in Thomas McEvilley, "Stages of Energy: Performance Art Ground Zero?" in *Marina Abramović: Artist Body*, 14–25; 15.

113. On *Relation in Space*, see *Marina Abramović*, 120–23; *Marina Abramović: Artist Body*, 130–37. On *Imponderabilia*, see *Marina Abramović*, 128–33; *Marina Abramović: Artist Body*, 150–57; and *Marina Abramović: Public Body*, 60–61.

114. See also Schimmel, "Leap into the Void," 101–2.

115. See *Marina Abramović*, 178–95; *Marina Abramović: Artist Body*, 258–95.

116. Janet A. Kaplan, "Deeper and Deeper: Interview with Marina Abramović," *Art Journal* 58, no. 2 (Summer 1999): 7–21; 13. See also Jennifer Fisher, "Interperformance: The Live Tableaux of Suzanne Lacy, Janine Antoni, and Marina Abramovic," *Art Journal* 56, no. 4 (Winter 1997): 28–33.

117. Germano Celant and Marina Abramović, "Towards a Pure Energy," in *Marina Abramović: Public Body*, 9–29; 22.

118. See *Marina Abramović: Public Body*, 162.

119. Doris van Drathen, "World Unity: Dream or Reality, A Question of Survival," trans. Lucinda Rennison, in *Marina Abramović*, 225–39; 225.

120. McEvilley, "Stages of Energy," 22.

121. Ibid., 23.

122. On *Dragon Heads*, see *Marina Abramović*, 293–99; *Marina Abramović: Artist Body*, 314–21. On *Balkan Baroque*, see *Marina Abramović: Artist Body*, 364–69; Kaplan, "Deeper and Deeper, 11–13; and Warr and Jones, *The Artist's Body*, 112–13.

123. Notable among the few art historians and critics who have examined the parallels between ritual and contemporary art practices is Thomas McEvilley, who investigates the overlap between many examples of contemporary visual art and not only religious content, but also ritual practices, in more depth than most authors; see especially his article "Art in the Dark" on these topics.

124. For a very different discussion of the museum as a site of ritual structures and practices, see Carol Duncan, *Civilizing Rituals: Inside Public Art Museums* (New York: Routledge, 1995).

125. Stiles, "Uncorrupted Joy," 283.

126. Ibid., 283–86.

127. Ibid., 283–86; my emphasis.

128. Ibid., 286.

129. Ibid., 283–86.

130. On these and related points, see also Bruce Lincoln, *Discourse and the Construction of Society: Comparative Studies of Myth, Ritual, and Classification* (New York: Oxford University Press, 1989).

CHAPTER 14: CONTEMPORARY MUSIC

1. http://www.dead.net/sites/deadbeta.rhino.com/files/deadvideos/greensboro.html. Accessed April 22, 2009.

2. Although it is not particularly accessible to a general audience unfamiliar with the technical jargon of academic scholarship, an especially excellent example of this can be found in the work of Michael Taussig. See Michael Taussig, *Defacement* (Stanford: Stanford University Press, 1999).

3. Series editor Vince Biondo, a scholar of Islam, adds that Michael Sells, Farid Esack, and other scholars have pointed out that, for most of the world's Muslims, the Qur'an is not read, but its sound is experienced, even when the literal meaning of all of the words is not understood. Additionally, the ethnomusicologist Scott Marcus has written an accessible introduction to the musical forms of Egypt.

4. Robert Bellah, Richard Madsen, William M. Sullivan, Ann Swidler, and Steven M. Tipton, *Habits of the Heart* (Berkeley: University of California Press, 1985).

CHAPTER 15: SPORT

1. The School of Letters, Art and Media (SLAM) at the University of Sydney provided research assistance to assist in the writing of this chapter. My thanks are due to Will Noonan, who was a great help in identifying relevant publications, borrowing books and photocopying articles, and otherwise easing my way into the research process. My love and gratitude to Don Barrett, whose critical contribution to the formation and clarification of my arguments is invaluable, is ongoing.

2. Shirl J. Hoffman, "The Sanctification of Sport: Can the Mind of Christ Co-Exist with the Killer Instinct?" *Christianity Today,* April 4, 1986, 17–21.

3. Barbara Tuchman, *A Distant Mirror: The Calamitous Fourteenth Century* (1978; London: Folio Society, 1997), 70.

4. Tuchman, *A Distant Mirror,* 65–66.

5. Robert J. Higgs, *God in the Stadium: Sport and Religion in America* (Lexington: University Press of Kentucky, 1995). See also John Savant, "The Saving Grace of Sport: Why We Watch & Play," *Commonweal,* September 26, 2003, 12–14.

6. Randolph Feezell, *Sport, Play, and Ethical Reflection* (Urbana: University of Illinois Press, 2004), 14. Feezell here references the classic works by Johan Huizinga (*Homo Ludens,* 1938) and Roger Caillois (*Les jeux et les hommes,* 1958).

7. Allen Guttmann, *From Ritual to Record: The Nature of Modern Sport* (New York: Columbia University Press, 1978), 5.

8. Simon Robinson, "Spirituality: A Story So Far," in *Sport and Spirituality: An Introduction,* ed. Jim Parry, Simon Robinson, Nick J. Watson, and Mark Nesti (New York: Routledge, 2007), 8.

9. Peter L. Berger, *The Social Reality of Religion* (London: Faber and Faber, 1969), 107.

10. Victor Turner, *The Ritual Process: Structure and Anti-Structure* (1969; New York: Aldine de Gruyter, 1995), 94–96.

11. Susan Birrell, "Sport as Ritual: Interpretations from Durkheim to Goffman," *Social Forces* 60, no. 2 (December 1981): 362.

12. Ian Reader, "Cleaning Floors and Sweeping the Mind: Cleaning as a Ritual Process," in *Ritual and Religious Belief: A Reader,* ed. Graham Harvey (London: Equinox, 2005), 87–104.

13. Higgs, *God in the Stadium,* 18. He is summarizing Harry Edwards, *Sociology of Sport* (Homewood, IL: Dorsey, 1973), 260–66.

14. Guttmann, *From Ritual to Record,* 16–55.

15. John Marshall Carter, "Sport, War and the Three Orders of Feudal Society" *Military Affairs* 49, no. 3 (July 1985): 136.

16. Joachim K. Rühl, "Time Might be Better Bestowed, and Besides We See Sin Acted," *British Journal of Sports History* 1, no. 2 (September 1984): 125.

17. Charles Kingsley, quoted in William J. Baker, *Playing with God: Religion and Modern Sport* (Cambridge, MA: Harvard University Press, 2007), 32.

18. Shirl James Hoffman, "Toward Narrowing the

Gulf between Sport and Religion," *Word & World* 23, no. 3 (Summer 2003): 306–7.

19. Mark Nesti, "Suffering, Sacrifice, Sport Psychology and the Spirit," in *Sport and Spirituality: An Introduction*, ed. Jim Parry, Simon Robinson, Nick J. Watson, and Mark Nesti (New York: Routledge, 2007), 161.

20. Charles S. Prebish, "'Heavenly Father, Divine Goalie': Sport and Religion," *Soundings* 81, no. 1–2 (Spring/Summer 1998): 307.

21. Baker, *Playing With God*, 1.

22. John Goodger, "Ritual Solidarity and Sport." *Acta Sociologica* 29, no. 3 (1986): 220.

23. Donald G. Kyle, *Sport and Spectacle in the Ancient World* (Oxford: Blackwell, 2007), 111.

24. William J. Baker, "Organized Greek Games," in *Sport: Critical Concepts in Sociology*, ed. Eric Dunning and Dominic Malcolm, vol. 2, *The Development of Sport* (New York: Routledge, 2003), 77.

25. Paul Cartledge, "The Greek Religious Festivals," in *Greek Religion and Society*, ed. P. Easterling and J. V. Muir (Cambridge: Cambridge University Press, 1985), 111.

26. Mark Golden, *Sport and Society in Ancient Greece* (Cambridge: Cambridge University Press, 1998), 40–45.

27. Nigel B. Crowther, *Sport in Ancient Times* (Westport CT: Praeger, 2007), 46.

28. Norbert Elias, "The Genesis of Sport as a Sociological Problem," in Dunning and Malcolm, *The Development of Sport*, 117.

29. Ibid., 114.

30. Baker, "Organized Greek Games," 83.

31. Kyle, *Sport and Spectacle*, 89.

32. David C. Young, *A Brief History of the Olympic Games* (Oxford: Blackwell, 2004), 120.

33. Matthew P. J. Dillon, "Did Parthenoi Attend the Olympic Games? Girls and Women Competing, Spectating, and Carrying Out Cult Roles at Greek Religious Festivals," *Hermes* 128, no. 4 (2000): 460.

34. Stephen G. Miller, "The Organization and Functioning of the Olympic Games," in *Sport and Festival in the Ancient Greek World*, ed. David J. Phillips and David Pritchard (Swansea: Classical Press of Wales, 2003), 4.

35. Ibid., 9.

36. Ibid., 11.

37. Kyle, *Sport and Spectacle*, 116.

38. Miller, "The Organization," 13.

39. John Gould, "On Making Sense of Greek Religion," in Easterling and Muir, *Greek Religion and Society*, 15–18.

40. Miller, "Organization," 18.

41. Ulrich Sinn, *Olympia: Cult, Sport, and Ancient Festival* (Princeton: Markus Wiener, 2000), 86.

42. Mark Golden, *Sport in the Ancient World from A to Z* (New York: Routledge, 2004), vii.

43. Miller, "The Organization," 23.

44. Louis A. Ruprecht, "The Ethos of Olympism: The Religious Meaning of the Modern Olympic Movement," *Soundings* 81, no. 1–2 (Spring/Summer 1998): 278.

45. Louis A. Ruprecht, "Greek Exercises: The Modern Olympics as Hellenic Appropriation and Reinvention," *Thesis Eleven* 93 (May 2008): 80.

46. Jürgen Moltmann, "Olympia between Politics and Religion," *Concilium* (October 1989): 101–9.

47. Ruprecht, "Greek Exercises," 81. He is quoting Pierre de Coubertin, *The Olympic Idea: Discourses and Essays* (Koln: Carl Diem Institut, 1967).

48. Jim Parry, "The *religio athletae*, Olympism and Peace," in Parry et al., *Sport and Spirituality*, 208.

49. Kyle, *Sport and Spectacle*, 99.

50. See Donald McRae, *Heroes without a Country: America's Betrayal of Joe Louis and Jesse Owens* (New York: Ecco/HarperCollins, 2003).

51. Amy Shipley, "Marion Jones Admits to Steroid Use," *Washington Post*, Friday October 5, 2007, www.washingtonpost.com/wp-dyn/content/article/2007/10/04/AR2007100401666.html.

52. Sally Magnusson, *The Flying Scotsman* (London: Quartet, 1981). Liddell's story is immortalized in the 1981 film *Chariots of Fire* (directed by Hugh Hudson, with Ian Charleson as Eric Liddell).

53. Wolfgang Vondey, "Christian Enthusiasm: Can the Olympic Flame Kindle the Fire of Christianity?" *Word & World* 23, no. 3 (Summer 2003): 319.

54. Harold Bolitho, "Sumo and Popular Culture: The Tokugawa Period," in Dunning and Malcolm, eds., *The Development of Sport*, 180–81.

55. Thomas P. Kasulis, *Shinto: The Way Home* (Honolulu: University of Hawaii Press, 2004), 71.

56. Yoshinobu Hamaguchi, "Innovation in Martial Arts," in *Japan, Sport and Society*, ed. Joseph Maguire and Masayoshi Nakayama, eds. (New York: Routledge, 2006), 9.

57. Crowther, *Sport in Ancient Times*, 9.

58. Bolitho, "Sumo and Popular Culture," 182.

59. P. L. Cuyler, *Sumo: From Rite to Sport* (New York: Weatherhill, 1979), 22.

60. Bolitho, "Sumo and Popular Culture," 185.

61. Cuyler, *Sumo*, 68–69.

62. Brian Bocking, *A Popular Dictionary of Shinto* (Lincolnwood, IL: NTC, 1997), 164.

63. Ann Fischer, "Flexibility in an Expressive Institution: *Sumo*," *Southwestern Journal of Anthropology* 22, 1 (Spring 1966): 32.

64. Cuyler, *Sumo*, 27.

65. Kasulis, *Shinto*, 60.

66. John K. Nelson, *Enduring Identities: The Guise of Shinto in Contemporary Japan* (Honolulu: University of Hawaii Press, 2000), 104.

67. Nelson, *Enduring Identities*, 106–9.

68. Fischer, "Flexibility," 32.

69. Kasulis, *Shinto*, 17–23.

70. Cuyler, *Sumo*, 74.

71. Bolitho, "Sumo and Popular Culture," 188–90.

72. Cuyler, *Sumo*, 81.

73. Cuyler, *Sumo*, 169.

74. Fischer, "Flexibility," 34.

75. Cuyler, *Sumo*, 175.

76. Fischer, "Flexibility," 34–36.

77. "Chiyonofuji: The Way of the Wolf" (Channel 4, UK: Cheerleader Productions, October 1991).

78. Clyde Haberman, "Wrestler Fails to Keep Hold on an Honorable Past," *New York Times*, January 2, 1988, at: www.juryo.net/newspaper/1980/19880102X.htm.

79. Ibid.

80. Richard Giulianotti, *Sport: A Critical Sociology* (Cambridge: Polity, 2005), 6.

81. Richard Sandomir, "Hits, Runs and Memories," *New York Times*, September 18, 1994, http://www.nytimes.com/1994/09/18/movies/hits-runs-and-memories.html?pagewanted=all&src=pm.

82. David Chidester, "The Church of Baseball, the Fetish of Coca-Cola, and the Potlatch of Rock 'n' Roll, in *Religion and Popular Culture in America*, ed. Bruce David Forbes and Jeffrey H. Mahan, rev. ed. (Berkeley: University of California Press, 2005), 218. I am grateful to Vince Biondo for personal anecdotes regarding the ritual significance of certain aspects of baseball.

83. Quoted in Joseph L. Price, "An American Apotheosis: Sport as Popular Religion," in Forbes and Mahan, *Religion and Popular Culture*, 206.

84. Price, "An American Apotheosis," 195.

85. Keith A. P. Sandiford, "Cricket and the Victorian Society," *Journal of Social History* 17, no. 2 (Winter 1983): 303–17.

86. P. Karvelas, "Race That Stops Nation Could Stop Your Citizenship," *The Weekend Australian* 29–30 (April 2005): 8.

87. Carole M. Cusack and Justine Digance, "The Melbourne Cup: Australian Identity and Secular Pilgrimage," *Sport and Society* 12, no. 7 (2009): 876–89.

CHAPTER 16: HUMOR

1. John Chrysostom, *Commentary on Matthew*, Homily 6.6 (*PG* 57:70D), as cited in Hugo Rahner, "Eutrapelia: A Forgotten Virtue," in *Holy Laughter; Essays on Religion in the Comic Perspective*, ed. M. Conrad Hyers (New York: Seabury, 1969), 185–97; 192.

2. *Buddhacarita* 4.59, as cited in Lee Siegel, *Laughing Matters: Comic Tradition in India* (Chicago: University of Chicago Press, 1987), 4.

3. Johan Huizinga, *Homo Ludens; A Study of the Play-Element in Culture* (Boston: Beacon, 1955), 6.

4. Alfred North Whitehead, quoted in *On Humour and the Comic in the Hebrew Bible*, ed. Yehuda T. Radday and Athalya Brenner (Sheffield: Almond, 1990), 21.

5. Gen. 17–18:15; 21:1–7, NRSV. See J. William Whedbee, *The Bible and the Comic Vision* (Cambridge University Press, 1998), 81.

6. Mark 10:25; Matt. 7:3. Gary A. Herion et al., "Humor and Wit: Ancient Egypt, Mesopotamia, Old Testament, New Testament," in *The Anchor Bible Dictionary*, ed. David Noel Freedman (New York: Doubleday, 1992), 325–33; 333.

7. Siegel, *Laughing Matters*, 279.

8. Nagendra Kr. Singh, "The Vasudevahindi," in *Encyclopaedia of Jainism*, ed. Nagendra Kr. Singh (New Delhi: Anmol, 2001), 6939–6987; 6947.

9. Richard Raskin, *Life Is Like a Glass of Tea: Studies of Classic Jewish Jokes* (Philadelphia: Jewish Publication Society, 1992), 45.

10. Ibid., 50.

11. Ibid., 57.

12. Ibid., 58.

13. Ronald P. Keeven, *A Joke, a Quote and the Word* (Mustang, OK: Tate, 2006), 152.

14. Ted Cohen, *Jokes: Philosophical Thoughts on Joking Matters* (Chicago: University of Chicago Press, 1999), 20. Italics mine.

15. Brendan Powell Smith, "The Brick Testament," http://www.thebricktestament.com/latest_additions/index.html. Accessed April 24, 2009.

16. For a theologically oriented discussion of humor in relation to transcendence, see Peter L. Berger, *Redeeming Laughter: The Comic Dimension of Human Experience* (New York: Walter de Gruyter, 1997), 205–15.

17. Mary Boyce, *A History of Zoroastrianism* (Leiden: Brill, 1975), 279.

18. Abdul Ali, *Arab Legacy to Humour Literature* (New Delhi: M.D., 1998), 3–4.

19. Siegel, *Laughing Matters*, 343–47.

20. Reginald Horace Blyth, *Oriental Humour* (Tokyo: Hokuseido, 1959), 93.

21. John Stevens, *Three Zen Masters: Ikkyū, Hakuin, and Ryōkan* (Tokyo: Kodansha, 1993), 79.

22. Massud Farzan, *Another Way of Laughter: A Collection of Sufi Humor* (New York: Dutton, 1973), 1.

23. *Wu-men kuan*, case 21, *T* 48.295c, as cited in Robert E. Buswell, "The 'Short-cut' Approach of *K'an-hua* Meditation: The Evolution of a Practical Subitism in Chinese Ch'an Buddhism," in *Sudden and Gradual: Approaches to Enlightenment in Chinese Thought*, ed. Peter N. Gregory (Honolulu: University of Hawaii Press, 1987), p. 335.

24. Kazuaki Tanahashi, *Penetrating Laughter: Hakuin's Zen and Art* (Woodstock, NY: Overlook, 1984), 109.

25. Joseph Telushkin, *Jewish Humor: What the Best Jewish Jokes Say about the Jews* (New York: W. Morrow, 1992), 158–59.

26. Sonja Arntzen, *Ikkyū and the Crazy Cloud Anthology: A Zen Poet of Medieval Japan* (Tokyo: University of Tokyo Press, 1986), 3.

27. Ibid., 90.

28. Bernard Faure, *The Red Thread: Buddhist Approaches to Sexuality* (Princeton: Princeton University Press, 1998), 114. Calling into question such dualistic (and thus problematic) distinctions is the prerogative and indeed the obligation of the enlightened *bodhisattva* in the Mahayana Buddhist tradition (which includes both Zen and Tibetan Buddhism). Unconstrained by conventional notions of morality, these saints obey a kind of "higher" morality, using *upaya* ("expedient means") to benefit others according to the needs of the situation and to bring them beyond a dualistic perception of the world and eventually to enlightenment.

29. Ibid., 110n37. The full story, from which Faure quotes, can be found in James H. Sanford, *Zen-Man Ikkyū* (Chico, CA: Scholars, 1981), 291–95.

30. Keith Dowman, *The Divine Madman: The Sublime Life and Songs of Drukpa Kunley*, 2nd ed. (Clearlake, CA: Dawn Horse, 1998), xxxiii.

31. Stevens, *Three Zen Masters: Ikkyū, Hakuin, and Ryōkan*, 33.

32. 1 Cor. 3:18-19; 4:10.

33. Alexander Y. Syrkin, "On the Behavior of the 'Fool for Christ's Sake,'" *History of Religions* 22, no. 2 (1982): 150–171; 163.

34. Ahmet T. Karamustafa, *God's Unruly Friends: Dervish Groups in the Islamic Later Middle Period, 1200–1550* (Salt Lake City: University of Utah Press, 1994), 13.

35. Ibid., 31.

36. David N. Lorenzen, "Śaivism: Paśupatas," in *Encyclopedia of Religion*, ed. Lindsay Jones, Mircea Eliade, and Charles J. Adams, 8049.

37. Lewis R. Lancaster and Jung-kwang, *The Mad Monk: Paintings of Unlimited Action* (Berkeley: Lancaster-Miller, 1979), 6.

38. Lewis R. Lancaster and Jung-kwang, *The Dirty Mop: Unlimited Action Paintings and Poems* (Berkeley: Asian Humanities, 1983), 84, 65.

39. Lancaster and Jung-kwang, *The Mad Monk*, 6.

40. Ibid.

41. Sally Belfrage, *Flowers of Emptiness: Reflections on an Ashram* (New York: Dial, 1981), 193, quoted in Ingvild Sælid Gilhus, *Laughing Gods, Weeping Virgins: Laughter in the History of Religion* (London: Routledge, 1997), 133.

42. Berger, *Redeeming Laughter*, 78.

43. Ibid.

44. Christopher Vecsey, "The Exception Who Proves the Rules: Ananse the Akan Trickster," in *Mythical Trickster Figures: Contours, Contexts, and Criticisms*, ed. William J. Hynes and William G. Doty (Tuscaloosa: University of Alabama Press, 1993), 106–21; 106–7.

45. Ibid., 113.

46. Ibid., 119.

47. "Paiyakyamu," in Kimberly A. Christen, *Clowns and Tricksters: An Encyclopedia of Tradition and Culture* (Denver: ABC-CLIO, 1998), 163.

48. Ibid.

49. Ibid., 164.

50. Barton Wright, *Clowns of the Hopi: Tradition Keepers and Delight Makers* (Flagstaff, AZ: Northland, 1994), 4.

51. Although neither of these figures is religious per se, their performances operate in the related spheres of social norms and ethics, providing antimodels of proper behavior.

52. Gideon Aran, "What's So Funny about Fundamentalism?" in *Fundamentalisms Comprehended*, ed. Martin E. Marty and R. Scott Appleby (Chicago: University of Chicago Press, 1995), 321–52; 325.

53. Ibid., 326.

54. Ibid.

55. Gilhus, *Laughing Gods, Weeping Virgins*, 88.

56. E. K. Chambers, *The Mediaeval Stage* (1903; London: Oxford University Press, 1954), 294, quoted in Gilhus, *Laughing Gods, Weeping Virgins*, 81.

57. Mikhail M. Bakhtin, *Rabelais and His World* (Cambridge, MA: MIT Press, 1968), 75.

58. John Lippitt, "Humour and Superiority," *Cogito* 9, no. 1 (1995): 54–61; 54, here summarizing the thought of Henri Bergson, *Laughter: An Essay on the Meaning of the Comic*, trans. Cloudesley Brereton and Fred Rothwell (1911; Los Angeles: Green Integer, 1999).

59. Ps. 37:13; Ps. 52:6; and 2 Kgs. 2:23–4.

60. Telushkin, *Jewish Humor*, 164.

61. Eric W. Gritsch, *The Wit of Martin Luther* (Minneapolis: Fortress Press, 2006), 29.

62. Joe Kissell, "The Wittenburg Door: The Strange World of Religious Satire," http://itotd.com/articles/340/the-wittenburg-door/. Accessed April 24, 2009. See also Michael McClymond, "The Wit and Wisdom of *The Door*," in *Religions of the United States in Practice*, ed. Colleen McDannell (Princeton: Chichester, 2002), 433–48.

63. *Subhāṣitāvali* of Vallabhadeva, 2402, as translated by Siegel, *Laughing Matters*, 211.

64. See Jawaharlal Handoo, "Folk Narrative and Ethnic Identity: The 'Sardarji' Joke Cycle," in *Storytelling in Contemporary Societies*, ed. Lutz Röhrich and Sabine Wienker-Piepho (Tübingen: Gunter Narr Verlag, 1990), 155–61.

65. Stephen J. Whitfield, "The Distinctiveness of American Jewish Humor," *Modern Judaism* 6, no. 3 (1986): 245–60; 249. Lawrence E. Mintz, "The Rabbi Versus the Priest and Other Jewish Stories," in *Jewish Humor*, ed. Avner Ziv (New Brunswick, NJ: Transaction, 1998), 125–31; 129.

66. David Chidester, *Savage Systems: Colonialism and Comparative Religion in Southern Africa* (Charlottesville: University Press of Virginia, 1996), 226.

67. Ibid., 227.

68. Vine Deloria, *Custer Died for Your Sins; an Indian Manifesto* (New York: Macmillan, 1969), 153–54.

69. Paul Lewis, *Cracking Up: American Humor in a Time of Conflict* (Chicago: University of Chicago Press, 2006), 9.

70. Ibid., 166, and http://www.rushlimbaugh.com/home/eibessential/illustrating_absurdity/clubgitmo.guest.html. Accessed April 25, 2009.

71. *The Late Late Show with Craig Ferguson*, Episode 2.45, 2005, http://www.imdb.com/title/tt0626276/. Accessed April 24, 2009.

Chapter 17: Religion and Film

1. See BBC article, "Film Trailer Voice-Over King Dies," at http://news.bbc.co.uk/2/hi/entertainment/7595352.stm. Accessed 25 June 2011.

2. Maya Deren, "Cinematography: The Creative Uses of Reality," in *The Avant-Garde Film*, ed. P. Adams Sitney (New York: Anthology Film Archives, 1987), 69.

3. Wendy Doniger, *The Implied Spider* (New York: Columbia University Press, 1998), 77.

4. Peter Berger, *The Sacred Canopy* (Garden City, NY: Doubleday, 1967), 27.

5. Ibid., 27–28.

6. Ibid., 27.

7. Nelson Goodman, *Ways of Worldmaking* (Indianapolis: Hackett, 1978), 7.

8. William Paden, *Religious Worlds: The Comparative Study of Religion*, 2nd ed. (Boston: Beacon, 1994), 51–52.

9. William Paden, "World," *Guide to the Study of Religion*, eds. Willi Braun and Russell T. McCutcheon (London: Cassell, 2000), 336.

10. Mary Douglas, *Purity and Danger* (New York: Routledge, 2002), 78.

11. Paden, *Religious Worlds*, 95–96.

12. Ibid., 73–74.

13. Yes, Hollywood creates predominantly heterosexual worlds.

14. Abraham Heschel, *The Sabbath: Its Meaning for Modern Man* (New York: Farrar, Straus, Giroux, 1951), 10.

15. Ibid., 14. Heschel is paraphrasing the Zohar here.

16. Judith Shulevitz, *The Sabbath World: Glimpses of a Different Order of Time* (New York: Random House, 2011).

17. Bobby Alexander, "Ritual and Current Studies of Ritual," in *Anthropology of Religion*, ed. Stephen D. Glazier (Westport, CT: Greenwood, 1997), 139.

18. A version of this section was originally published by S. Brent Plate as, "Something Borrowed, Something Blue: *Avatar* and the Myth of Originality" in *Religion Dispatches*, January 28, 2010, http://www.religiondispatches.org/archive/culture/2228/something_borrowed%2C_something_blue%3A_avatar_and_the_myth_of_originality/. Accessed July 10, 2011.

19. Dave Itzkoff, "You Saw What in 'Avatar'? Pass Those Glasses!" in *New York Times*, January 20, 2010.

http://www.nytimes.com/2010/01/20/movies/20avatar .html?. Accessed July 10, 2011.

20. See more on all this in S. Brent Plate, *Religion and Film*.

21. Berger, *Sacred Canopy*, 33–34.

22. Siegfried Kracauer, *Theory of Film: The Redemption of Physical Reality* (Princeton: Princeton University Press, 1997), 48. Relatedly, see Walter Benjamin's suggestions in *Selected Writings III*, ed. Howard Eiland and Michael W. Jennings (Cambridge, MA: Belknap Press of Harvard University Press, 2002), 117; and my own comments on the subject in *Walter Benjamin, Religion, and Aesthetics* (New York: Routledge, 2004), 105–12.

23. Paul Hirsch, "Percussive Editing," in *First Cut: Conversations with Film Editors*, ed. Gabriella Oldham (Berkeley: University of California Press, 1992), 188–89. The philosopher Stanley Cavell was way ahead of some of this argument as he turned to the projections of film as a way of understanding the world. His book *The World Viewed,* enlarged ed. (Cambridge, MA: Harvard University Press, 1979) argues that the world as it is holds a distinct relation to the "world viewed" on screen, and that the two are not entirely distinguishable, even if the screened world goes out of existence when the film is over. Yet, just below the surface of Cavell's writings is a suggestion that cinema is ultimately a private, anonymous experience.

24. These levels are quoted from Warren Buckland, *The Cognitive Semiotics of Film* (Cambridge: Cambridge University Press, 2000), 47. See Etienne Souriau, *L'Univers filmique* (Paris: Flammarion, 1953). Souriau's work has not been translated into English, but good overviews include chapter 3 of Edward Lowry's *The Filmology Movement and Film Study in France* (Ann Arbor, MI: UMI Research Press, 1985).

25. Clifford Geertz, "Religion as a Cultural System," in *The Interpretation of Cultures* (New York: Basic Books, 1973), 90.

26. Charles McGrath, "Terry Gilliam's Feel-Good Endings," *New York Times*, August 14, 2005. http://www.nytimes.com/2005/08/14/movies/14mcgr .html?ex=1124769600&en=b8eac6b20a90d575&ei=5070&emc=eta1. Accessed 15 August 2005.

Chapter 18: Memorialization

1. Robert Pogue Harrison, *Dominion of the Dead* (Chicago: University of Chicago Press, 2003), 158.

2. Ibid., xi.

3. Ibid.

4. Maurice Halbwachs, *On Collective Memory*, trans. Lewis Coser (Chicago: University of Chicago Press, 1922), 43.

5. See Søren Kierkegaard, *Fear and Trembling and Repetition*, trans. Robert Perkins (Atlanta: Mercer University Press, 1993); and Martin Marty, "We Might Know What to Do and How to Do It: On the Usefulness of the Religious Past," *Westminster Tanner-McMerrin Lecture on the History and Philosophy of Religion* (Salt Lake: Westminster College of Salt Lake, 1989); and Henry Steele Commager, *The Search for a Usable Past, and Other Essays in Historiography* (New York: Alfred A. Knopf, 1967), for more on this understanding of the need for the past to speak the present in order to be called forth from the reserves of memory.

6. Daniele Hervieu-Léger, *Religion as a Chain of Memory*, trans. Simon Lee (New Brunswick, NJ: Rutgers University Press, 2000), 4.

7. Ibid., 126.

8. Edward Linenthal, "The Predicament of Aftermath: Oklahoma City and September 11," in *The Resilient City: How Modern Cities Recover from Disaster,* ed. Lawrence J. Yale and Thomas I. Campanella (New York: Oxford University Press, 2005), 55.

9. Edward Linenthal, *Preserving Memory: The Struggle to Create America's Holocaust Museum* (New York: Columbia University Press, 2001), xiii.

10. James E. Young, *The Texture of Memory: Holocaust Memorials and Meaning* (New Haven, CT: Yale University Press, 1993), xi.

11. Judith Butler, *Precarious Life: The Powers of Mourning and Violence* (New York: Verso, 2004), 34.

12. Ibid., 20.

13. Linenthal, *Preserving Memory*, xiii.

14. Jonathan Z. Smith, *Imagining Religion: From Babylon to Jonestown* (Chicago: University of Chicago Press, 1988), 20.

15. Jacques Derrida, *Acts of Religion* (New York: Routledge, 2001), 74.

16. Martin Heidegger, *Being and Time*, trans. J. Macquarrie and E. Robinson (San Francisco: HarperSanFrancisco, 1962), 211.

17. Harrison, *Dominion of the Dead,* 102.

18. Ibid., 98.

Chapter 19: The Disney Way of Death

1. Steven Watts, *The Magic Kingdom: Walt Disney*

and the *American Way of Life* (Boston: Houghton Mifflin, 1997), 163.

2. See, for example, Lawrence E. Sullivan, ed., *Death, Afterlife, and the Soul* (New York: Macmillan, 1989).

3. Alan Bryman, *Disney and His Worlds* (London: Routledge, 1995); Elizabeth Bell, Lynda Haas, and Laura Sells, eds., *From Mouse to Mermaid: The Politics of Film, Gender, and Culture* (Bloomington: Indiana University Press, 1995); and Susan Willis, ed., "The World according to Disney," *South Atlantic Quarterly* 92, no. 1 (1993 Special Issue).

4. A recent NEH summer institute on the history of death in America, with participants from such fields as history, anthropology, and religious studies, is one expression of this growing interest. New and forthcoming books on a range of topics, including cemeteries, cremation, funerals, and disasters, also captures this interest.

5. Some recent discussions about this label can be found in David Wendell Moller, *Confronting Death: Values, Institutions, and Human Mortality* (New York: Oxford University Press, 1996); Lynne Ann DeSpelder and Albert Lee Strickland, *The Last Dance: Encountering Death and Dying* (Mountain View, CA: Mayfield, 1999); and Kathy Charmaz, *The Social Reality of Death: Death in Contemporary America* (New York: Random, 1980).

6. Herman Feifel, ed. *The Meaning of Death* (New York: McGraw Hill, 1959), v.

7. Ibid., xii.

8. Ibid., xv.

9. Elisabeth Kübler-Ross, *On Death and Dying* (New York: Macmillan, 1969).

10. Ibid., 6–7.

11. Robert Fulton, ed., *Death and Identity* (New York: Wiley, 1965), 4.

12. Philippe Aries, *The Hour of Our Death*, trans. Helen Weaver (New York: Vintage, 1982), 596. My next book, titled *Death in Modern America: A Cultural History of the Funeral Industry in the Twentieth Century* (New York: Oxford University Press) will address this very question.

13. Moller, *Confronting Death*, 22.

14. Douglas W. Churchill, "Disney's 'Philosophy,'" *New York Times Magazine,* March 6, 1938, 9.

15. Bob Thomas, *Walt Disney: An American Original* (New York: Simon and Schuster, 1976), 28.

16. Kathy Merlock Jackson, *Walt Disney: A Bio-Bibliography* (Westport: Greenwood, 1993), 18.

17. Watts, *Magic Kingdom*, 38.

18. Thomas, *Walt Disney*, 99.

19. Ibid.

20. Ann Douglas, *The Feminization of American Culture* (New York: Anchor, 1988); Colleen McDannell and Bernhard Lang, *Heaven: A History* (New Haven: Yale University Press, 1988).

21. Leonard Mosley, *Disney's World: A Biography* (New York: Arno, 1985), 123. See also Thomas, *Walt Disney*, 100.

22. Mosley, *Disney's World*, 124.

23. Thomas, *Walt Disney*, 100.

24. Watts, *Magic Kingdom*, 113–19.

25. Richard Schickel, *The Disney Vision: The Life, Times, Art, and Commerce of Walt* Disney, rev. ed. (New York: Simon and Schuster, 1985), 440.

26. Ibid., 11.

27. Ibid., 146.

28. Mosley, *Disney's World*, 253.

29. Thomas, *Walt Disney*, 225

30. Mosley, *Disney's World*, 287–88.

31. Watts, *Magic Kingdom*, 447.

32. Ibid., 452.

33. Ibid., 453.

34. Maria Tartar, *The Hard Facts of the Grimms' Fairy Tales* (Princeton: Princeton University Press, 1987), xiv.

35. Ibid., xv.

36. Ibid., 3.

37. Ibid., xiii–xx.

38. Robert Darnton, *The Great Cat Massacre and Other Stories in French Cultural History* (New York: Vintage, 1985), 13.

39. Robert Bellah, *The Broken Covenant: American Civil Religion in Time of Trial* (New York: Seabury, 1975); David Chidester, "The Church of Baseball, the Fetish of Coca-Cola, and the Potlatch of Rock 'n' Roll: Theoretical Models for the Study of Religion in American Popular Culture," *Journal of the American Academy of Religion* 64, no. 4 (Winter 1996): 743–65; Colleen McDannell, *Material Christianity: Religion and Popular Culture in America* (New Haven, CT: Yale University Press, 1996); Leonard Primiano, "Vernacular Religion and the Search for Method in Religious Folklife," *Western Folklore* 54 (1995): 37–56.

40. Catherine Albanese, *America: Religions and Religion*, 3rd ed. (Belmont: Wadsworth, 1999), 499.

41. Robert Jewett and John Shelton Lawrence, *The American Monomyth*, 2nd ed. (Lanham: University Press of America, 1988), xi.

42. Ibid., 141.

43. Ibid., 140.

44. Paul Boyer, *When Time Shall Be No More: Prophecy Belief in Modern America* (Cambridge, MA: Belknap Press of Harvard University Press, 1992); McDannell and Lang, *Heaven*, 326–32.

45. Marian S. Pyles, *Death and Dying in Children's and Young People's Literature: A Survey and Bibliography* (Jefferson: McFarland, 1988); Tatar, *Hard Facts of the Grimms' Fairy Tales*.

46. Nicholas Tucker, "Who's Afraid of Walt Disney?" *New Society* 288 (1968): 502.

47. Robert D. Feild, *The Art of Walt Disney* (New York: Macmillan, 1942), 122.

48. Jewett and Lawrence, *American Monomyth*, 136; John Culhane, *Walt Disney's Fantasia* (New York: Harry N. Abrams, 1983), 182.

49. Ibid., 137.

50. Many thanks to my colleague Wendy Farley, who gave me a spellbinding theological analysis of this film.

51. Manny Farber, "Saccharine *Symphony-Bambi!*," in *The American Animated Cartoon: A Critical Anthology*, ed. Danny Peary and Gerald Peary (New York: Dutton, 1980), 90.

52. David Payne, "*Bambi*," in *From Mouse to Mermaid: The Politics of Film, Gender, and Culture*, ed. Elizabeth Bell et al. (Bloomington: Indiana University Press, 1995), 140. This was unequivocally confirmed in the many conversations I had with friends, colleagues, and audience members at conferences. Although the memory was repressed, nearly everyone remembered the formative, traumatic experience of witnessing the death of Bambi's mother.

53. Aries, *Hour of Our Death*, 409–556.

54. Thomas, *Walt Disney*, 135–36.

55. Payne, "*Bambi*," 145.

56. Watts, *Magic Kingdom*, 326.

About the Editors
and Contributors

GENERAL EDITORS:

Richard D. Hecht (PhD, University of California, Los Angeles) is professor of religious studies, northwest Semitic languages, Hebrew Judaic studies, and history of religion at the University of California, Santa Barbara. In addition to his teaching at UCLA and UCSB, he served as visiting associate professor at the Hebrew University of Jerusalem. Richard is a long-term member of several professional societies, including the American Academy of Religion, the Society of Biblical Literature, and the American Society for the Study of Religion, and has served on numerous editorial boards. He received a prestigious Ford Foundation grant to study religious pluralism, and he has published broadly in the areas of religious and Jewish studies. Richard is the author, with Ninian Smart, of The *Sacred Texts of the World: A Universal Anthology* (first published in 1982 and reprinted many times), and is coauthor with Roger Friedland of *To Rule Jerusalem*, which is now in its second edition by Cambridge University Press.

Vincent F. Biondo III (PhD, University of California, Santa Barbara) is associate professor of western religious traditions at California State University, Fresno. At the University of California, Santa Barbara, he co-coordinated a three-year research project for the Ford Foundation on religious pluralism in Southern California and earned a grant to visit the riot towns of northern England. This research was published in the *Journal of Muslim Minority Affairs* and *The Muslim World*. In 2009 he served as Fulbright Scholar to the UK in Cardiff researching Jewish-Christian-Muslim relations. In 2010, he was named an Irmgard Coninx Scholar by the Social Science Research Center in Berlin. Vincent secured a National Endowment for the Humanities Research Grant in 2011 to study ethics, religion, and civil discourse, and he has organized conferences around this program of study. In addition to publishing several articles in comparative religion, he is the co-editor, with Richard D. Hecht, of the three-volume reference work, *Religion and Everyday Life and Culture*, published by ABC-CLIO.

Contributors

Elizabeth Adan received an interdisciplinary PhD in contemporary art, religion, and cultural analysis with a doctoral emphasis in women's studies from the University of California, Santa Barbara, in 2006. She also holds an MA in rhetoric from the University of California, Berkeley, and an MFA in studio art from the University of California, Santa Barbara. In 2000–2001, she was a Helena Rubenstein Fellow in Critical Studies at the Whitney Museum Independent Study Program, and she is currently assistant professor of modern and contemporary art history in the Department of Art and Design at Cal Poly, San Luis Obispo.

Evan Berry is an assistant professor in the Department of Philosophy and Religion at American University, where he is also the co-director for the MA program in Ethics, Philosophy, and Global Affairs. His recent research—part of a collaborative, interdisciplinary project called Ecotopia Revisited—uses ethnographic methodologies to explore environmental utopianism in the Pacific Northwest. This focus on intentional communities and outdoor recreation organizations is part of a broader effort to understand the role that nature plays in contemporary American spirituality.

David Chidester is professor and head of the Department of Religious Studies at the University of Cape Town, South Africa. A prolific writer and an internationally acclaimed scholar in the field of comparative religion, Chidester's interests lie in the relationships between religion and globalization, religion and popular culture, religion in society and the problems of social cohesion. He has written extensively on religion in South Africa and North America, as well as religion and education. He is a two-time winner of the American Academy of Religion's Award for Excellence in Religious Studies. In 2005, he was evaluated as an A-rated researcher by the National Research Foundation and received the Alan J. Pifer Award for Social Research.

David J. Cooper is a graduate student with an emphasis on Tibetan Buddhism in the Department of Religious Studies at the University of California, Santa Barbara. His research interests include humor, religious literature and folklore, and monastic life.

Carole M. Cusack is associate professor and departmental chair of studies in religion at the University of Sydney. Her research interests include theories of religious conversion, northern European mythology and religion, medieval Christianity, secularization and contemporary Western religious trends, and medievalism. She is the author of *Conversion among the Germanic Peoples* (Cassell, 1998) and *The Essence of Buddhism* (Lansdowne, 2001). With Christopher Hartney, she is editor of the *Journal of Religious History* (published by Wiley).

Roger Friedland, a cultural sociologist and social theorist, is professor of religious studies and sociology at the University of California, Santa Barbara. He is coauthor, with Richard Hecht, of an historical ethnography of Jerusalem, To Rule Jerusalem. Friedland has been working for several years developing an institutional approach on the case of politicized religion as a vehicle to understand attempted transformation in the institutional architecture of society. This has eventuated in a series of essays, including "Money, Sex and God: The Erotic Logic of Religious Nationalism" (2002) and "The Constitution of Religious Nationalist Violence" (2009).

Robert M. Geraci is assistant professor of religious studies at Manhattan College in New York City. His research focuses upon the interaction of religion, science, and technology, and he has published extensively on the ways in which religious practices and beliefs intertwine with digital technologies such as robotics, artificial intelligence, and video games. To support this work, he has been a visiting researcher at Carnegie Mellon University's Robotics Institute and has done ethnographic fieldwork in *World of Warcraft* and *Second Life*.

Stephen Hunt is a reader in the sociology of religion, based at the University of the West of England, Bristol, UK. His specialized interest in contemporary Christianity has led to research in such areas as religion and the life course, Christianity and political mobilization, Christianity and non-heterosexualities, and the interface between sociology and theology. Dr. Hunt's publications include the volumes *Religion in the West: A Sociological Perspective* (MacMillan, 2001), *Alternative Religion: A Sociological Introduction* (Ashgate, 2003), *The Alpha Enterprise: Evangelism in the Post-Christian Era* (Ashgate, 2004), and *Religion in Everyday Life* (Routledge, 2005).

Gary Laderman is professor and chairperson of the Department of Religion at Emory University. He is the author of *Sacred Matters: Celebrity Worship, Sexual Ecstasies, the Living Dead, and Other Signs of Religious Life in the United States* (The New Press, 2009), *The Sacred Remains: American Attitudes Toward Death, 1799–1883* (Yale University Press, 1996), and *Rest in Peace: A Cultural History of Death and the Funeral Home in Twentieth-Century America* (Oxford University Press, 2003). He also has coedited two encyclopedias, *Religion and American Cultures: An Encyclopedia of Traditions, Diversity, and Popular Expressions* (3 vols., ABC-Clio, 2003; voted best reference by *Library Journal* in same year) and *Science, Religion, Societies: Histories, Cultures, Controversies* (2 vols., 2006; ME Sharpe). Over the last decade, Laderman has been interviewed on topics ranging from death and funerals to horror films and televangelists in a variety of media, including the *New York Times, Los Angeles Times, Washington Post*, and other newspapers; *US News and World Reports, Ebony, The Lutheran*, and other magazines; *On Point, Odyssey, Charles Osgood CBS Morning Show*, and other radio shows; as well as on the *NBC Evening News, The Today Show*, and other television and documentary broadcasts. Additionally, Laderman is editor of the new online religion magazine, ReligionDispatches.org. He has been involved in a variety of collaborative projects that have received funding from the Lilly Endowment, Center for Theology and Natural Sciences, and the Ford Foundation. In fall 2006, Laderman was a visiting fellow at the University of Victoria, BC, and in summer 2007, he participated in the Nanzan American Studies Summer Seminar as a Fulbright Distinguished Lecturer.

Alex Norman is a PhD candidate, tutor, and research assistant at the Department of Studies in Religion at the University of Sydney. His research interests include tourism and religion, new religious movements, and the practice of secular spirituality in the everyday. His current doctoral thesis research examines the intersection of travel and secular spiritual practice in the contemporary Western world. He hopes to make tourism a more thoroughly examined topic in the subject of religion. He has also been a leader of the University of Sydney's Tutors Development Program and has been awarded for excellence in teaching.

Atalia Omer is an assistant professor of religion, conflict, and peace studies at the Joan B. Kroc Institute for International Peace Studies in the University of Notre Dame, where she is also a faculty affiliate with the Center for the Study of Religion and Society. She earned her PhD from the Committee on the Study of Religion at Harvard University. Her research has focused primarily on a systematic study of the dynamics of ethno-national conflicts, political and social theory, the theoretical study of religion and society, and the theoretical study of the interrelation between religion, nationalism, and questions of justice, peace, and conflict. She is currently coediting the *Oxford Handbook of Religion, Conflict, and Peace* and working on a book manuscript titled *After Peace: How Does the Israeli Peace Camp Think about Religion, Nationalism, and Justice?*

S. Brent Plate is currently visiting associate professor of religious studies at Hamilton College, and has taught previously at Texas Christian University, the University of Vermont, and the University of Glasgow. He is the author or editor of several books, including most recently *Religion and Film: Cinema and the Re-Creation of the World*. Earlier books include *Blasphemy: Art that Offends*; *Walter Benjamin, Religion, and Aesthetics*; *Representing Religion in World Cinema*; *Religion, Art, and Visual Culture*; and *The Religion and Film Reader*. He is co-founder and managing editor of *Material Religion: The Journal of Objects, Art, and Belief*.

Jason A. Springs is assistant professor of religion, ethics and peace studies at the Joan B. Kroc Institute for International Peace Studies at the University of Notre Dame, where he also holds an appointment as faculty affiliate in the Center for the Study of Religion and Society. His research and teaching focus on conceptions of religious toleration and the challenges posed by religious pluralism for transforming conflict in European and North American contexts. His journal articles addressing issues in modern religion in public life appear in such journals as the *Journal of Religious Ethics, Modern Theology, Journal of the American Academy of Religion*, and *Contemporary Pragmatism*.

Stephanie J. Stillman-Spisak is a researcher at the Meadows Center for the Prevention of Educational Risk at the University of Texas in Austin. She has delivered numerous public lectures on the politics of memory, particularly with regard to the aftermath of school shootings in the United States. She is the recipient of several distinguished awards for her interdisciplinary research on religion and politics in the United States.

Masen Uliss is a doctoral candidate in the Department of Religious Studies at the University of California, Santa Barbara. His dissertation, an analysis of the White House Conferences on Aging, reevaluates relationships between religion, government, and national culture. His teaching and research interests focus on the confluence of religion and culture outside of religious institutions, especially in music, film, and the political arena.

Sarah W. Whedon has a PhD in religious studies, with an emphasis in women's studies, from the University of California, Santa Barbara. She currently teaches in the Department of Theology and Religious History at Cherry Hill Seminary, and has taught at Newbury College in Brookline, Massachusetts and in the Department of Women's Studies at Simmons College in Boston. Her recent publications include "The Wisdom of the Indigo Children: An Emphatic Restatement of the Value of American Children" in *Nova Religio: The Journal of Alternative and Emergent Religions*. She is currently conducting research on media representations of fundamentalist Mormon women and girls.

Colleen Windham-Hughes is a doctoral candidate in religious studies at the University of California, Santa Barbara, where she studies intersections between Christian thought, contemporary philosophy, and political theory. She also serves as a consultant to elementary schools that seek to integrate study of religion into school curriculum.

INDEX

Index